Picture Chord Encyclopedia

ISBN 978-0-634-05828-2

Visit Hal Leonard Online at
www.halleonard.com

Contact us:
Hal Leonard
7777 West Bluemound Road
Milwaukee, WI 53213
Email: info@halleonard.com

In Europe, contact:
Hal Leonard Europe Limited
42 Wigmore Street
Marylebone, London, W1U 2RN
Email: info@halleonardeurope.com

In Australia, contact:
Hal Leonard Australia Pty. Ltd.
4 Lentara Court
Cheltenham, Victoria, 3192 Australia
Email: info@halleonard.com.au

CONTENTS

HOW TO USE THIS BOOK

Just a century ago, the average popular pianist had relatively few chords to worry about. Things have changed great deal since then. Today, pianists must know how to construct an astounding assortment of chords. The *cture Chord Encyclopedia* is a valuable resource that will help in a number of ways:

- **as a chord dictionary**
  If you find a chord you're not familiar with in a piece of music, look it up in this book. If you compose music and create chords, this book will also help you to determine proper chord spelling.

- **as a fingering guide**
  If you're uncertain how to play a chord, just look at its accompanying photo. The *Picture Chord Encyclopedia* takes the guesswork out of fingering by including a photo with every chord. You'll learn to play even the most advanced chords comfortably and naturally.

- **as a music reading tool**
  Observe each chord's notation on the staff as you learn to play it. Routine practice at this will improve your note reading and chord recognition skills tremendously.

- **as a resource for improvisers and non-pianists**
  A working knowledge of chords is essential to becoming an effective improviser. This book will help you to visualize possible note choices when improvising. Non-pianists may want to practice outlining the chords in the book as a way to better understand and conceptualize chords and harmony.

The Chord Chart on pages 10-11 lists all the chord types included in the *Picture Chord Encyclopedia*, in the der that they appear. You'll find that three-note chords (triads) appear first, then chords with four notes (seventh ords and sixth chords), and then more unusual chords (extensions, alterations, power chords, etc.). To find a ord, first notice its position on the chart, and then turn to the root of your choice (C, C♯/D♭, D, D♯/E♭, E, etc.) thin the encyclopedia to locate the actual keyboard voicings.

To become more familiar with chord reading, here's a suggested practice routine.

1. **Learn triads.** Triads are three-note chords, and are the basis of keyboard harmony. Each triad is shown in three positions, or "inversions." Practice playing each of these up and down the keyboard.

2. **Learn seventh chords.** Seventh chords are a little more advanced. They consist of four notes, so each is shown in four positions or "inversions." Practice all positions.

3. **Try the rest.** If you're comfortable with triads and seventh chords, the remaining chords will come more easily. Extensions, alterations, and other chord types are all considered variations on basic triads or seventh chords.

BASIC CHORDS & INTERVALS

INTERVALS

Learning about intervals is a key element in learning how to construct chords. An *interval* describes the distance between two notes. For example, the distance from the note C to the note D is the interval of a "second." The distance from C to E is the interval of a "third," and so on. The reason intervals are so helpful is that, once yo are comfortable visualizing intervals, it will be easy to construct any type of chord in any key. The real difficulty wi intervals is determining whether an interval is major, minor, perfect, augmented, or diminished. It is important to understand that all similar chords contain similar intervals. For example, a C major triad contains a root, major third, and perfect fifth. Therefore, any major triad will contain a root, major third, and perfect fifth. Look at the example below. You will notice that, in a C major scale (or any other major scale), some intervals are *perfect* anc some intervals are *major*. The reason for this is beyond the scope of this book. Suffice it to say that the intervals presented in this chapter are the results of many centuries of theory development. Just remember that fourths, fifth and octaves are perfect, and all other intervals in a major scale are major.

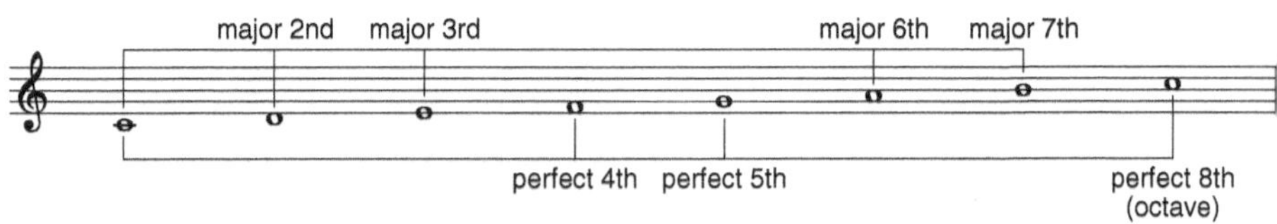

A critical point to consider when learning about intervals is what happens when we alter an interval such as a perfect fifth. Consider the perfect fifth from the note C and G. What happens if we change the G to a G sharp? In this case, the interval becomes an *augmented* fifth. In other words, the space (or *interval*) between notes has bee augmented, or increased. In this example, if the note G were a G flat, the interval would still be a fifth (C to G is always a fifth), but in this instance, the interval would be a *diminished* fifth. In other words, the interval between notes has been diminished, or decreased. The following example shows the terminology for altering major and perfect intervals. Note that the only difference between the two types of intervals is that when you make a major interval smaller, it becomes *minor*. When you make a perfect interval smaller, it becomes *diminished*. Other than this one distinction, the terminology for major and perfect intervals is the same. Note that the minor interval becomes diminished when made smaller.

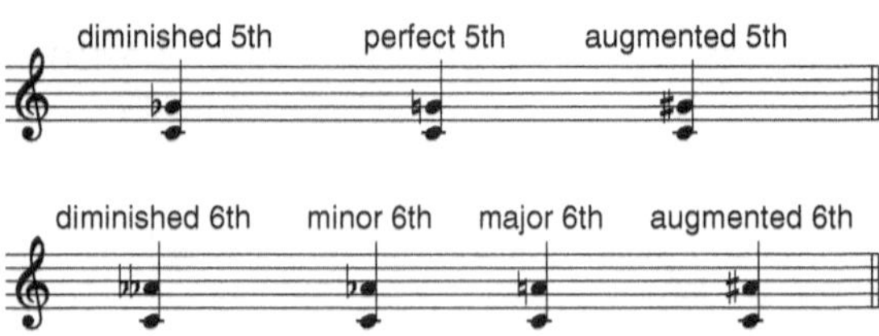

Understanding the theory behind intervals is one thing, being able to utilize intervals in your playing is 1other. You may find it helpful to use some tricks to be able to comfortably visualize intervals. Begin by learning erfect fifths and major thirds. All other intervals can easily be related to these primary intervals. Regarding erfect fifths: with only two exceptions, both notes in a perfect fifth will share the same accidental. In the following kample, you can see that the only fifths that don't follow this rule are B♭ to F and B to F♯.

Major thirds are also easy to find. To find a major third, count up two whole steps from any note. The llowing example illustrates common major thirds:

The following is a list of tricks to find common intervals:

- Major second: Count up one whole step from any note.
- Minor third: Lower the top note of any major third by one half step.
- Perfect fourth: Count down one whole step from the top note of any perfect fifth.
- Major sixth: Count up one whole step from any perfect fifth interval.
- Minor seventh: A whole step "shy" of an octave.
- Major seventh: A half step "shy" of an octave.
- Major ninth: Same note as a major second but an octave higher.
- Perfect eleventh: Same note as a perfect fourth but one octave higher.
- Major thirteenth: Same as a sixth but an octave higher.

As you can see, intervals are relatively easy to learn. The next step is to learn to construct chords using tervals.

RIADS

Triads are chords consisting of three notes. The primary triads are *major*, *minor*, *diminished*, and *igmented*. Major and minor triads are most prevalent in music today. Note that in the figure below, both the ajor and minor triads contain a perfect fifth interval. The only difference is the interval of a third: major triads ntain a major third, minor triads contain a minor third. As you can see, a diminished triad contains a minor third d a diminished fifth. The augmented triad contains a major third and an augmented fifth.

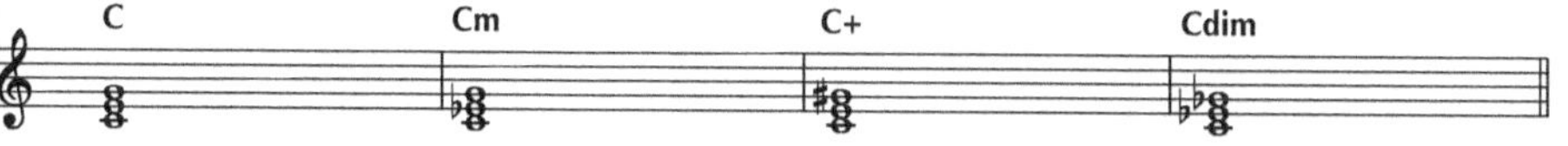

In the previous example, the root of each triad was the note C. This brings up an important point regarding construction of chords: Is the root always the lowest note? Unlike figured bass chord construction in traditional theory, the root may not always be the lowest note in popular music chord nomenclature. The root is always the lowest note in terms of chord construction (building a chord using intervals), but the root may not always be placed as the lowest note of the chord. Play the following chords:

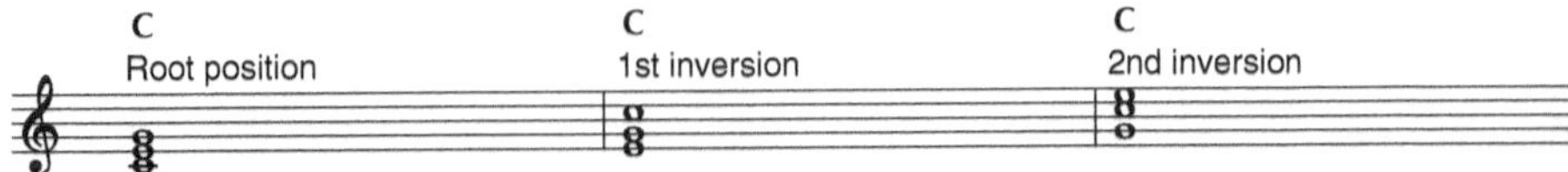

In this example, the order of notes in the original C major triad has changed, but the chords still sound like the original C major chord. These new varieties of C major triads are called *inversions*. In the previous example, the triads may be described as *root position, first inversion*, and *second inversion*. **To invert any chord, raise the bottom note one octave or lower the top note one octave**. Generally, triads and seventh chords are the only chords that may be practically inverted. More complex chord inversions may be easily handled by adding notes to a simple triad or seventh chord inversion. As you will see, it is also common to omit some notes when inverting more complex chords.

There may be occasions where you would like to hear a chord with a tone other than the root in the bass register. In these cases, notate the name of the chord and use a slash to signify the bass note. C/G would be interpreted as a C major triad over the bass note G. Incidentally, notes other than chord tones may also be used. The chord F/G, for example, is common in popular music today. When inverting chords, be aware that the quality of chord may change if a note other than the root occurs in the bass register. A first inversion C major chord may sound different if placed below middle C on the piano. In this case, the lowest note (E) may start to sound like a root. The best way to determine the difference between a simple inversion and an actual change of chord type is through experimentation. Play chords and inversions in the lower register of the piano. You will start to get a sense of how range can alter the quality of a chord.

SEVENTH CHORDS

Seventh chords are common in many styles of music. The term "seventh chords" refers to triads that also contain an interval of a seventh. If you can construct basic triads, seventh chords are relatively easy to spell. Here are some common seventh chords:

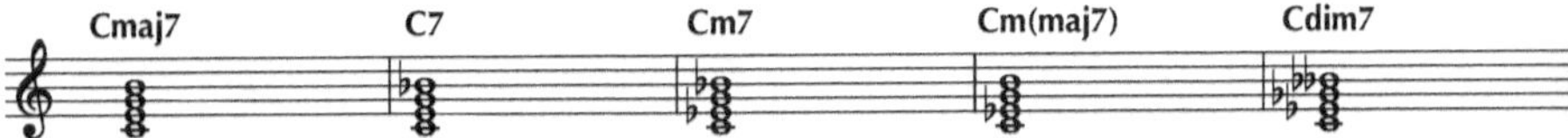

Some tricks to remember:

- Major 7 chord: major triad and major seventh interval (Remember: a major seventh is a half step shy of an octave)
- Minor 7 chord: minor triad and minor seventh
- Major/minor 7: minor triad and major seventh
- 7 chord: major triad with minor seventh interval
- Diminished 7: diminished triad with diminished seventh interval (chord is constructed entirely from minor third intervals)

To this point, we have considered a variety of triads and seventh chords. Students would be advised to study construction of these chord types as well as inversions for the basic triads and seventh chords. Inversions for these chords may be found in the dictionary portion of the *Picture Chord Encyclopedia*. In the next few pages, we will look at concepts relating to extensions and alterations.

EXTENSIONS AND ALTERATIONS

An *extension* refers to an interval greater than a seventh that is added to a chord. Examples of extensions re ninths, elevenths, and thirteenths. The term *alteration* refers to a chord where one of the primary intervals has een altered. We have already seen examples of altered chords. In the preceding section, a major triad had been tered to include an augmented (altered) fifth. The resulting chord was a C augmented (+) triad.

Questions often arise around the concept of extensions. An interval of a ninth is the same as a major second us one octave. Why is it that ninth chords are not notated as "2nd" chords? The answer lies in the fact that our ord system is built around a concept of *tertian* harmony – chords built in thirds. A triad may contain a root, third, d fifth. A seventh chord contains a root, third, fifth, and seventh. A ninth chord contains a root, third, fifth, seventh, d ninth, and so on. Although there are a few exceptions, the basic rule is as follows: the higher the extension umber, the more potential chord tones may be included in a voicing. To better understand this concept, visualize e difference between a C6 chord and a C13 chord. Although these chords might seem similar, the C6 chord is a mple major triad with an interval of a major sixth added. The C13 chord contains a minor seventh and major ninth terval in addition to a major triad. In the following example, note that no eleventh is present in the C13 chord. In e strictest technical sense the eleventh could be used. In this case, the reason for excluding it is simple – it sounds d.

NTH CHORDS

Ninth chords are chords that contain an interval of a ninth. In most cases, these chords are four-note seventh ords that also contain an interval of a major ninth. An important concept to remember when dealing with ninth ords is the following: major ninths are always added to chords unless otherwise specified. In the following ample, notice how all of the example chords use the same major ninth interval – a D in this case.

There will be occasions where a minor or augmented ninth will be used, but this will always be specified with qualifier such as + or ♯9, - or flat 9. Ninth chords can often be a point of confusion for students. With a chord ch as a Cm9, you might expect that the ninth of this chord would be a minor ninth. In this case, the ninth is still major ninth. Just remember that ninths are always major unless otherwise specified. An easy way to tell the type underlying chord quality for any ninth chord is to replace 9 with 7. For example, an Fm9 is really an Fm7 with a ajor ninth added. A B9 is really a B7 with major ninth added.

ELEVENTH CHORDS

Eleventh chords are not as common as ninth chords. An easy way to find a perfect eleventh is to count down one whole step from the top note of a perfect fifth interval. An eleventh is the same as a perfect fourth plus an octave. It is interesting to note that the interval of an eleventh is typically altered. In common practice, the only tim a perfect eleventh is added is over a minor seventh or minor ninth chord. A Cm11 chord, major ninth, and a perfe eleventh.

An augmented eleventh is more common, and is often in conjunction with major ninth chords and dominant ninth chords. Although the interval of an augmented eleventh is an enharmonic equivalent to a diminished fifth, in the following example, you can see that both a perfect fifth and augmented eleventh are used.

There is one other variety of eleventh chord that may cause some confusion. A C11 chord looks as if it may have evolved from a C7 or C9 chord. This is true, but unlike other examples to this point, the third is always omitt for this type of chord. A better way to describe this type of chord would be Gm7/C or C9sus.

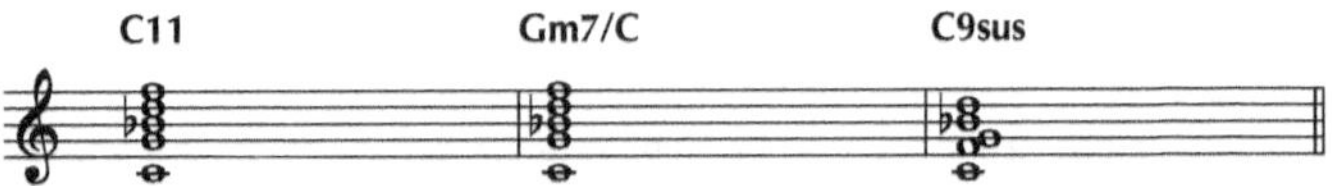

THIRTEENTH CHORDS

The last type of extended chord we will look at are thirteenth chords. Like ninth chords, the interval of a thirteenth will always be a major thirteenth unless otherwise noted. The most common thirteenth chord is the "dominant thirteenth." A major thirteenth chord is also fairly common.

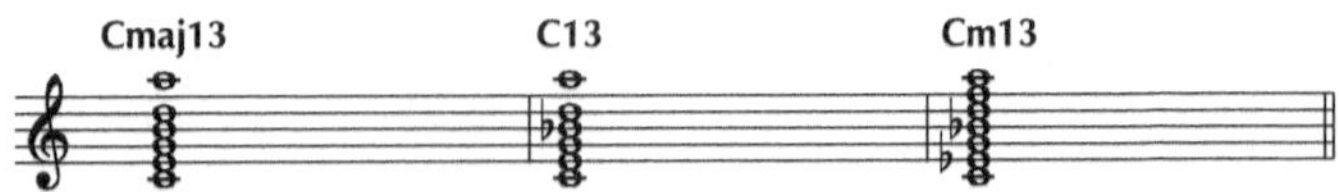

Notice the absence of an eleventh in these chords. It is customary to omit the eleventh on dominant or majo thirteenth chords because the eleventh conflicts with the third.

OTHER CHORD TYPES

There are a great many chords that don't fit nicely into a major or minor category. Unlike major and minor iads and seventh chords, many of these chords may not be built in thirds. Sus4 and sus2 chords are two such camples. The sus4 chord has its roots in Renaissance harmony. At that point in time, *suspensions* were a common evice. In a 4-3 suspension, an interval of a perfect fourth resolves to an interval of a third. In our modern quivalent, a perfect fourth is used instead of a major or minor third. The sus2 chord is similar. Here, a major cond is used instead of a major or minor third.

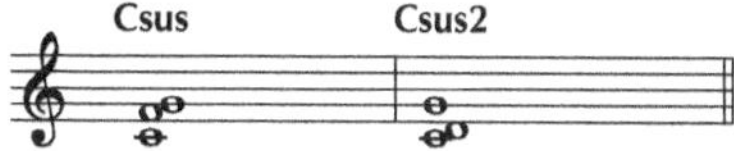

DD9 CHORDS

Intervals are sometimes added to a simple triad. In a C(add9) chord for example, an interval of a major ninth added to a simple major triad. This chord is similar to a Csus2 with the exception that a C(add9) chord contains major third.

XTH CHORDS

The interval of a sixth is another common interval that may be added to triads. This is so common that the dd6" qualifier is not needed. A C6 may be interpreted as a C major triad with a major sixth added. A Cm6 would a C minor triad with major sixth added. A major ninth may also be added. Note that in all of the following ords, sixths and ninths are added to basic major or minor triads – no seventh is used.

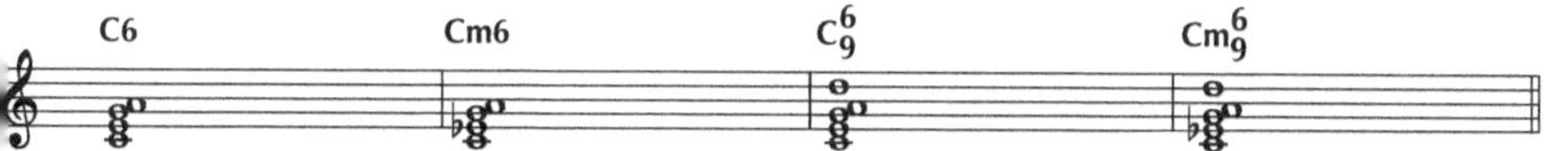

OWER CHORDS

There is one other chord variety that should be mentioned in this section on chord construction. In some les of popular music, it is customary to use "power chords" – chords that are not major or minor. In these ses, only a root and perfect fifth are used. A C5 chord, for example, would contain only the notes C and G.

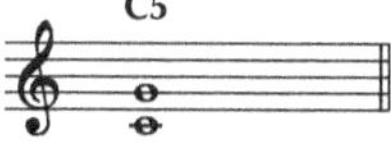

To conclude this portion of the text, let's review some of the important concepts.

- Intervals are key to learning proper chord construction.
- Perfect fifths and major thirds are two helpful intervals – most other intervals can be found by counting up or down whole and half steps from these intervals.
- Triads are three-note chords.
- The most common triads are major, minor, diminished, and augmented.
- Seventh chords extend basic triads by adding the interval of a seventh. There are a great variety of seventh chords, but the most helpful to learn are: major 7, minor 7, 7, and diminished 7.
- Extensions may be added to seventh chords. Possible extension notes are the ninth, eleventh, and thirteenth.
- Chord tones may be altered. Augmented and diminished fifths are two examples of altered chord tones.

ADVANCED CHORD VOICINGS

Learning the notes of chords is only one facet of actually using chords effectively. Deciding how to "voice" or organize the notes of a given chord can be a daunting task. Many variables must be considered — range, spacing, complexity, and context. This section will provide some suggestions on common voicing techniques.

An important concept to understand when voicing chords is the fact that no specific order of notes is implied. For example, although a C9 chord does contain the note D (the ninth), the D may not actually be placed a ninth higher than the root. In some cases, it might be next to the root. The key here is to understand that a chord name describes the construction (in root position) of the chord. It does not imply a specific order of notes as they might actually be played.

OPEN VS. CLOSE

Close or "tight" voicings generally work fine in the mid and upper range of the piano, but as you move to the lower register the voicings will need to "open up." Below are a few common left hand structures. Notice how the interval between notes is fairly large in these examples.

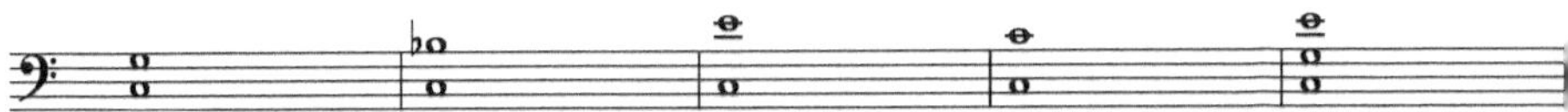

In the next example, the right hand is voiced using "close" harmony. This works well because the right hand is in the middle register of the piano.

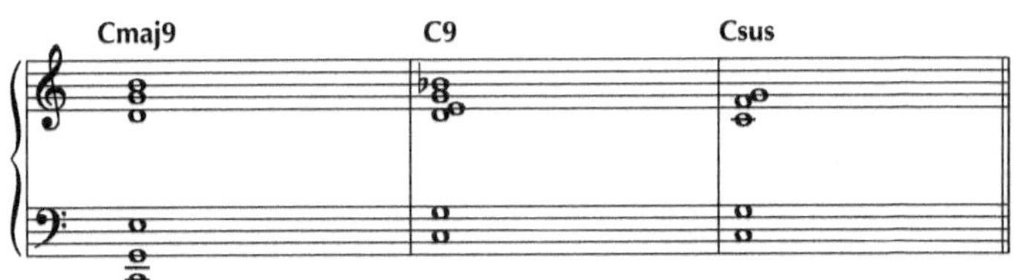

It is important to avoid changing the quality of chord by placing notes other than the root in the bass register. In the following example, the first chord will sound like an Am7, not a C6. The reason for this is that the note A sounds like a root because of its position in the chord.

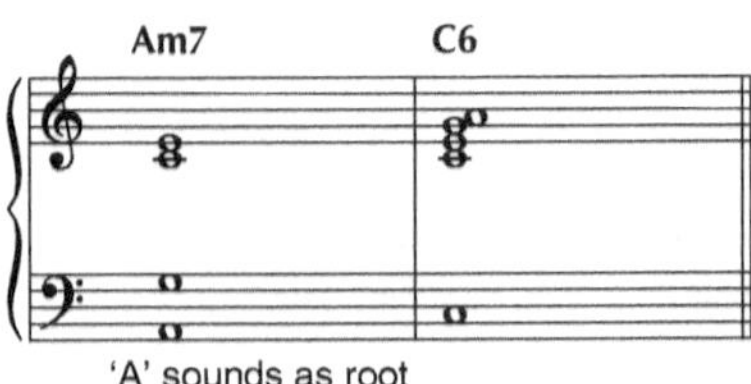

'A' sounds as root

OP VOICINGS

One of the best ways to learn about voicing chords is to work with four-note seventh chords. The *Picture* *ord Encyclopedia* lists inversions for the primary seventh chords. Learn these inversions and you will find it is y to voice more complex chords by adding tones to these primary inversions. The next few suggestions will apply our-note voicings in the right hand. These suggestions are also applicable to mid-range left hand voicings as well.

- To add a ninth, drop the root.
- To add a thirteenth, drop the fifth.
- To add a ♯11, drop the fifth.

The term "drop" can mean two different things. You can drop the note to the left hand or you may even omit note. The next example demonstrates this concept. Notice how each of the chords derives from a more basic enth chord inversion.

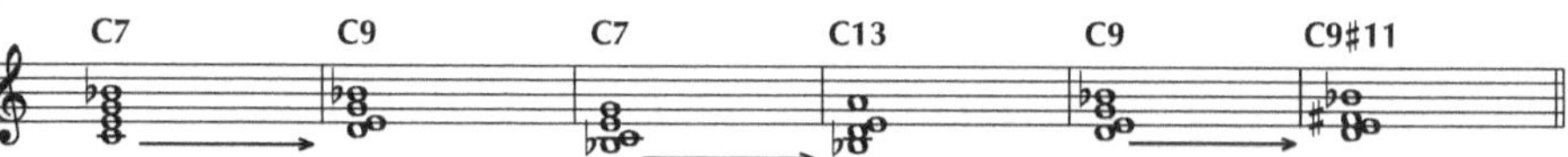

The following demonstrates some possible voicings using a variety of notes in both the left and right hand. In se voicings, "dropped" notes are placed in the left hand.

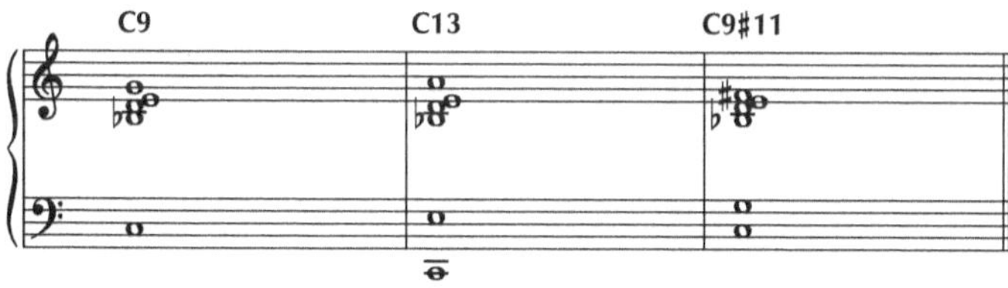

Another approach to voicing a complex chord such as a ninth, eleventh, or thirteenth, is to begin with the third, , seventh, and ninth in the right hand. This is always a good starting point. Extensions and alterations may be lied to this basic structure.

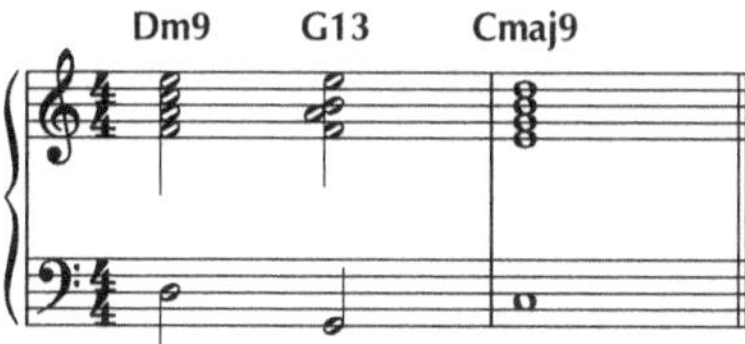

Another common structure are "drop 2" voicings. To make a drop 2, lower the second note from the top ny close position voicing one octave. Two inversions are particularly helpful: 3-7-9-5 and 7-3-5-9.

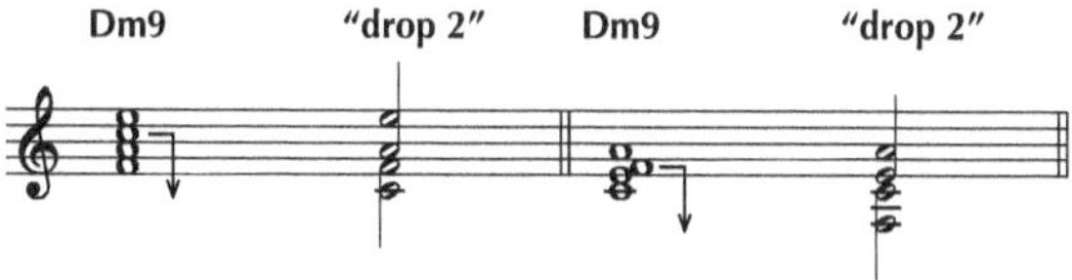

As you can see, learning to construct and voice chords is not an easy task. The *Picture Chord Encyclopedia* will be luable reference for learning chords. You will find an extensive listing of chords and inversions of primary triads and enth chords. Learn the inversions, and it will be relatively easy to construct and voice even the most complex chord.

CHORD CHART

m = minor interval   d = diminished interval   a = augmented interval
All other intervals are major or perfect

Chord	Alternate Names	Spelling
C	CM, Cmaj., C∆, Cmajor	1, 3, 5
Cm	Cmi., Cmin., C-	1, m3, 5
C+	Caug., C+5, C(♯5)	1, 3, ♯5
Cdim	C°, C diminished	1, m3, d5
Csus	Csus4	1, 4, 5
C(♭5)	C(-5)	1, 3, d5
Csus2	C2	1, 2, 5
C6	Cmaj.6, Cadd6	1, 3, 5, 6
C(add2)	C(add9)	1, 2, 3, 5
Cmaj7	C∆7, CM7, CMa7	1, 3, 5, 7
Cmaj7♭5	C∆7♭5, CM7(-5), Cma7(♭5)	1, 3, d5, 7
Cmaj7♯5	C∆7♯5, CM7(+5), Cma7(♯5)	1, 3, a5, 7
C7	none	1, 3, 5, m7
C7♭5	C7-5	1, 3, d5, m7
C7♯5	C+7, C7+, C7+5	1, 3, a5, m7
C7sus	C7sus4	1, 4, 5, m7
Cm(add2)	Cm2, C-2	1, 2, m3, 5
Cm6	Cm(add6), C-6	1, m3, 5, 6
Cm7	C-7, Cmi7, Cmin7	1, m3, 5, m7
Cm(maj7)	C-(∆7), Cmi(ma7)	1, m3, 5, 7
Cm7♭5	Cø7, Cm7-5	1, m3, d5, m7
Cdim7	C°7	1, m3, d5, d7
Cdim(maj7)	C°(maj7)	1, m3, d5, 7
C5	C(no 3rd)	1, 5
C6/9	C6/9, C6(add9)	1, 3, 5, 6, 9
Cmaj6/9	C∆9(add6)	1, 3, 5, 6, 7, 9
Cmaj7♯11	C∆7(♯11)	1, 3, 5, 7, a11
Cmaj9	C∆9, CM9, Cma9	1, 3, 5, 7, 9
Cmaj9♭5	C∆9♭5, Cma9(-5)	1, 3, d5, 7, 9
Cmaj9♯5	C∆9♯5, Cma9(+5)	1, 3, a5, 7, 9
Cmaj9♯11	C∆9♯11, Cma9(+11)	1, 3, 5, 7, 9, a11
Cmaj13	C∆13, Cma13	1, 3, 5, 7, 9, 13
Cmaj13♭5	C∆13♭5, Cma13(-5)	1, 3, d5, 7, 9, 13
Cmaj13♯11	C∆13♯11, Cma13(+11)	1, 3, 5, 7, 9, a11, 13
C7♭9	C7(-9)	1, 3, 5, m7, m9

hord	Alternate Names	Spelling
7♯9	C7(+9)	1, 3, 5, m7, a9
7♯11	C7(+11)	1, 3, 5, m7, a11
7♭5(♭9)	C7(-5,-9)	1, 3, d5, m7, m9
7♭5(♯9)	C7(-5,+9)	1, 3, d5, m7, a9
7♯5(♭9)	C7(+5,-9)	1, 3, a5, m7, m9
7♯5(♯9)	C7(+5,+9)	1, 3, a5, m7, a9
7♭9(♯9)	C7(-9,+9)	1, 3, 5, m7, m9, a9
7(add13)	C13(no 9)	1, 3, 5, m7, 13
7♭13	C7(-13)	1, 3, 5, m7, m13
7♭9(♯11)	C7(-9,+11)	1, 3, 5, m7, m9, a11
7♯9(♯11)	C7(+9,+11)	1, 3, 5, m7, a9, a11
7♭9(♭13)	C7(-9,-13)	1, 3, 5, m7, m9, m13
7♯9(♭13)	C7(+9,-13)	1, 3, 5, m7, a9, m13
7♯11(♭13)	C7(+11,-13)	1, 3, 4, m7, a11, m13
7♭9(♯9,♯11)	C7(-9,+9,+11)	1, 3, 5, m7, m9, a9, a11
9	none	1, 3, 5, m7, 9
9(♭5)	C9(-5)	1, 3, d5, m7, 9
9♯5	C9+, C+9	1, 3, a5, m7, 9
9♯11	C9(+11)	1, 3, 5, m7, 9, a11
9♭13	C9(-13)	1, 3, 5, m7, 9, m13
9♯11(♭13)	C9(+11,-13)	1, 3, 5, m7, 9, a11, m13
11	C9sus4, Gm7/C	1, 5, m7, 9, 11
13	none	1, 3, 5, m7, 9, 13
13♭5	C13(-5)	1, 3, d5, m7, 9, 13
13♭9	C13(-9)	1, 3, 5, m7, m9, 13
13♯9	C13(+9)	1, 3, 5, m7, a9, 13
13♯11	C13(+11)	1, 3, 5, m7, 9, a11, 13
13(sus4)	C13sus	1, 4, 5, m7, 9, 13
n(♯5)	Cm+5	1, m3, a5
m6/9	Cmi6(add9)	1, m3, 5, 6, 9
n7(add4)	Cm7(add11)	1, m3, 5, m7, 11
n7♭5(♭9)	Cø7(-9)	1, m3, d5, m7, m9
m9	C-9, Cmin9	1, m3, 5, m7, 9
n9(maj7)	C-(Δ7), Cmi(ma7)	1, m3, 5, 7
n9(♭5)	Cø9, C-7(-5)	1, m3, d5, m7, 9
m11	Cmin11, C-11	1, m3, 5, m7, 9, 11
n13	C-13, Cmin13	1, m3, 5, m7, 9, 11, 13
dim7(add9)	C°7(add9)	1, m3, d5, d7, 9
m11♭5	Cø11, C-11(♭5)	1, m3, d5, m7, 9, 11
n11(maj7)	C-11(maj7), C-11(Δ7)	1, m3, 5, 7, 9, 11
7alt.	C7altered	1, 3, 5, m7, m9, a9, a11, m13

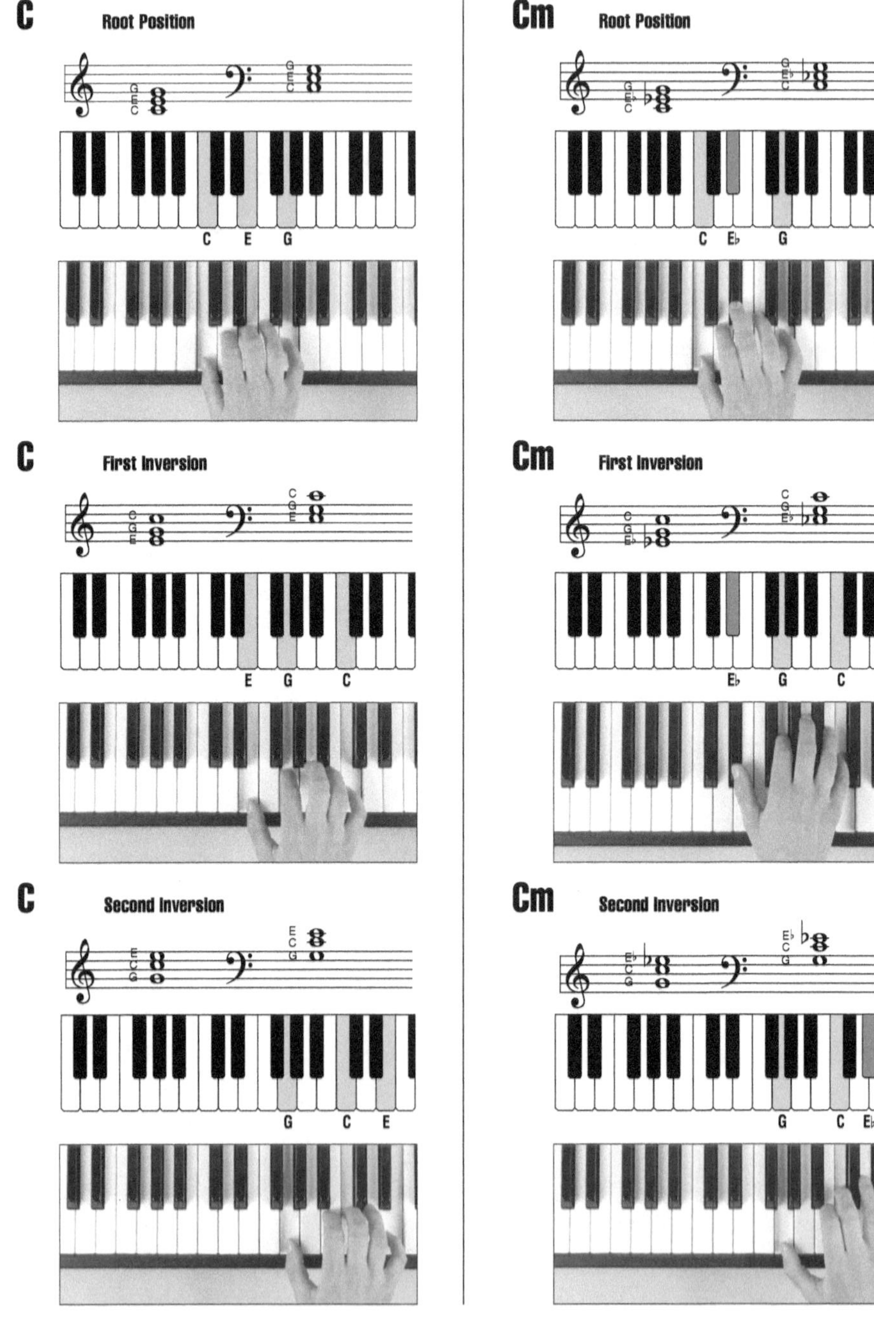
C
Root Position
C E G
Cm
Root Position
C E♭ G
C
First Inversion
E G C
Cm
First Inversion
E♭ G C
C
Second Inversion
G C E
Cm
Second Inversion
G C E♭

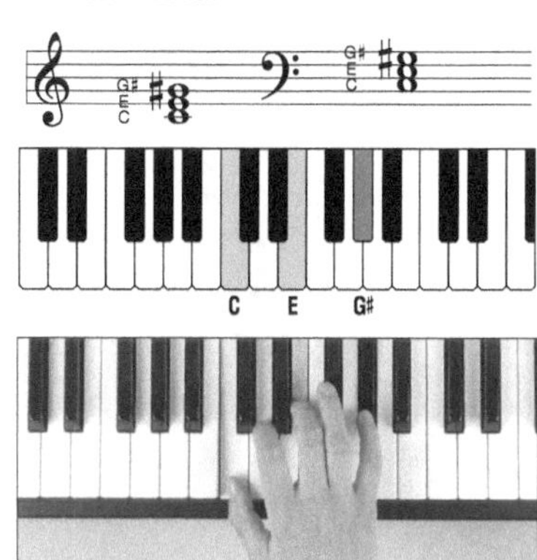

C+ First Inversion

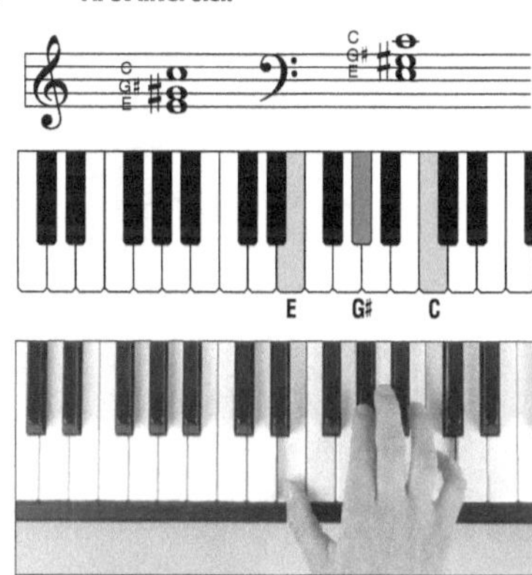

C+ Second Inversion

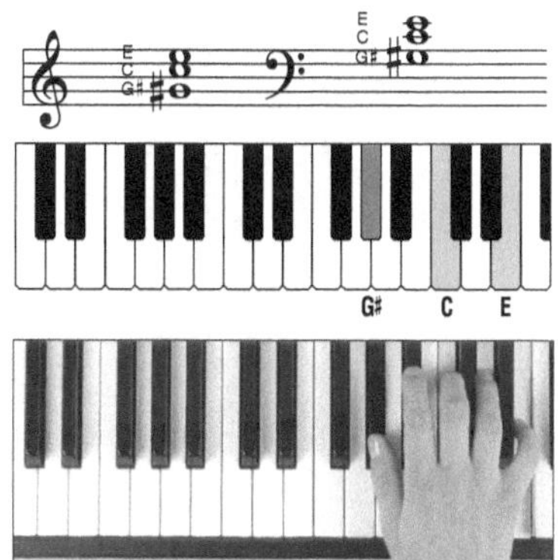

Cdim Root Position

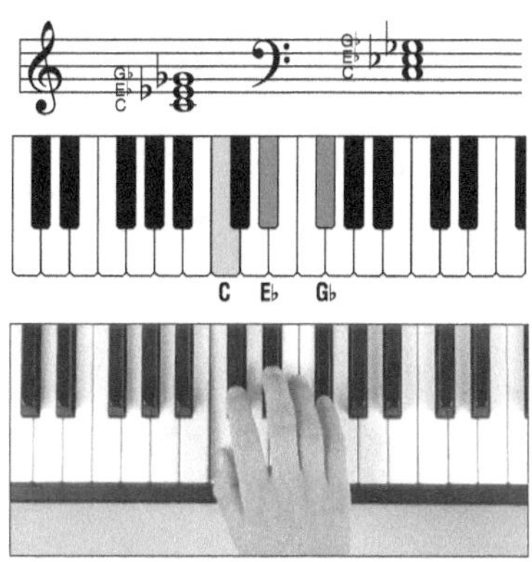

Cdim First Inversion

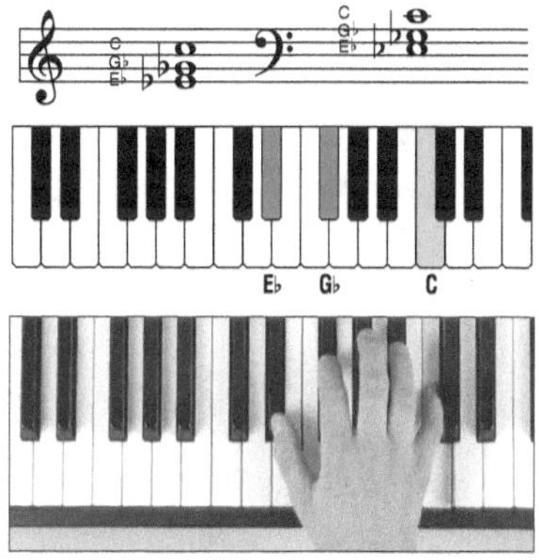

Cdim Second Inversion

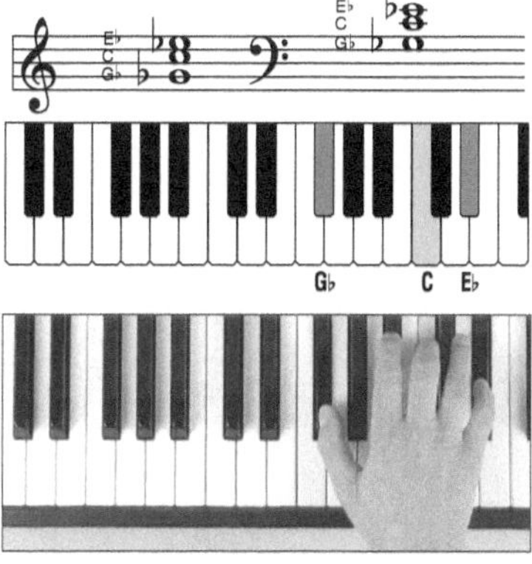

Csus Root Position

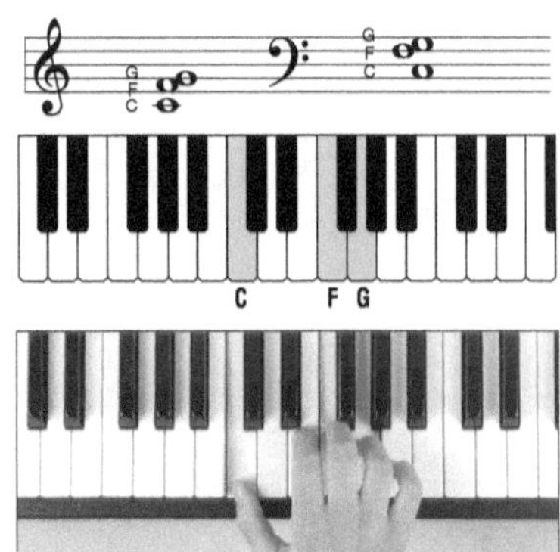

Csus First Inversion

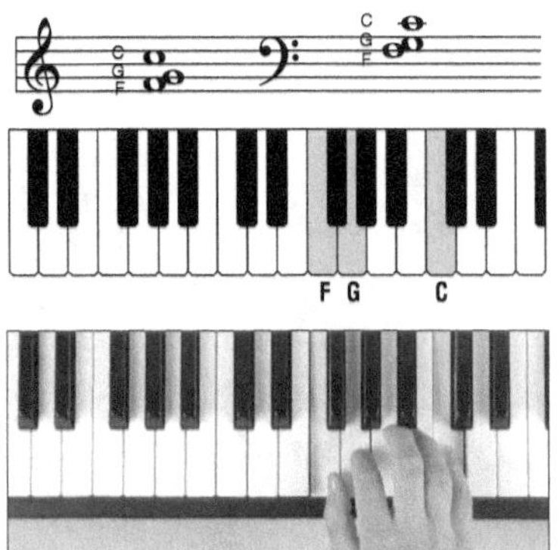

Csus Second Inversion

C(♭5) Root Position

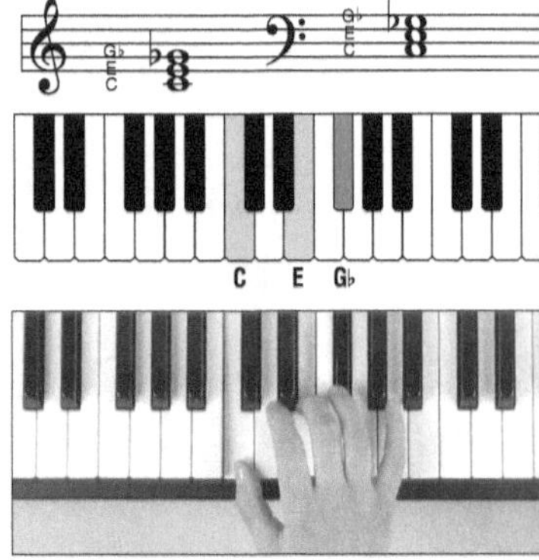

C(♭5) First Inversion

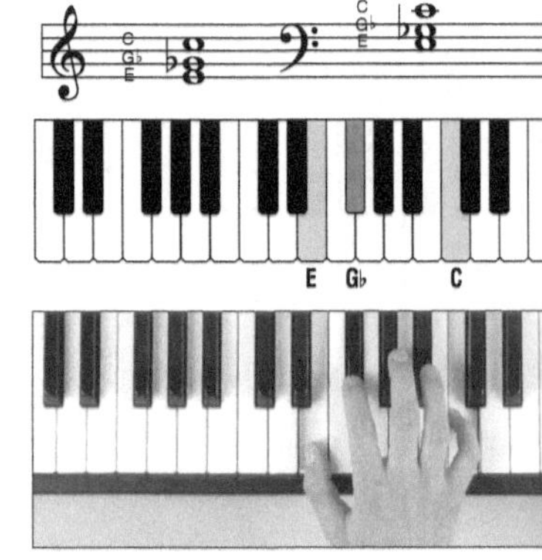

C(♭5) Second Inversion

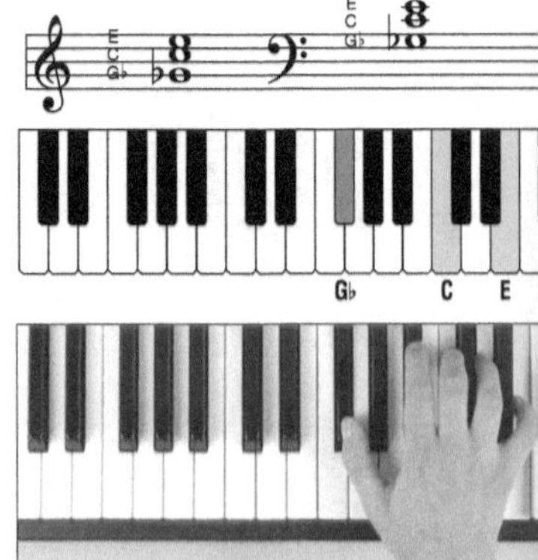

Csus2 Root Position

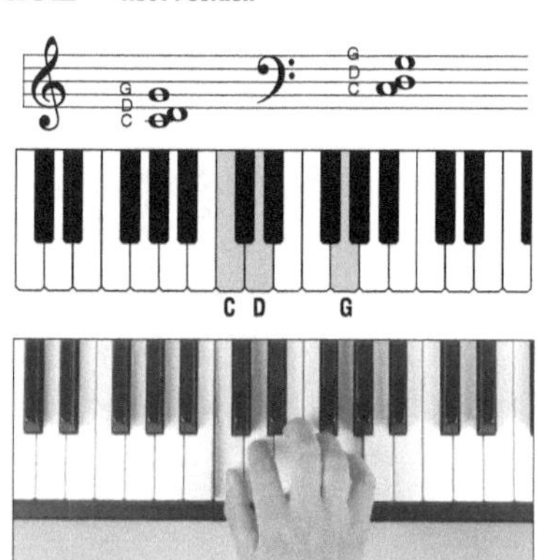

Csus2 First Inversion

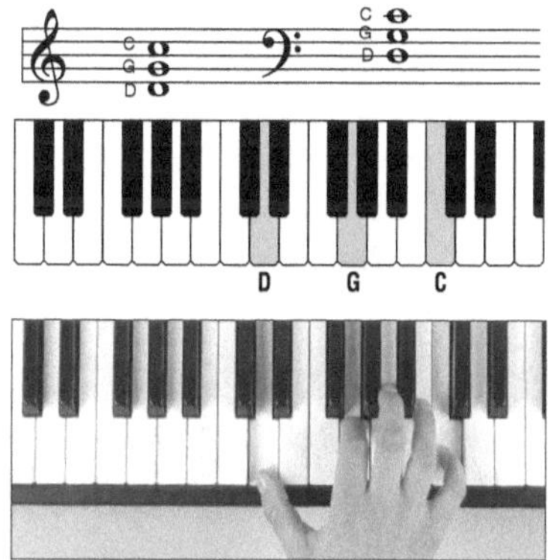

Csus2 Second Inversion

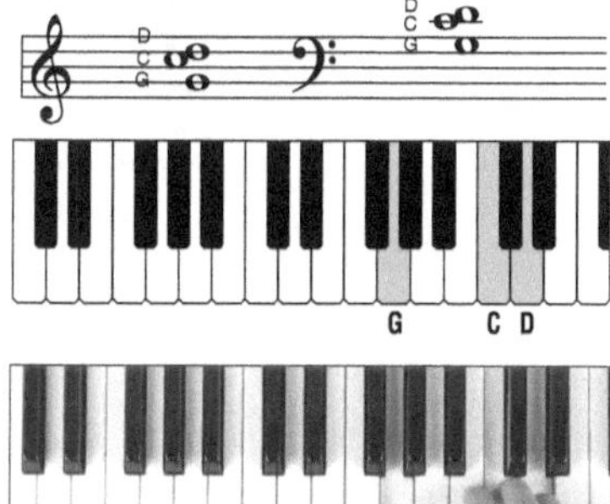

C6 Root Position

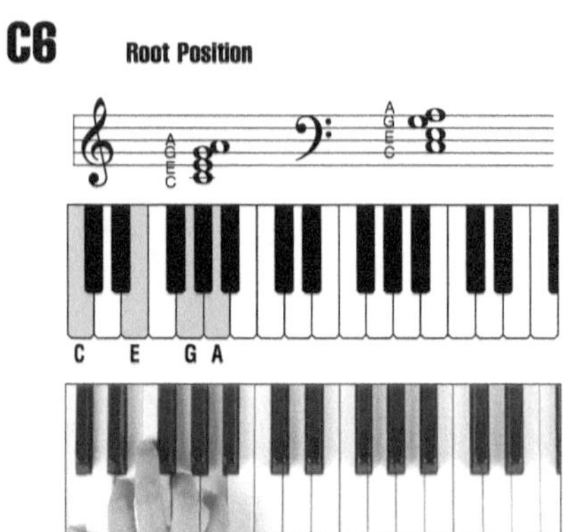

C6 First Inversion

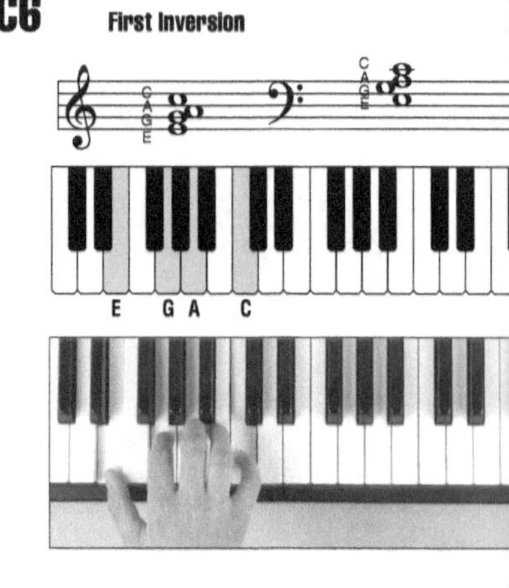

C6 Second Inversion

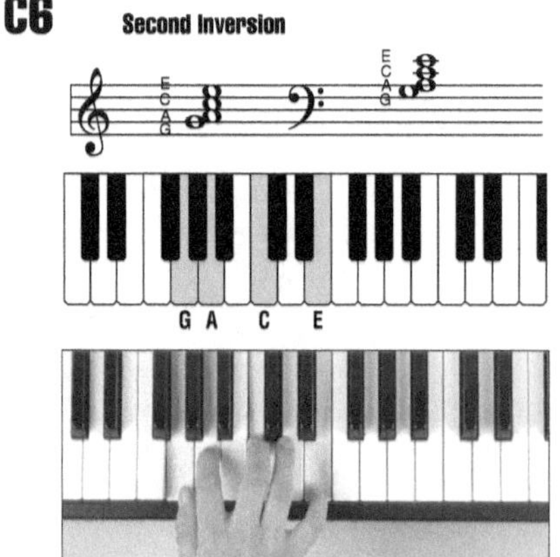

C6 Third Inversion

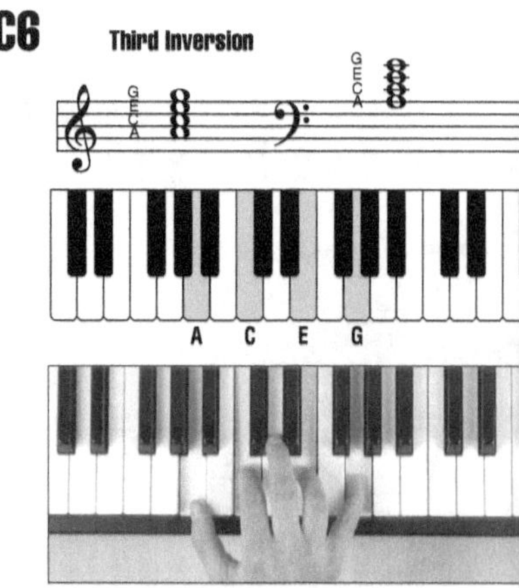

C(add2), C(add9) Root Inversion

C(add2), C(add9) First Inversion

C(add2), C(add9) Second Inversion

C(add2), C(add9) Third Inversion

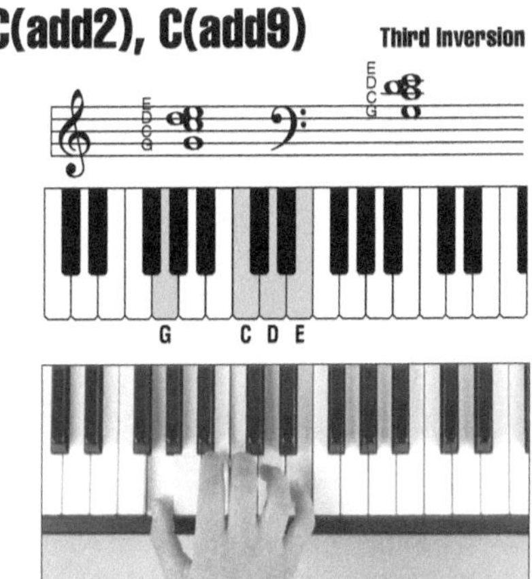

Cmaj7 Root Position

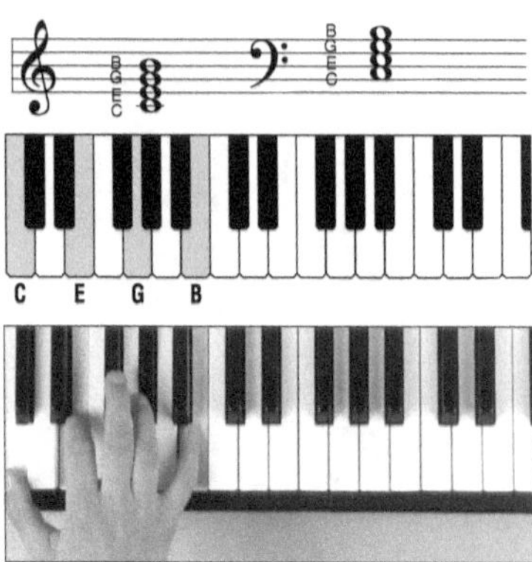

Cmaj7 First Inversion

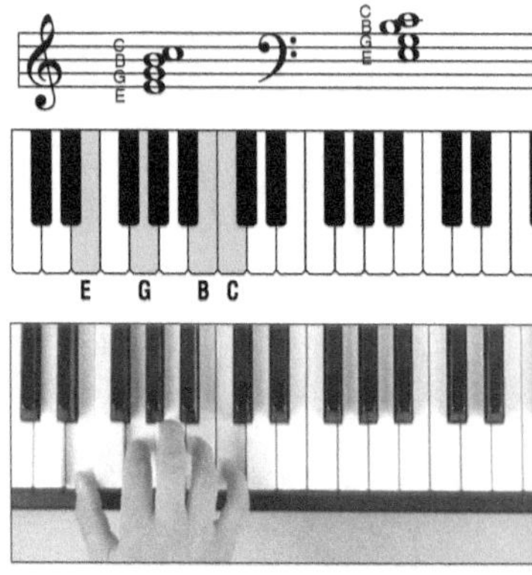

Cmaj7 Second Inversion

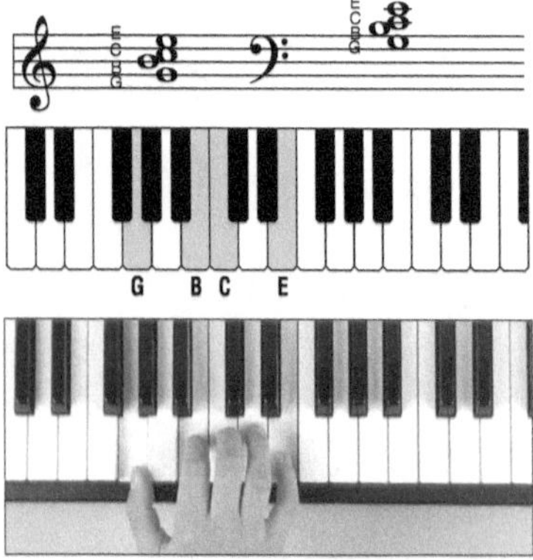

Cmaj7 Third Inversion

Cmaj7♭5 Root Position

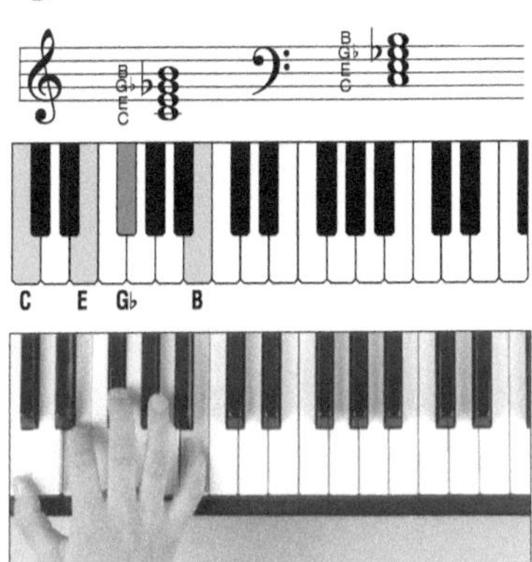

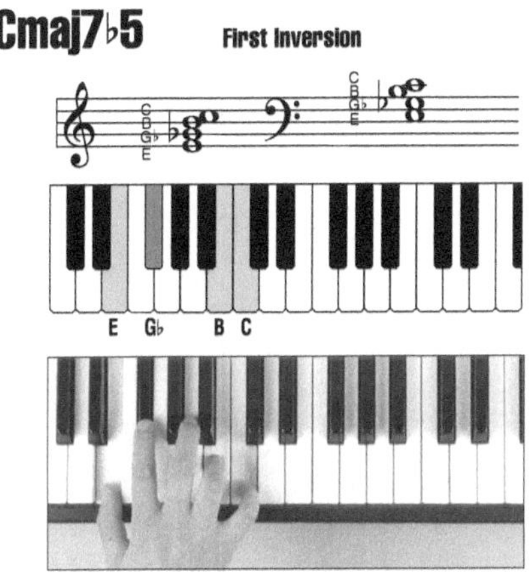

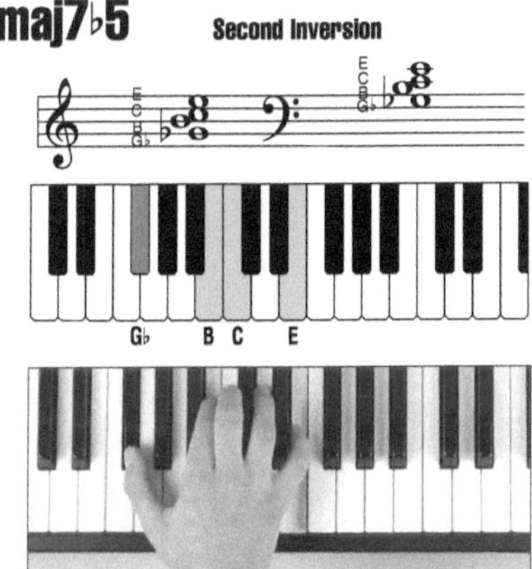

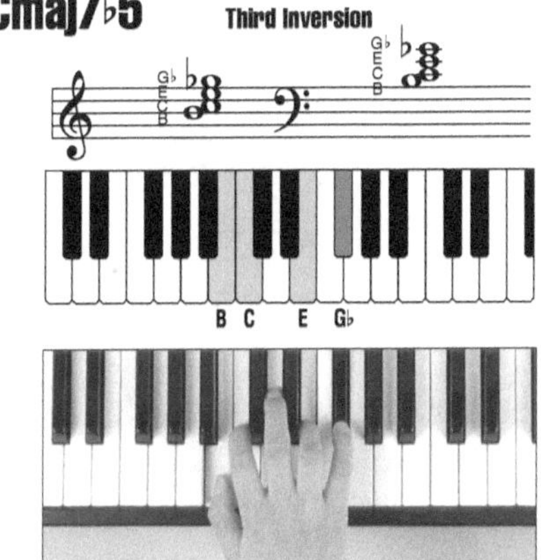

Cmaj7♯5 Root Position

Cmaj7♯5 First Inversion

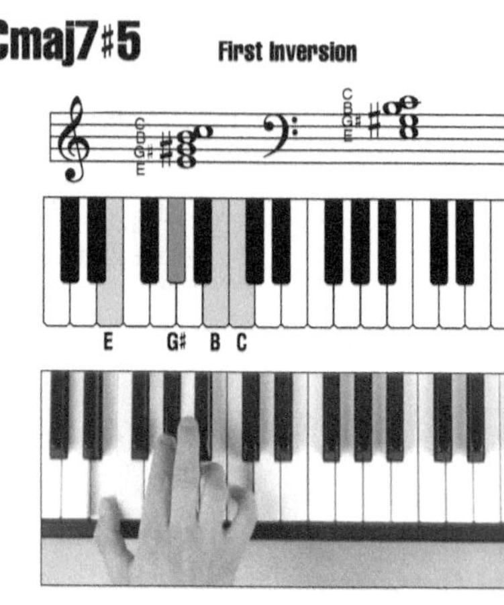

Cmaj7♯5 Second Inversion

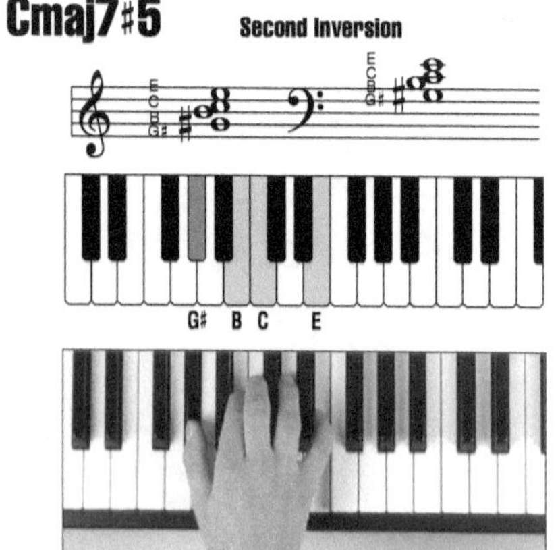

Cmaj7♯5 Third Inversion

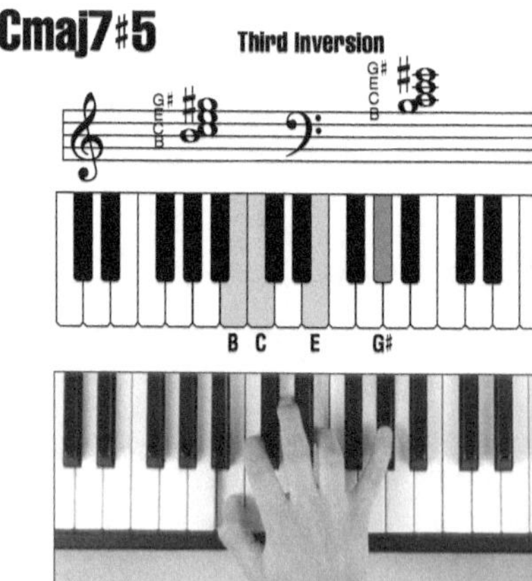

C7 Root Position

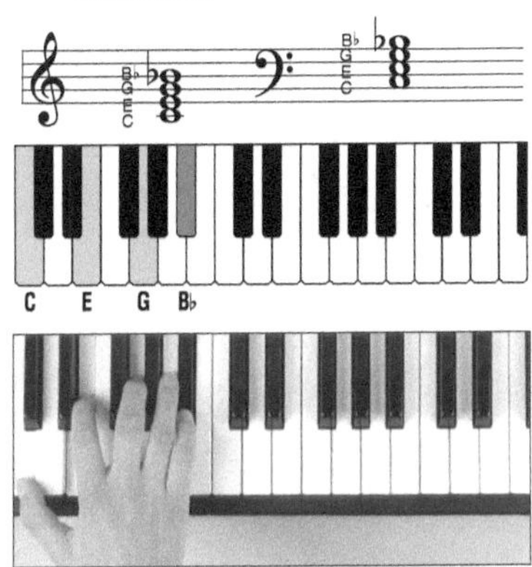

C7 First Inversion

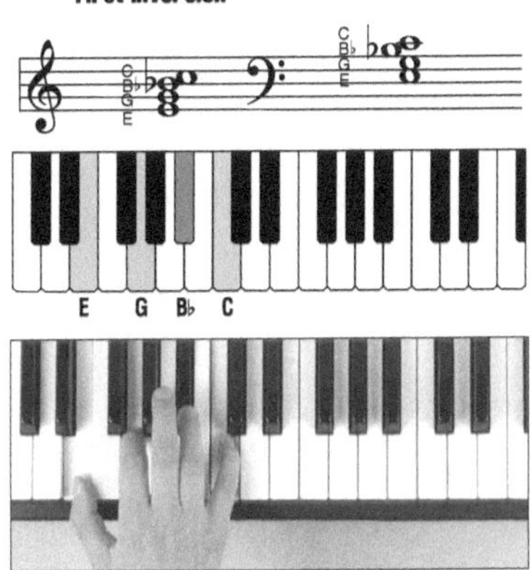

C7 Second Inversion

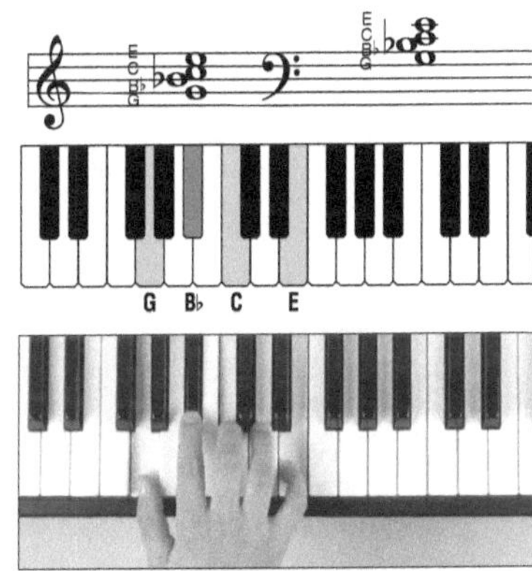

C7 Third Inversion

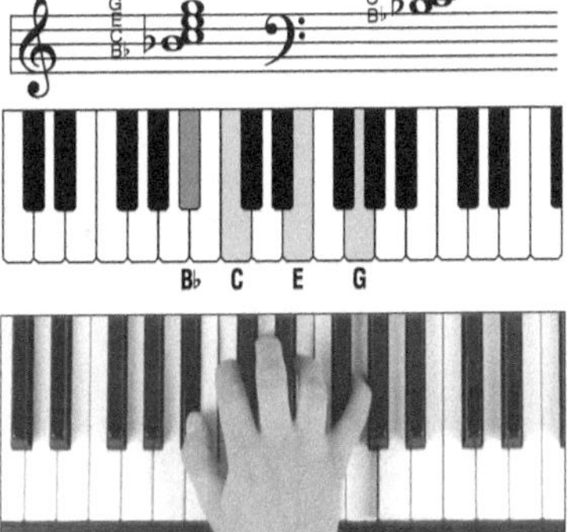

C7♭5 Root Position

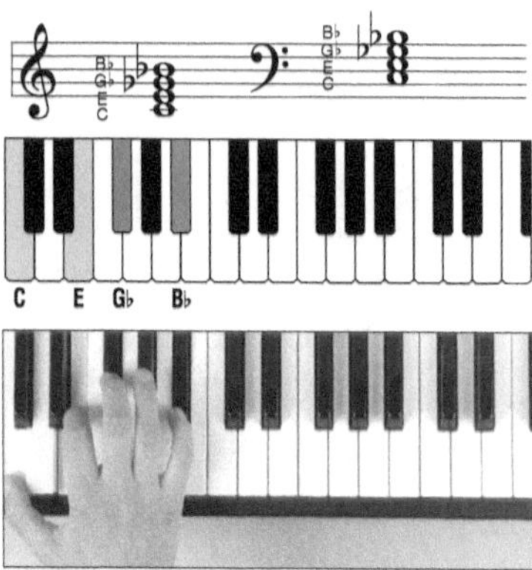

C7♭5 First Inversion

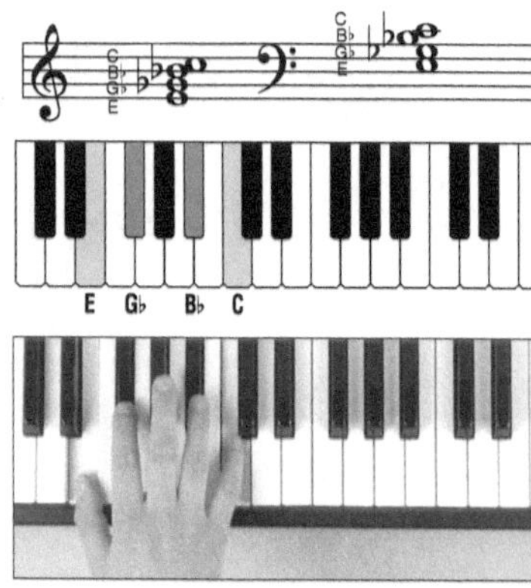

C7♭5 Second Inversion

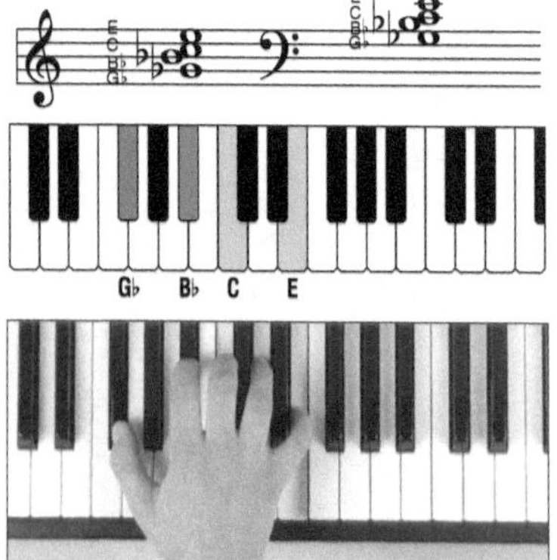

C7♭5 Third Inversion

B♭ C E G♭

C7♯5 Root Position

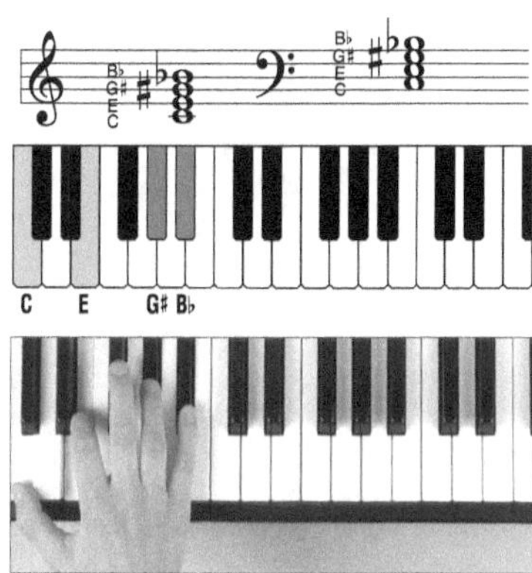

C7♯5 First Inversion

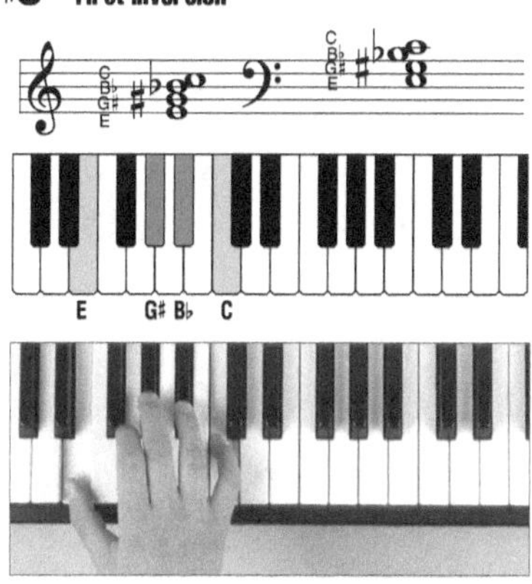

C7♯5 Second Inversion

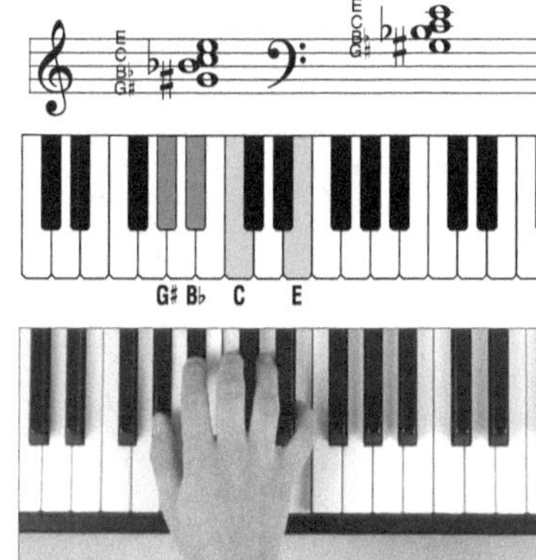

C7♯5 Third Inversion

C7sus Root Position

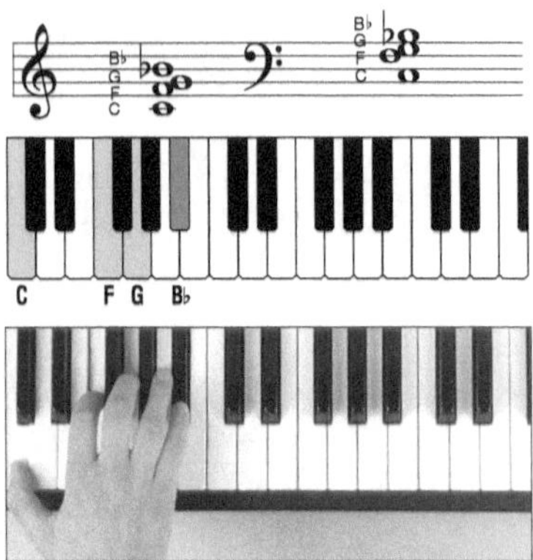

C7sus First Inversion

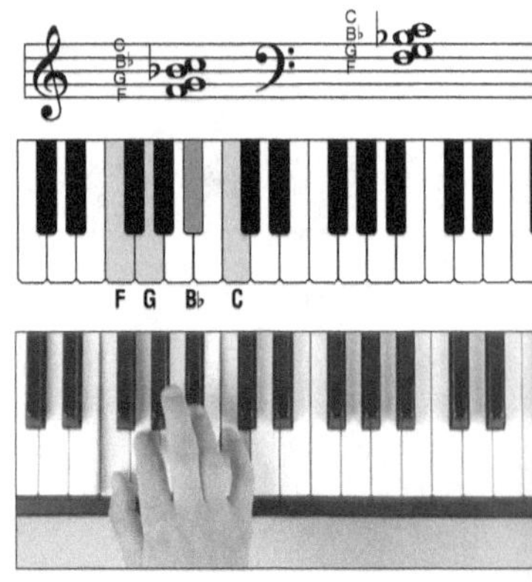

C7sus Second Inversion

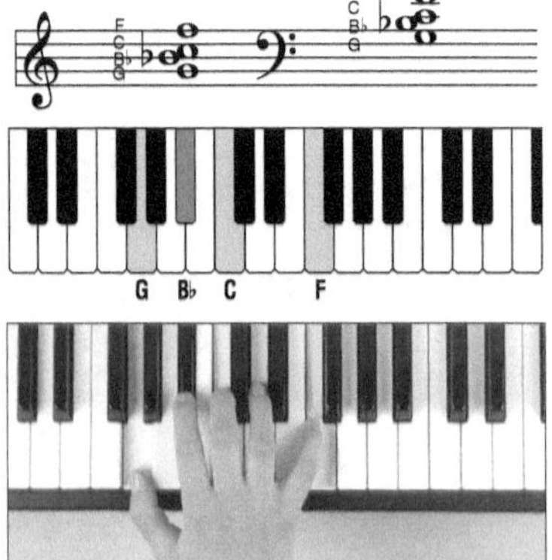

C7sus Third Inversion

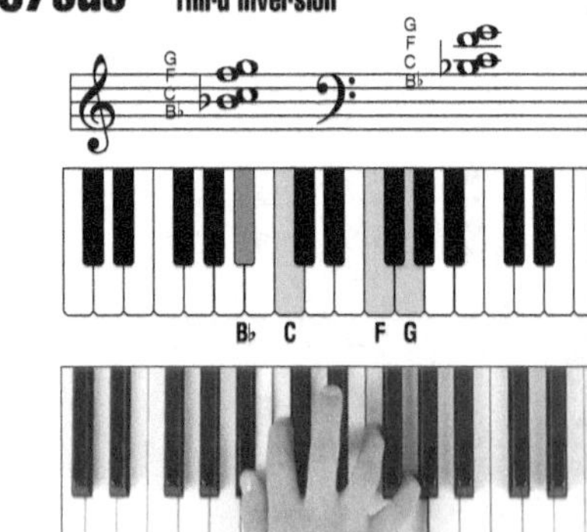

Cm(add2), Cm(add9) Root Position

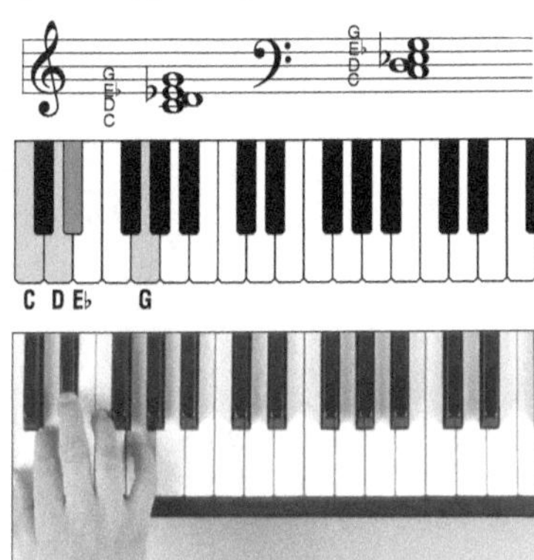

Cm(add2), Cm(add9) First Inversion

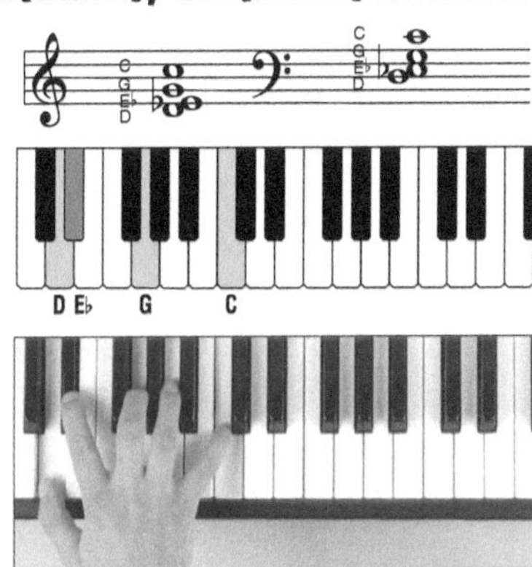

Cm(add2), Cm(add9) Second Inversion

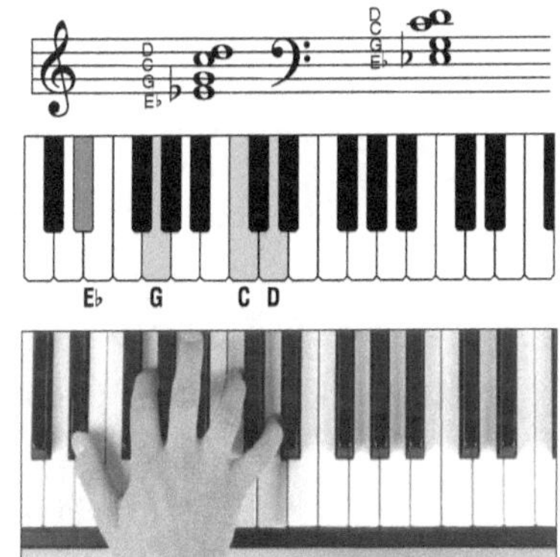

Cm(add2), Cm(add9) Third Inversion

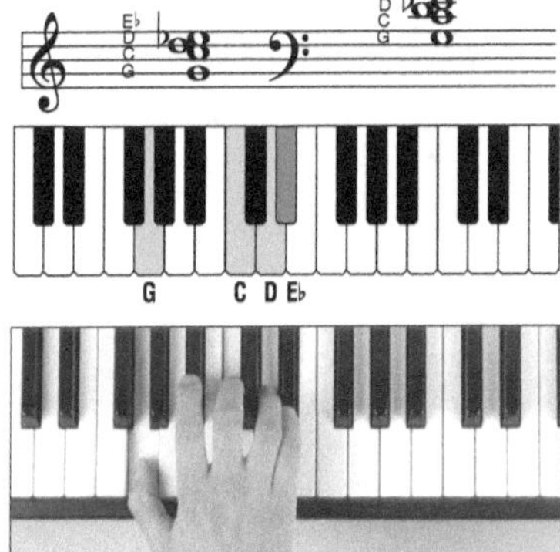

Cm6 Root Position

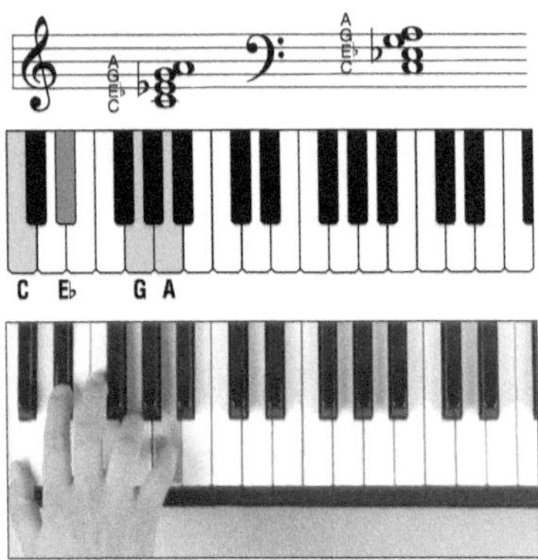

Cm6 First Inversion

Cm6 Second Inversion

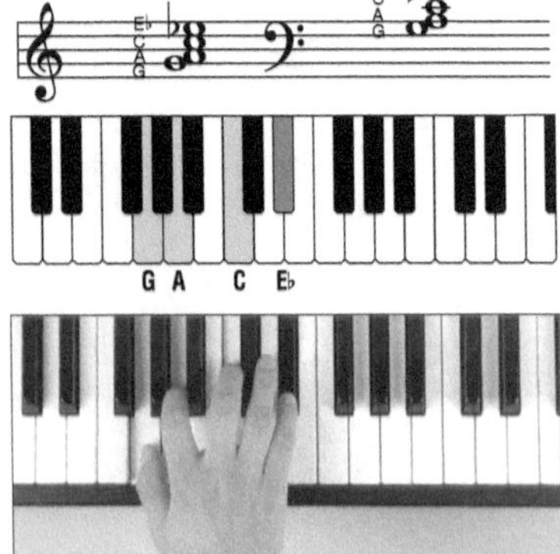

Cm6 Third Inversion

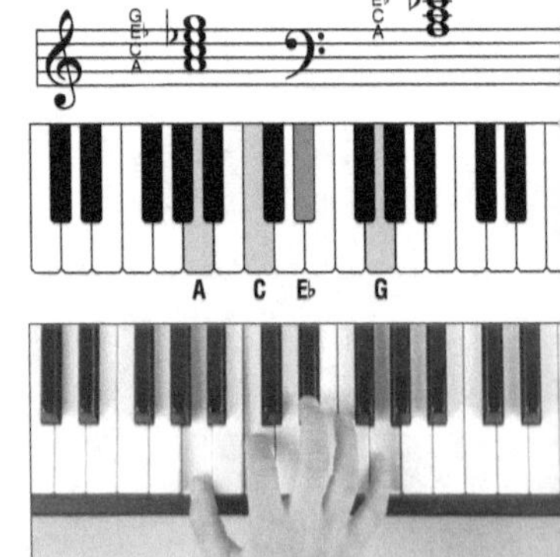

Cm7 Root Position

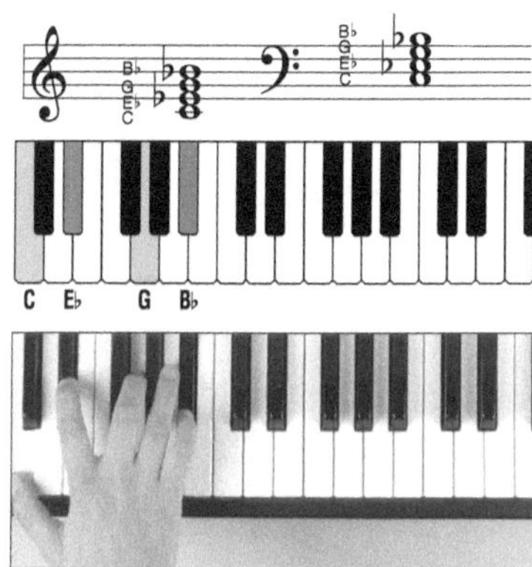

Cm7 First Inversion

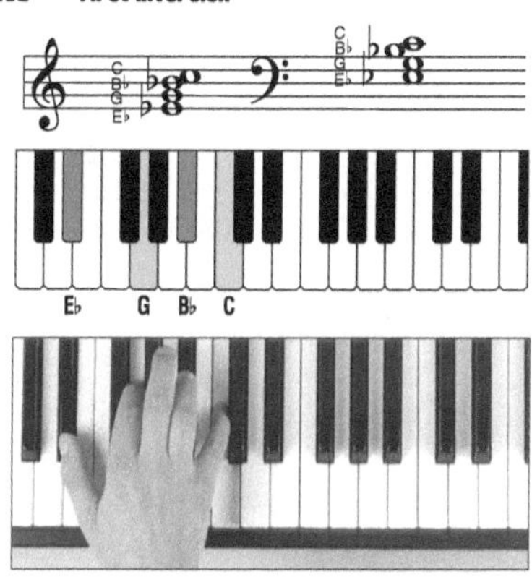

Cm7 Second Inversion

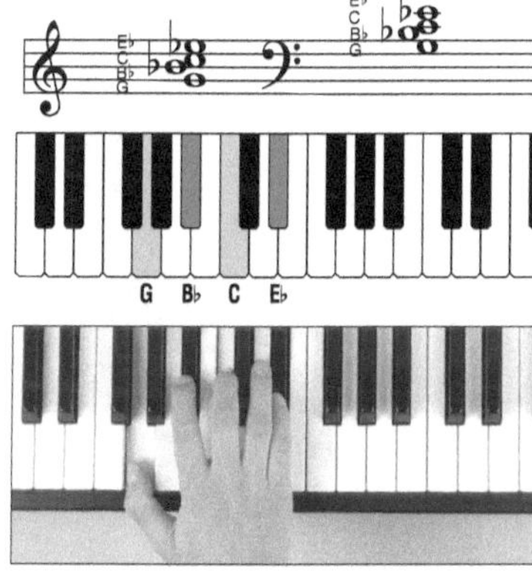

Cm7 Third Inversion

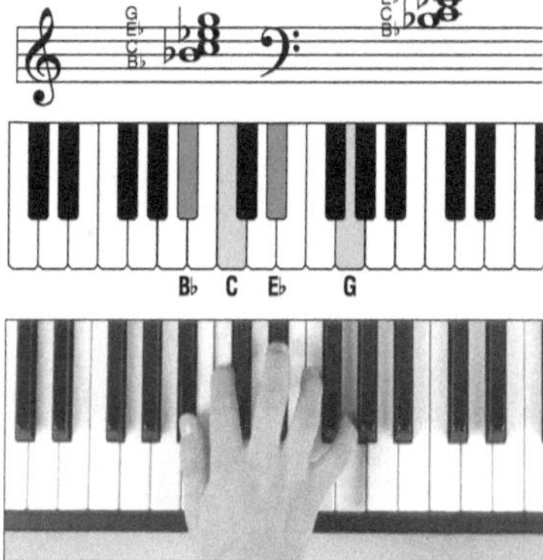

Cm(maj7) Root Position

B G E♭ C

B G E♭ C

C E♭ G B

Cm(maj7) First Inversion

Cm(maj7) Second Inversion

Cm(maj7) Third Inversion

Cm7♭5 Root Position

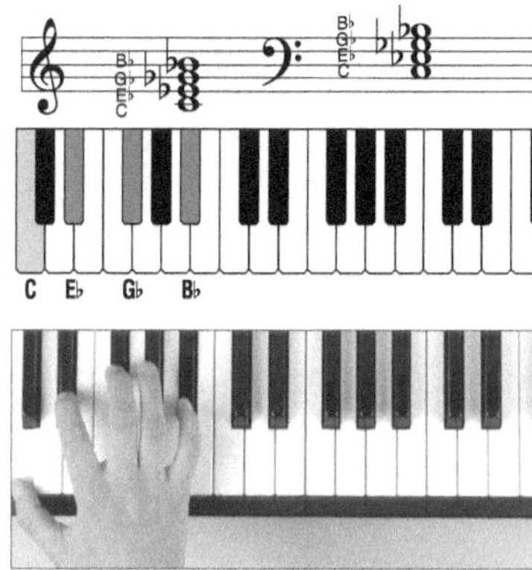

Cm7♭5 First Inversion

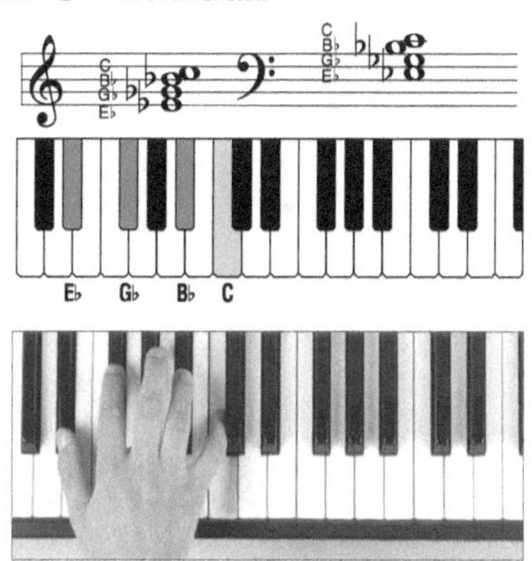

Cm7♭5 Second Inversion

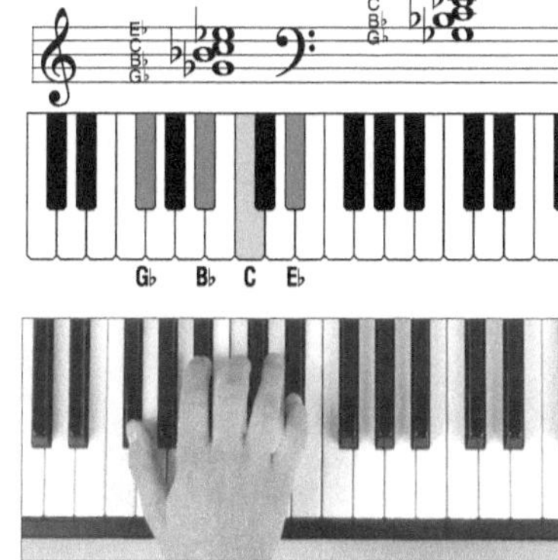

Cm7♭5 Third Inversion

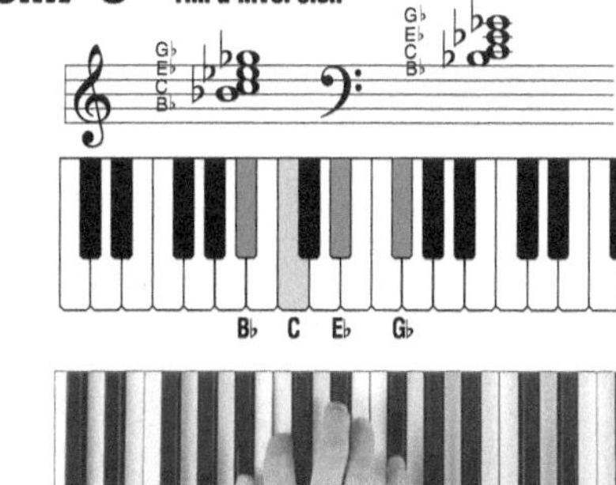

Cdim7 Root Position

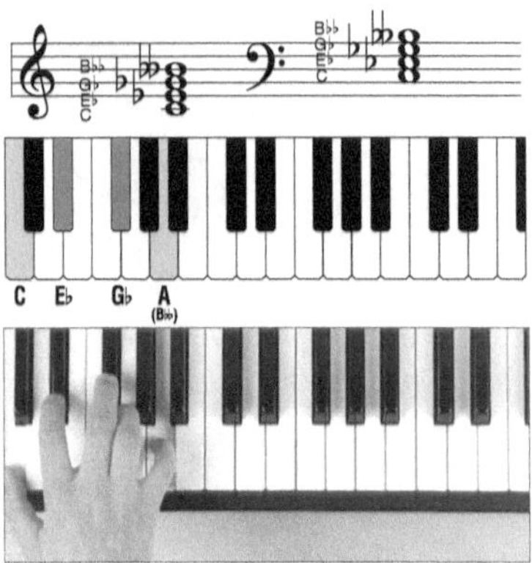

Cdim7 First Inversion

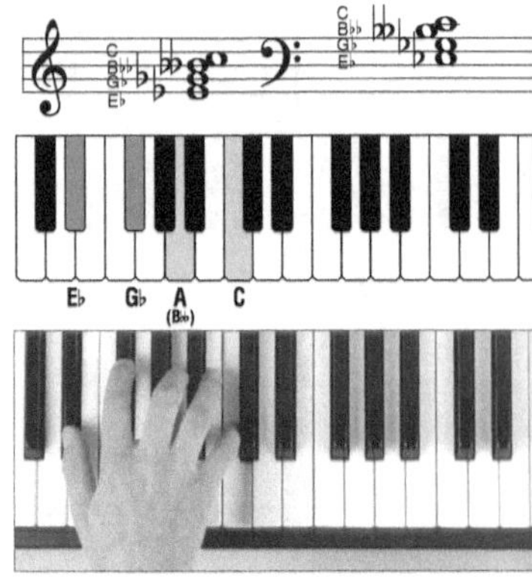

Cdim7 Second Inversion

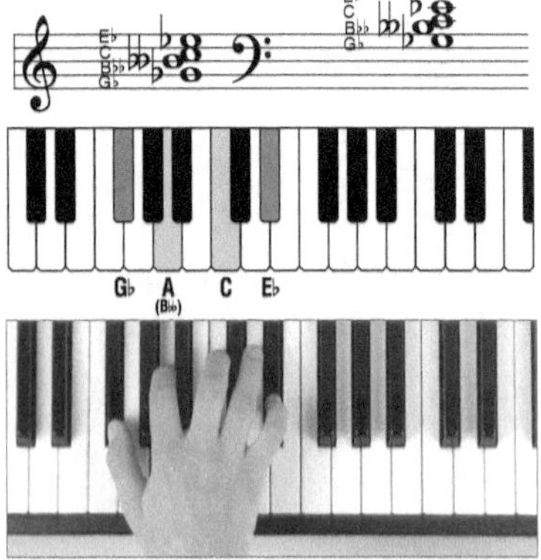

Cdim7 Third Inversion

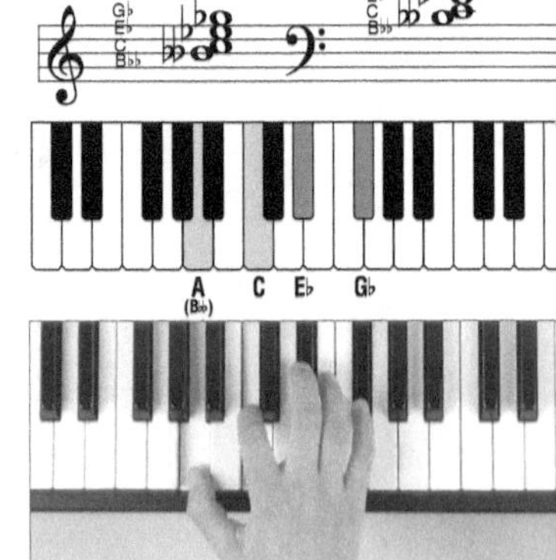

Cdim(maj7) Root Position

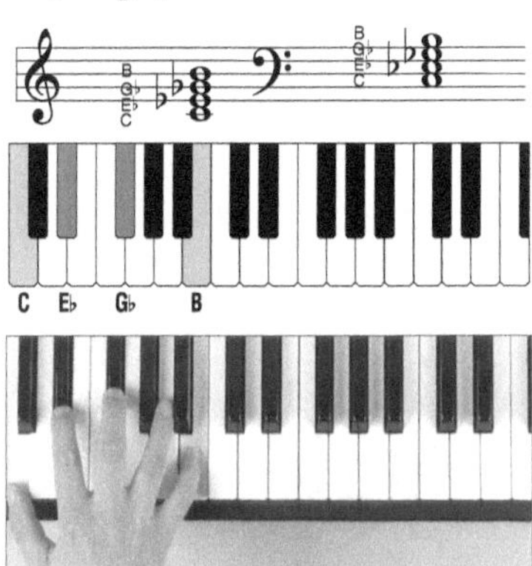

Cdim(maj7) First Inversion

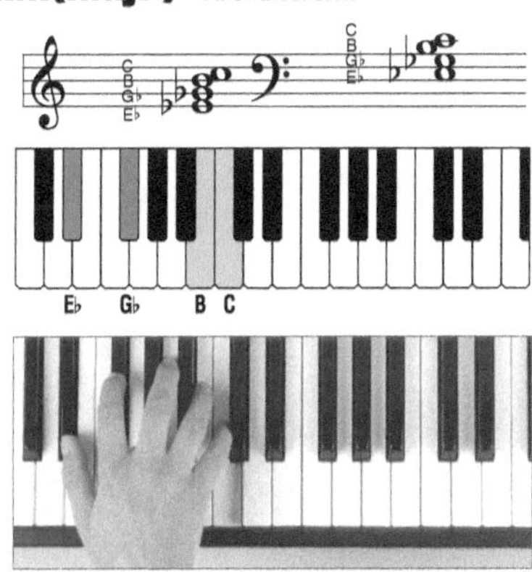

Cdim(maj7) Second Inversion

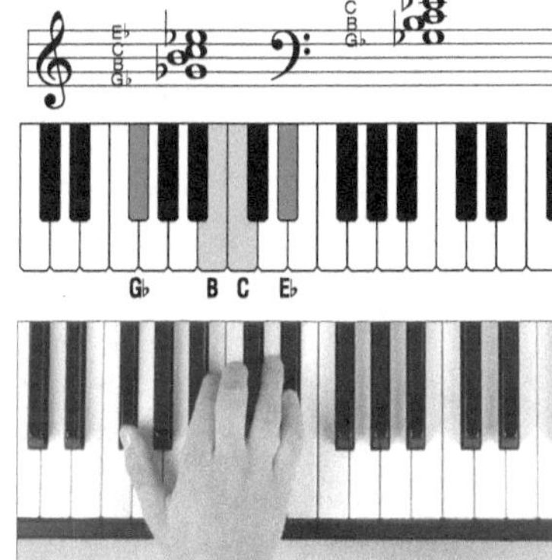

Cdim(maj7) Third Inversion

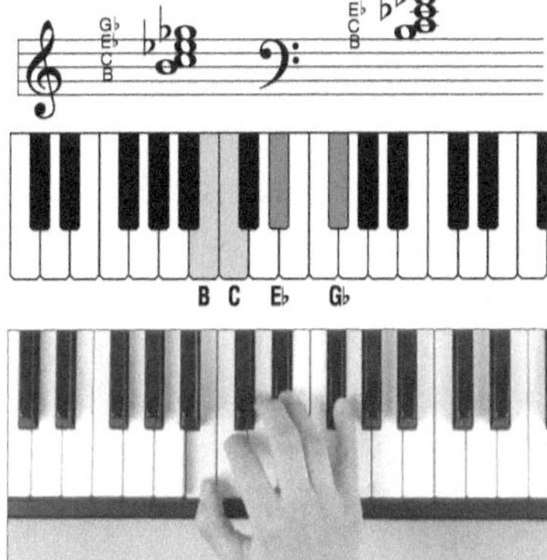

C5

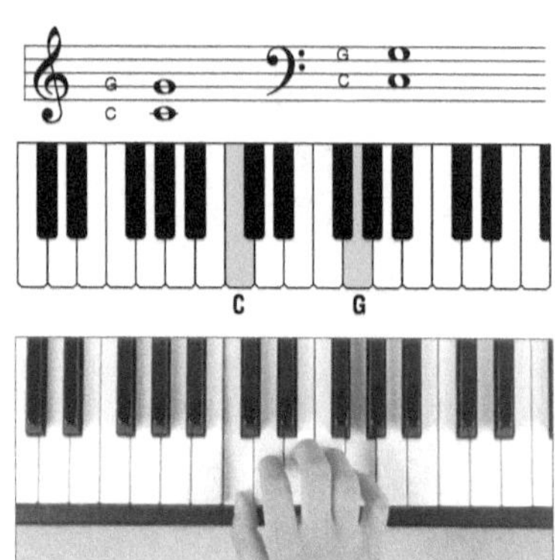

C6/9

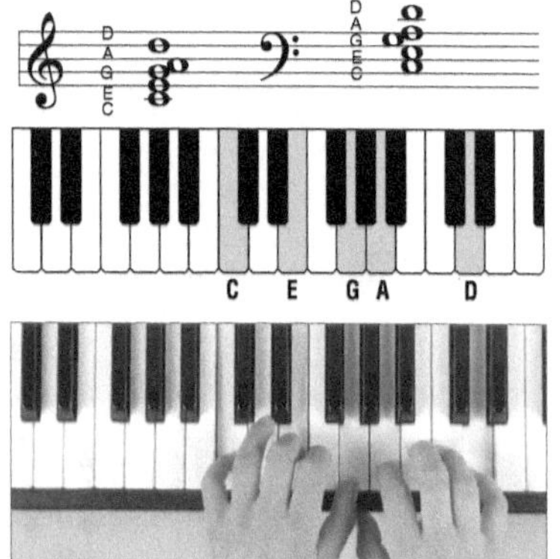

Cmaj6/9

Cmaj7♯11

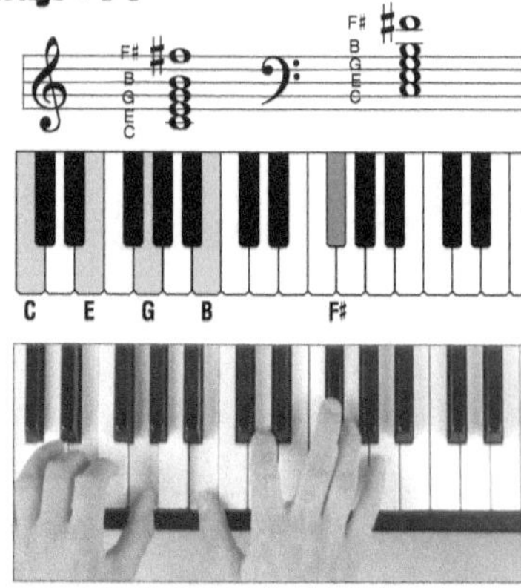

Cmaj9

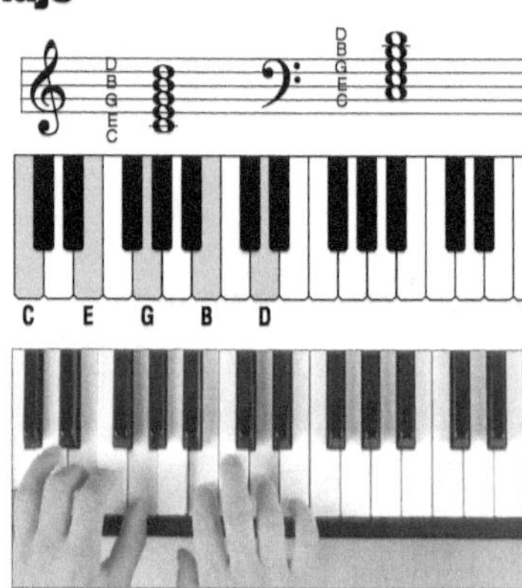

Cmaj9♭5

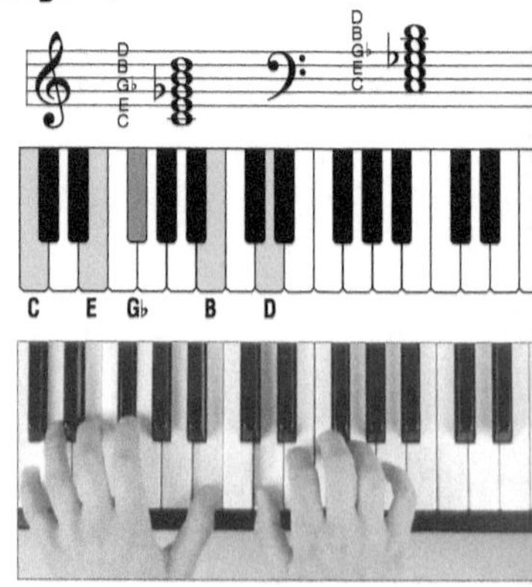

Cmaj9♯5

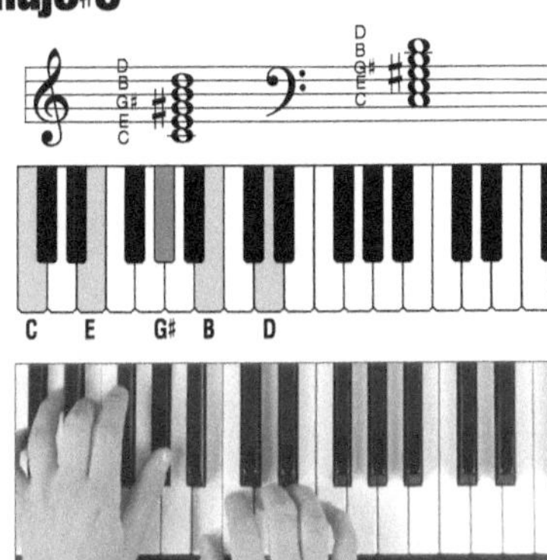

Cmaj9♯11

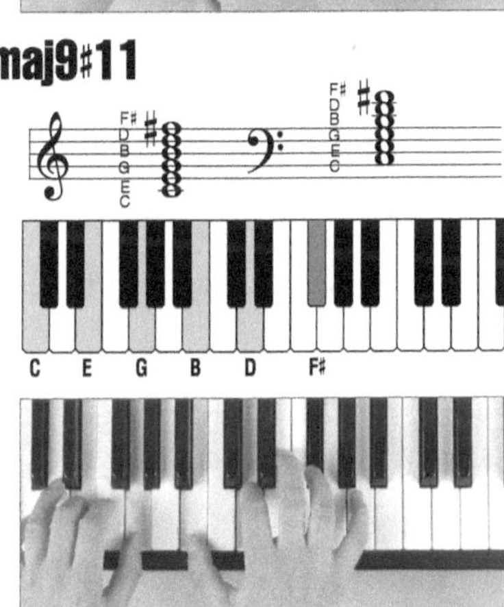

Cmaj13

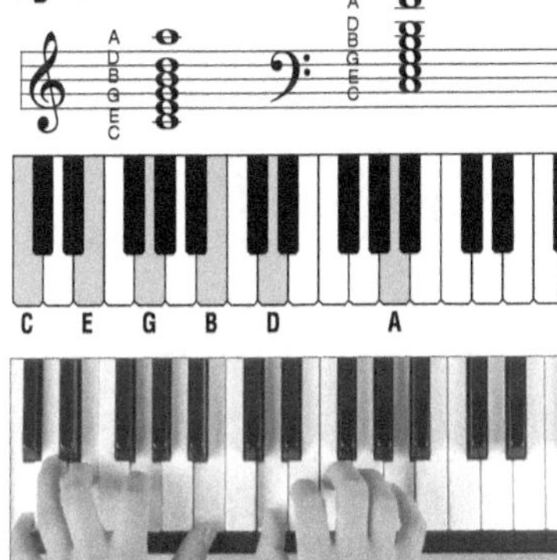

Cmaj13♭5

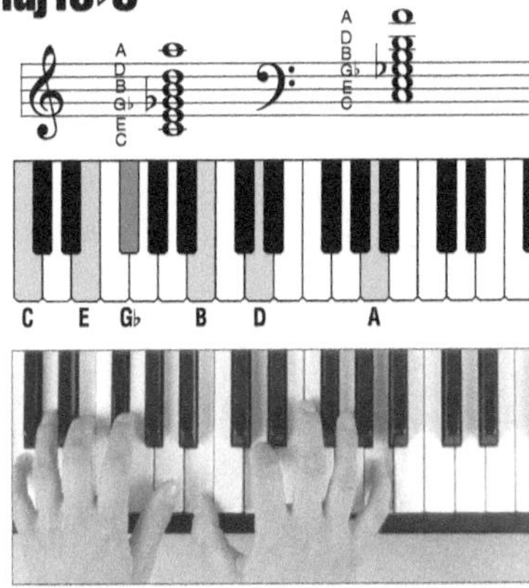

Cmaj13♯11

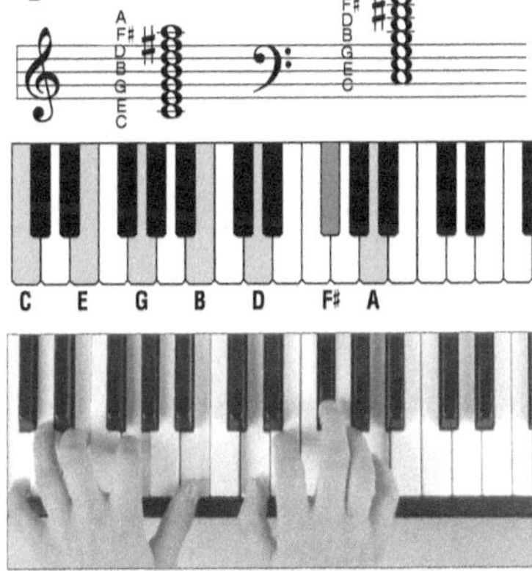

C7♭9

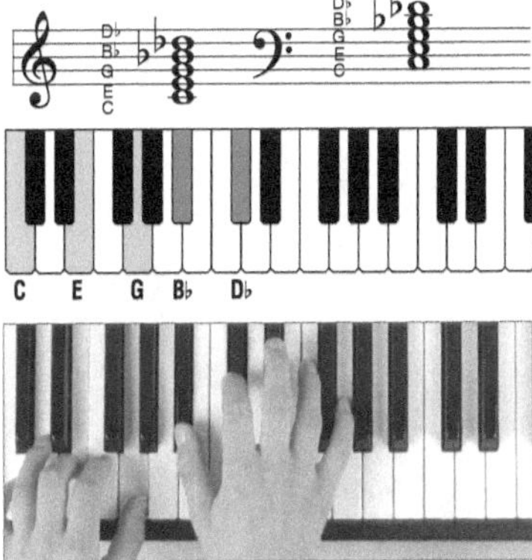

C7♯9

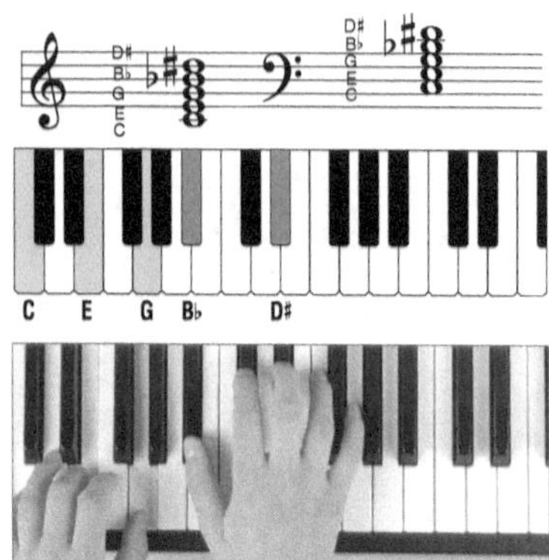

C7♯11

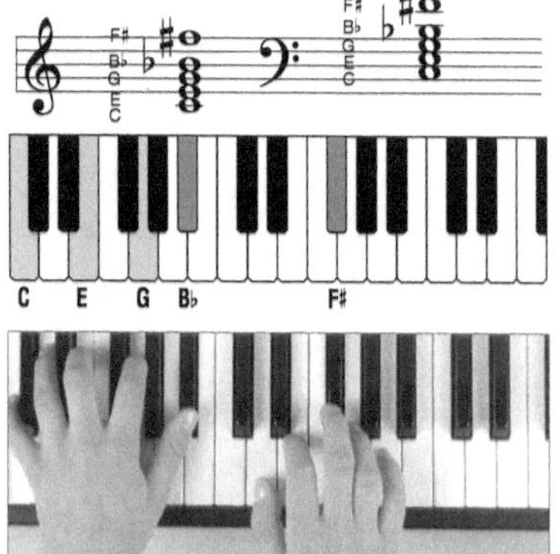

C7♭5(♭9)

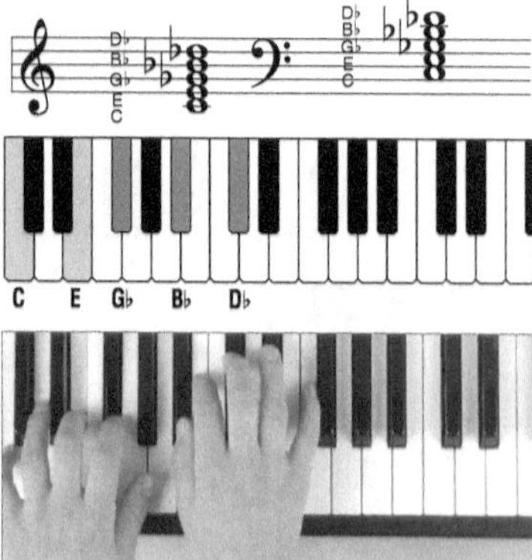

C7♭5(♯9)

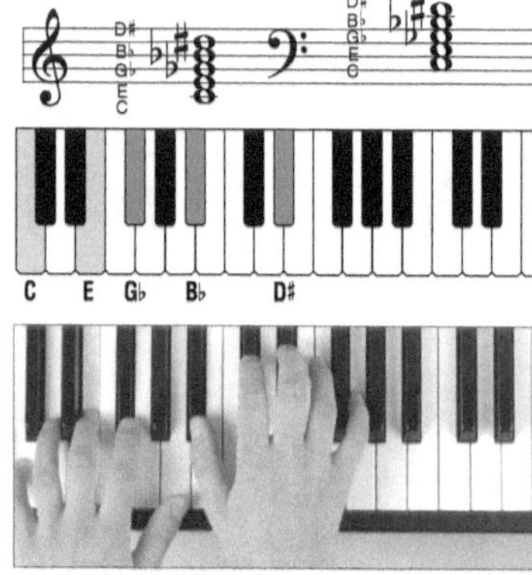

C7♯5(♭9)

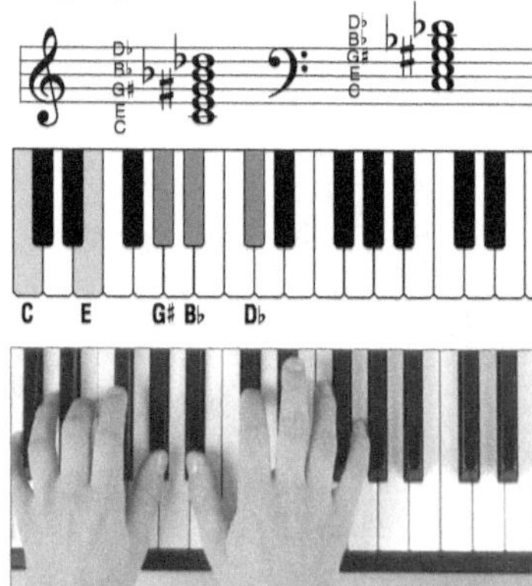

C7♯5(♯9)

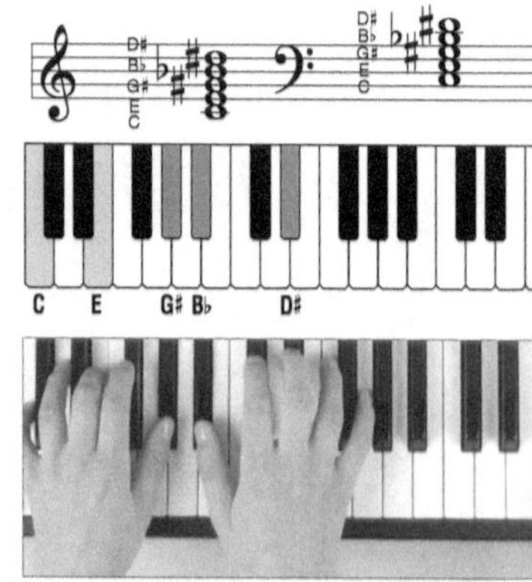

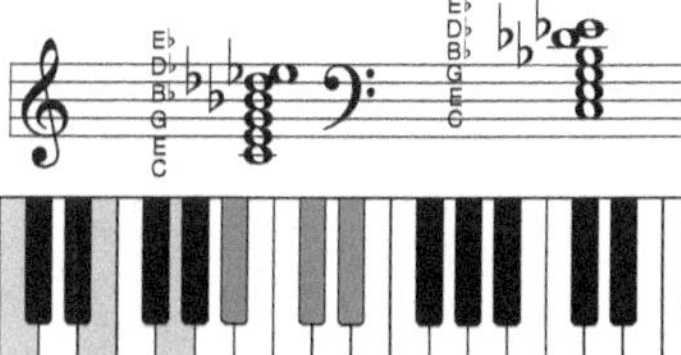

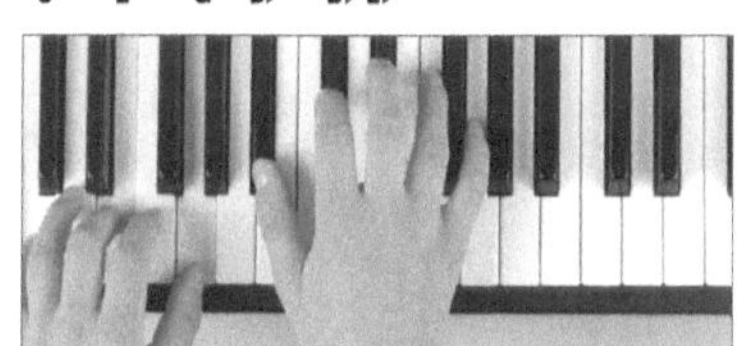

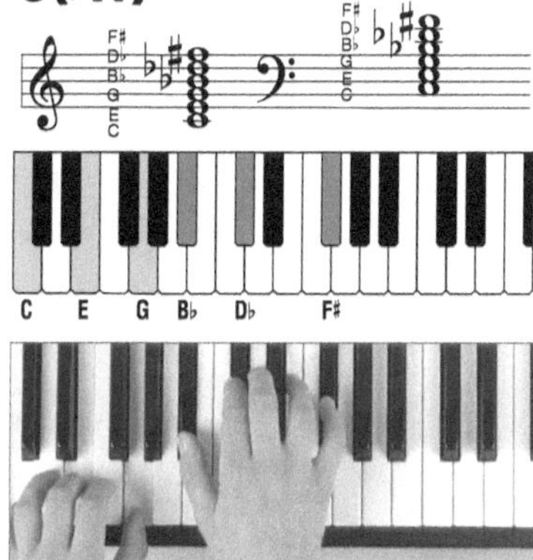

C7(add13)

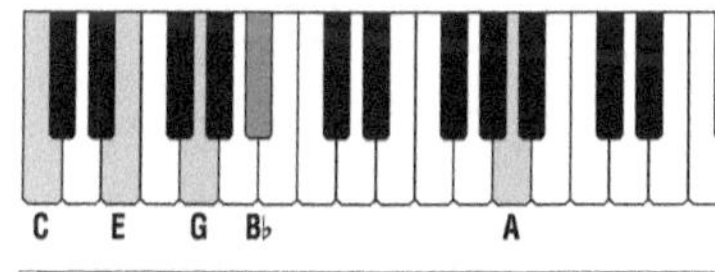

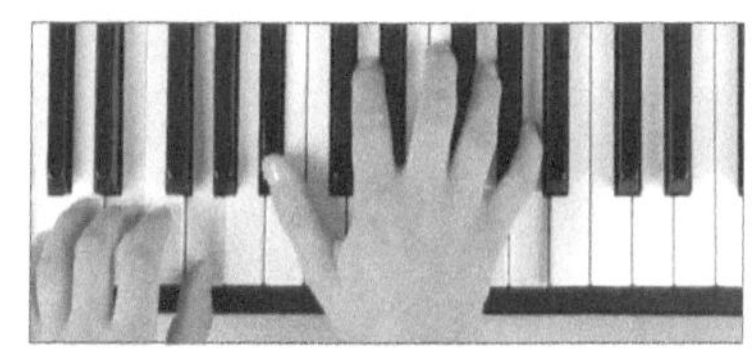

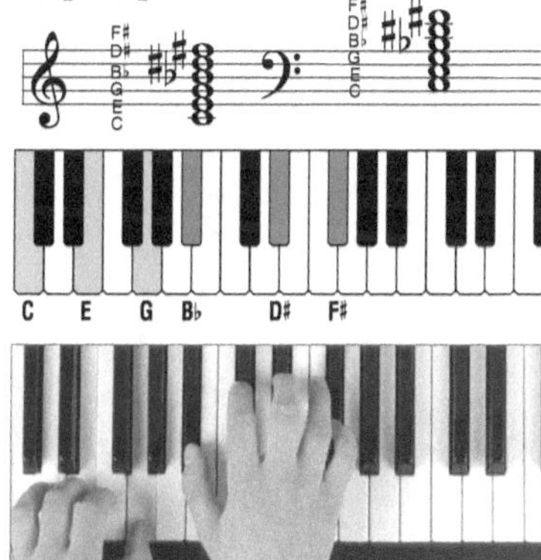

C7♭13

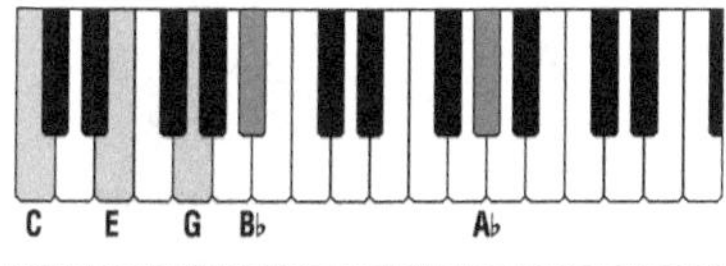

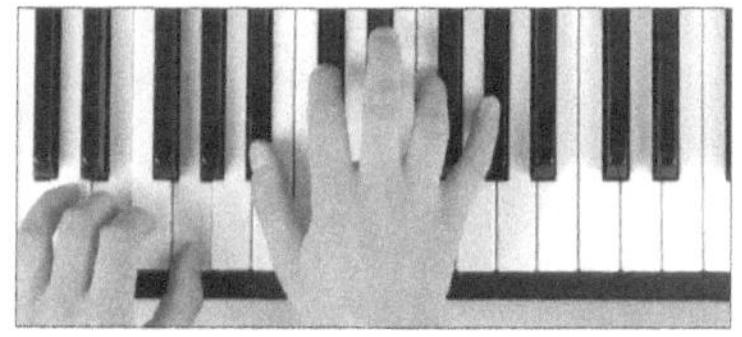

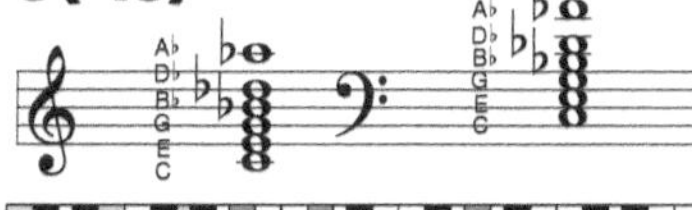

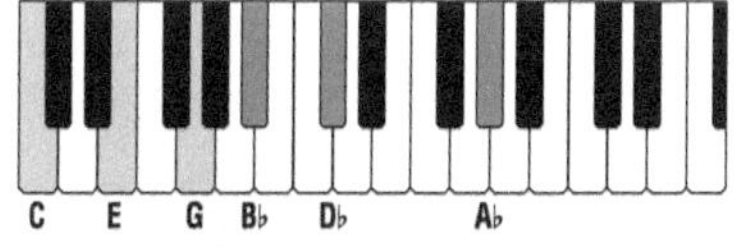

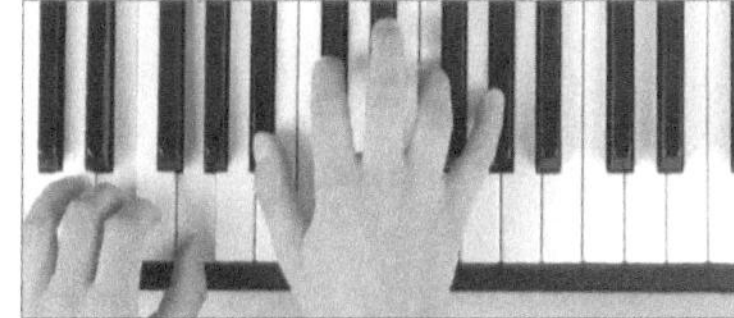

C7♯9(♭13)

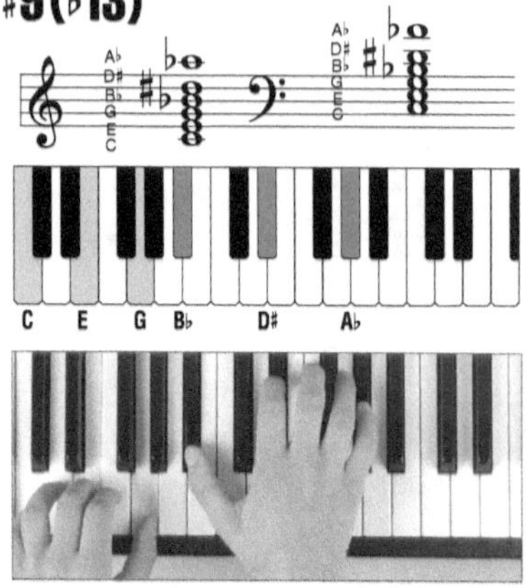

A♭ D♯ B♭ G E C
A♭ D♯ B♭ G E C
C E G B♭ D♯ A♭

C7♯11(♭13)

A♭ F♯ B♭ G E C
A♭ F♯ B♭ G E C
C E G B♭ F♯ A♭

C7♭9(♯9, ♯11)

F♯ E♭ D♭ B♭ G E C
F♯ E♭ D♭ B♭ G E C
C E G B♭ D♭ E♭ F♯

C9

D B♭ G E C
D B♭ G E C
C E G B♭ D

C9(♭5)

D B♭ G♭ E C
D B♭ G♭ E C
C E G♭ B♭ D

C9♯5

D B♭ G♯ E C
D B♭ G♯ E C
C E G♯ B♭ D

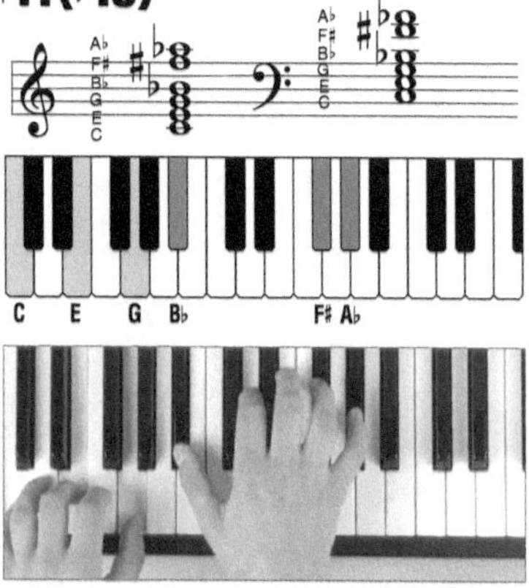

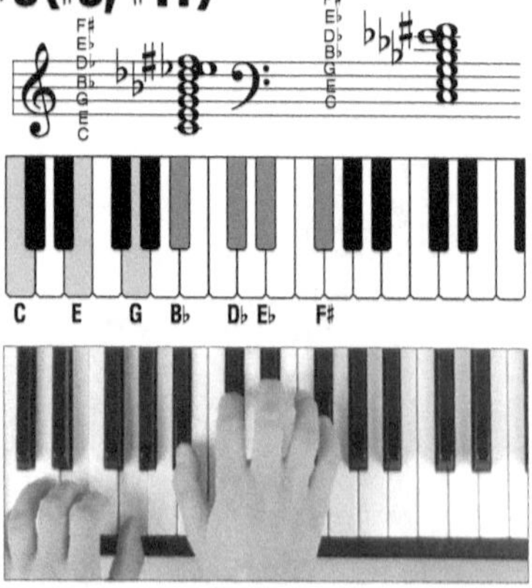

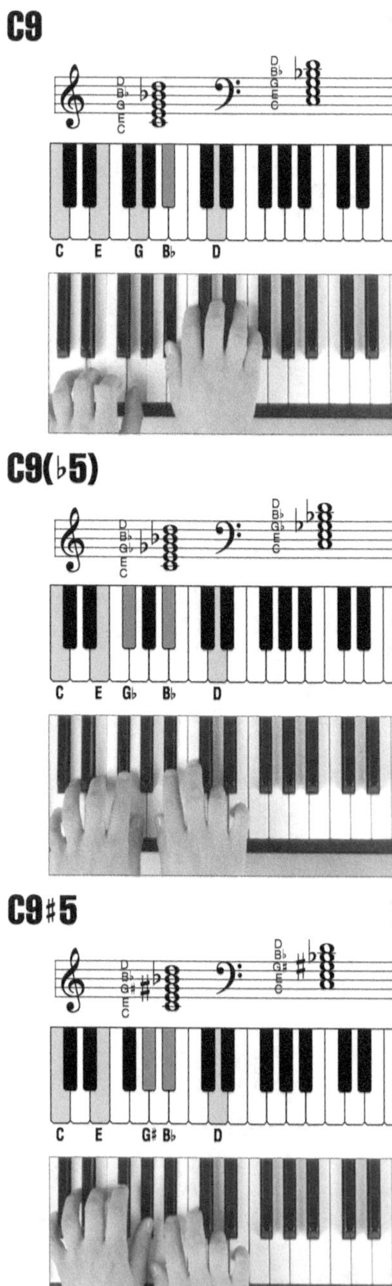

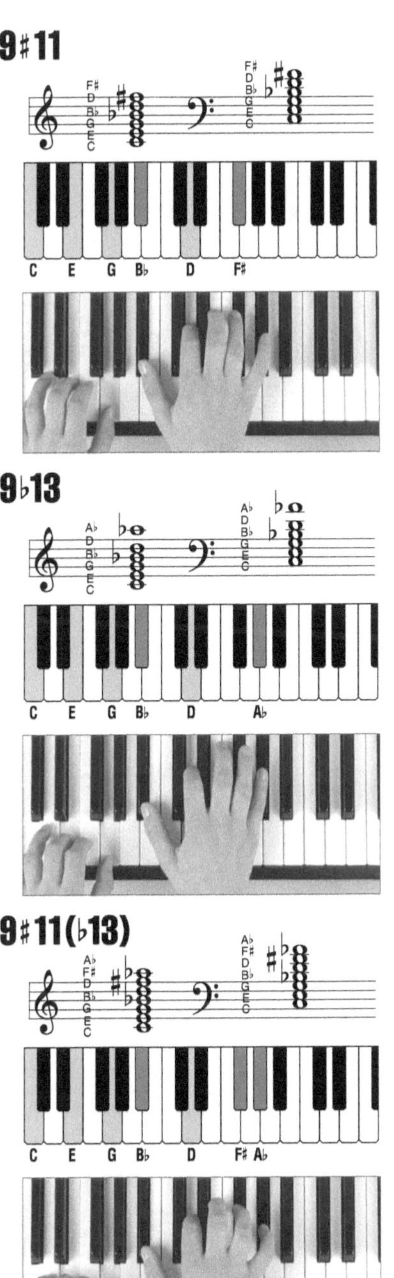
C9♯11
F♯
D
B♭
G
E
C
C E G B♭ D F♯
C9♭13
A♭
D
B♭
G
E
C
C E G B♭ D A♭
C9♯11(♭13)
A♭
F♯
D
B♭
G
E
C
C E G B♭ D F♯ A♭

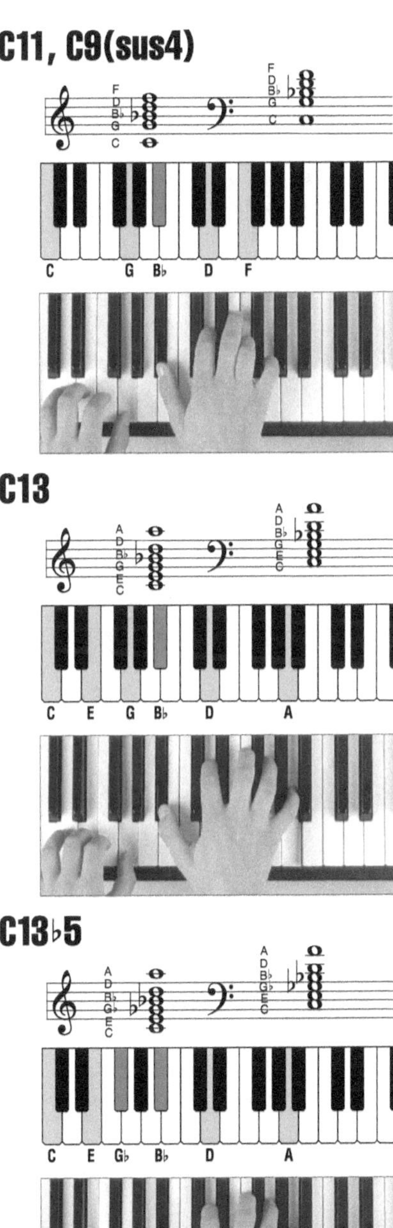
C11, C9(sus4)
F
D
B♭
G
C
C G B♭ D F
C13
A
D
B♭
G
E
C
C E G B♭ D A
C13♭5
A
D
B♭
G♭
E
C
C E G♭ B♭ D A

C13♭9

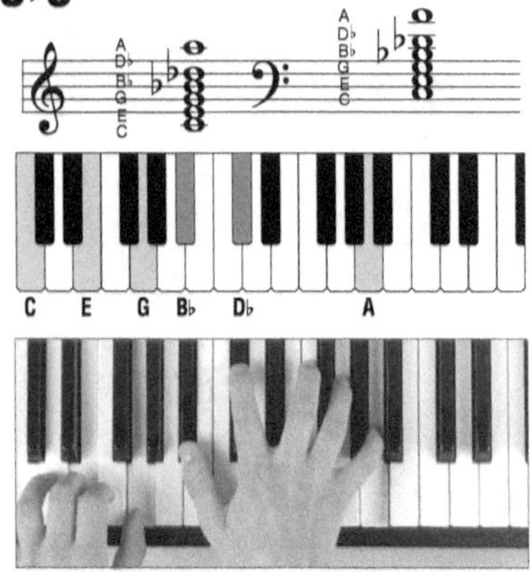

A D♭ B♭ G E C
A D♭ B♭ G E C
C E G B♭ D♭ A

C13♯9

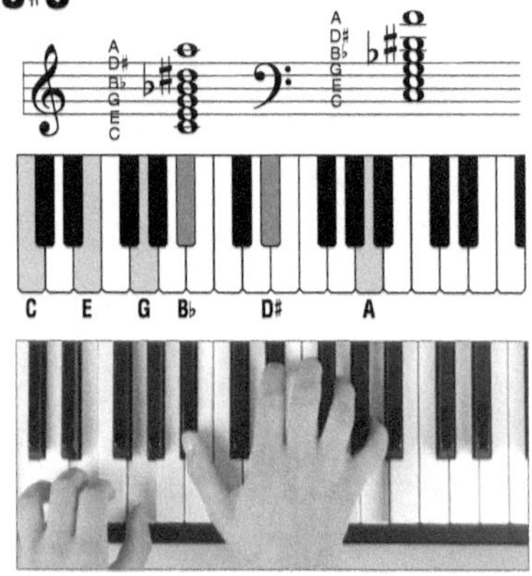

A D♯ B♭ G E C
A D♯ B♭ G E C
C E G B♭ D♯ A

C13♯11

A F♯ D B♭ G E C
A F♯ D B♭ G E C
C E G B♭ D F♯ A

C13(sus4)

A D B♭ G F C
A D B♭ G F C
C F G B♭ D A

Cm(♯5)

G♯ E♭ C
G♯ E♭ C
C E♭ G♯

Cm$^{6}_{9}$

D A G E♭ C
D A G E♭ C
C E♭ G A D

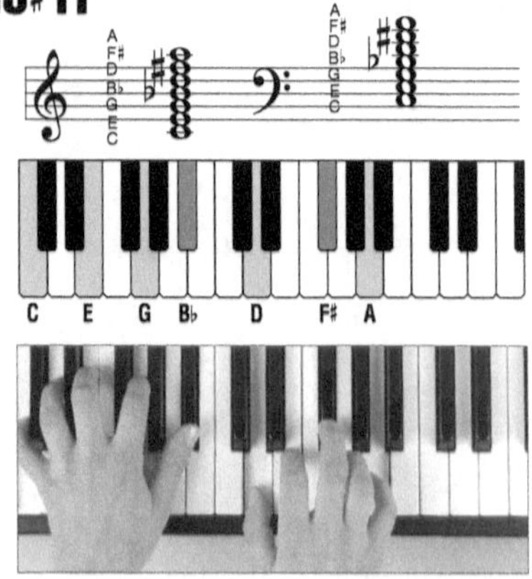

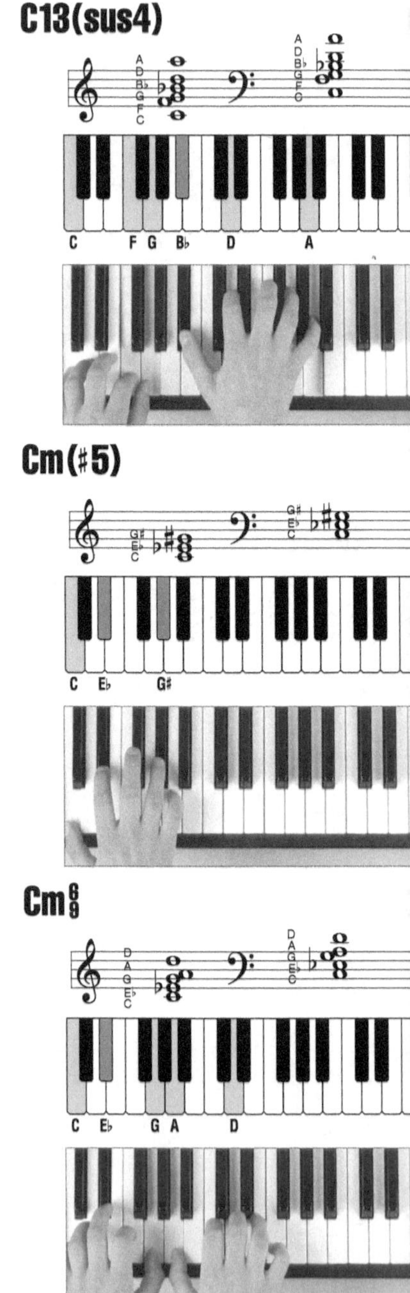

Cm7(add4)

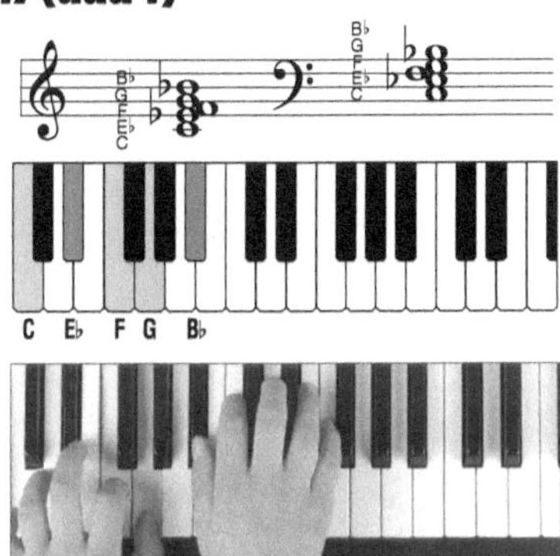

Cm7(add11)

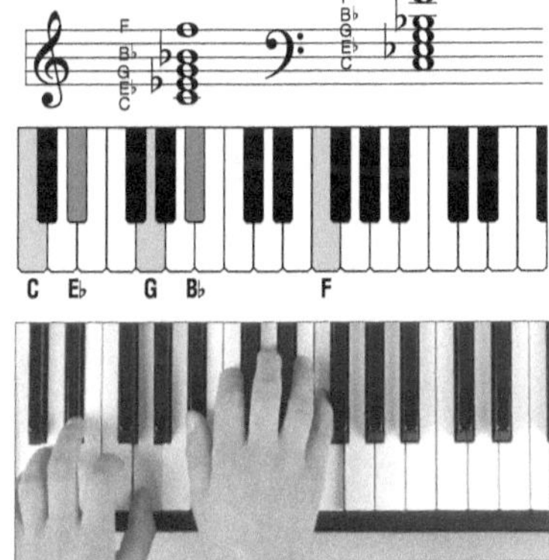

Cm7♭5(♭9)

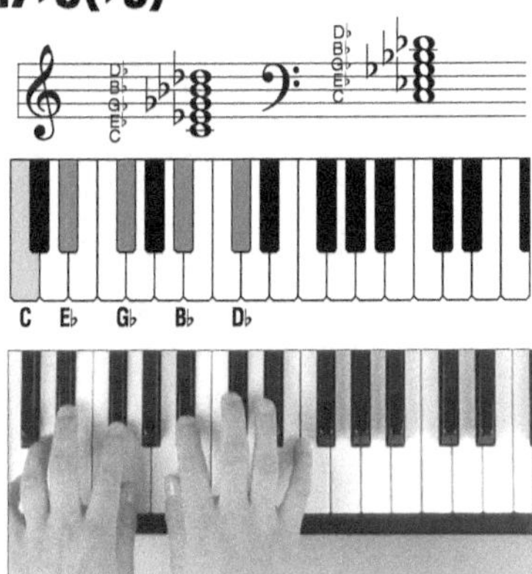

Cm9

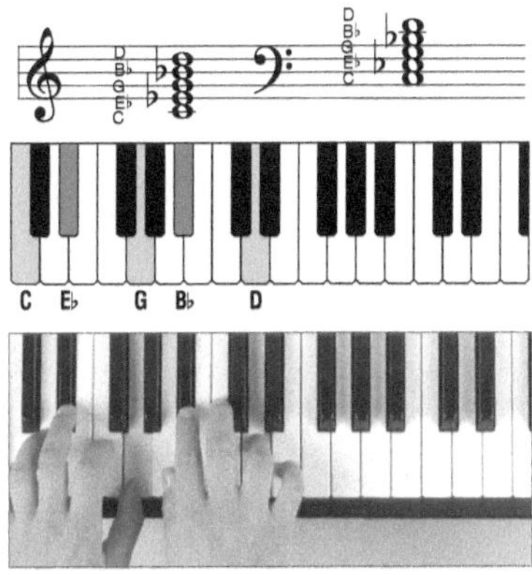

Cm9(maj7)

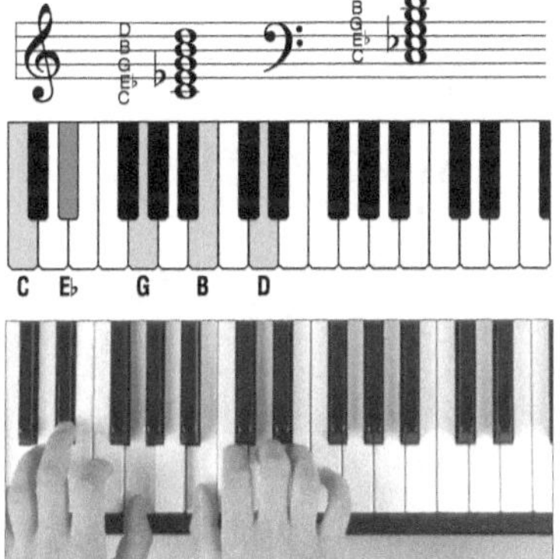

Cm9♭5

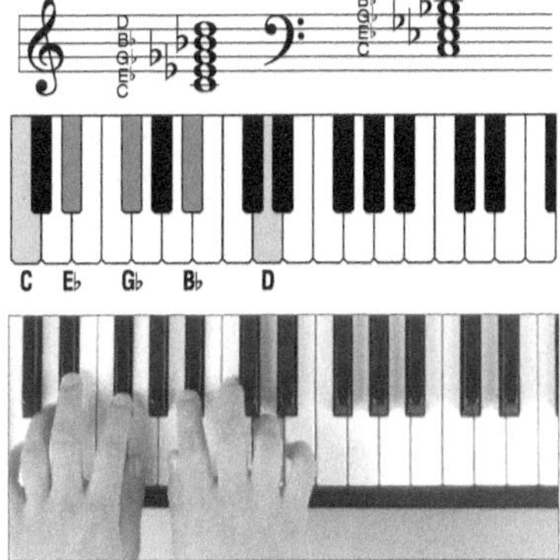

Cm11

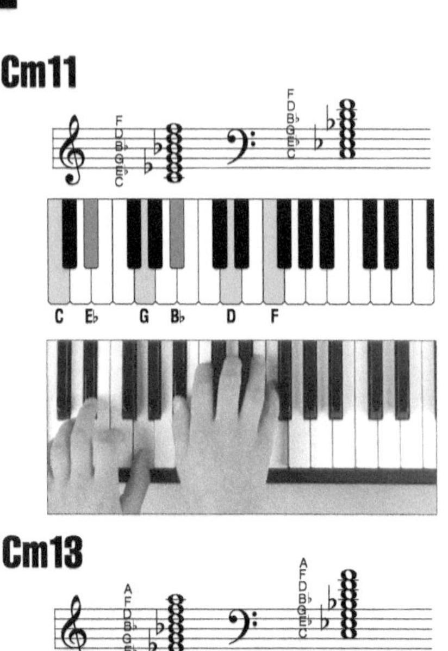

Cm13

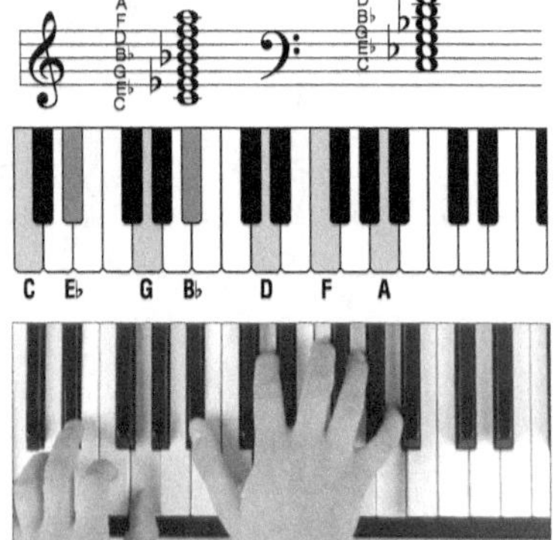

Cdim7(add9)

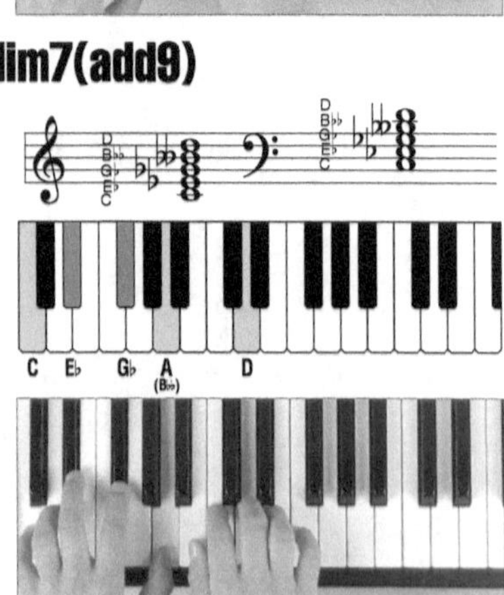

Cm11♭5

Cm11(maj7)

C7alt.

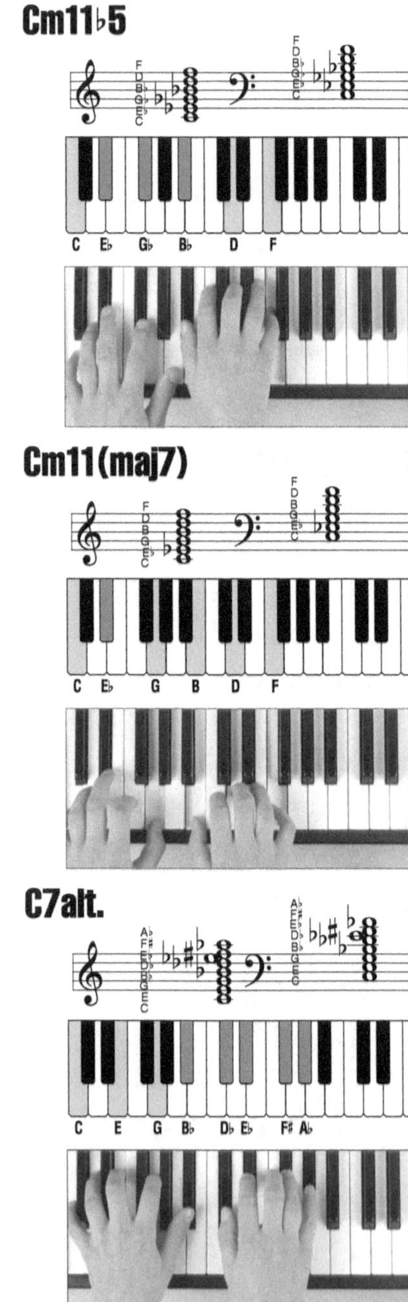

C# Root Position

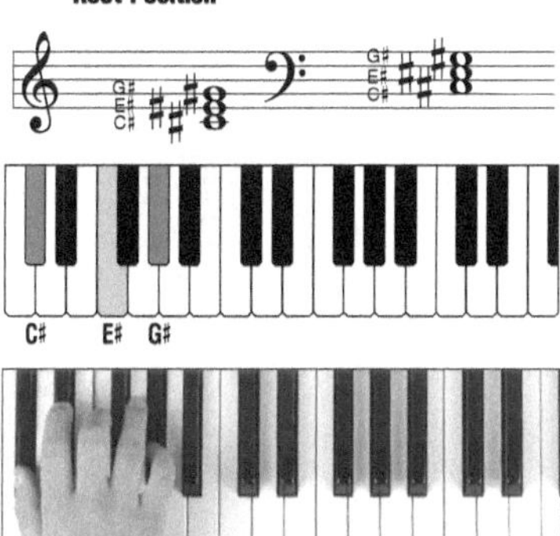

C# First Inversion

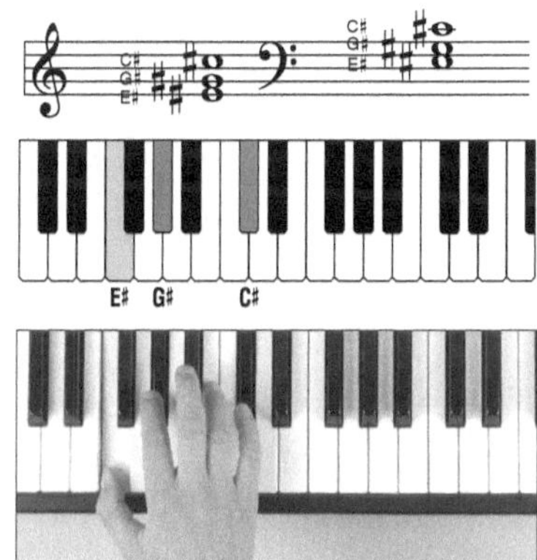

C# Second Inversion

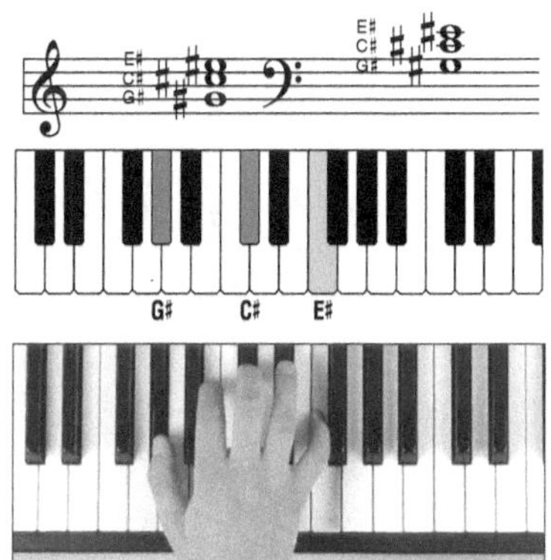

C#m Root Position

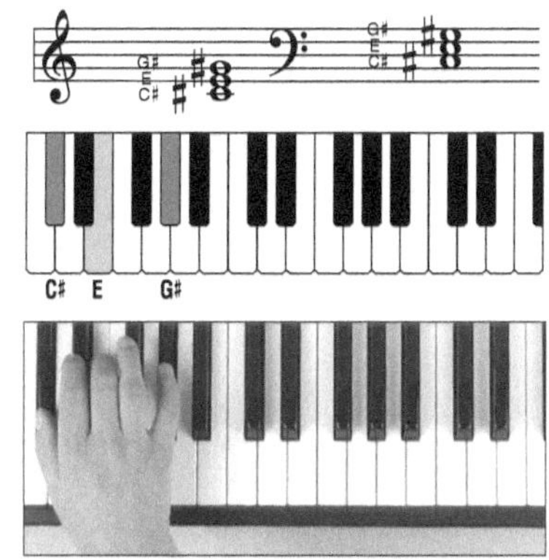

C#m First Inversion

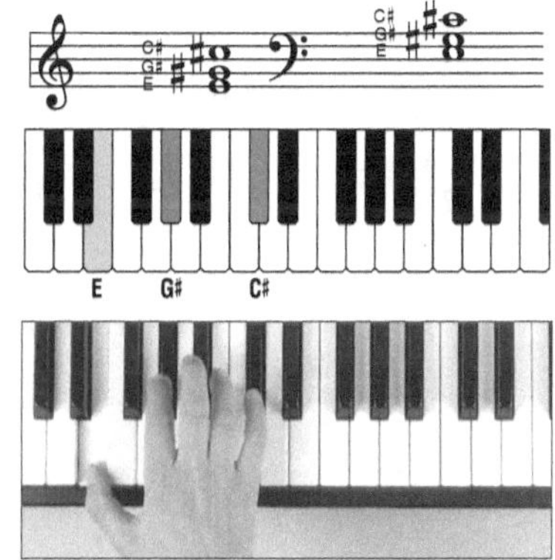

C#m Second Inversion

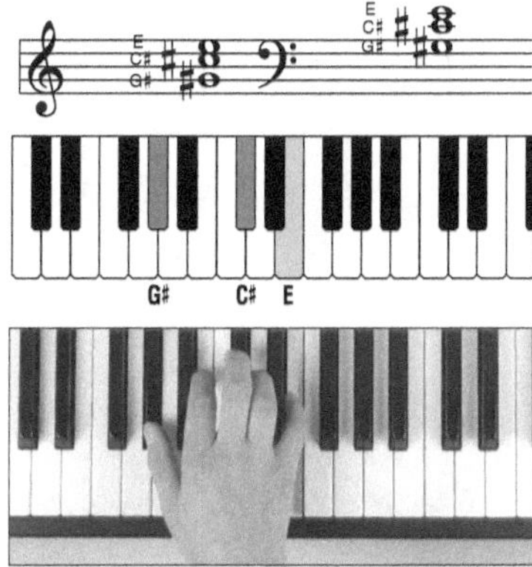

C♯+ Root Position

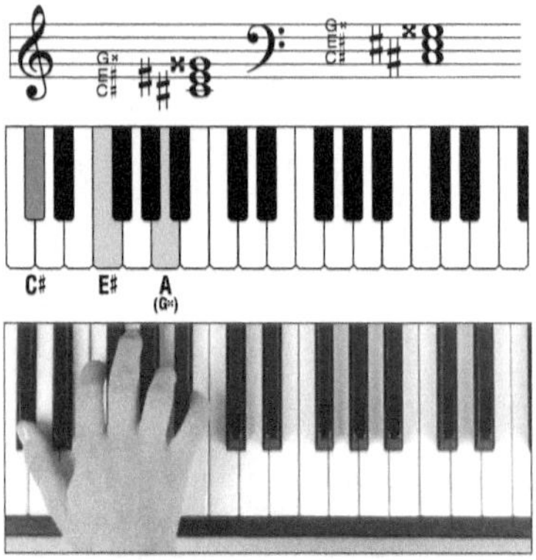

C♯ E♯ A (G𝄪)

C♯+ First Inversion

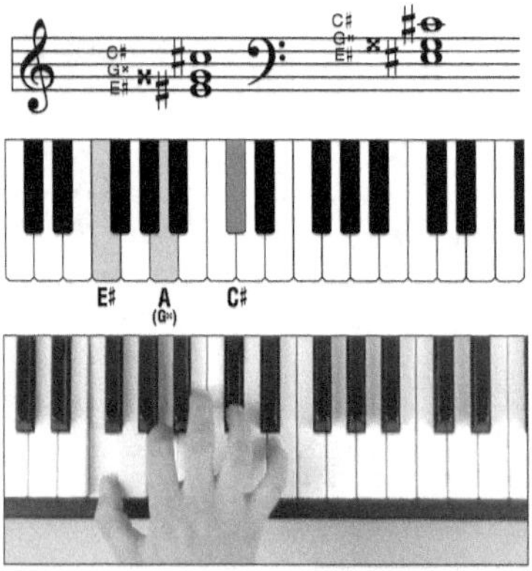

E♯ A (G𝄪) C♯

C♯+ Second Inversion

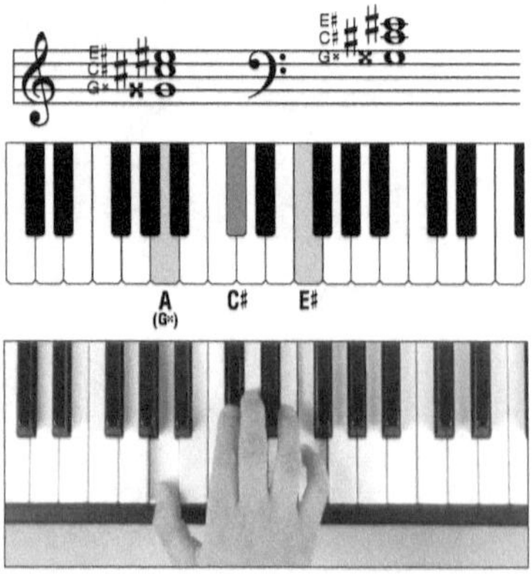

A (G𝄪) C♯ E♯

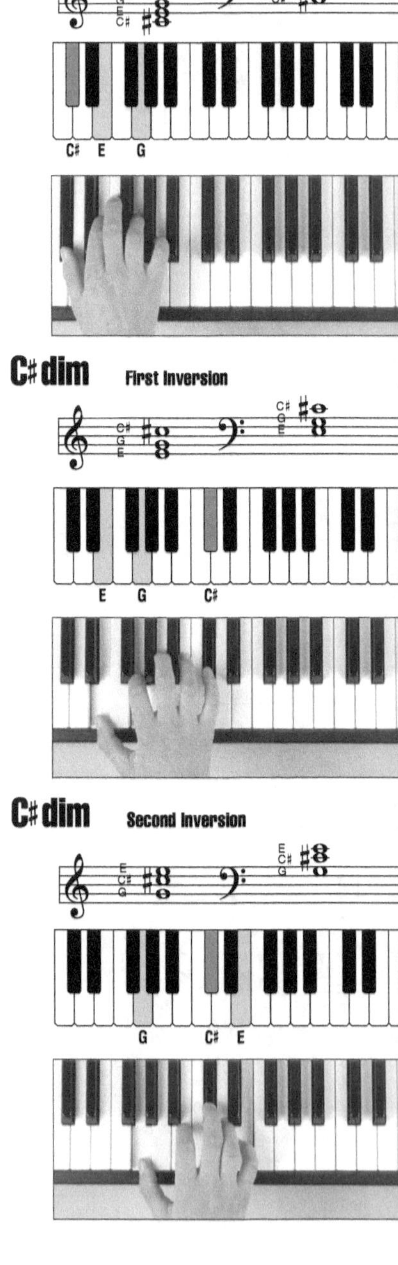

C♯sus Root Position

C♯sus First Inversion

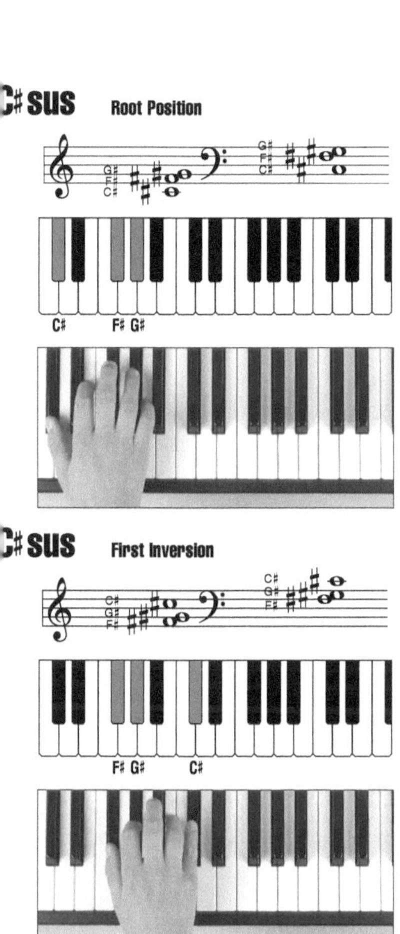

C♯sus Second Inversion

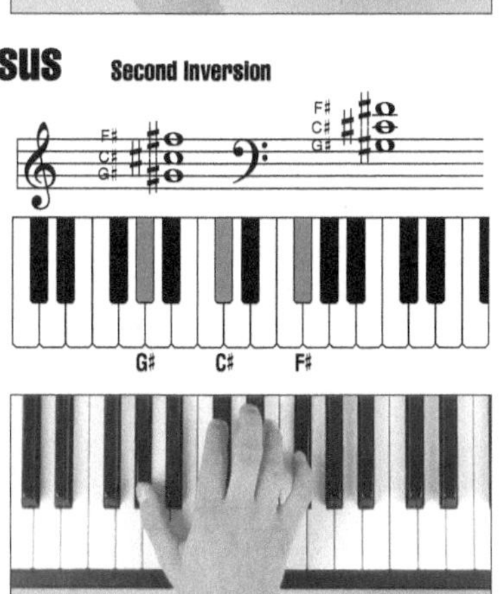

C♯(♭5) Root Position

C♯(♭5) First Inversion

C♯(♭5) Second Inversion

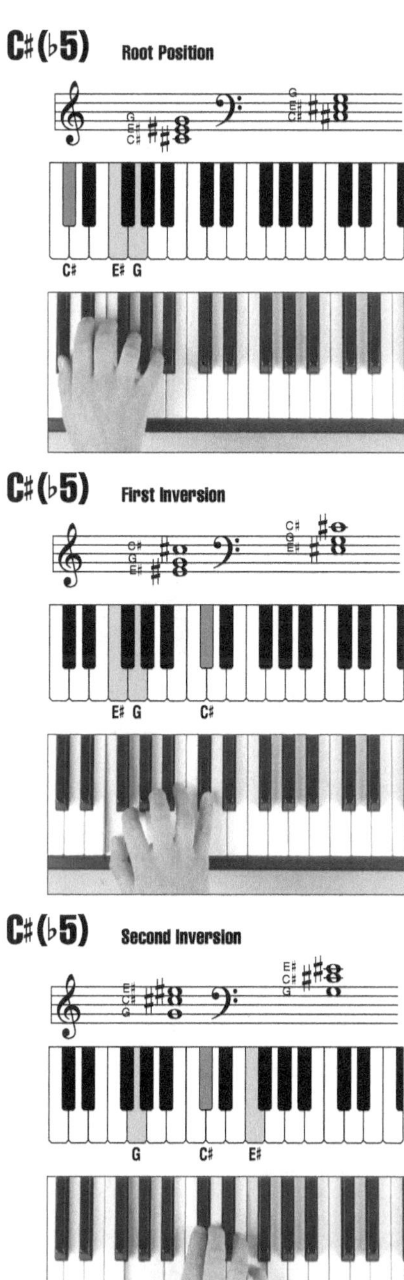

C♯sus2 Root Position

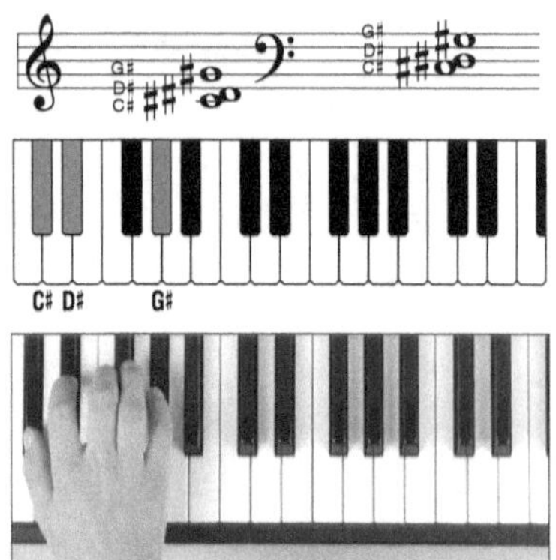

C♯sus2 First Inversion

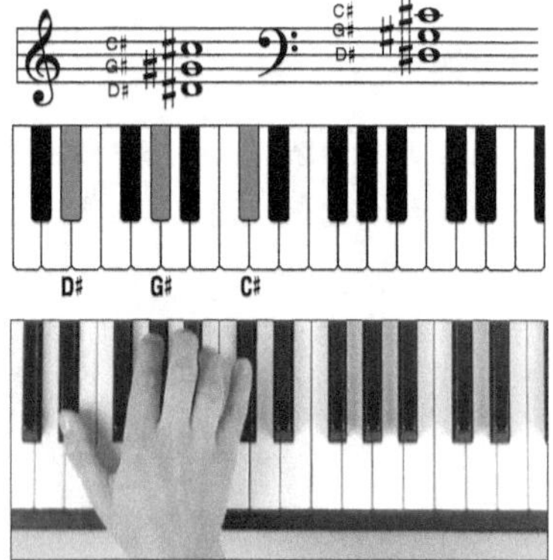

C♯sus2 Second Inversion

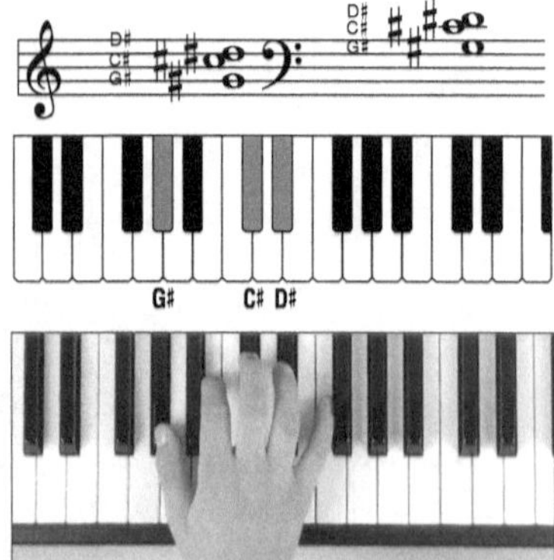

C♯6 Root Position

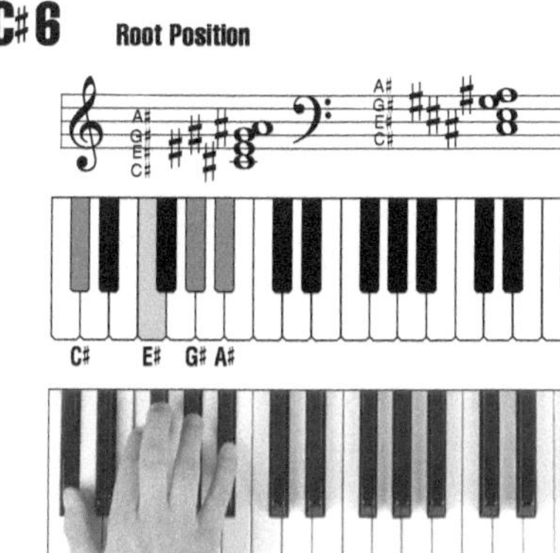

C♯6 First Inversion

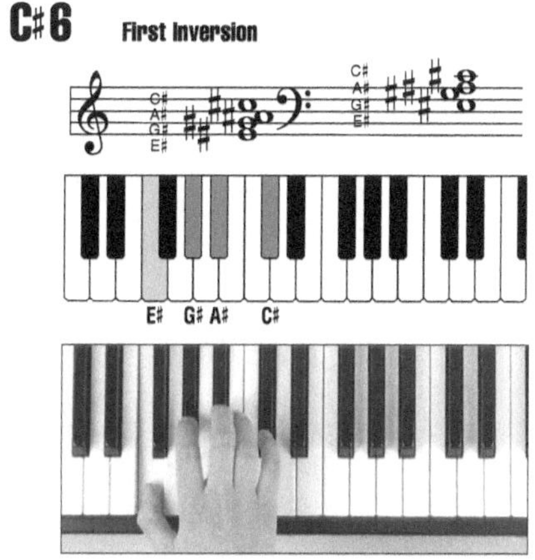

C♯6 Second Inversion

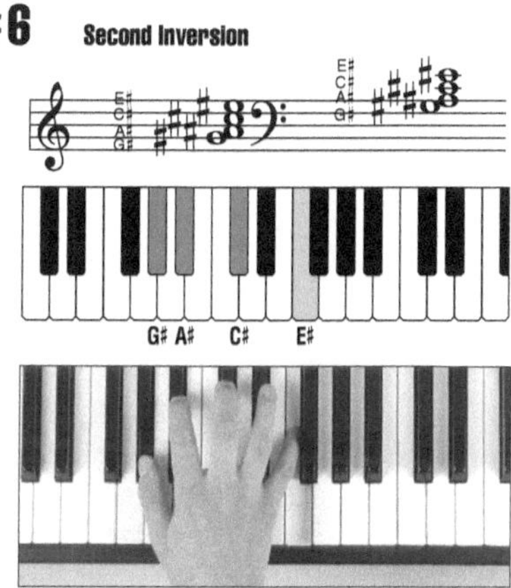

C♯6 Third Inversion

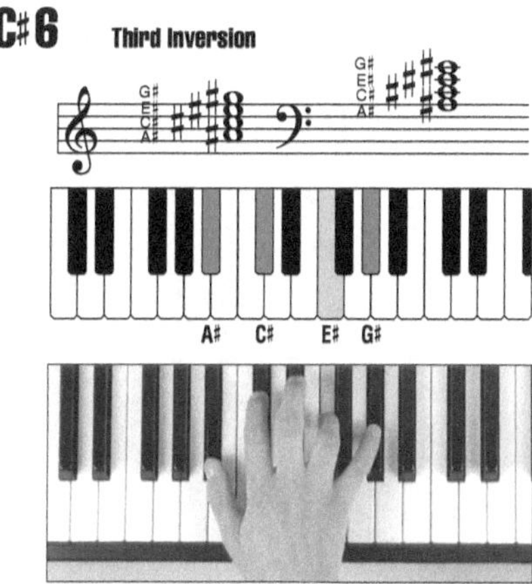

C♯(add2), C♯(add9) Root Position

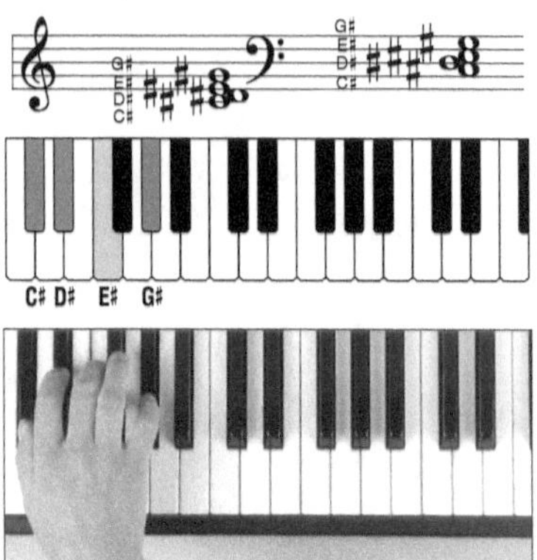

C♯(add2), C♯(add9) First Inversion

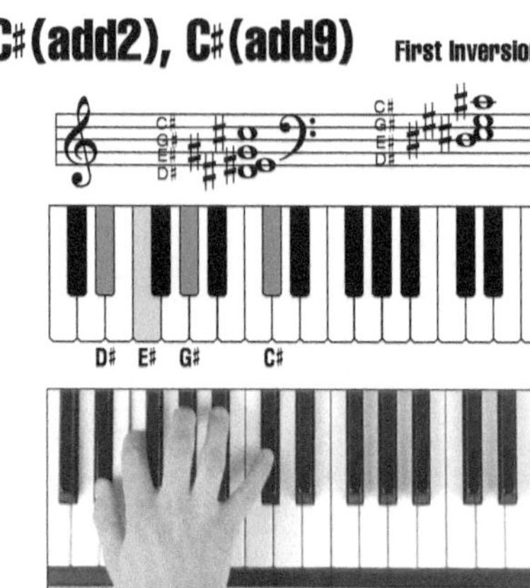

C♯(add2), C♯(add9) Second Inversion

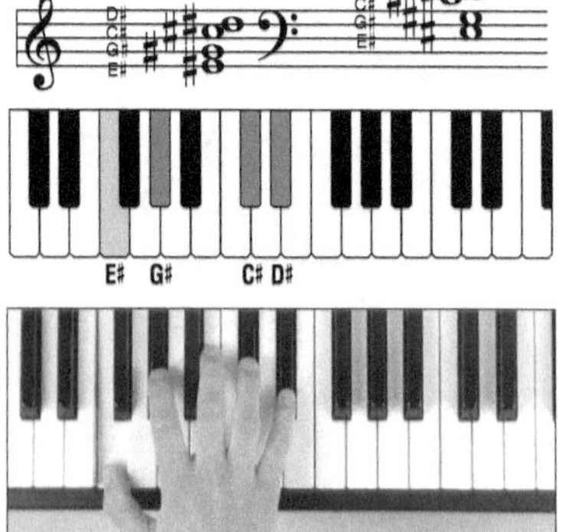

C♯(add2), C♯(add9) Third Inversion

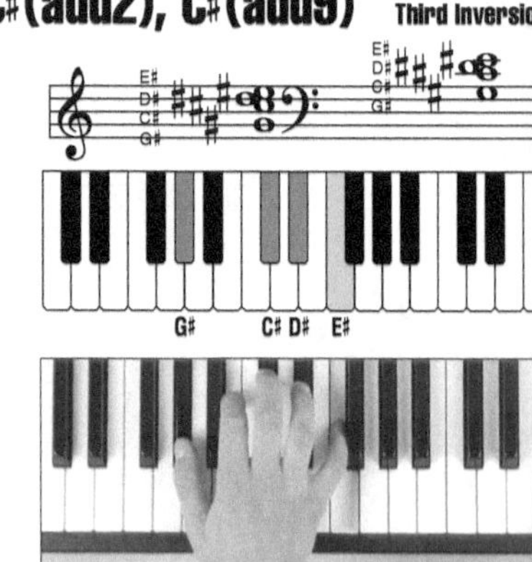

C♯ maj7 Root Position

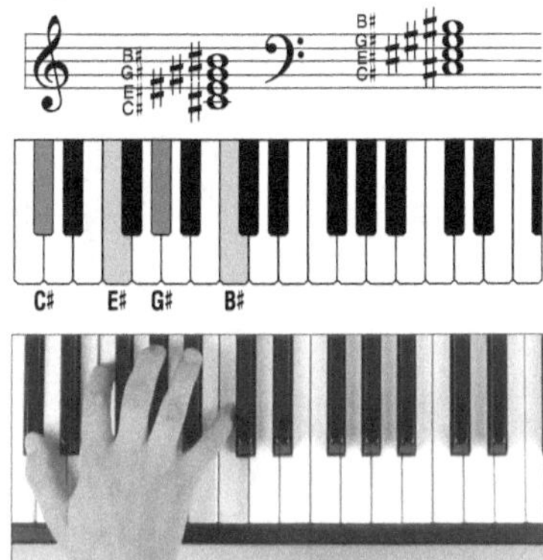

C♯ maj7 First Inversion

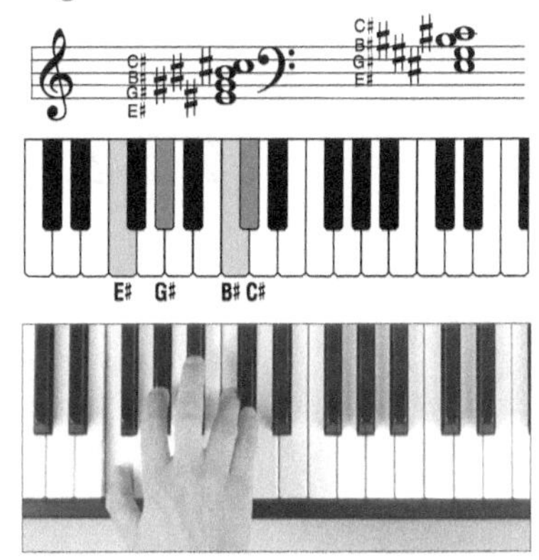

C♯ maj7 Second Inversion

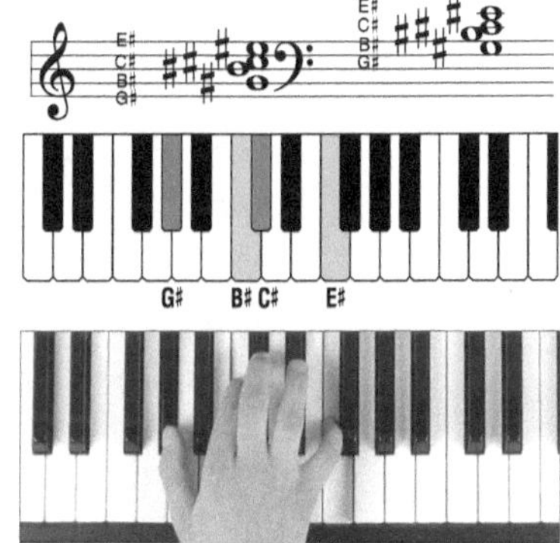

C♯ maj7 Third Inversion

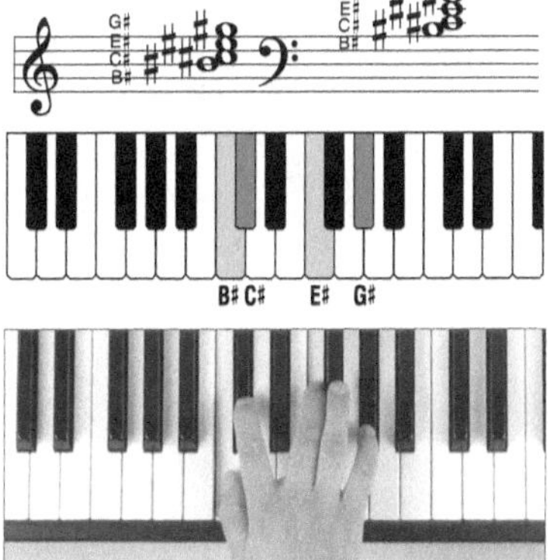

C♯maj7♭5 Root Position

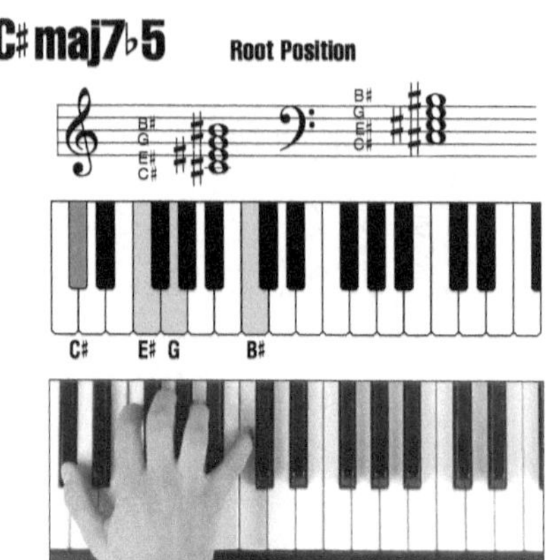

C♯maj7♭5 First Inversion

C♯maj7♭5 Second Inversion

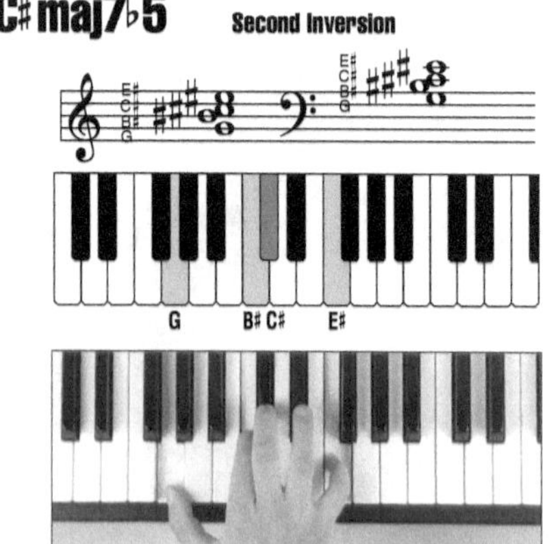

C♯maj7♭5 Third Inversion

C♯maj7♯5 Root Position

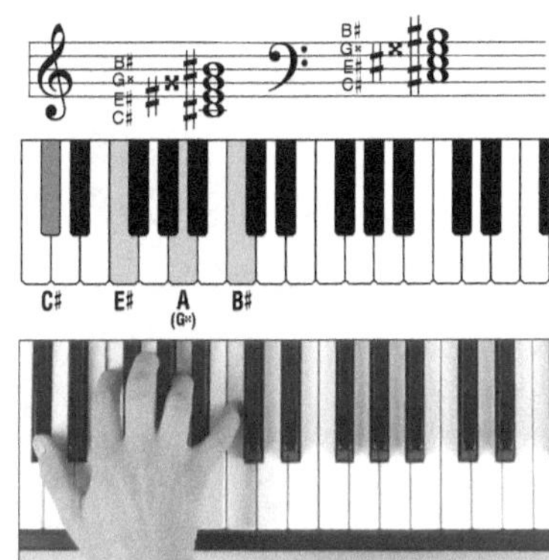

C♯maj7♯5 First Inversion

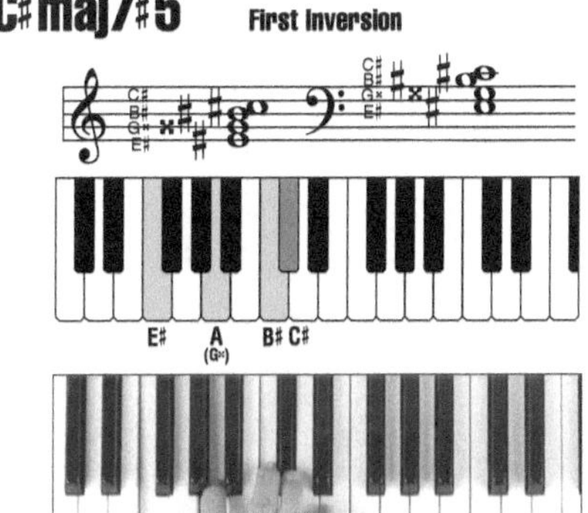

C♯maj7♯5 Second Inversion

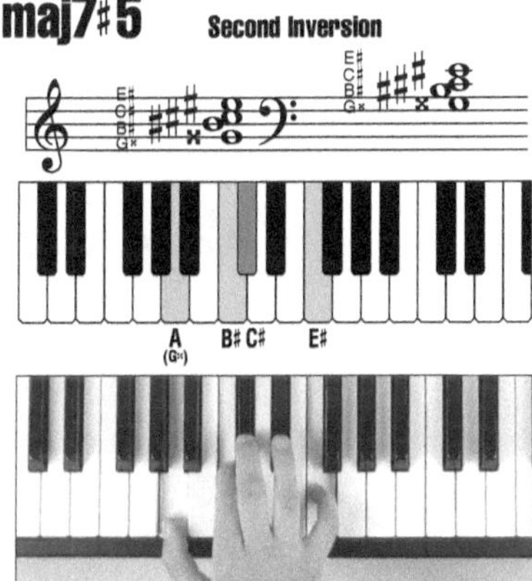

C♯maj7♯5 Third Inversion

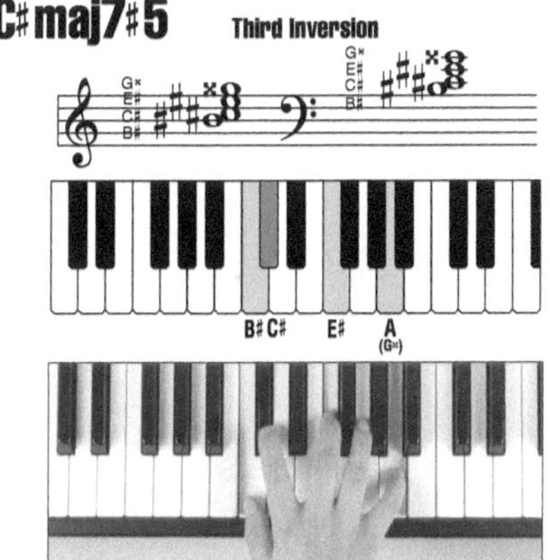

C♯7 Root Position

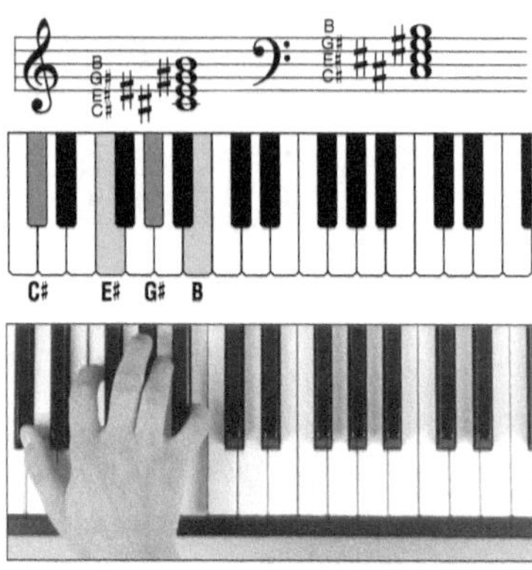

C♯7 First Inversion

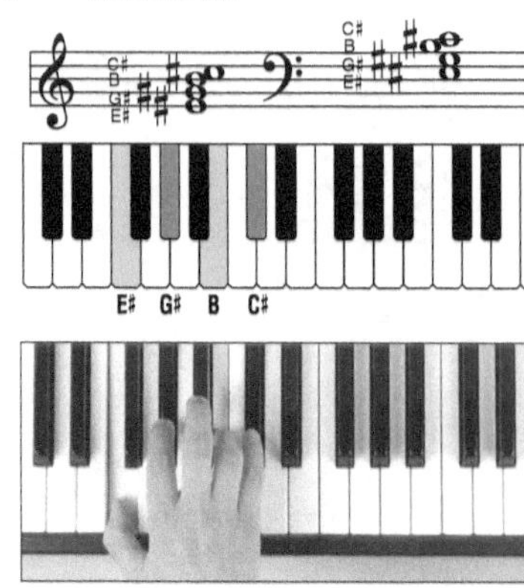

C♯7 Second Inversion

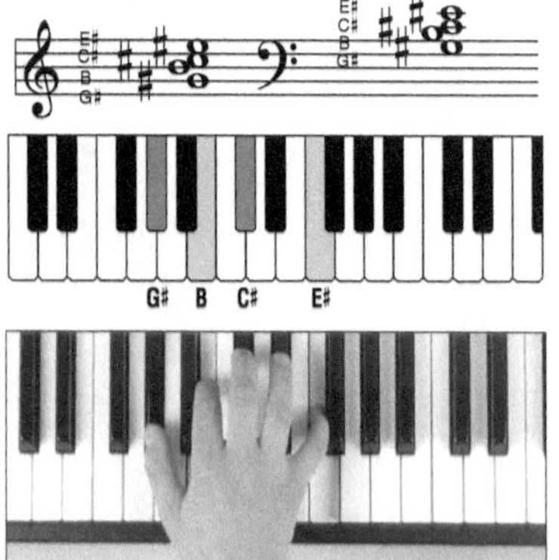

C♯7 Third Inversion

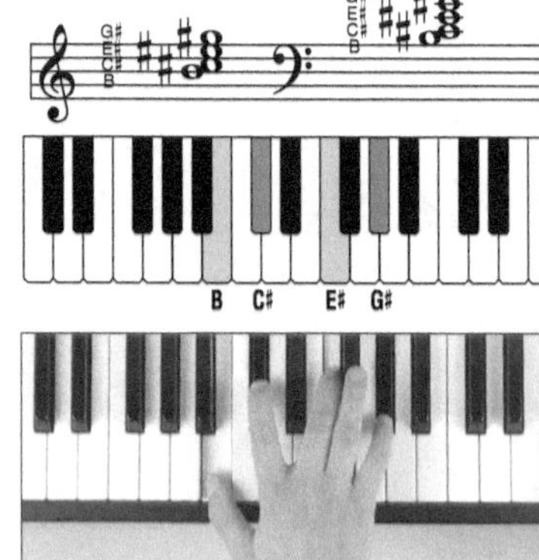

C♯7♭5 Root Position

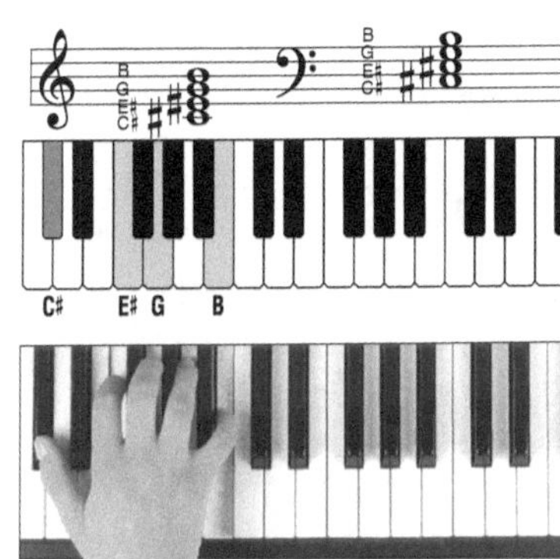

C♯7♭5 First Inversion

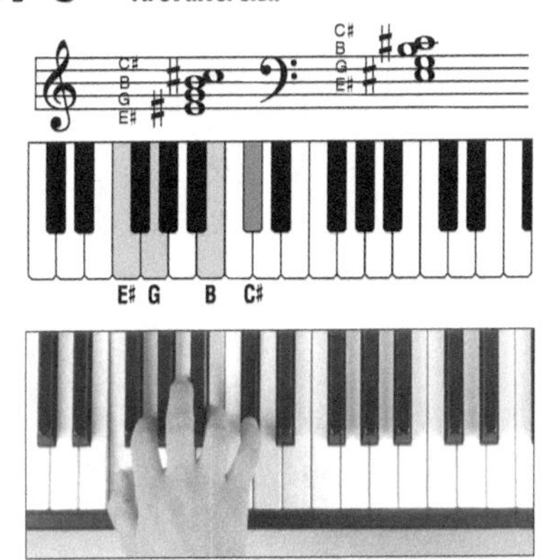

C♯7♭5 Second Inversion

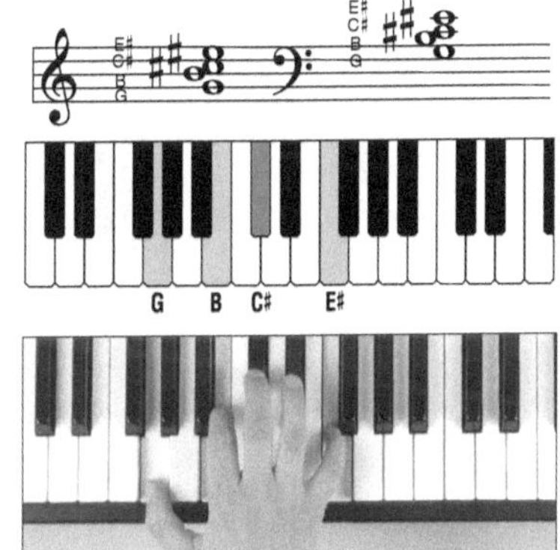

C♯7♭5 Third Inversion

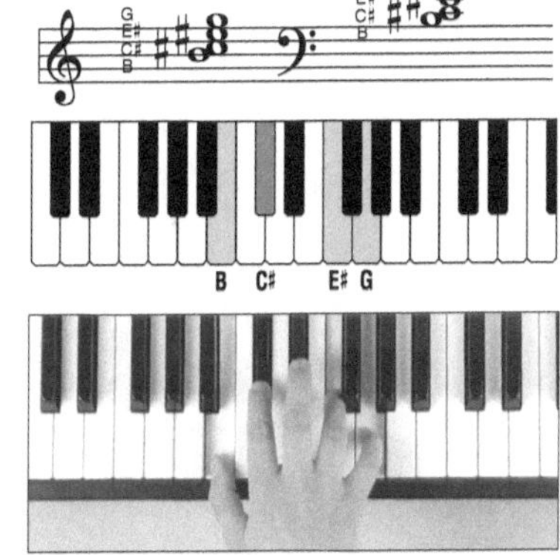

C♯7♯5 Root Position

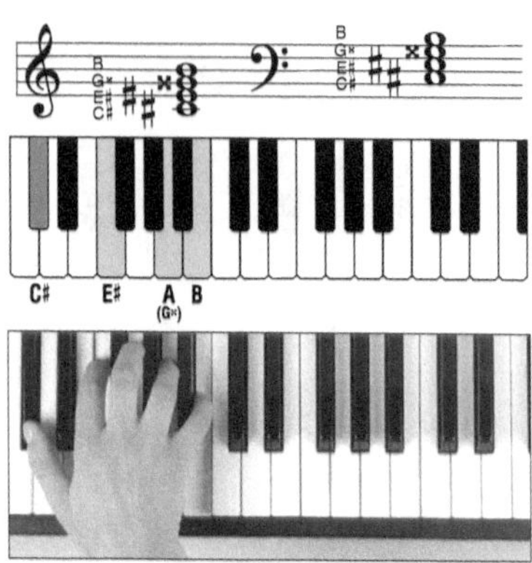

C♯7♯5 First Inversion

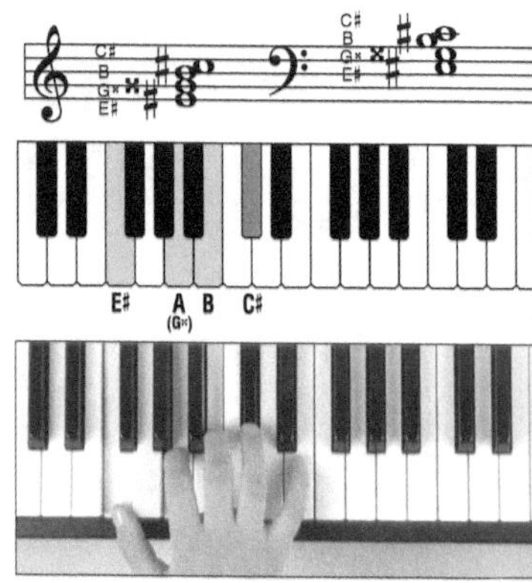

C♯7♯5 Second Inversion

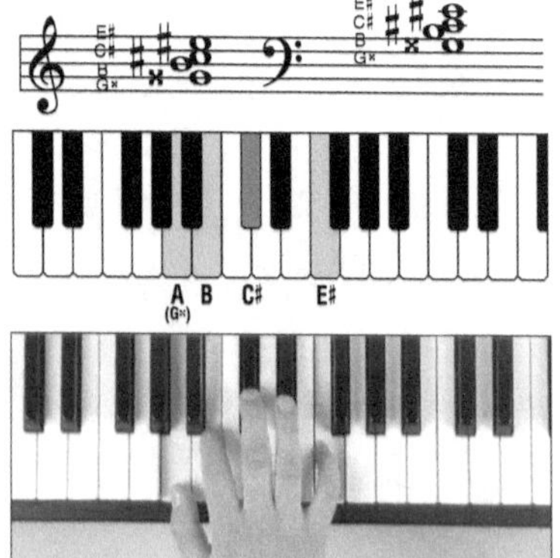

C♯7♯5 Third Inversion

G×
E♯
C♯
B

B C♯ E♯ A
(G×)

C♯7sus Root Position

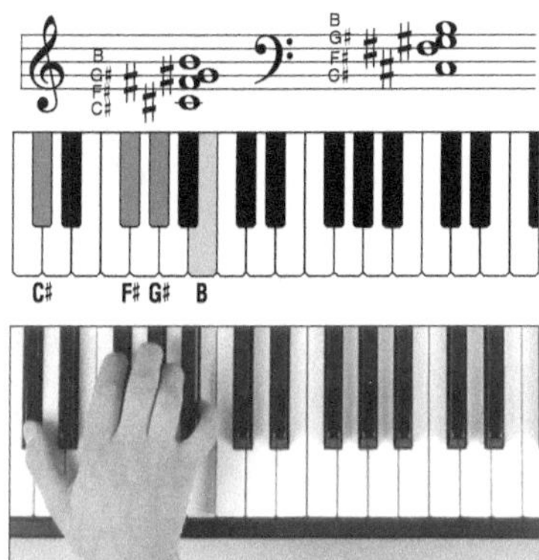

C♯7sus First Inversion

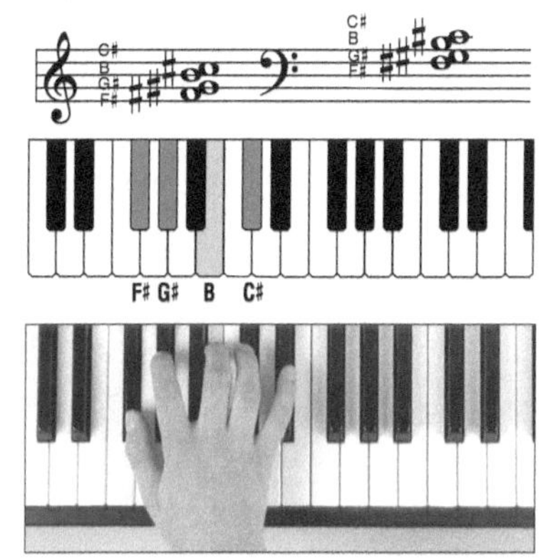

C♯7sus Second Inversion

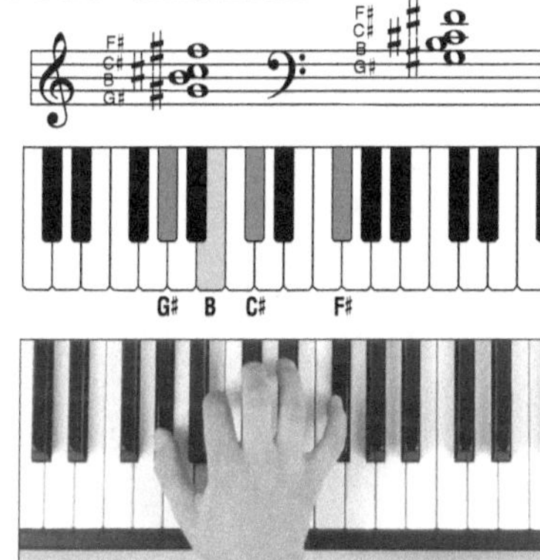

C♯7sus Third Inversion

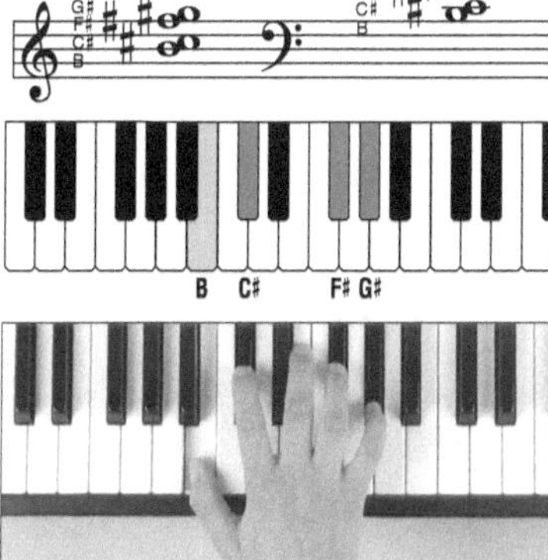

C♯m(add2), C♯m(add9) Root Position

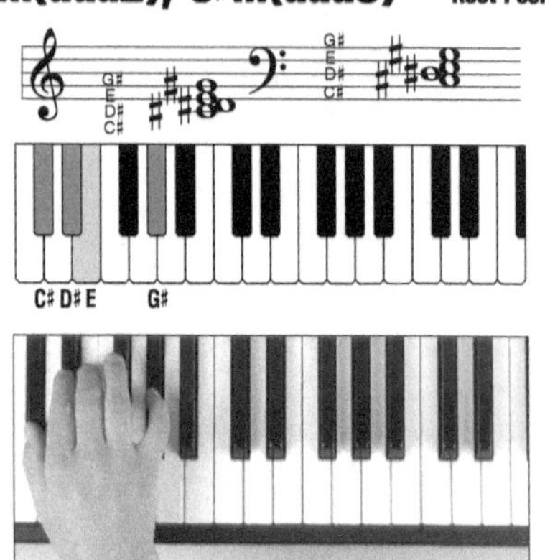

C♯m(add2), C♯m(add9) First Inversion

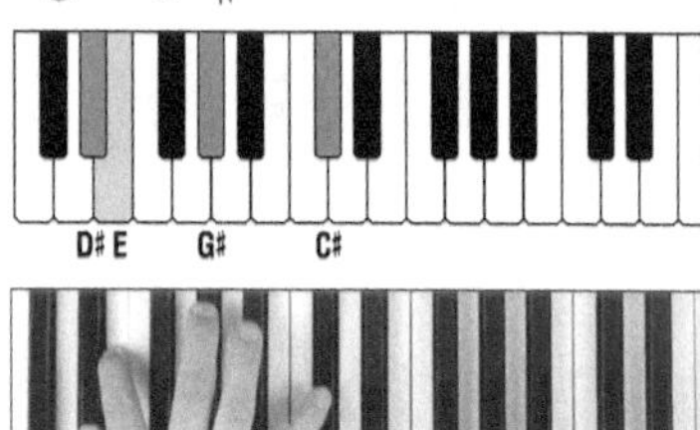
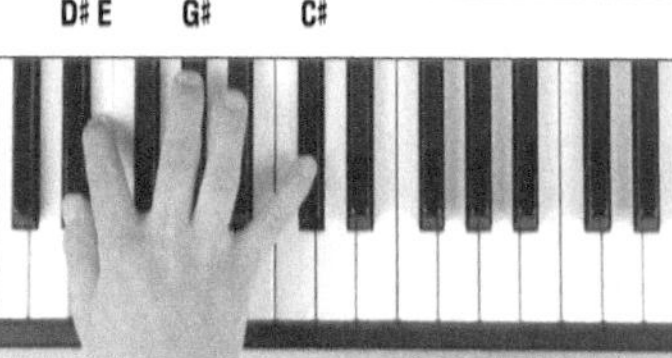

C♯m(add2), C♯m(add9) Second Inversion

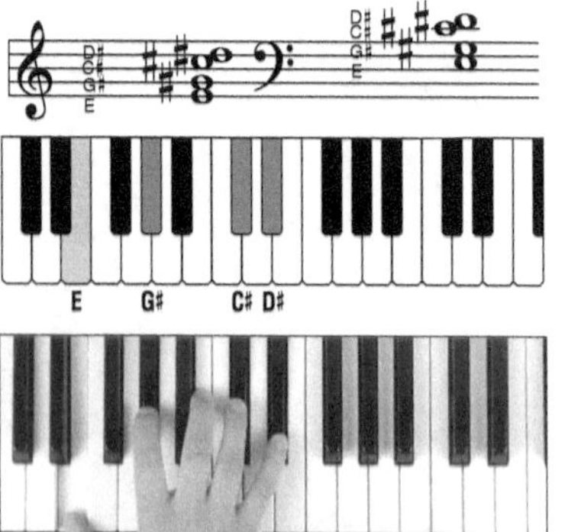

C♯m(add2), C♯m(add9) Third Inversion

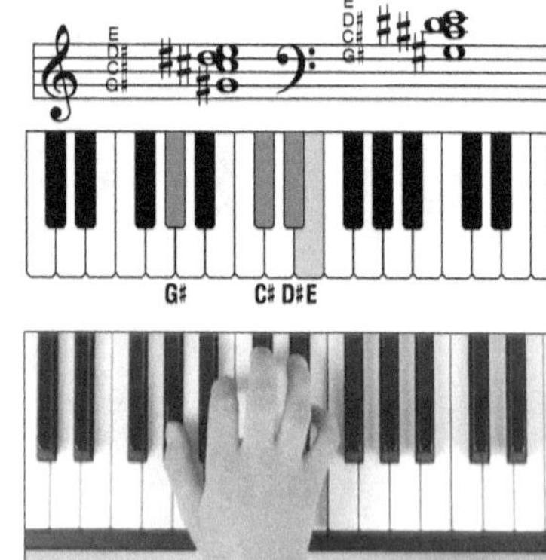

C♯m6 Root Position

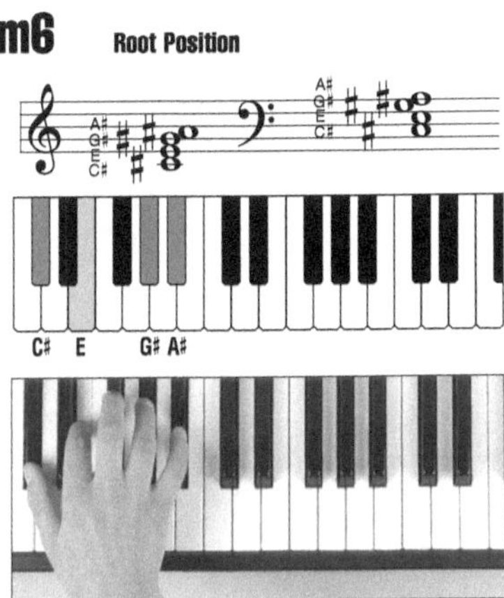

C♯m6 First Inversion

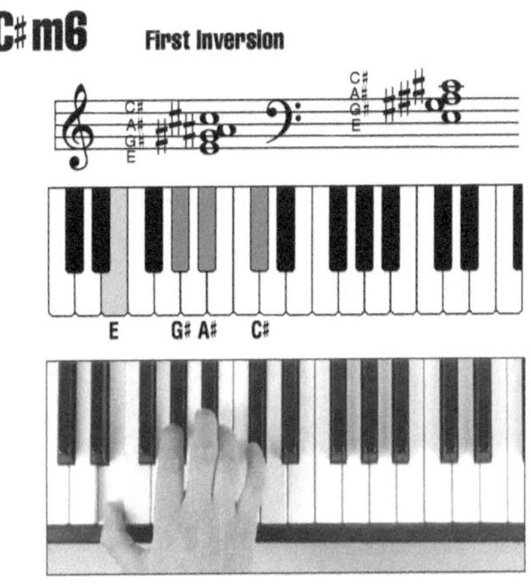

C♯m6 Second Inversion

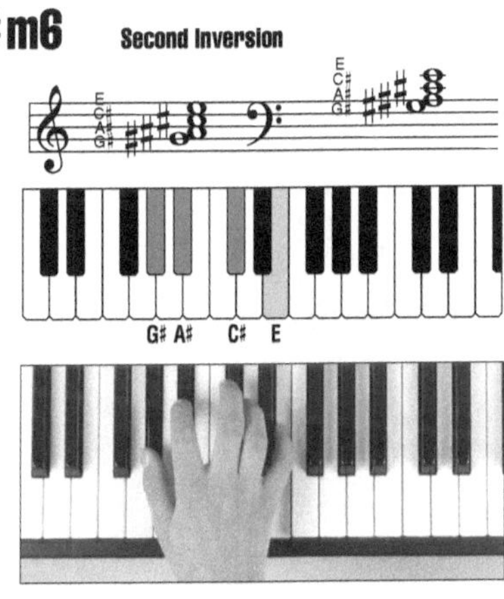

C♯m6 Third Inversion

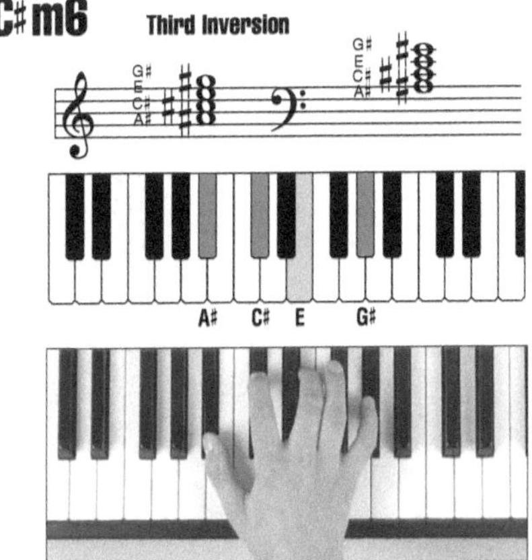

C♯m7 Root Position

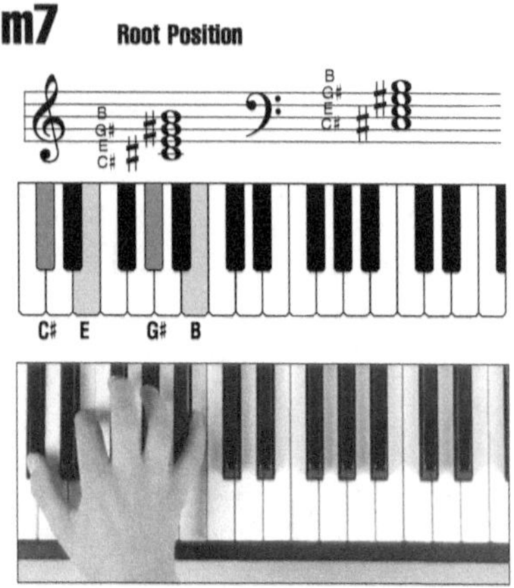

C♯m7 First Inversion

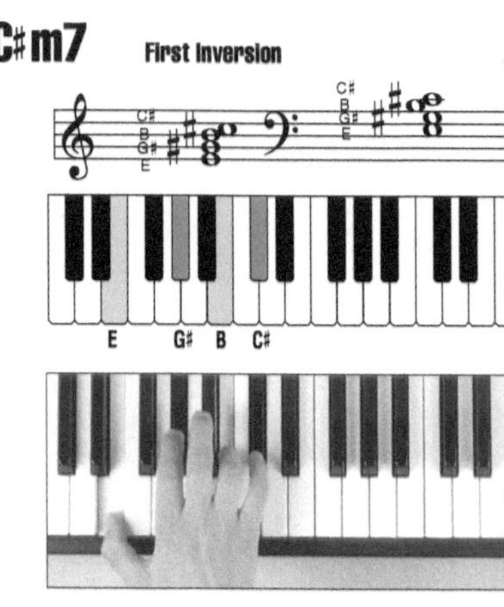

C♯m7 Second Inversion

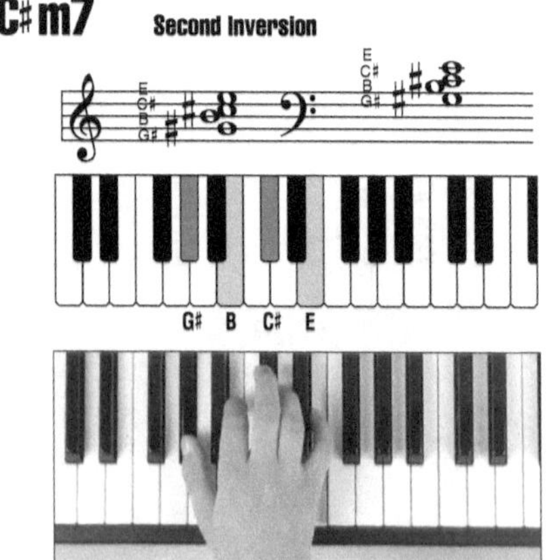

C♯m7 Third Inversion

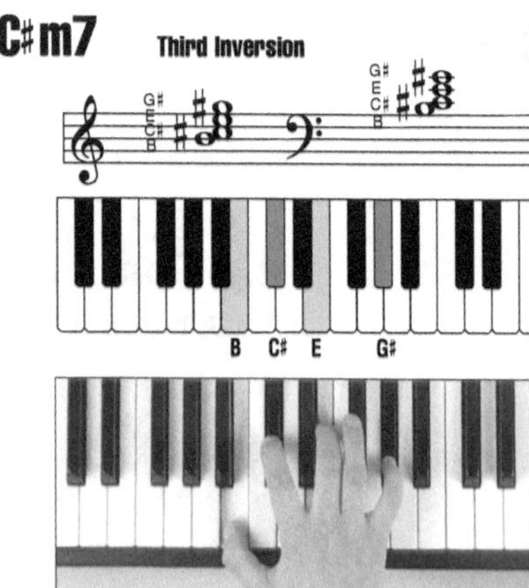

C♯m(maj7) Root Position

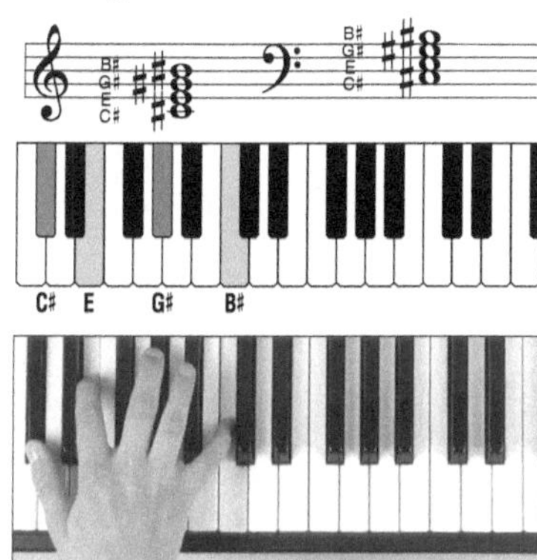

C♯m(maj7) First Inversion

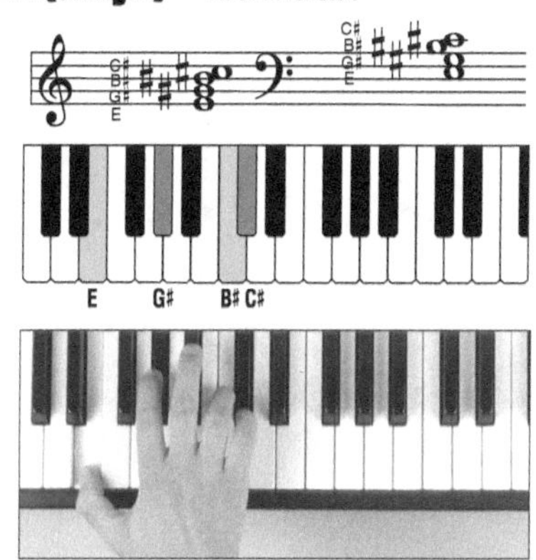

C♯m(maj7) Second Inversion

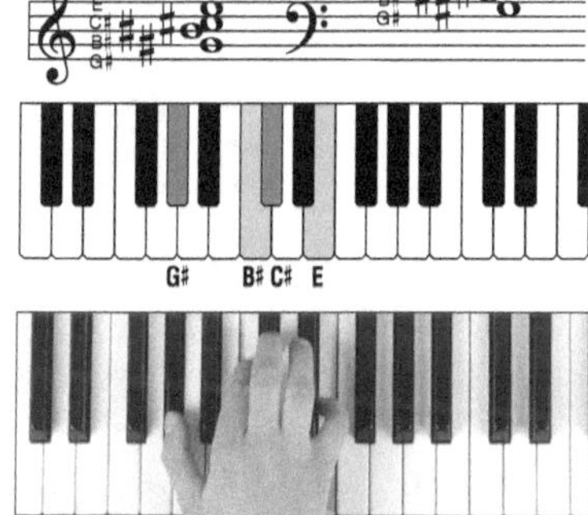

C♯m(maj7) Third Inversion

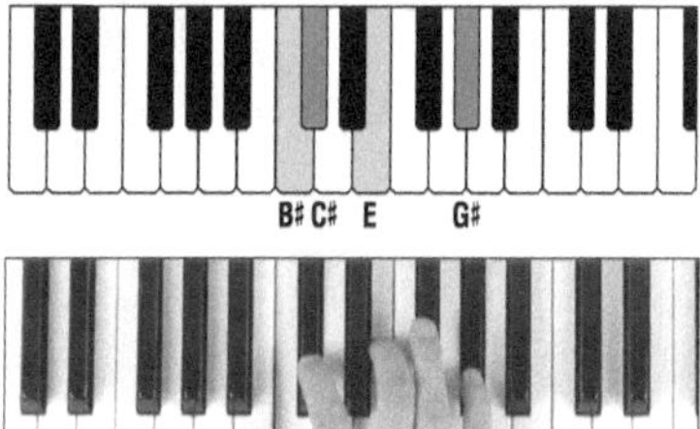

C♯m7♭5 Root Position

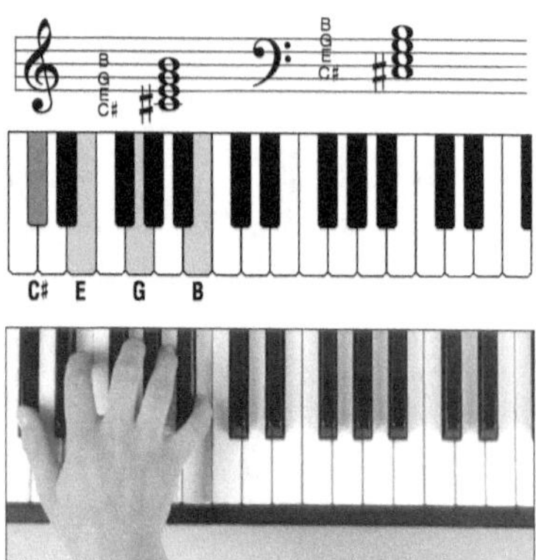

C♯m7♭5 First Inversion

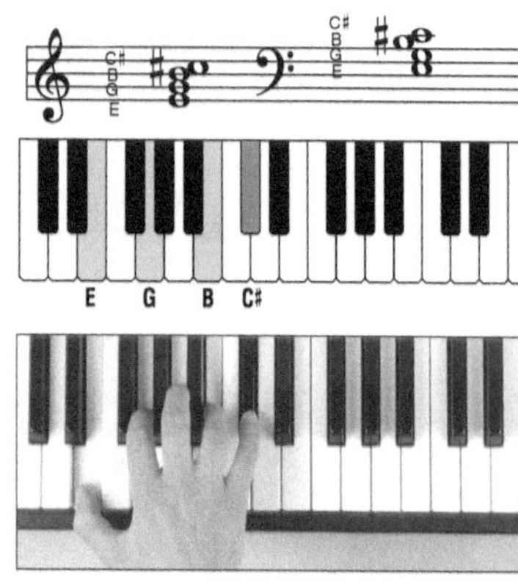

C♯m7♭5 Second Inversion

C♯m7♭5 Third Inversion

C♯dim7 Root Position

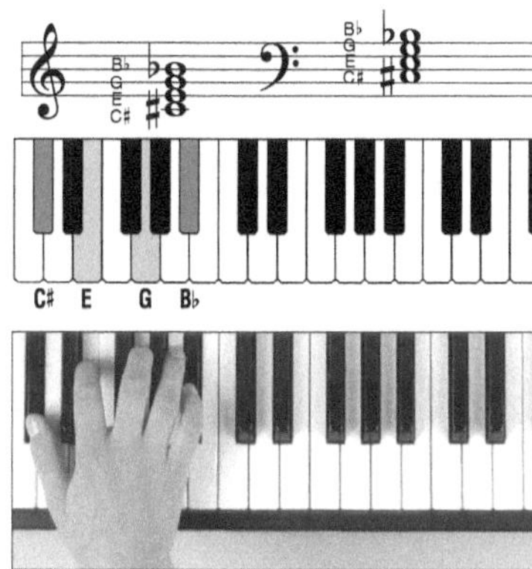

C♯dim7 First Inversion

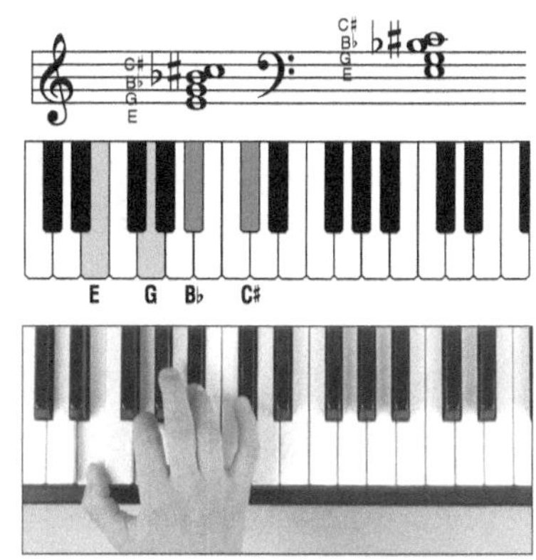

C♯dim7 Second Inversion

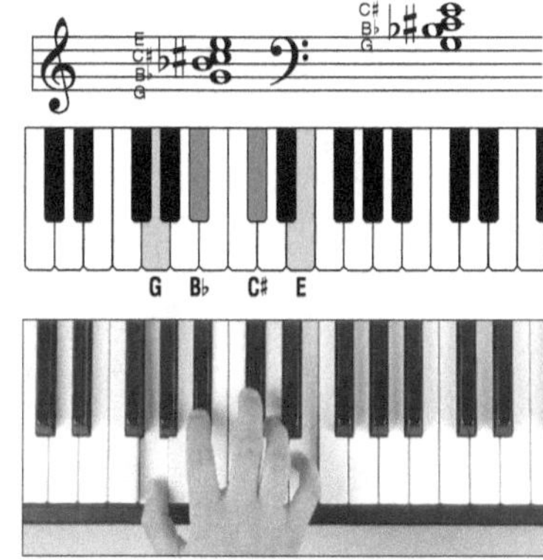

C♯dim7 Third Inversion

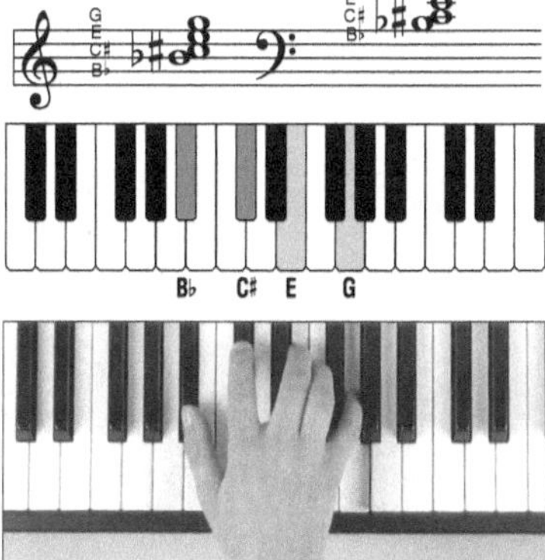

C♯ dim(maj7) — Root Position

C♯ dim(maj7) — First Inversion

C♯ dim(maj7) — Second Inversion

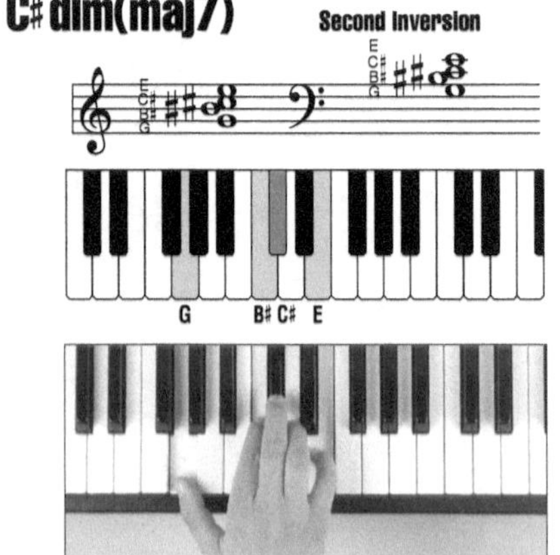

C♯ dim(maj7) — Third Inversion

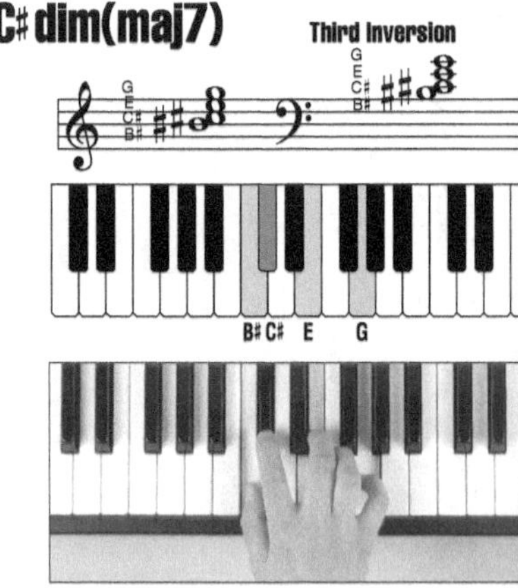

C♯5

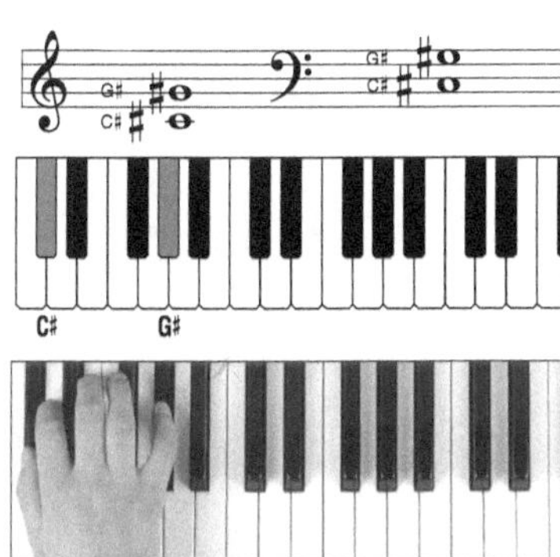

C♯6/9

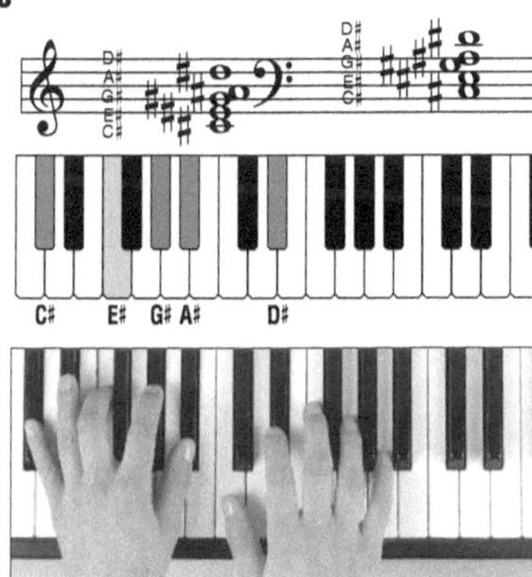

C♯maj6/9

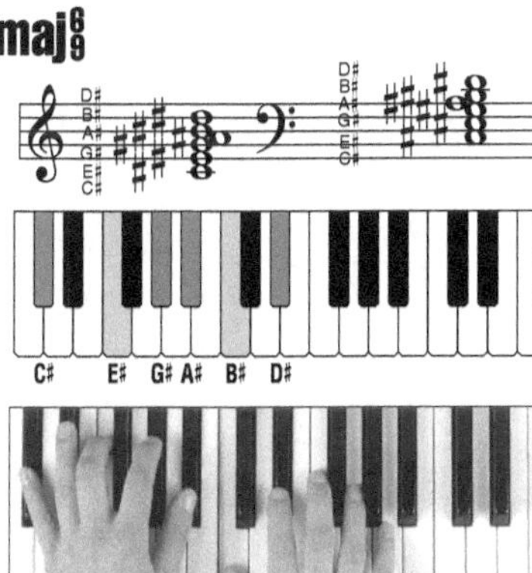

C♯maj7♯11

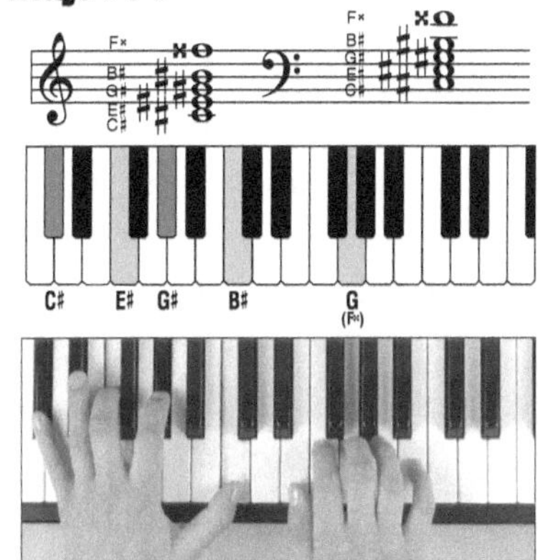

C♯maj9

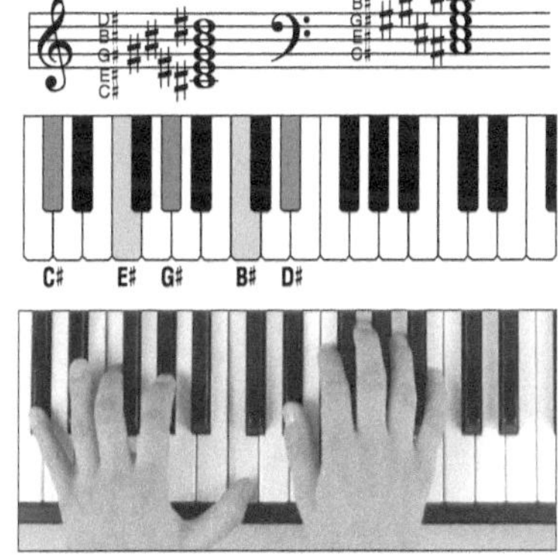

C♯maj9♭5

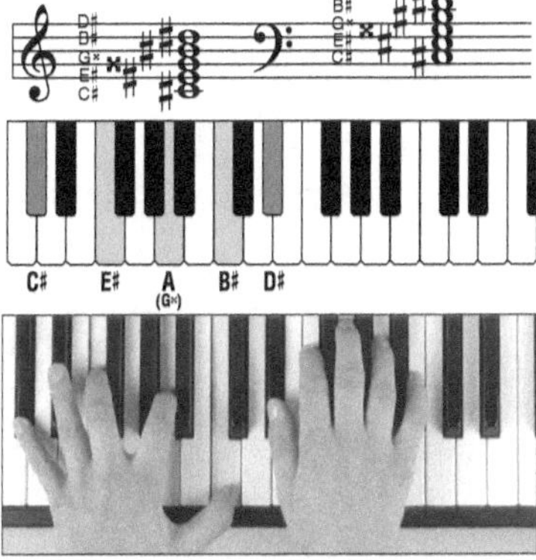

C♯maj9♯5

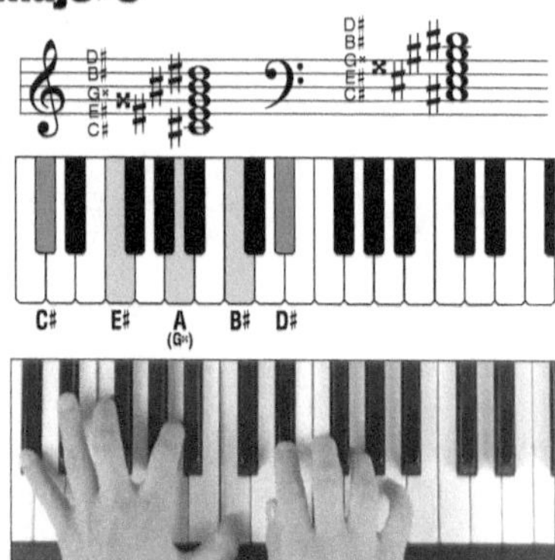

C♯maj9♯11

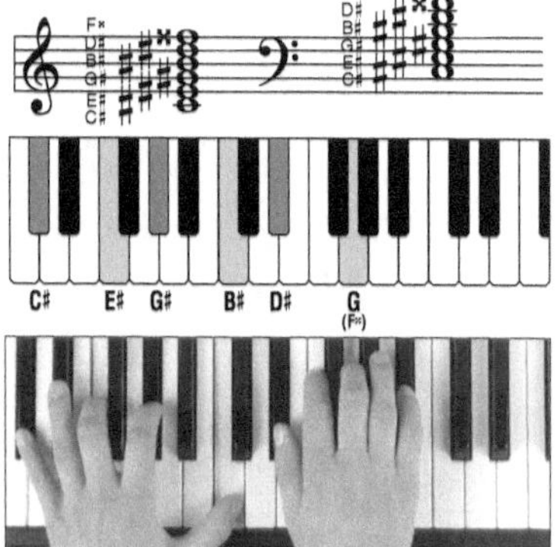

C♯maj13

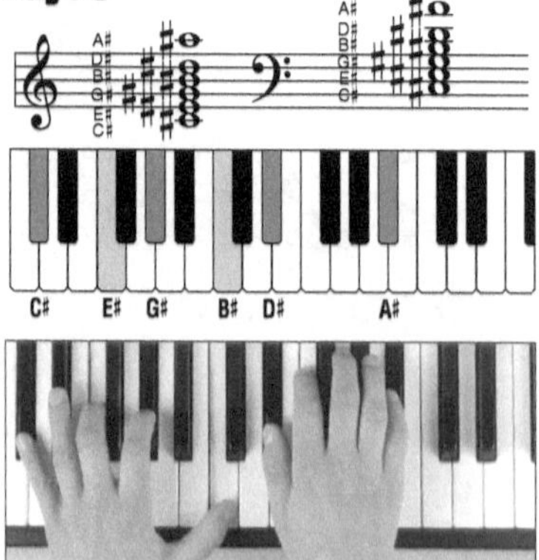

C♯maj13♭5

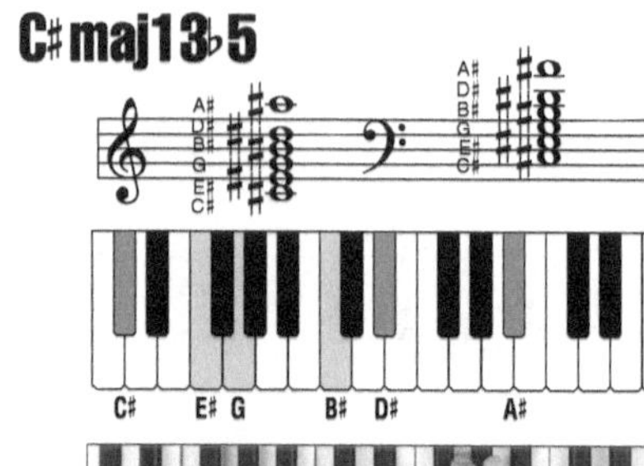

C♯maj13♯11

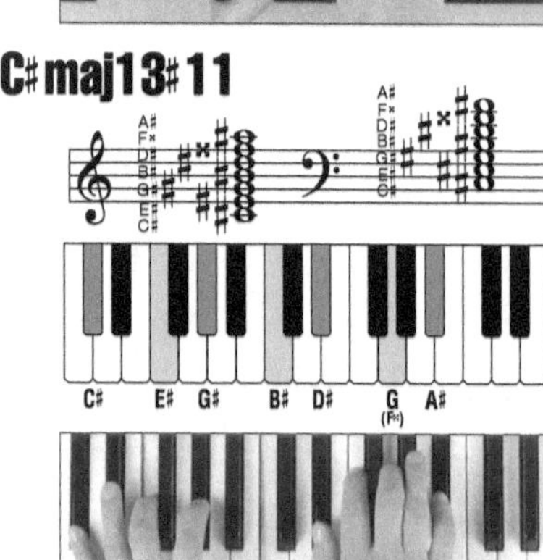

C♯7♭9

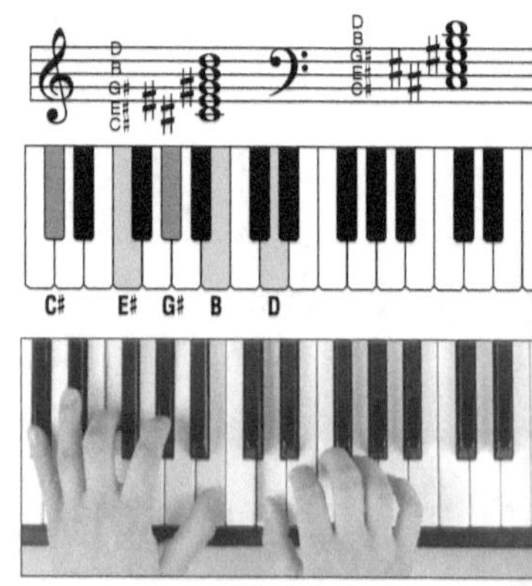

C♯7♯9

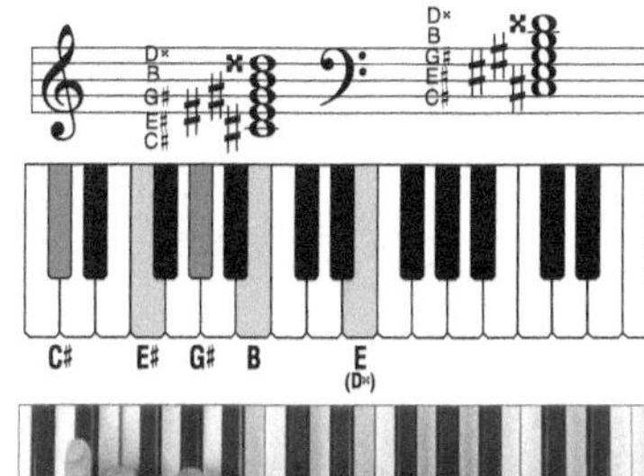

C♯7♯11

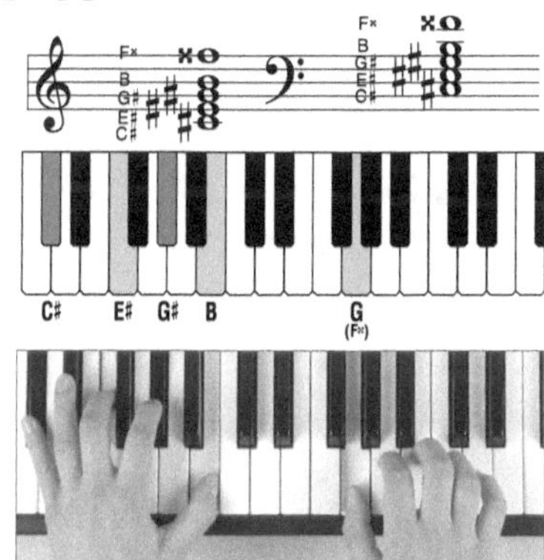

C♯7♭5(♭9)

C♯7♭5(♯9)

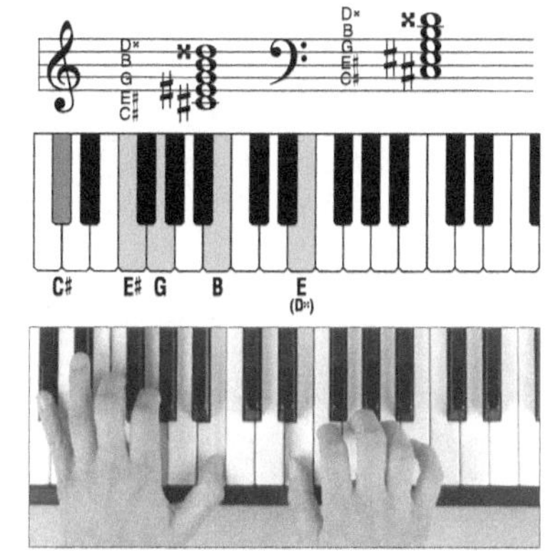

C♯7♯5(♭9)

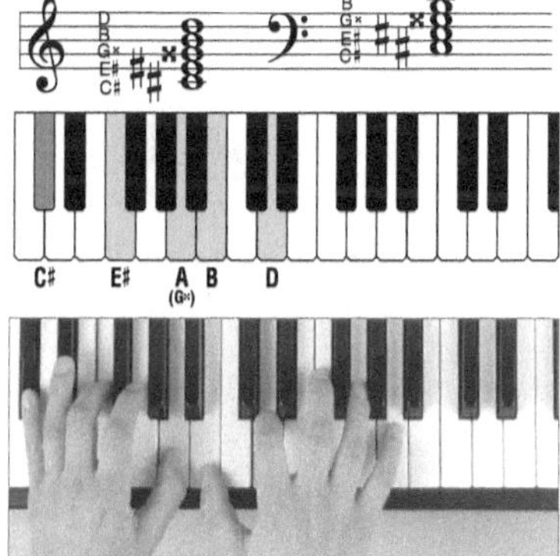

C♯7♯5(♯9)

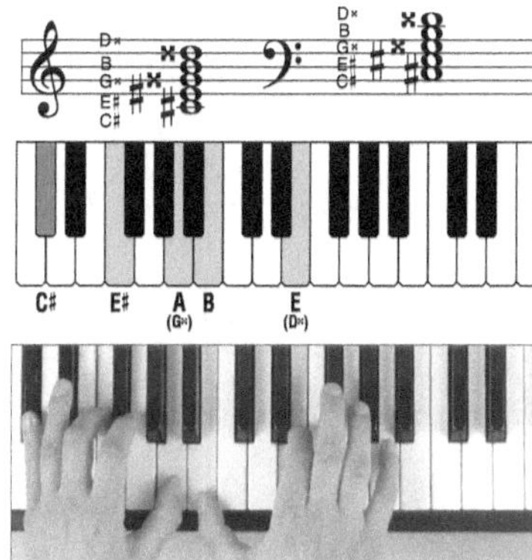

C♯7♭9(♯9)

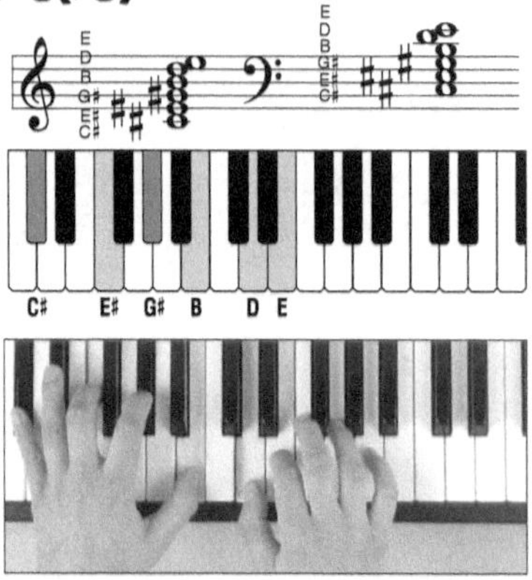

C♯ E♯ G♯ B D E

C♯7(add13)

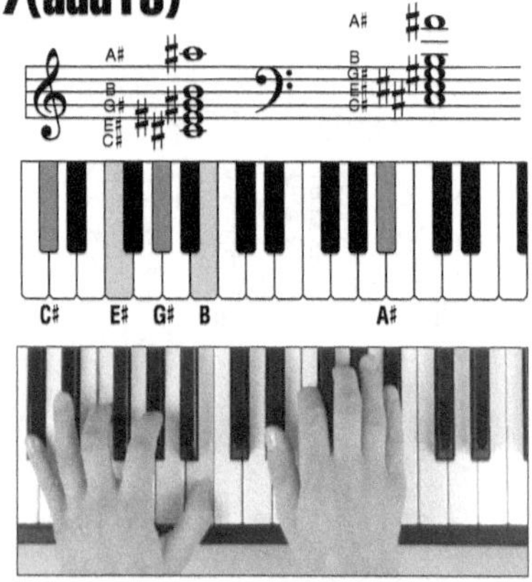

C♯ E♯ G♯ B A♯

C♯7♭13

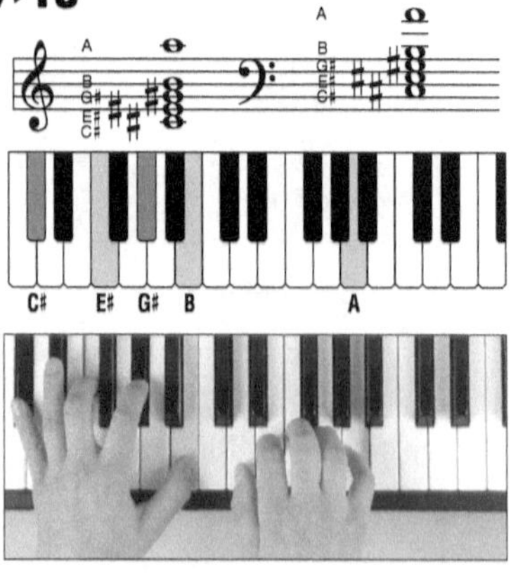

C♯ E♯ G♯ B A

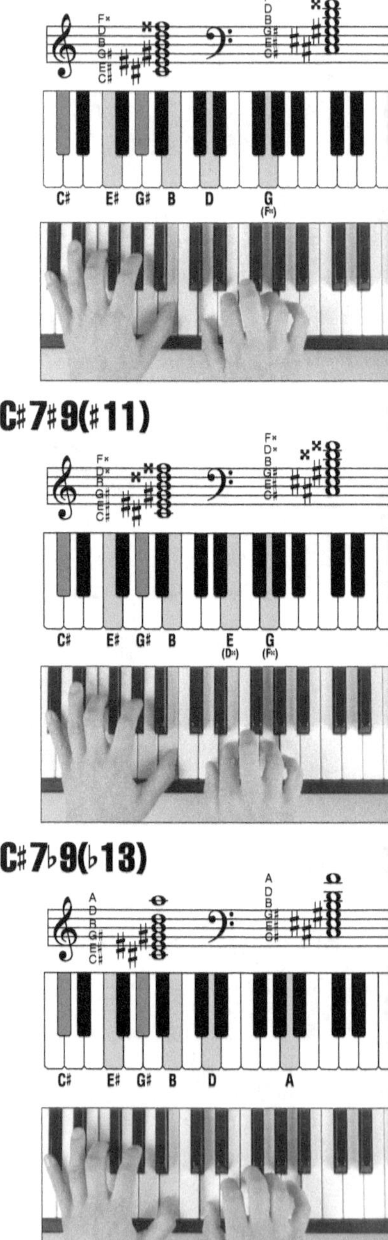

C♯7♯9(♭13)

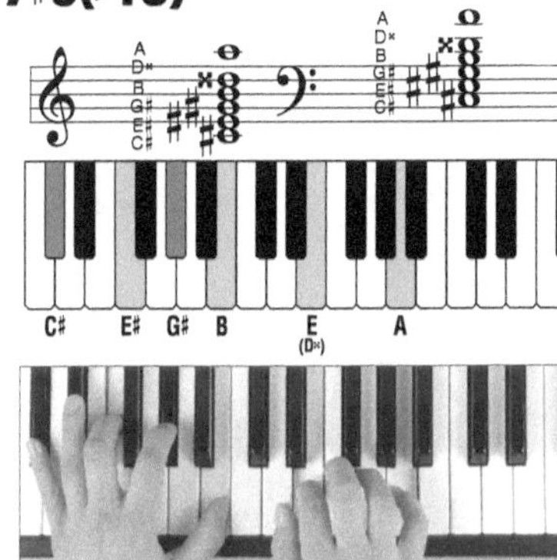

C♯7♯11(♭13)

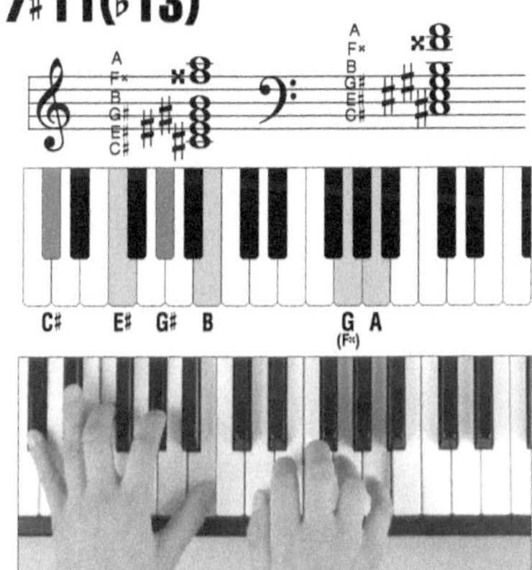

C♯7♭9(♯9, ♯11)

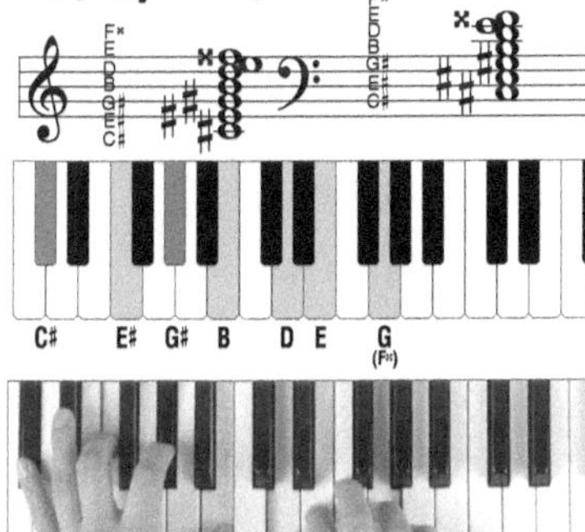

C♯9

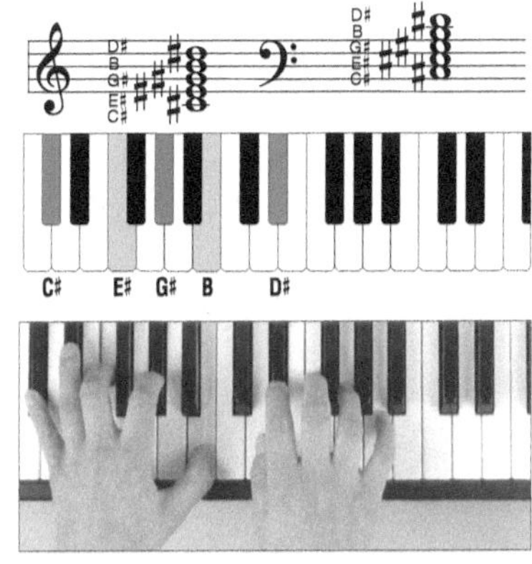

C♯9(♭5)

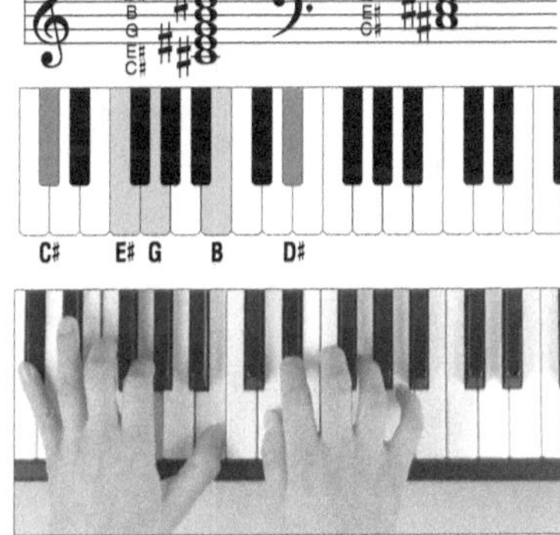

C♯9♯5

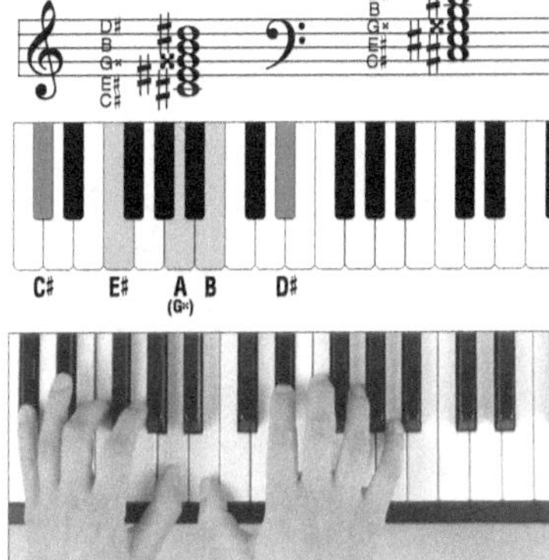

C♯9♯11

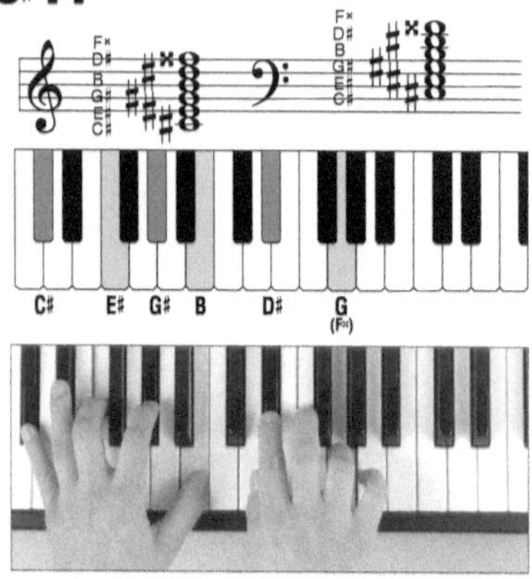

F×
D♯
B
G♯
E♯
C♯
C♯ E♯ G♯ B D♯ G
(F×)

C♯11, C♯9(sus4)

F♯
D♯
B
G♯
C♯
C♯ G♯ B D♯ F♯

C♯9♭13

A
D♯
B
G♯
E♯
C♯
C♯ E♯ G♯ B D♯ A

C♯13

A♯
D♯
B
G♯
E♯
C♯
C♯ E♯ G♯ B D♯ A♯

C♯9♯11(♭13)

A
F×
D♯
B
G♯
E♯
C♯
C♯ E♯ G♯ B D♯ G A
(F×)

C♯13♭5

A♯
D♯
B
G
E♯
C♯
C♯ E♯ G B D♯ A♯

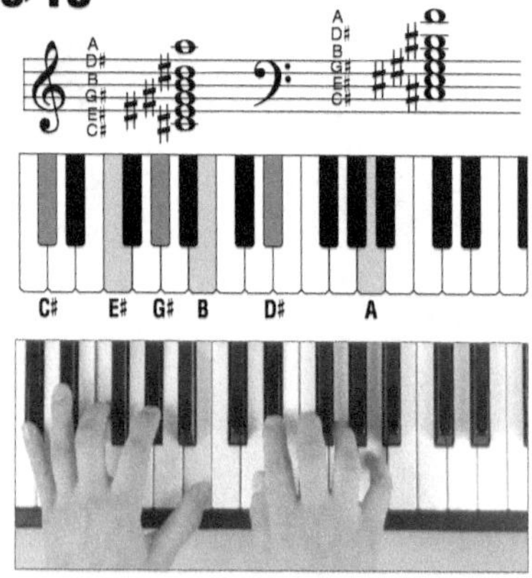

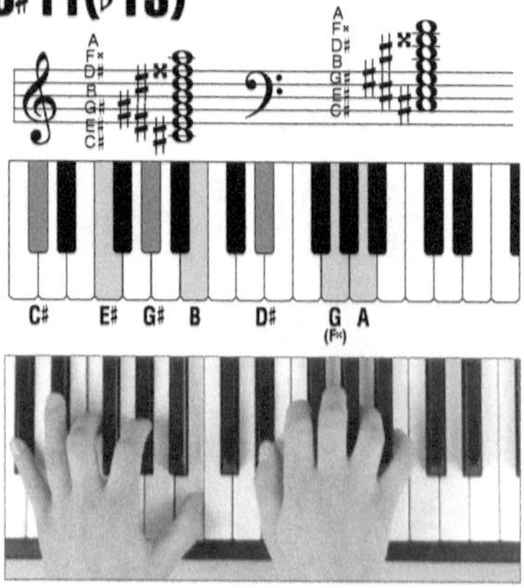

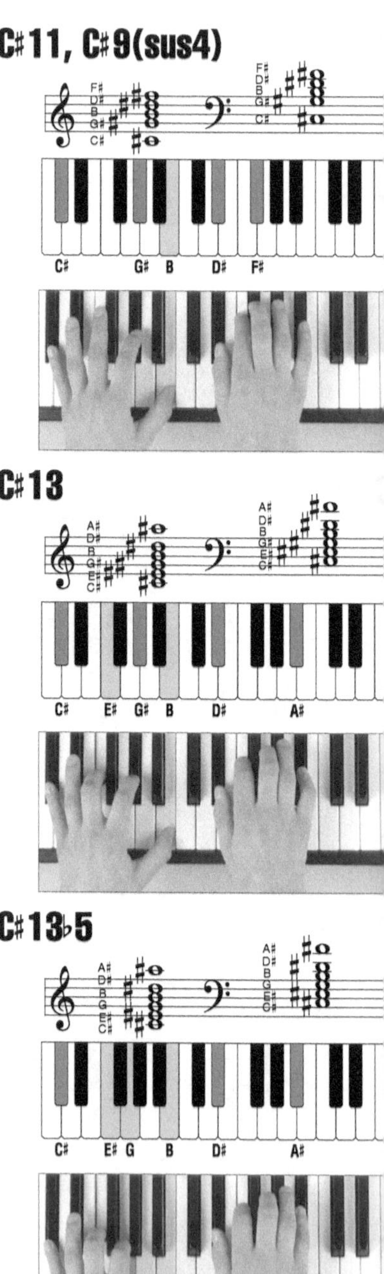

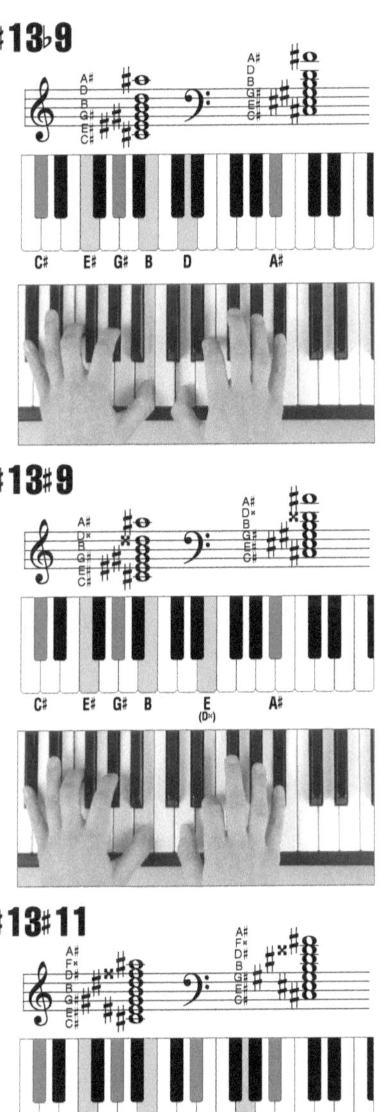
C♯13♭9
A♯
D
B
G♯
E♯
C♯
C♯ E♯ G♯ B D A♯
C♯13♯9
A♯
D×
B
G♯
E♯
C♯
C♯ E♯ G♯ B E (D×) A♯
C♯13♯11
A♯
F×
D♯
B
G♯
E♯
C♯
C♯ E♯ G♯ B D♯ G (F×) A♯

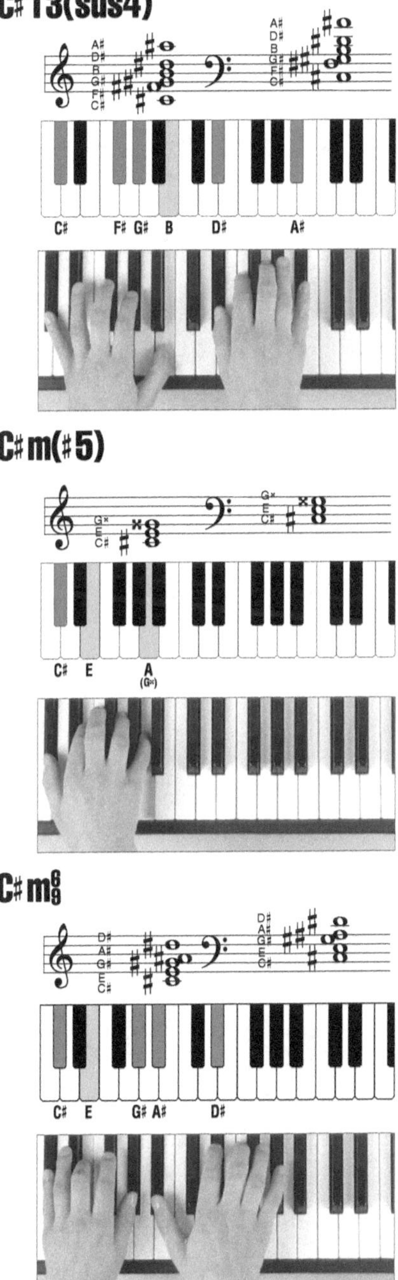
C♯13(sus4)
A♯
D♯
B
G♯
F♯
C♯
C♯ F♯ G♯ B D♯ A♯
C♯m(♯5)
G×
E
C♯
C♯ E A (G×)
C♯m6/9
D♯
A♯
G♯
E
C♯
C♯ E G♯ A♯ D♯

C♯m7(add4)

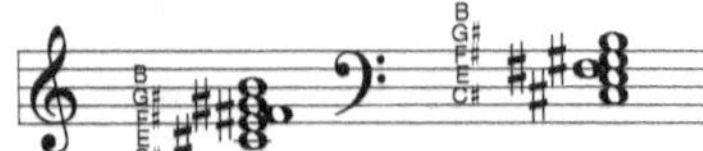

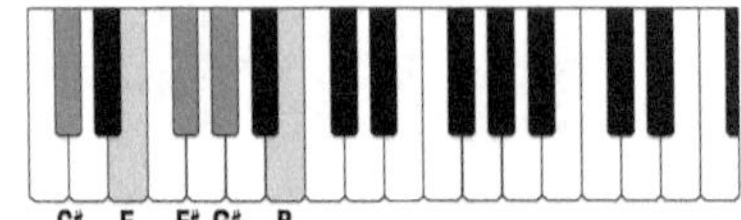

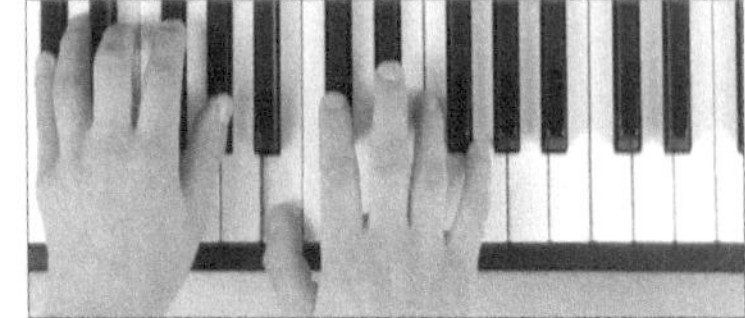

C♯m7(add11)

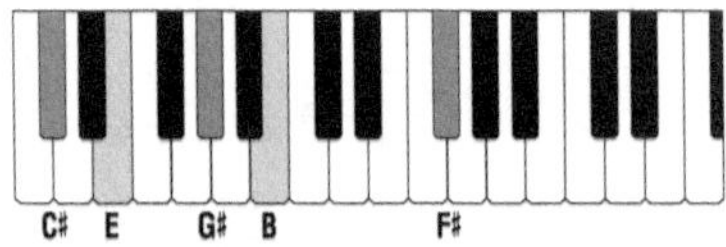

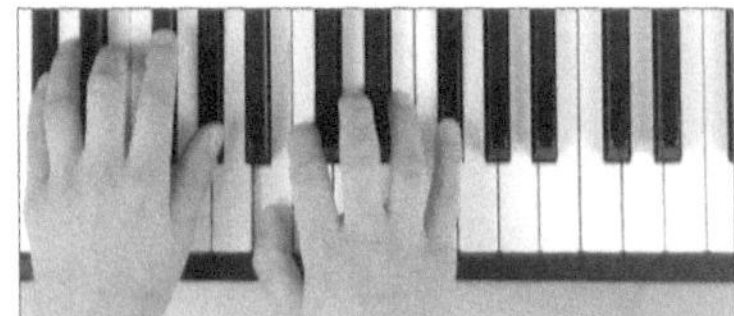

C♯m7♭5(♭9)

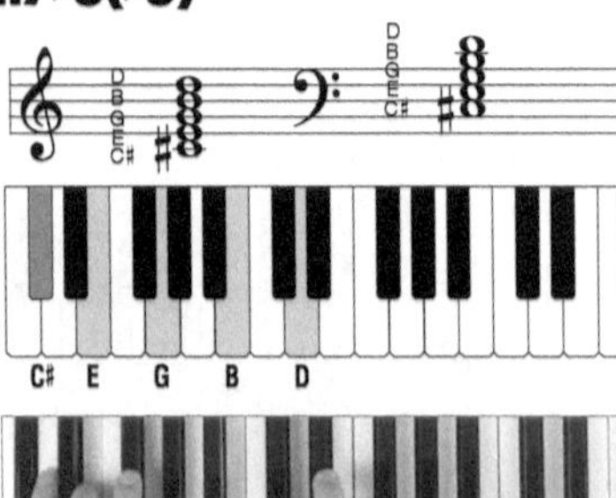

C♯m9

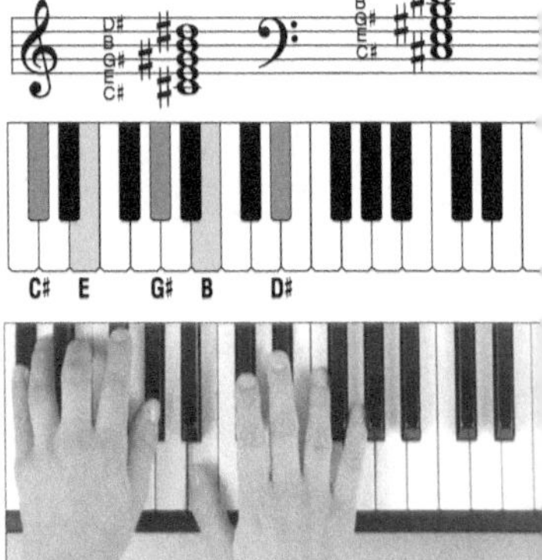

C♯m9(maj7)

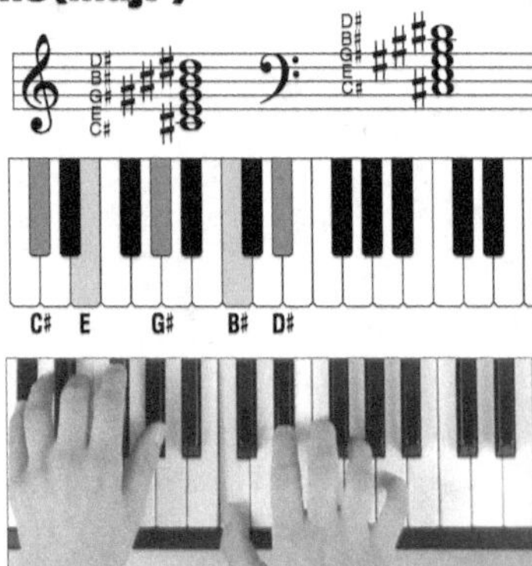

C♯m9♭5

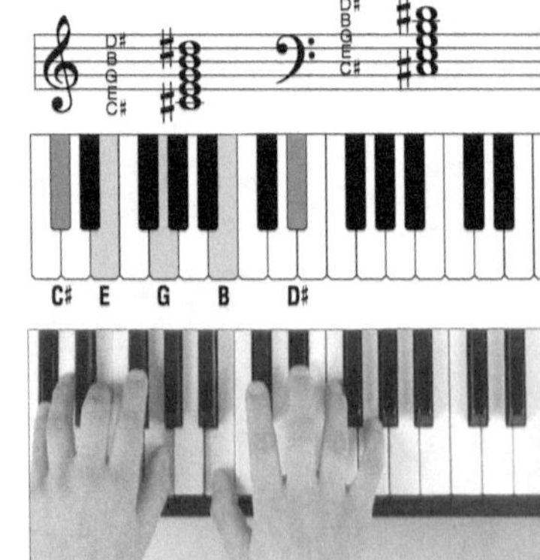

C♯m11

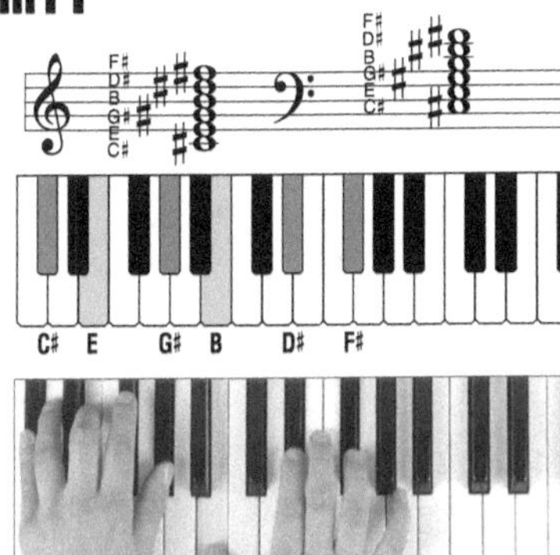

C♯m11♭5

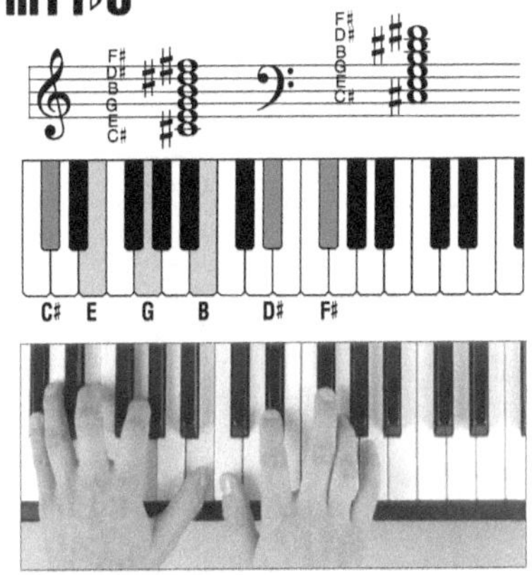

C♯m13

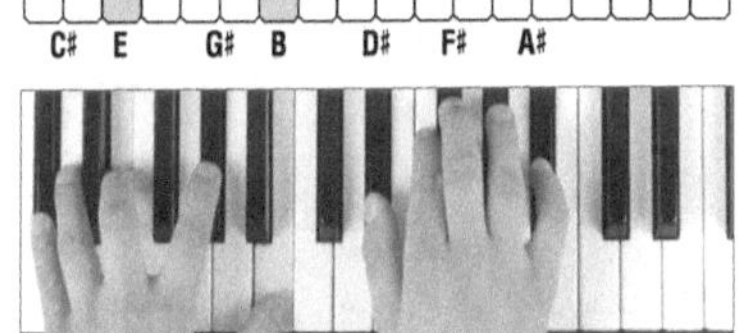

C♯m11(maj7)

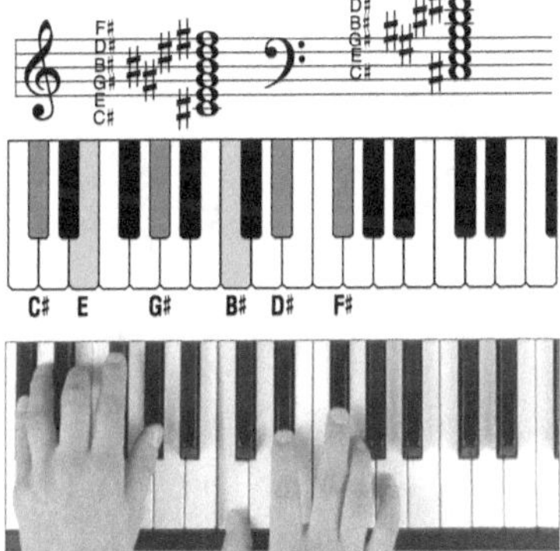

C♯dim7(add9)

C♯7alt

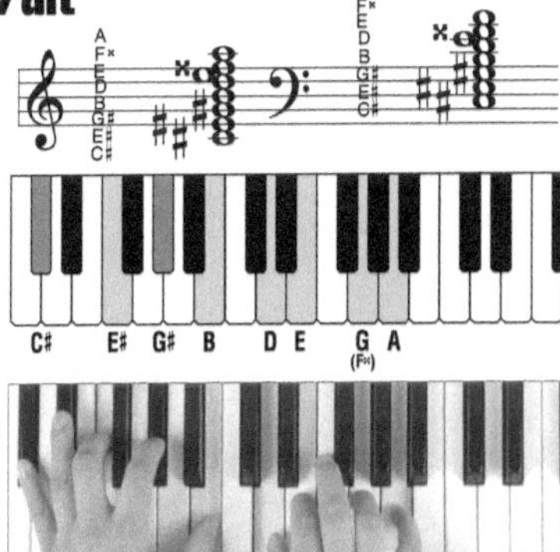

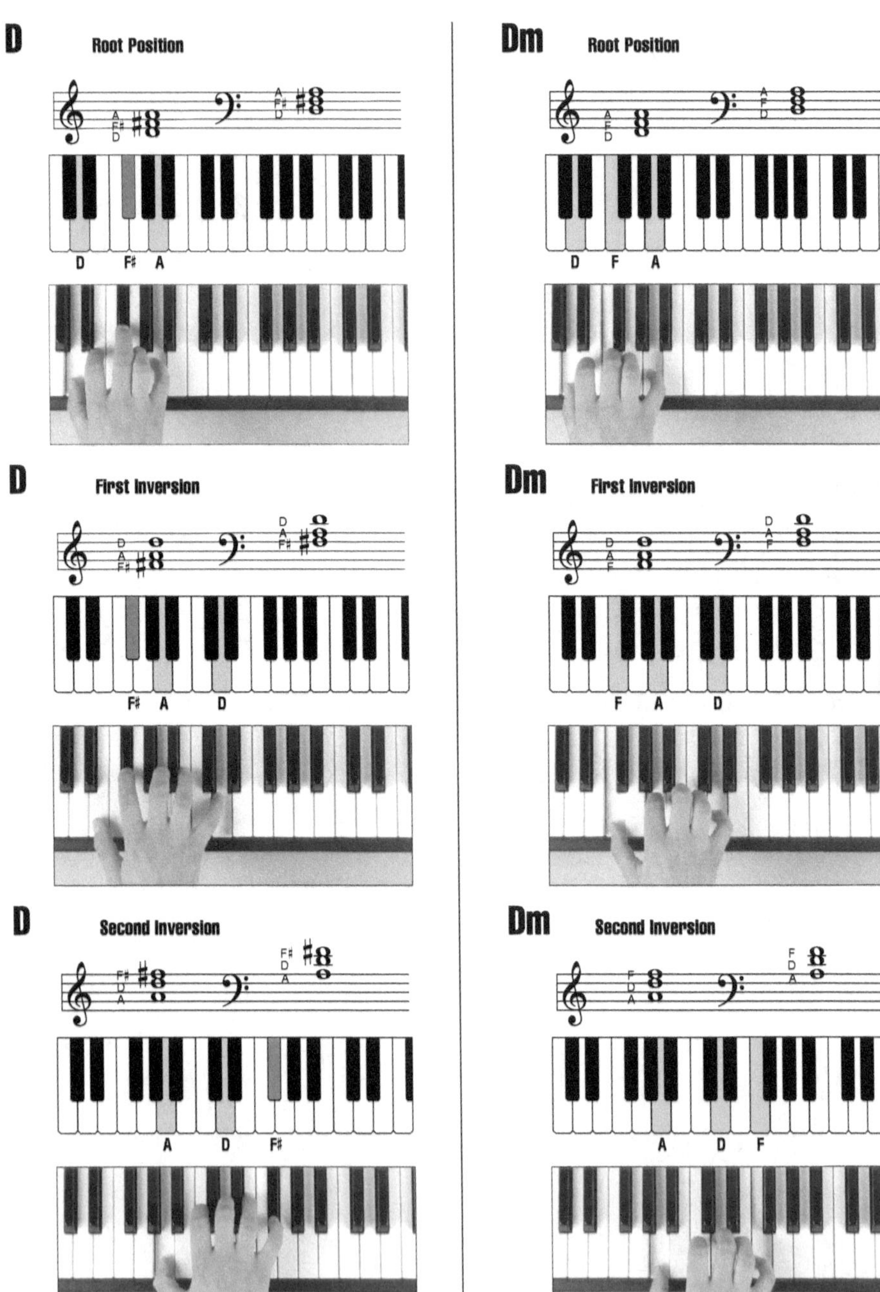
D
Root Position
A
F♯
D
D F♯ A
Dm
Root Position
A
F
D
D F A
D
First Inversion
D
A
F♯
F♯ A D
Dm
First Inversion
D
A
F
F A D
D
Second Inversion
F♯
D
A
A D F♯
Dm
Second Inversion
F
D
A
A D F

D+ Root Position

D+ First Inversion

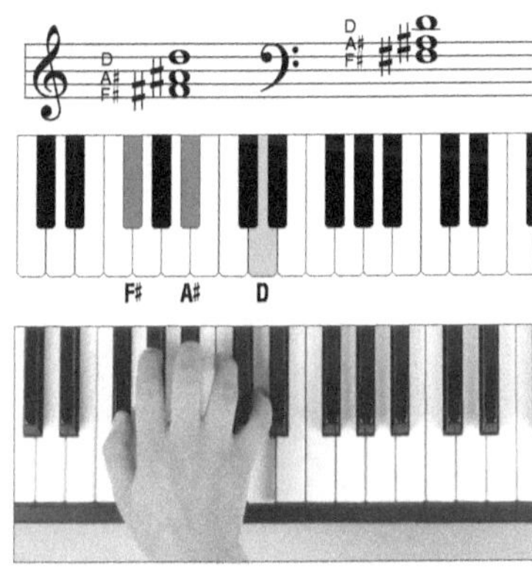

D+ Second Inversion

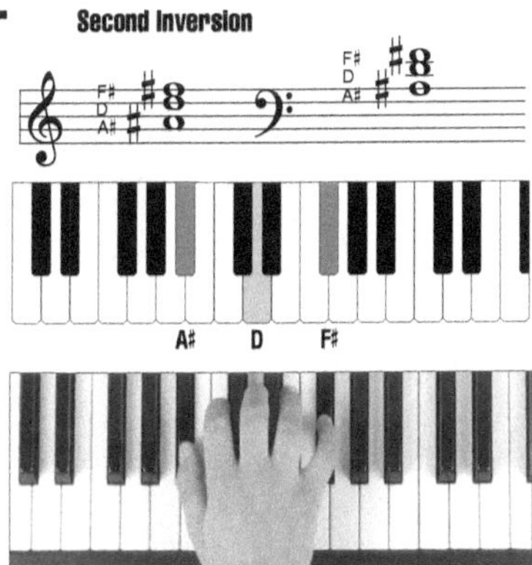

Ddim Root Position

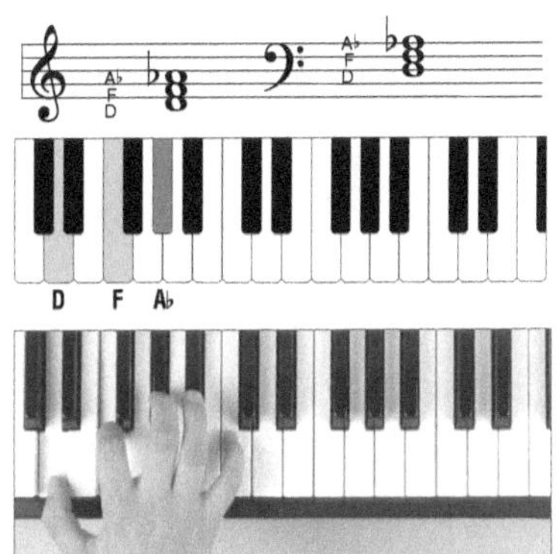

Ddim First Inversion

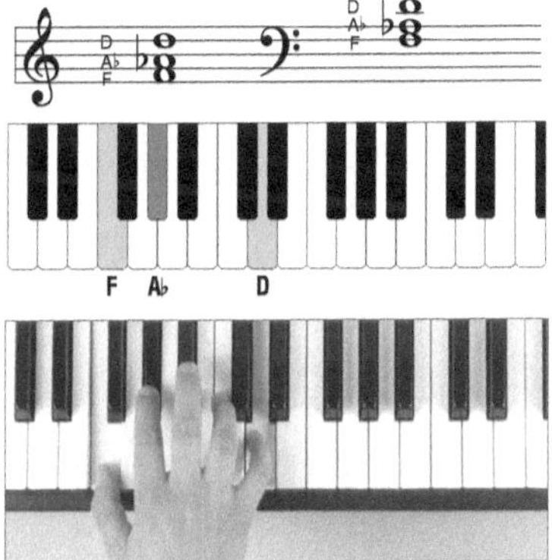

Ddim Second Inversion

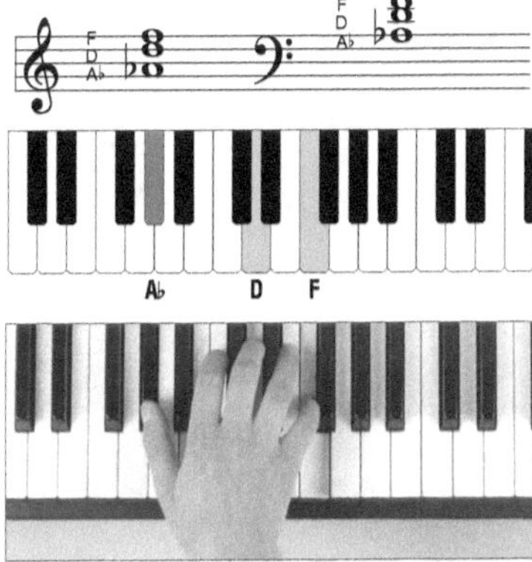

Dsus Root Position

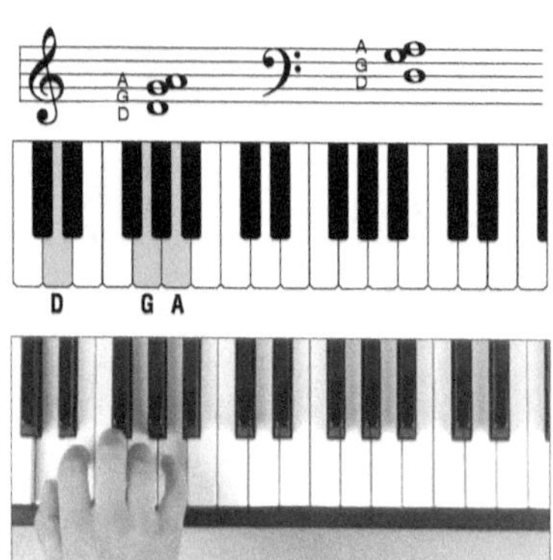

Dsus First Inversion

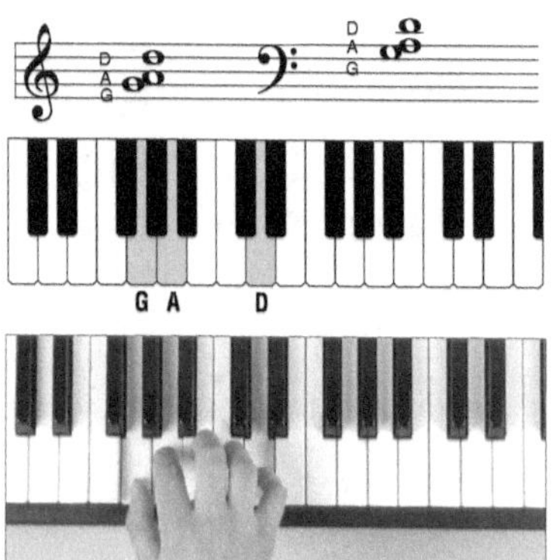

Dsus Second Inversion

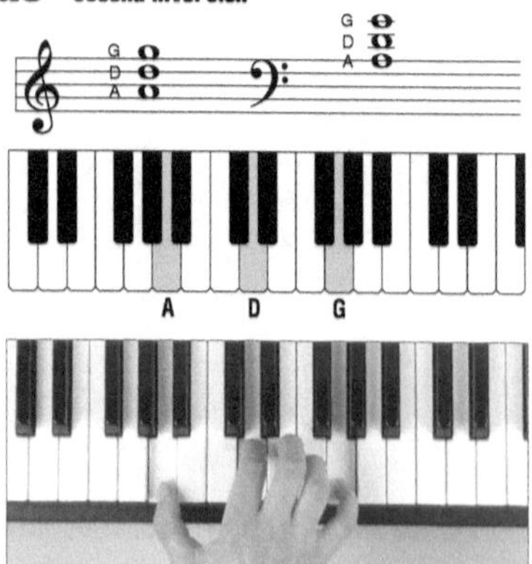

D(♭5) Root Position

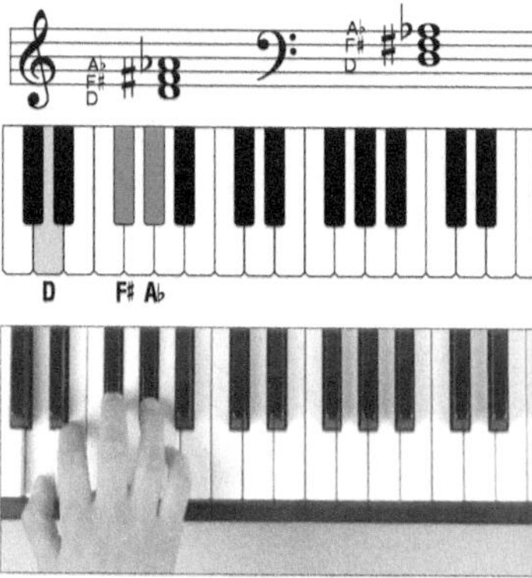

D(♭5) First Inversion

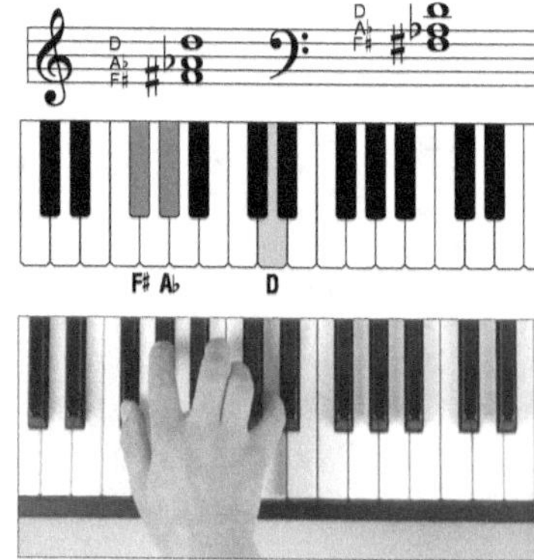

D(♭5) Second Inversion

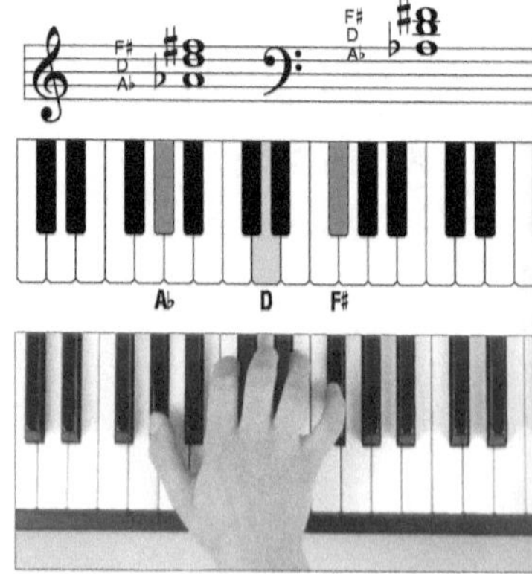

Dsus2 Root Position

Dsus2 First Inversion

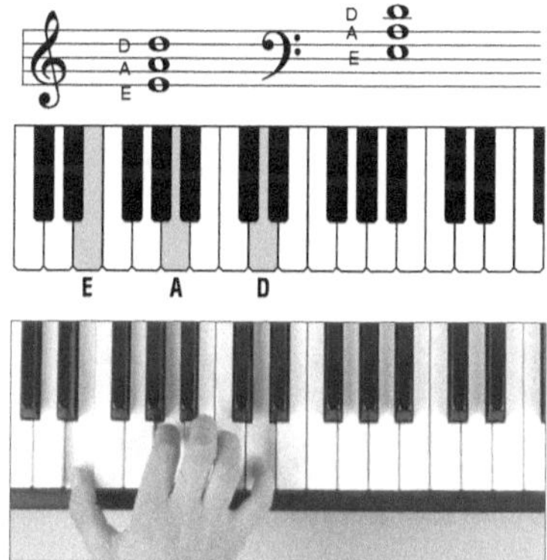

Dsus2 Second Inversion

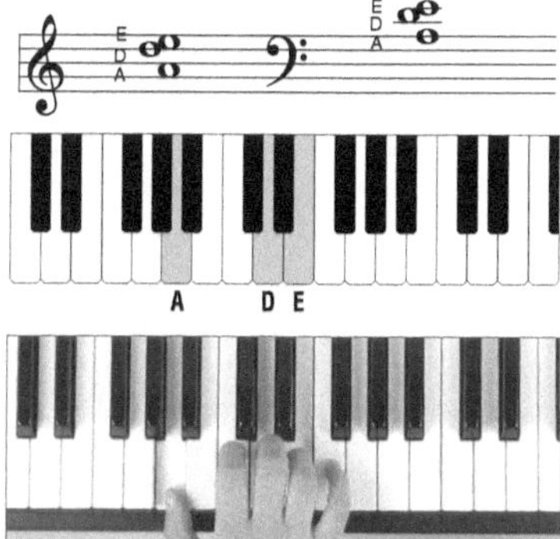

D6 Root Position

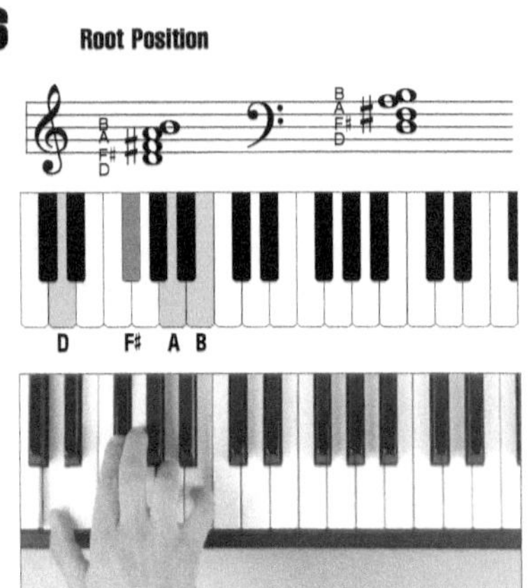

D6 First Inversion

D6 Second Inversion

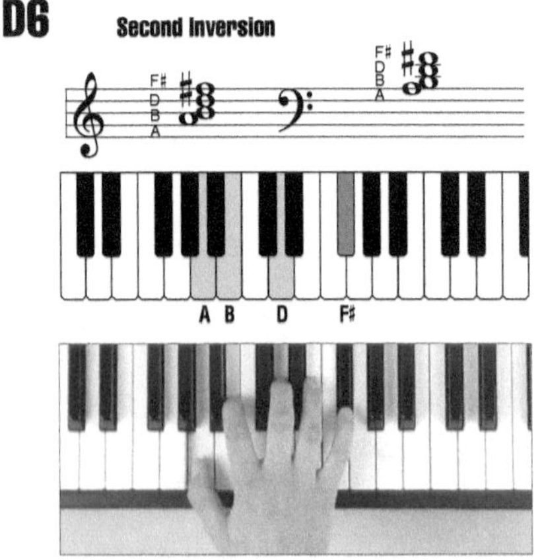

D6 Third Inversion

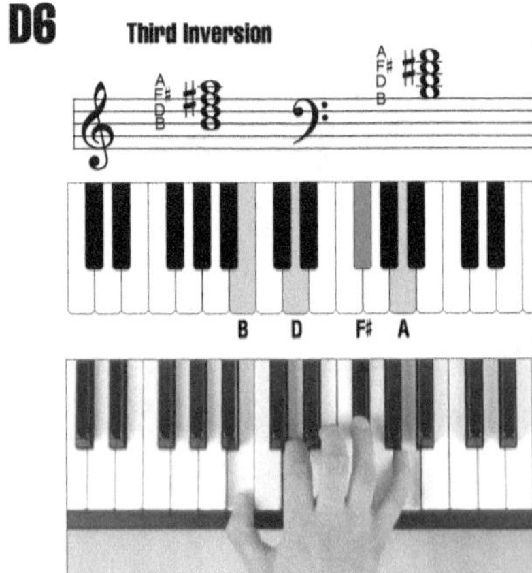

D(add2), D(add9) Root Position

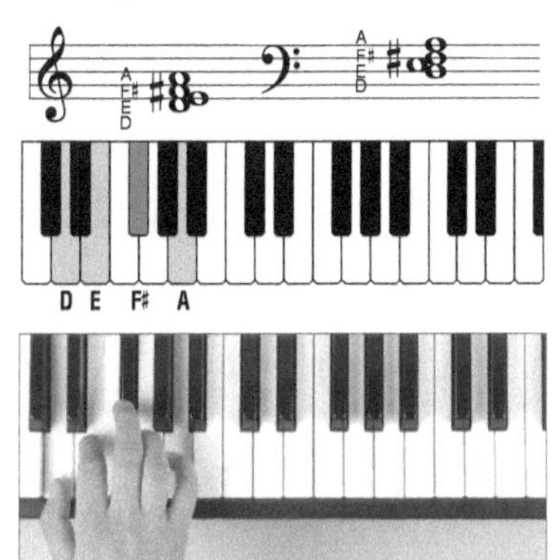

D(add2), D(add9) First Inversion

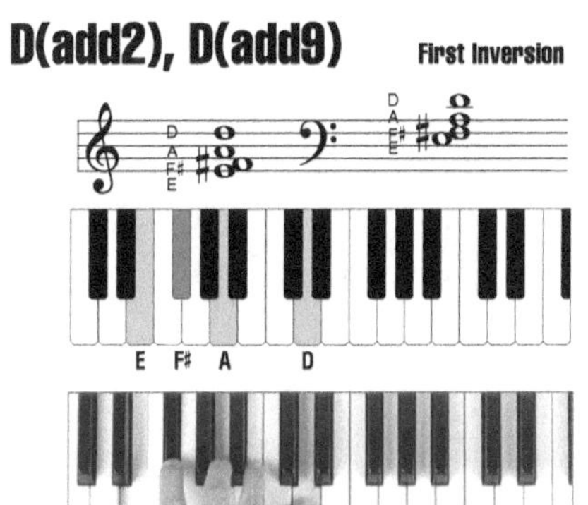

D(add2), D(add9) Second Inversion

F♯ A D E

D(add2), D(add9) Third Inversion

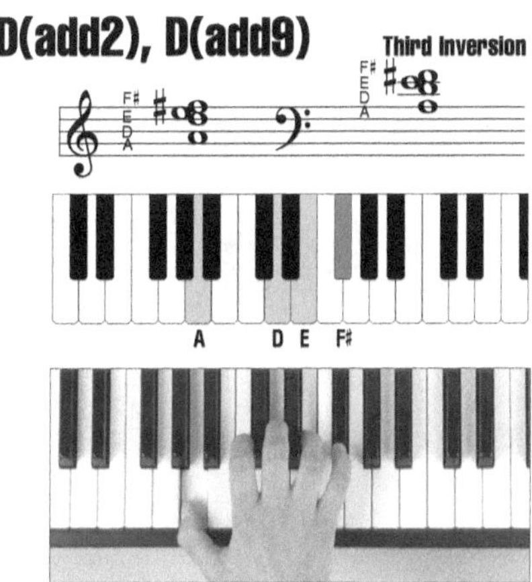

Dmaj7 Root Position

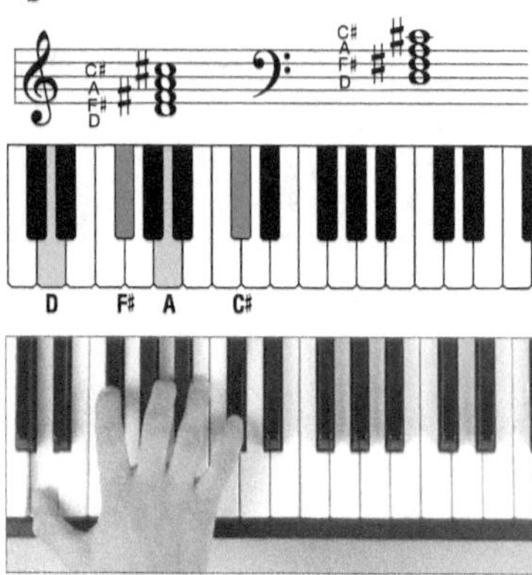

Dmaj7 First Inversion

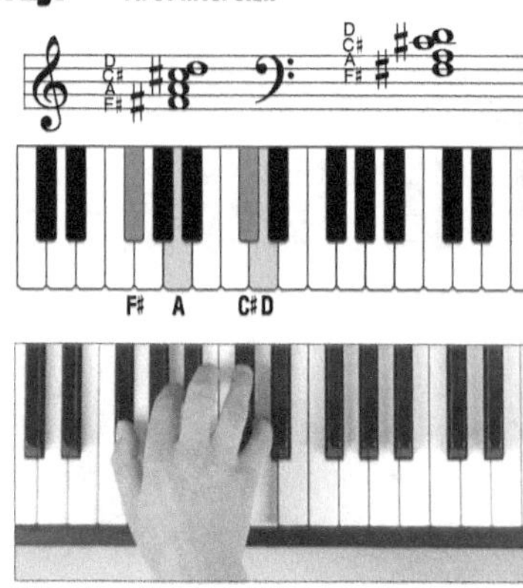

Dmaj7 Second Inversion

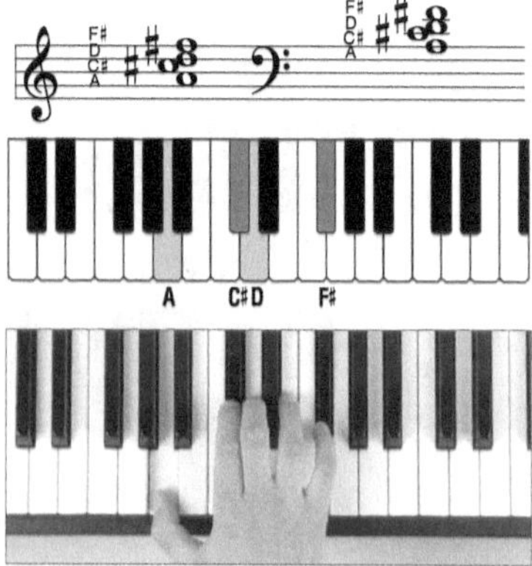

Dmaj7 Third Inversion

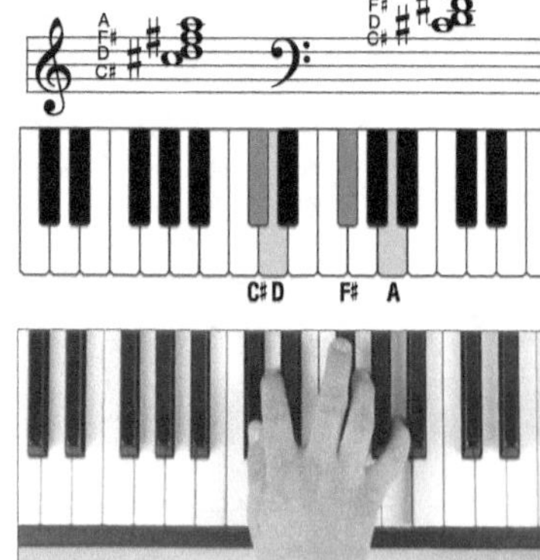

Dmaj7♭5 Root Position

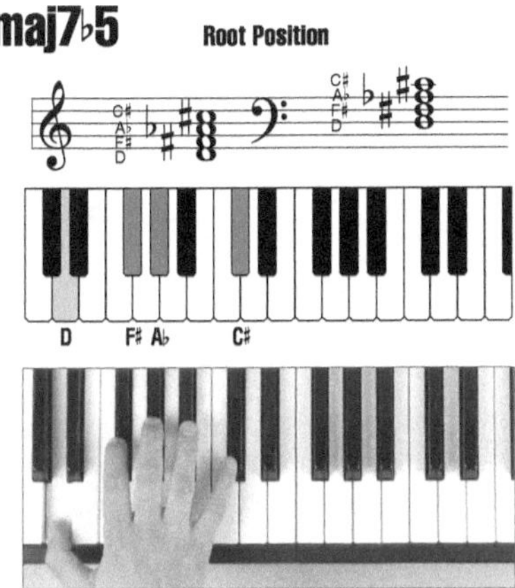

Dmaj7♭5 First Inversion

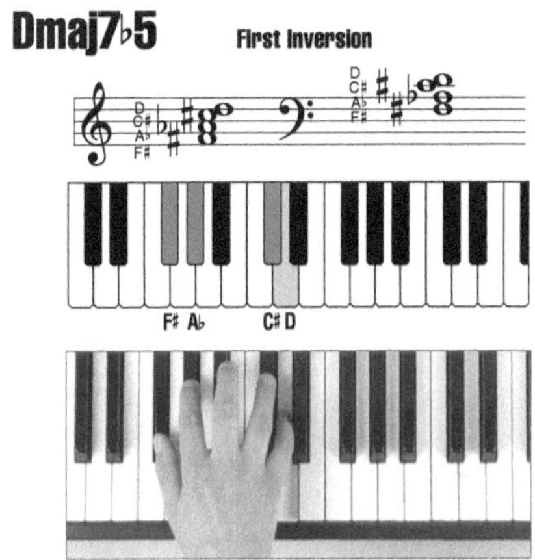

Dmaj7♭5 Second Inversion

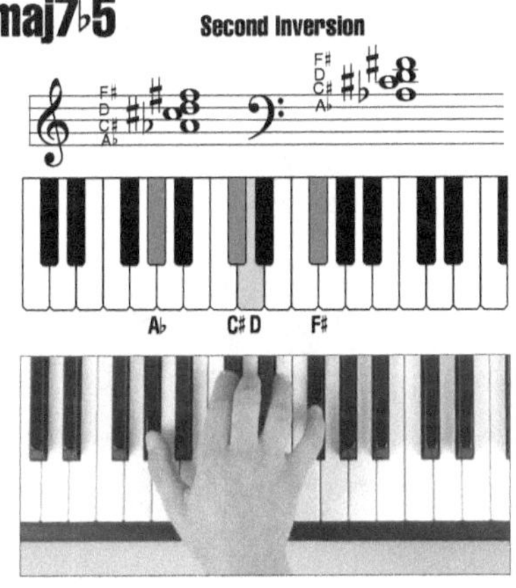

Dmaj7♭5 Third Inversion

Dmaj7♯5 Root Position

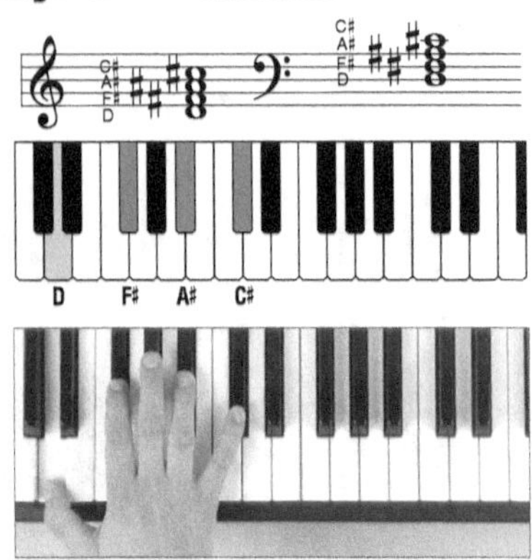

Dmaj7♯5 First Inversion

D
C♯
A♯
F♯

F♯ A♯ C♯ D

Dmaj7♯5 Second Inversion

F♯
D
C♯
A♯

A♯ C♯ D F♯

Dmaj7♯5 Third Inversion

A♯
F♯
D
C♯

C♯ D F♯ A♯

D7 Root Position

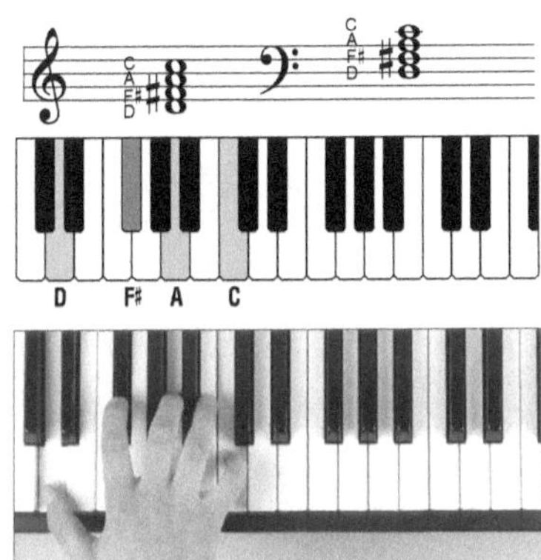

D7 First Inversion

D

D7 Second Inversion

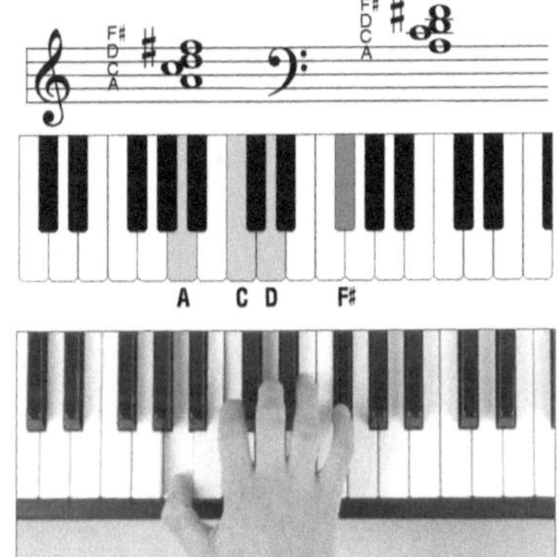

D7 Third Inversion

A
F♯
D
C

A
F♯
D
C

C D F♯ A

D7♭5 Root Position

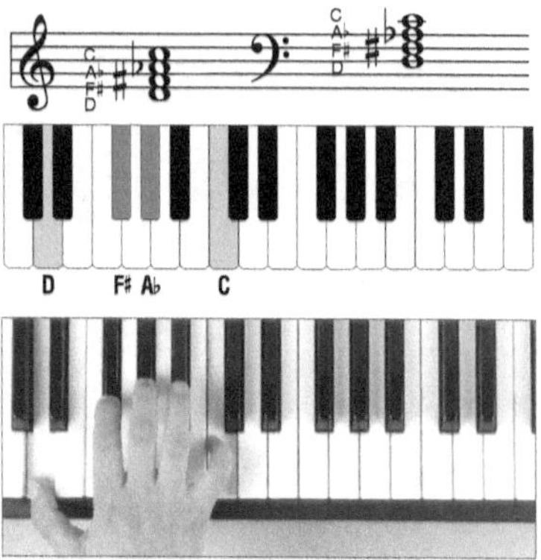

D7♭5 First Inversion

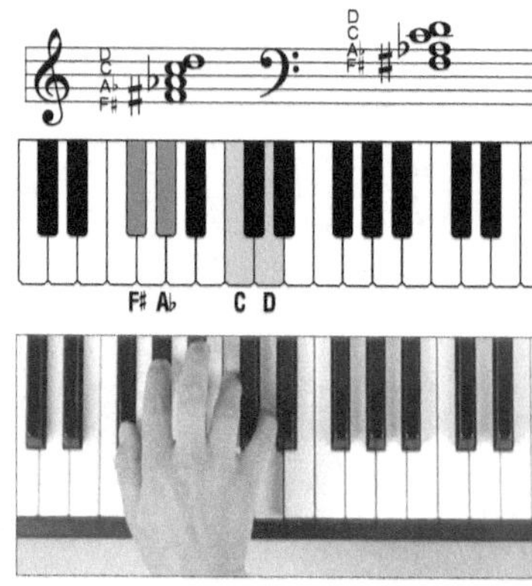

D7♭5 Second Inversion

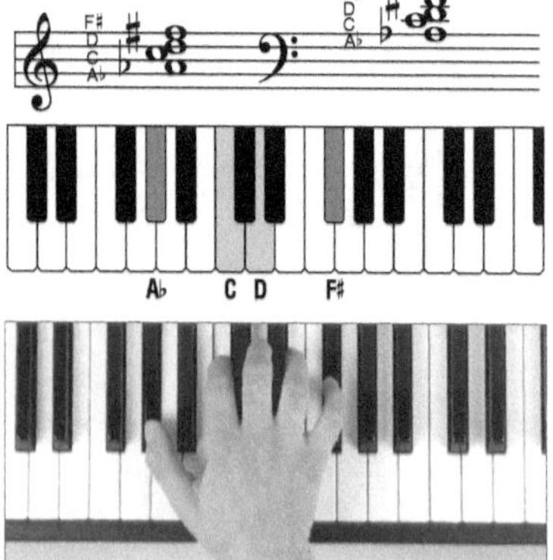

D7♭5 Third Inversion

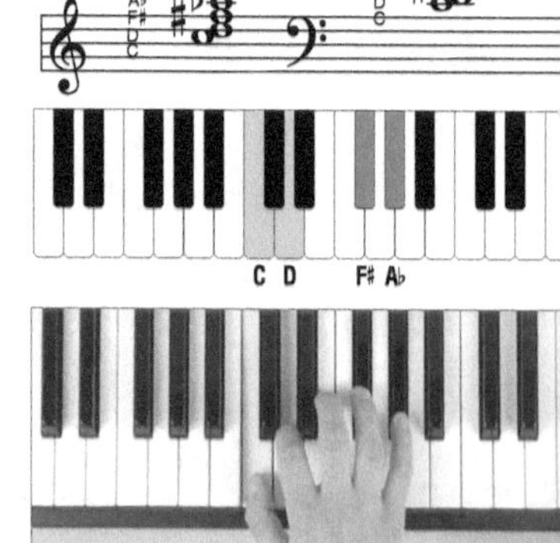

D7♯5 Root Position

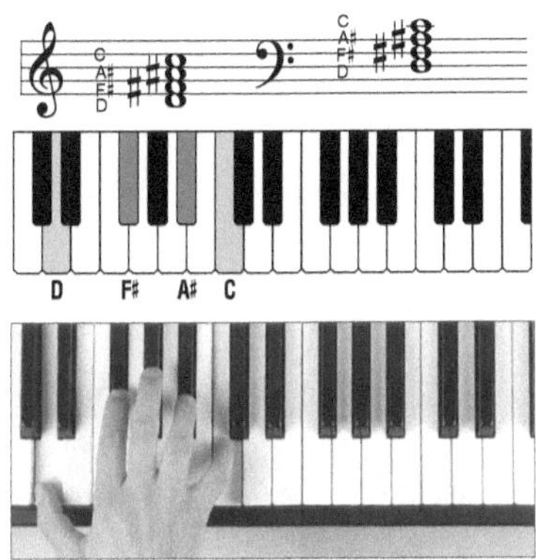

D7♯5 First Inversion

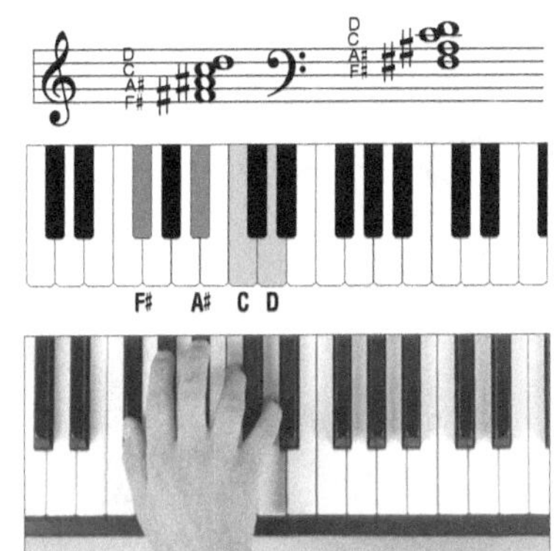

D7♯5 Second Inversion

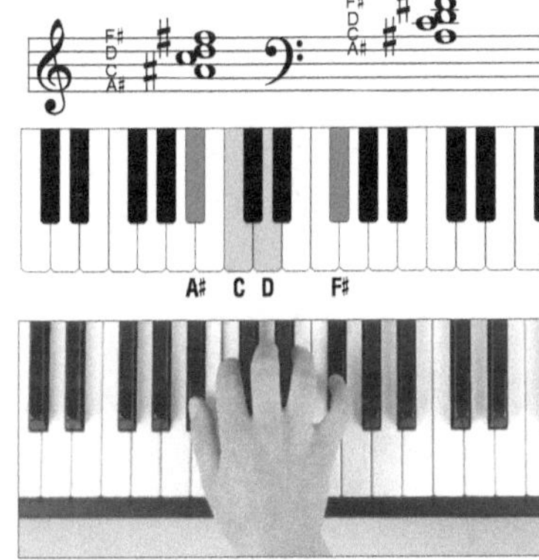

D7♯5 Third Inversion

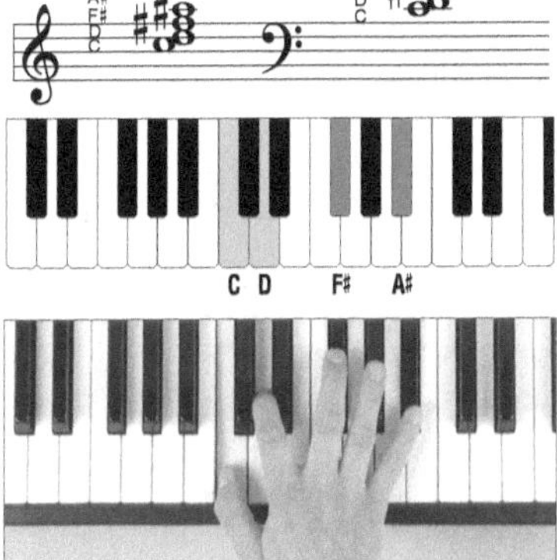

D7sus Root Position

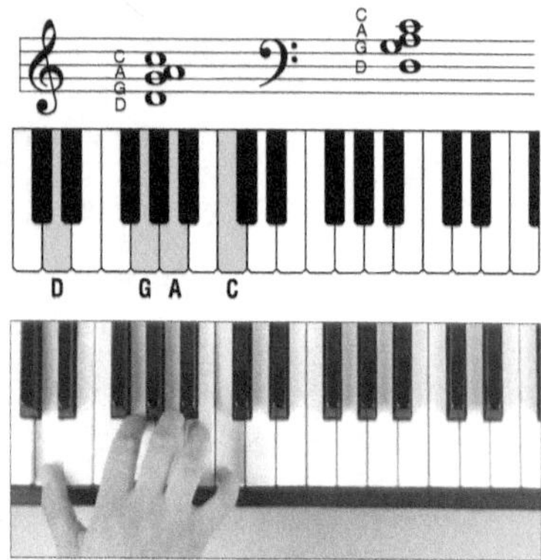

D7sus First Inversion

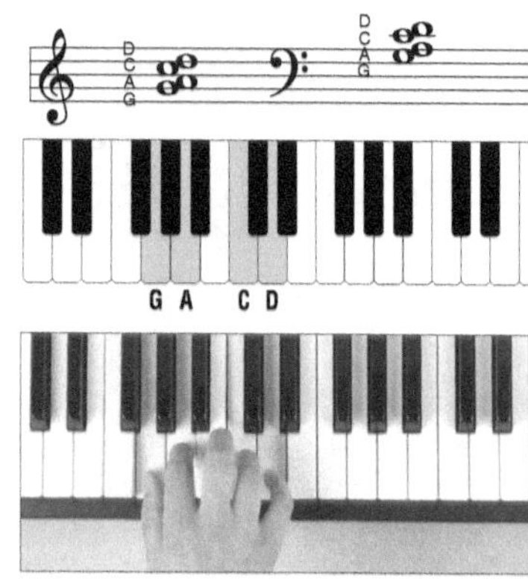

D7sus Second Inversion

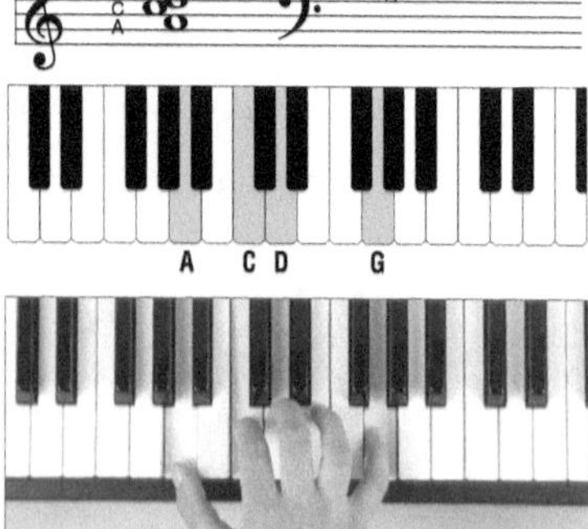

D7sus Third Inversion

Dm(add2), Dm(add9) Root Position

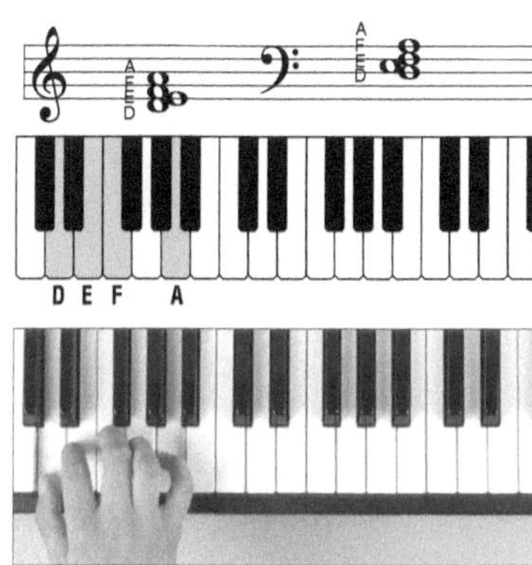

Dm(add2), Dm(add9) First Inversion

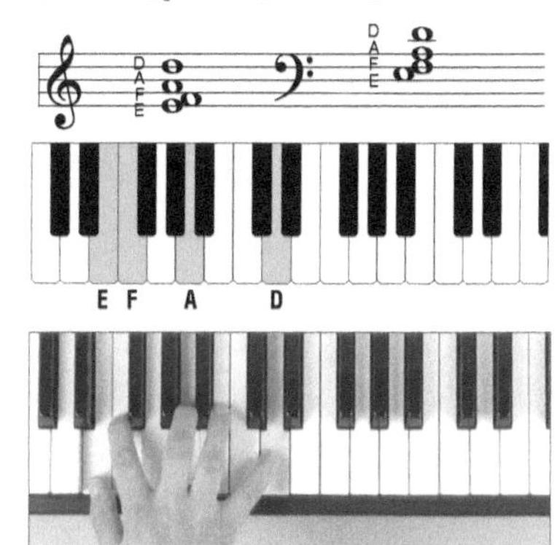

Dm(add2), Dm(add9) Second Inversion

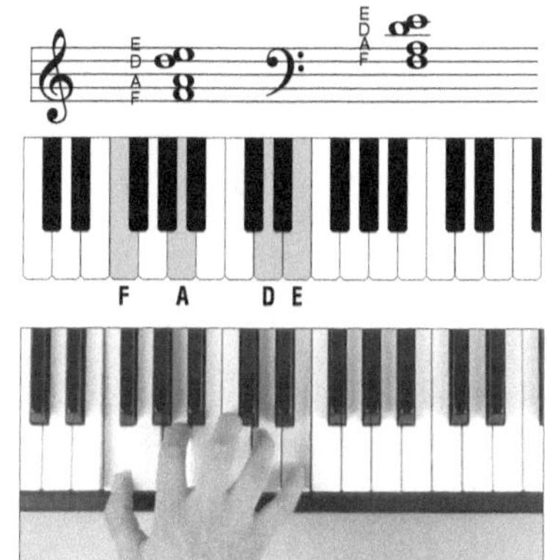

Dm(add2), Dm(add9) Third Inversion

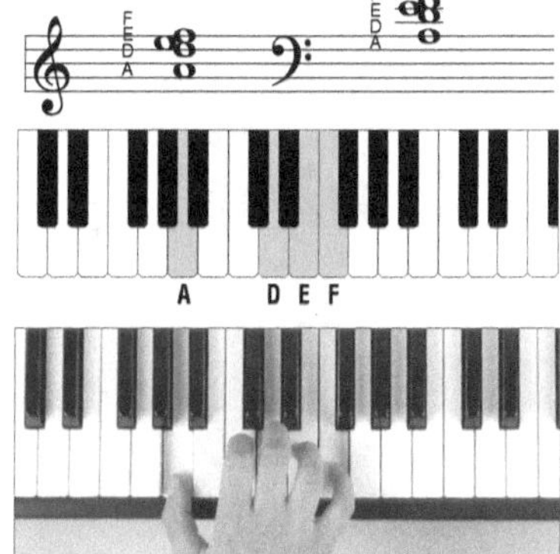

Dm6 Root Position

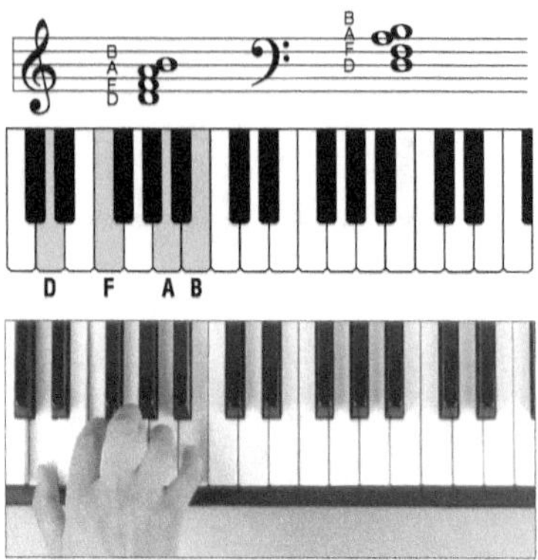

Dm6 First Inversion

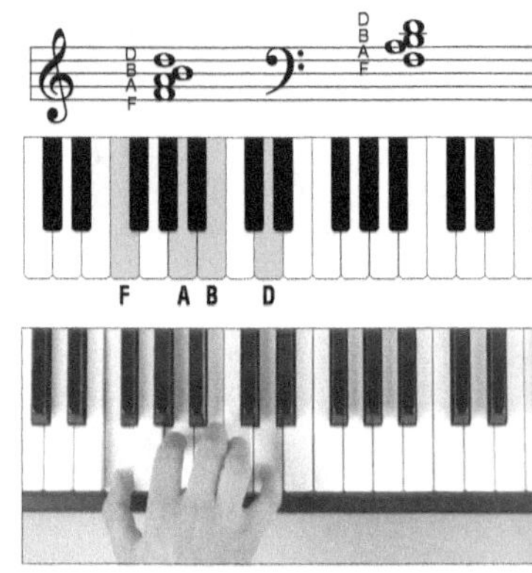

Dm6 Second Inversion

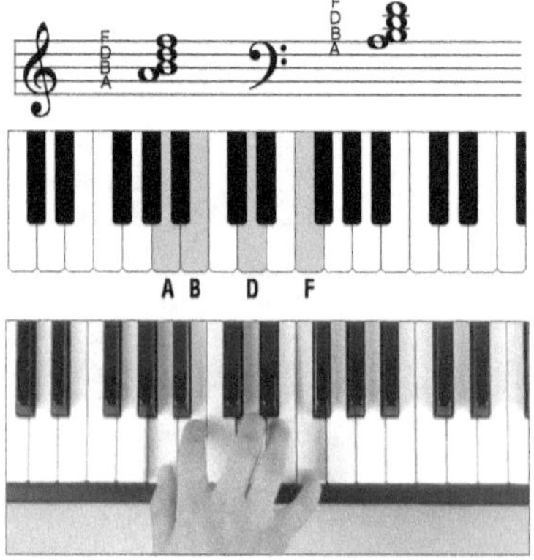

Dm6 Third Inversion

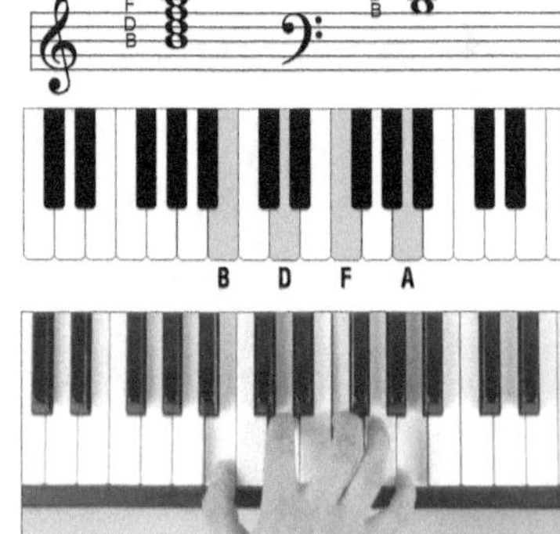

Dm7 Root Position

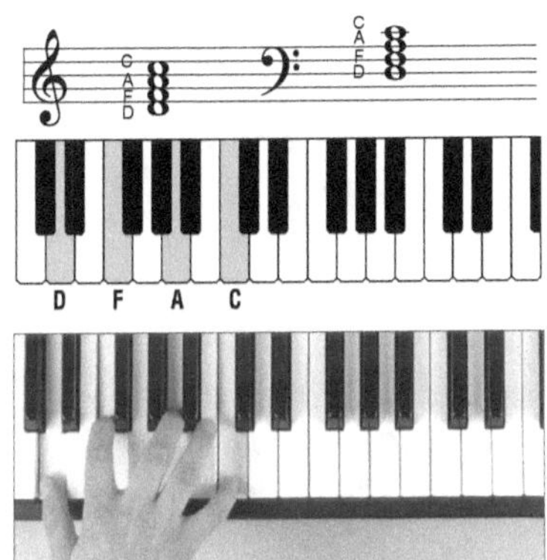

Dm7 First Inversion

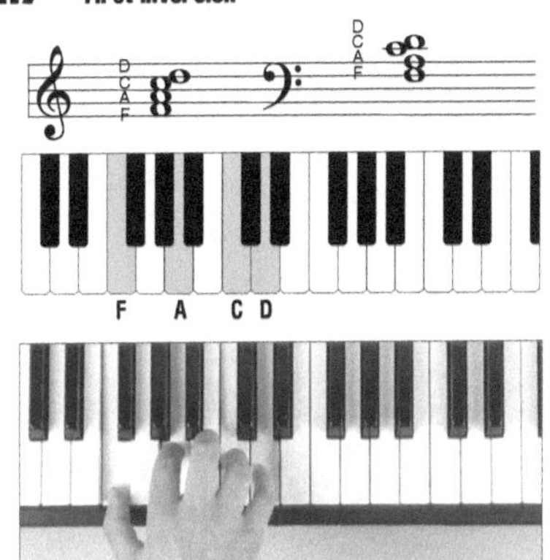

Dm7 Second Inversion

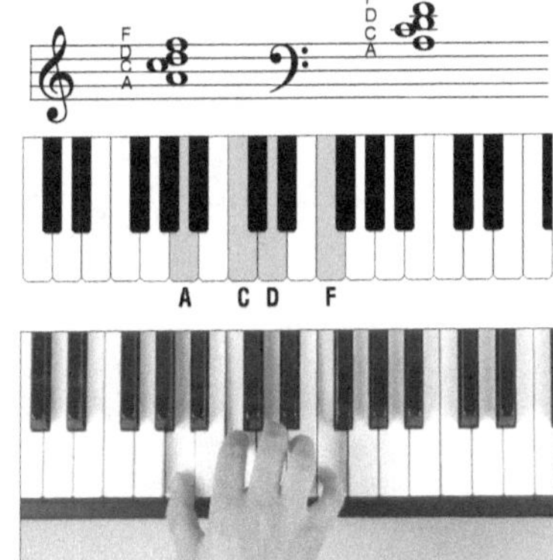

Dm7 Third Inversion

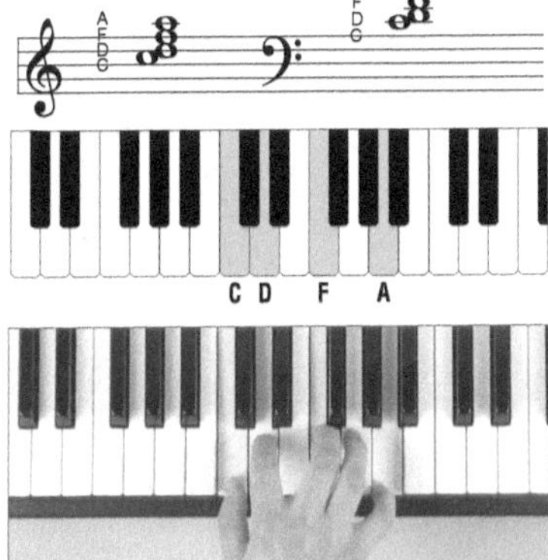

Dm(maj7) Root Position

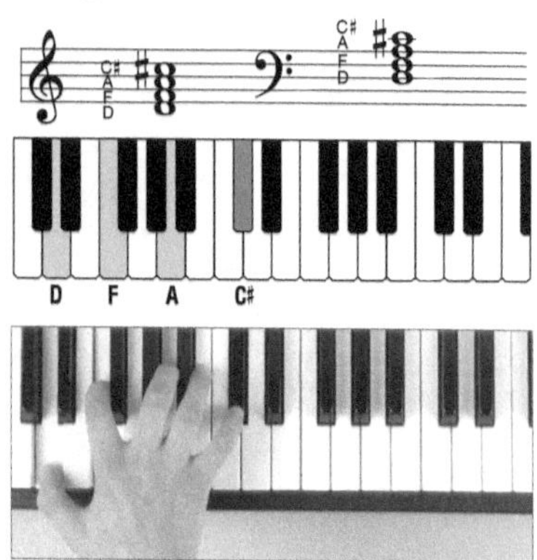

Dm(maj7) First Inversion

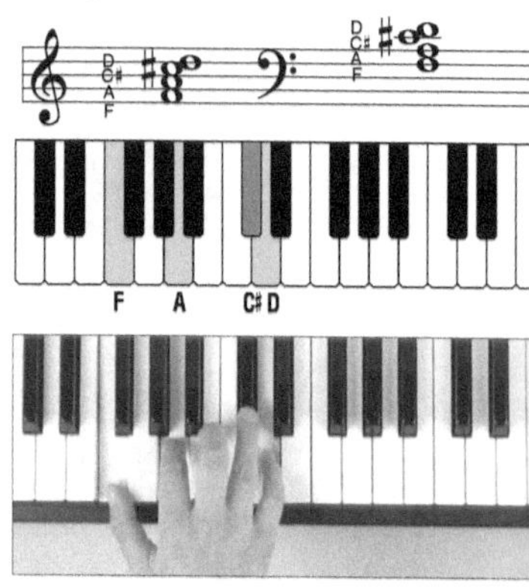

Dm(maj7) Second Inversion

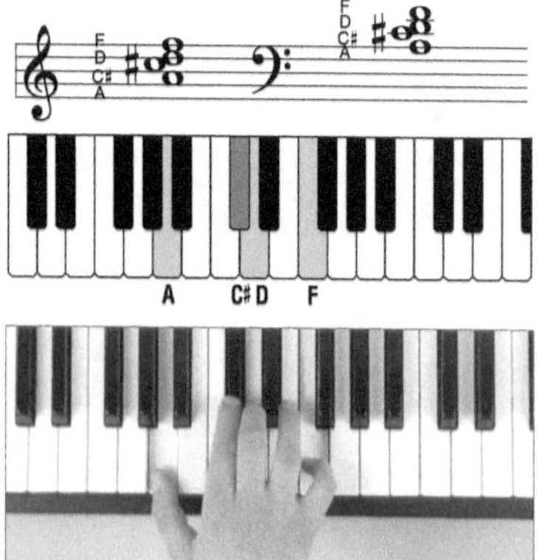

Dm(maj7) Third Inversion

A
F
D
C♯

C♯ D F A

Dm7♭5 Root Position

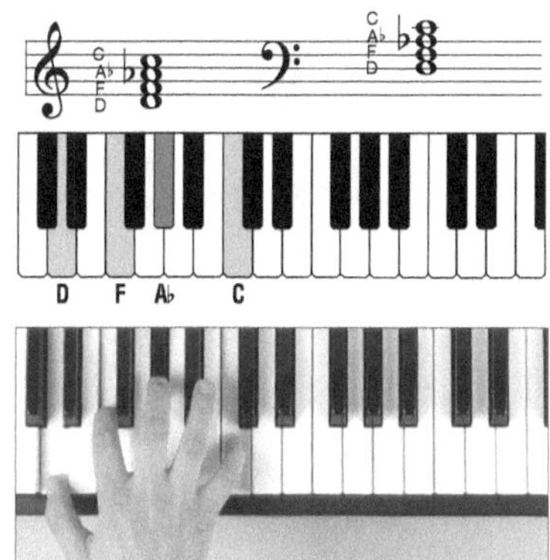

Dm7♭5 First Inversion

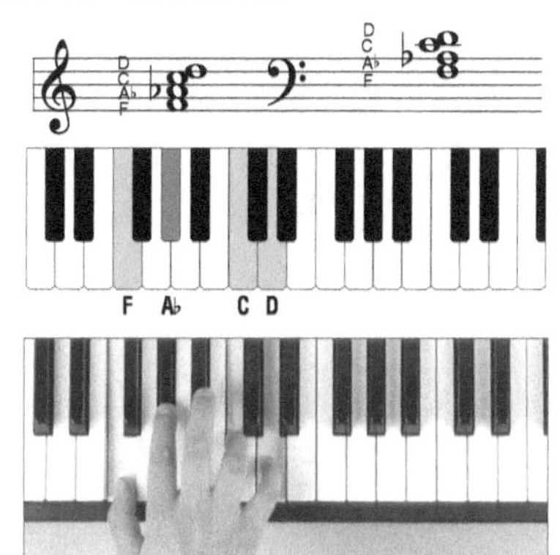

Dm7♭5 Second Inversion

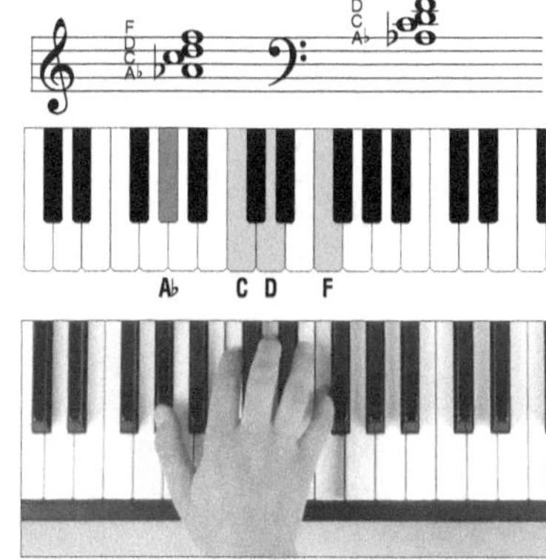

Dm7♭5 Third Inversion

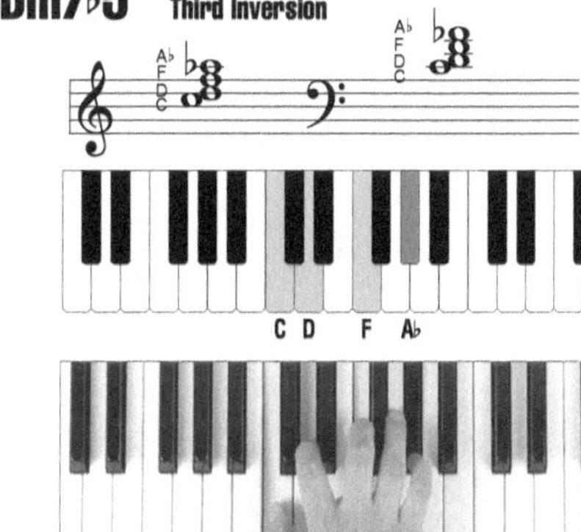

Ddim7 Root Position

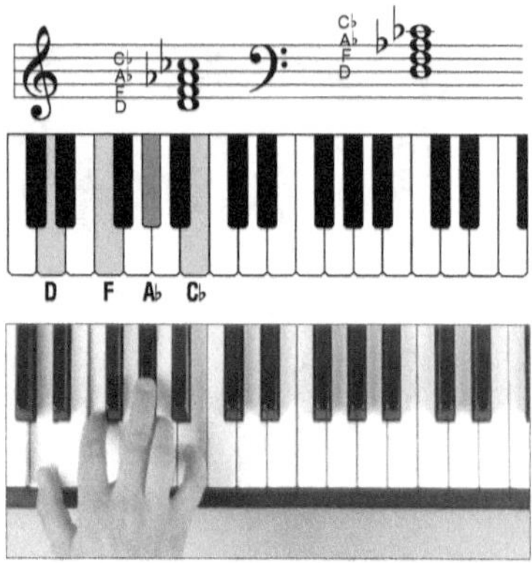

Ddim7 First Inversion

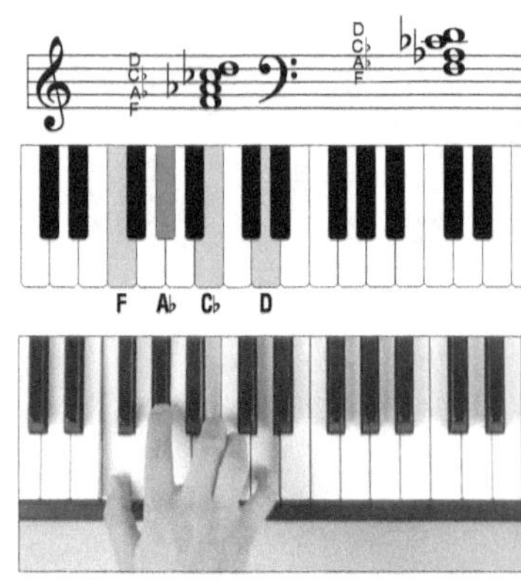

Ddim7 Second Inversion

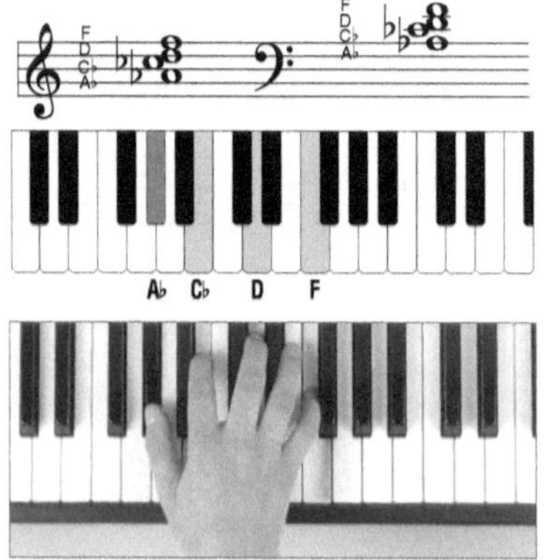

Ddim7 Third Inversion

A♭
F
D
C♭

A♭
F
D
C♭

C♭ D F A♭

Ddim(maj7) Root Position

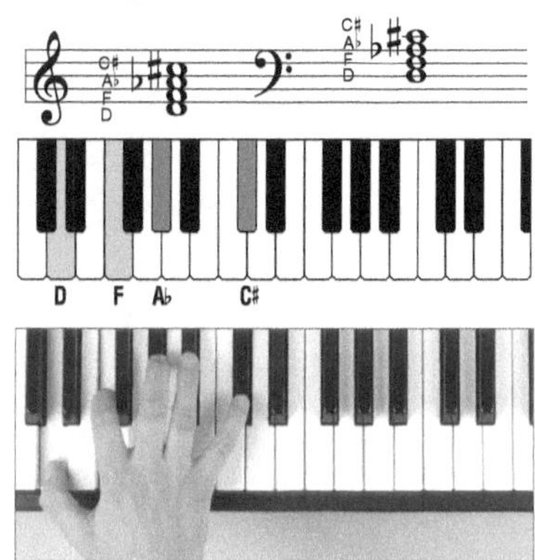

Ddim(maj7) First Inversion

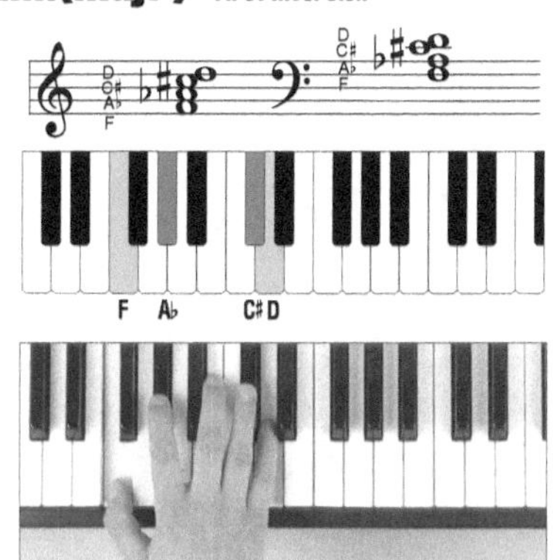

Ddim(maj7) Second Inversion

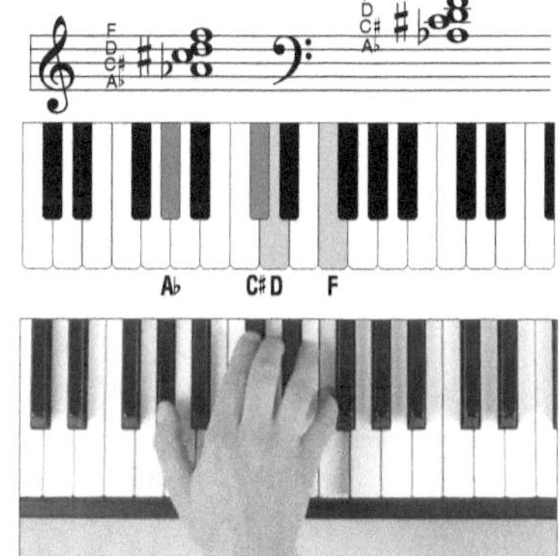

Ddim(maj7) Third Inversion

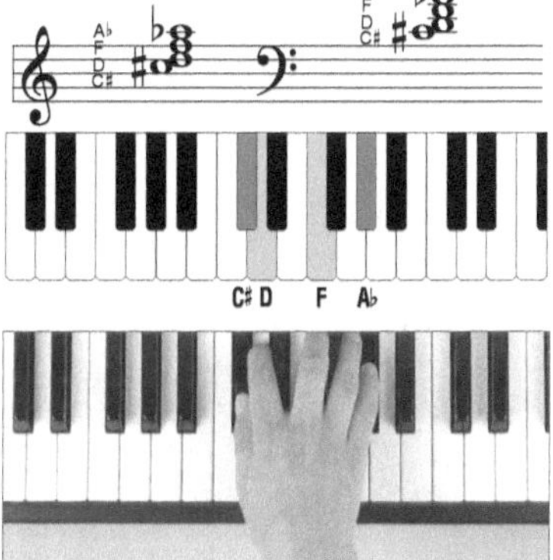

D5

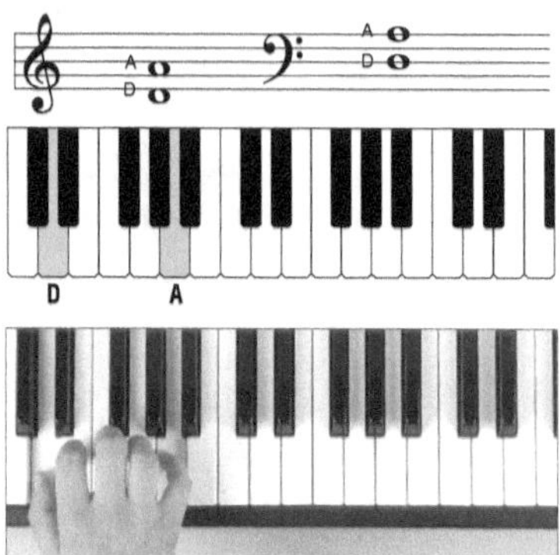

Dmaj7♯11

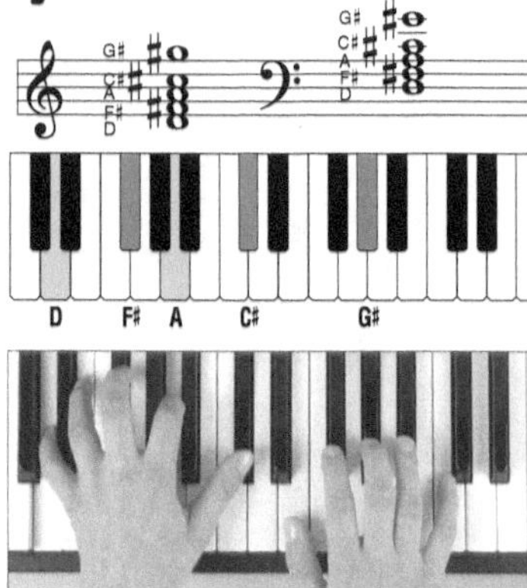

D6/9

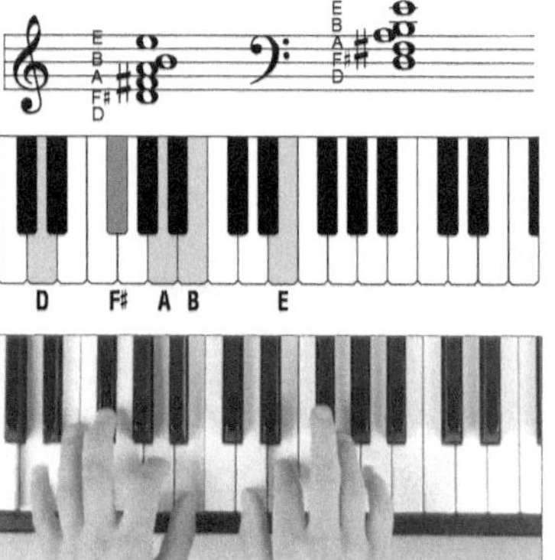

Dmaj9

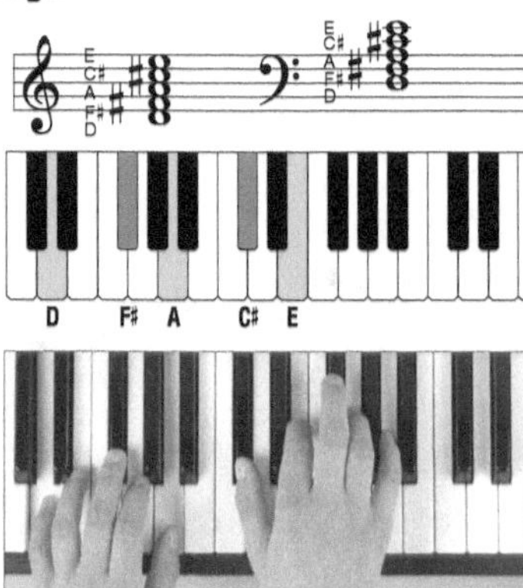

Dmaj6/9

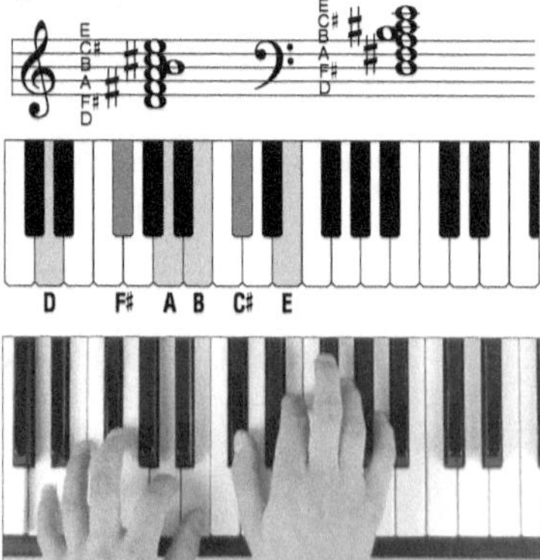

Dmaj9♭5

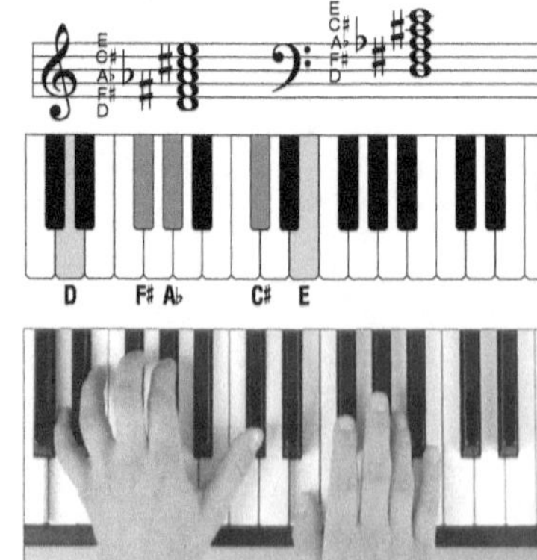

Dmaj9♯5

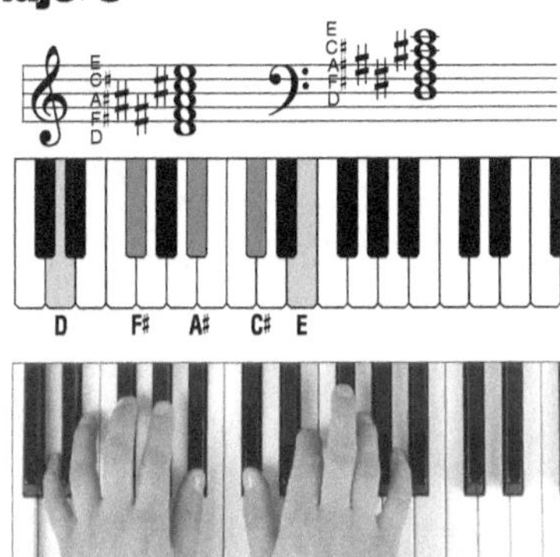

Dmaj9♯11

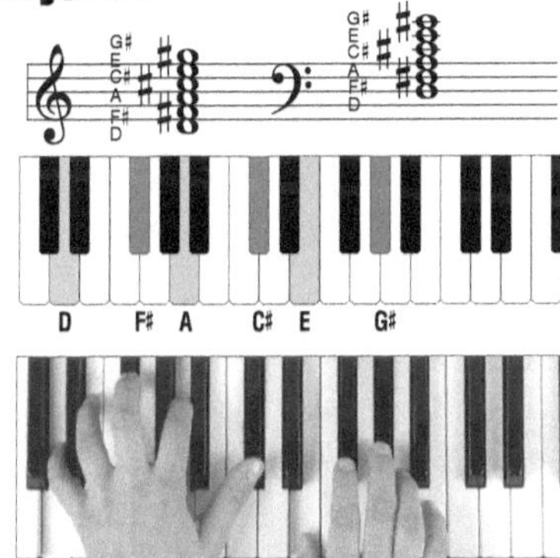

Dmaj13

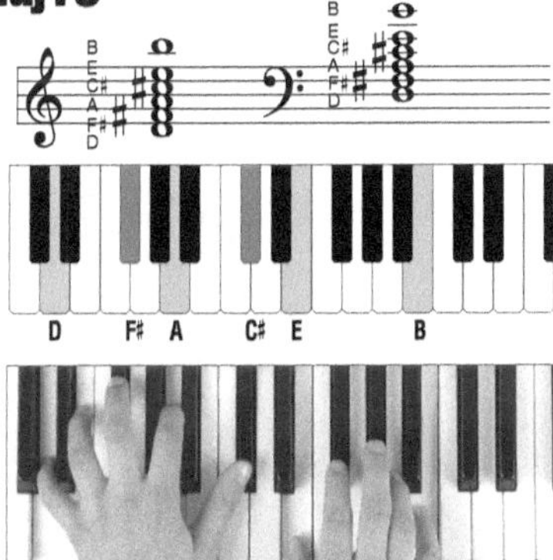

Dmaj13♭5

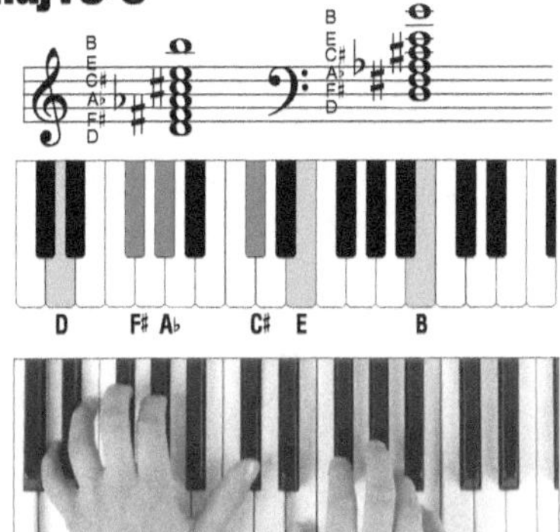

Dmaj13♯11

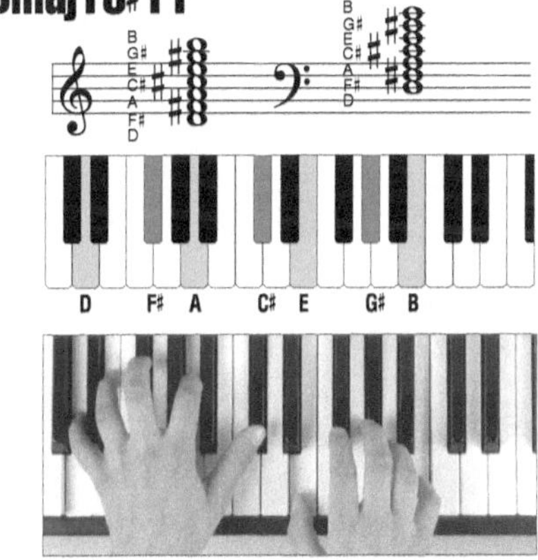

D7♭9

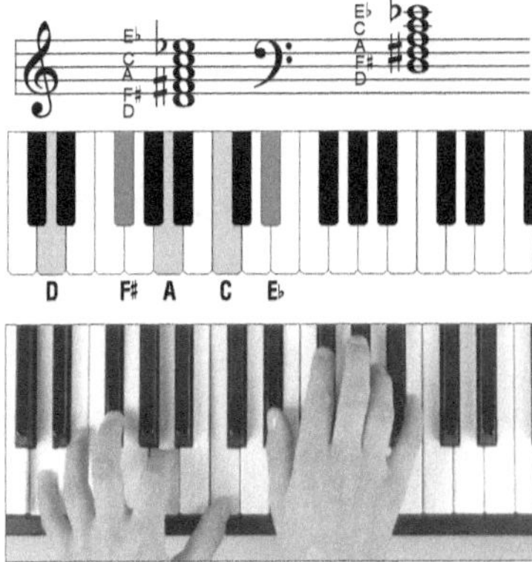

D7♯9

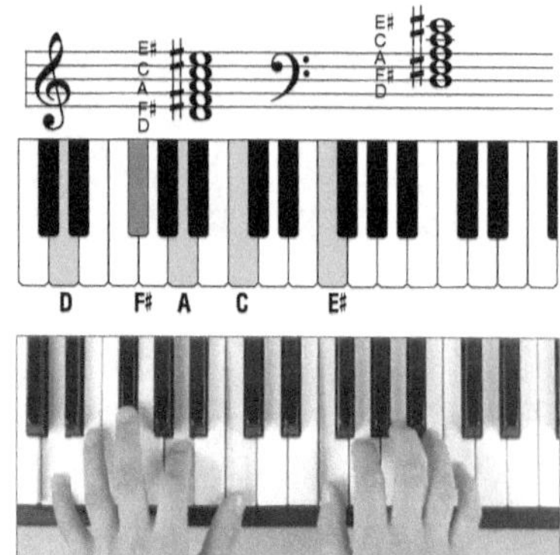

D7♯11

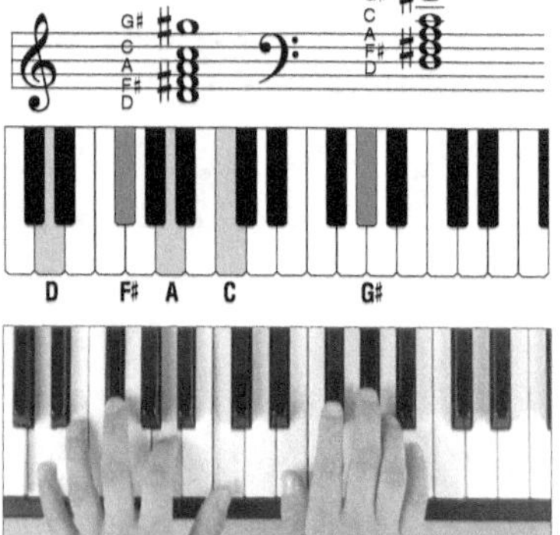

D7♭5(♭9)

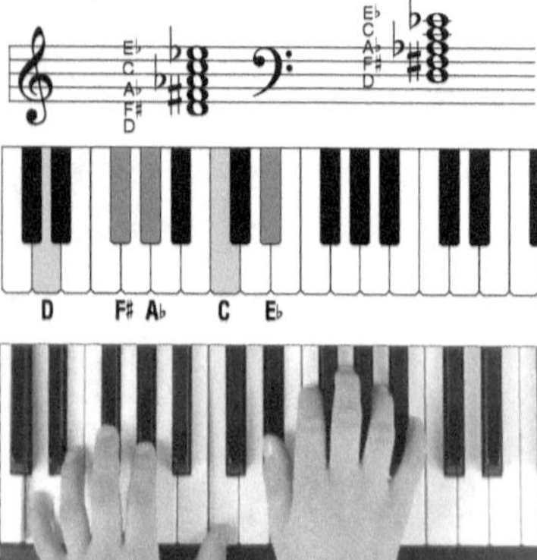

D7♭5(♯9)

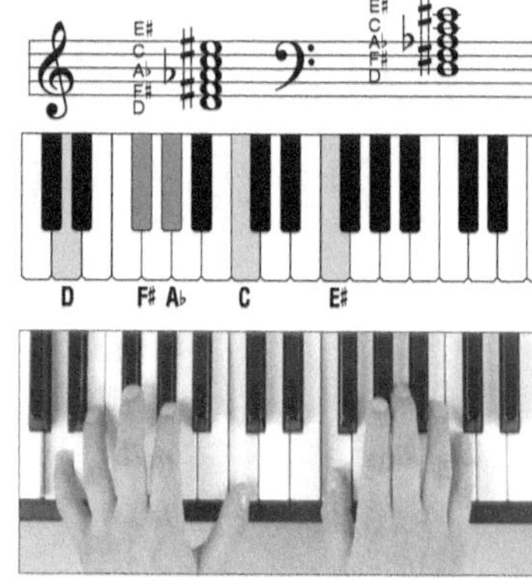

D7♯5(♭9)

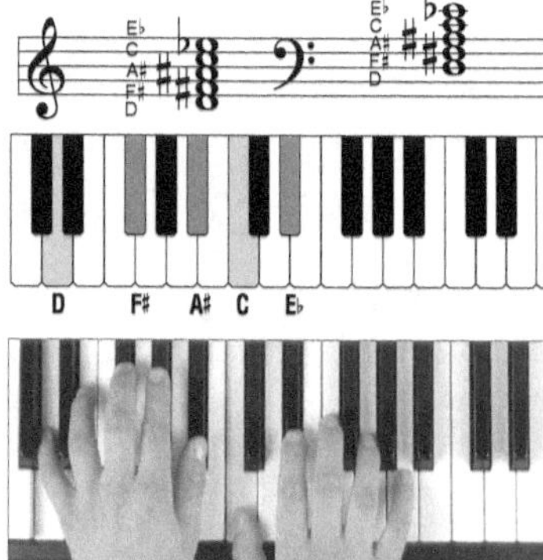

D7♯5(♯9)

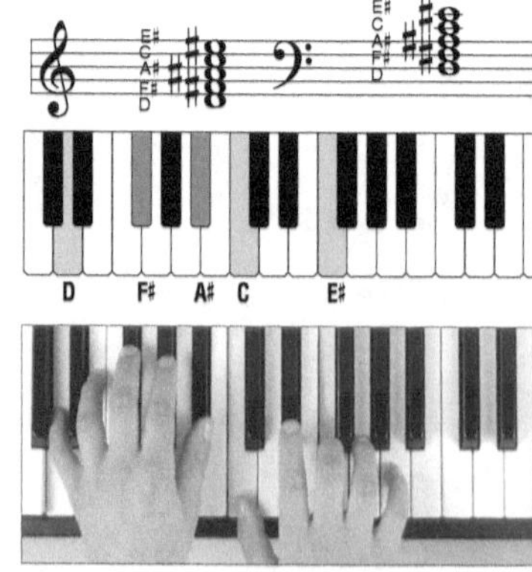

D7♭9(♯9)

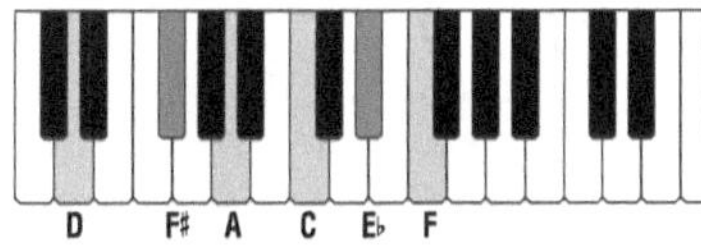

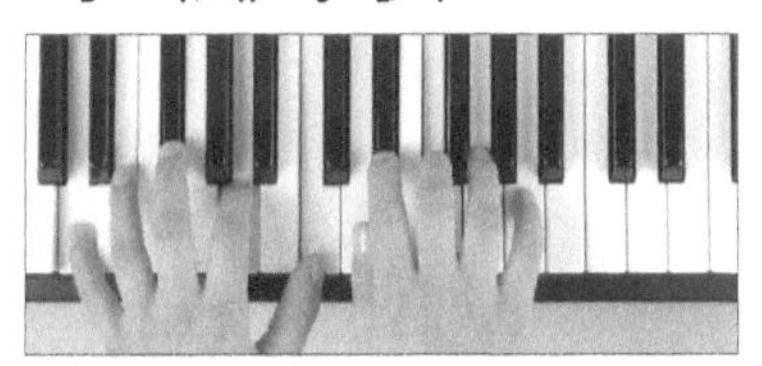

D7(add13)

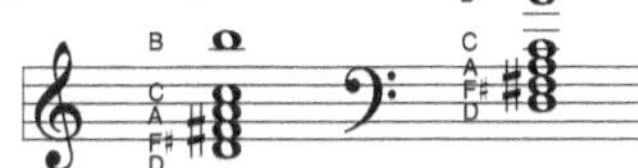

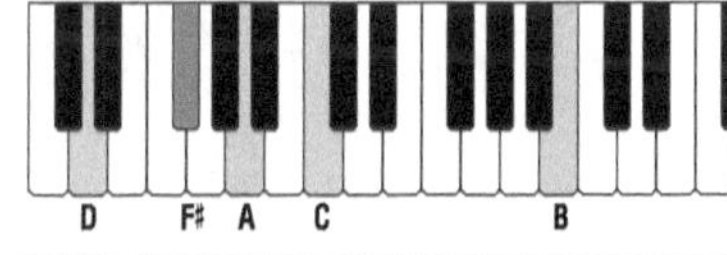

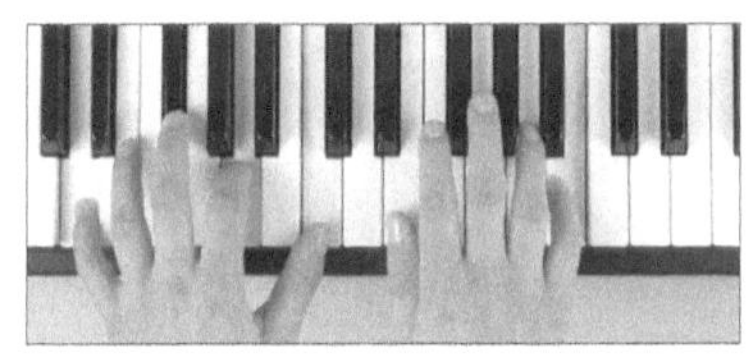

D7♭13

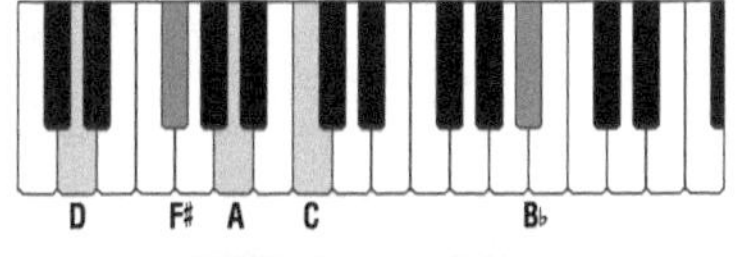

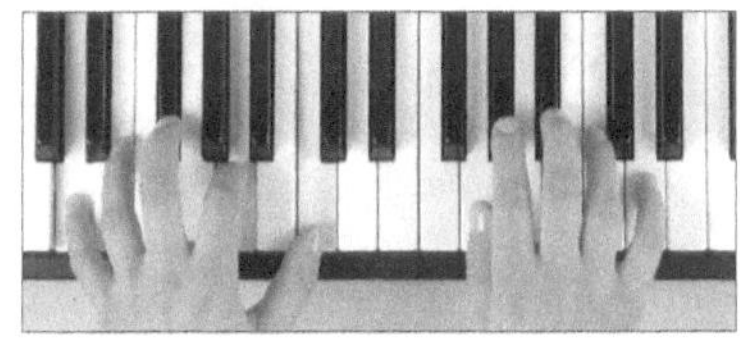

D7♭9(♯11)

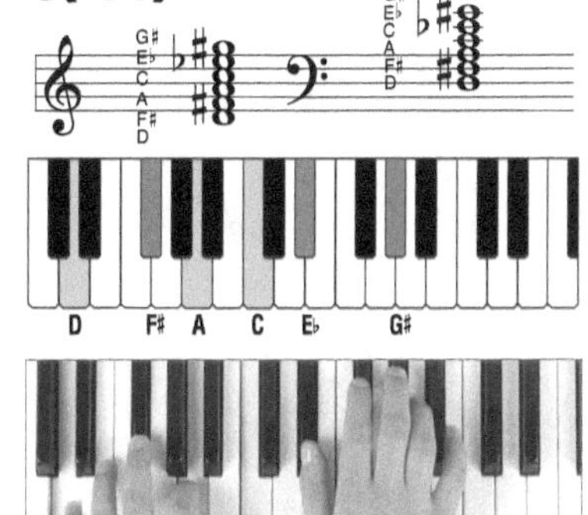

D7♯9(♯11)

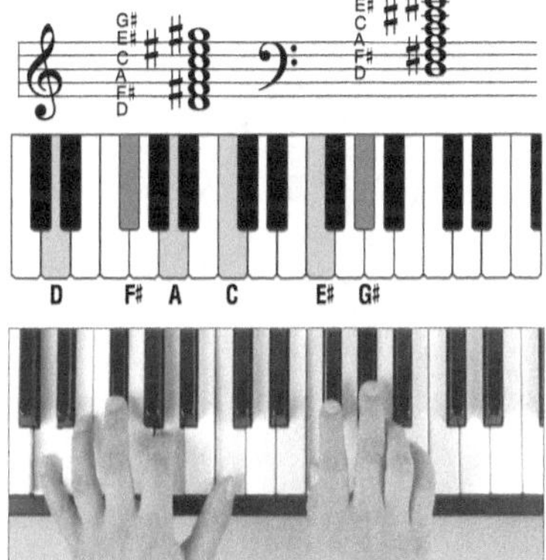

D7♭9(♭13)

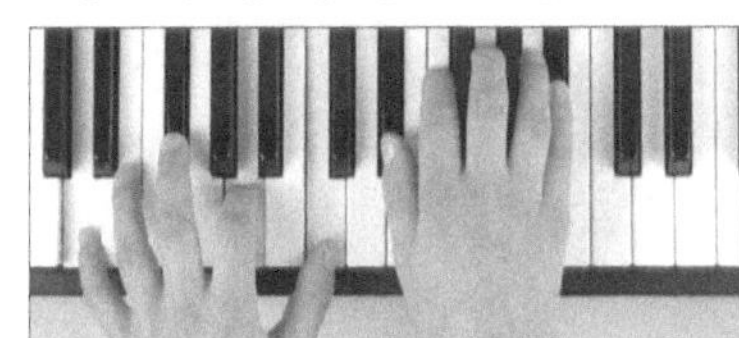

D7♯9(♭13)

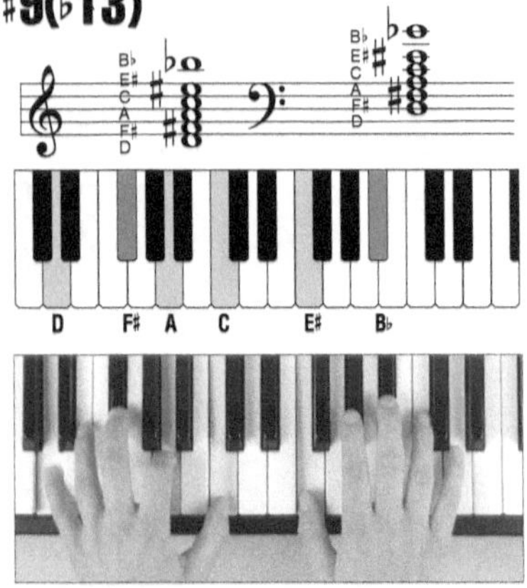

B♭
E♯
C
A
F♯
D

B♭
E♯
C
A
F♯
D

D F♯ A C E♯ B♭

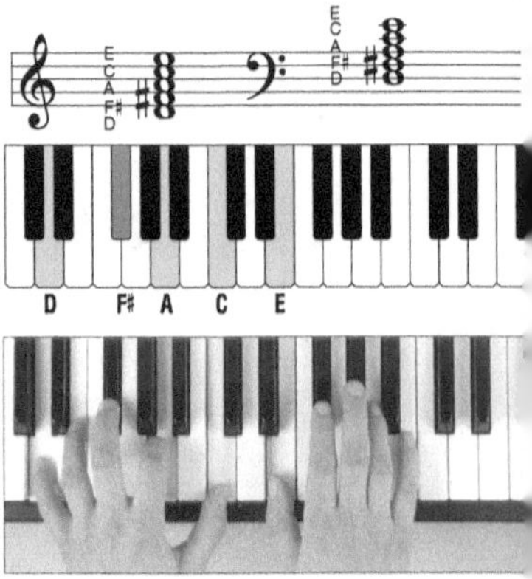

D7♯11(♭13)

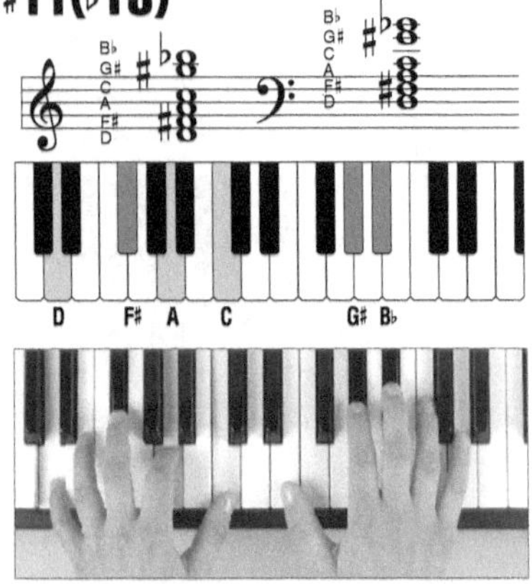

B♭
G♯
C
A
F♯
D

B♭
G♯
C
A
F♯
D

D F♯ A C G♯ B♭

D7♭9(♯9, ♯11)

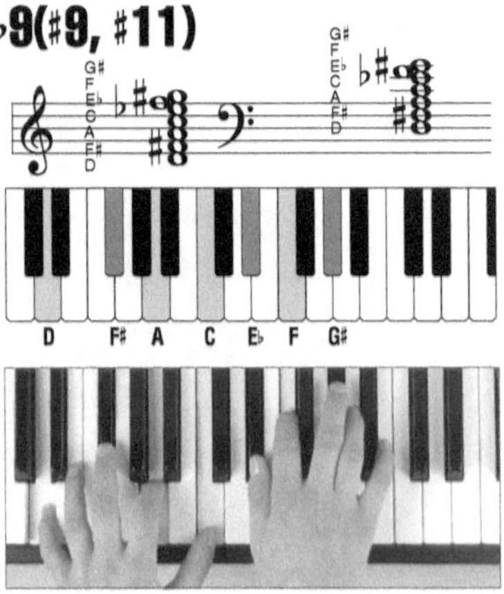

G♯
F
E♭
C
A
F♯
D

G♯
F
E♭
C
A
F♯
D

D F♯ A C E♭ F G♯

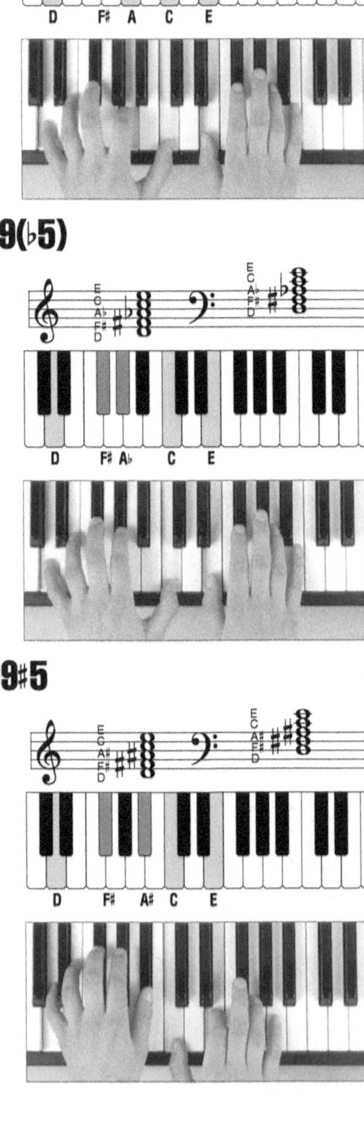

D9♯11

D9♭13

D9♯11(♭13)

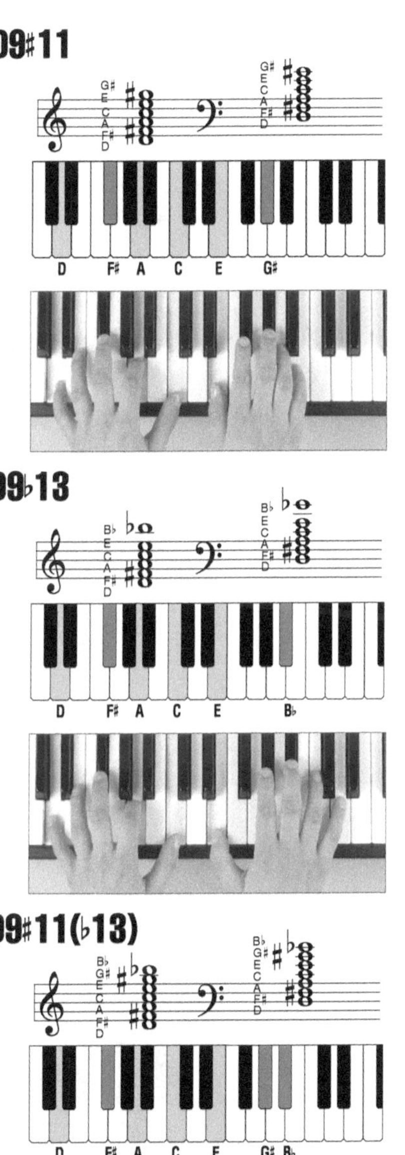

D11, D9(sus4)

D13

D13♭5

D13♭9

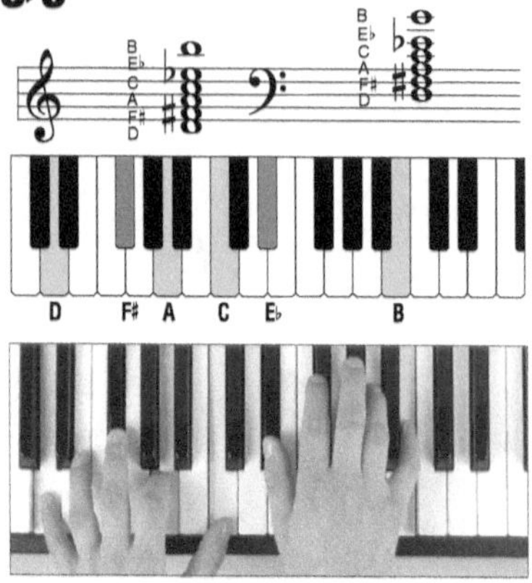

B
E♭
C
A
F♯
D
B
E♭
C
A
F♯
D
D F♯ A C E♭ B

D13(sus4)

B
E
C
A
G
D
B
E
C
A
G
D
D G A C E B

D13♯9

B
E♯
C
A
F♯
D
B
E♯
C
A
F♯
D
D F♯ A C E♯ B

Dm(♯5)

A♯
F
D
A♯
F
D
D F A♯

D13♯11

B
G♯
E
C
A
F♯
D
B
G♯
E
C
A
F♯
D
D F♯ A C E G♯ B

Dm$^{6}_{9}$

E
B
A
F
D
E
B
A
F
D
D F A B E

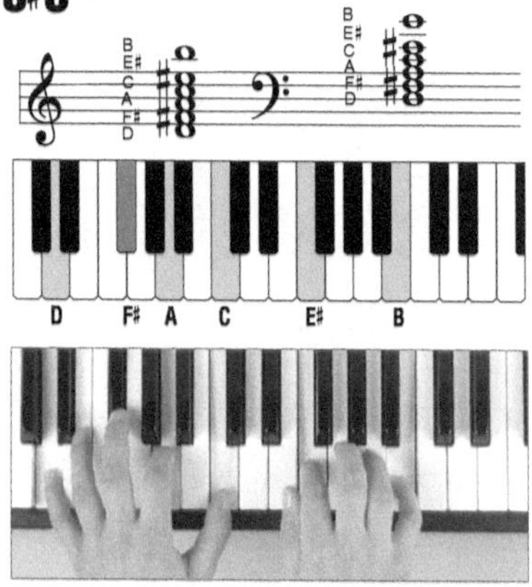

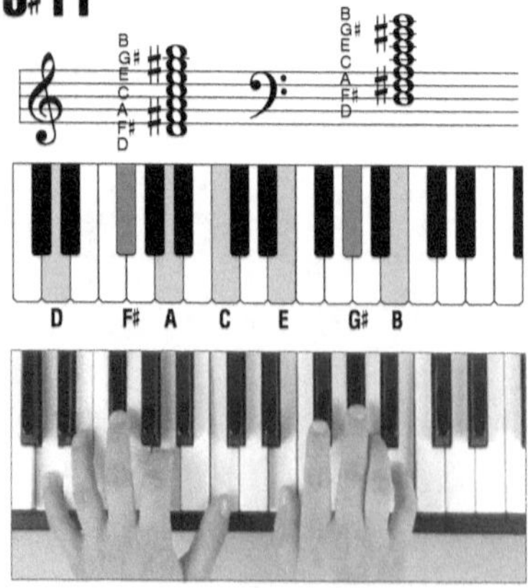

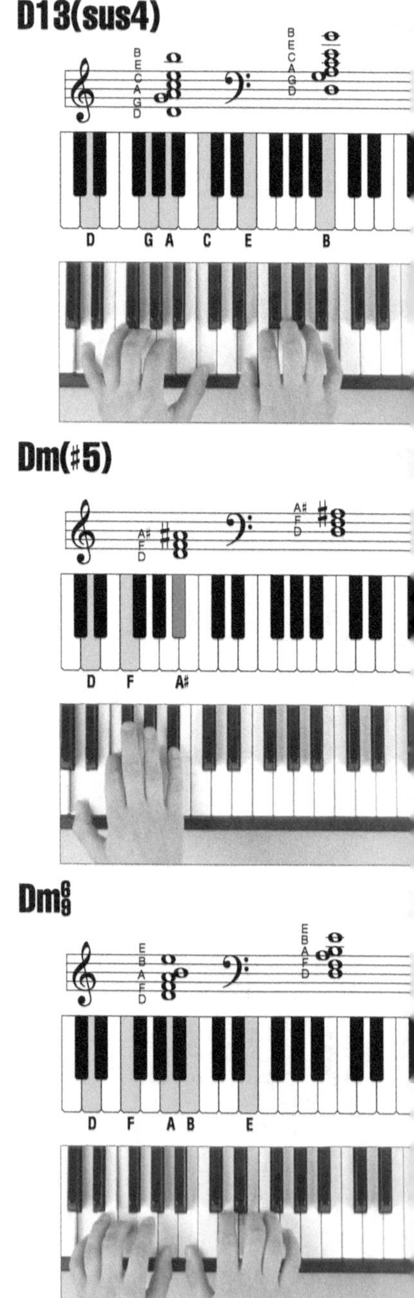

Dm7(add4)

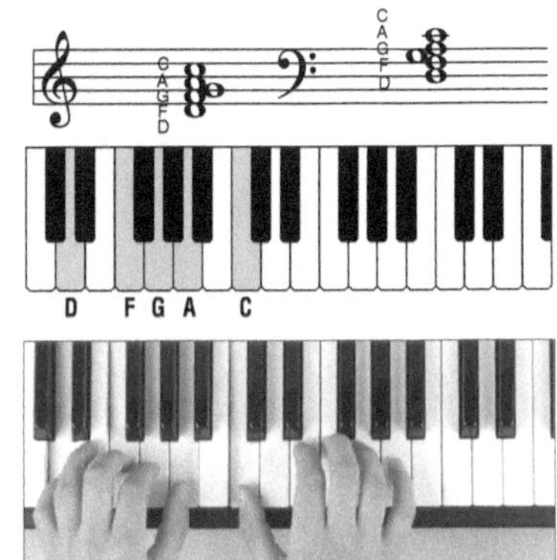

Dm9

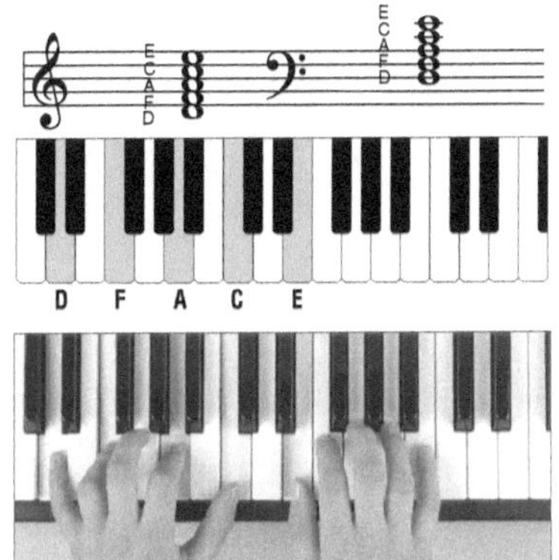

Dm7(add11)

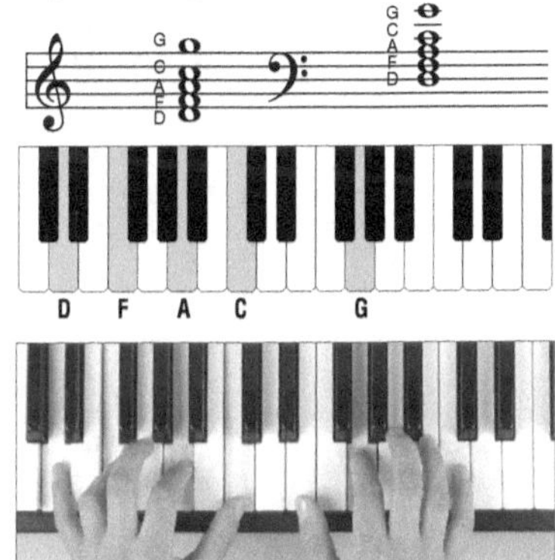

Dm9(maj7)

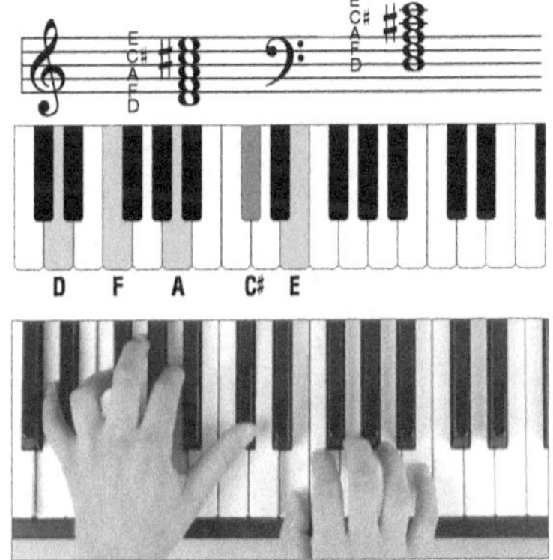

Dm7♭5(♭9)

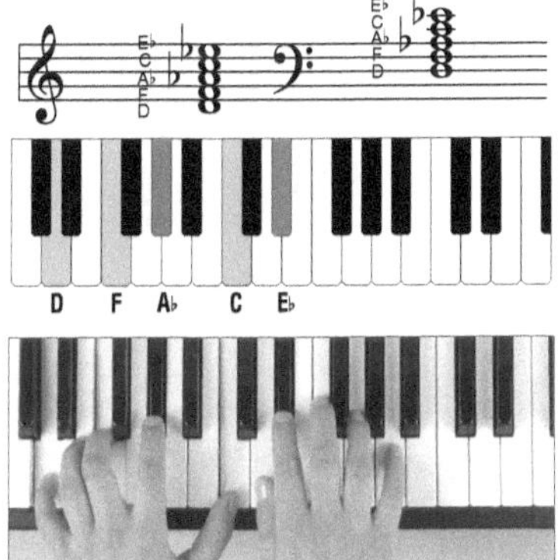

Dm9♭5

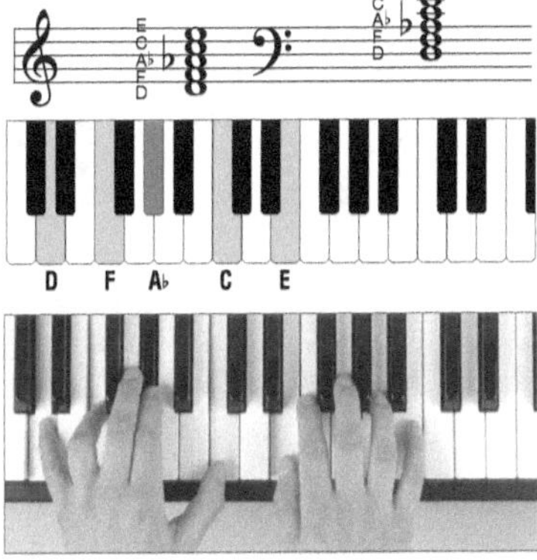

Dm11

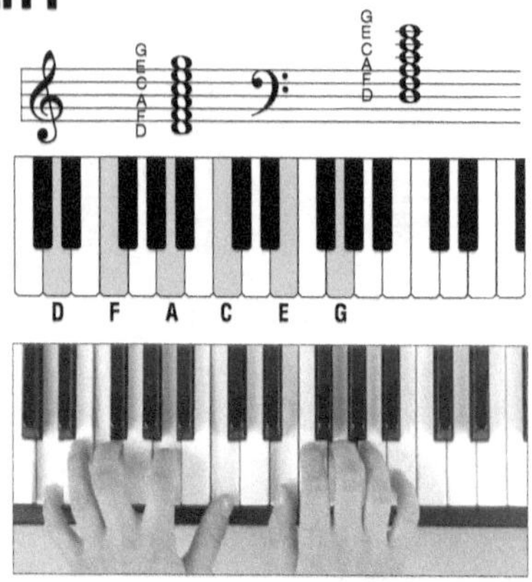

D F A C E G

Dm11♭5

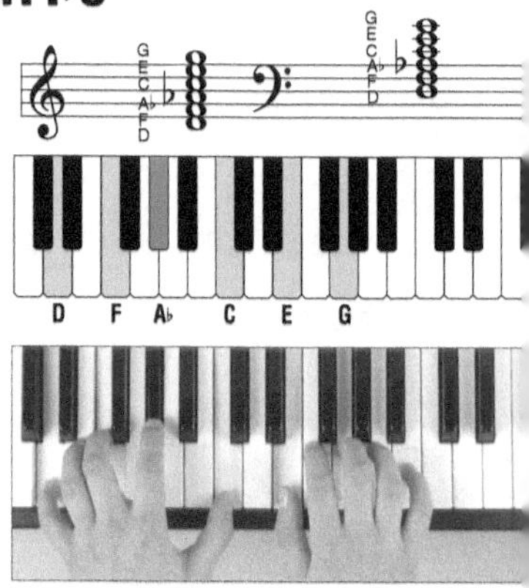

D F A♭ C E G

Dm13

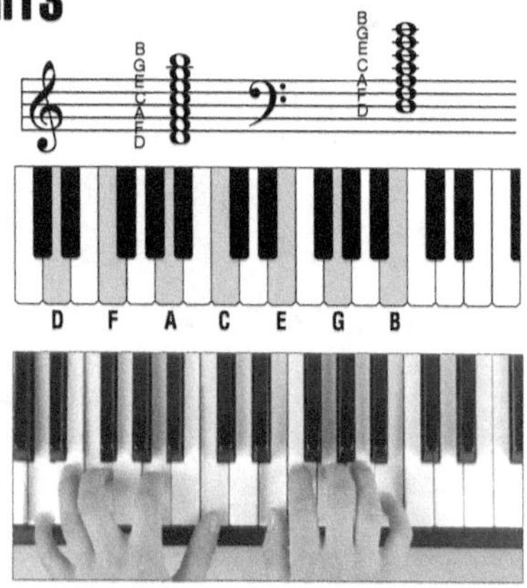

D F A C E G B

Dm11(maj7)

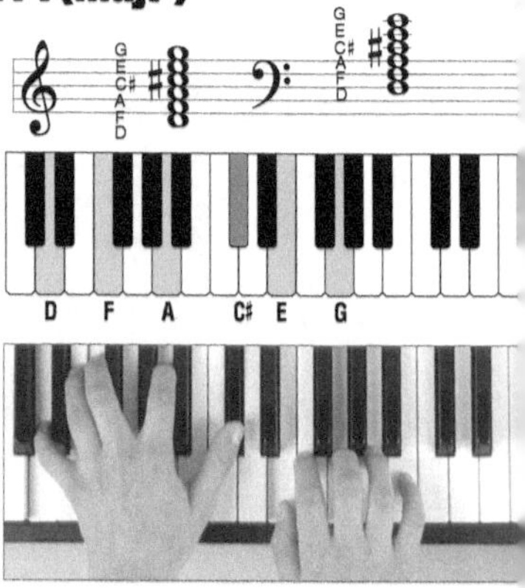

D F A C♯ E G

Ddim7(add9)

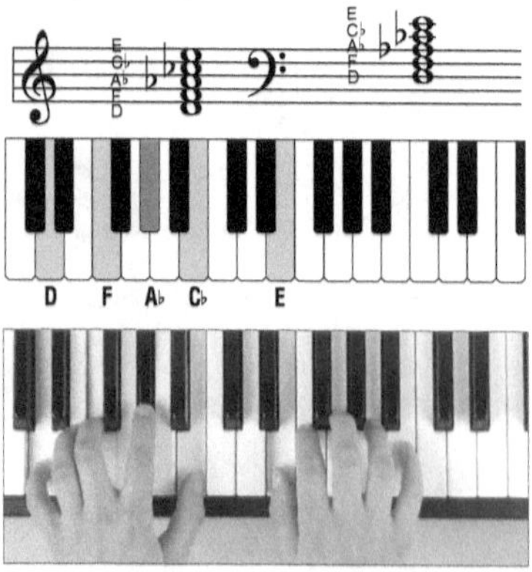

D F A♭ C♭ E

D7alt.

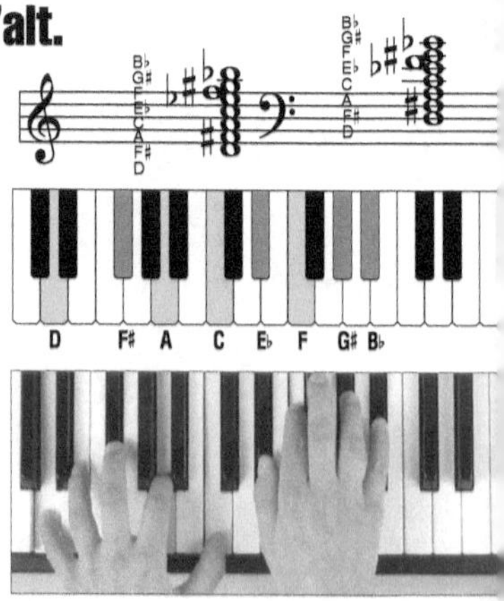

D F♯ A C E♭ F G♯ B♭

E♭ Root Position

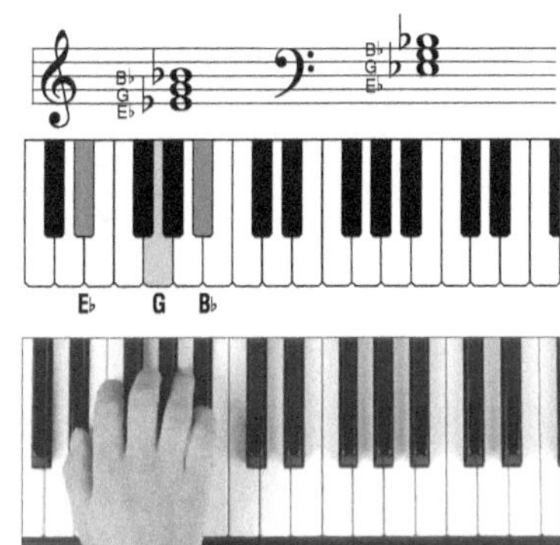

E♭ First Inversion

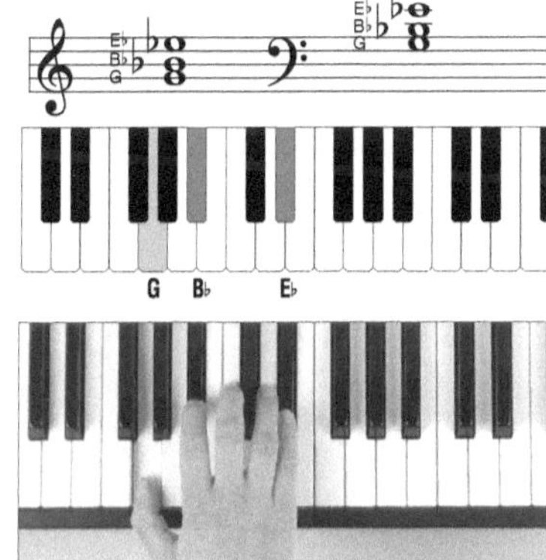

E♭ Second Inversion

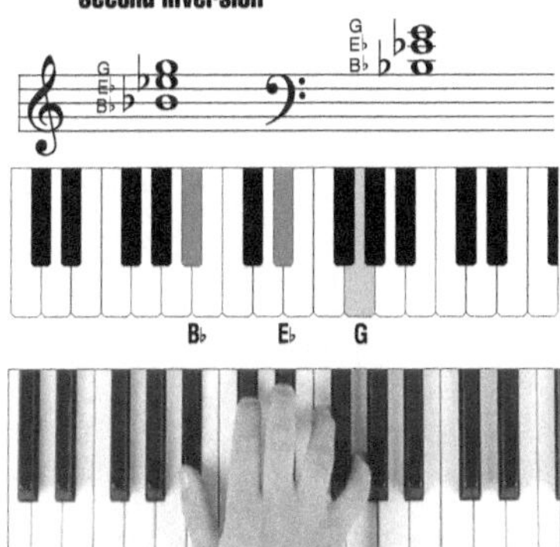

E♭m Root Position

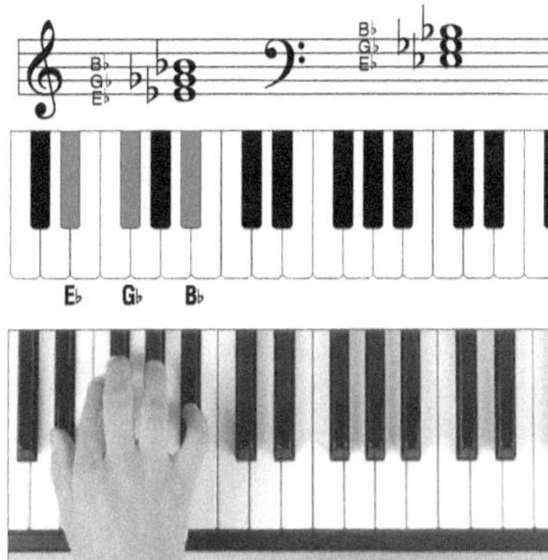

E♭m First Inversion

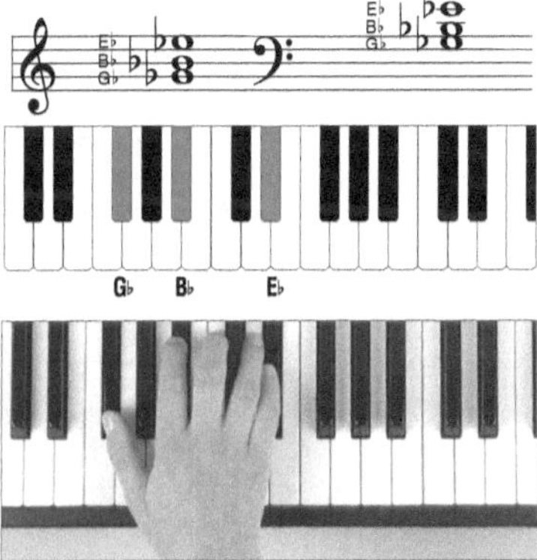

E♭m Second Inversion

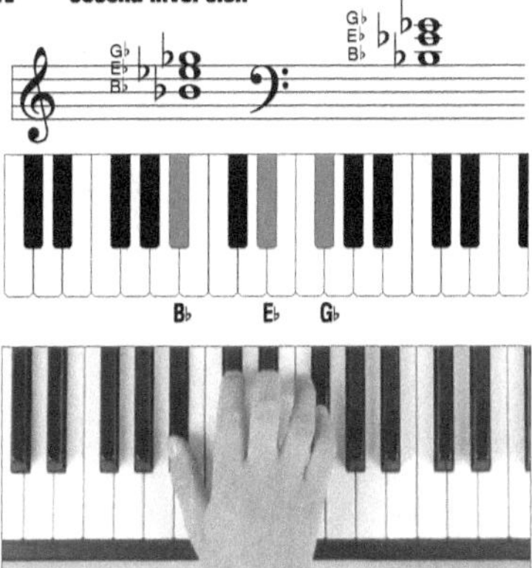

E♭+ Root Position

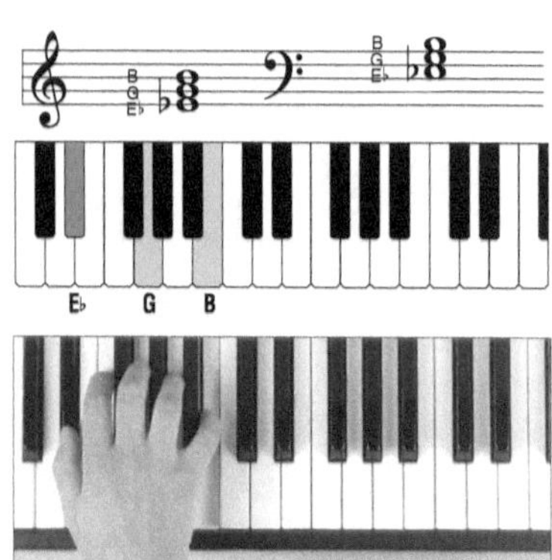

E♭+ First Inversion

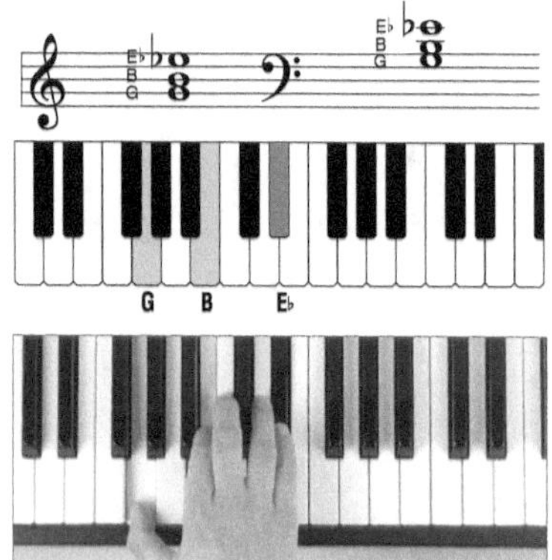

E♭+ Second Inversion

E♭dim Root Position

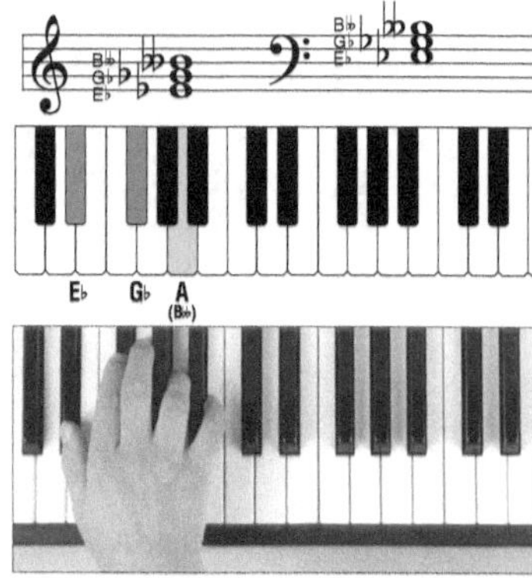

E♭dim First Inversion

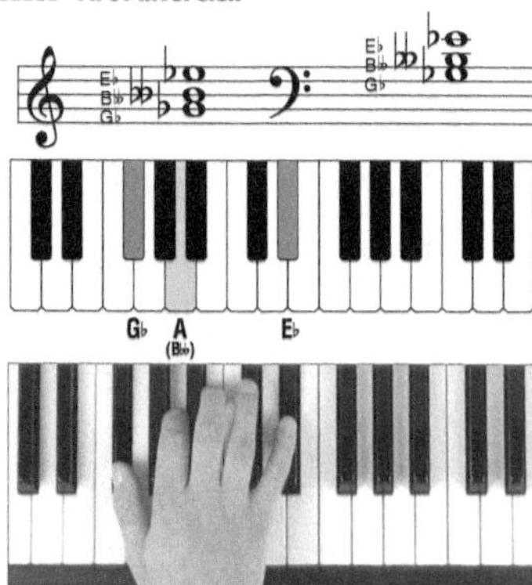

E♭dim Second Inversion

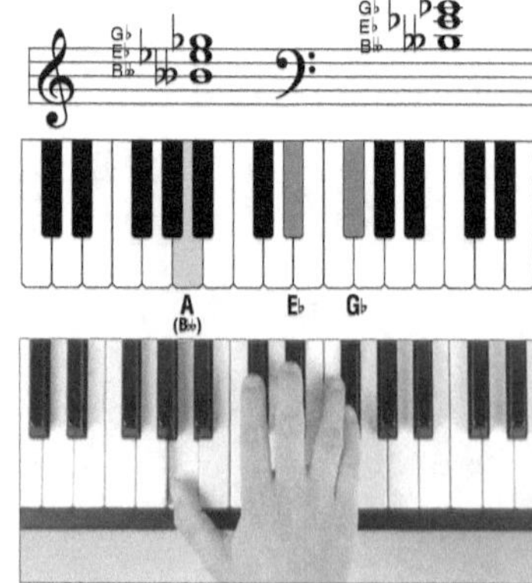

E♭sus Root Position

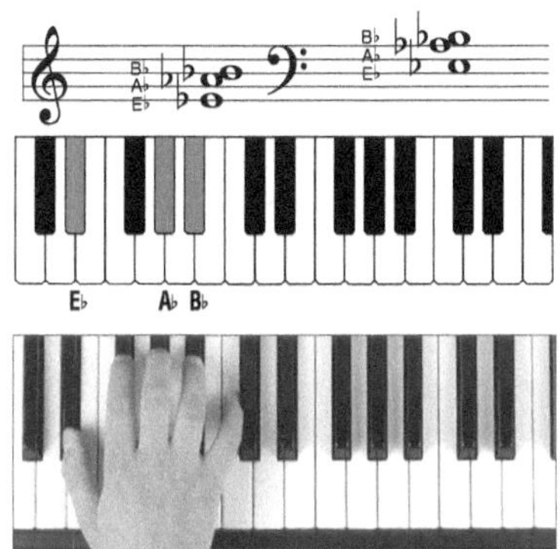

E♭sus First Inversion

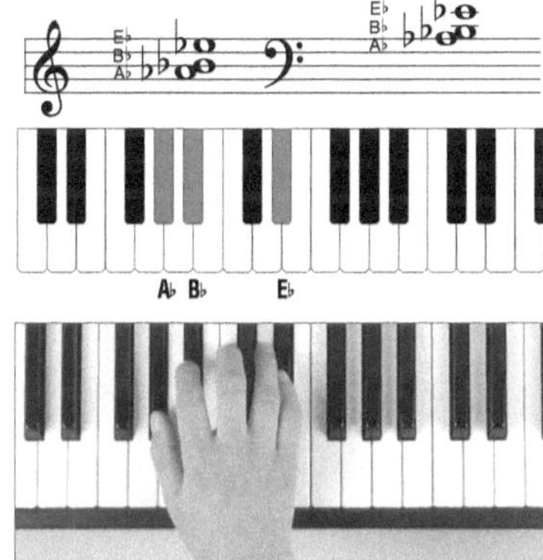

E♭sus Second Inversion

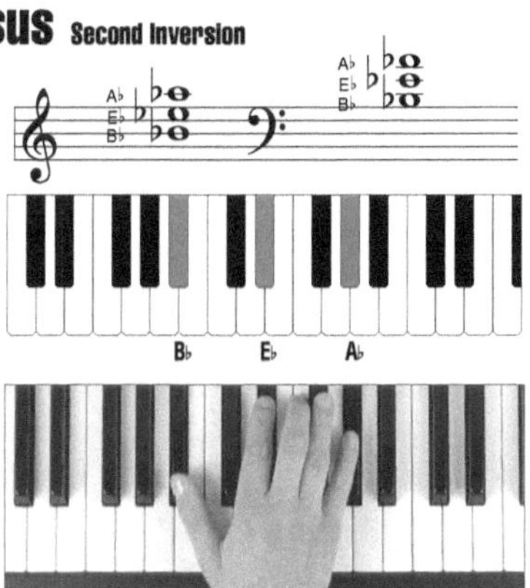

E♭(♭5) Root Position

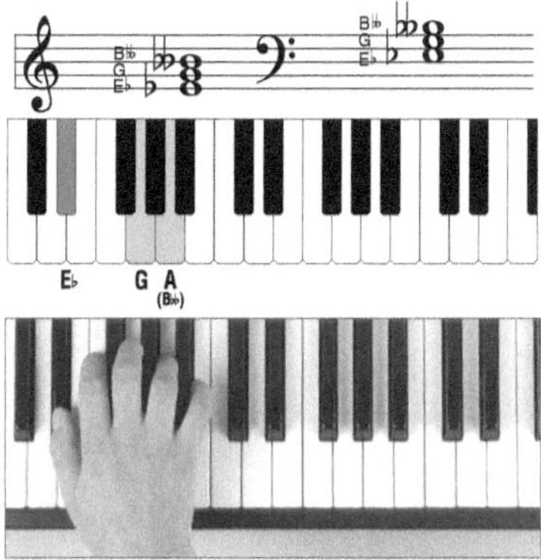

E♭(♭5) First Inversion

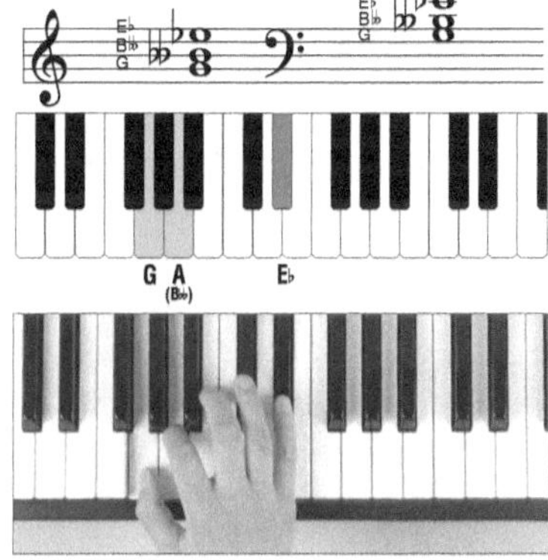

E♭(♭5) Second Inversion

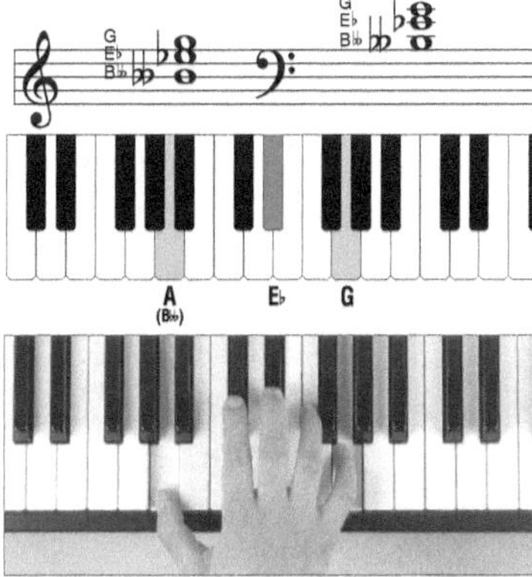

E♭sus2 Root Position

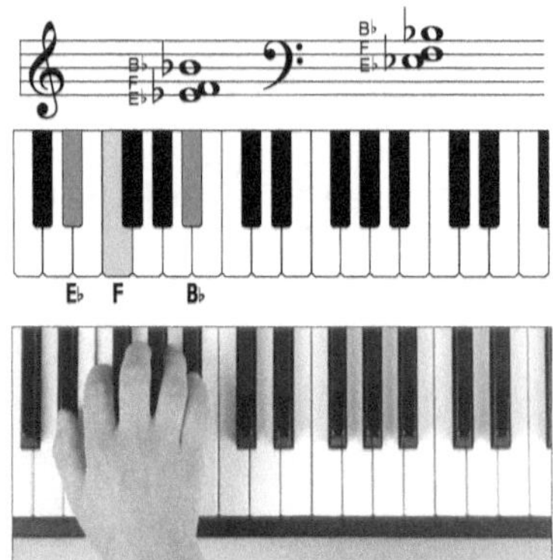

E♭sus2 First Inversion

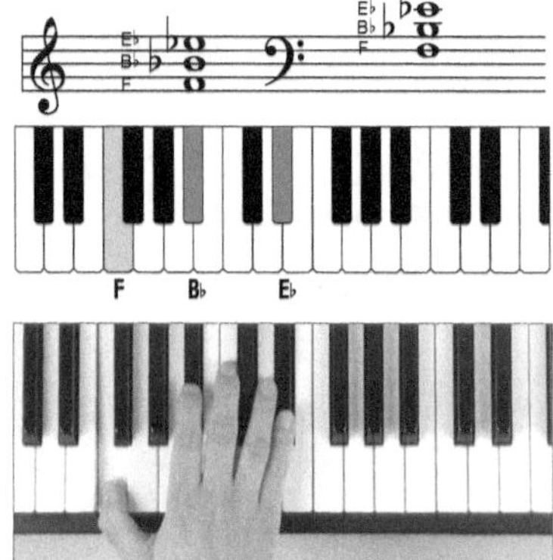

E♭sus2 Second Inversion

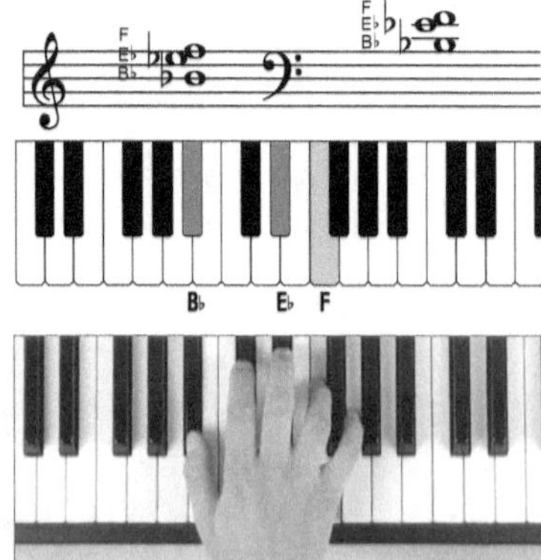

E♭6 Root Position

E♭6 First Inversion

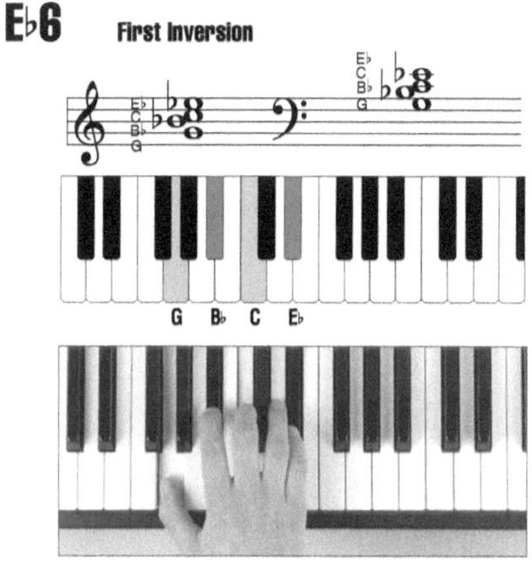

E♭6 Second Inversion

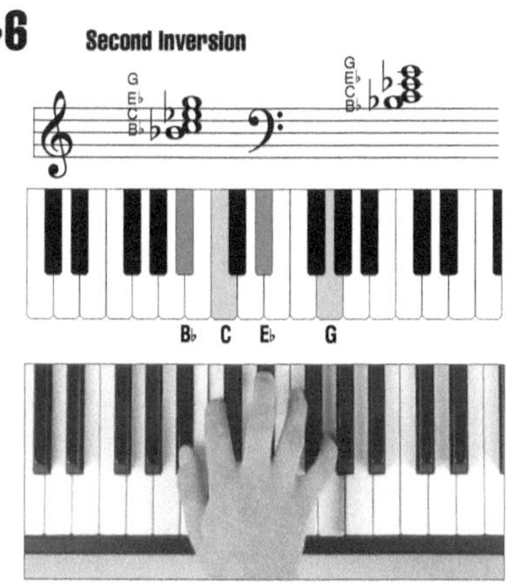

E♭6 Third Inversion

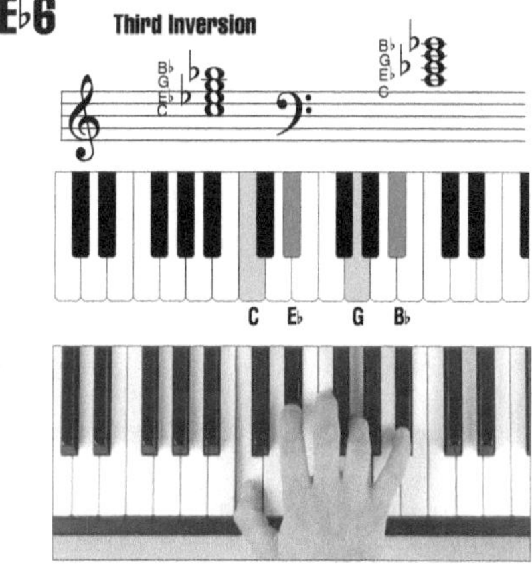

E♭(add2), E♭(add9) Root Position

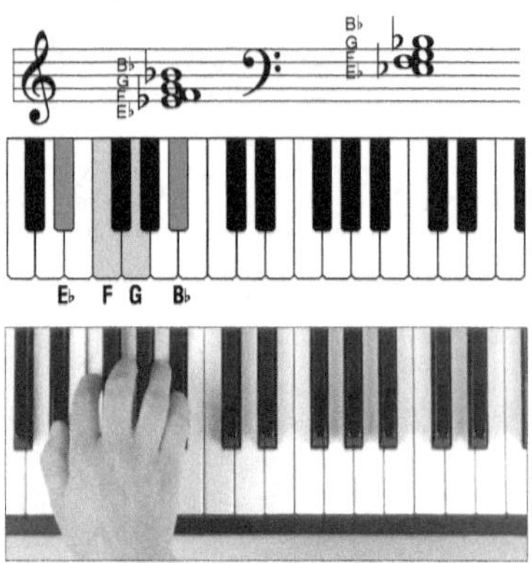

E♭(add2), E♭(add9) First Inversion

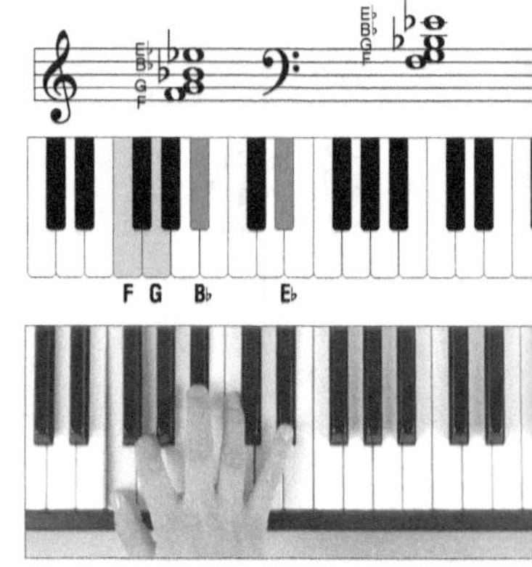

E♭(add2), E♭(add9) Second Inversion

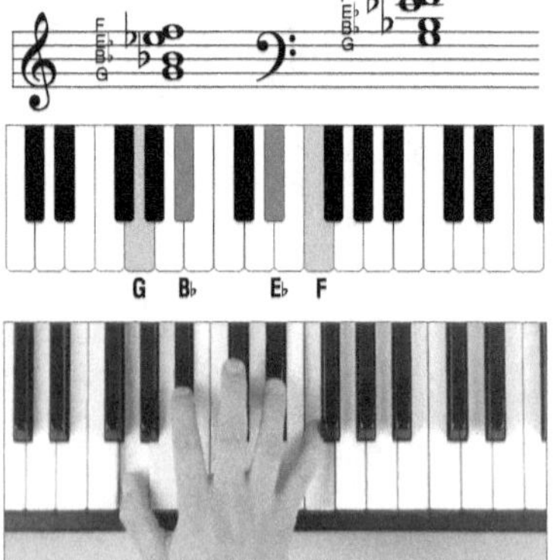

E♭(add2), E♭(add9) Third Inversion

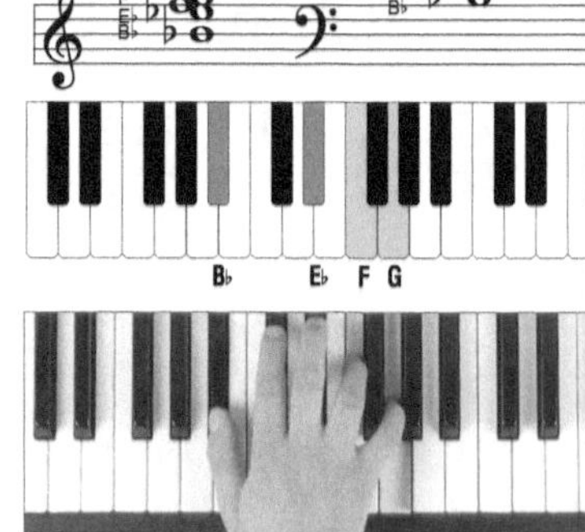

E♭maj7 Root Position

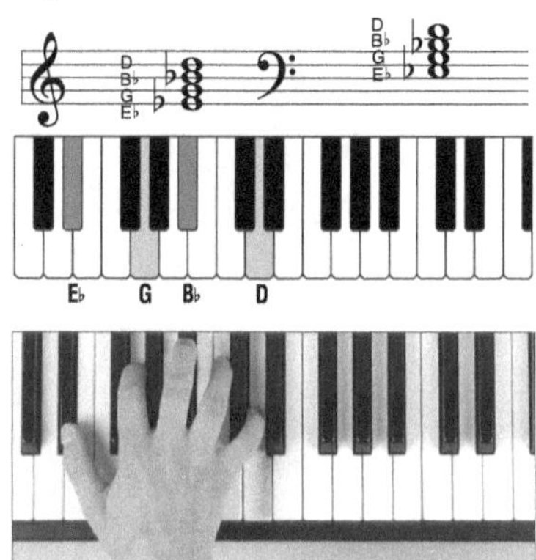

E♭maj7 First Inversion

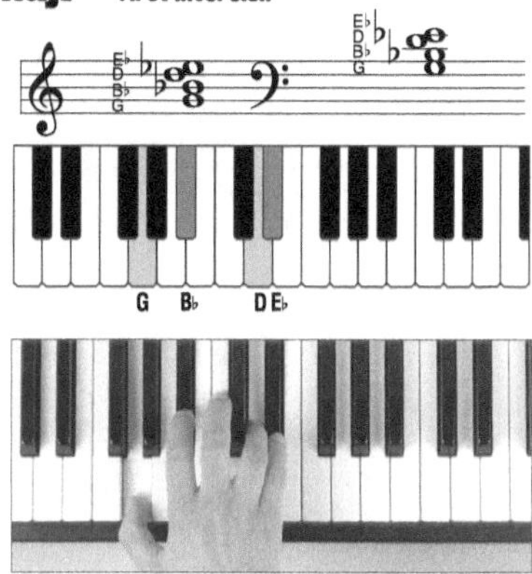

E♭maj7 Second Inversion

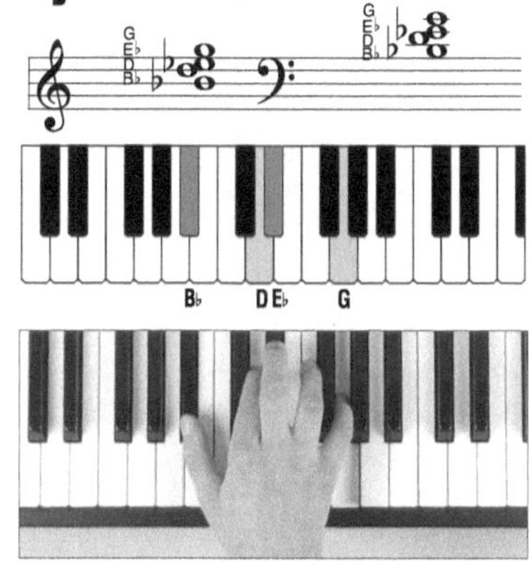

E♭maj7 Third Inversion

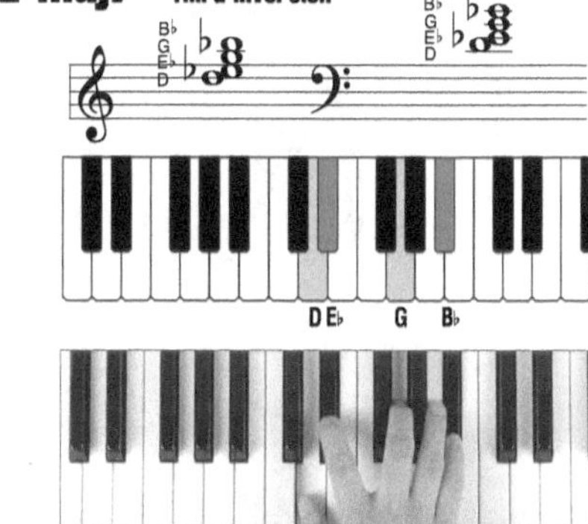

E♭maj7♭5 Root Position

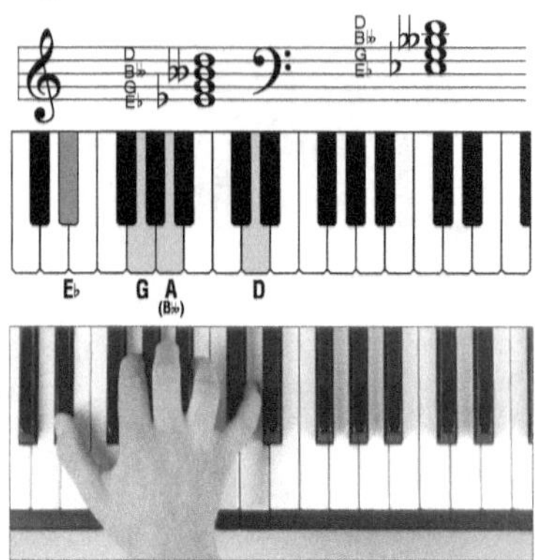

E♭maj7♭5 First Inversion

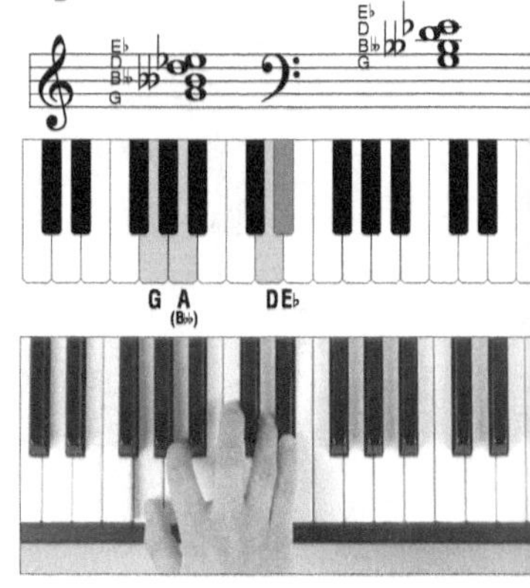

E♭maj7♭5 Second Inversion

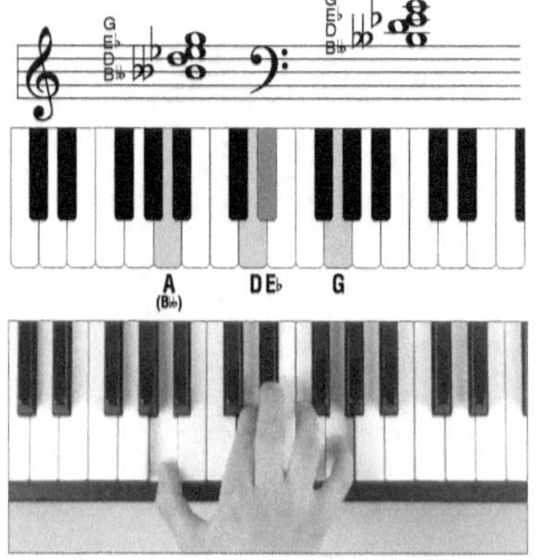

E♭maj7♭5 Third Inversion

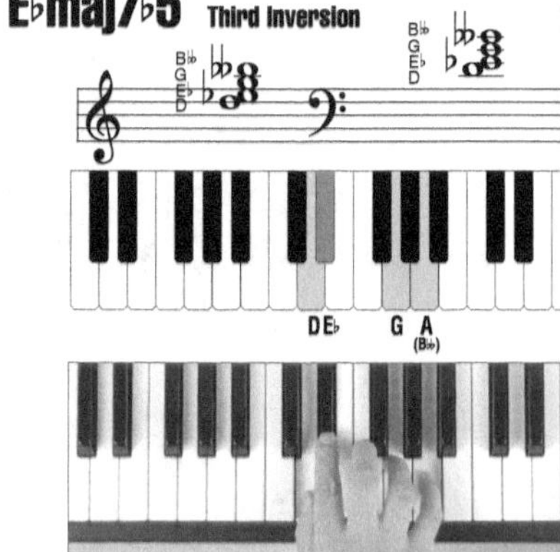

E♭maj7♯5 Root Position

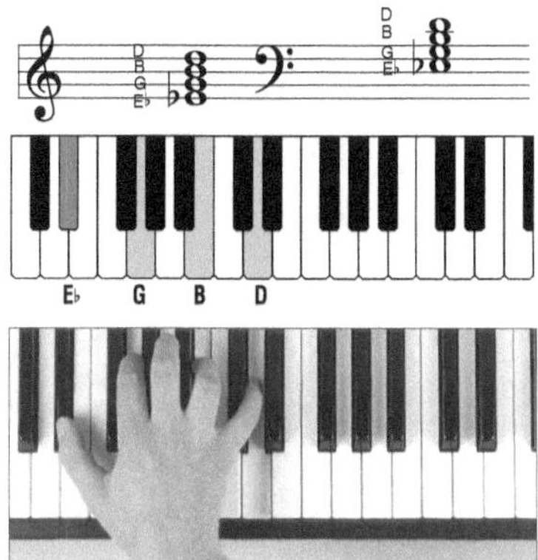

E♭maj7♯5 First Inversion

E♭maj7♯5 Second Inversion

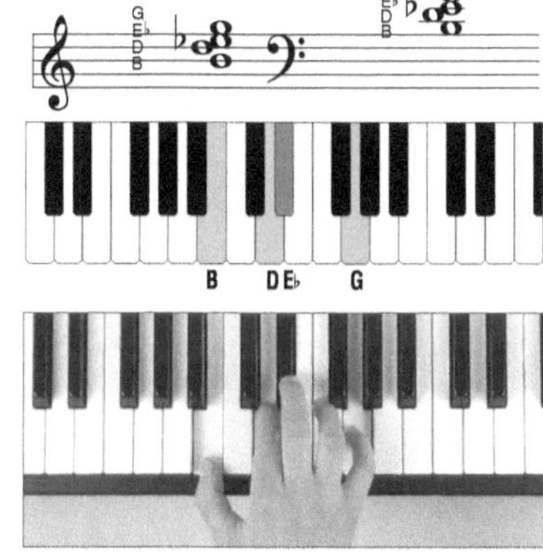

E♭maj7♯5 Third Inversion

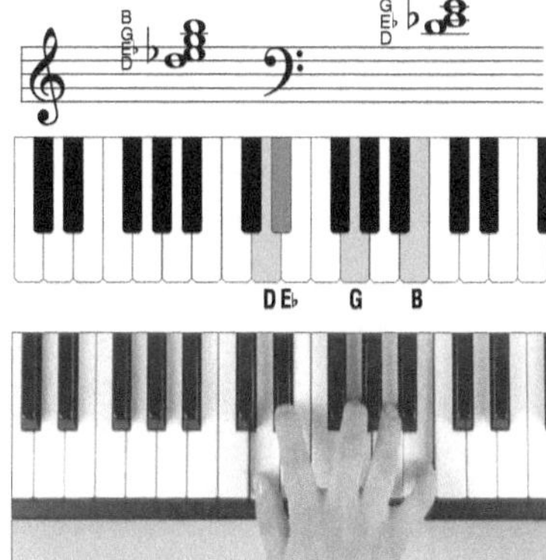

E♭7 Root Position

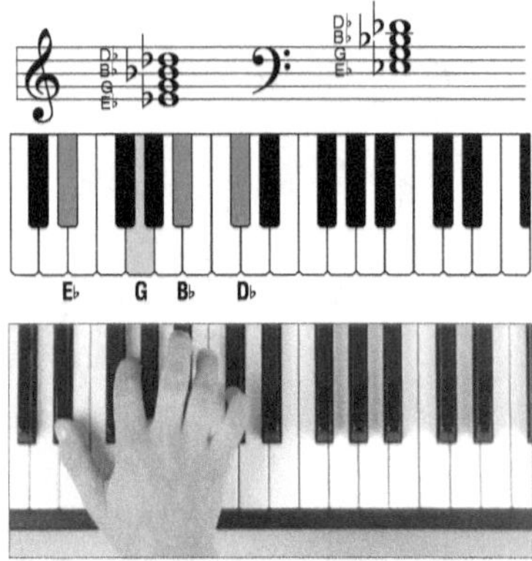

E♭7 First Inversion

E♭ D♭ B♭ G

G B♭ D♭ E♭

E♭7 Second Inversion

E♭7 Third Inversion

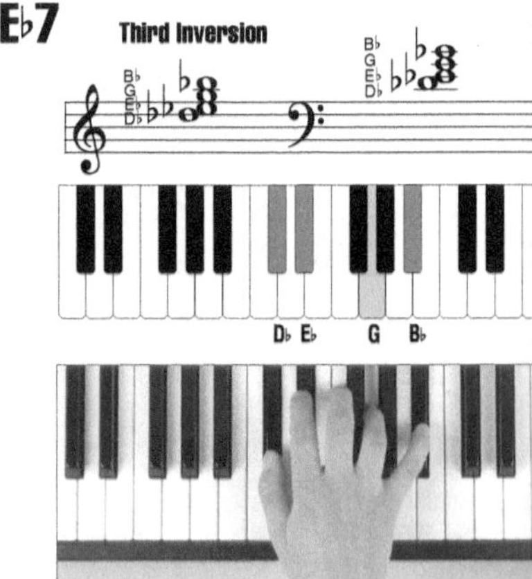

E♭7♭5 Root Position

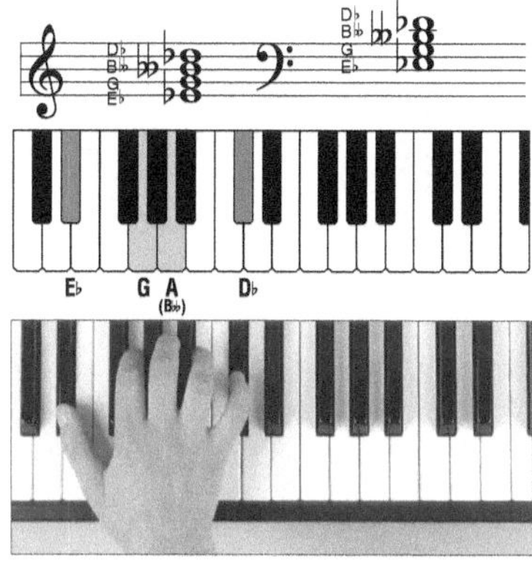

E♭7♭5 First Inversion

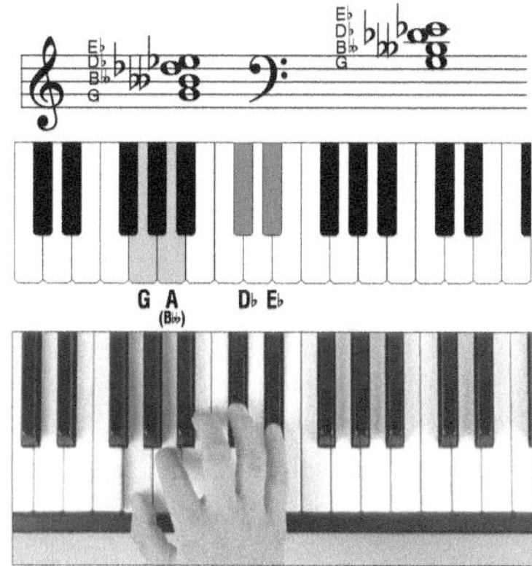

E♭7♭5 Second Inversion

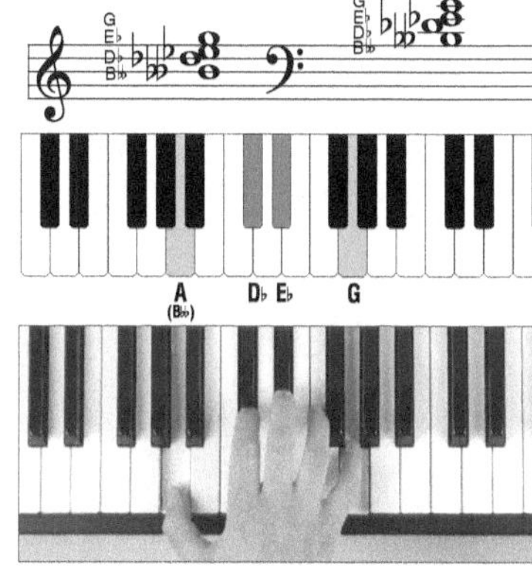

E♭7♭5 Third Inversion

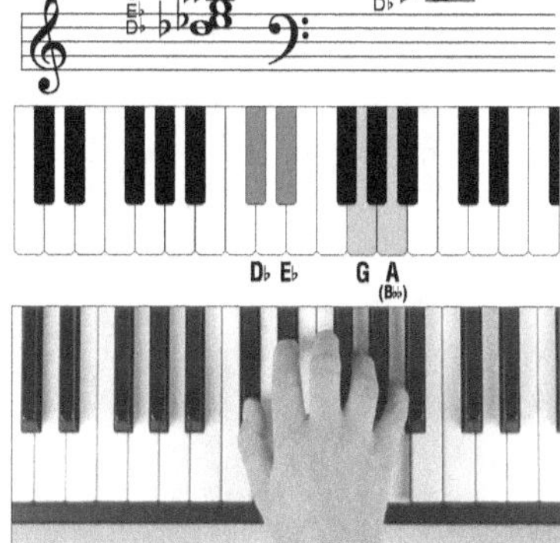

E♭7♯5 Root Position

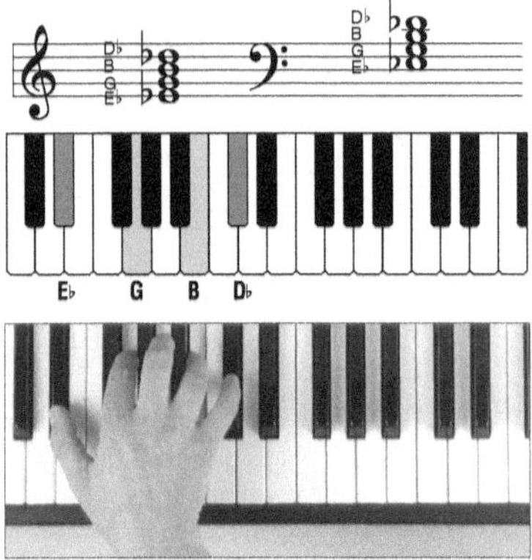

E♭7♯5 First Inversion

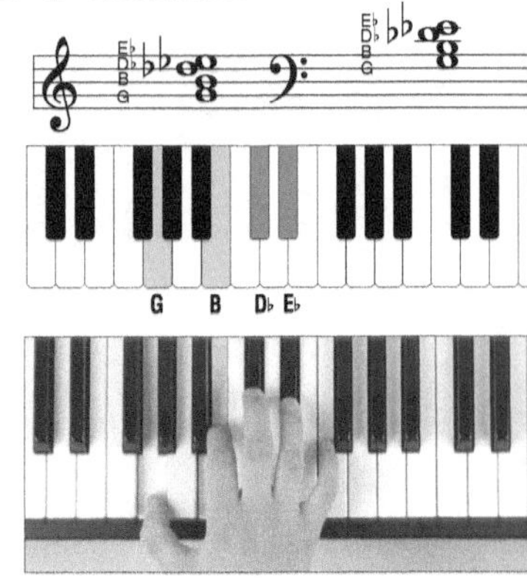

E♭7♯5 Second Inversion

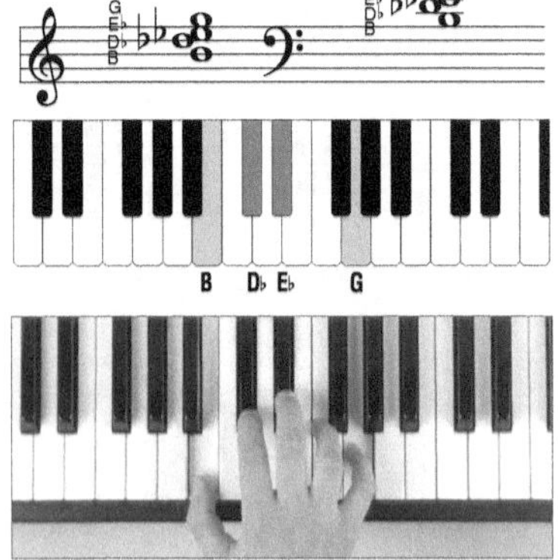

E♭7♯5 Third Inversion

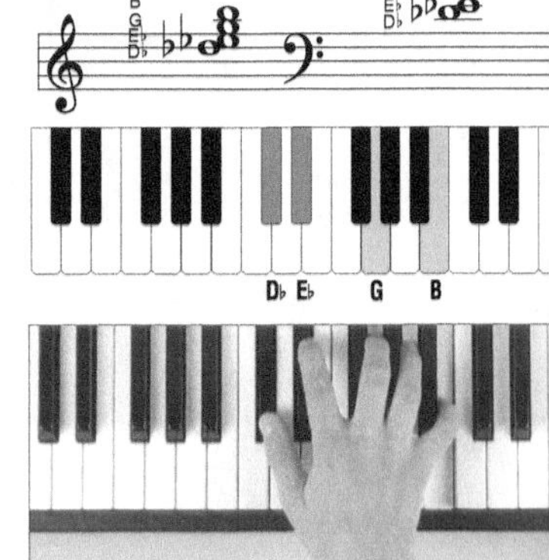

E♭7sus Root Position

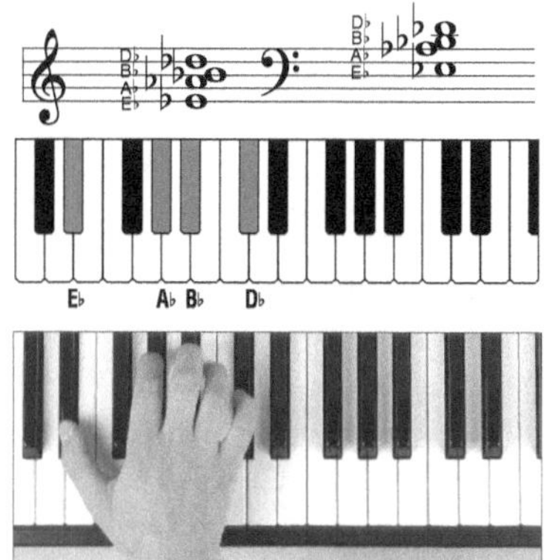

E♭7sus First Inversion

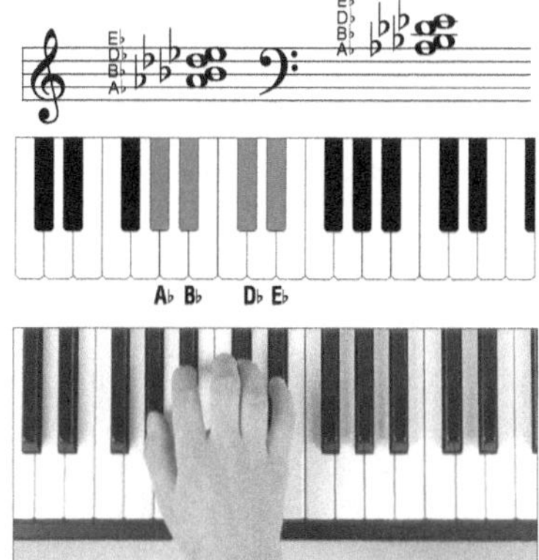

E♭7sus Second Inversion

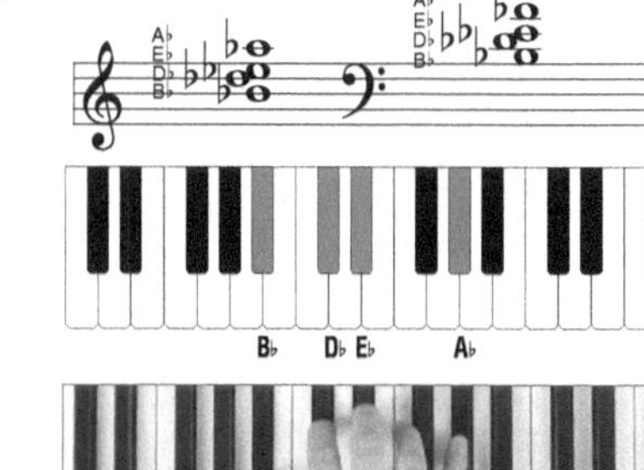

E♭7sus Third Inversion

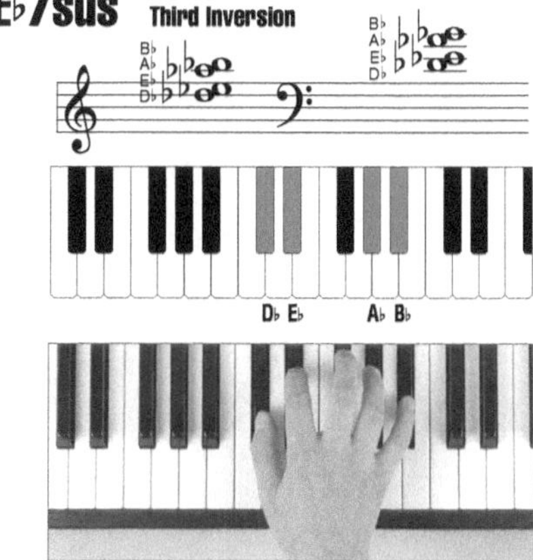

E♭m(add2), E♭m(add9) Root Position

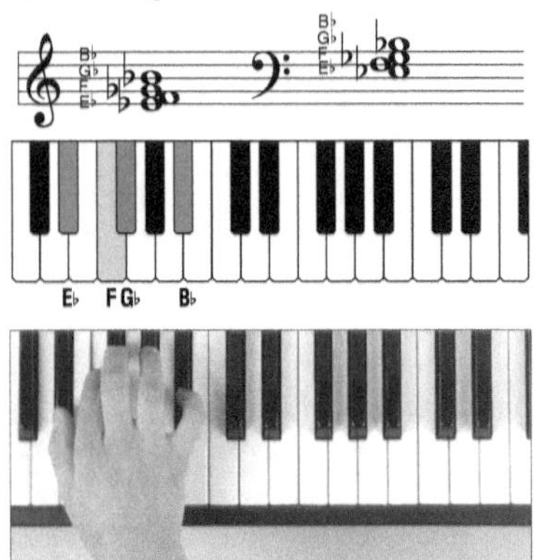

E♭m(add2), E♭m(add9) First Inversion

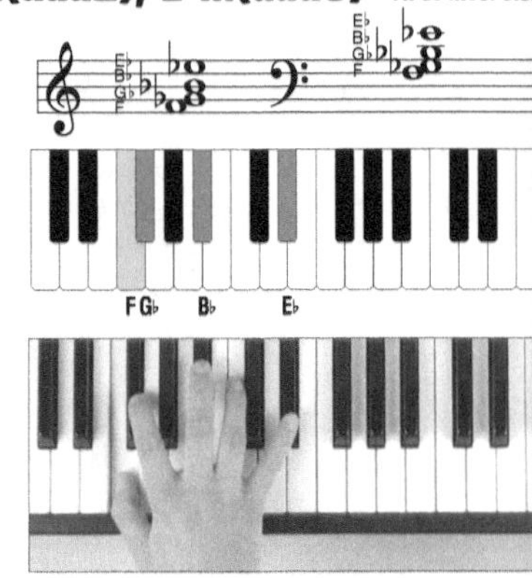

E♭m(add2), E♭m(add9) Second Inversion

E♭m(add2), E♭m(add9) Third Inversion

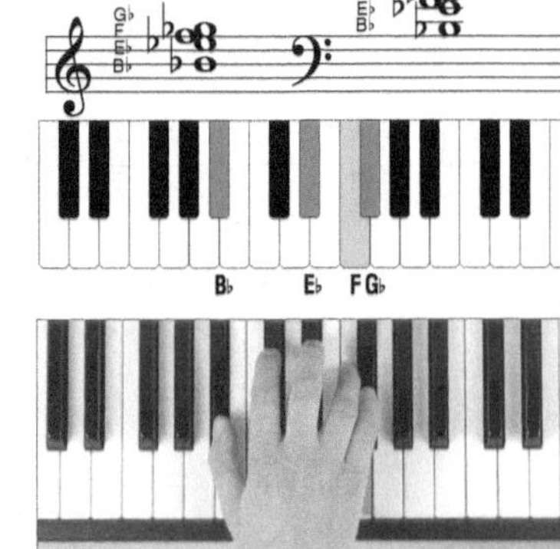

E♭m6 Root Position

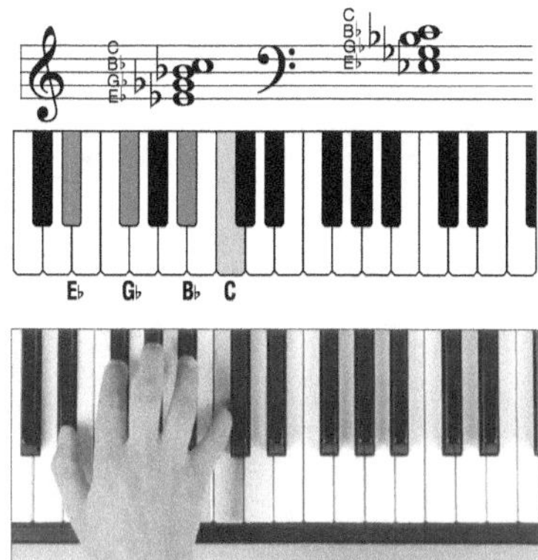

E♭m6 First Inversion

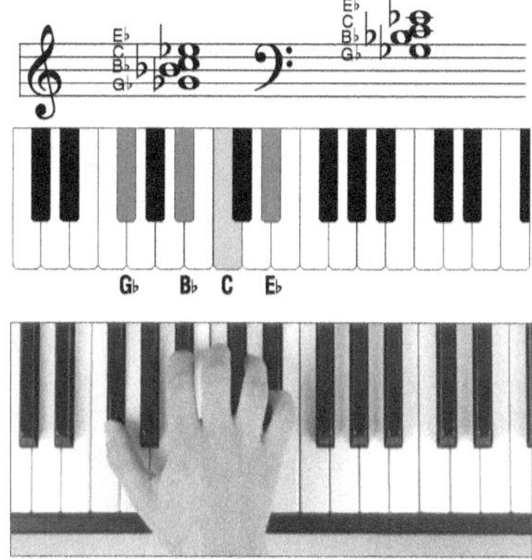

E♭m6 Second Inversion

E♭m6 Third Inversion

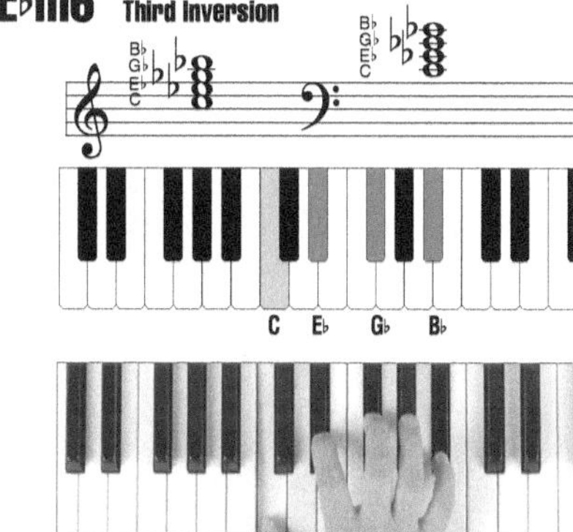

E♭m7 Root Position

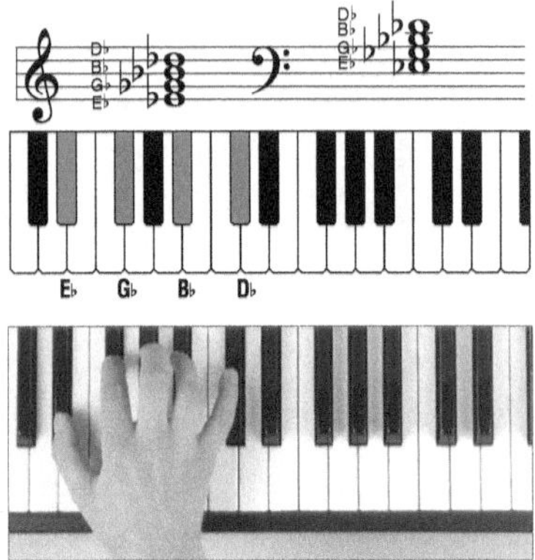

E♭m7 First Inversion

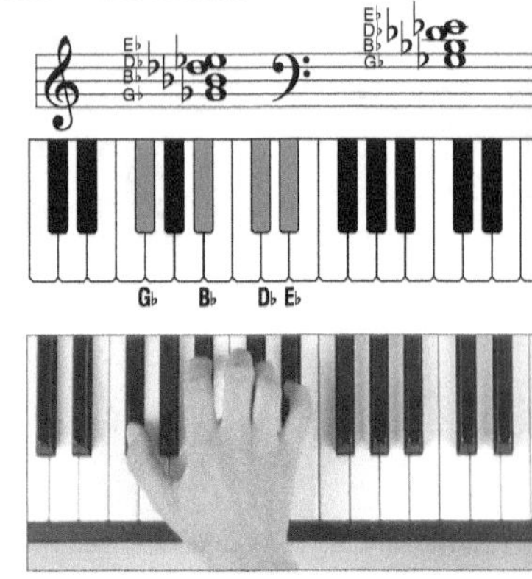

E♭m7 Second Inversion

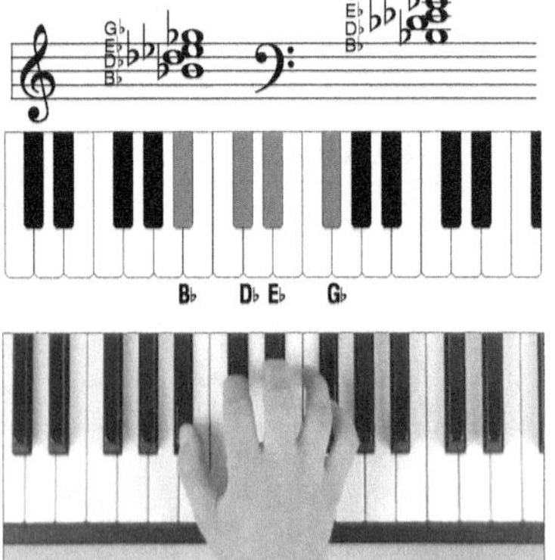

E♭m7 Third Inversion

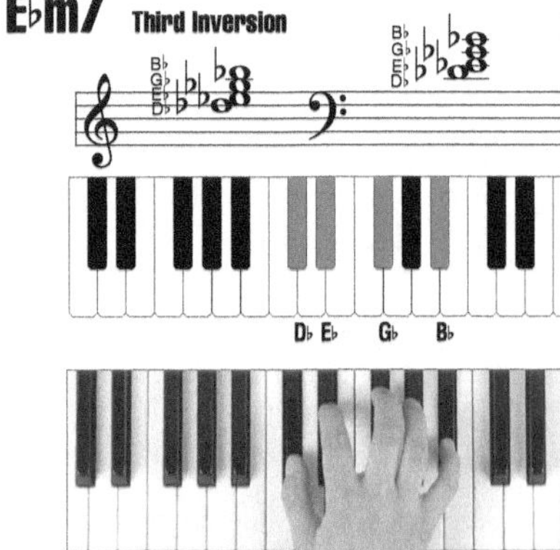

E♭m(maj7) Root Position

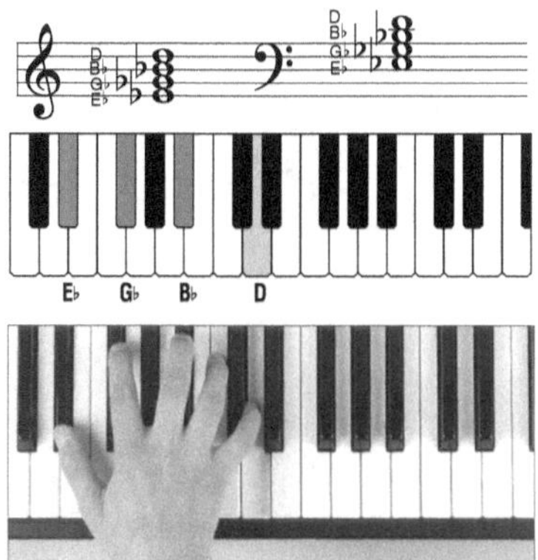

E♭m(maj7) First Inversion

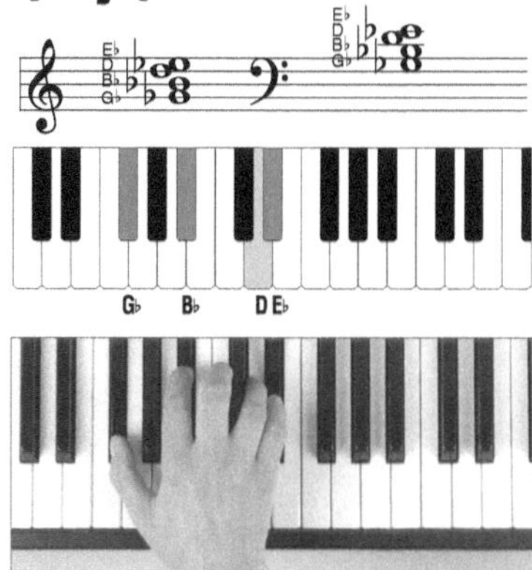

E♭m(maj7) Second Inversion

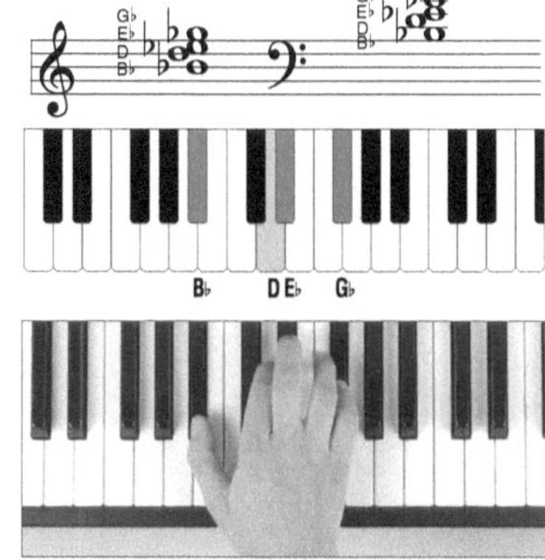

E♭m(maj7) Third Inversion

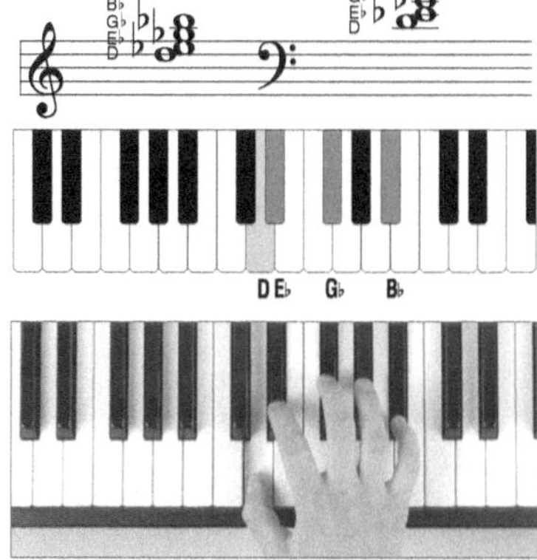

E♭m7♭5 Root Position

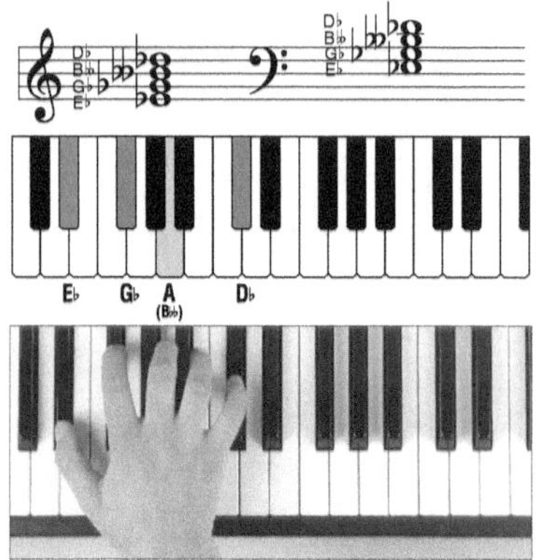

E♭m7♭5 First Inversion

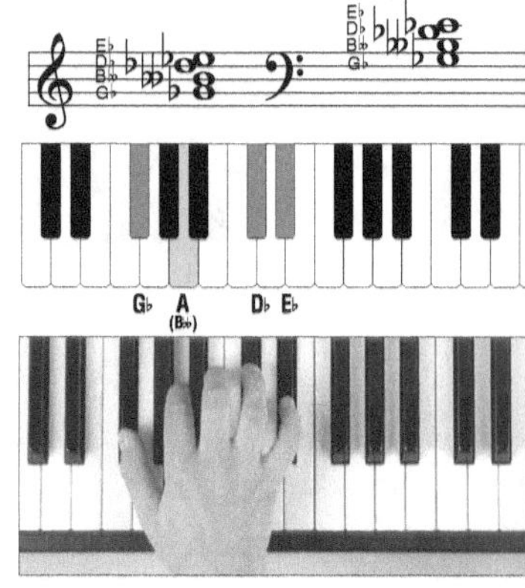

E♭m7♭5 Second Inversion

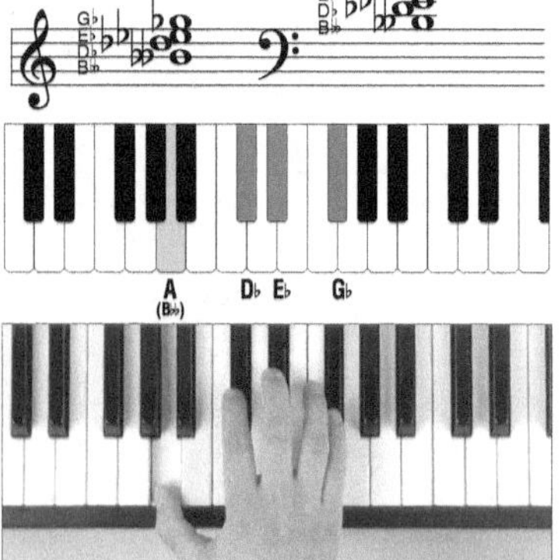

E♭m7♭5 Third Inversion

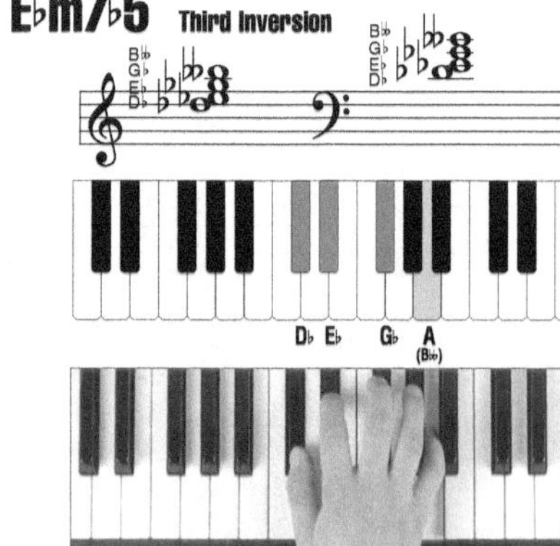

E♭dim7 Root Position

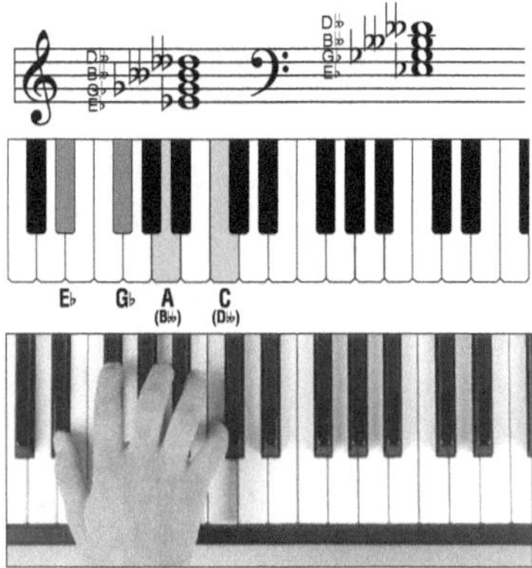

E♭dim7 First Inversion

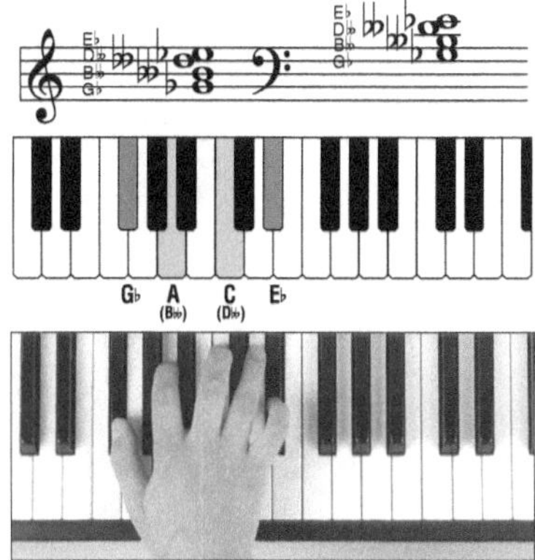

E♭dim7 Second Inversion

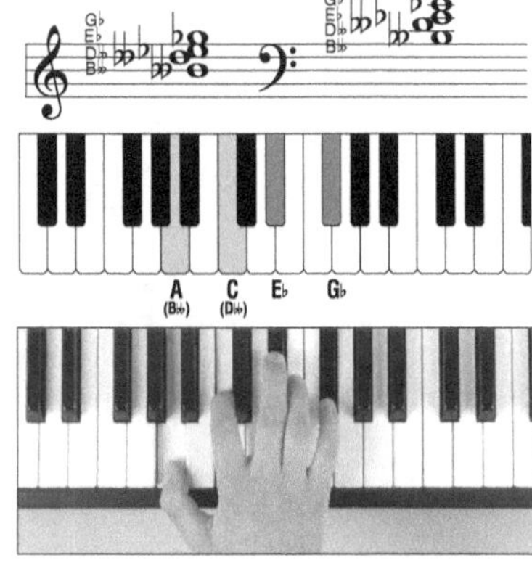

E♭dim7 Third Inversion

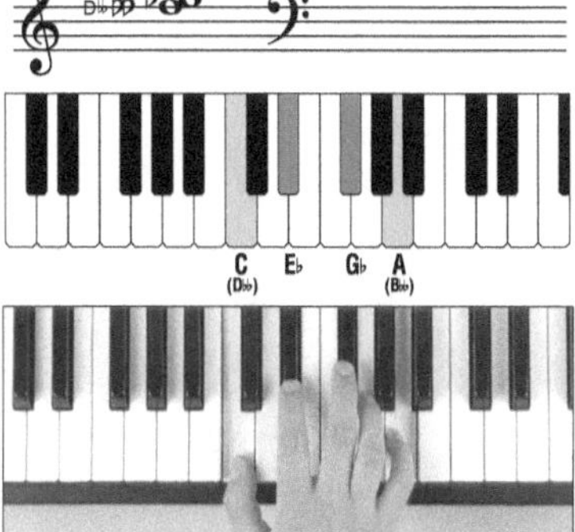

E♭dim(maj7) Root Position

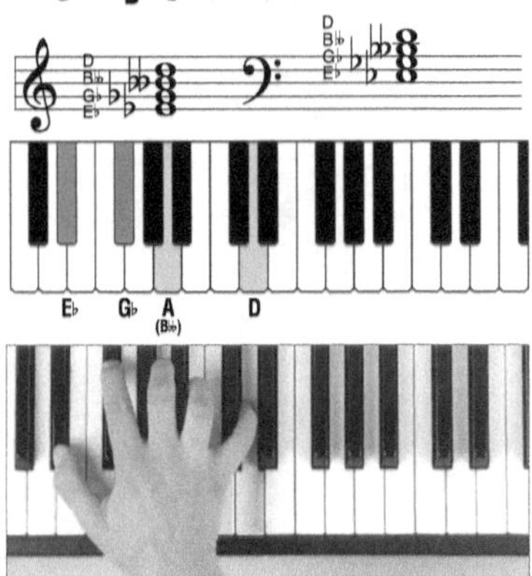

E♭dim(maj7) First Inversion

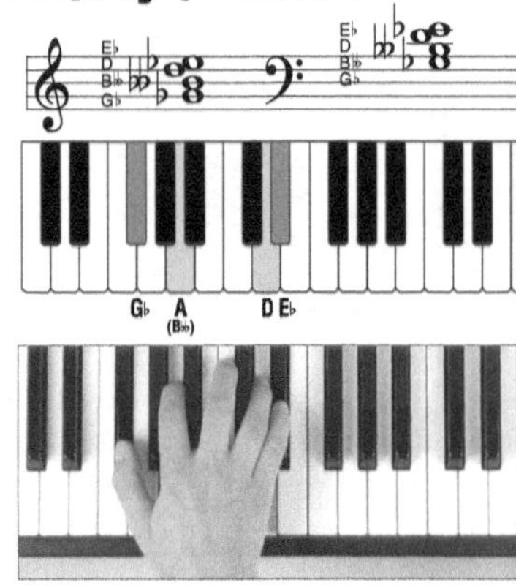

E♭dim(maj7) Second Inversion

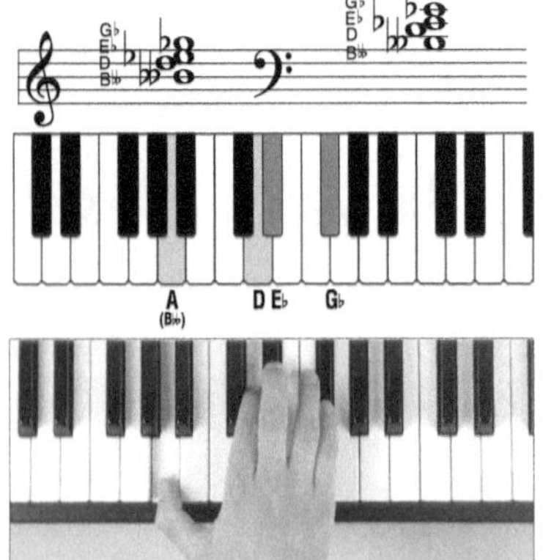

E♭dim(maj7) Third Inversion

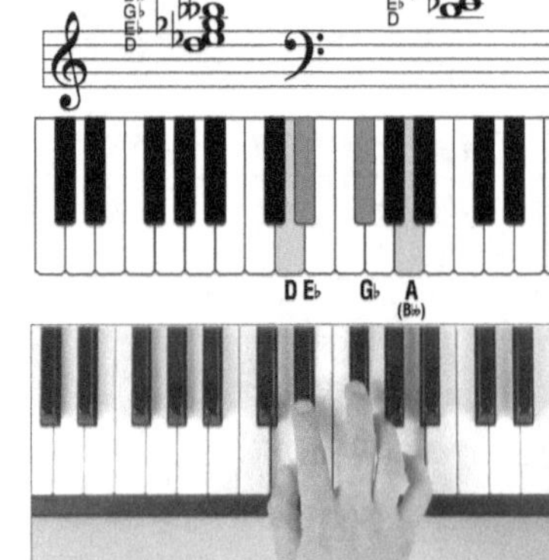

E♭5

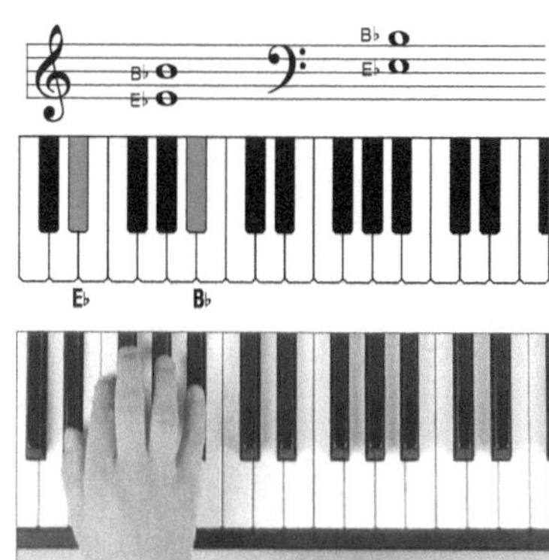

E♭6/9

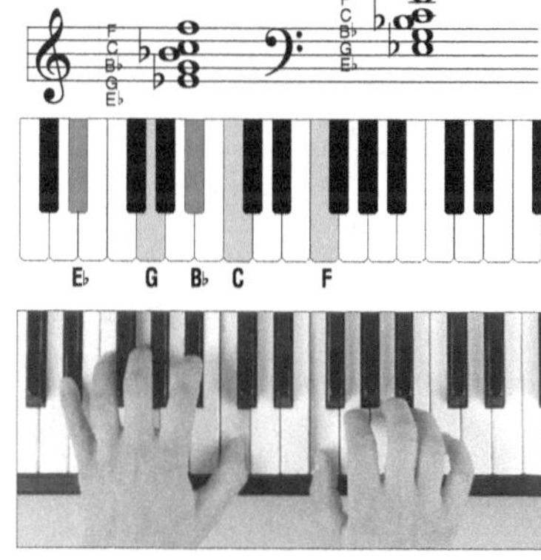

E♭maj6/9

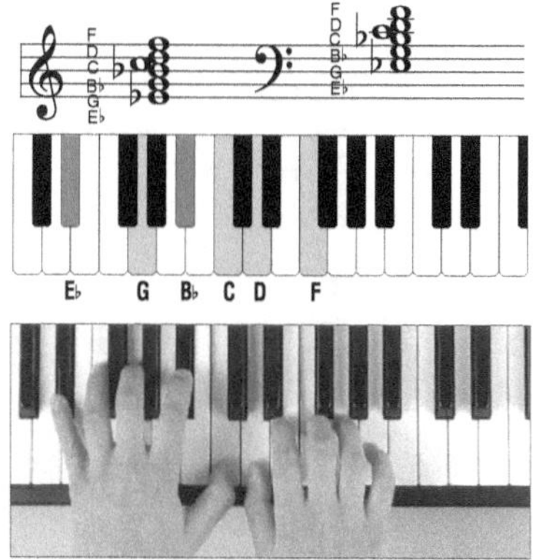

E♭maj7♯11

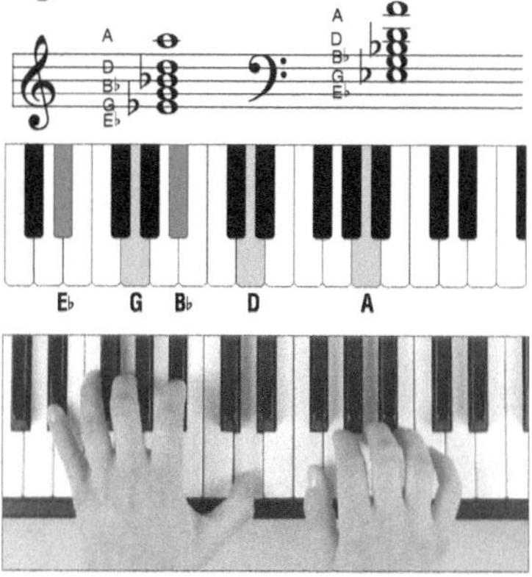

E♭maj9

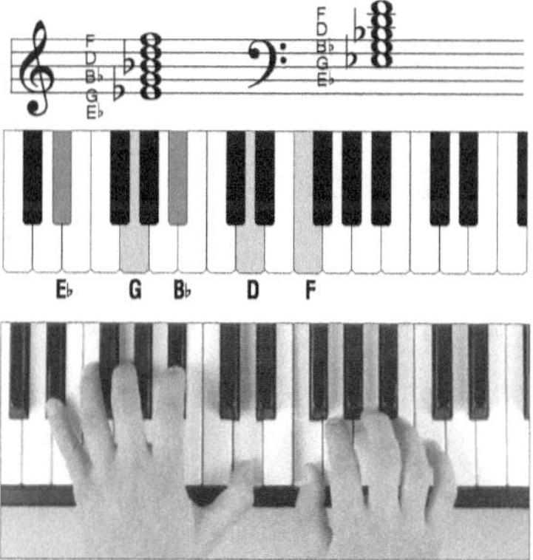

E♭maj9♭5

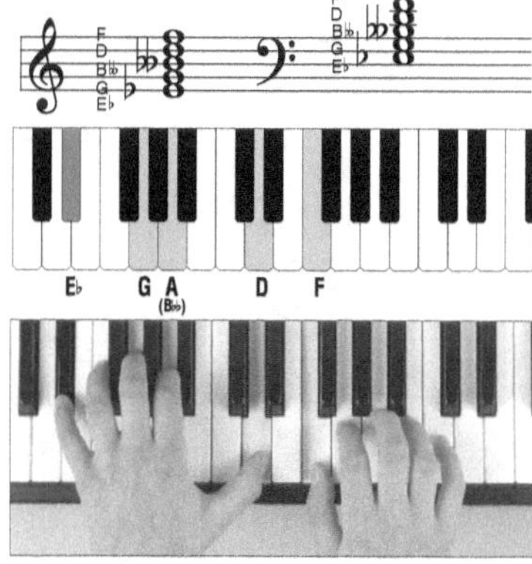

E♭maj9♯5

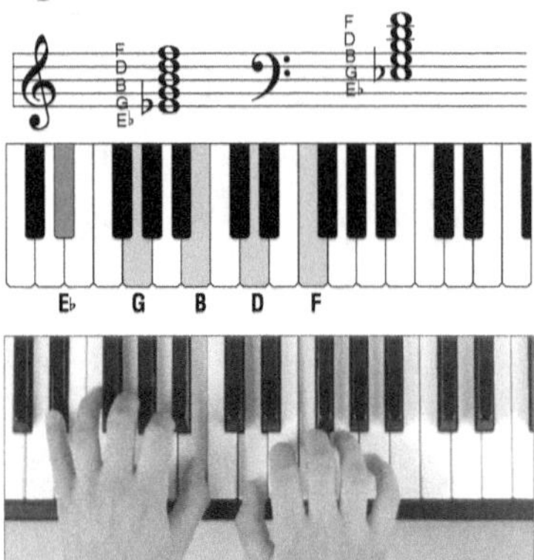

E♭maj9♯11

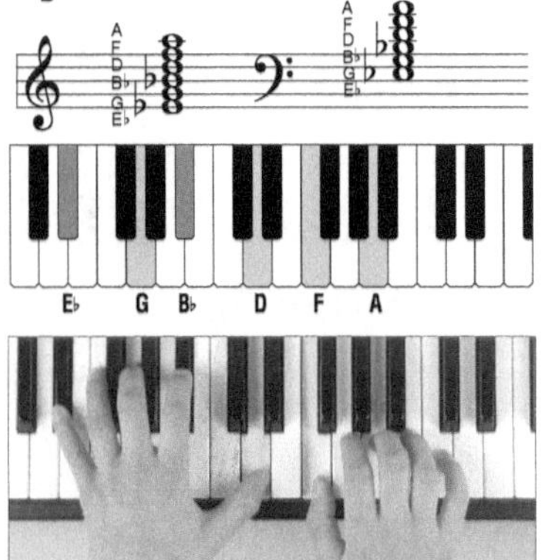

E♭maj13

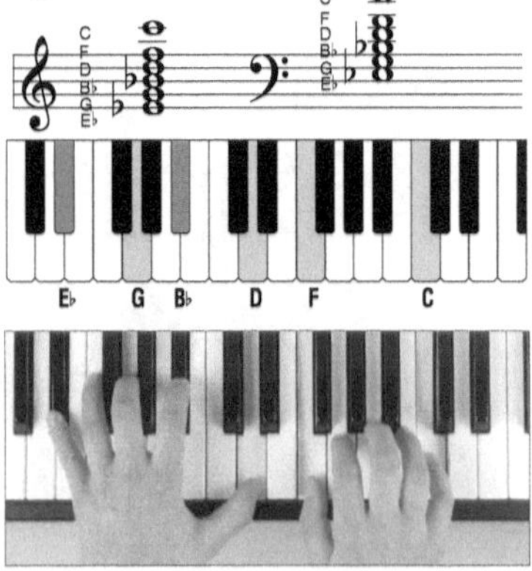

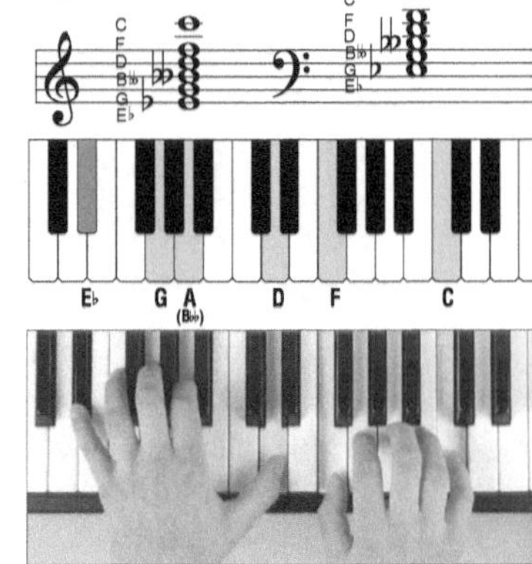

E♭maj13♯11

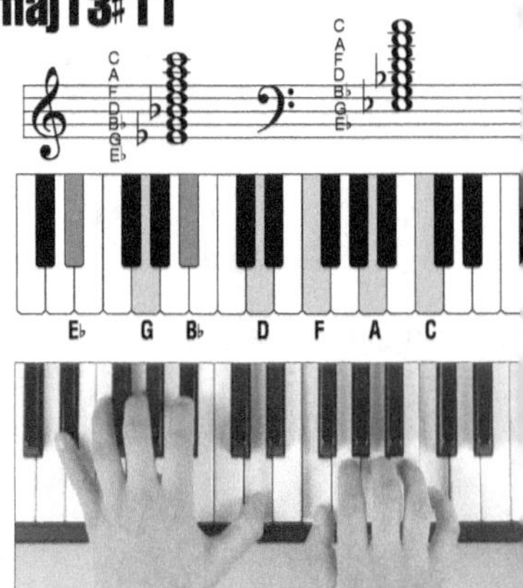

E♭7♭9

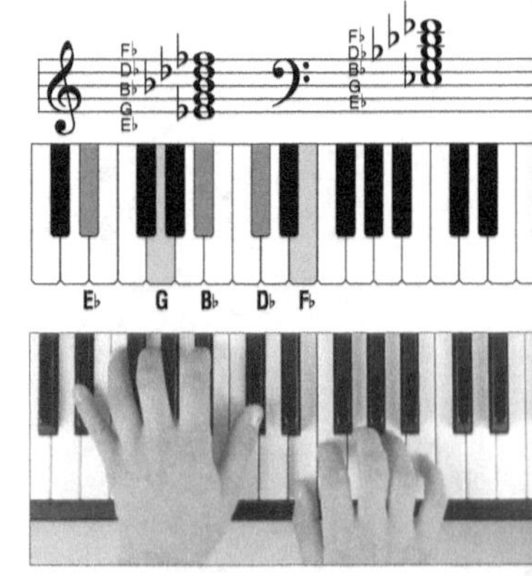

E♭7♯9

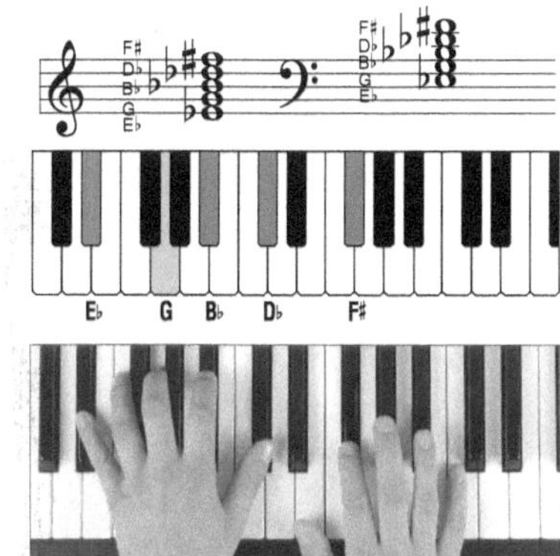

E♭7♭5(♯9)

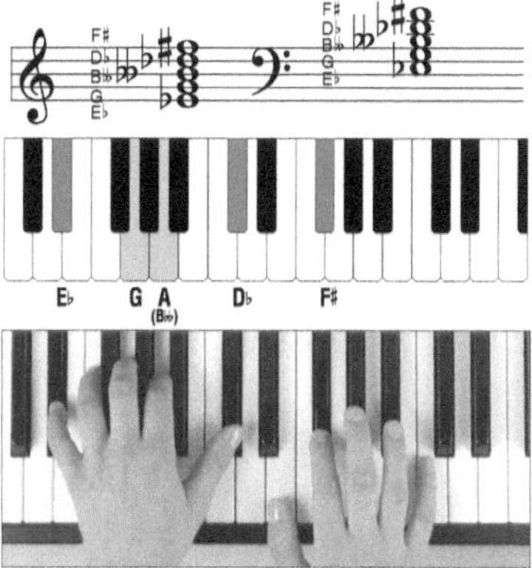

E♭7♯11

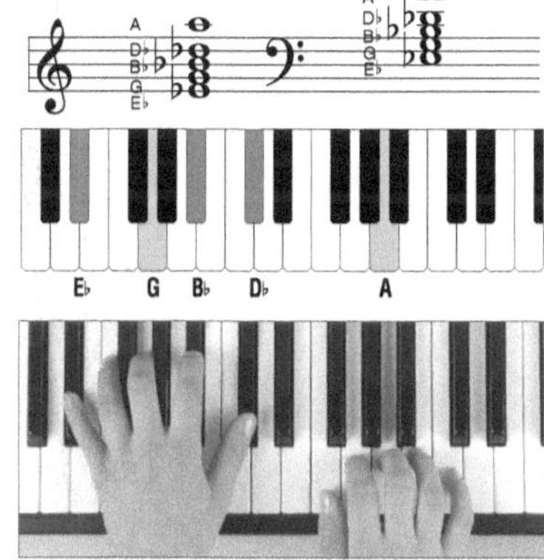

E♭7♯5(♭9)

E♭7♭5(♭9)

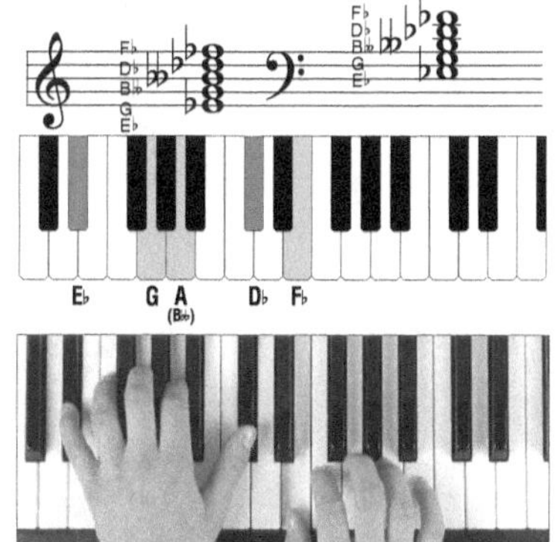

E♭7♯5(♯9)

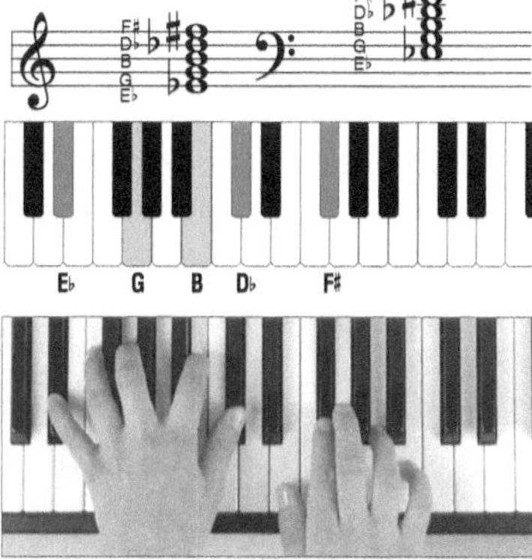

E♭7♭9(♯9)

E♭ G B♭ D♭ F♭ G♭

E♭7♭9(♯11)

E♭ G B♭ D♭ F♭ A

E♭7(add13)

E♭ G B♭ D♭ C

E♭7♯9(♯11)

E♭ G B♭ D♭ F♯ A

E♭7♭13

E♭ G B♭ D♭ C♭

E♭7♭9(♭13)

E♭ G B♭ D♭ F♭ C♭

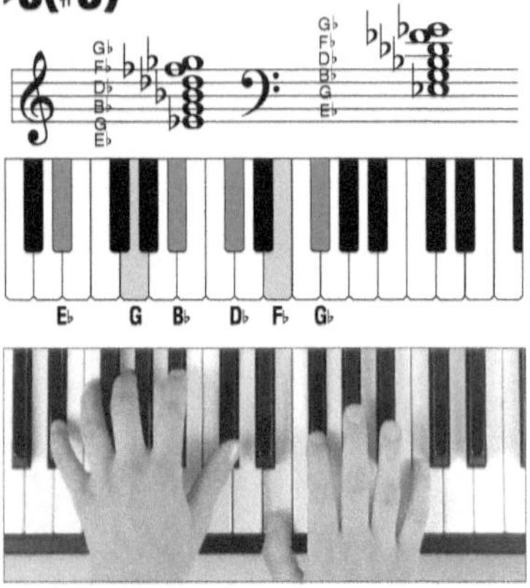

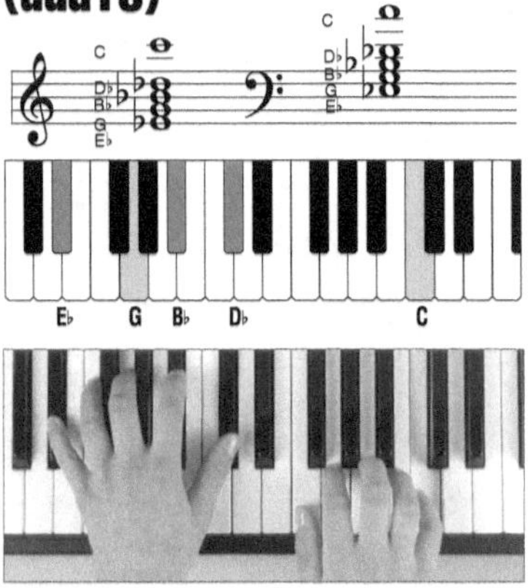

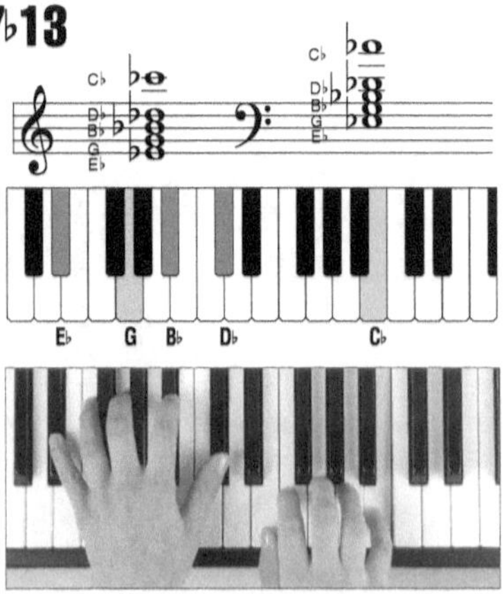

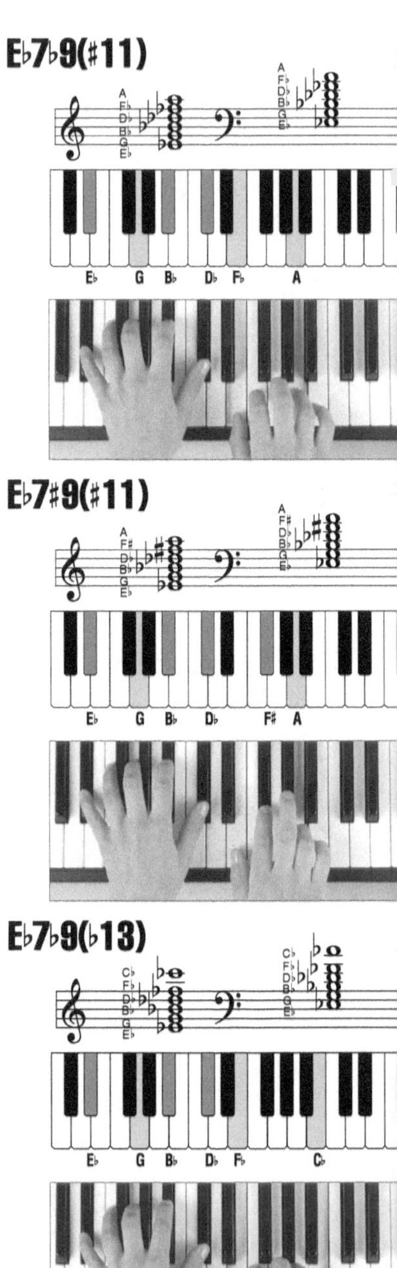

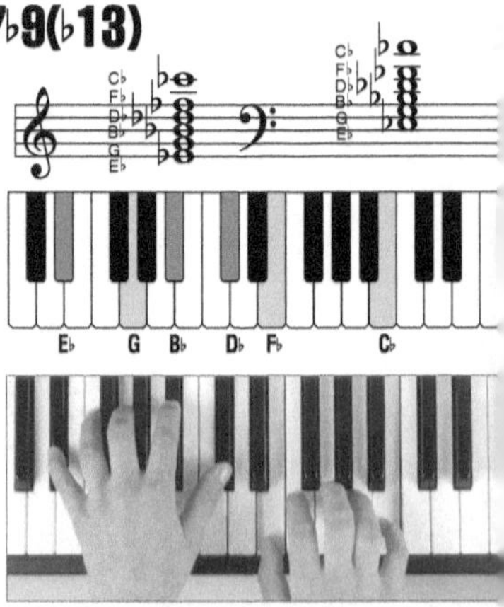

♭7♯9(♭13)

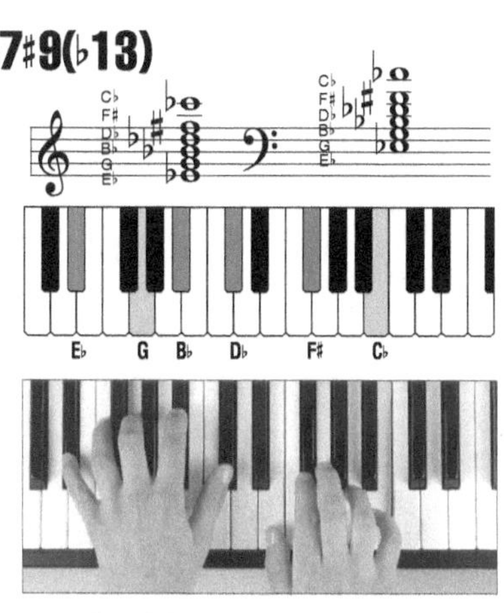

♭7♯11(♭13)

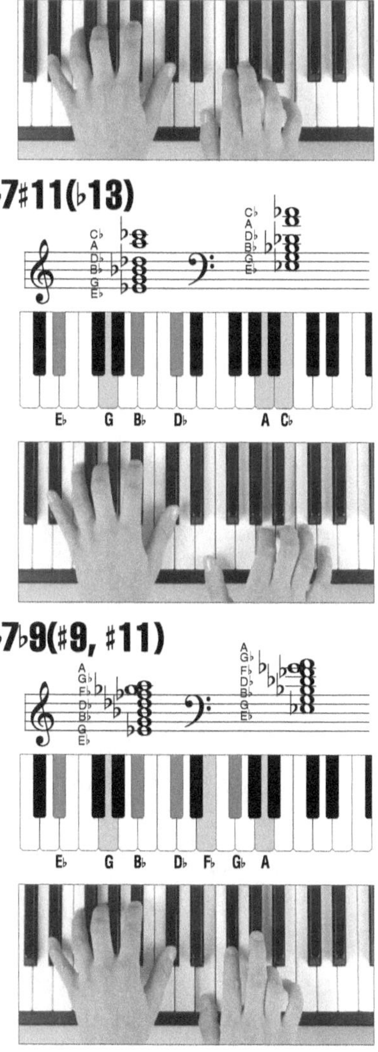

♭7♭9(♯9, ♯11)

E♭9

E♭9(♭5)

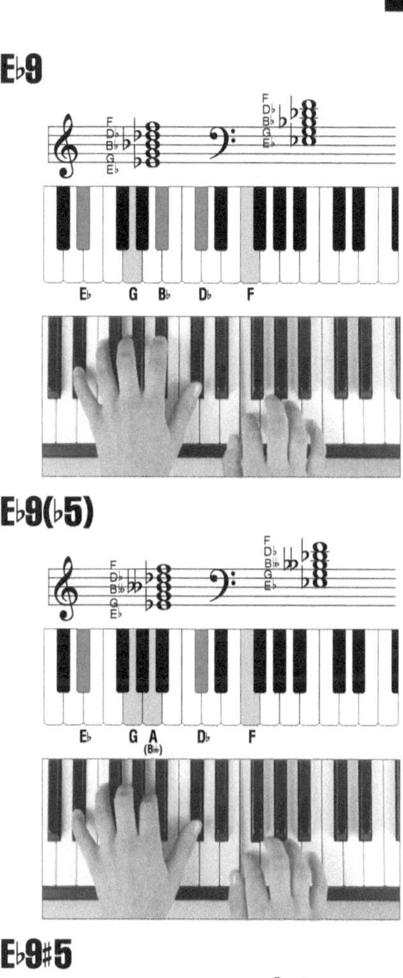

E♭9♯5

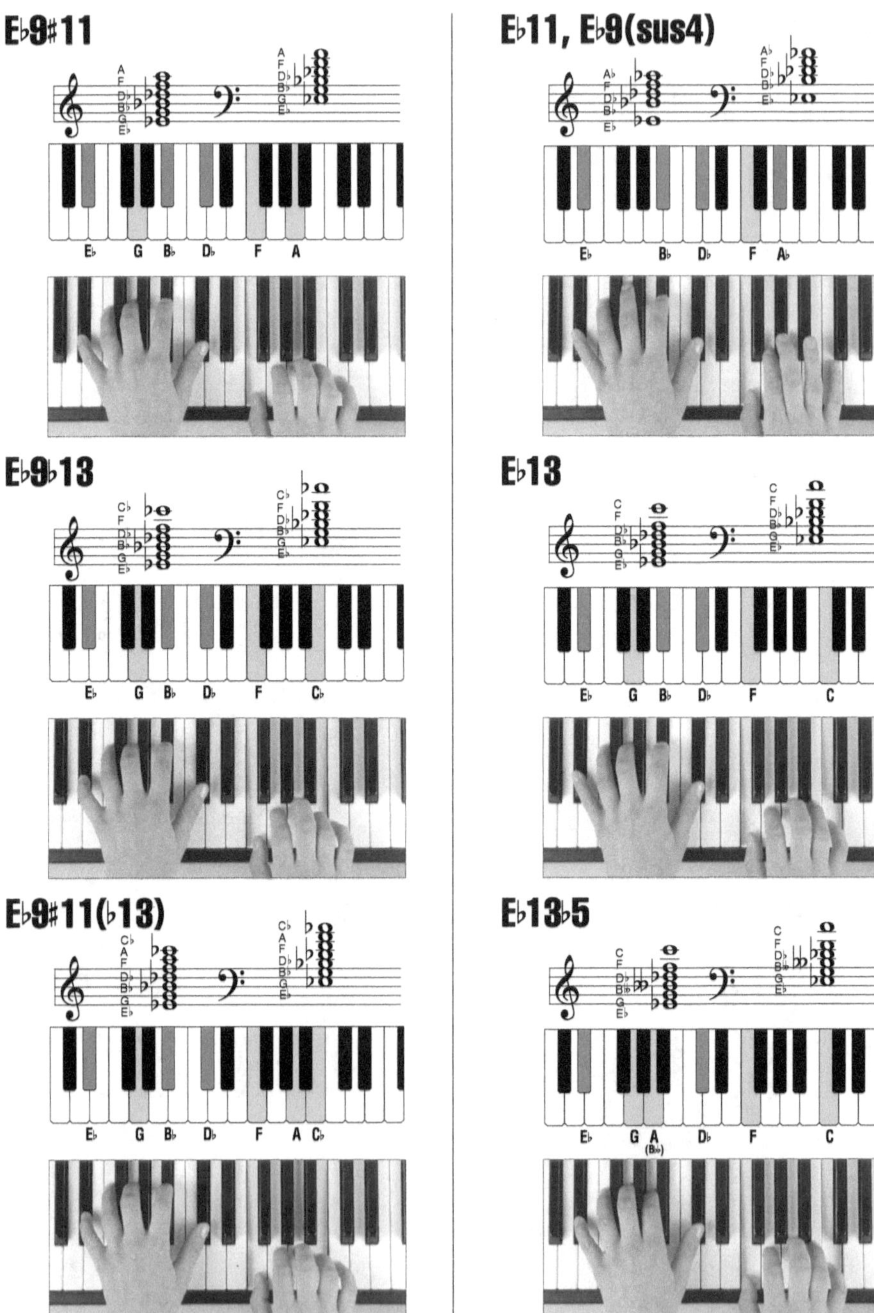
E♭9♯11
E♭ G B♭ D♭ F A
E♭11, E♭9(sus4)
E♭ B♭ D♭ F A♭
E♭9♭13
E♭ G B♭ D♭ F C♭
E♭13
E♭ G B♭ D♭ F C
E♭9♯11(♭13)
E♭ G B♭ D♭ F A C♭
E♭13♭5
E♭ G A (B♭♭) D♭ F C

E♭13♭9

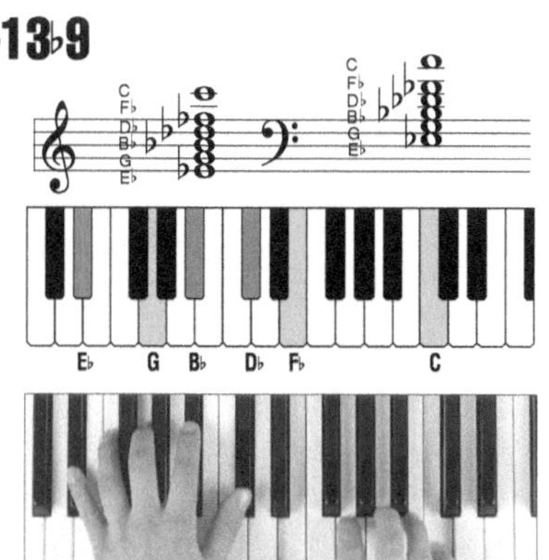

E♭13♯9

E♭13♯11

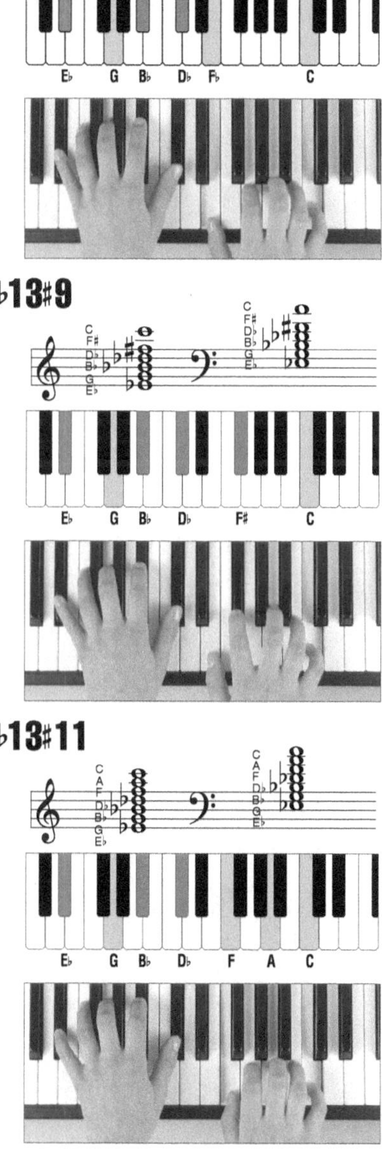

E♭13(sus4)

E♭m(♯5)

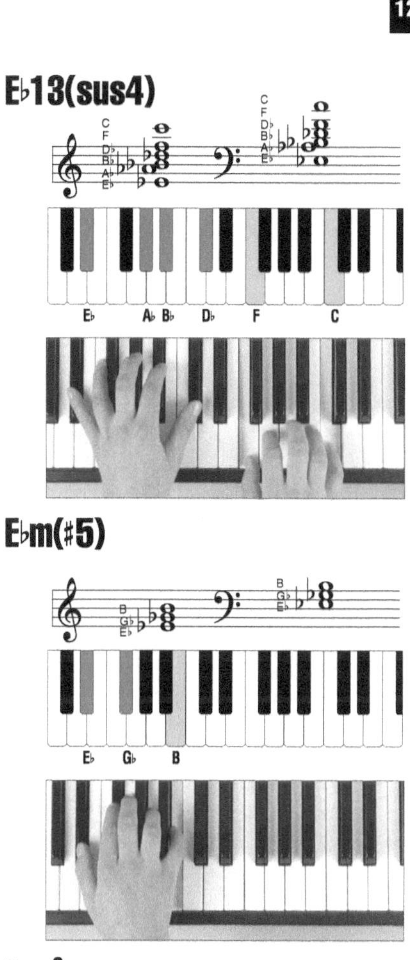

E♭m$^{6}_{9}$

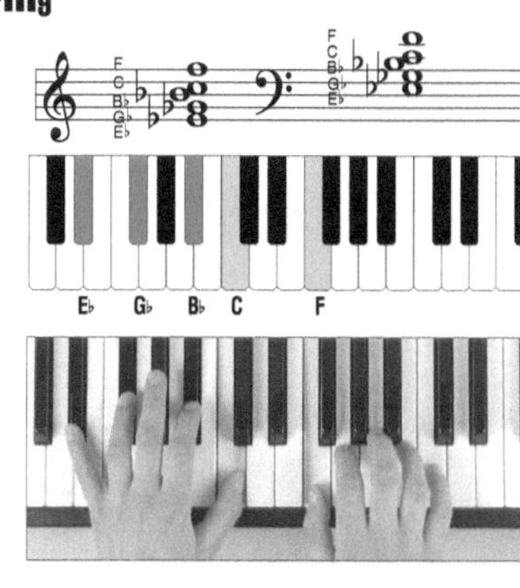

E♭m7(add4)

E♭m7(add11)

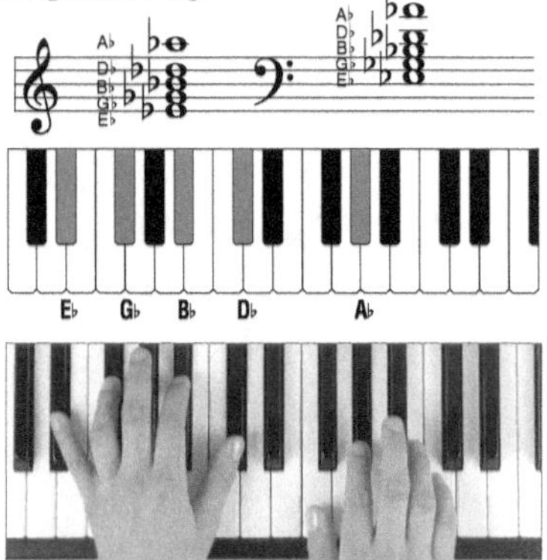

E♭m7♭5(♭9)

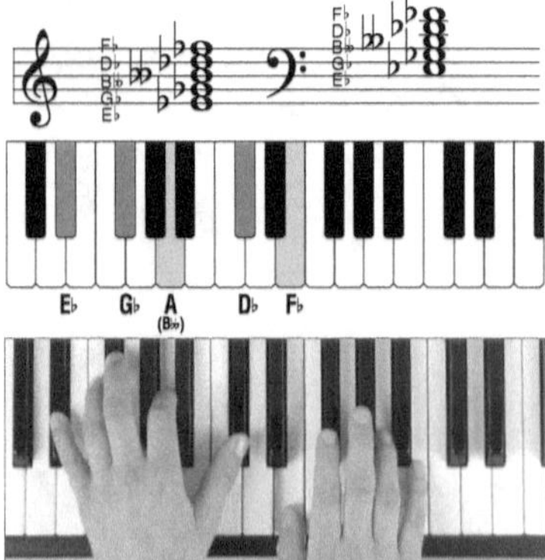

E♭m9

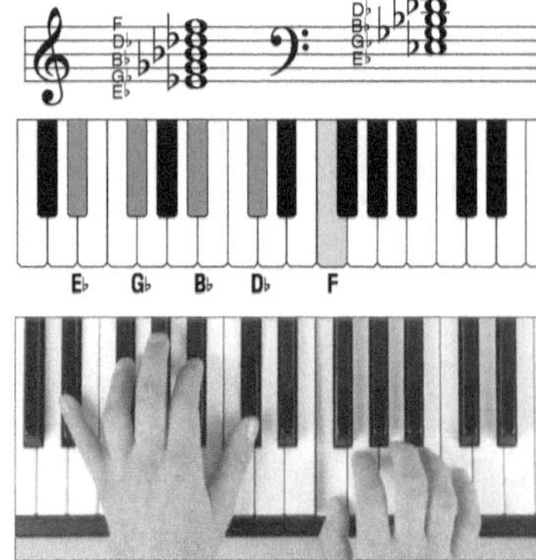

E♭m9(maj7)

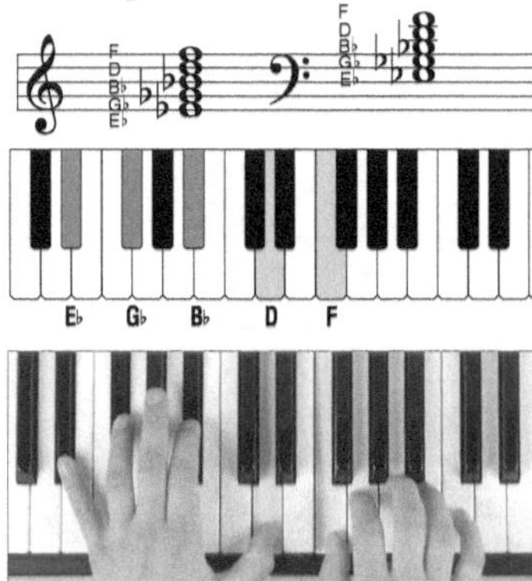

E♭m9♭5

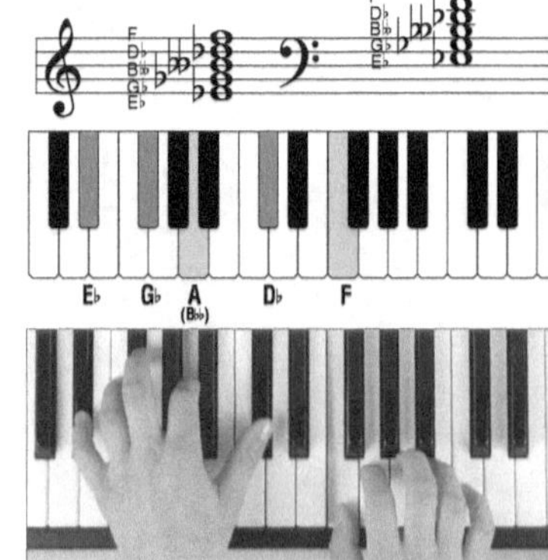

E♭m11

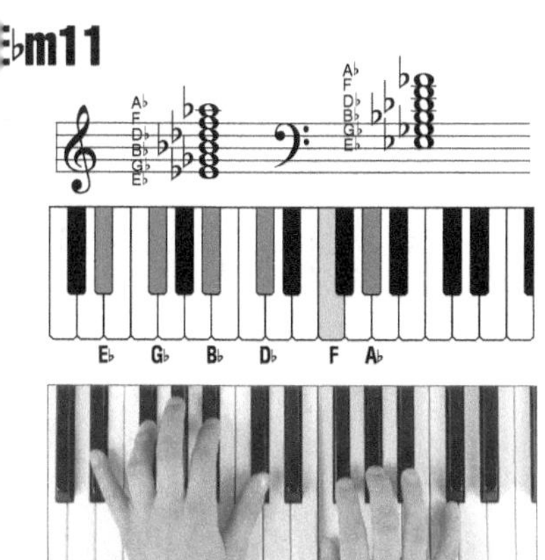

E♭m13

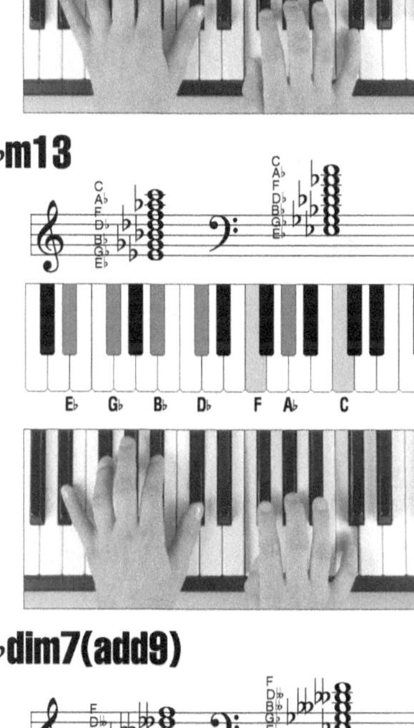

E♭dim7(add9)

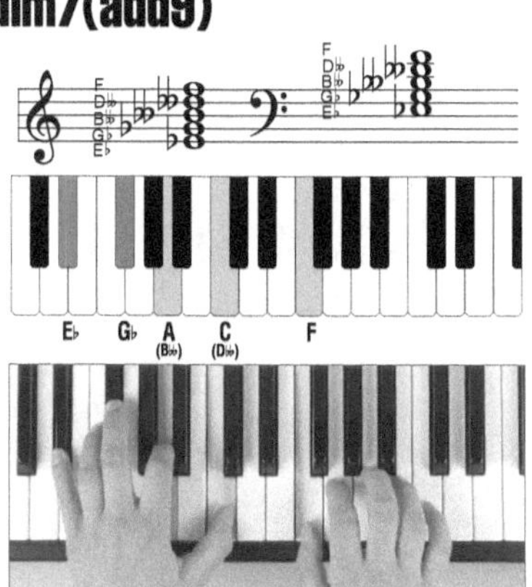

E♭m11♭5

E♭m11(maj7)

E♭7alt.

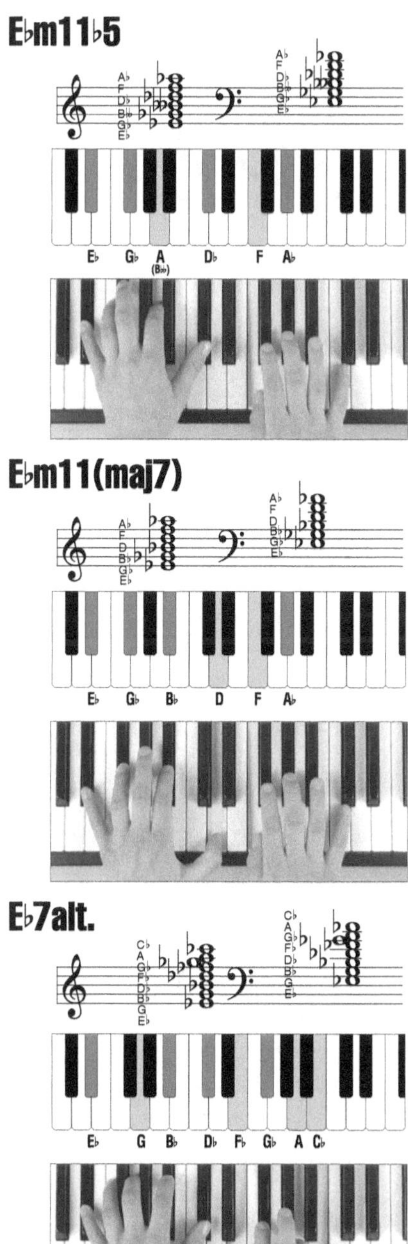

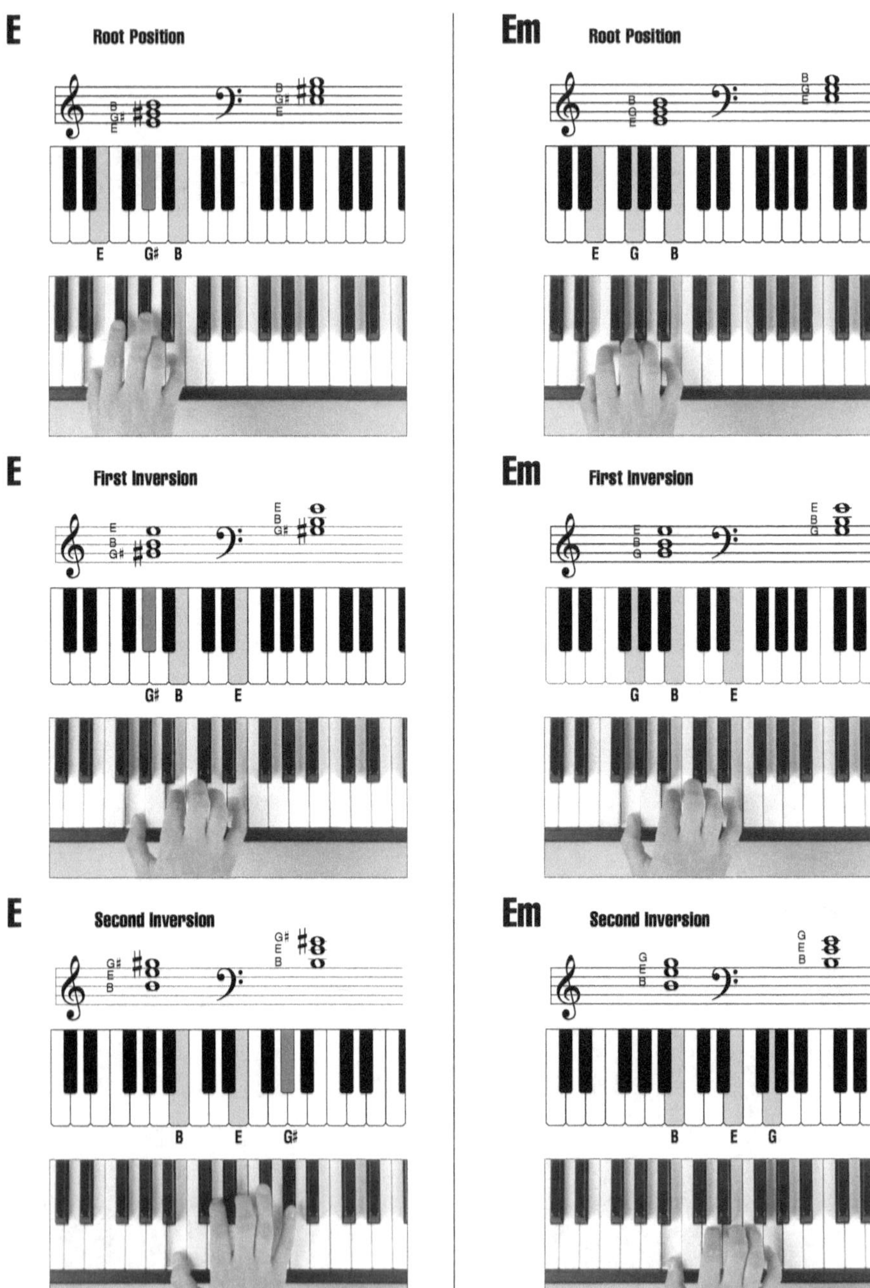
E
Root Position
E G♯ B
Em
Root Position
E G B
E
First Inversion
G♯ B E
Em
First Inversion
G B E
E
Second Inversion
B E G♯
Em
Second Inversion
B E G

E+ Root Position

E+ First Inversion

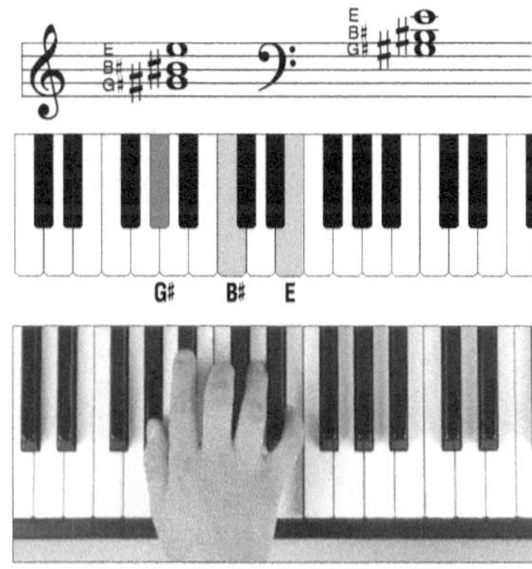

E+ Second Inversion

Edim Root Position

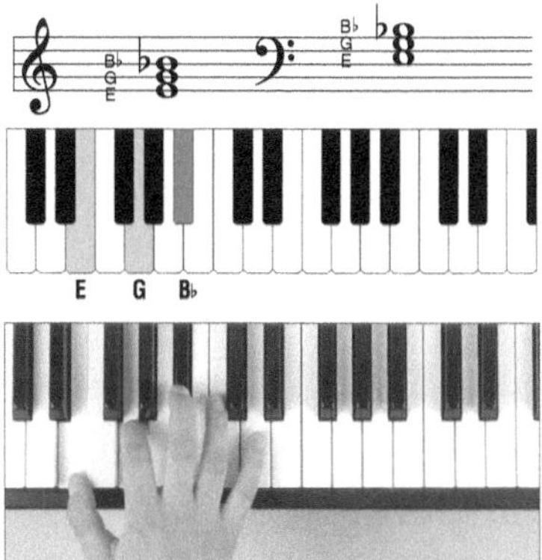

Edim First Inversion

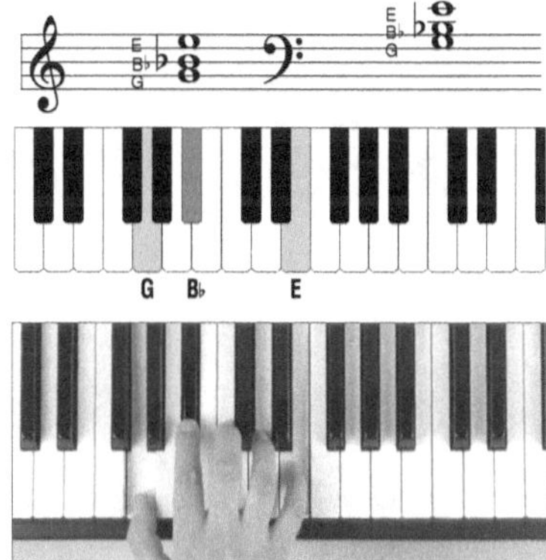

Edim Second Inversion

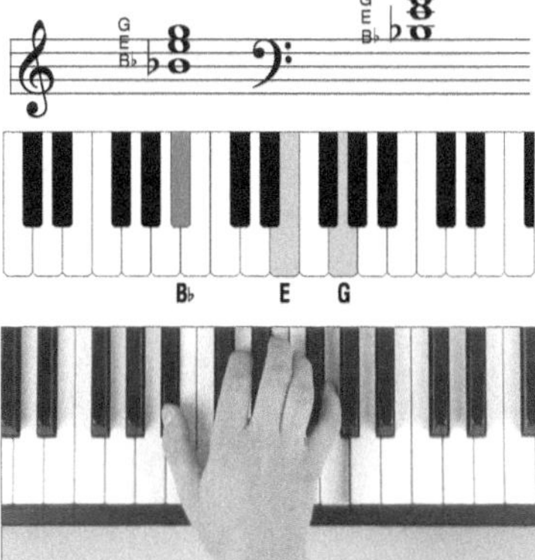

Esus Root Position

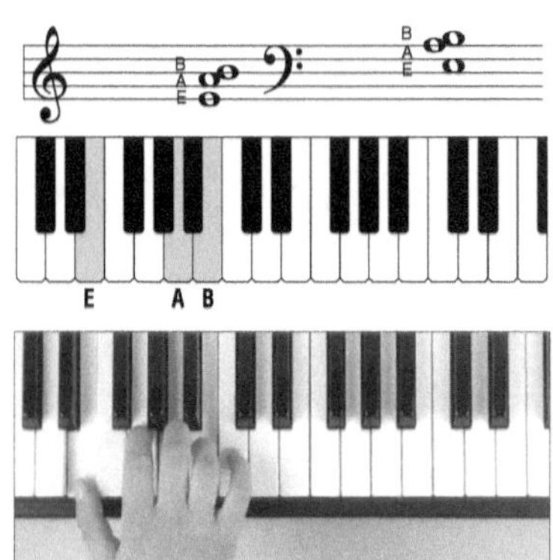

Esus First Inversion

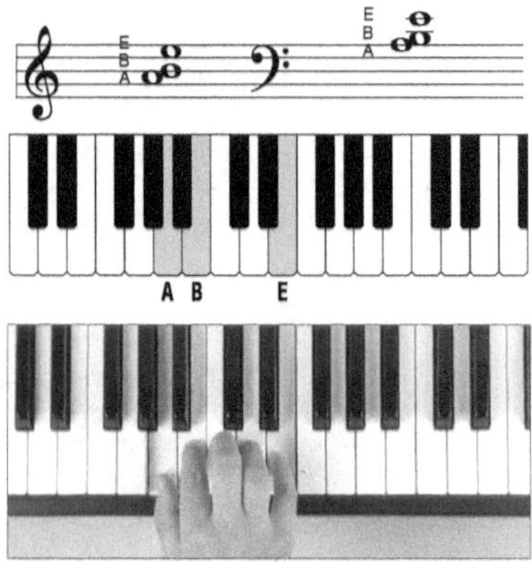

Esus Second Inversion

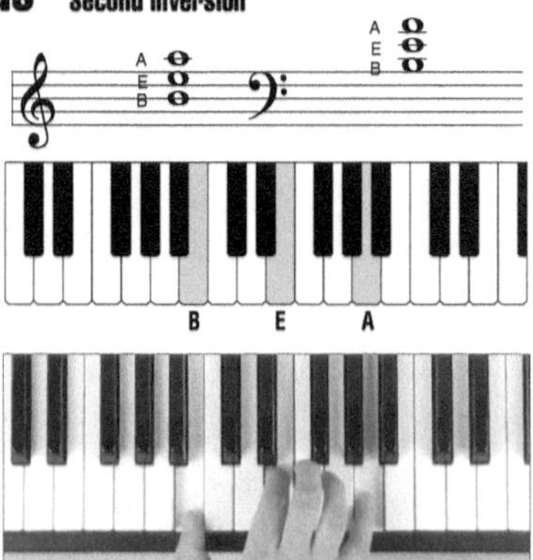

E(♭5) Root Position

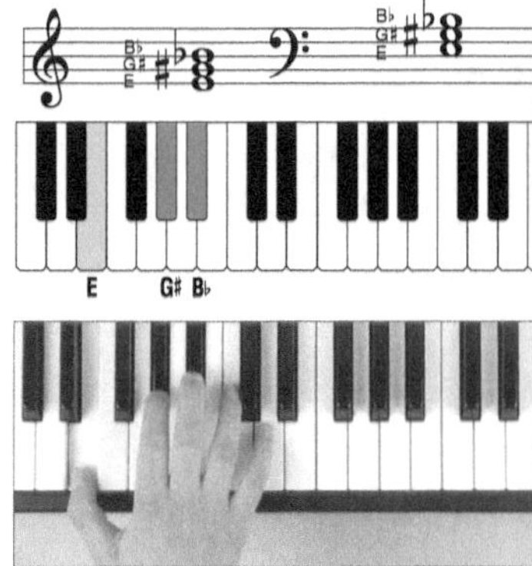

E(♭5) First Inversion

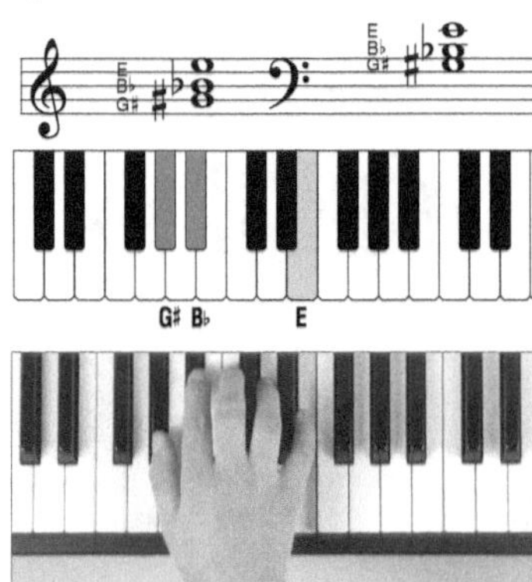

E(♭5) Second Inversion

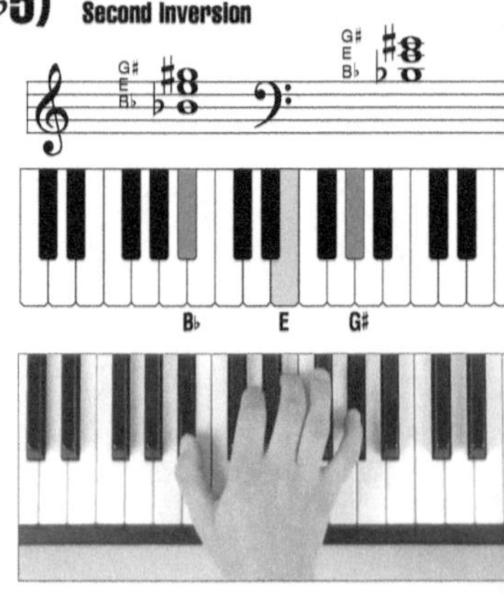

Esus2 Root Position

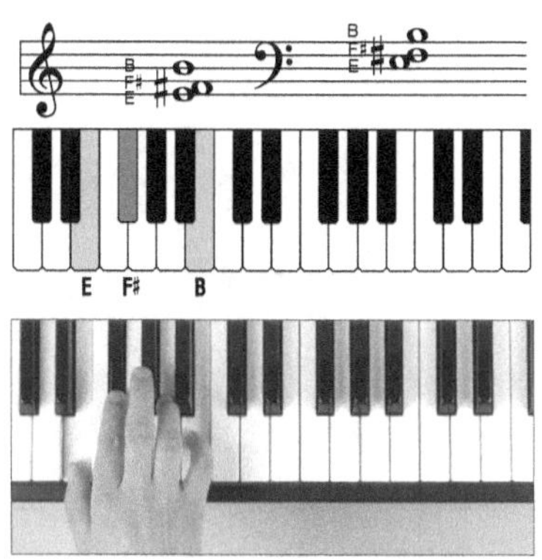

Esus2 First Inversion

Esus2 Second Inversion

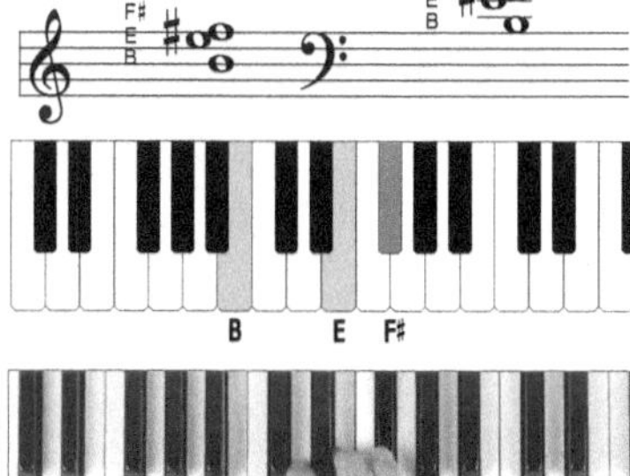

E6 Root Position

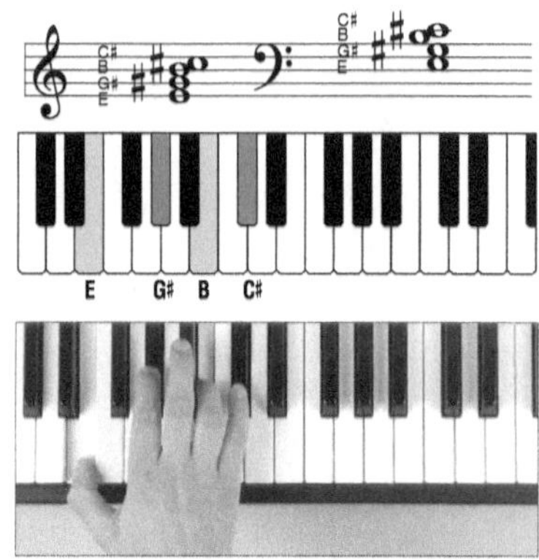

E6 First Inversion

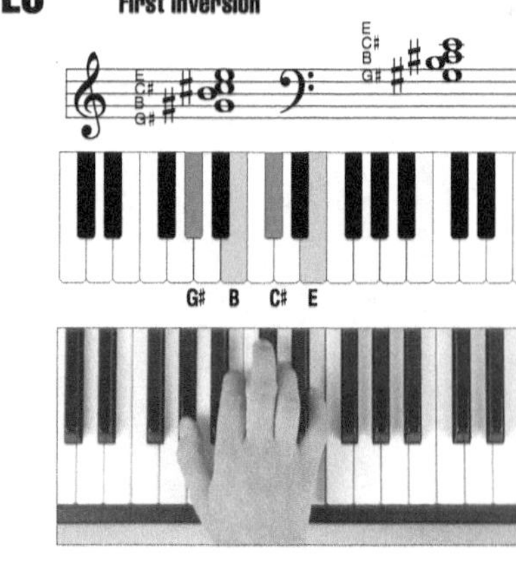

E6 Second Inversion

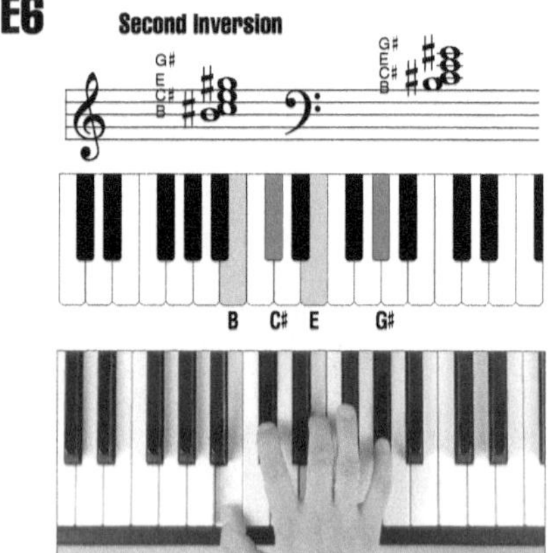

E6 Third Inversion

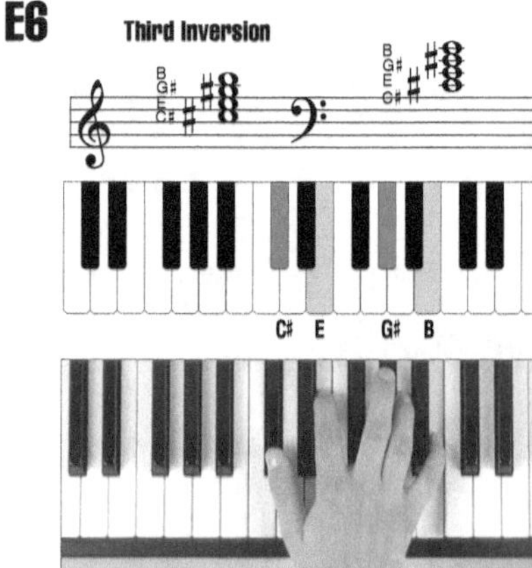

E(add2), E(add9) Root Position

E(add2), E(add9) First Inversion

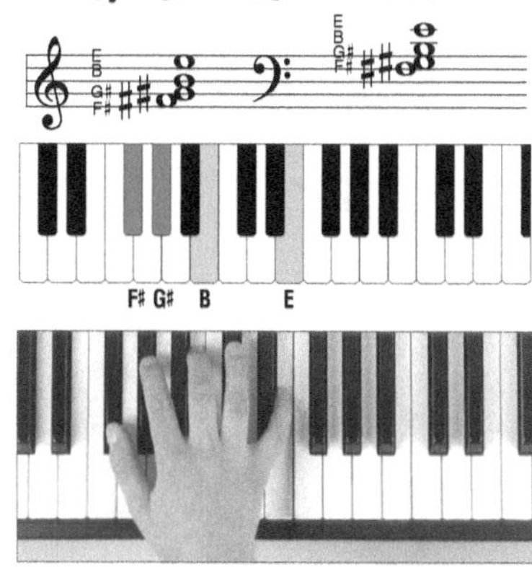

E(add2), E(add9) Second Inversion

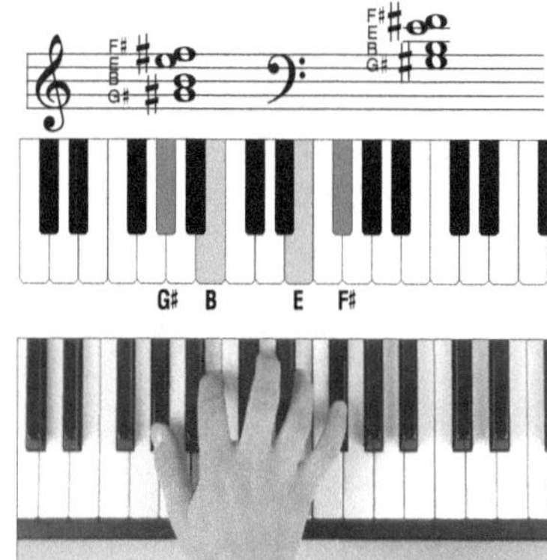

E(add2), E(add9) Third Inversion

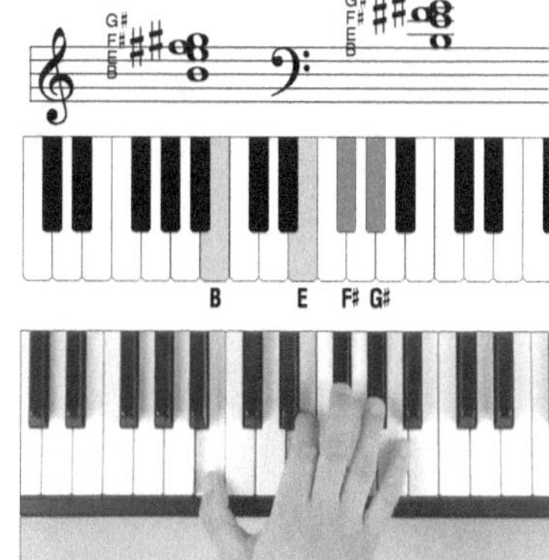

Emaj7 Root Position

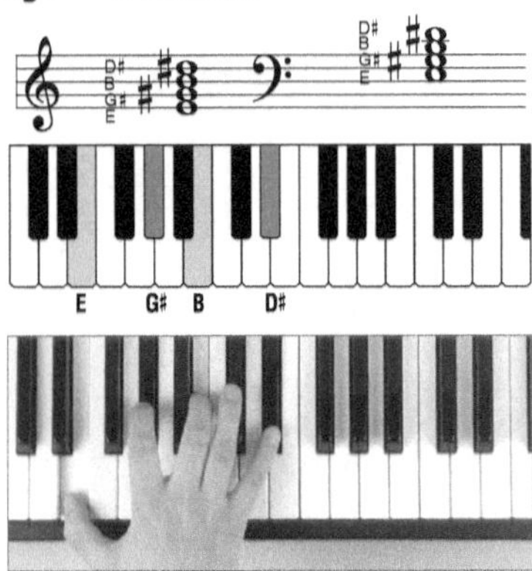

Emaj7 First Inversion

E
D♯
B
G♯

G♯ B D♯E

Emaj7 Second Inversion

G♯
E
D♯
B

B D♯E G♯

Emaj7 Third Inversion

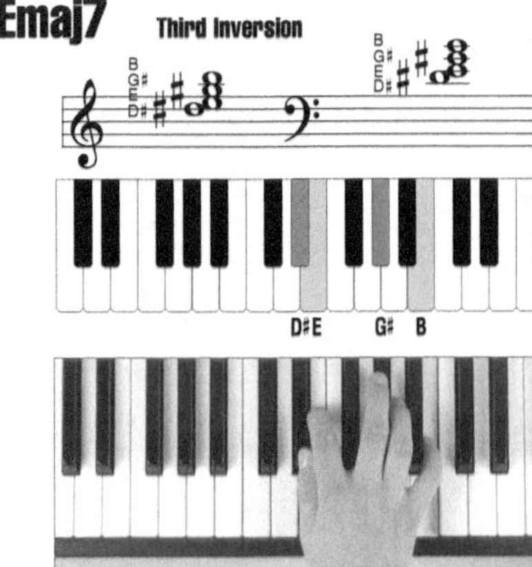

Emaj7♭5 Root Position

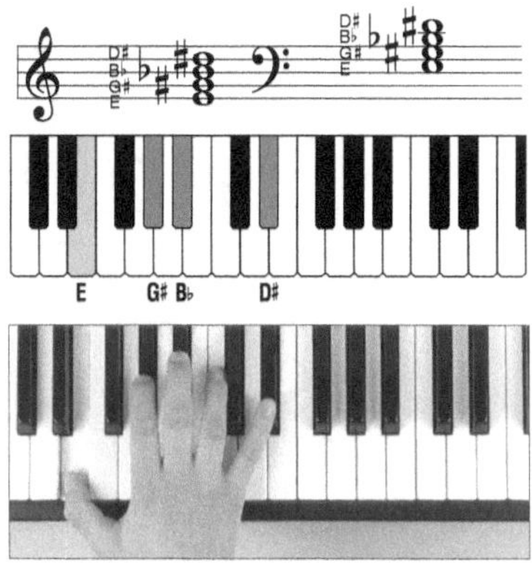

Emaj7♭5 First Inversion

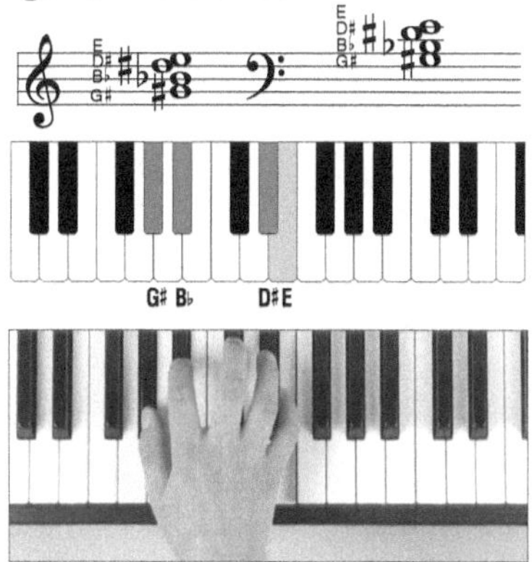

Emaj7♭5 Second Inversion

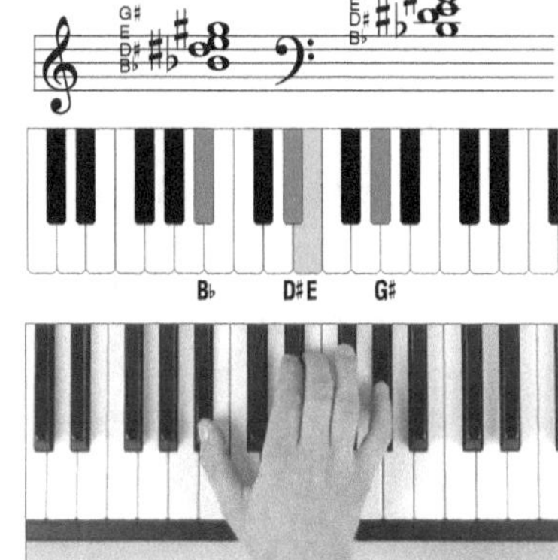

Emaj7♭5 Third Inversion

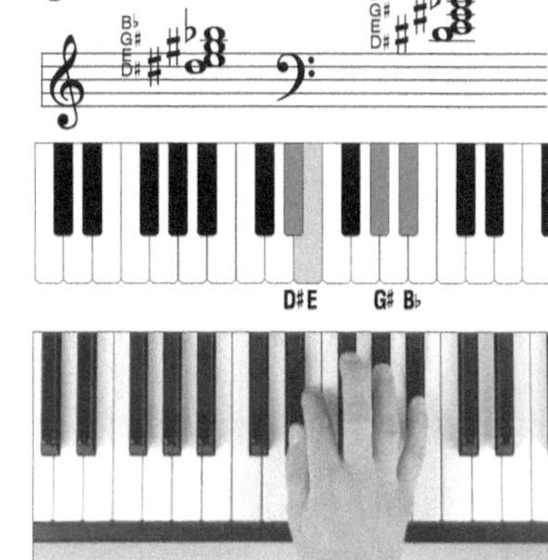

Emaj7♯5 Root Position

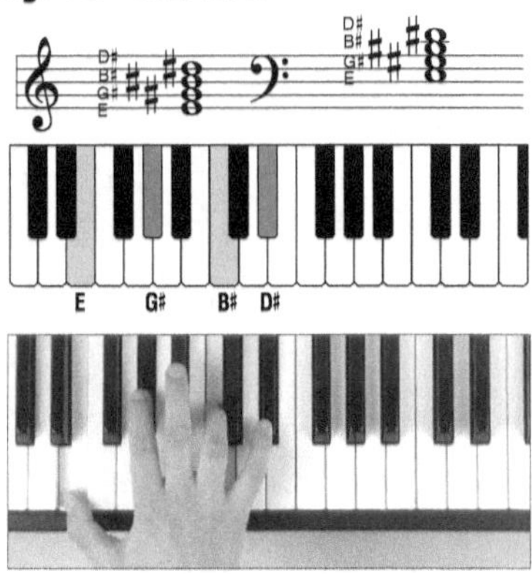

Emaj7♯5 First Inversion

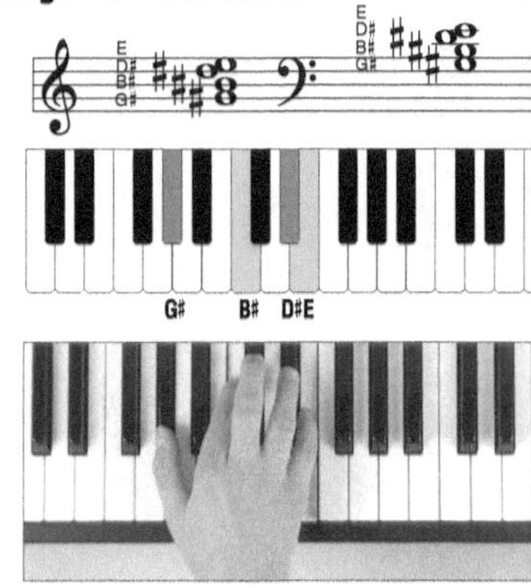

Emaj7♯5 Second Inversion

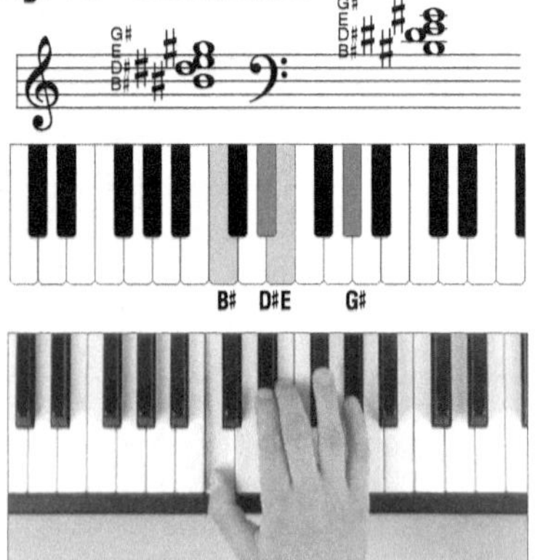

Emaj7♯5 Third Inversion

B♯
G♯
E
D♯

D♯E G♯ B♯

E7 Root Position

E7 First Inversion

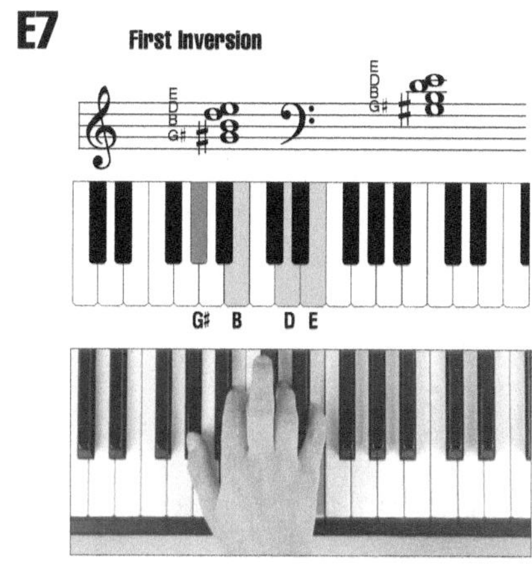

E7 Second Inversion

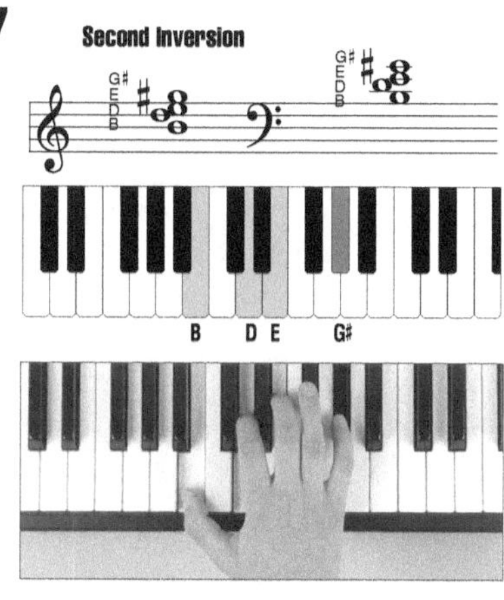

E7 Third Inversion

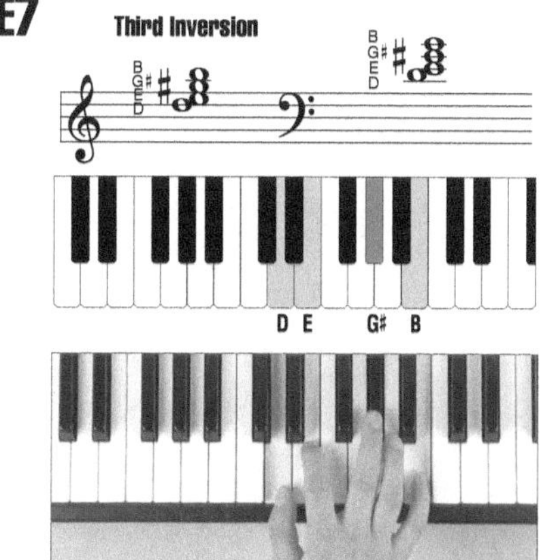

E7♭5 Root Position

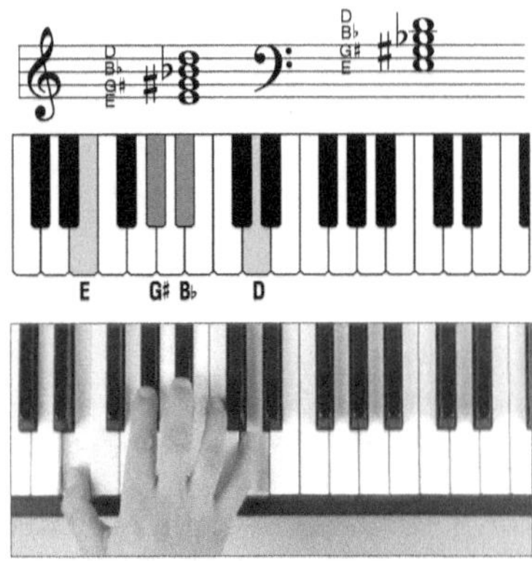

E7♭5 First Inversion

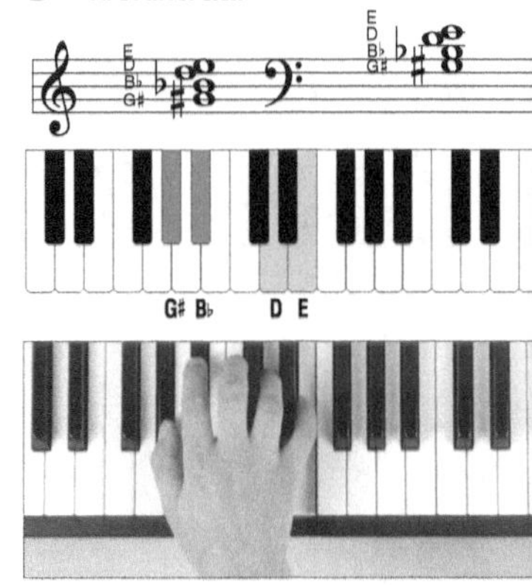

E7♭5 Second Inversion

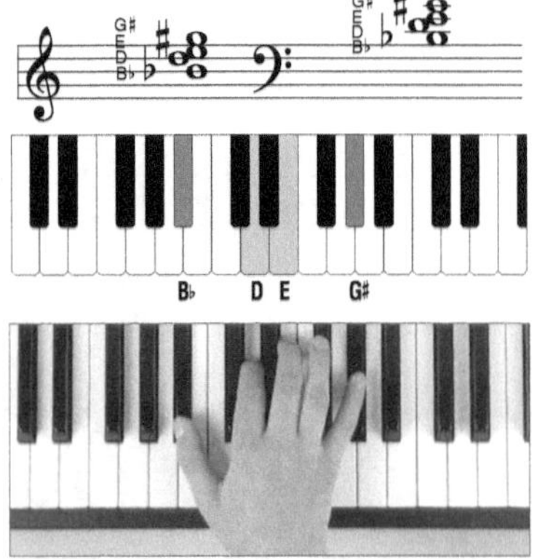

E7♭5 Third Inversion

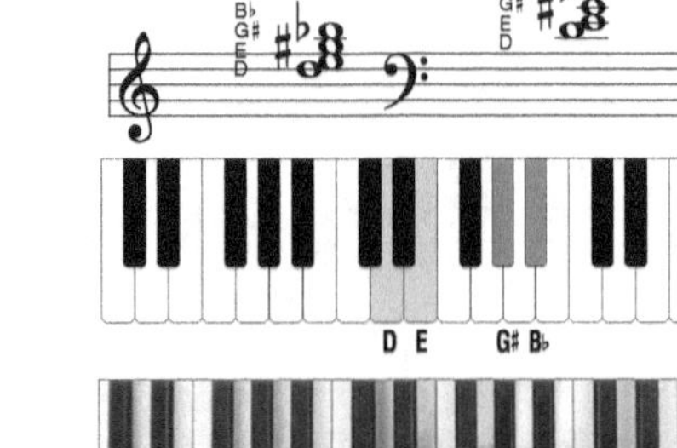

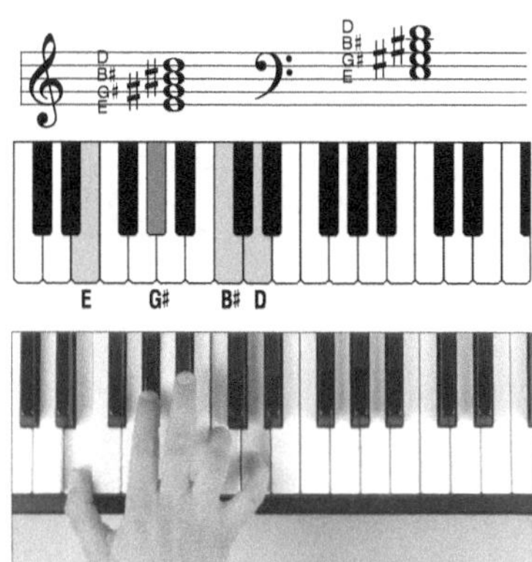

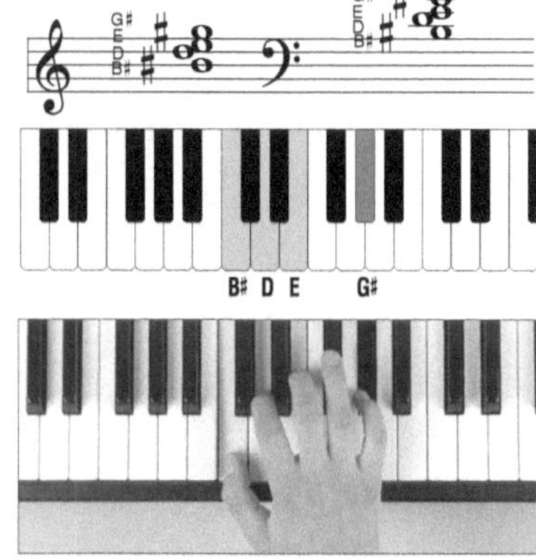

E7♯5 Third Inversion

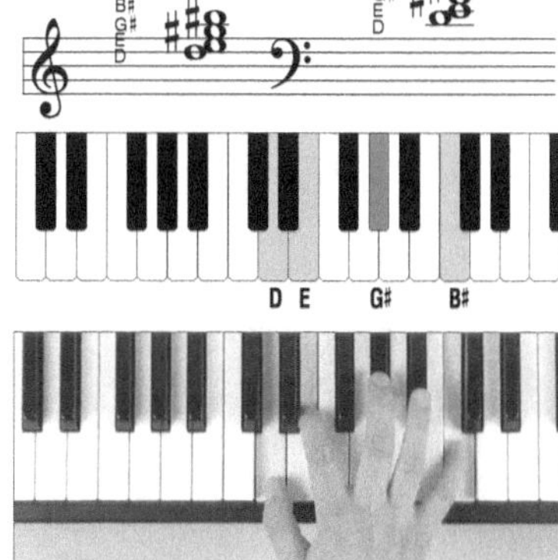

E7sus Root Position

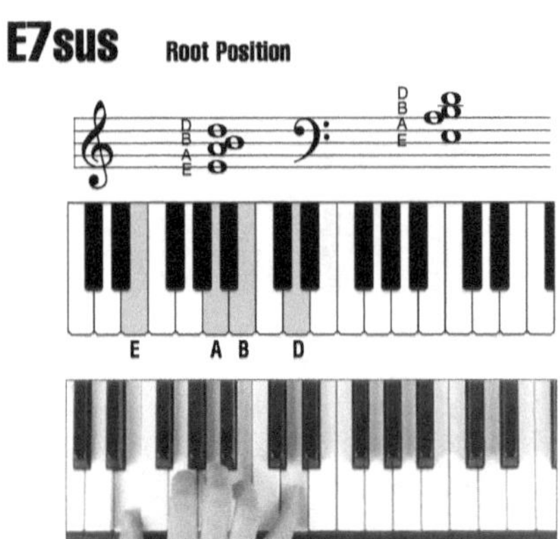

E7sus First Inversion

E7sus Second Inversion

E7sus Third Inversion

Em(add2), Em(add9) Root Position

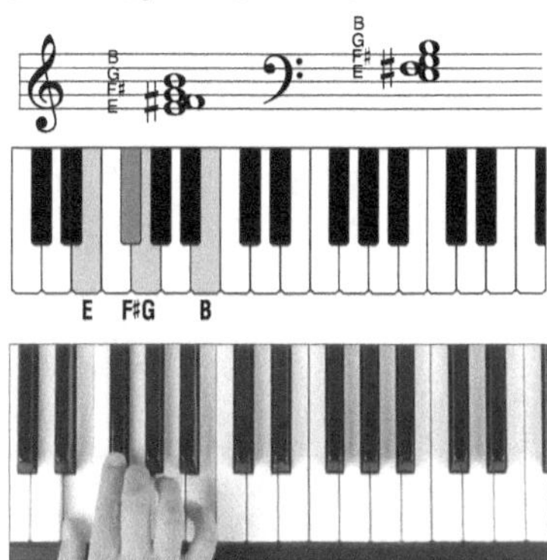

Em(add2), Em(add9) First Inversion

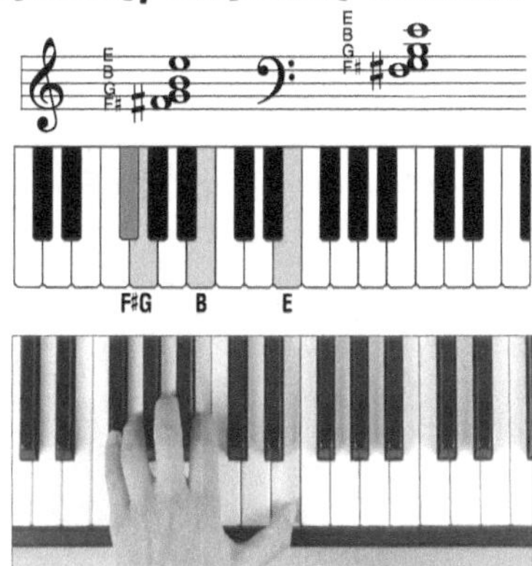

Em(add2), Em(add9) Second Inversion

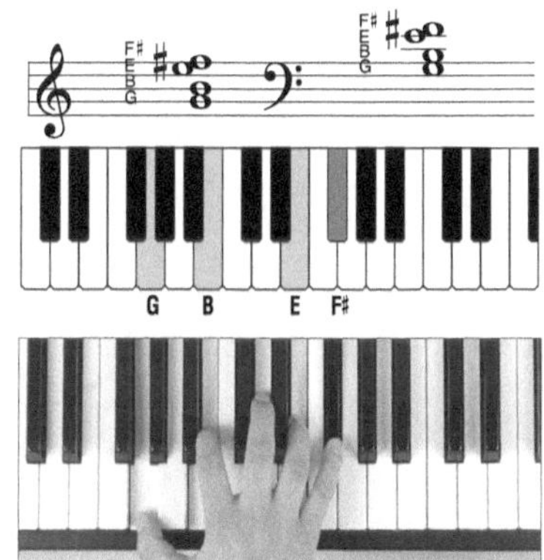

Em(add2), Em(add9) Third Inversion

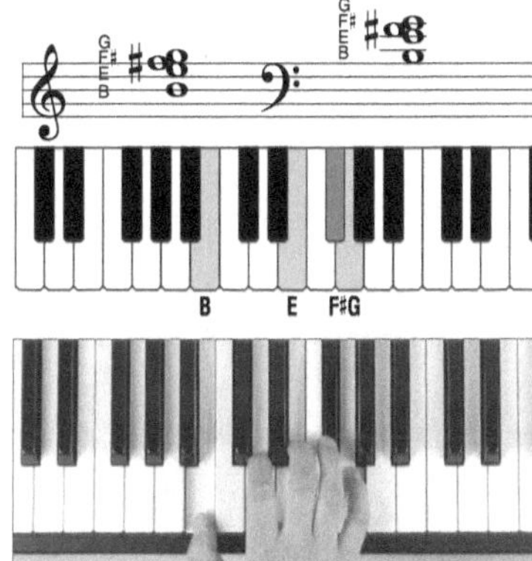

Em6 Root Position

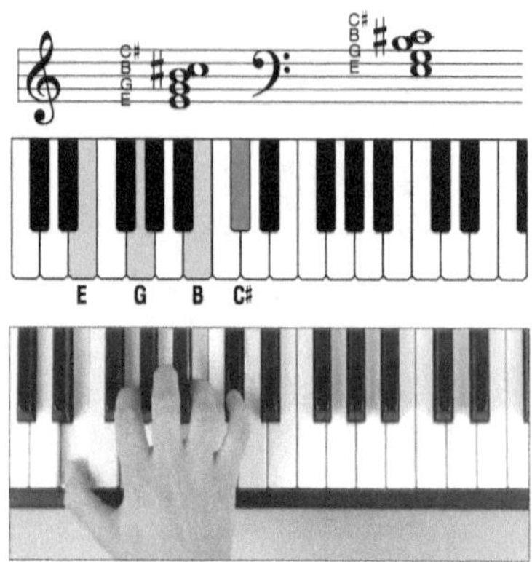

Em6 First Inversion

Em6 Second Inversion

Em6 Third Inversion

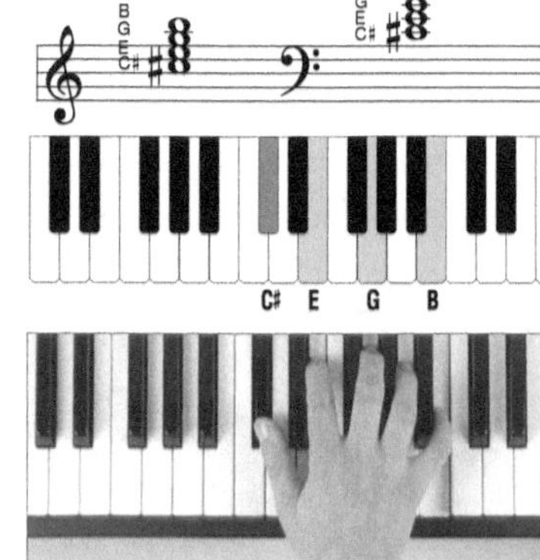

Em7 Root Position

Em7 First Inversion

Em7 Second Inversion

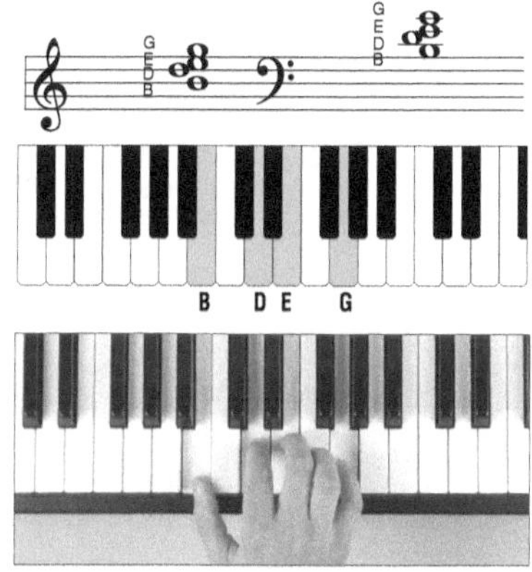

Em7 Third Inversion

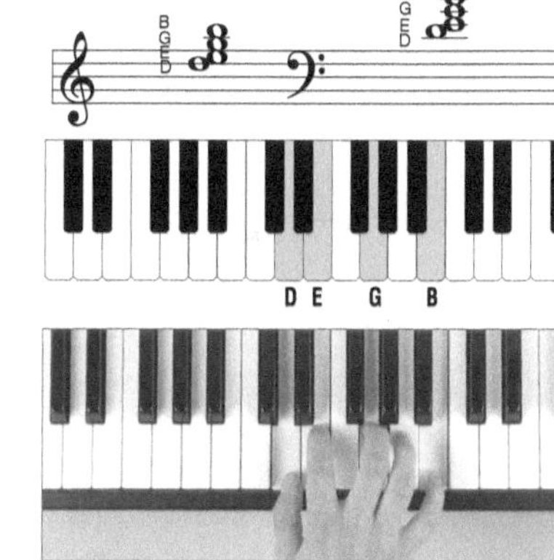

Em(maj7) Root Position

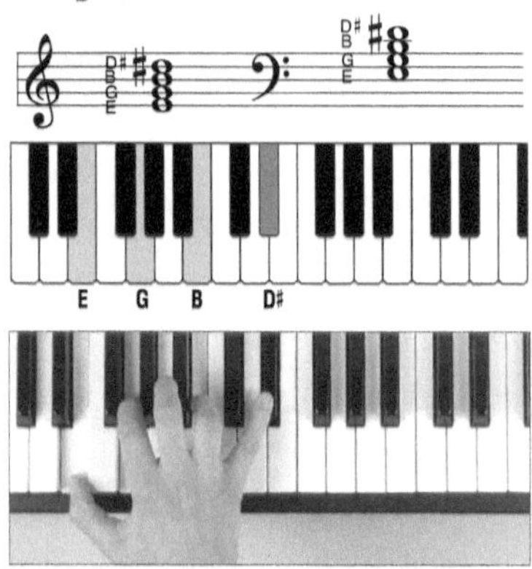

Em(maj7) First Inversion

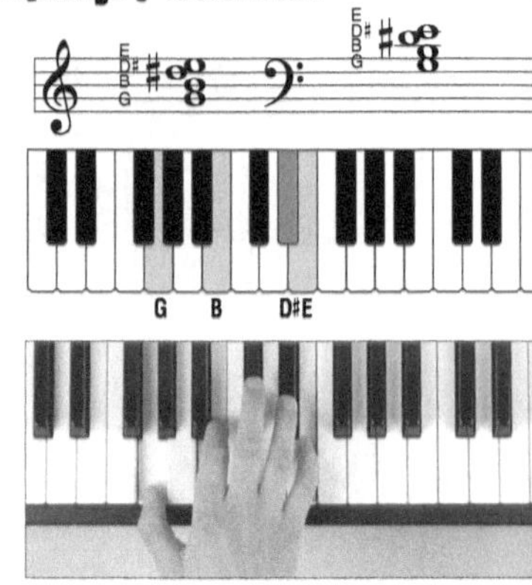

Em(maj7) Second Inversion

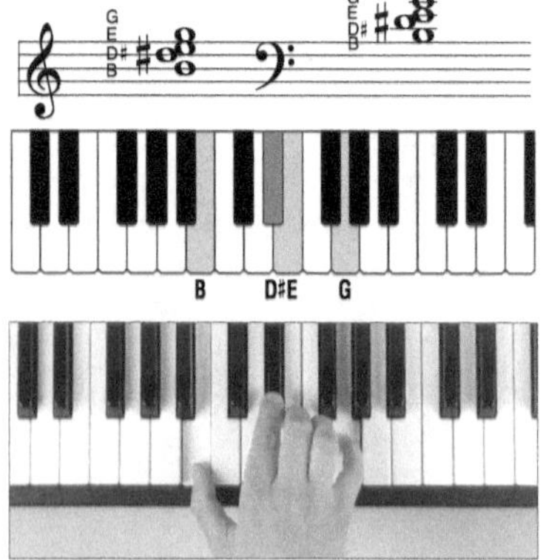

Em(maj7) Third Inversion

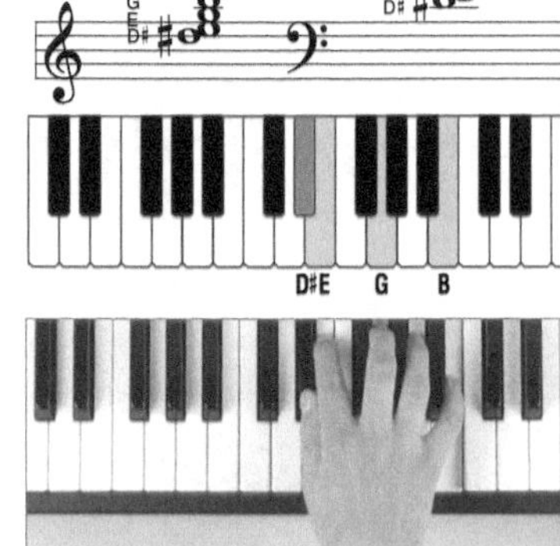

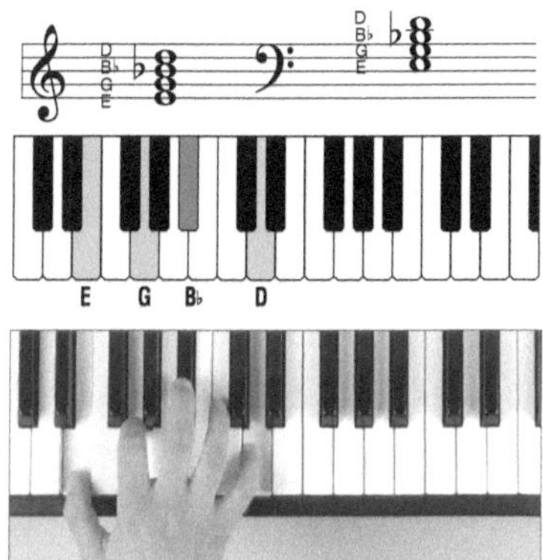

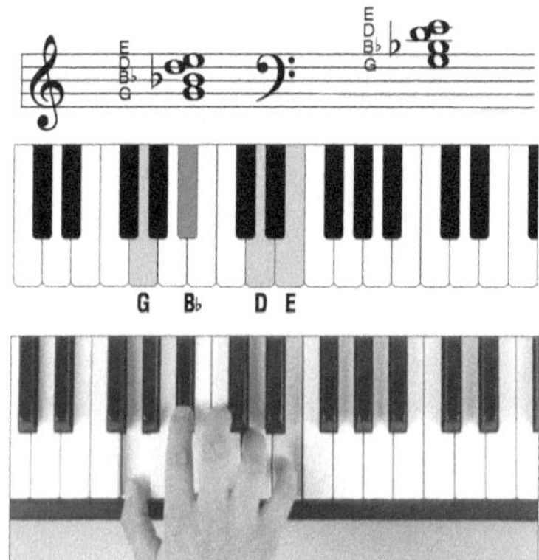

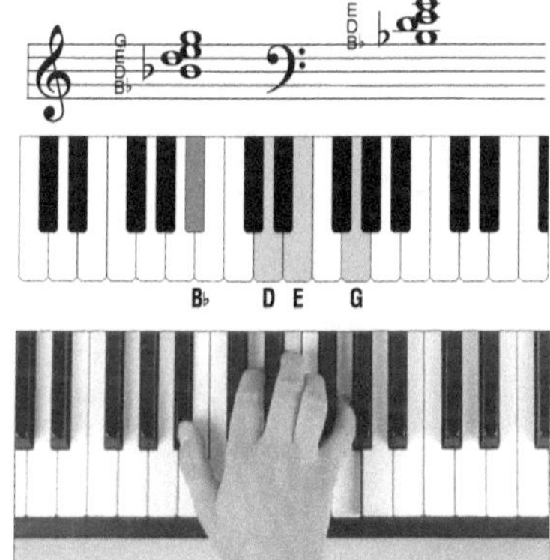

Em7♭5 Third Inversion

Edim7 Root Position

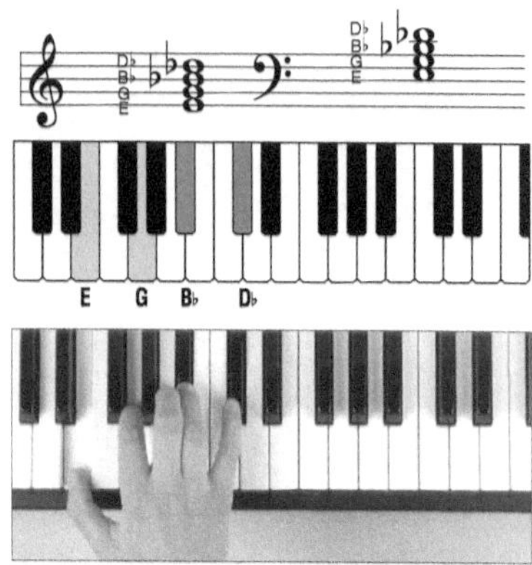

Edim7 First Inversion

E
D♭
B♭
G

G B♭ D♭ E

Edim7 Second Inversion

G
E
D♭
B♭

B♭ D♭ E G

Edim7 Third Inversion

Edim(maj7) Root Position

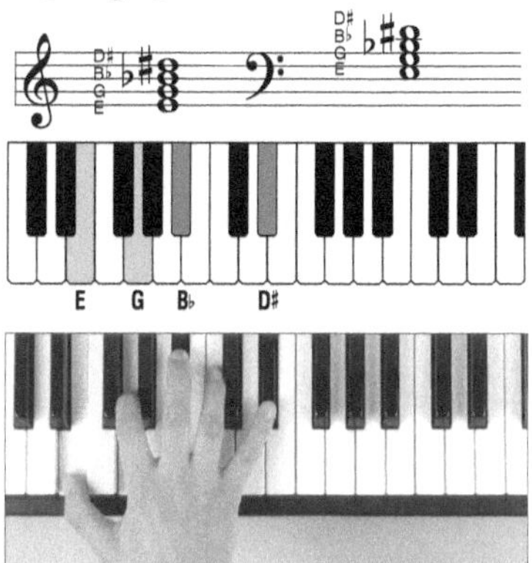

Edim(maj7) First Inversion

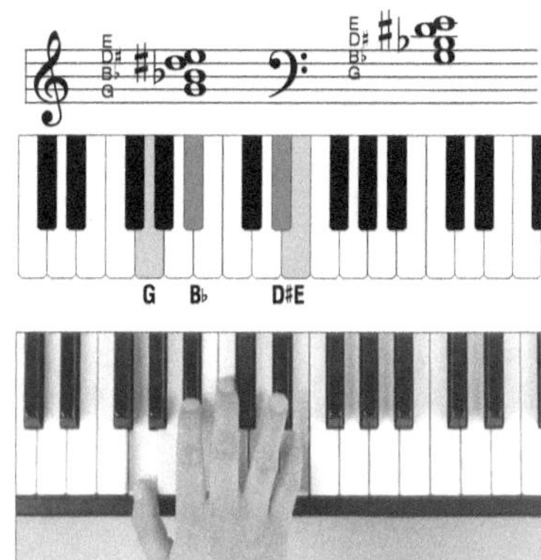

Edim(maj7) Second Inversion

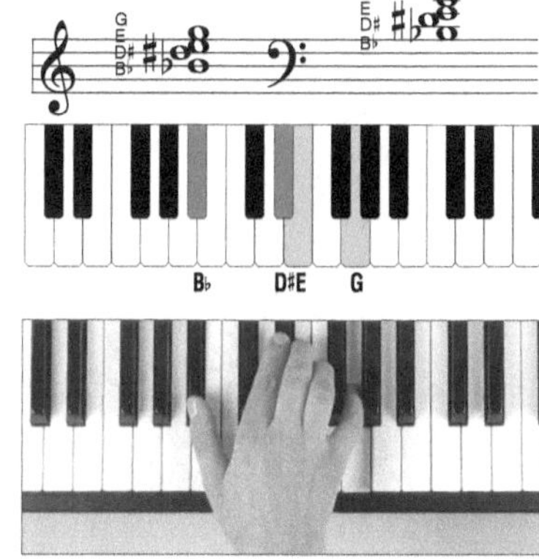

Edim(maj7) Third Inversion

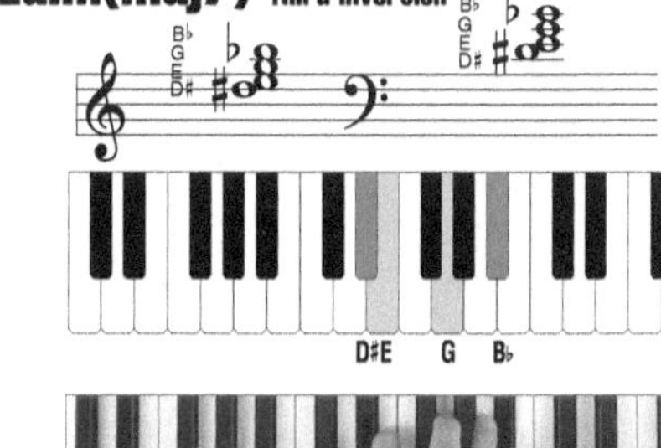

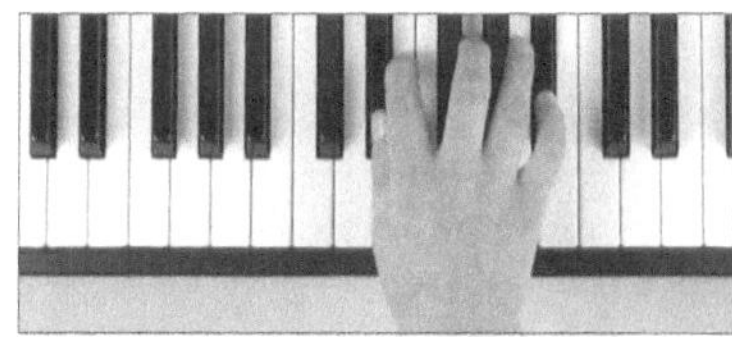

E5

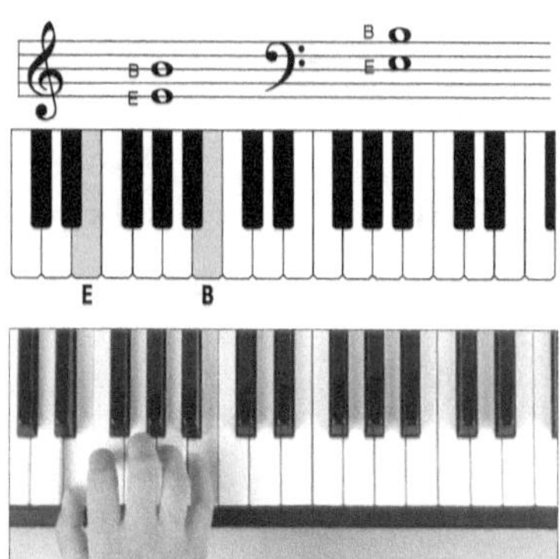

E$^{6}_{9}$

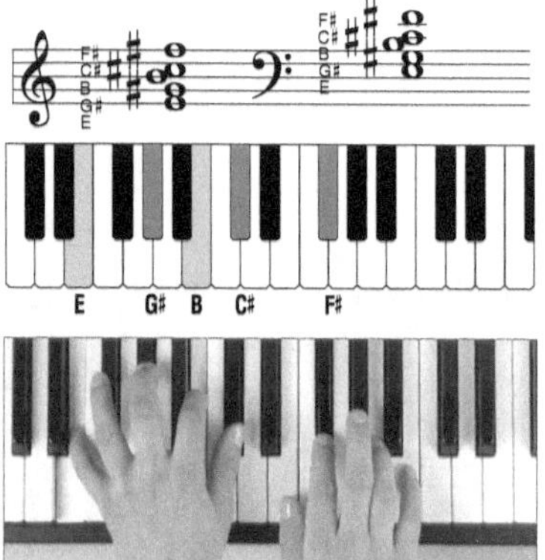

Emaj$^{6}_{9}$

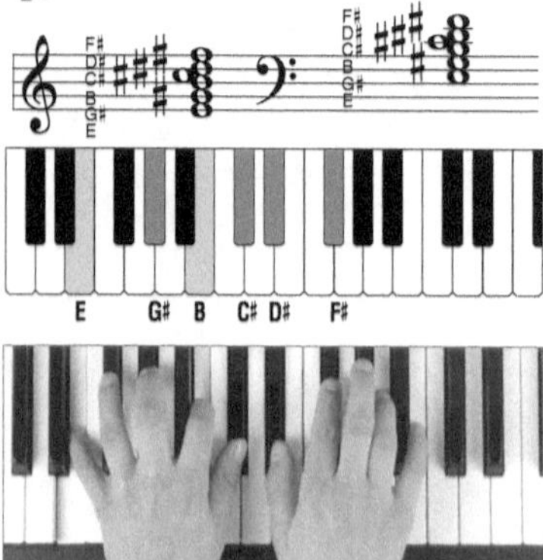

Emaj7♯11

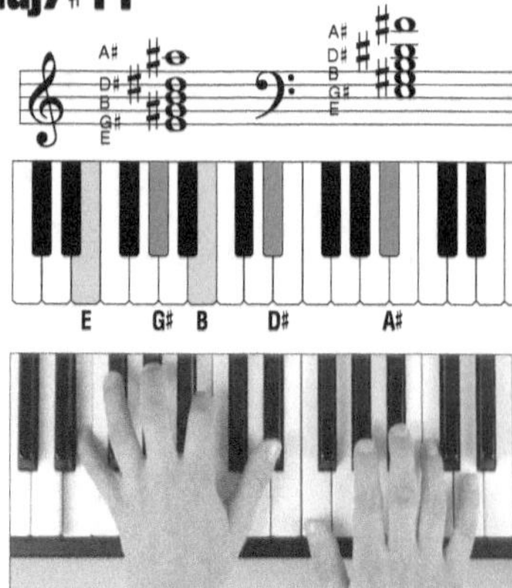

Emaj9

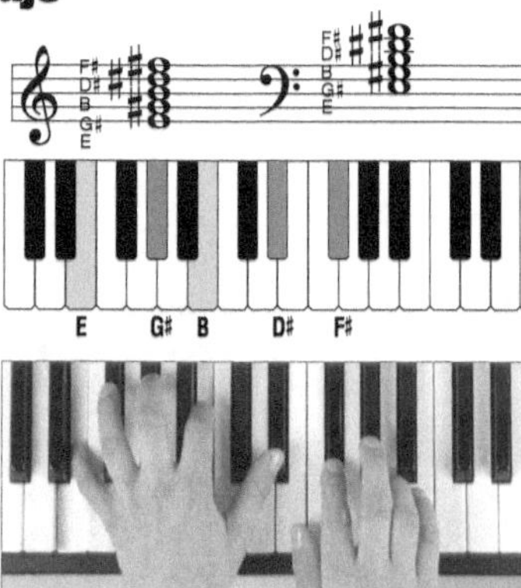

Emaj9♭5

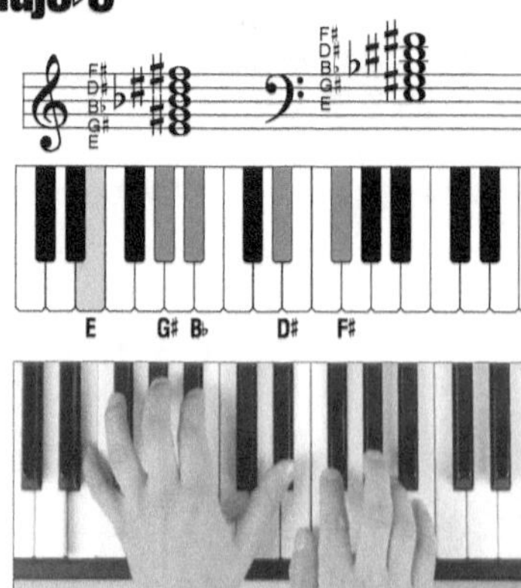

Emaj9♯5

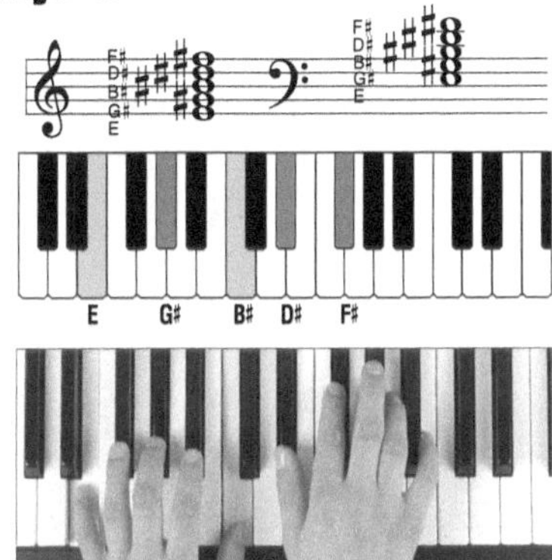

Emaj13♭5

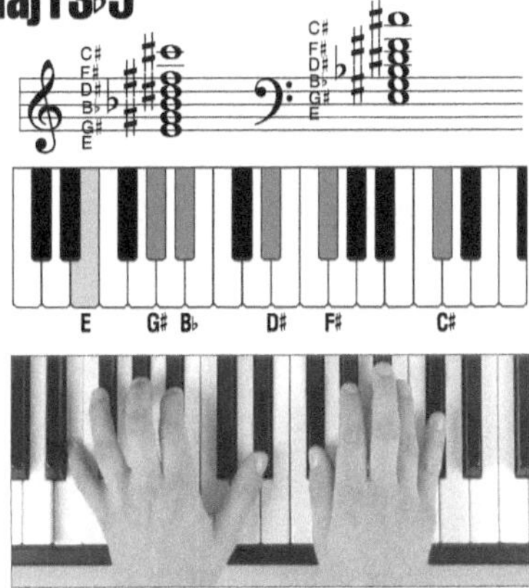

Emaj9♯11

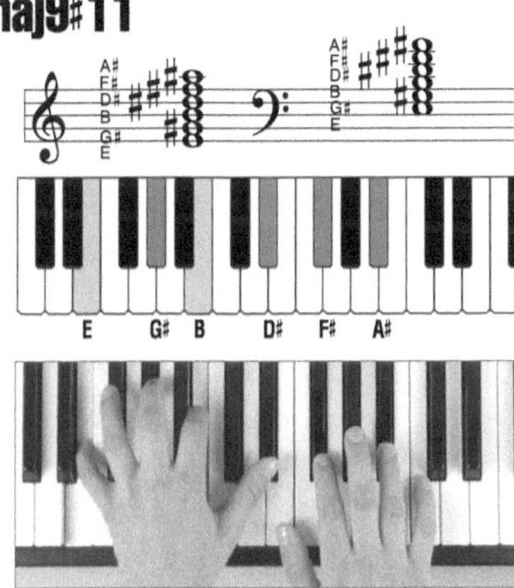

Emaj13♯11

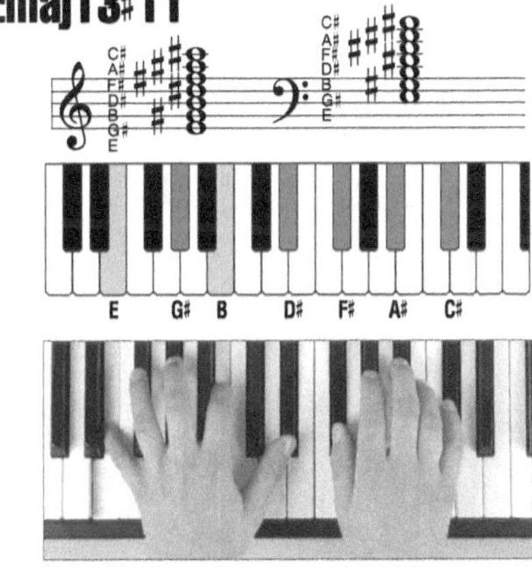

Emaj13

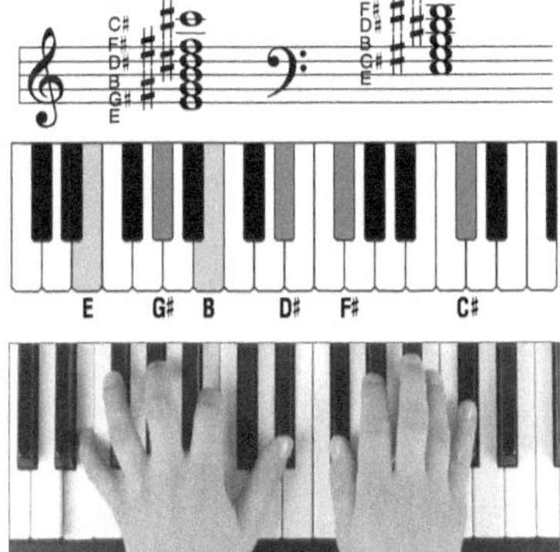

E7♭9

E7♯9

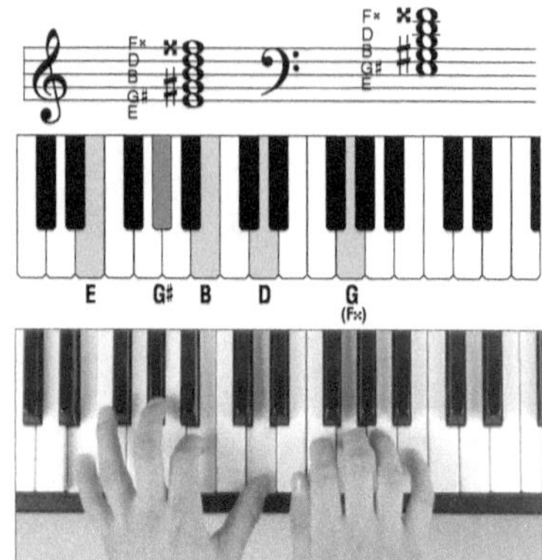

E7♯11

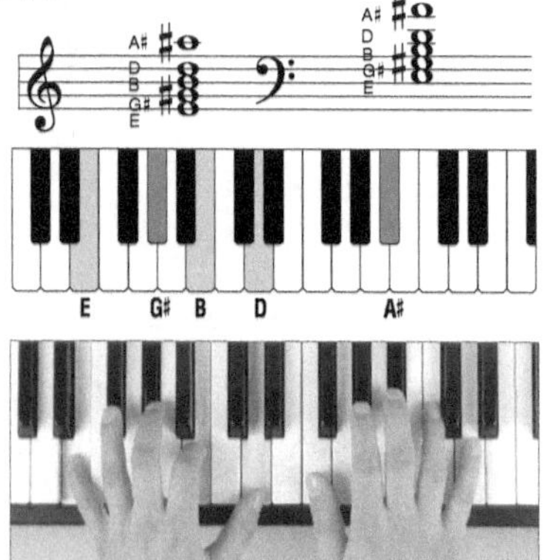

E7♭5(♭9)

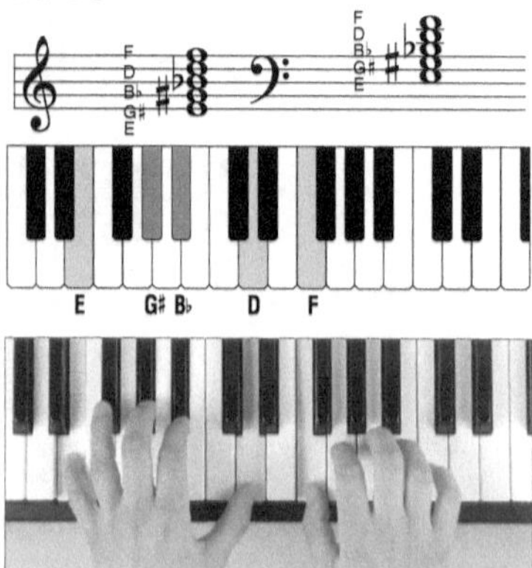

E7♭5(♯9)

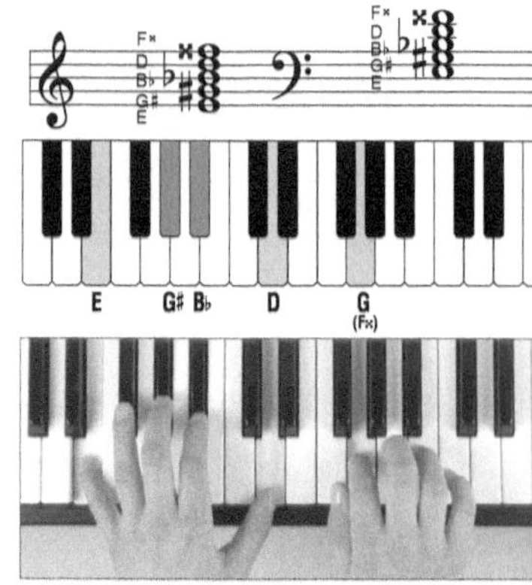

E7♯5(♭9)

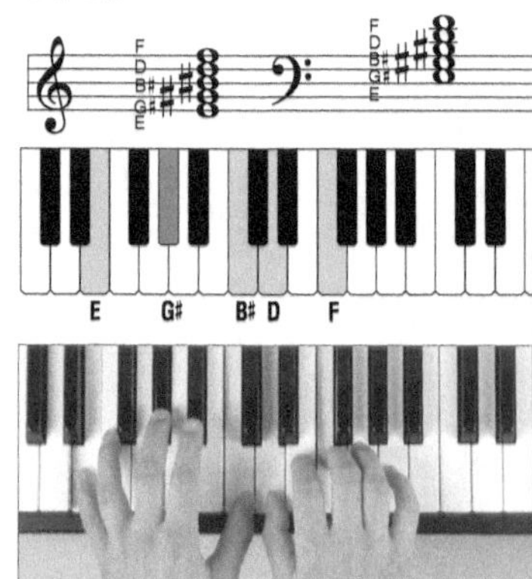

E7♯5(♯9)

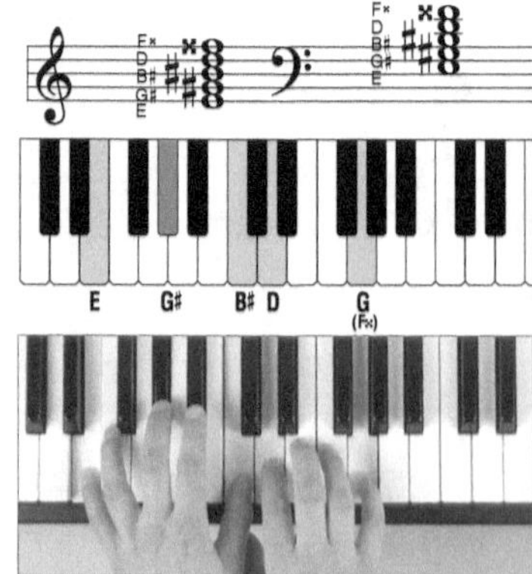

E7♭9(♯9)

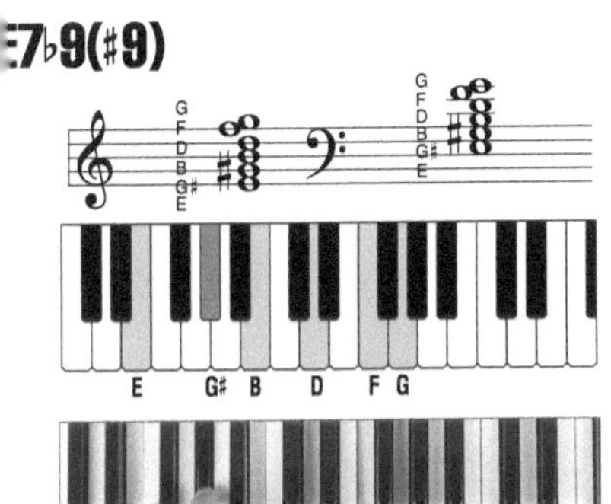

E7(add13)

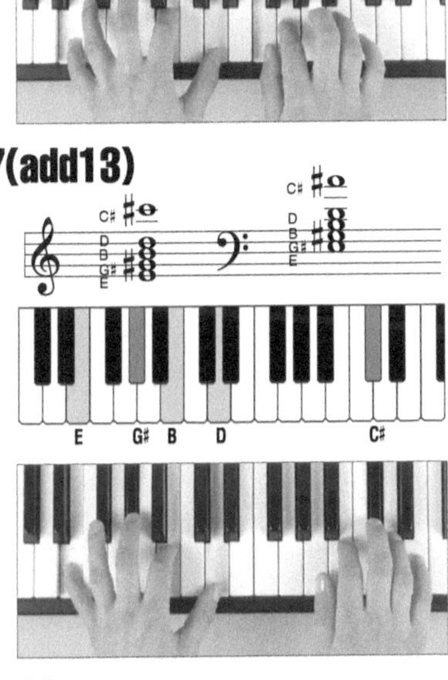

E7♭13

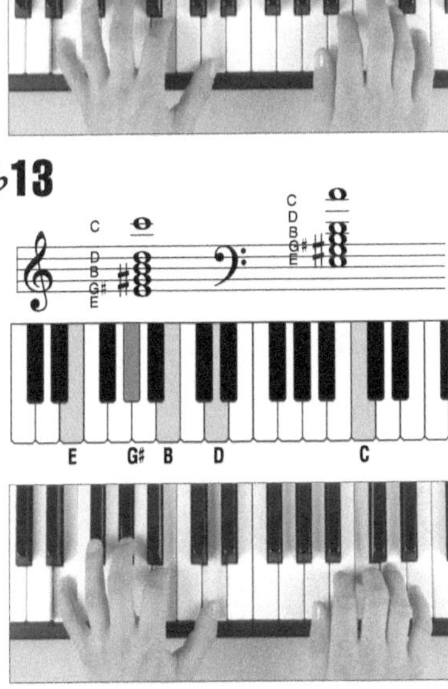

E7♭9(♯11)

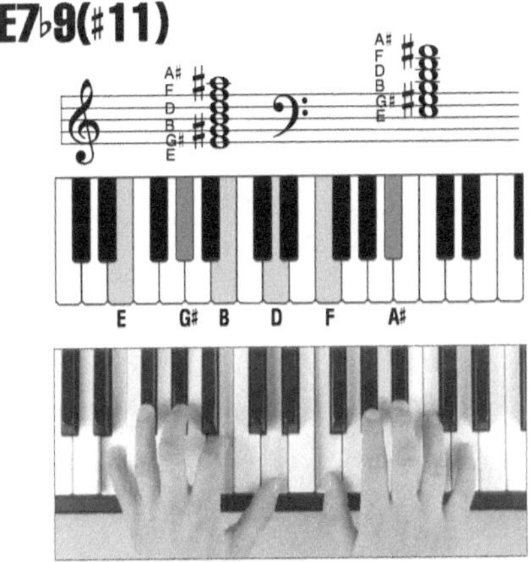

E7♯9(♯11)

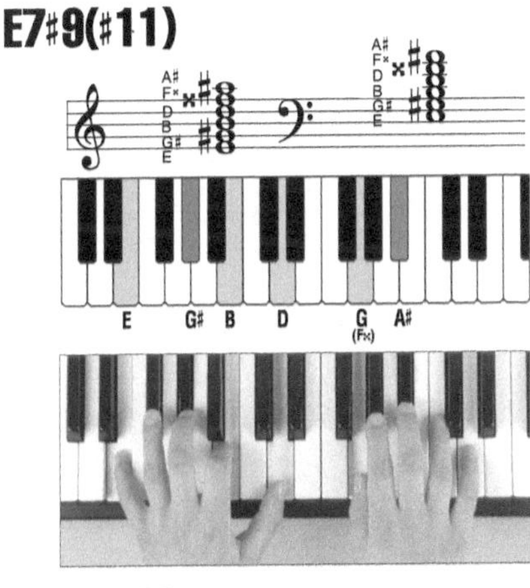

E7♭9(♭13)

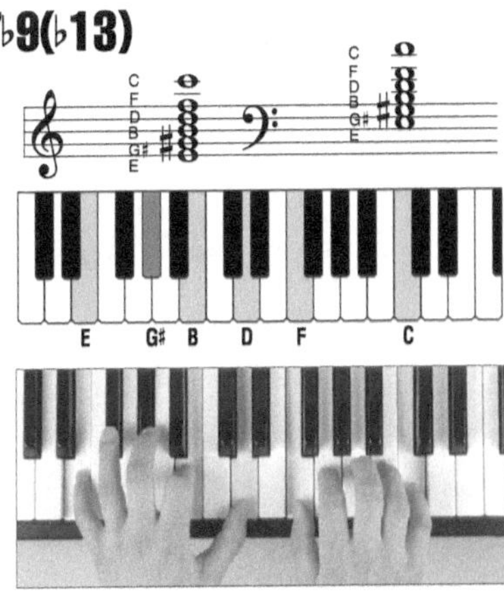

E7♯9(♭13)

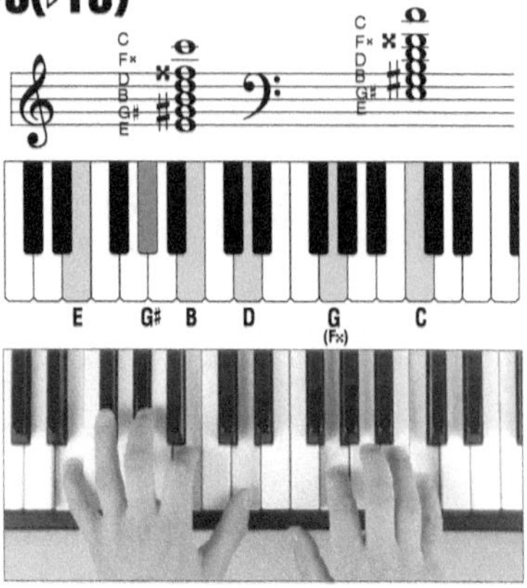

C
F×
D
B
G♯
E
C
F×
D
B
G♯
E
E
G♯
B
D
G
(F×)
C

E9

F♯
D
B
G♯
E
F♯
D
B
G♯
E
E
G♯
B
D
F♯

E7♯11(♭13)

C
A♯
D
B
G♯
E
C
A♯
D
B
G♯
E
E
G♯
B
D
A♯
C

E9(♭5)

F♯
D
B♭
G♯
E
F♯
D
B♭
G♯
E
E
G♯
B♭
D
F♯

E7♭9(♯9, ♯11)

A♯
G
F
D
B
G♯
E
A♯
G
F
D
B
G♯
E
E
G♯
B
D
F
G
A♯

E9♯5

F♯
D
B♯
G♯
E
F♯
D
B♯
G♯
E
E
G♯
B♯
D
F♯

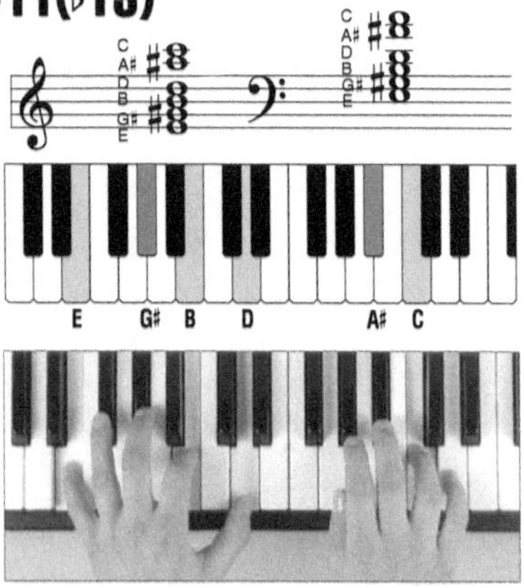

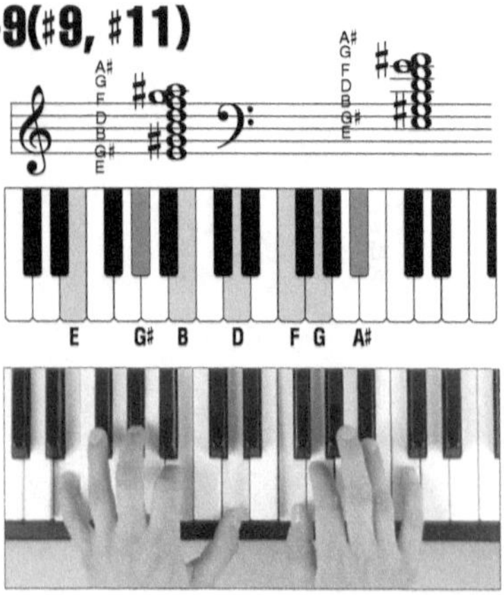

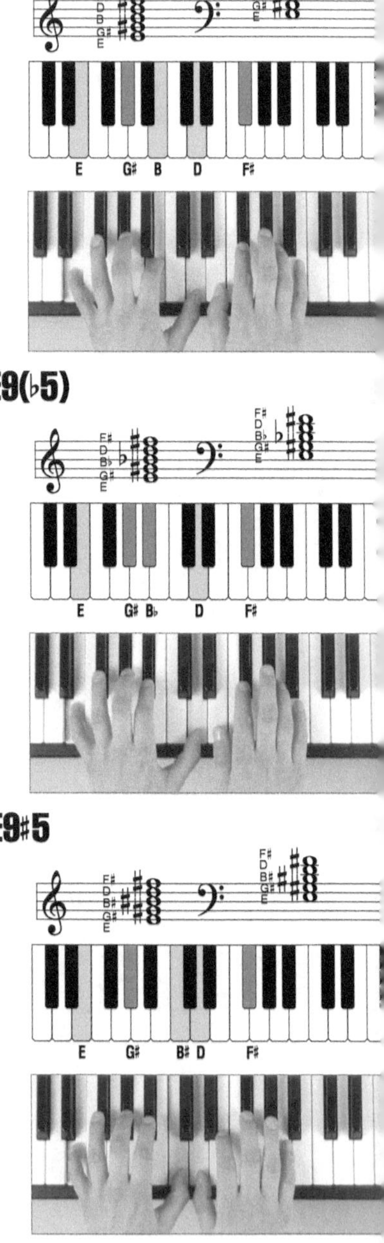

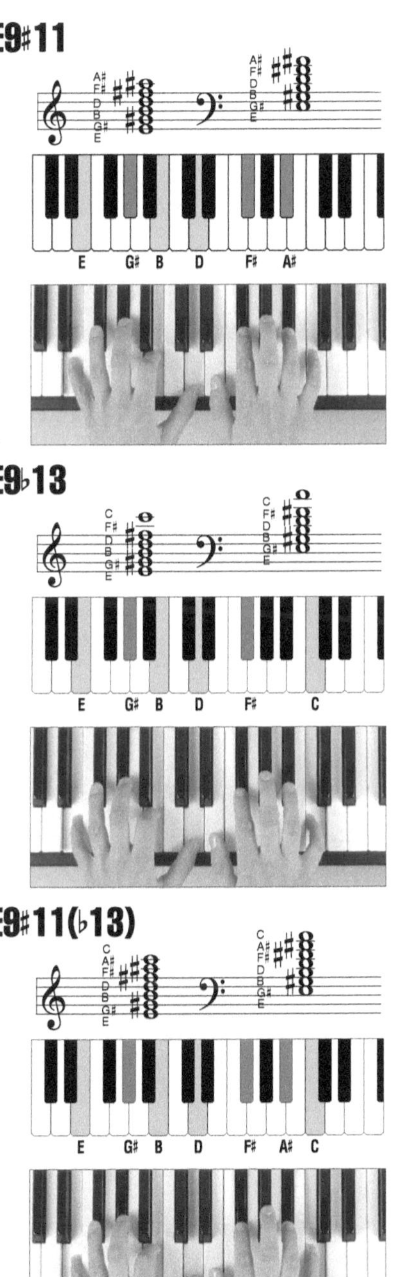
E9♯11
E G♯ B D F♯ A♯
E9♭13
E G♯ B D F♯ C
E9♯11(♭13)
E G♯ B D F♯ A♯ C

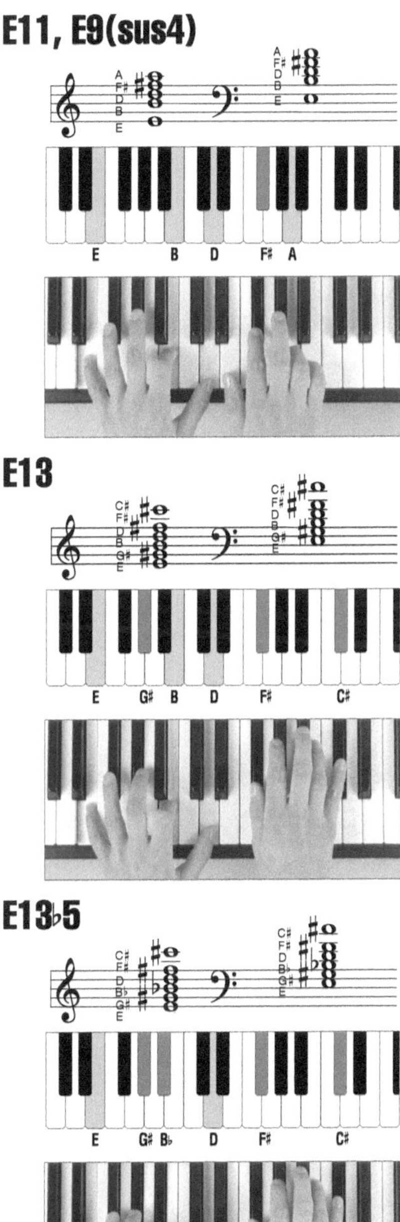
E11, E9(sus4)
E B D F♯ A
E13
E G♯ B D F♯ C♯
E13♭5
E G♯ B♭ D F♯ C♯

E13♭9

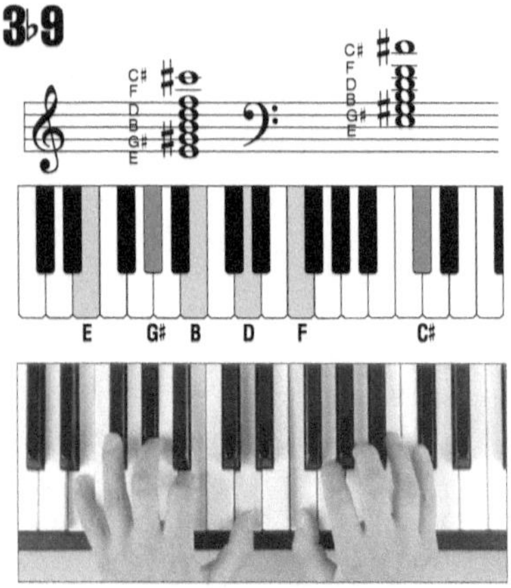

E G♯ B D F C♯

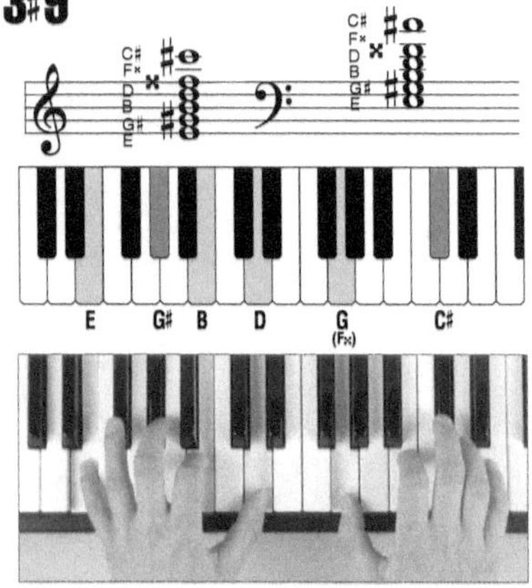

E13♯9

E G♯ B D G (F𝄪) C♯

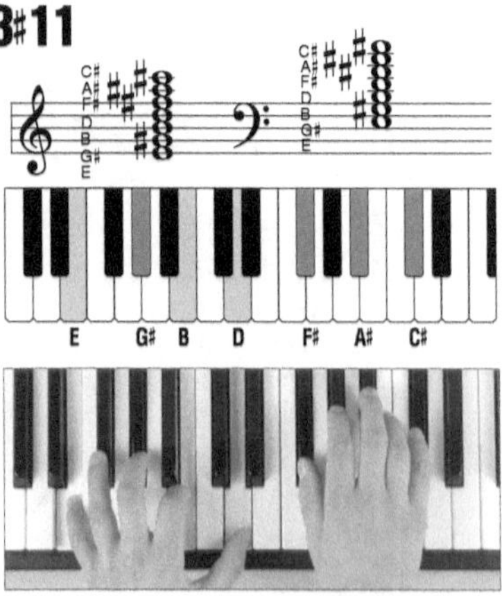

E13♯11

E G♯ B D F♯ A♯ C♯

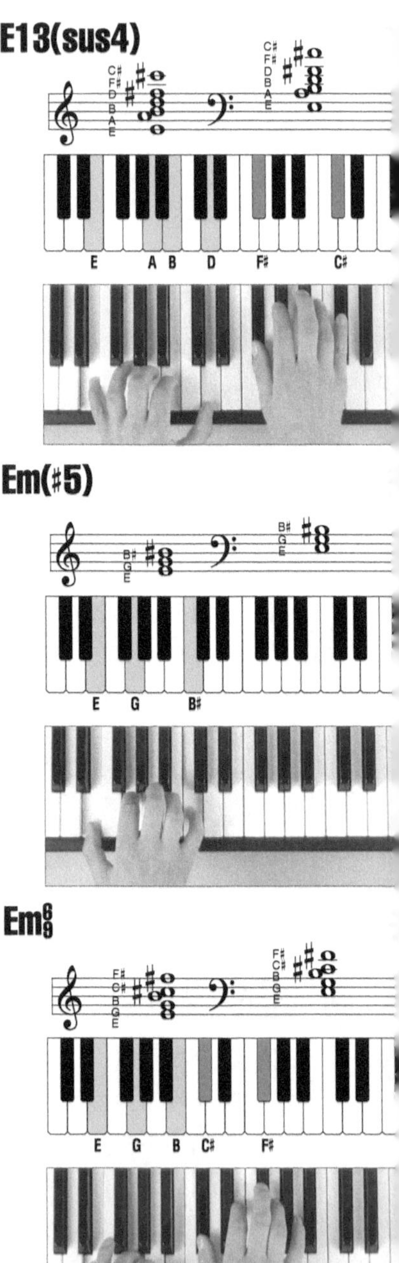

Em7(add4)

Em9

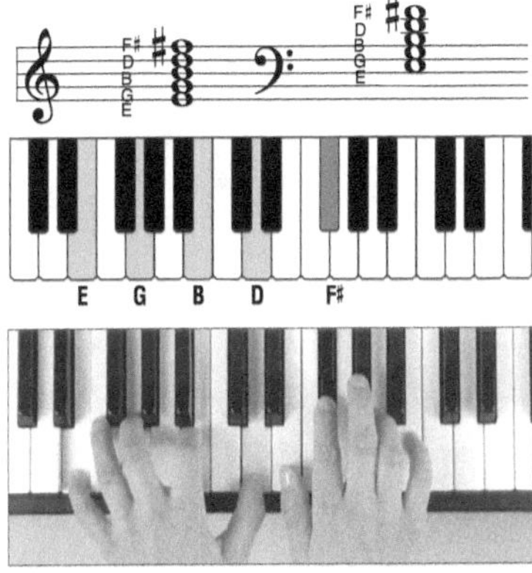

Em7(add11)

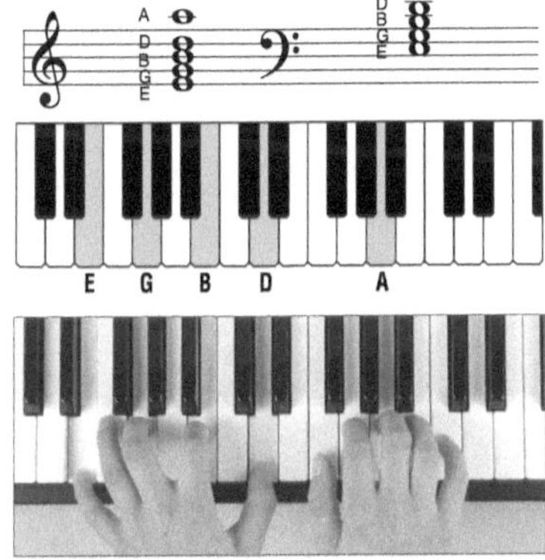

Em9(maj7)

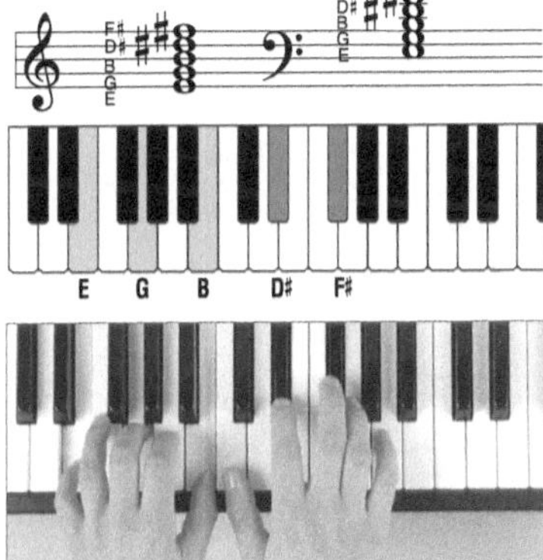

Em7♭5(♭9)

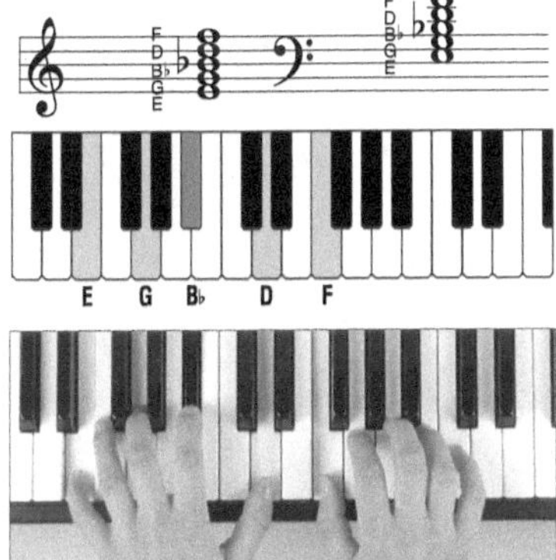

Em9♭5

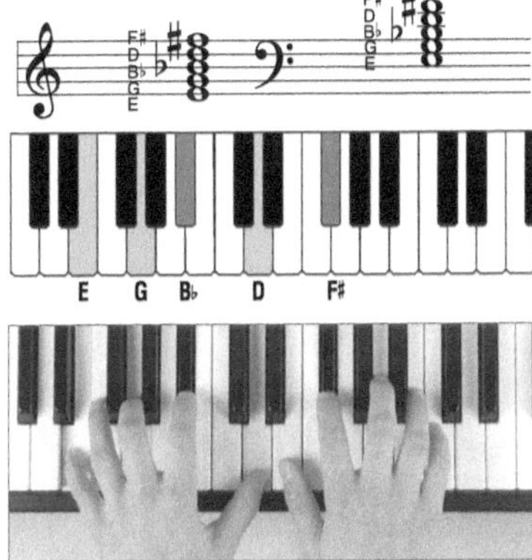

Em11

A F♯ D B G E

A F♯ D B G E

E G B D F♯ A

Em13

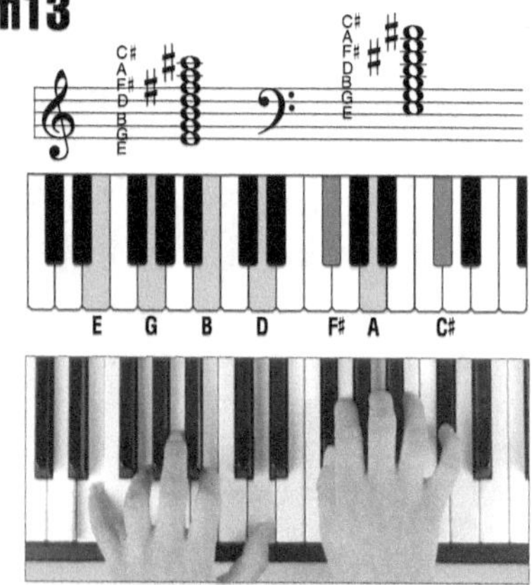

Edim7(add9)

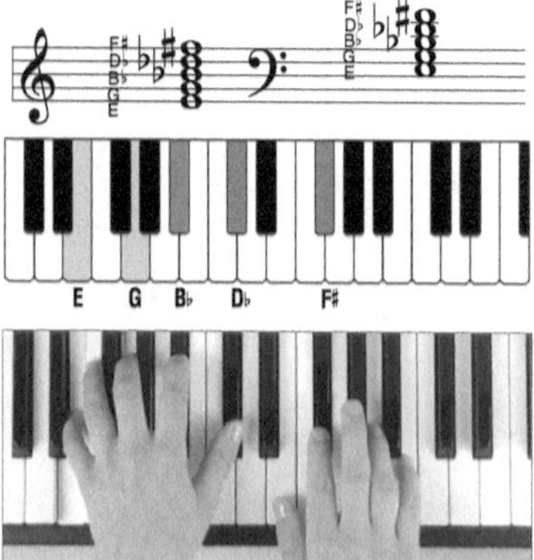

Em11♭5

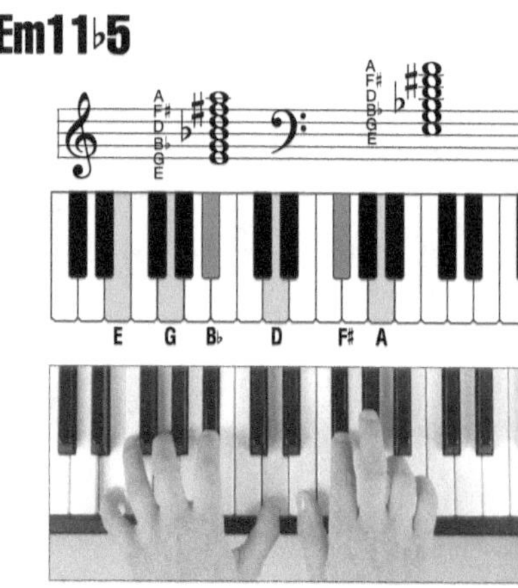

Em11(maj7)

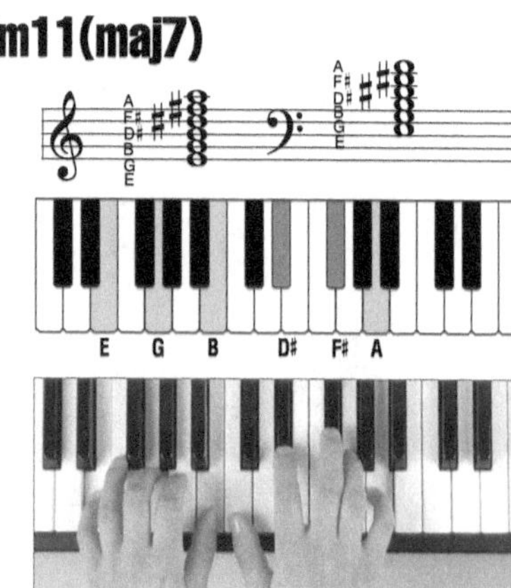

E7alt.

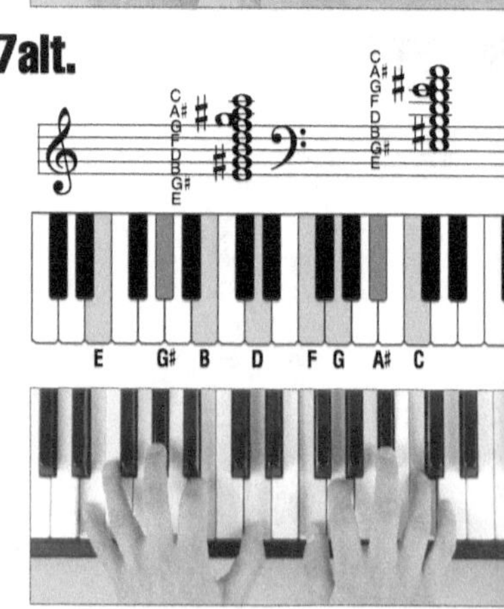

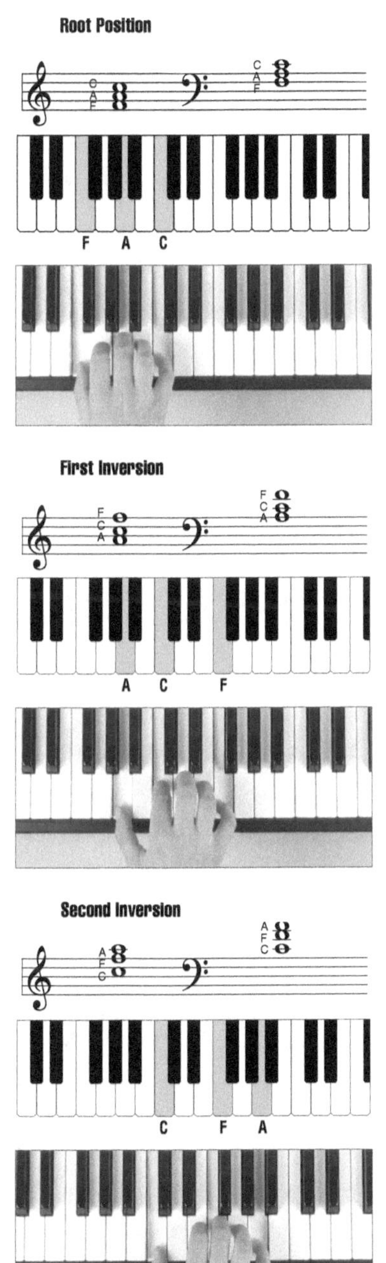
Root Position
C
A
F
C
A
F
F
A
C
First Inversion
F
C
A
F
C
A
A
C
F
Second Inversion
A
F
C
A
F
C
C
F
A

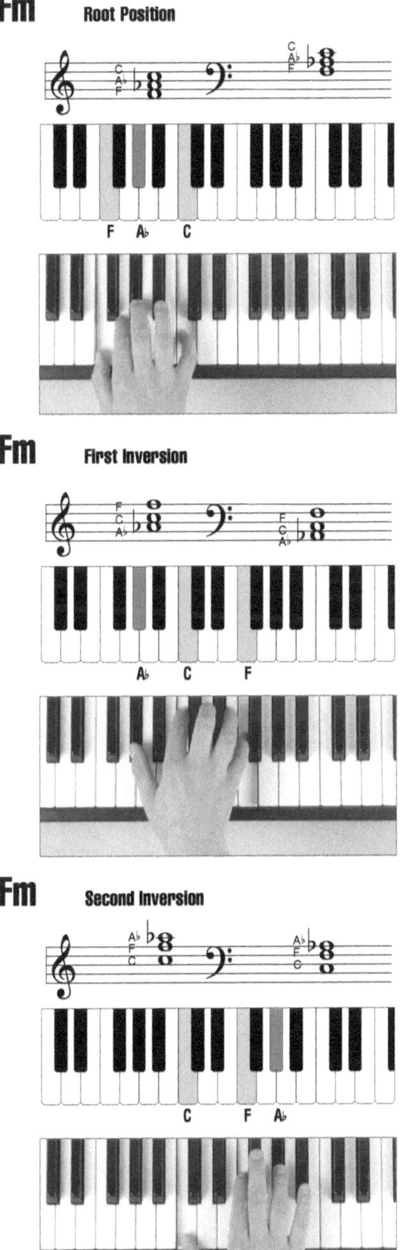
Fm
Root Position
C
A♭
F
C
A♭
F
F
A♭
C
Fm
First Inversion
F
C
A♭
F
C
A♭
A♭
C
F
Fm
Second Inversion
A♭
F
C
A♭
F
C
C
F
A♭

F+ Root Position

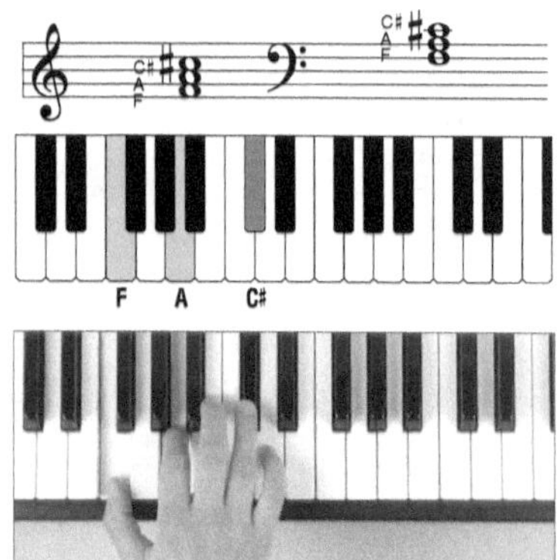

F+ First Inversion

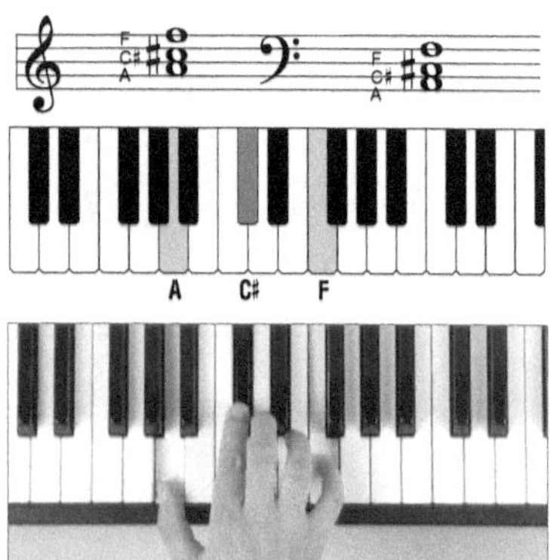

F+ Second Inversion

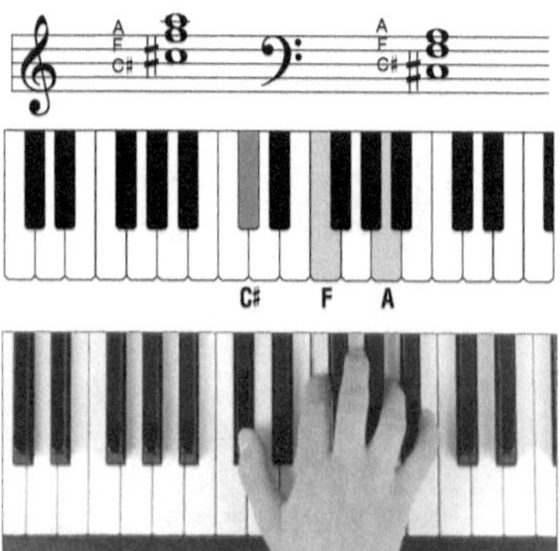

Fdim Root Position

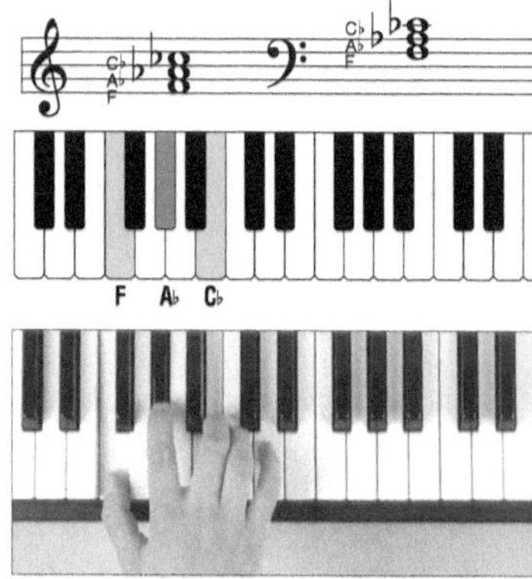

Fdim First Inversion

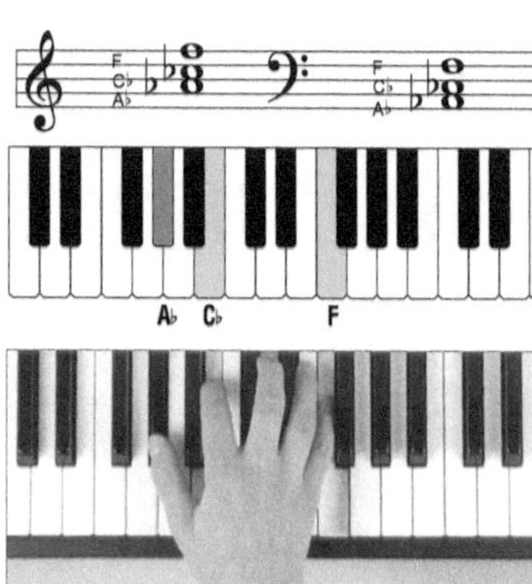

Fdim Second Inversion

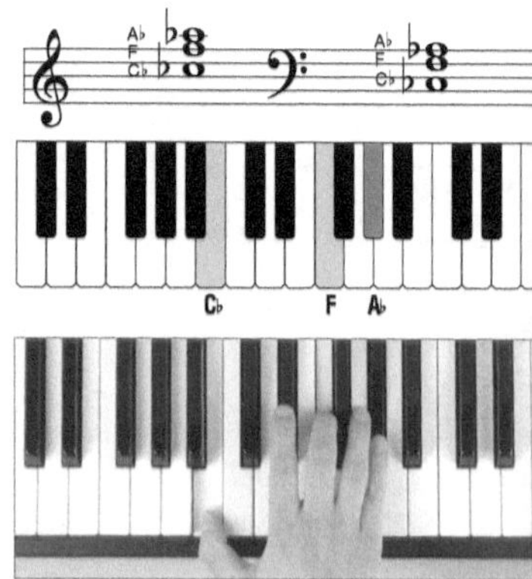

Fsus Root Position

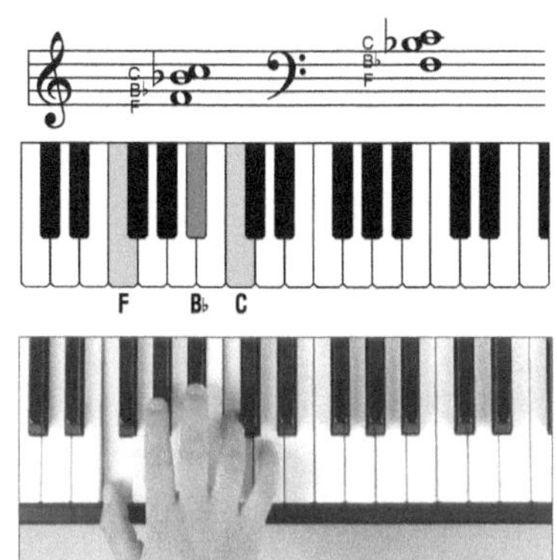

Fsus First Inversion

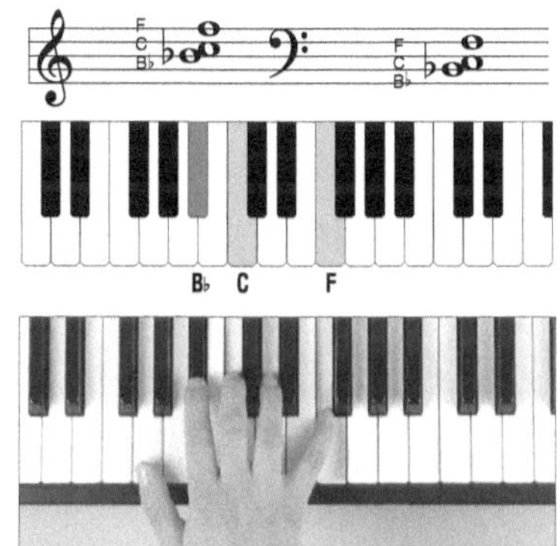

Fsus Second Inversion

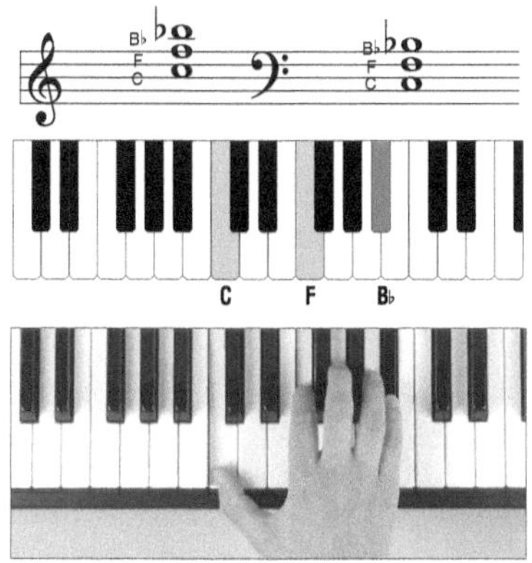

F(♭5) Root Position

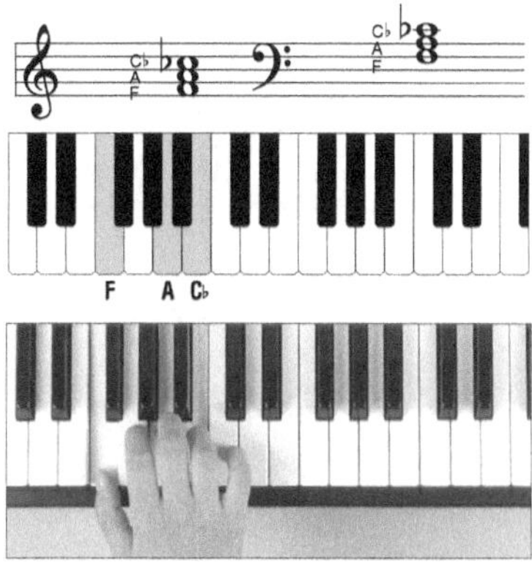

F(♭5) First Inversion

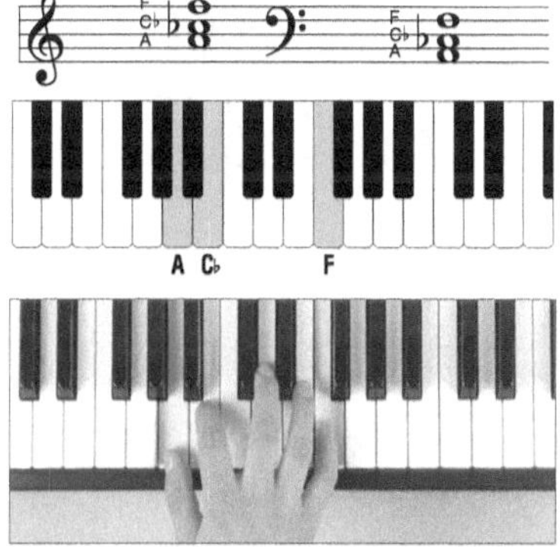

F(♭5) Second Inversion

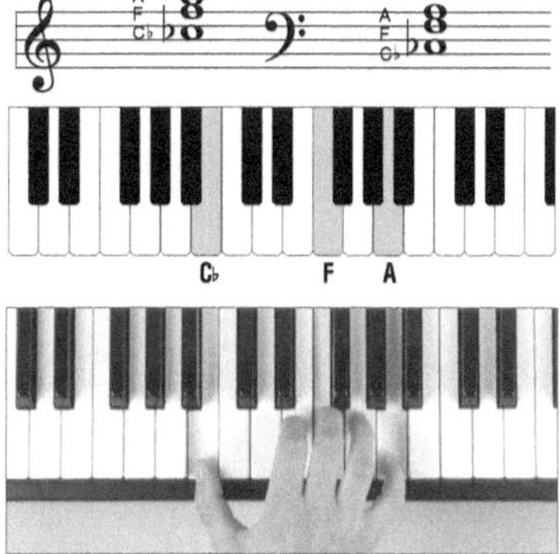

Fsus2 Root Position

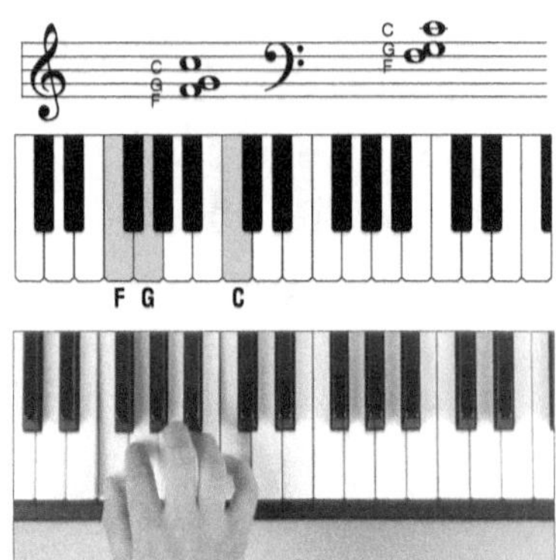

Fsus2 First Inversion

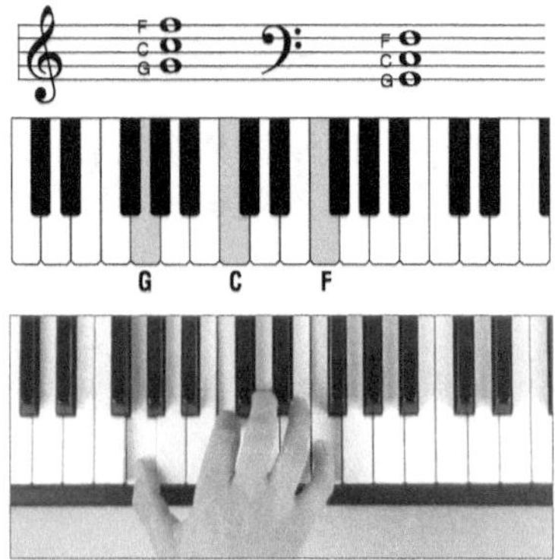

Fsus2 Second Inversion

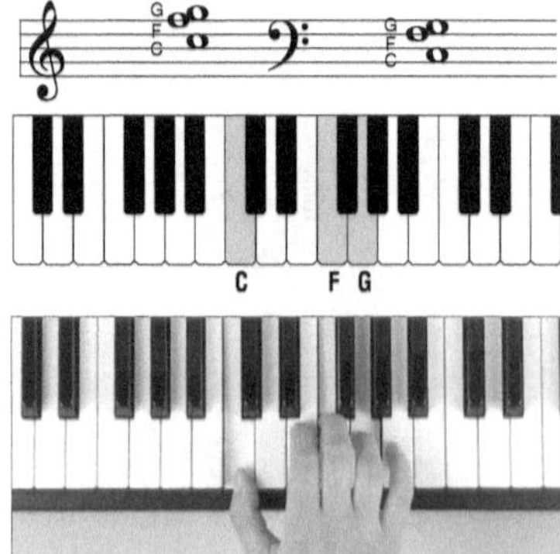

F6 Root Position

F6 First Inversion

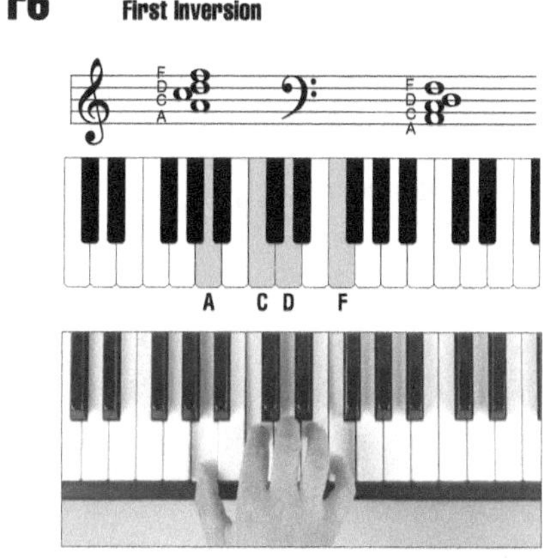

F6 Second Inversion

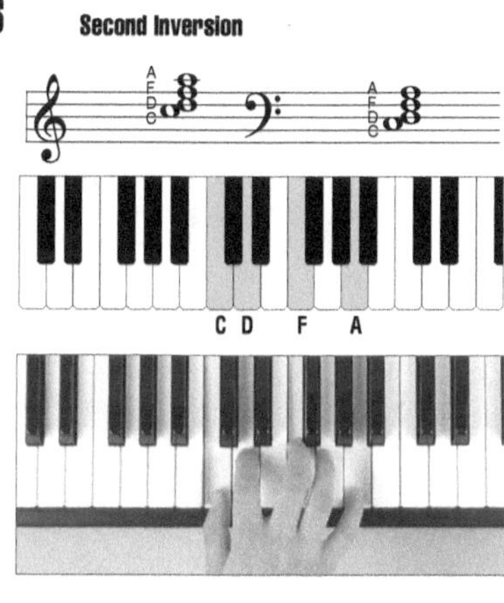

F6 Third Inversion

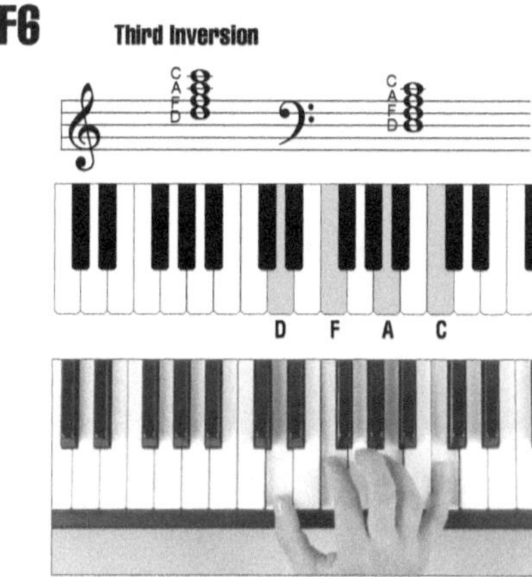

F(add2), F(add9) Root Position

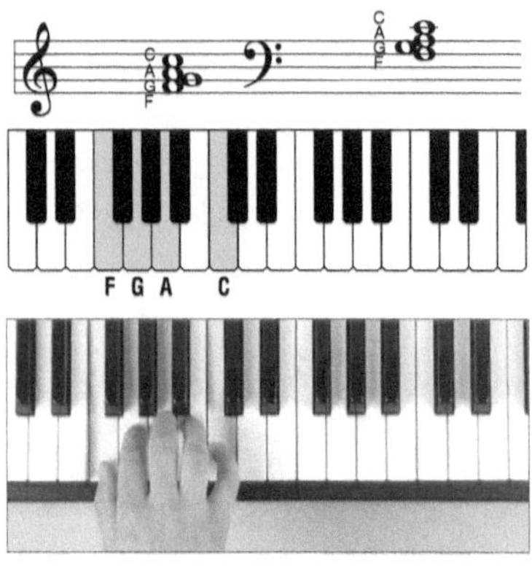

F(add2), F(add9) First Inversion

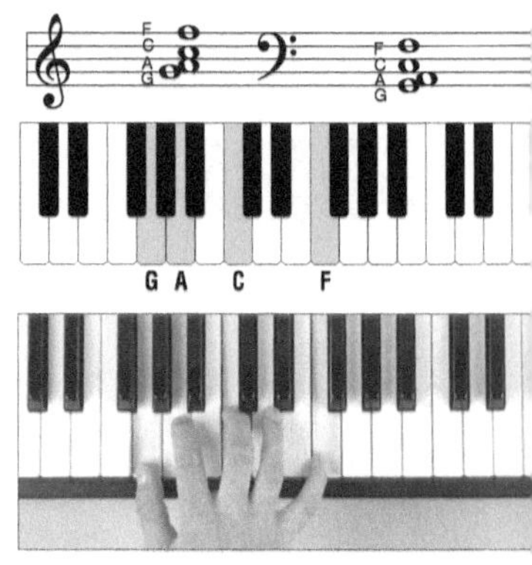

F(add2), F(add9) Second Inversion

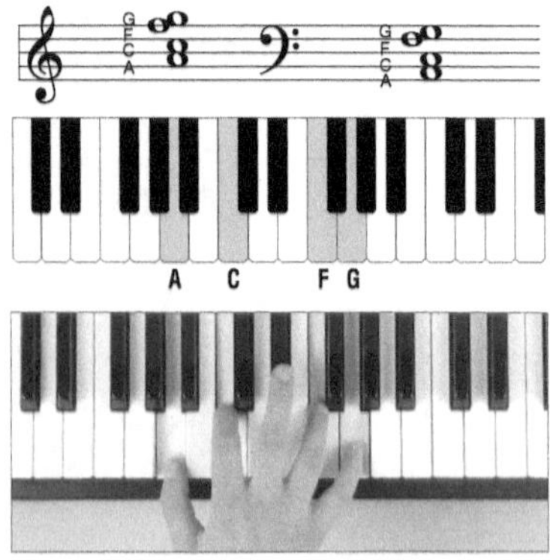

F(add2), F(add9) Third Inversion

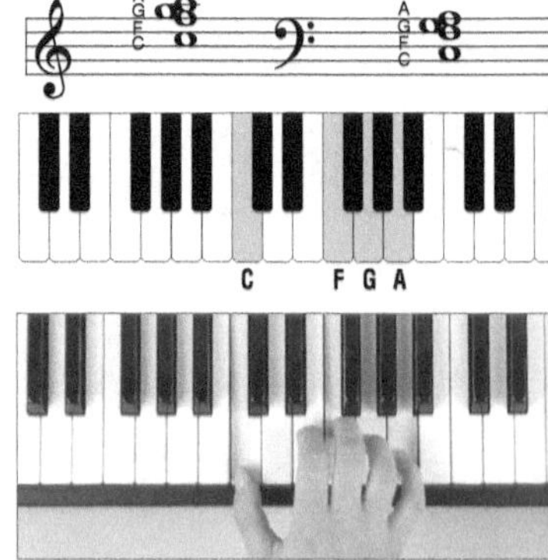

Fmaj7 Root Position

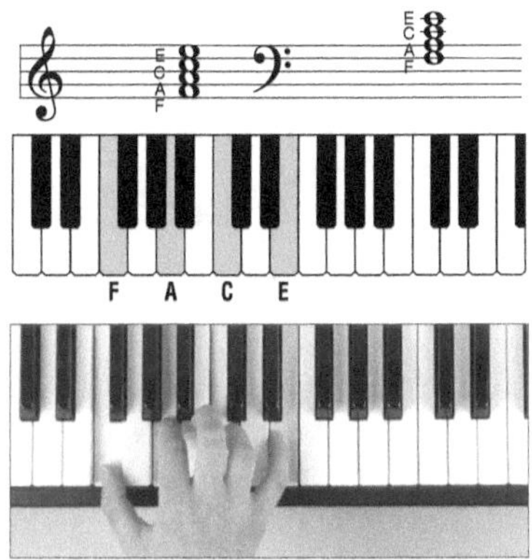

Fmaj7 First Inversion

Fmaj7 Second Inversion

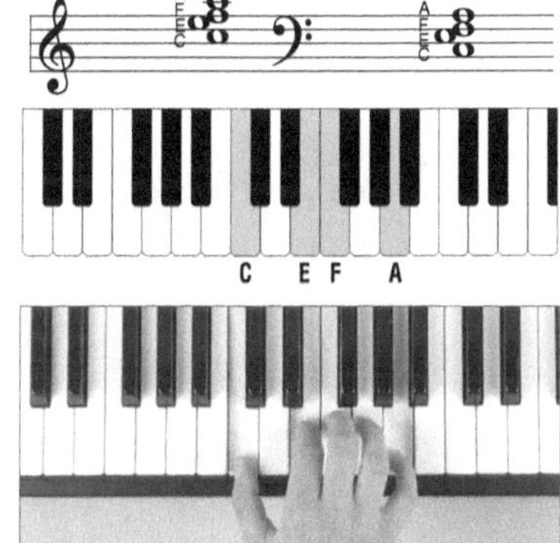

Fmaj7 Third Inversion

Fmaj7♭5 Root Position

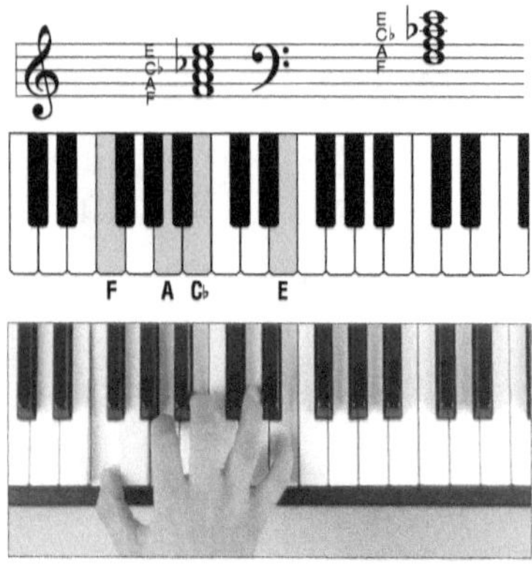

Fmaj7♭5 First Inversion

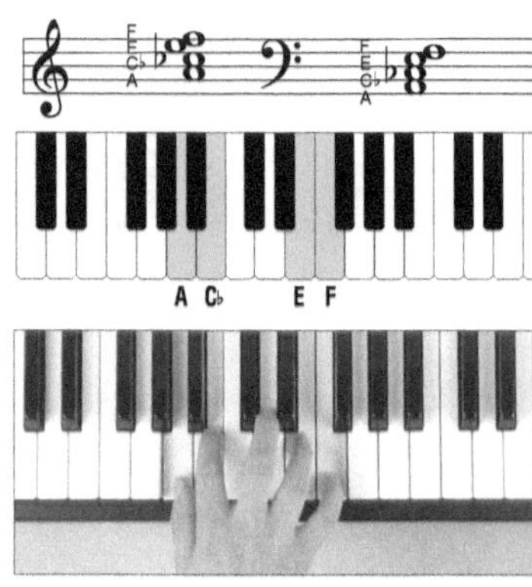

Fmaj7♭5 Second Inversion

Fmaj7♭5 Third Inversion

C♭
A
F
E
C♭
A
F
E
E F A C♭

Fmaj7♯5 Root Position

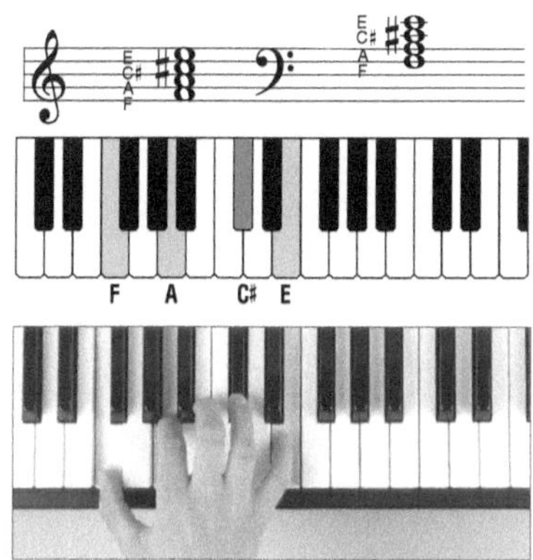

Fmaj7♯5 First Inversion

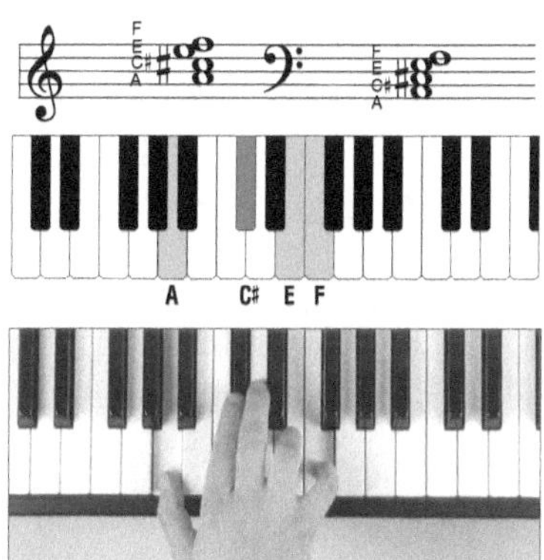

Fmaj7♯5 Second Inversion

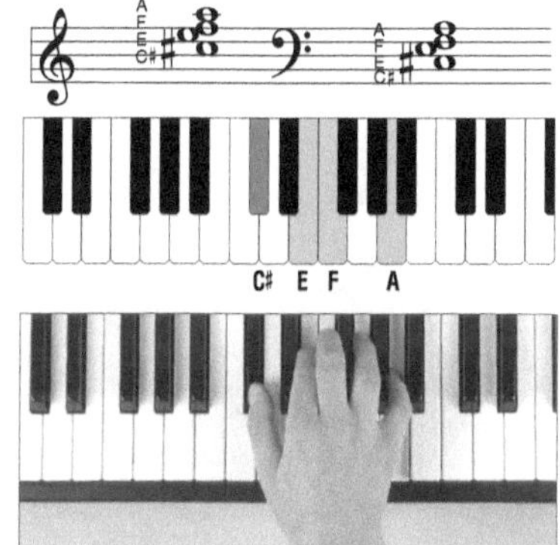

Fmaj7♯5 Third Inversion

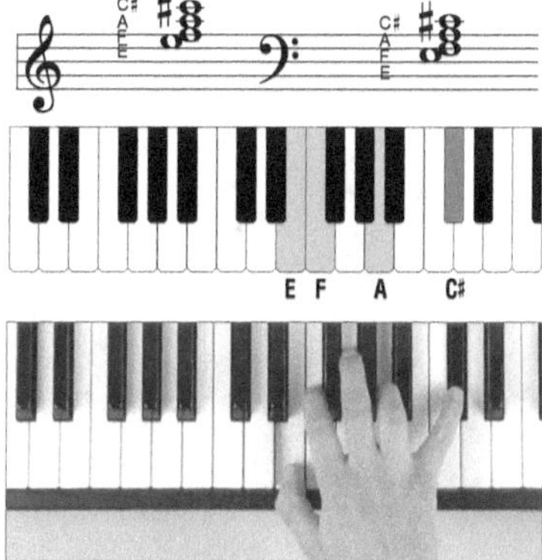

F7 Root Position

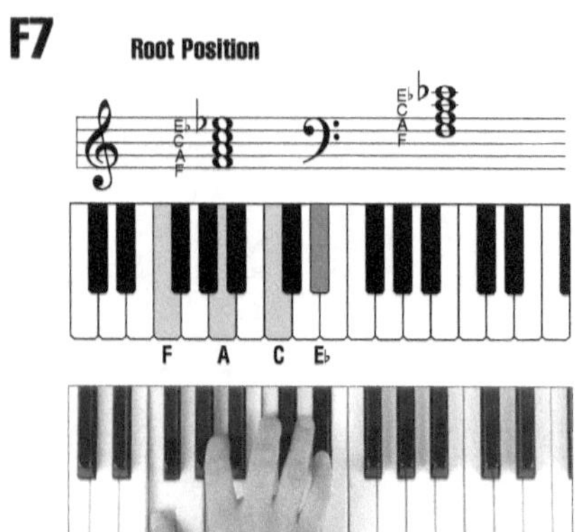

F7 First Inversion

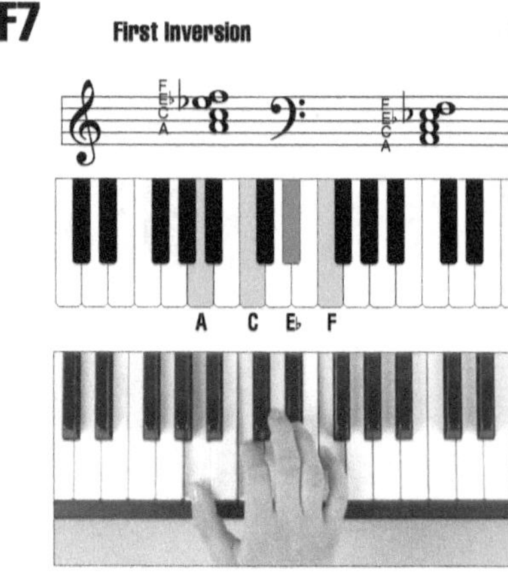

F7 Second Inversion

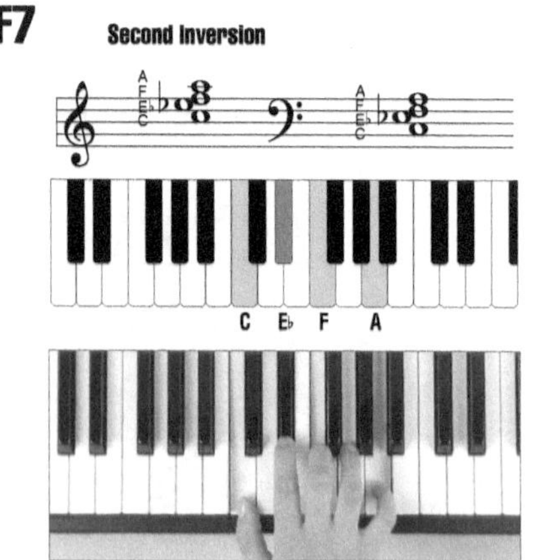

F7 Third Inversion

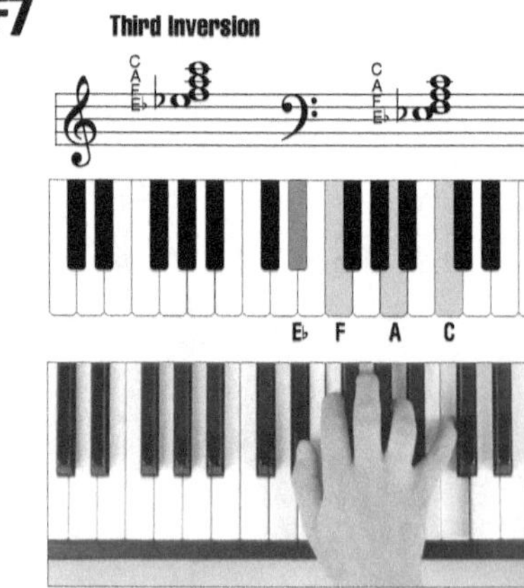

F7♭5 Root Position

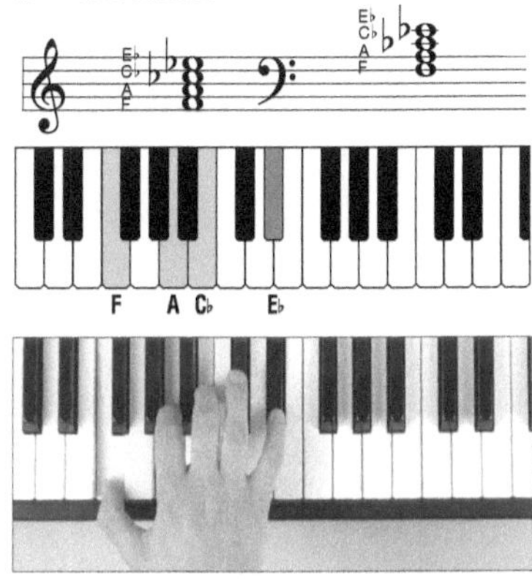

F7♭5 First Inversion

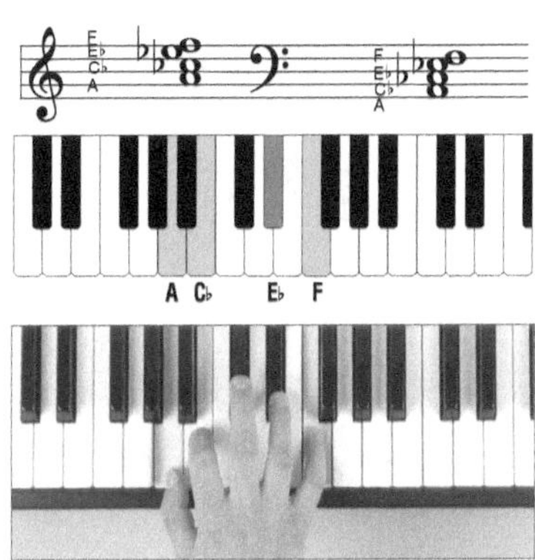

F7♭5 Second Inversion

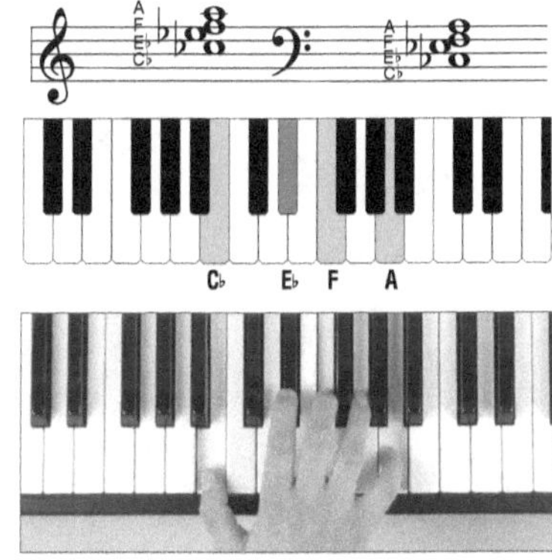

F7♭5 Third Inversion

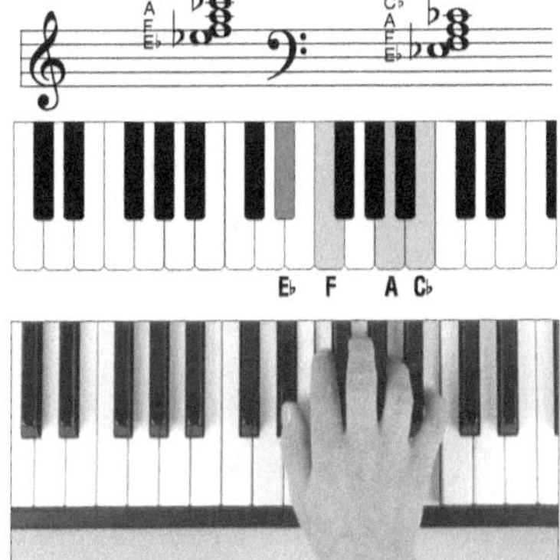

F7♯5 Root Position

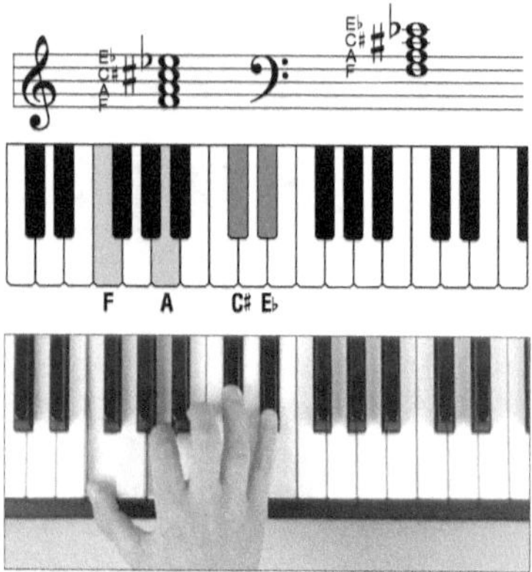

F7♯5 First Inversion

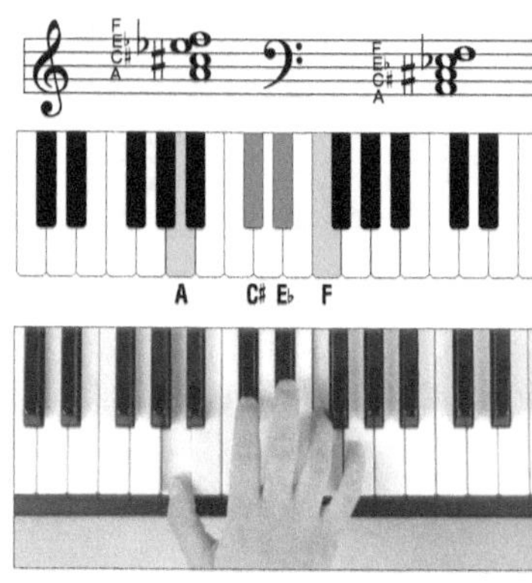

F7♯5 Second Inversion

F7♯5 Third Inversion

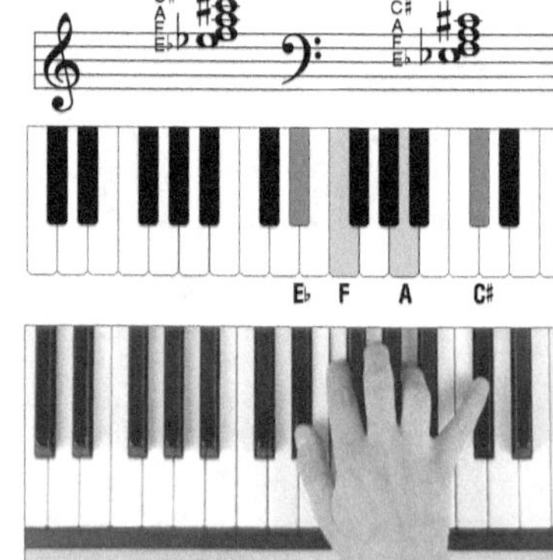

F7sus Root Position

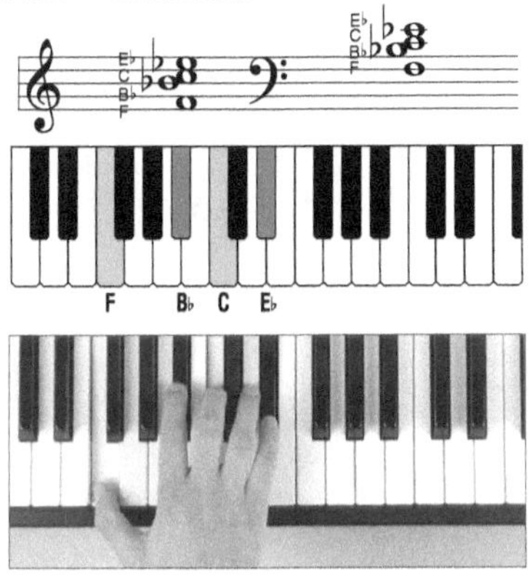

F7sus First Inversion

F7sus Second Inversion

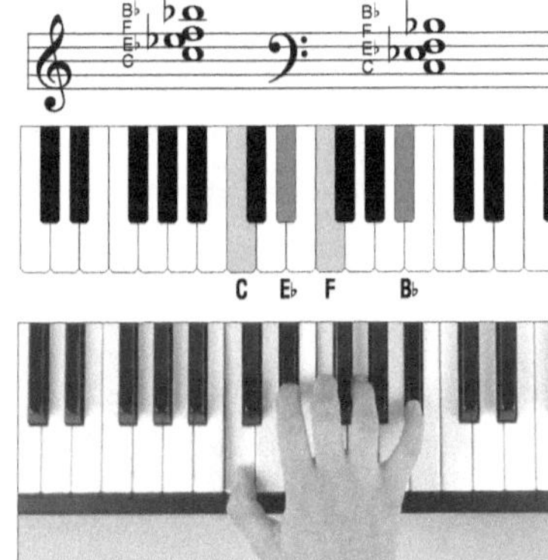

F7sus Third Inversion

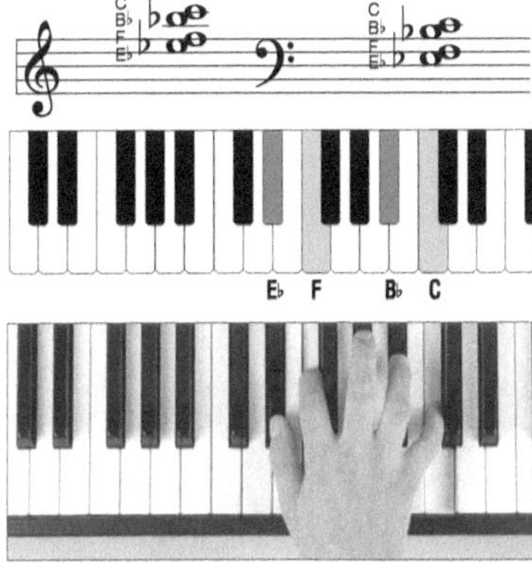

Fm(add2), Fm(add9) Root Position

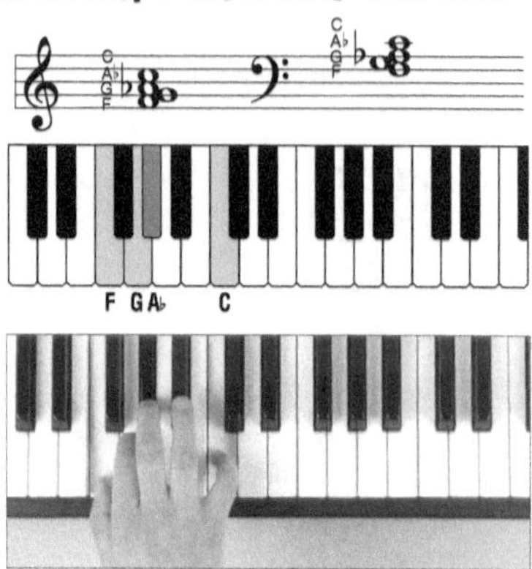

Fm(add2), Fm(add9) First Inversio

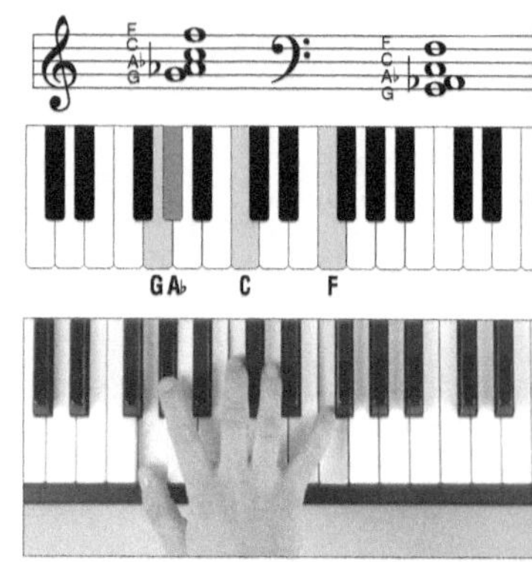

Fm(add2), Fm(add9) Second Inversion

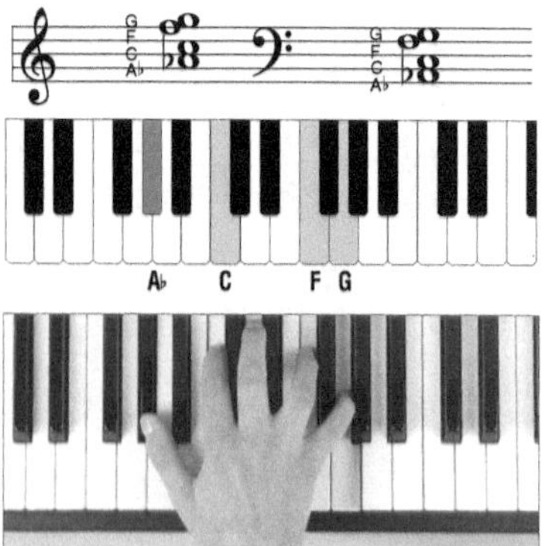

Fm(add2), Fm(add9) Third Inversio

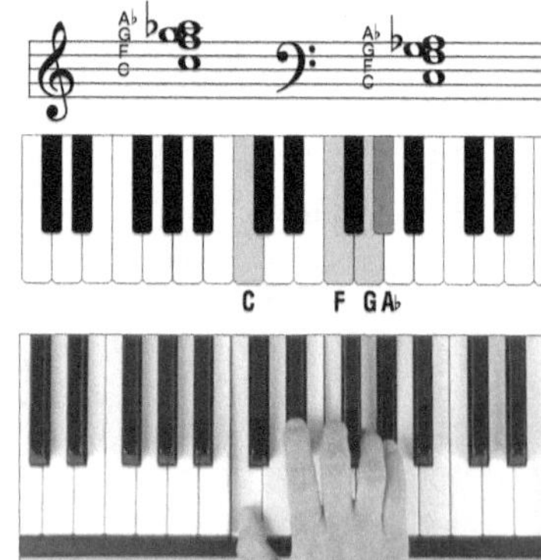

Fm6 Root Position

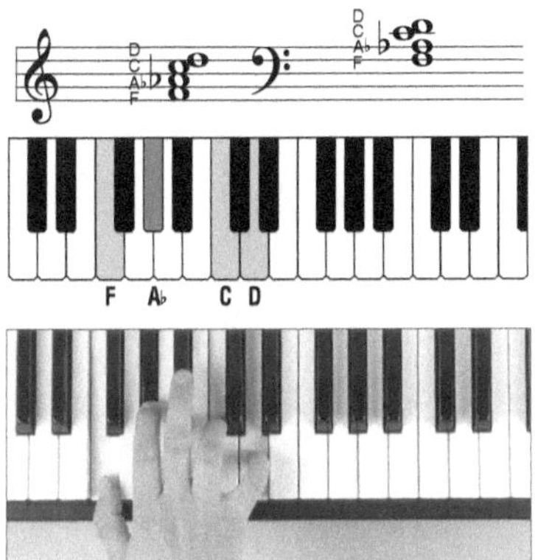

Fm6 First Inversion

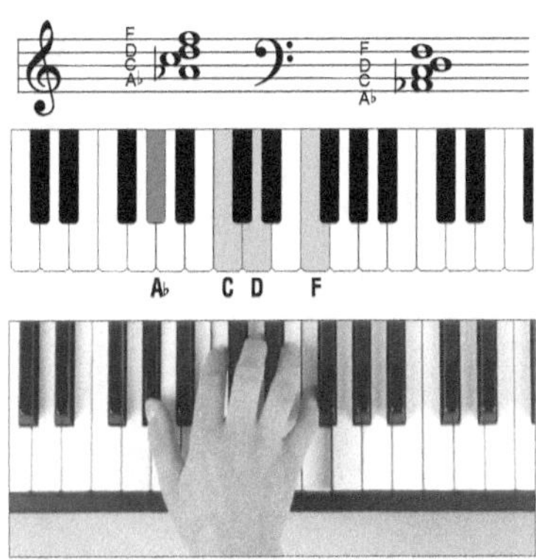

Fm6 Second Inversion

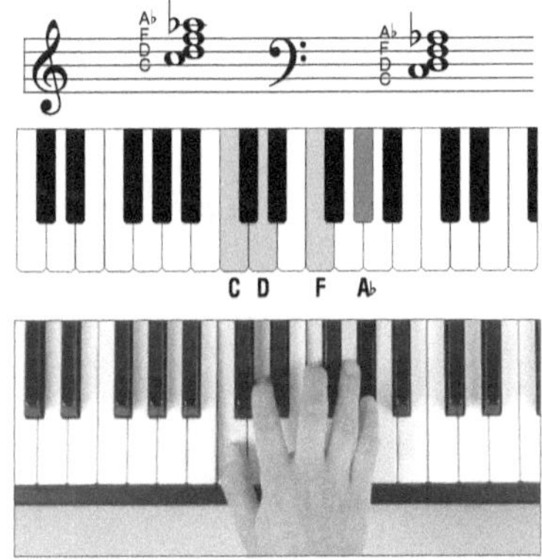

Fm6 Third Inversion

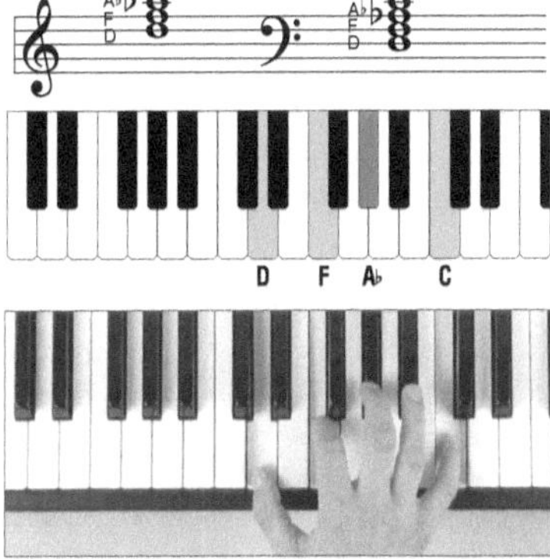

Fm7 Root Position

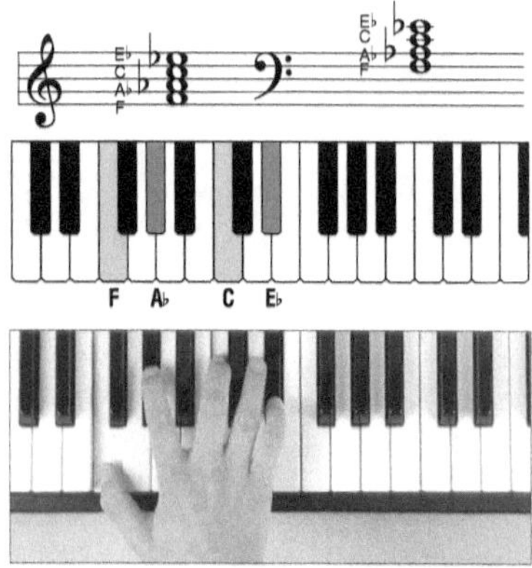

Fm7 First Inversion

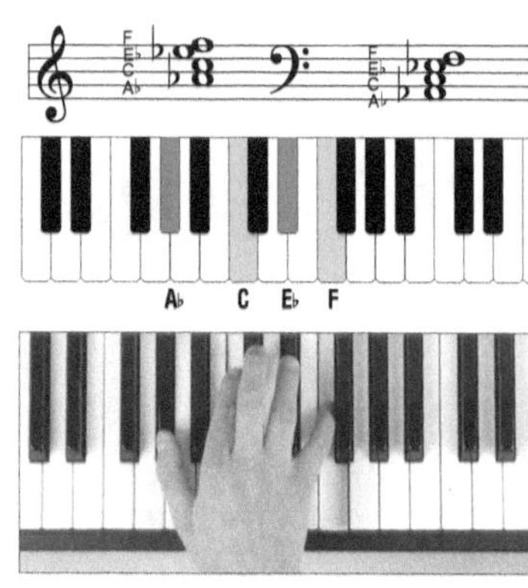

Fm7 Second Inversion

Fm7 Third Inversion

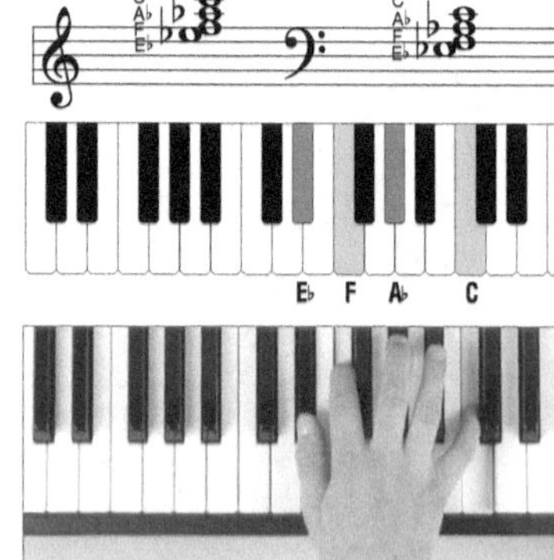

Fm(maj7) Root Position

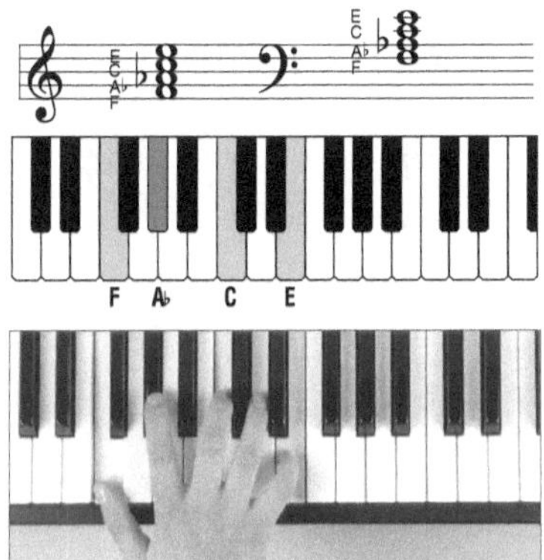

Fm(maj7) First Inversion

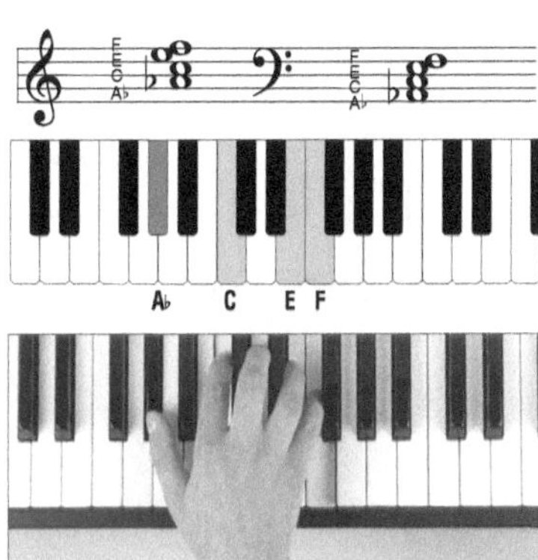

Fm(maj7) Second Inversion

Fm(maj7) Third Inversion

Fm7♭5 Root Position

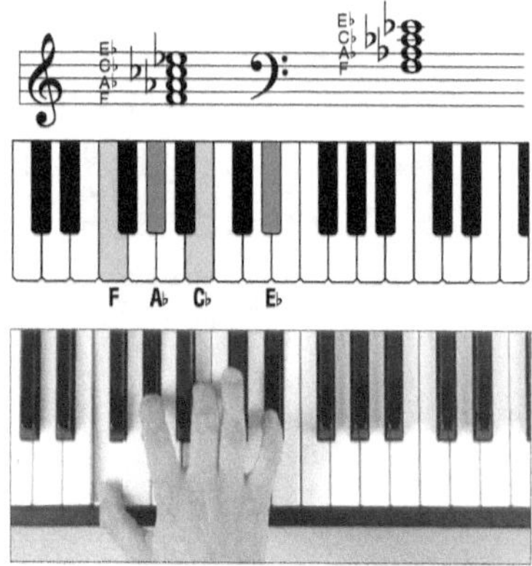

Fm7♭5 First Inversion

Fm7♭5 Second Inversion

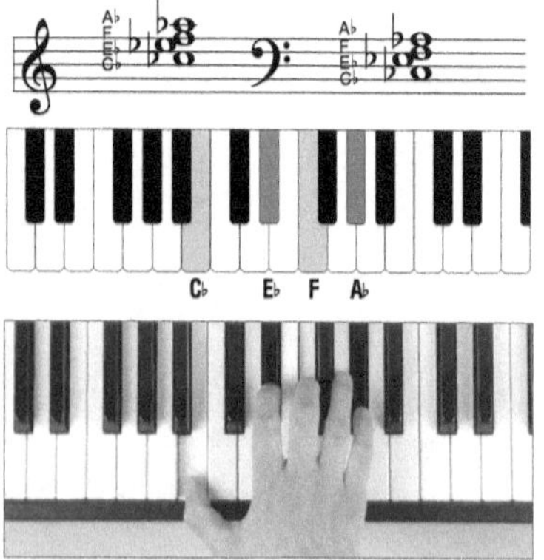

Fm7♭5 Third Inversion

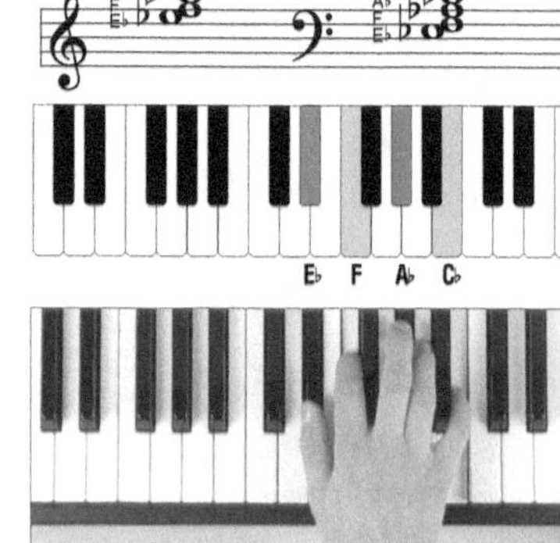

Fdim7 Root Position

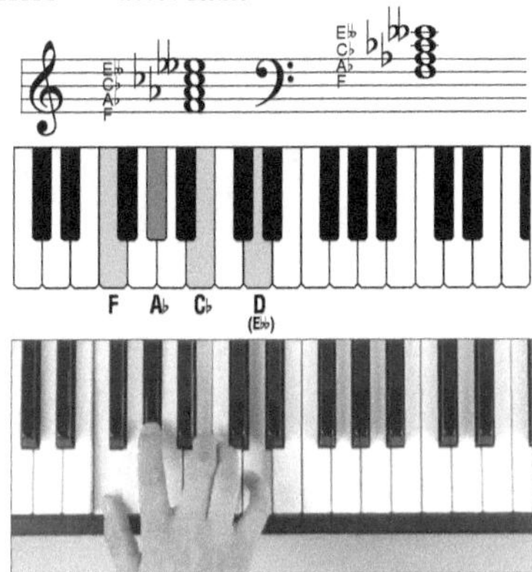

Fdim7 First Inversion

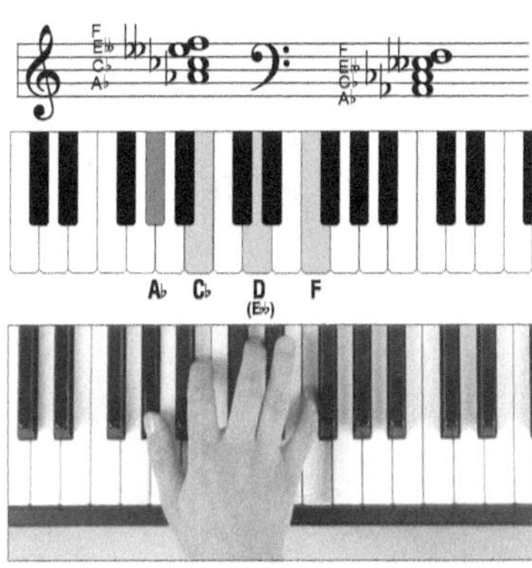

Fdim7 Second Inversion

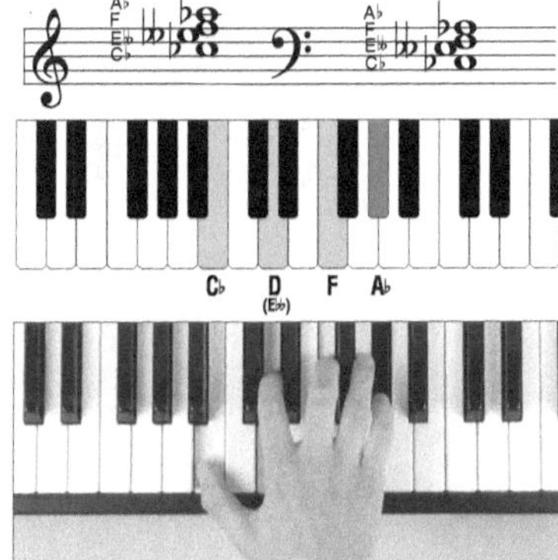

Fdim7 Third Inversion

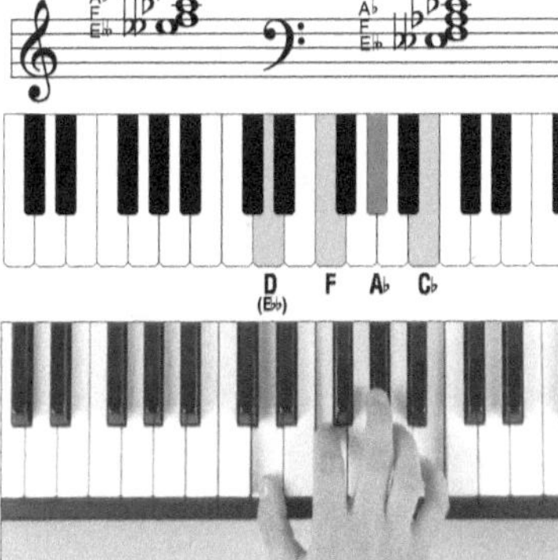

Fdim(maj7) Root Position

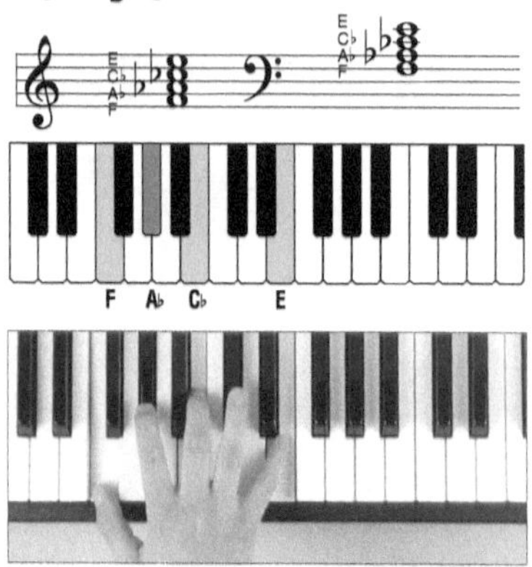

Fdim(maj7) First Inversion

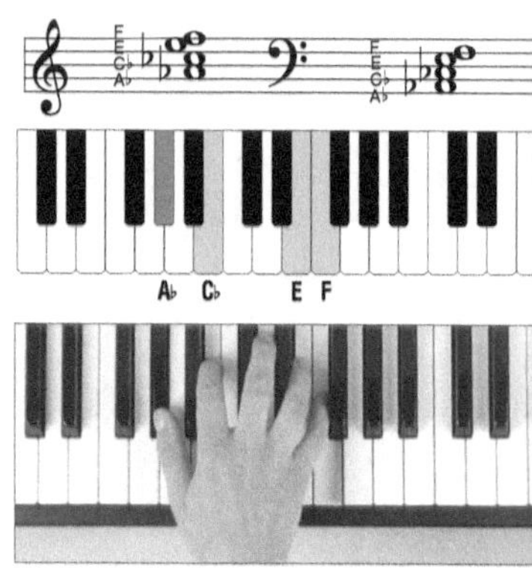

Fdim(maj7) Second Inversion

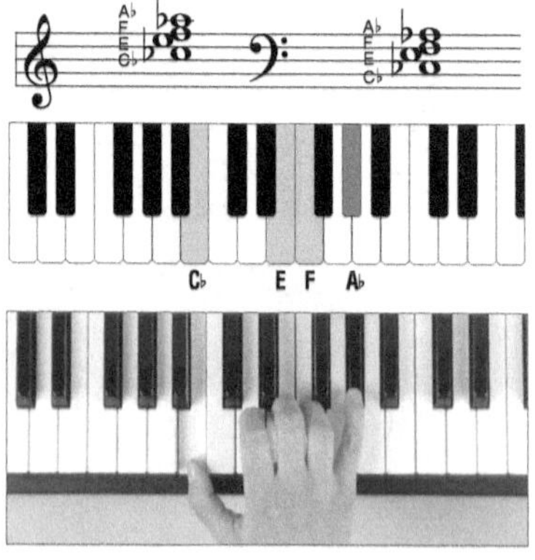

Fdim(maj7) Third Inversion

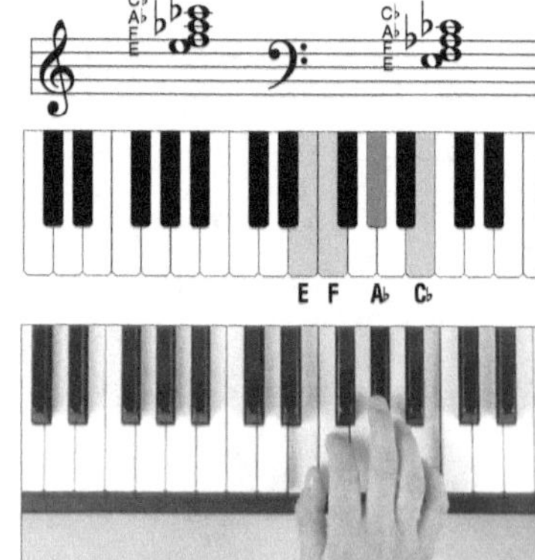

F5

F6/9

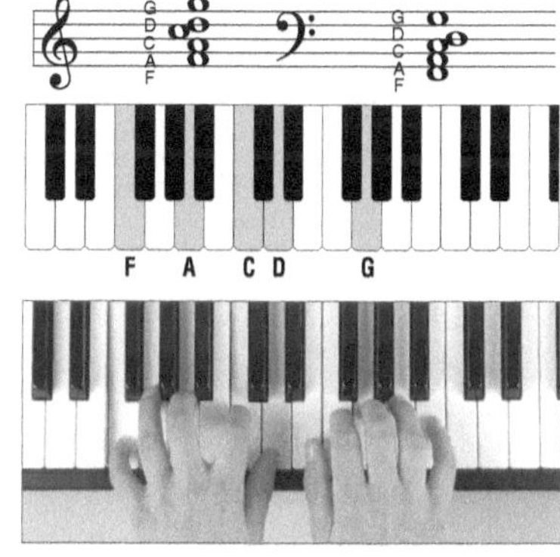

Fmaj6/9

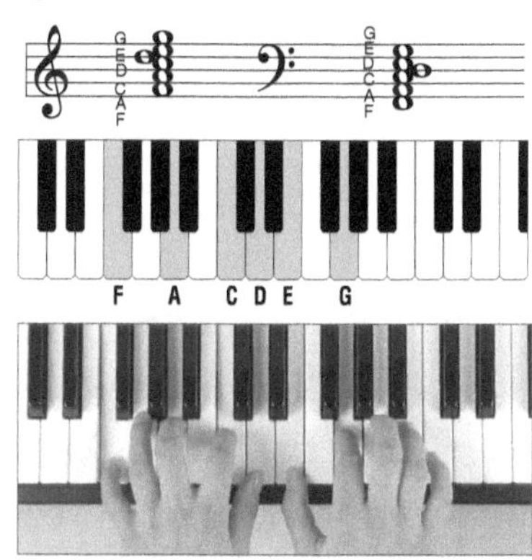

Fmaj7♯11

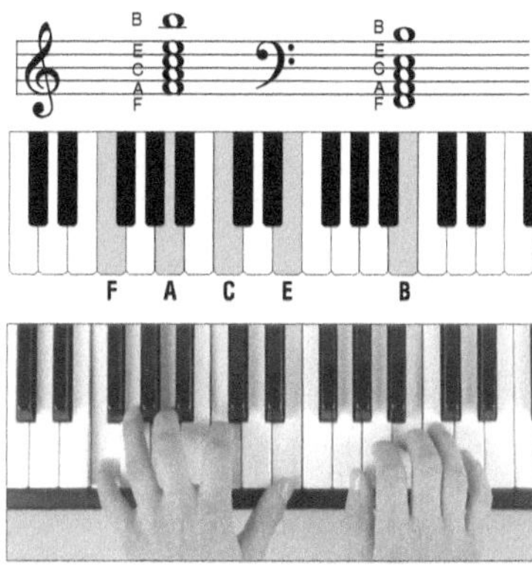

Fmaj9

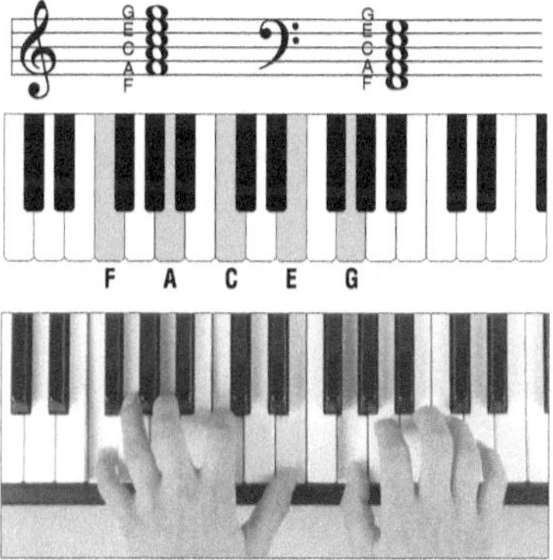

Fmaj9♭5

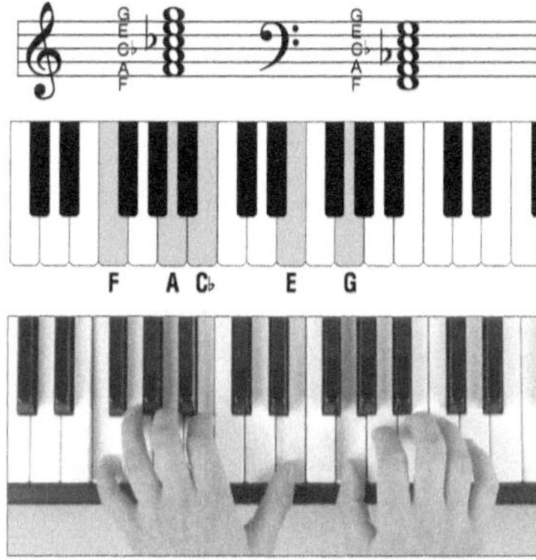

F

Fmaj9♯5

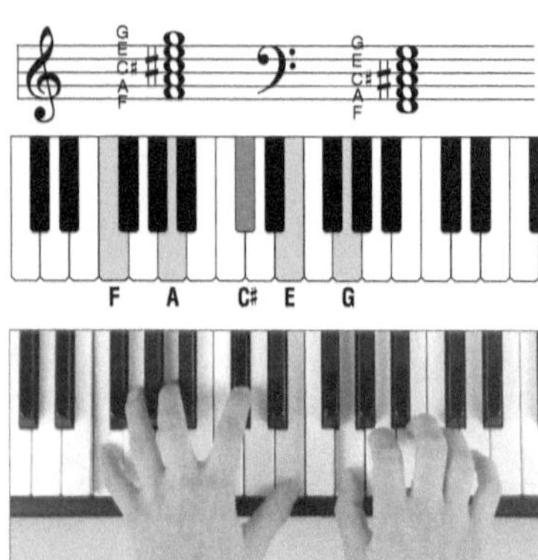

Fmaj9♯11

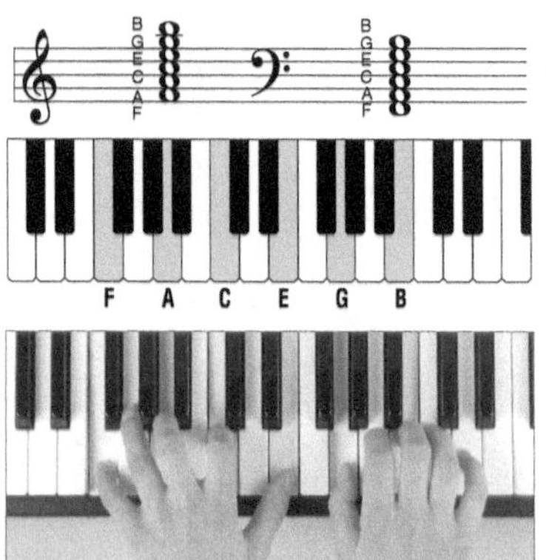

Fmaj13

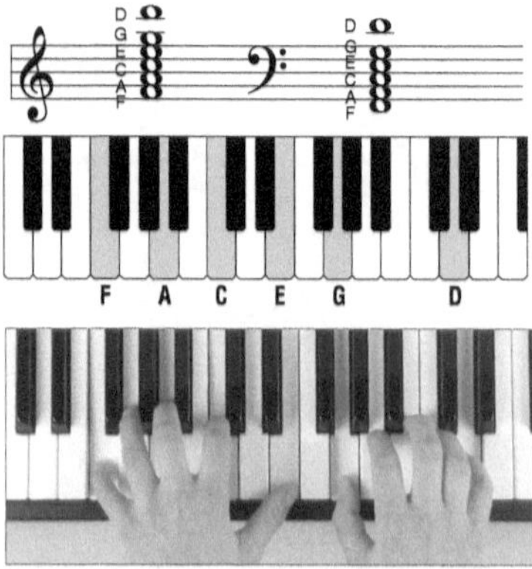

Fmaj13♭5

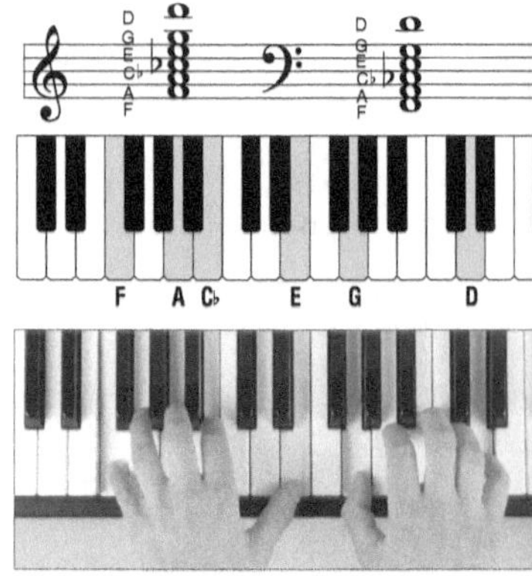

Fmaj13♯11

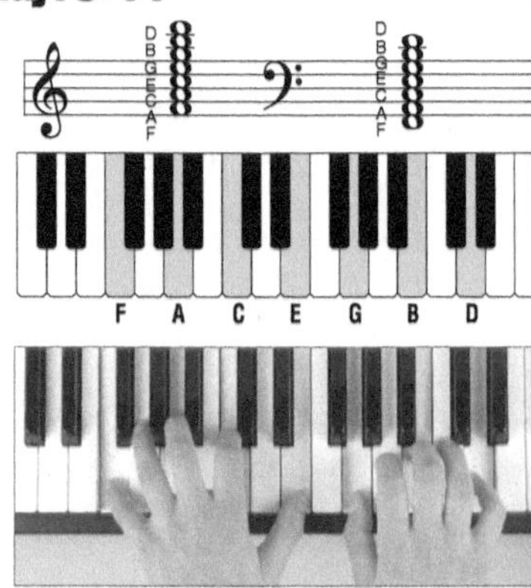

F7♭9

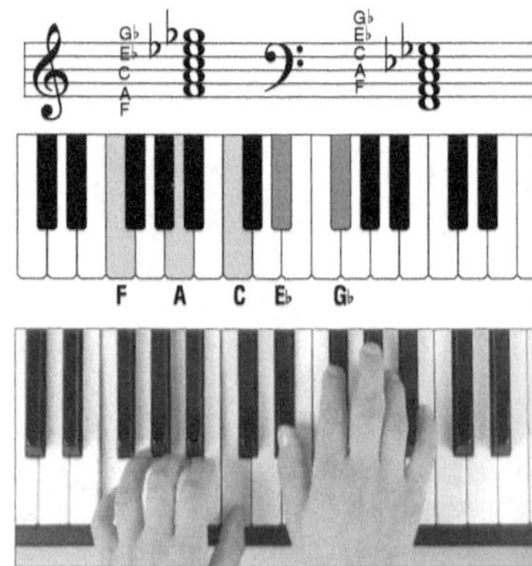

F7♯9

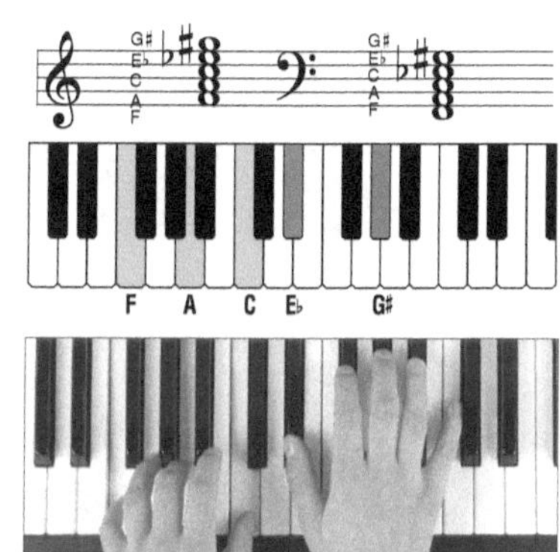

F7♭5(♯9)

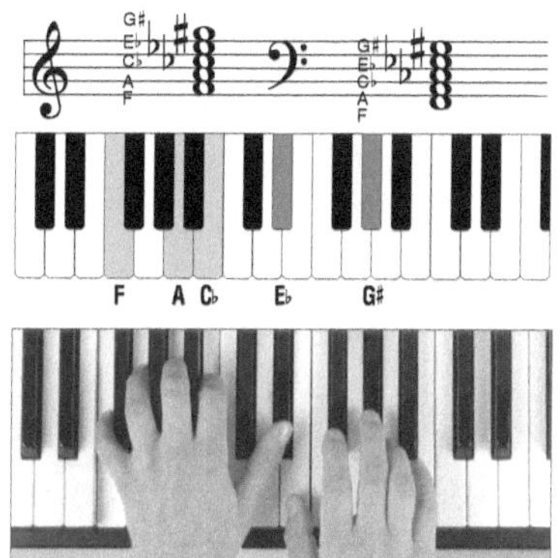

F7♯11

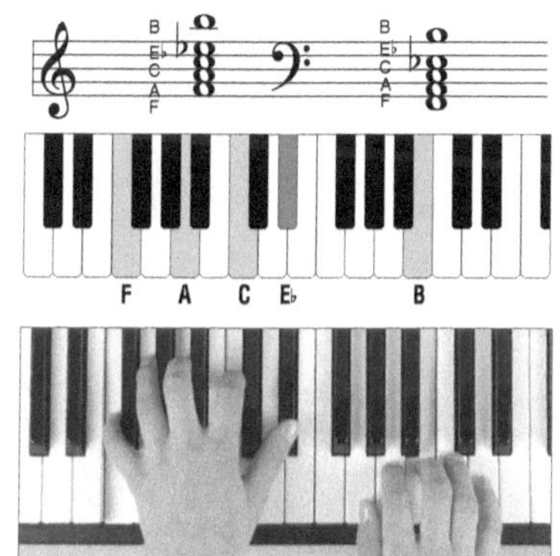

F7♯5(♭9)

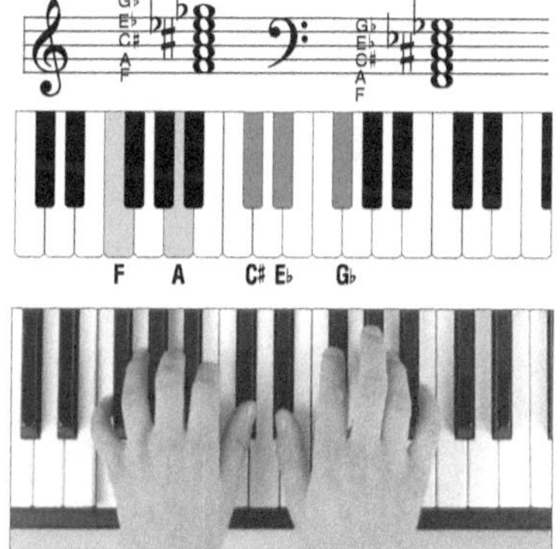

F7♭5(♭9)

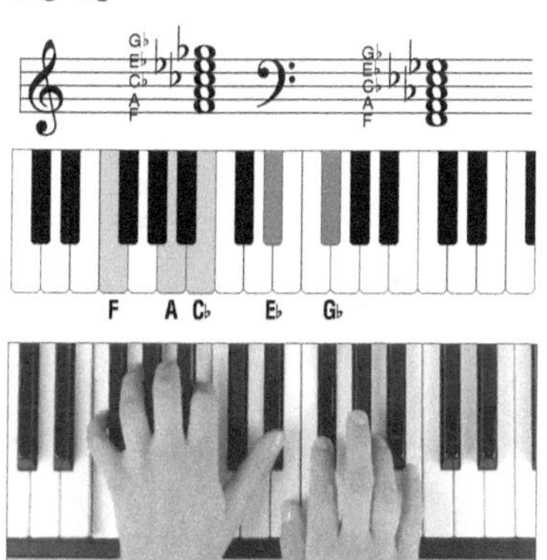

F7♯5(♯9)

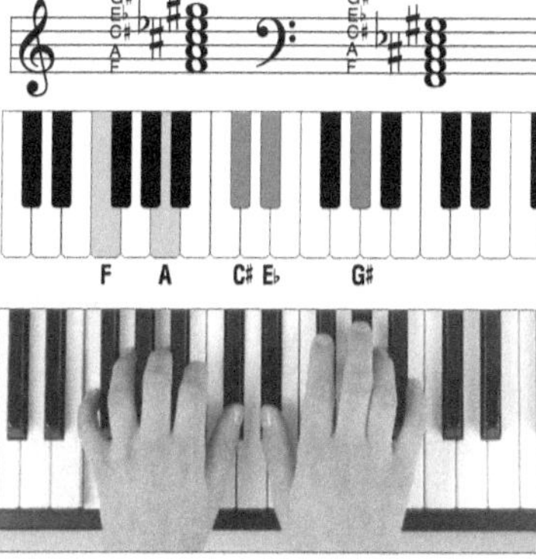

F7♭9(♯9)

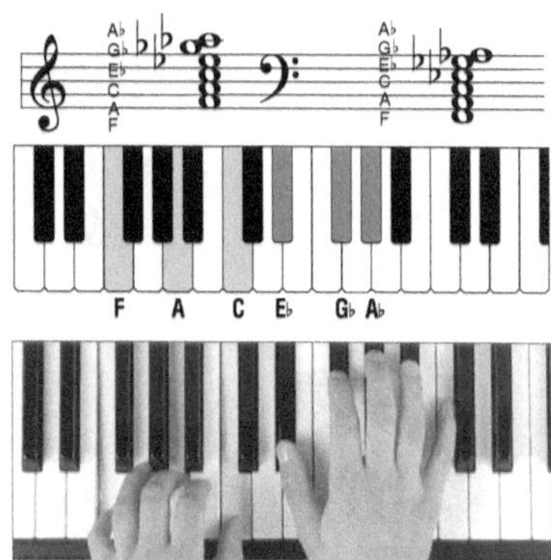

F7(add13)

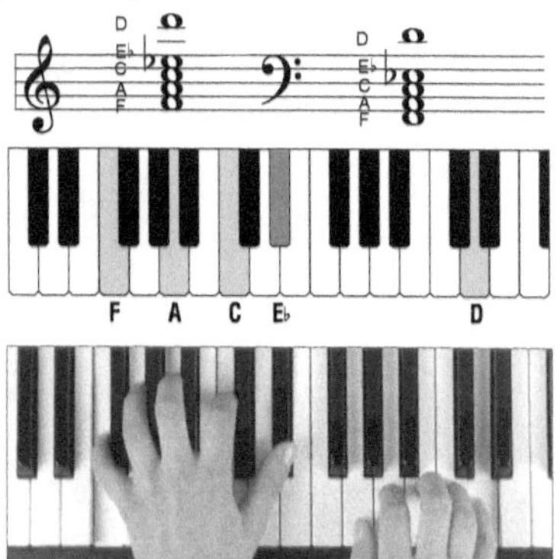

F7♭13

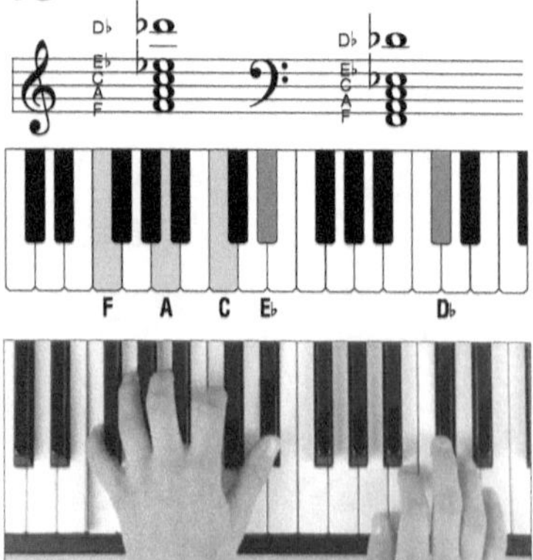

F7♭9(♯11)

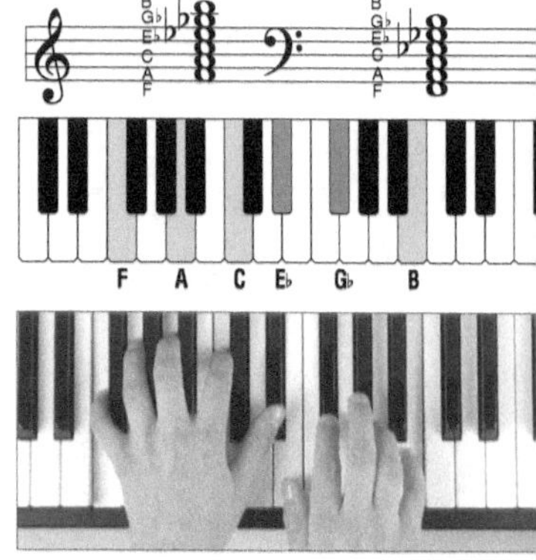

F7♯9(♯11)

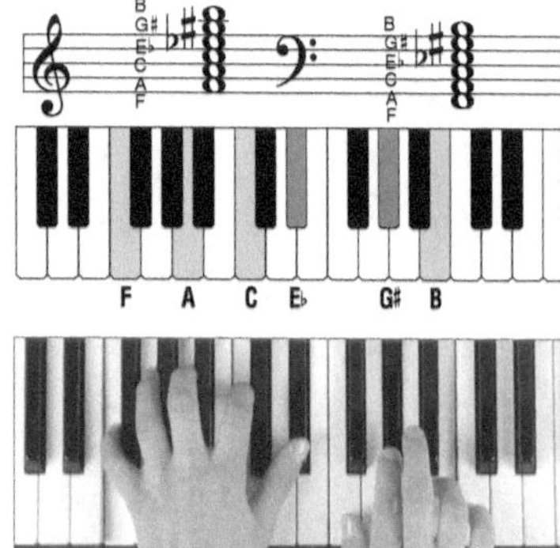

F7♭9(♭13)

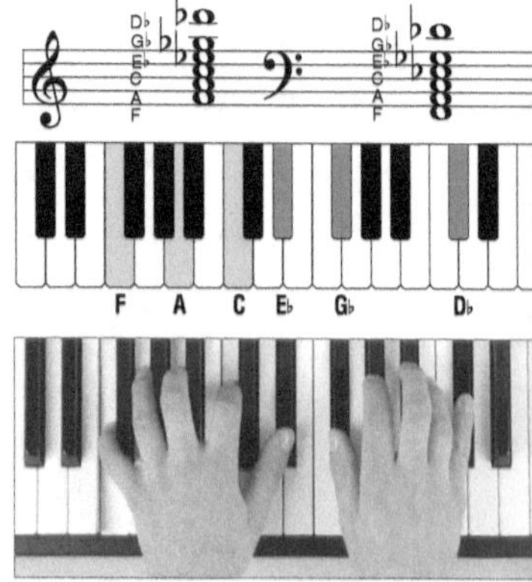

F7♯9(♭13)

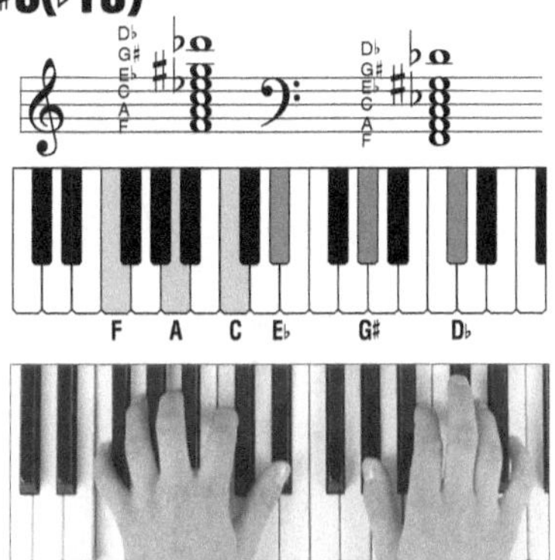

F9

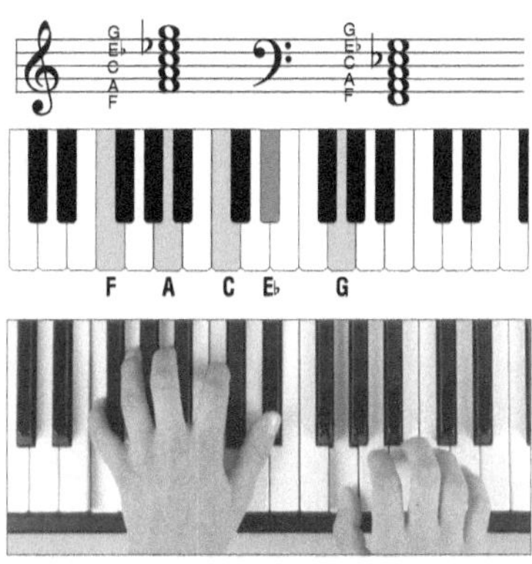

F7♯11(♭13)

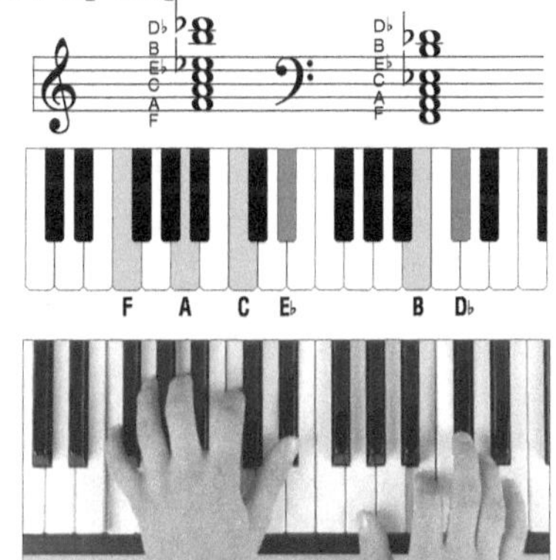

F9(♭5)

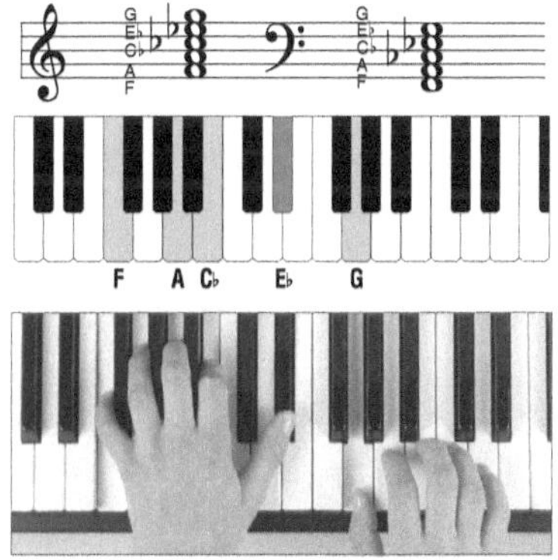

F7♭9(♯9, ♯11)

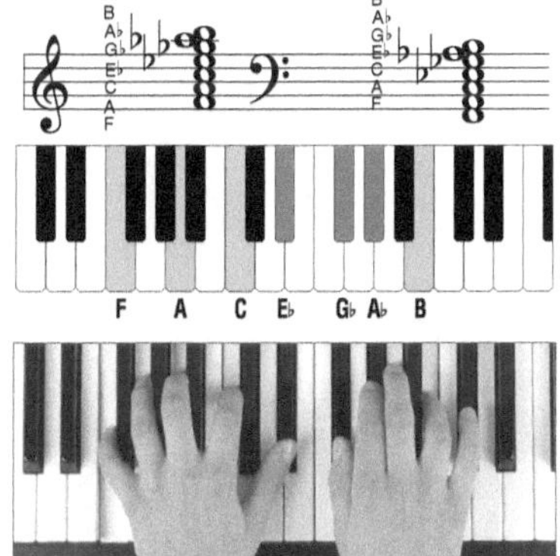

F9♯5

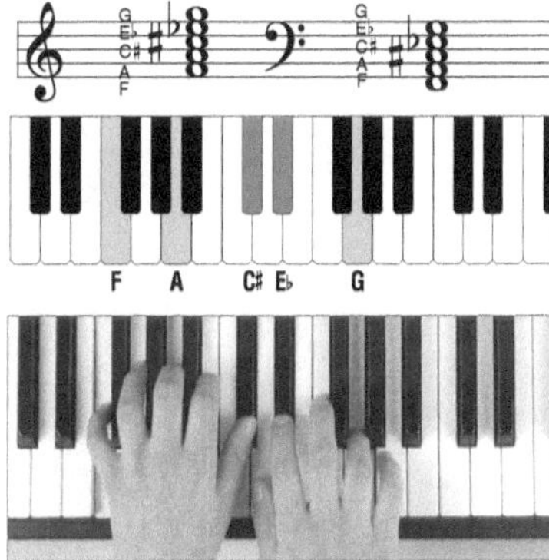

F9♯11

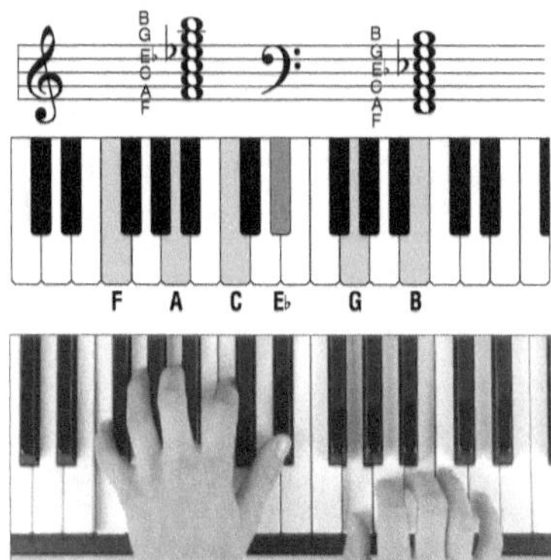

F11, F9(sus4)

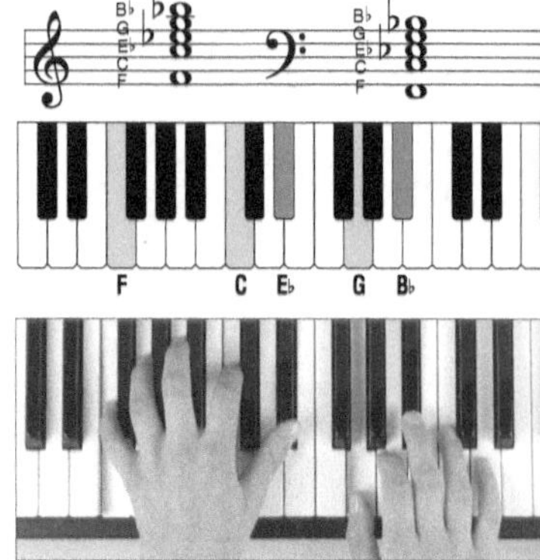

F9♭13

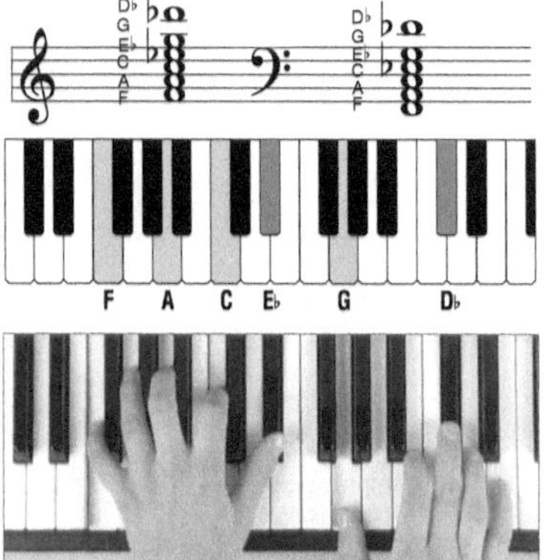

F13

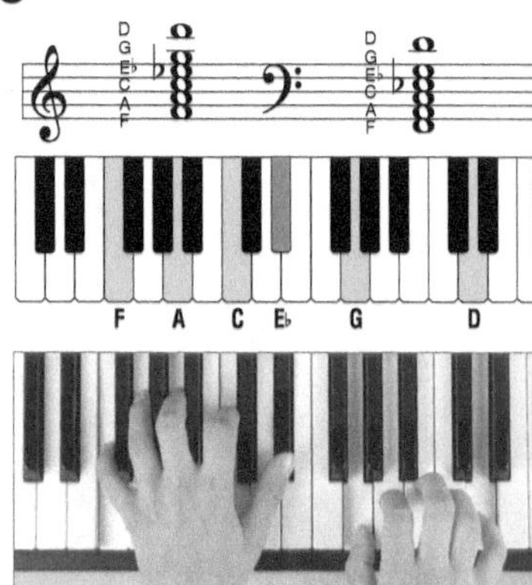

F9♯11(♭13)

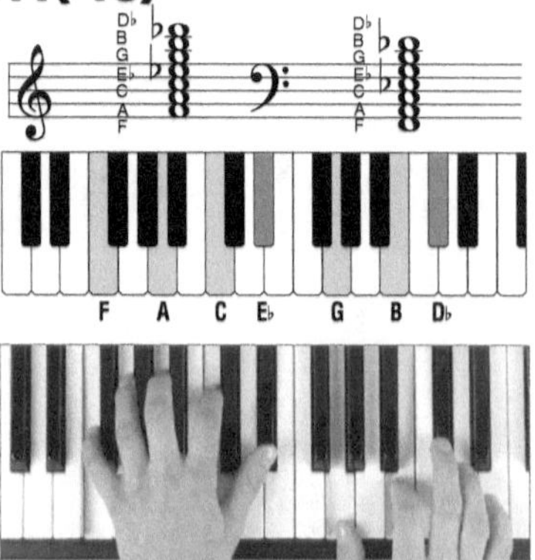

F13♭5

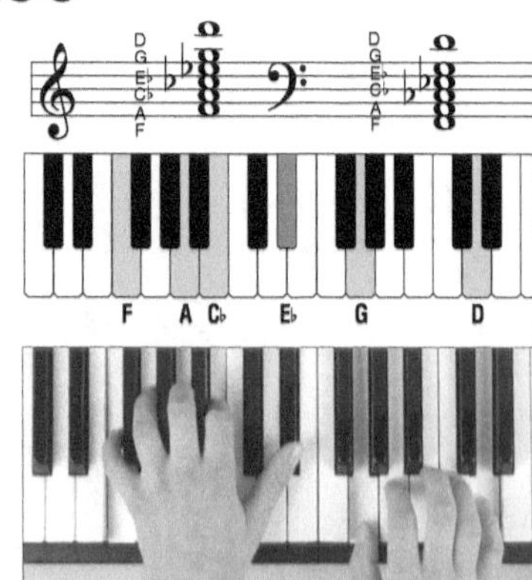

F13♭9

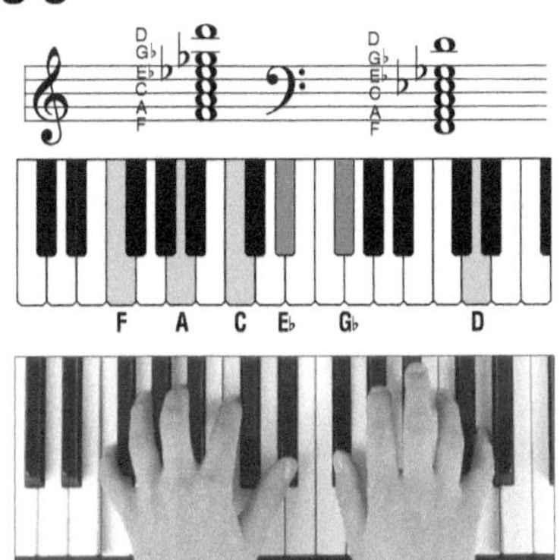

F13♯9

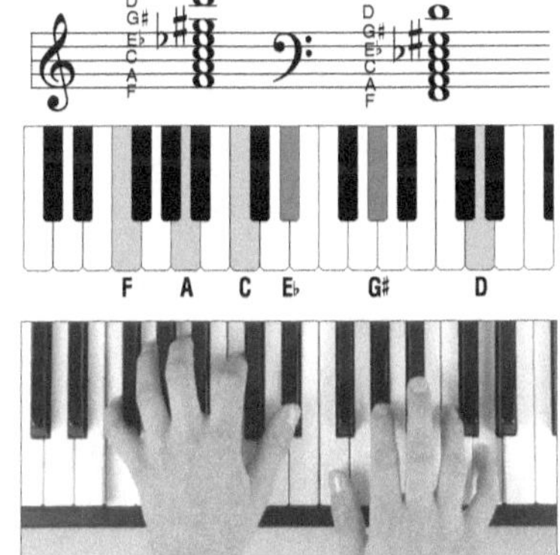

F13♯11

F13(sus4)

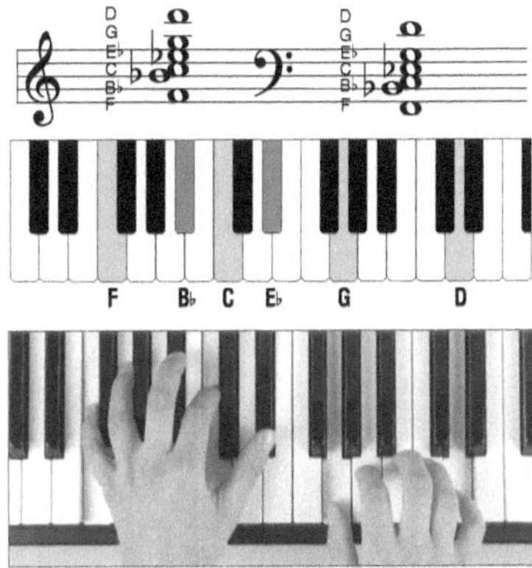

Fm(♯5)

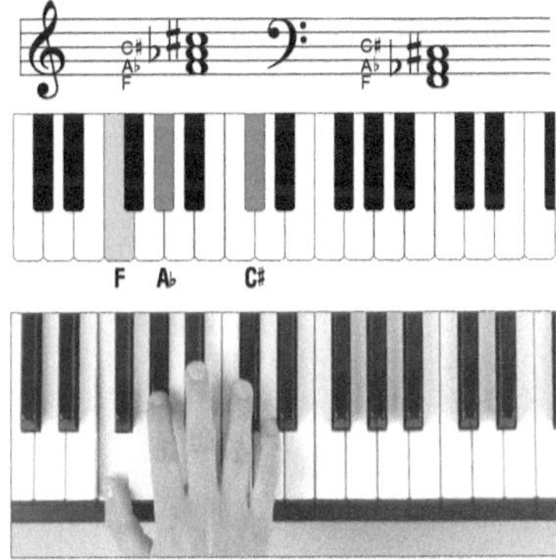

Fm$^{6}_{9}$

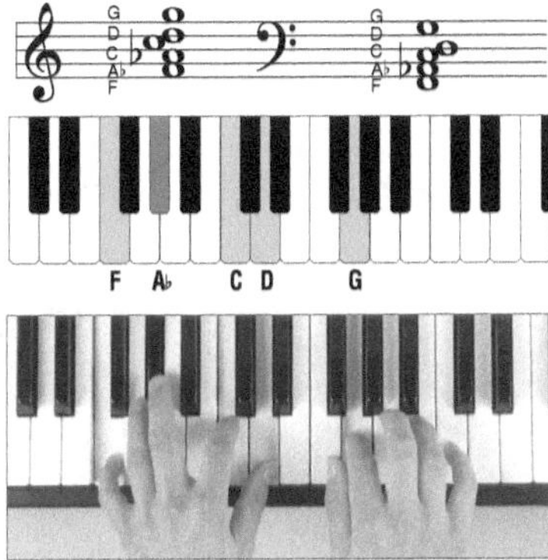

F

Fm7(add4)

Fm9

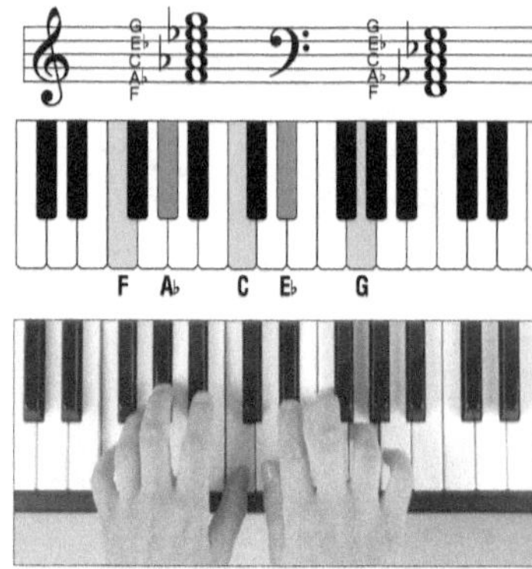

Fm7(add11)

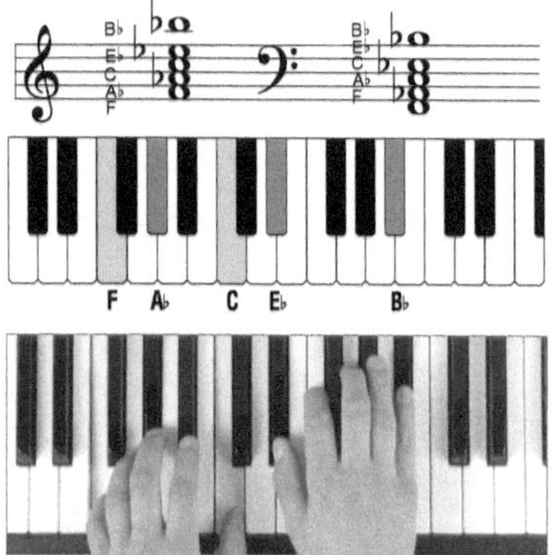

Fm9(maj7)

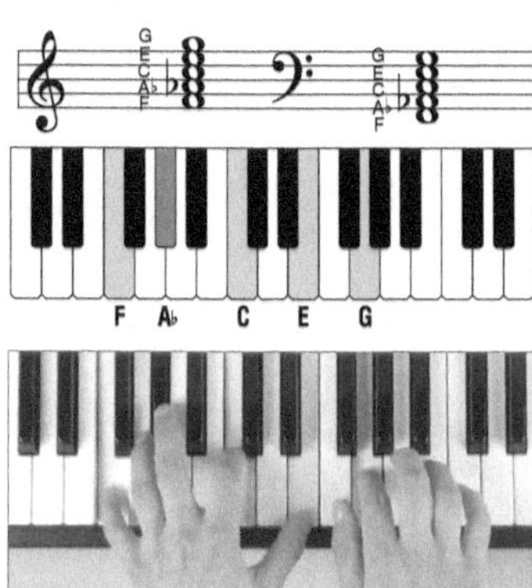

Fm7♭5(♭9)

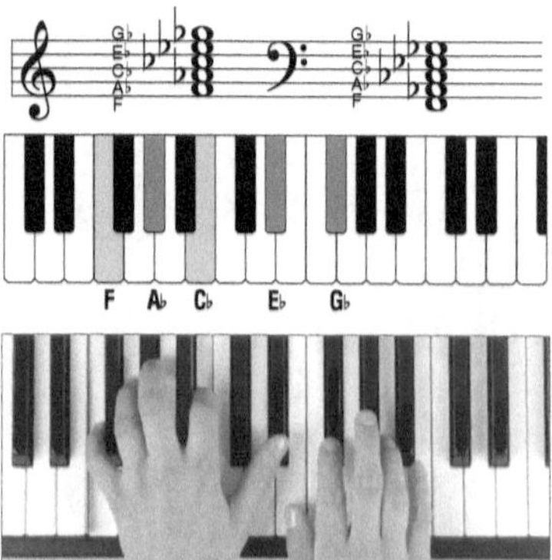

Fm9♭5

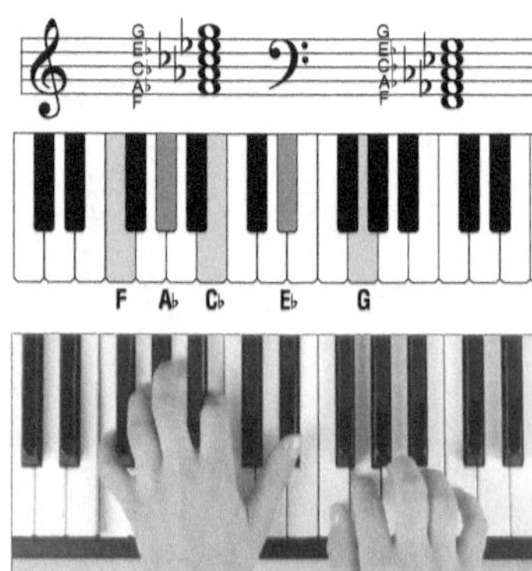

Fm11

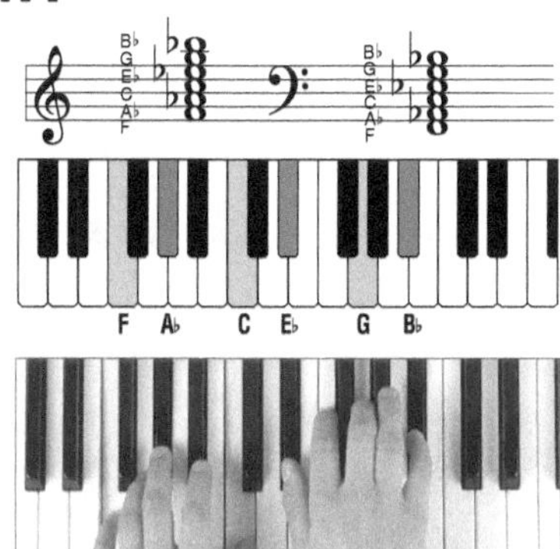

Fm13

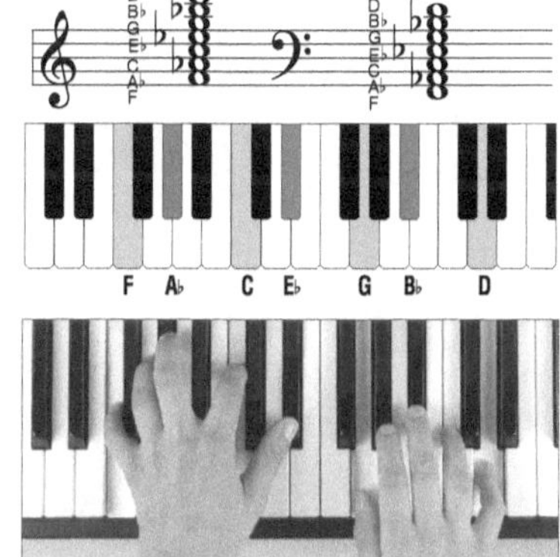

Fdim7(add9)

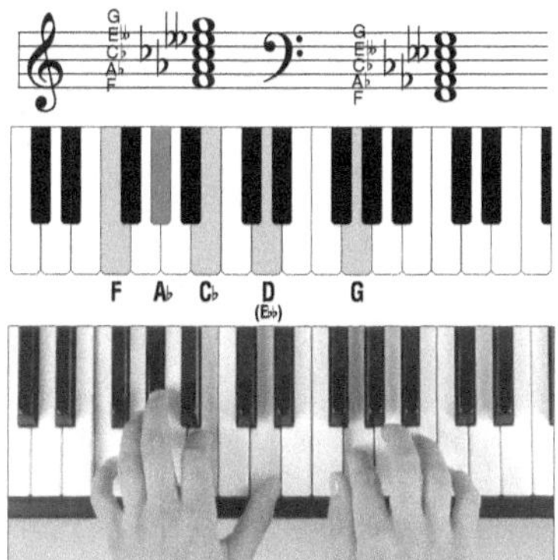

Fm11♭5

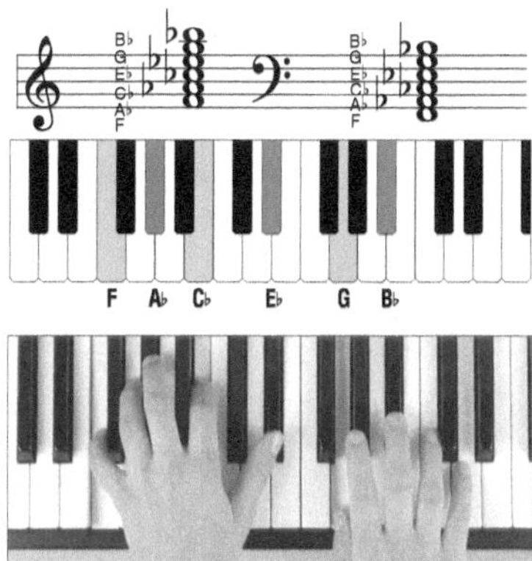

Fm11(maj7)

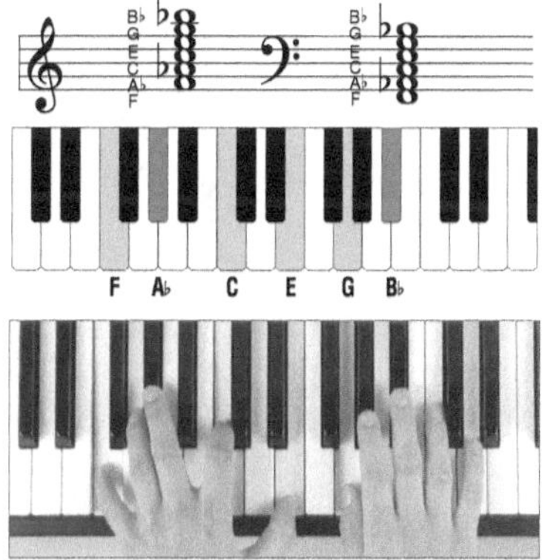

F7alt.

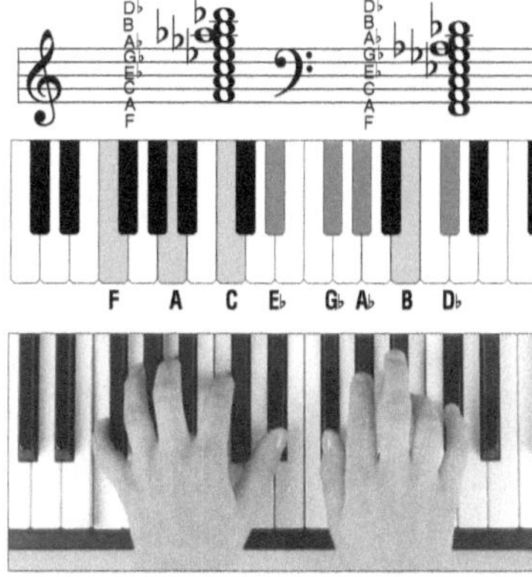

F♯

Root Position

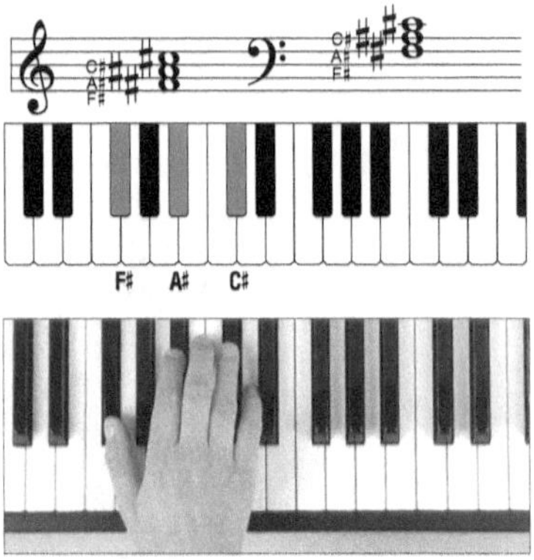

F♯ A♯ C♯

F♯

First Inversion

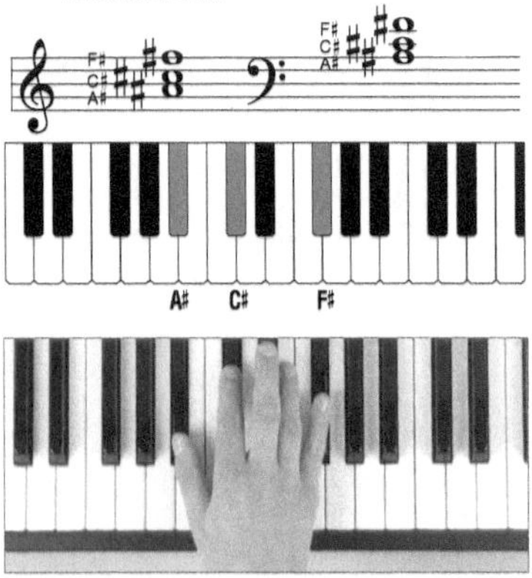

A♯ C♯ F♯

F♯

Second Inversion

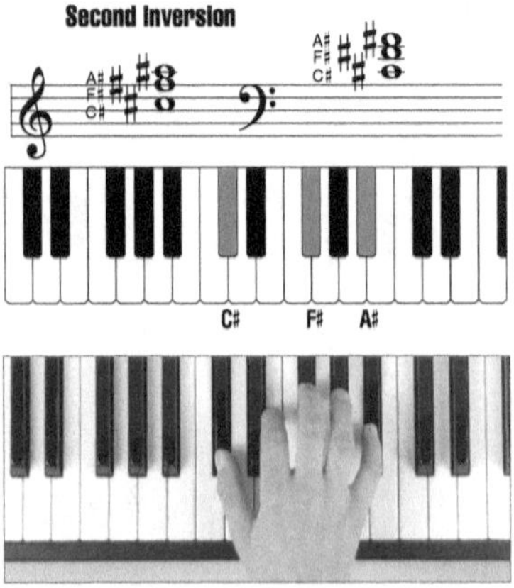

C♯ F♯ A♯

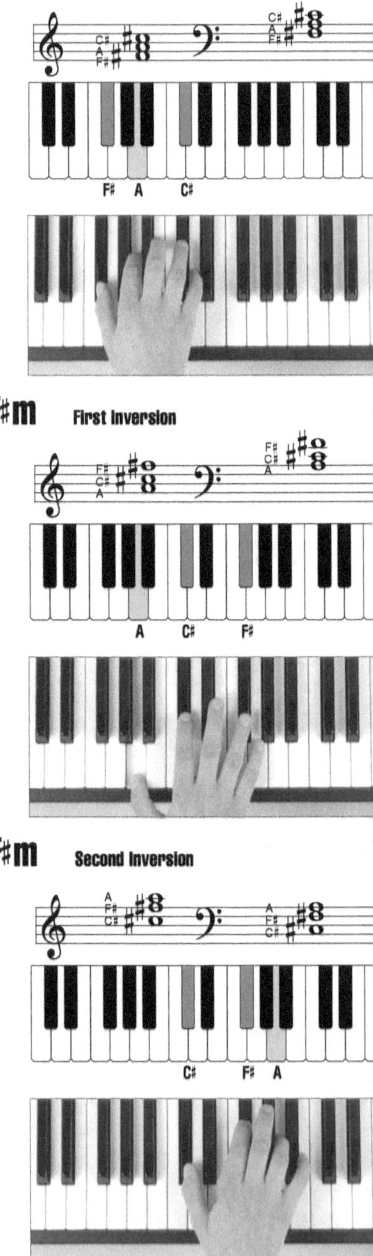

♯+ Root Position

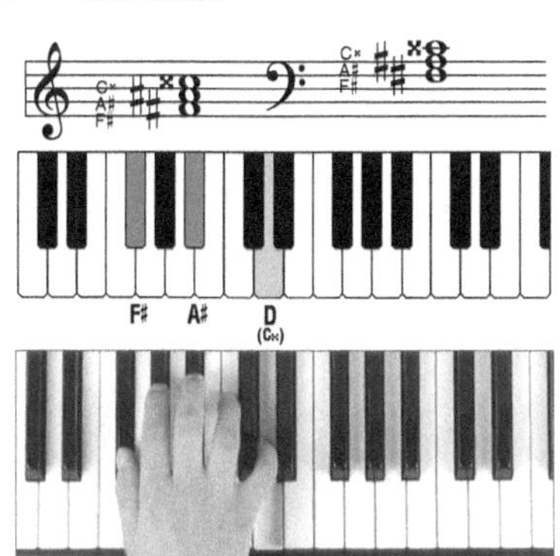

F♯dim Root Position

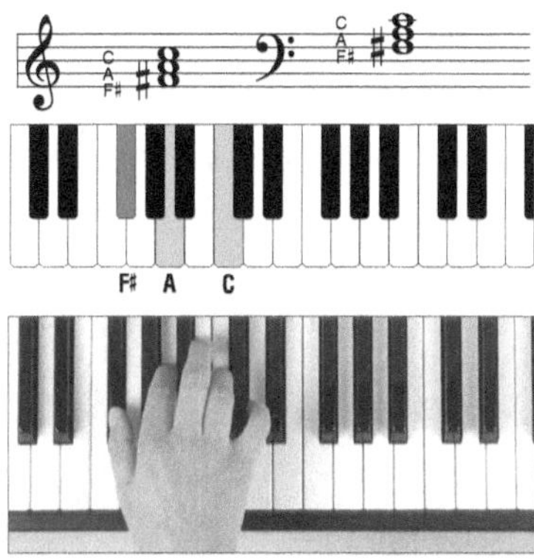

♯+ First Inversion

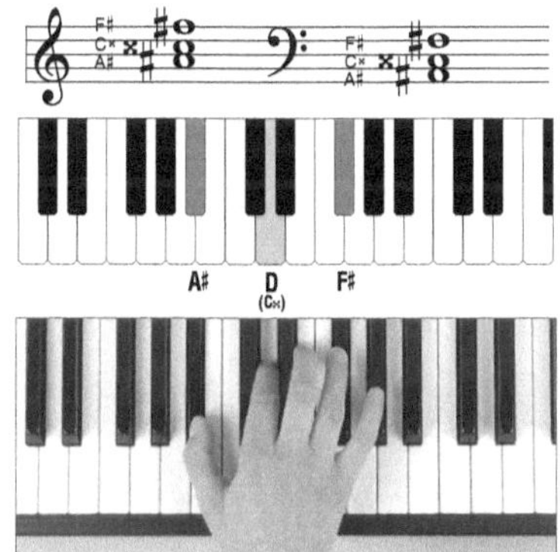

F♯dim First Inversion

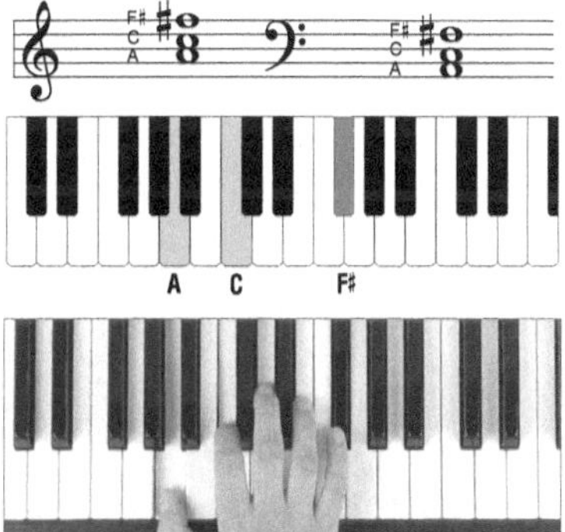

♯+ Second Inversion

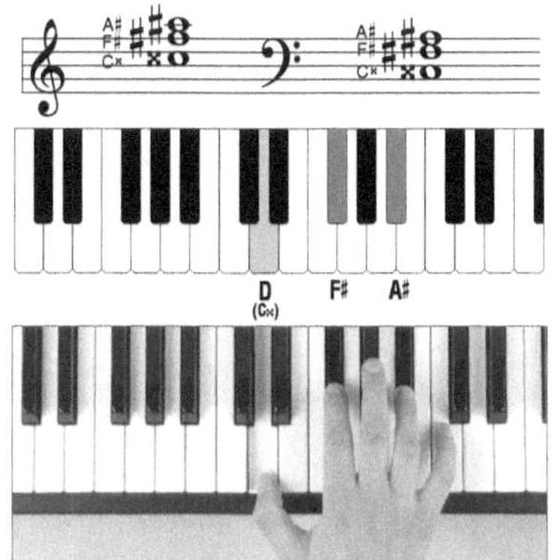

F♯dim Second Inversion

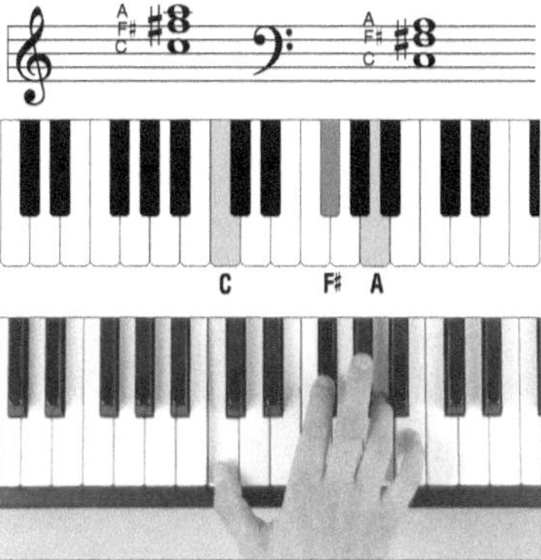

F♯sus Root Position

F♯sus First Inversion

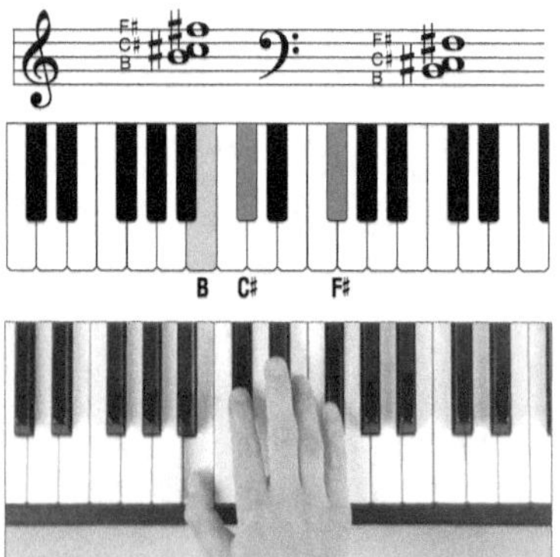

F♯sus Second Inversion

F♯(♭5) Root Position

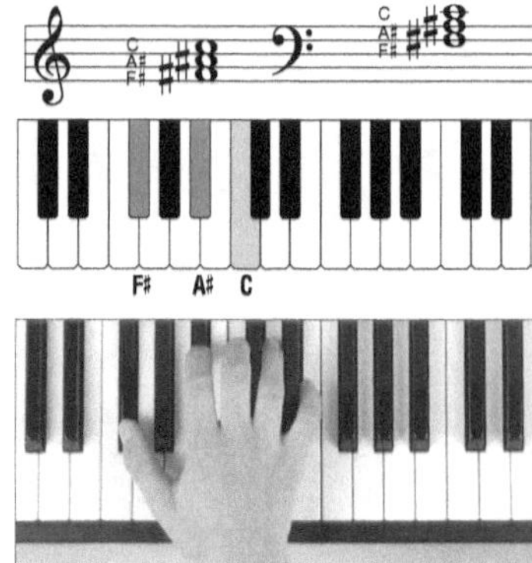

F♯(♭5) First Inversion

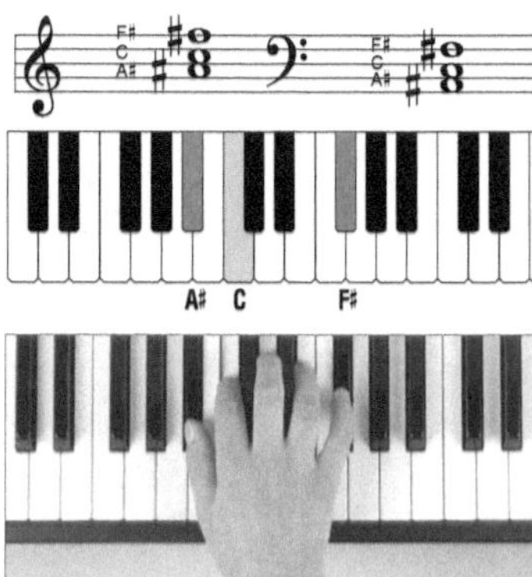

F♯(♭5) Second Inversion

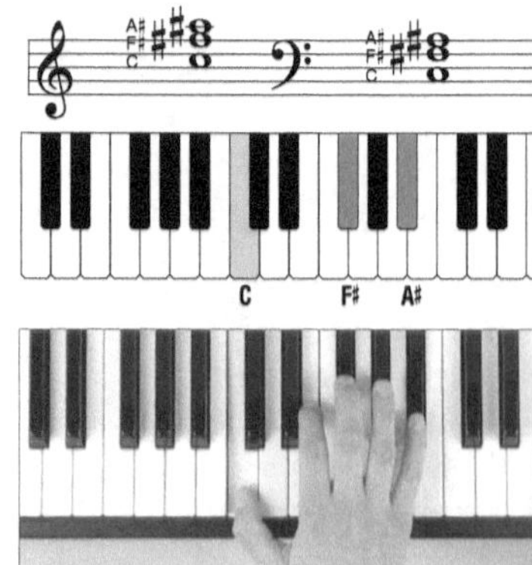

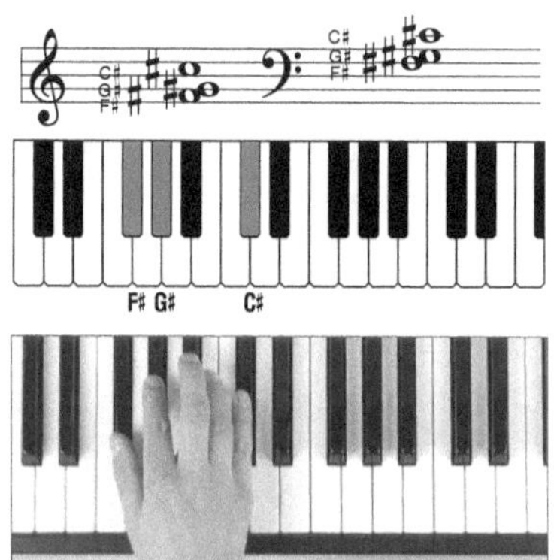

F#sus2 First Inversion

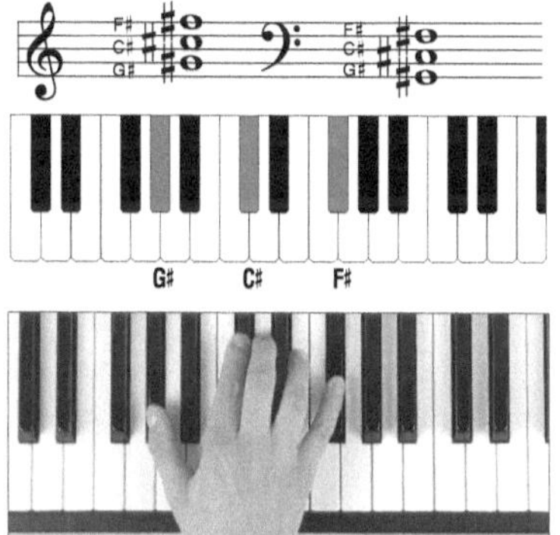

F#sus2 Second Inversion

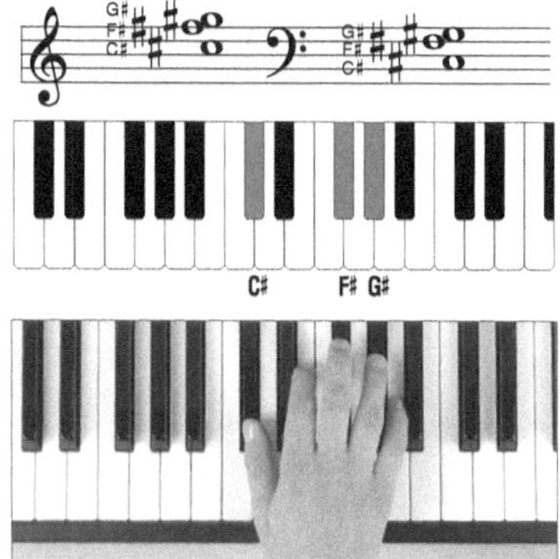

F♯6 Root Position

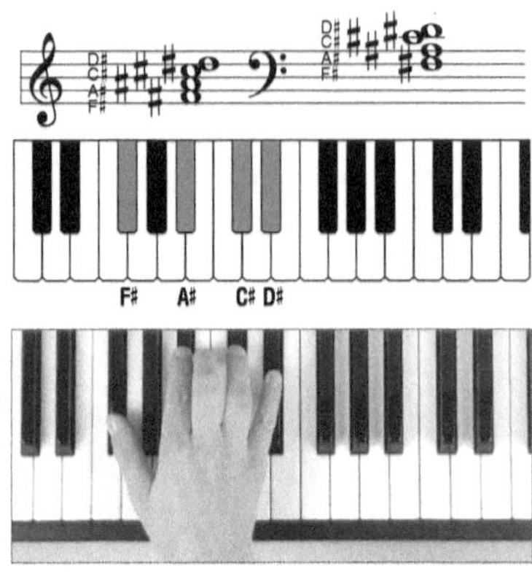

F♯6 First Inversion

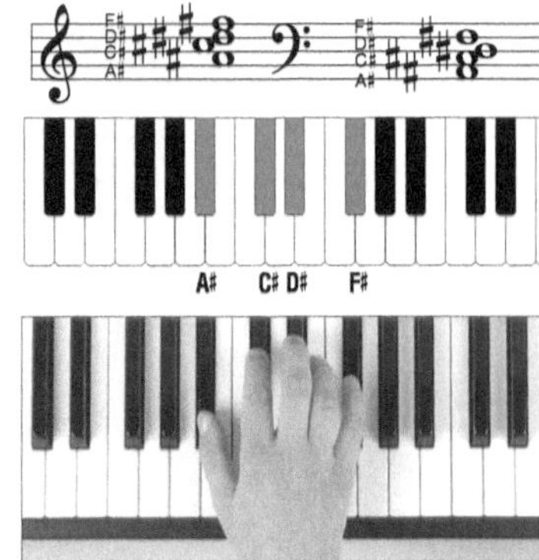

F♯6 Second Inversion

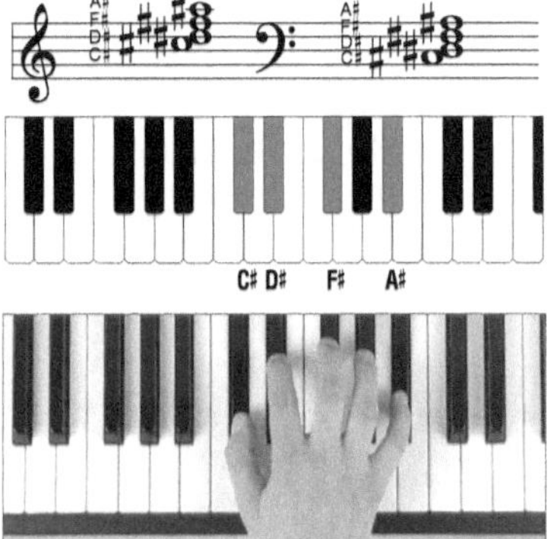

F♯6 Third Inversion

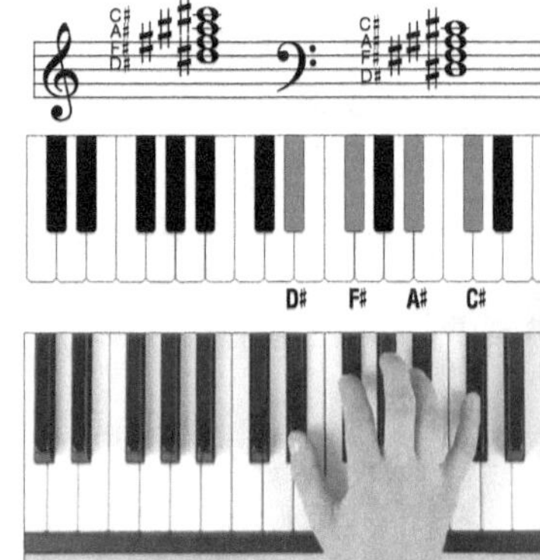

F♯(add2), F♯(add9) Root Position

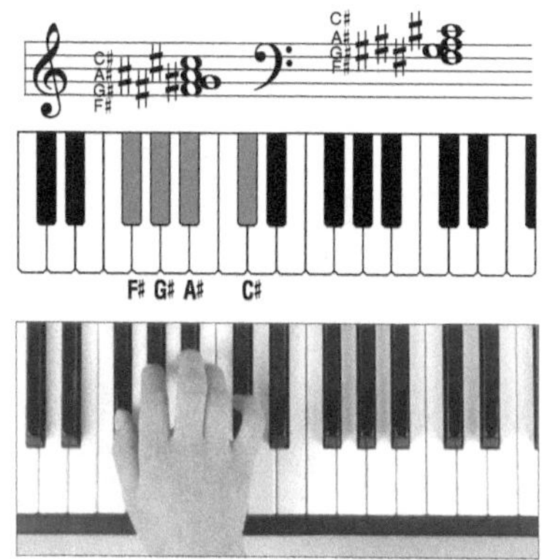

F♯(add2), F♯(add9) First Inversion

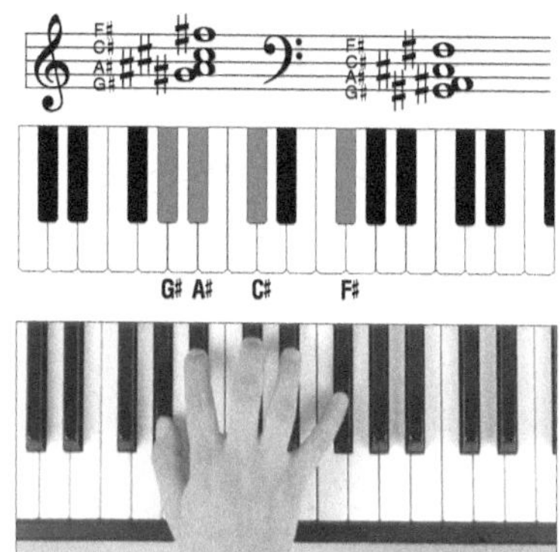

F♯(add2), F♯(add9) Second Inversion

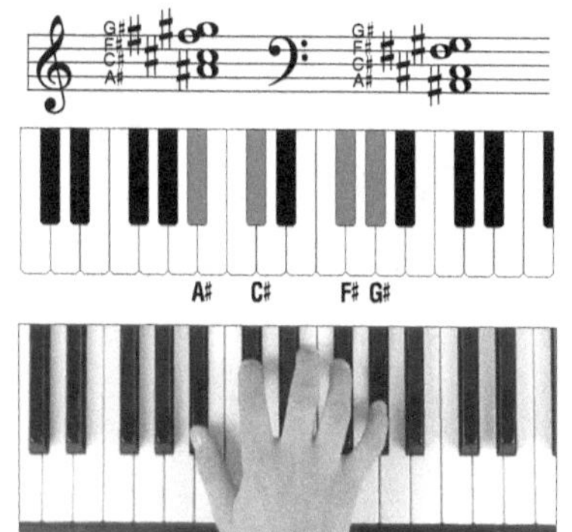

F♯(add2), F♯(add9) Third Inversion

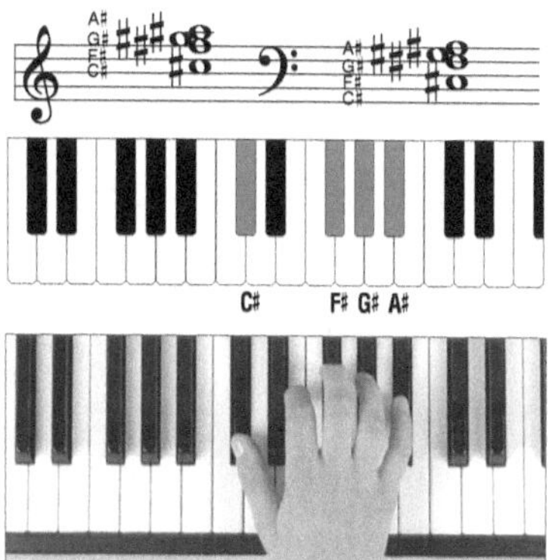

F♯maj7 Root Position

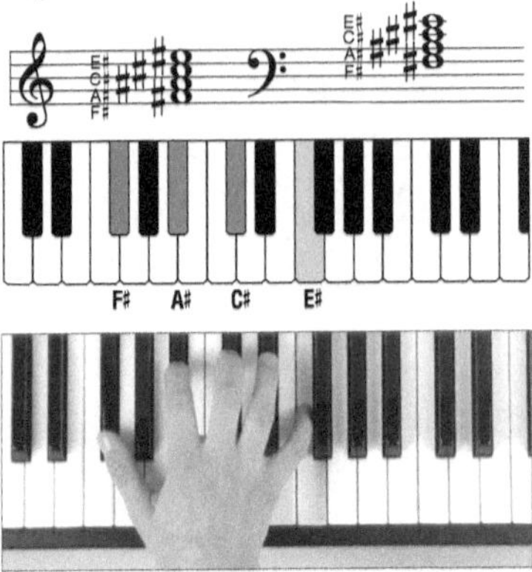

F♯maj7 First Inversion

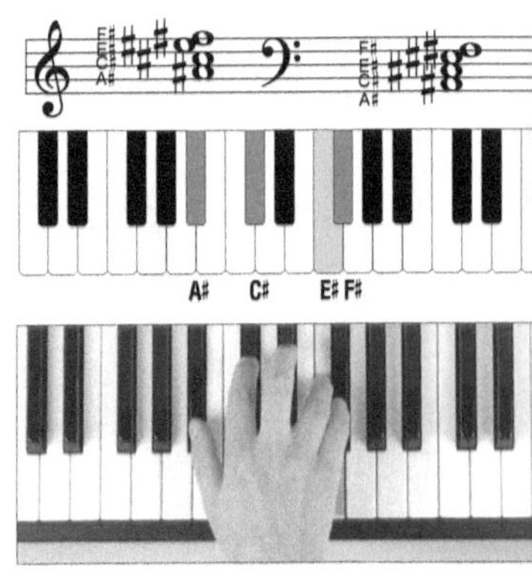

F♯maj7 Second Inversion

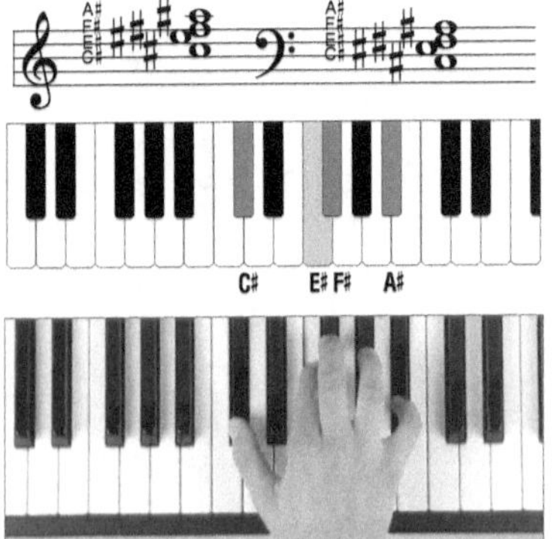

F♯maj7 Third Inversion

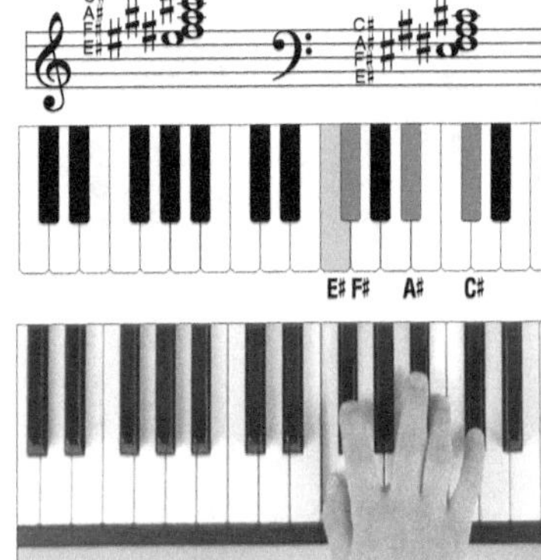

F♯maj7♭5 Root Position

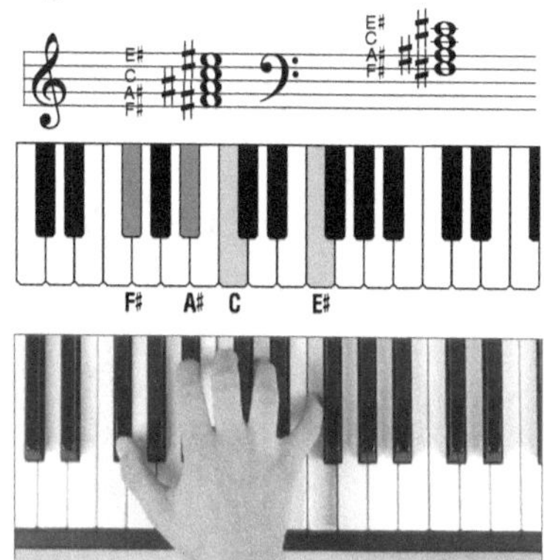

F♯maj7♭5 First Inversion

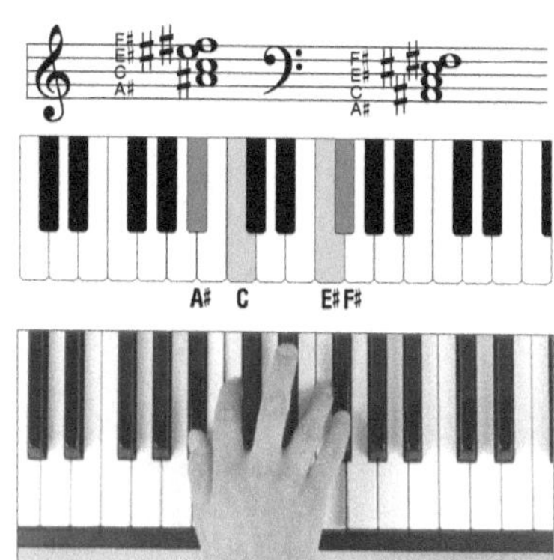

F♯maj7♭5 Second Inversion

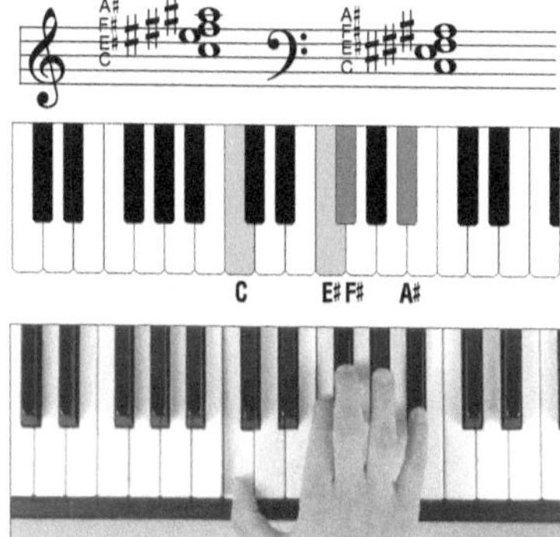

F♯maj7♭5 Third Inversion

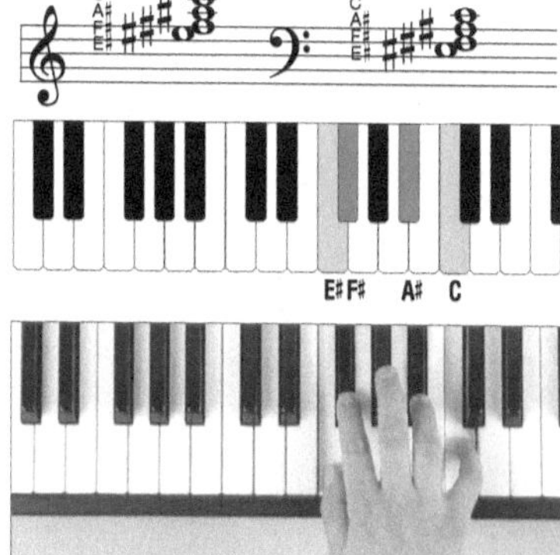

F♯maj7♯5 Root Position

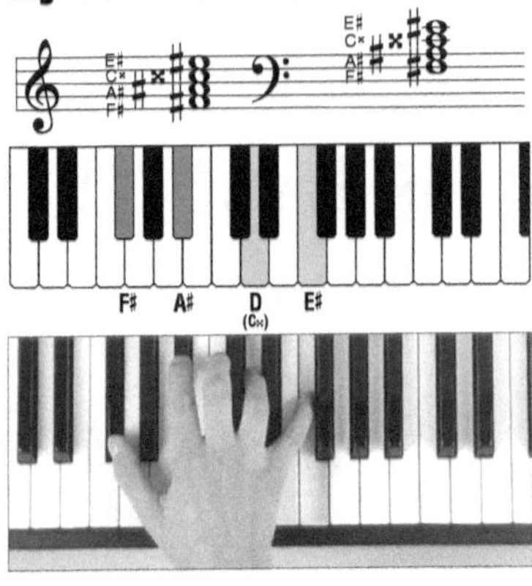

F♯maj7♯5 First Inversion

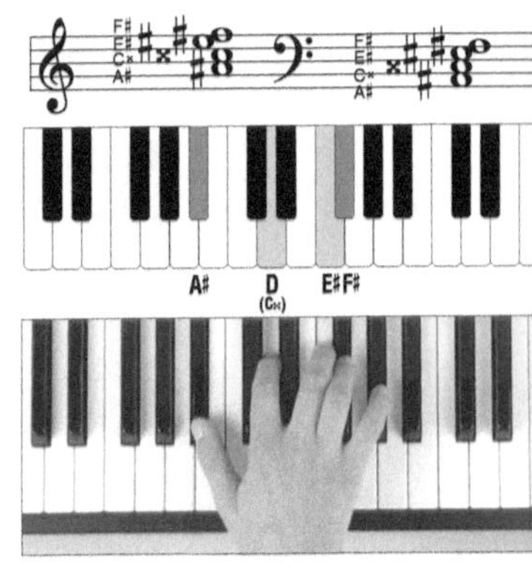

F♯maj7♯5 Second Inversion

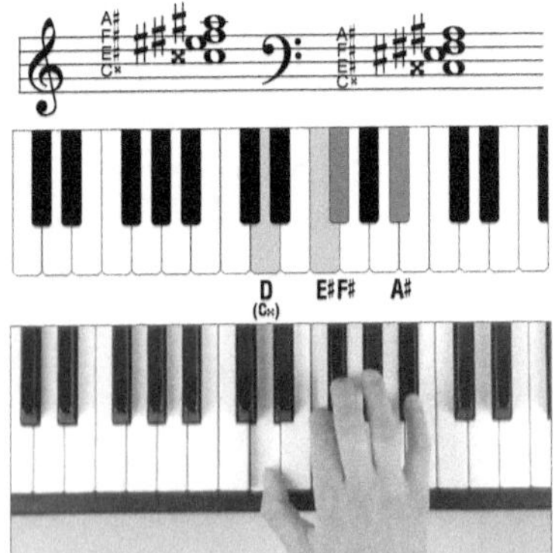

F♯maj7♯5 Third Inversion

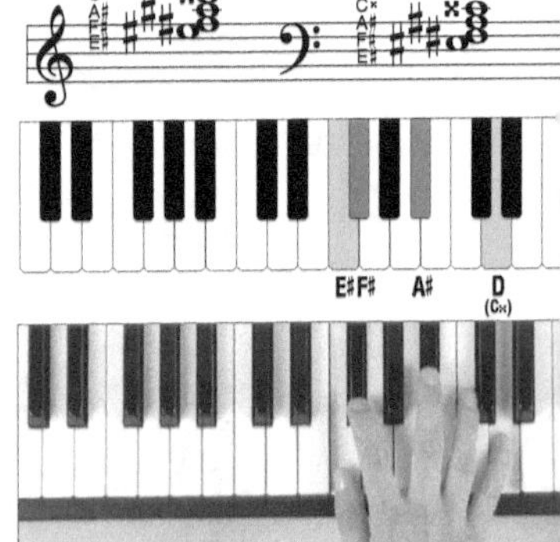

F♯7

Root Position

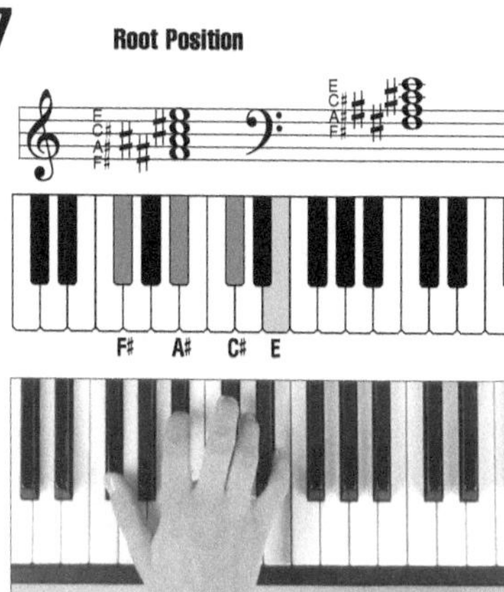

F♯7

First Inversion

F♯7

Second Inversion

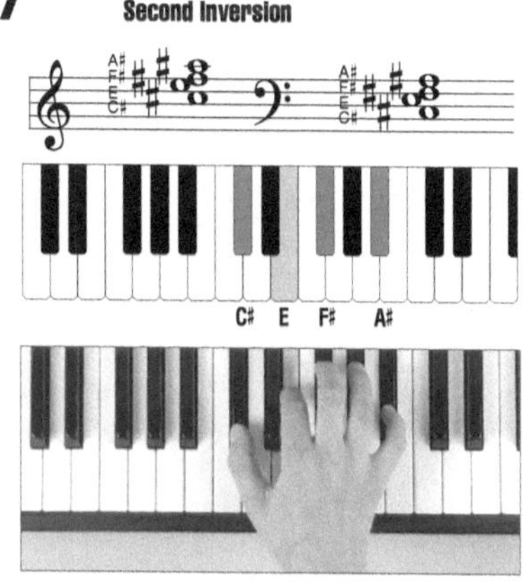

F♯7

Third Inversion

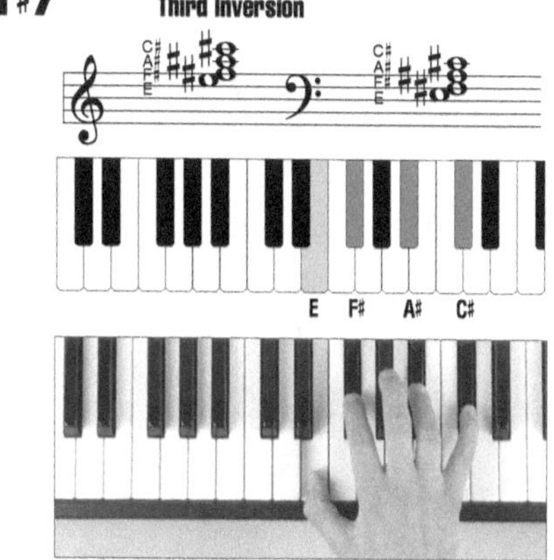

F♯7♭5 Root Position

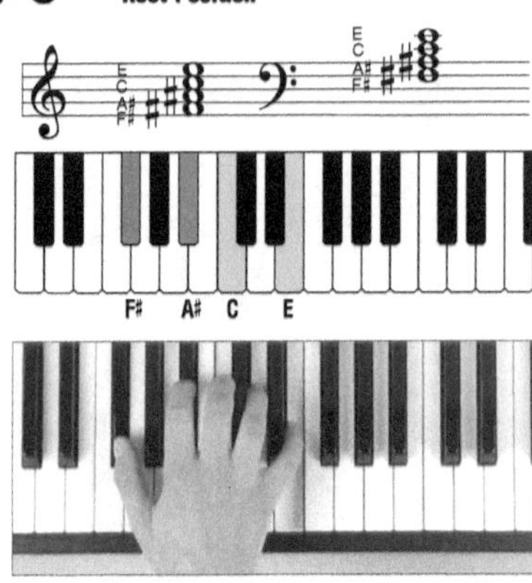

F♯7♭5 First Inversion

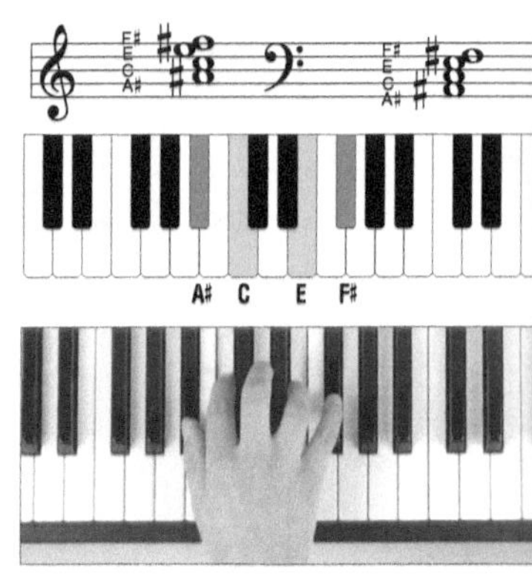

F♯7♭5 Second Inversion

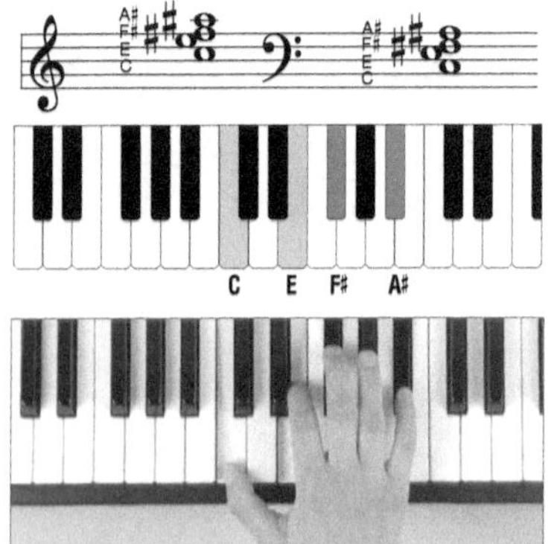

F♯7♭5 Third Inversion

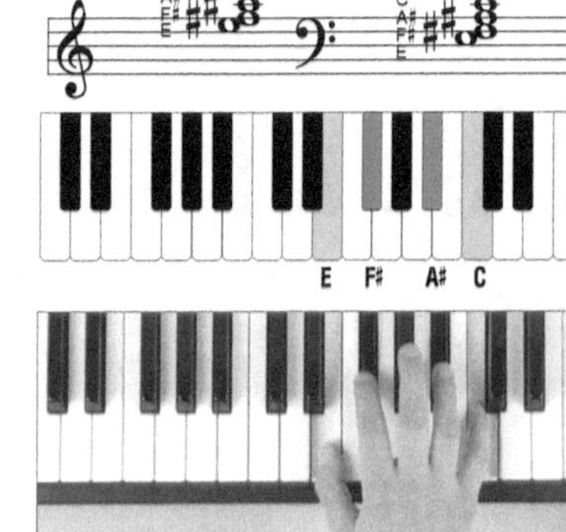

F♯7♯5 Root Position

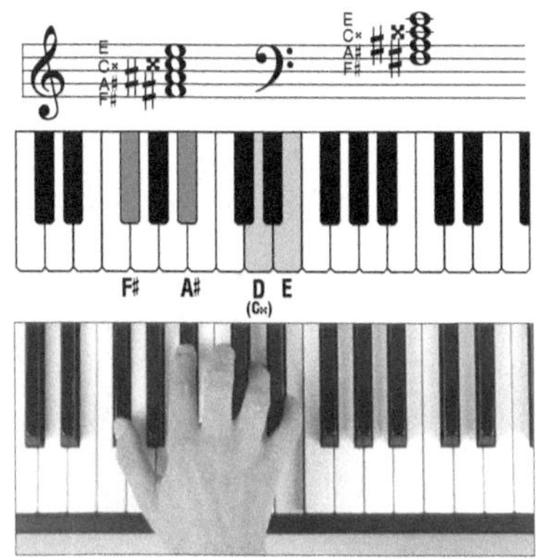

F♯7♯5 First Inversion

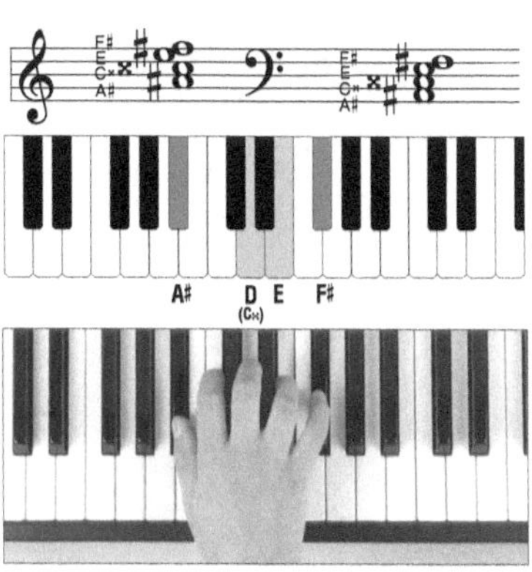

F♯7♯5 Second Inversion

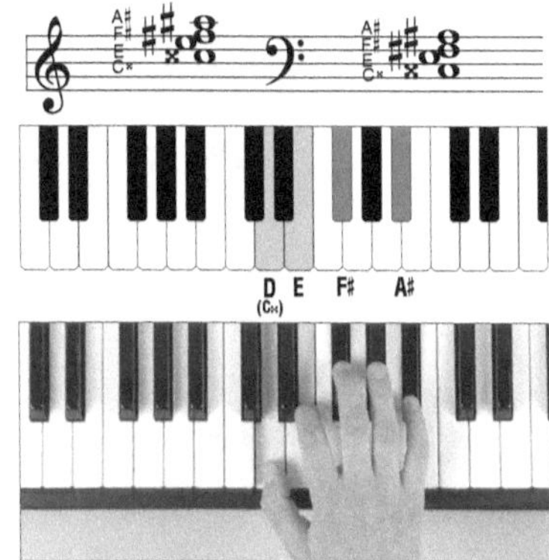

F♯7♯5 Third Inversion

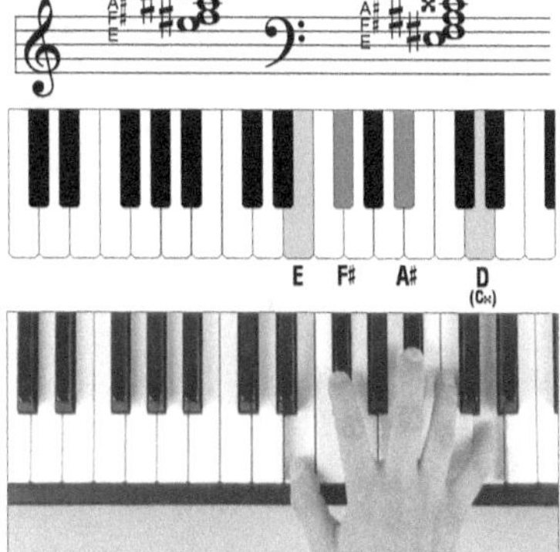

F♯7sus Root Position

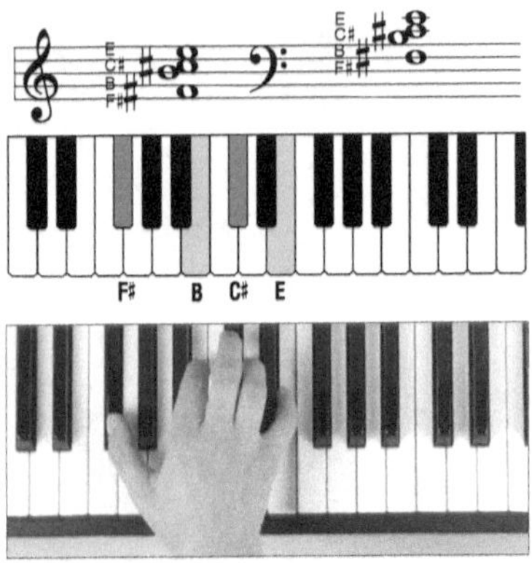

F♯7sus First Inversion

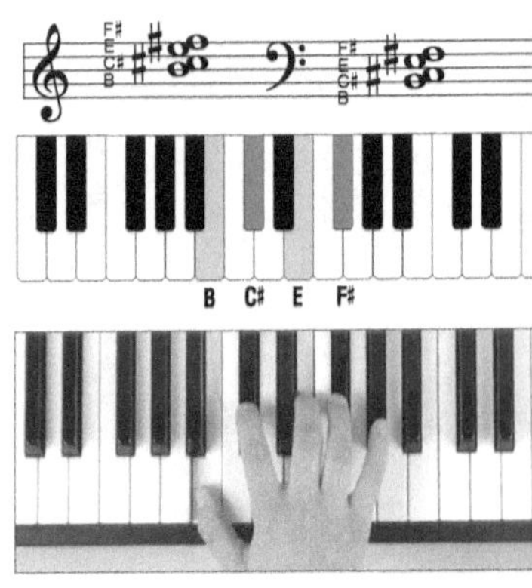

F♯7sus Second Inversion

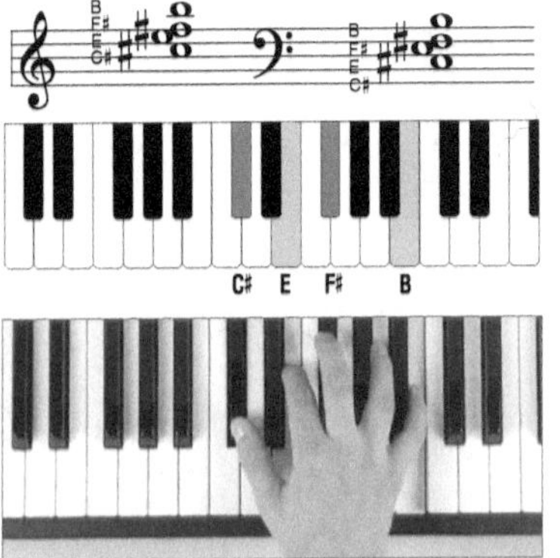

F♯7sus Third Inversion

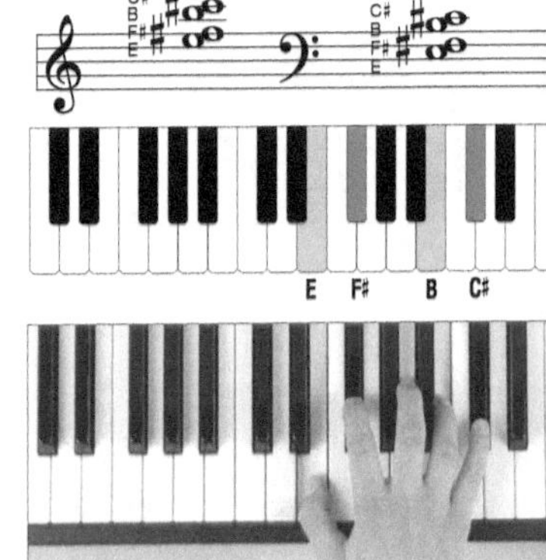

F♯m(add2), F♯m(add9) Root Position

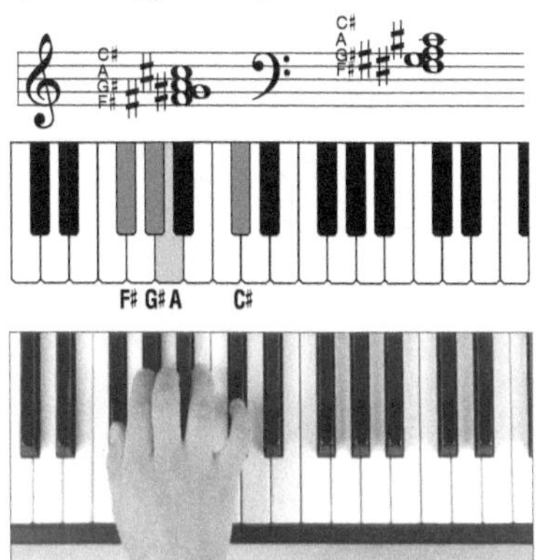

F♯m(add2), F♯m(add9) First Inversion

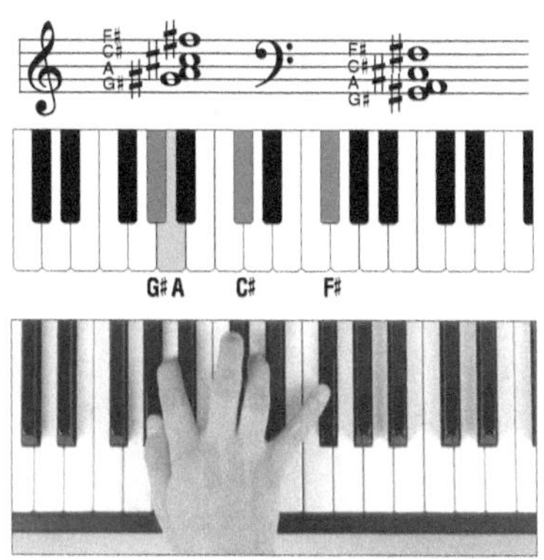

F♯m(add2), F♯m(add9) Second Inversion

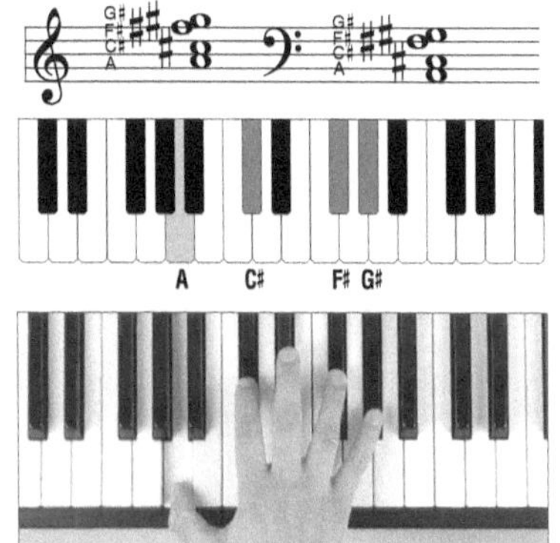

F♯m(add2), F♯m(add9) Third Inversion

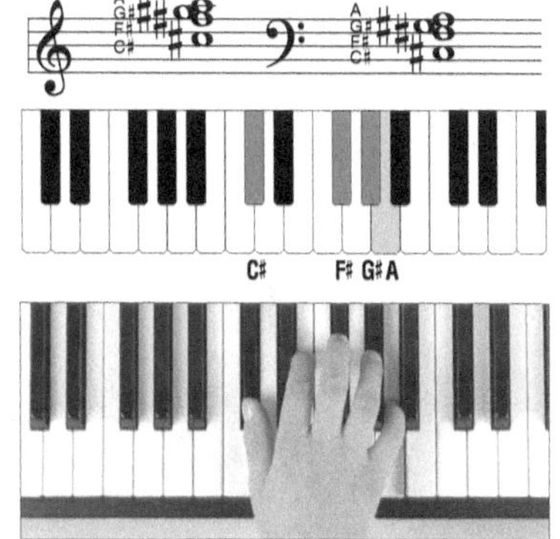

F♯m6 Root Position

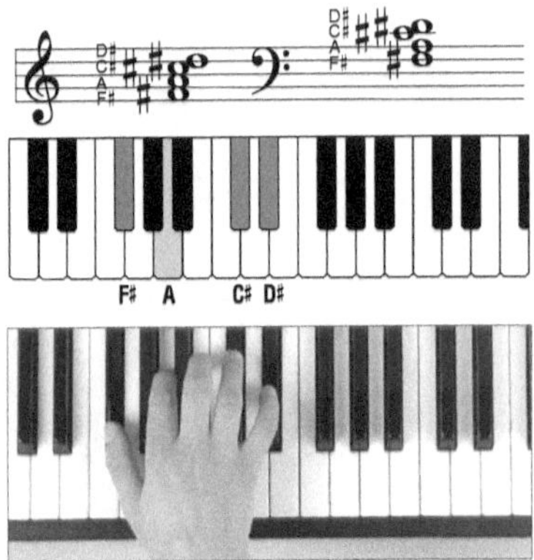

F♯m6 First Inversion

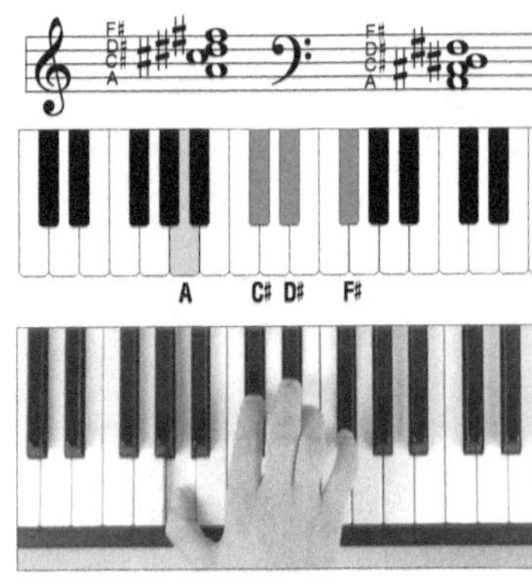

F♯m6 Second Inversion

F♯m6 Third Inversion

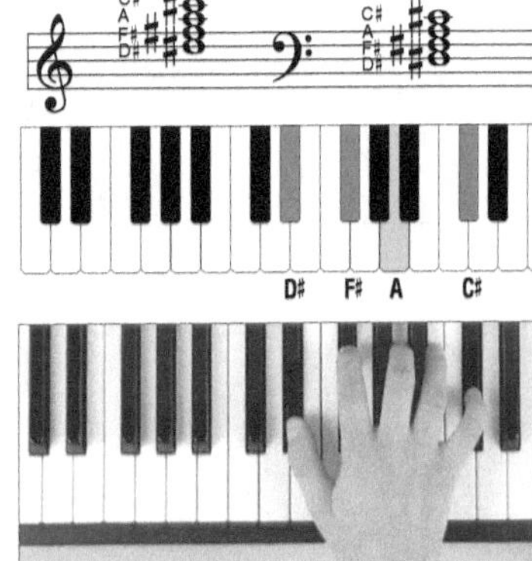

F♯m7 Root Position

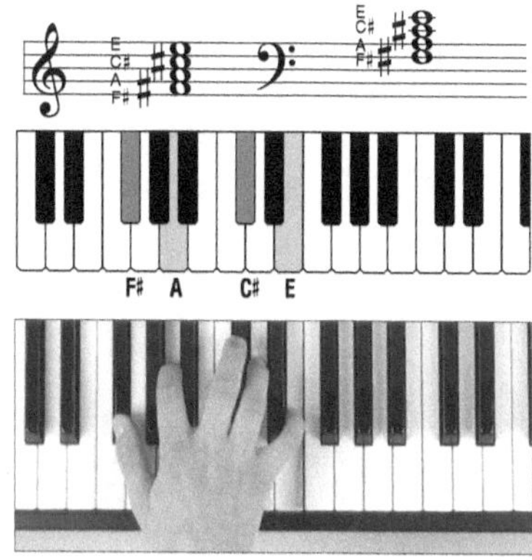

F♯m7 First Inversion

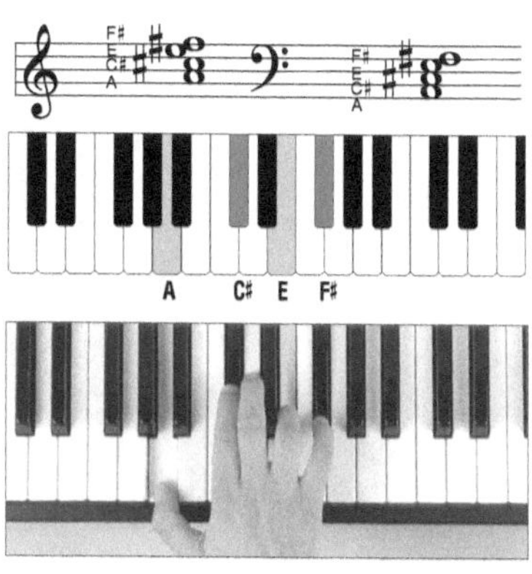

F♯m7 Second Inversion

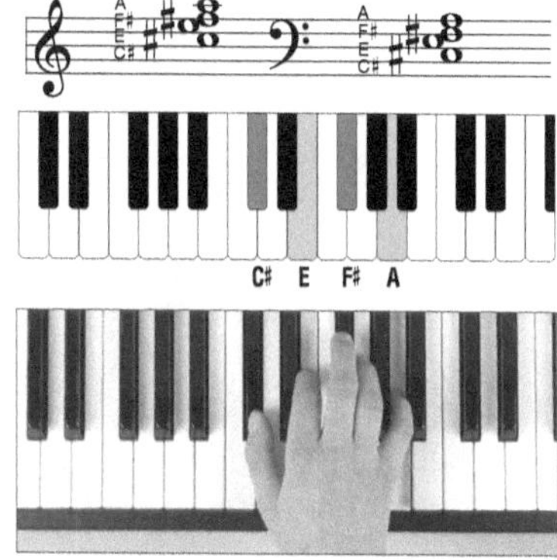

F♯m7 Third Inversion

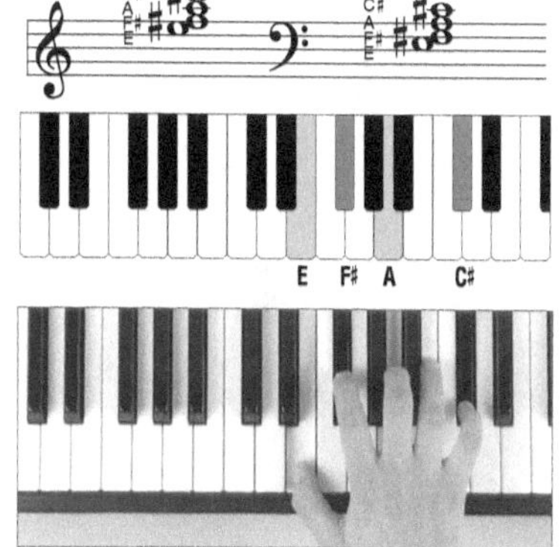

F♯m(maj7) Root Position

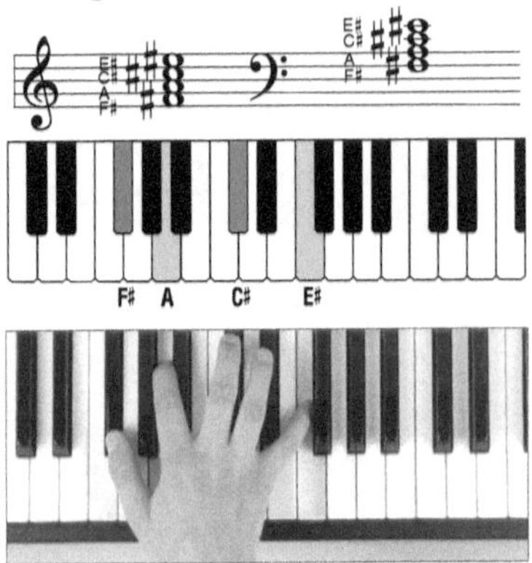

F♯m(maj7) First Inversion

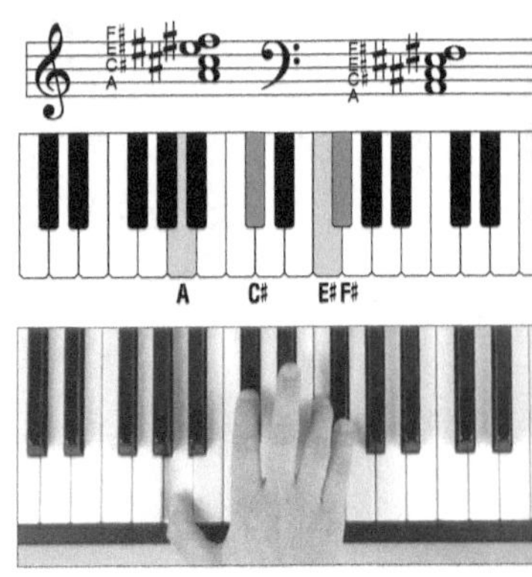

F♯m(maj7) Second Inversion

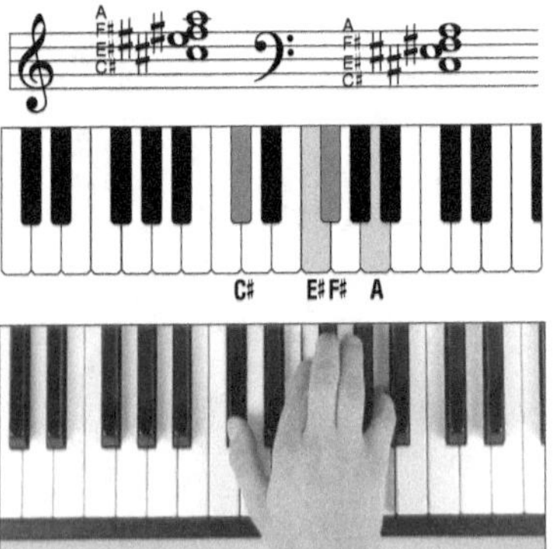

F♯m(maj7) Third Inversion

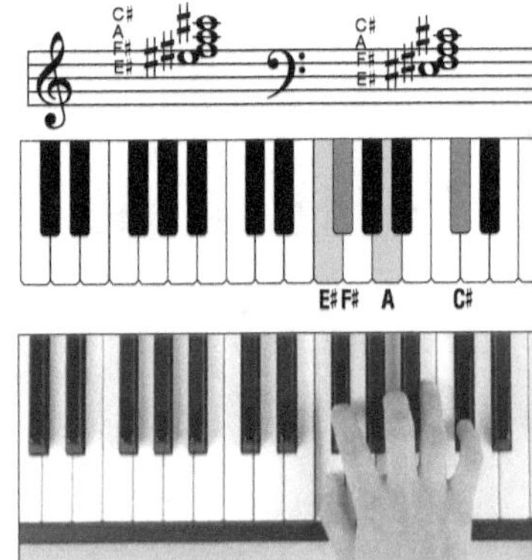

♯m7♭5 Root Position

F♯m7♭5 First Inversion

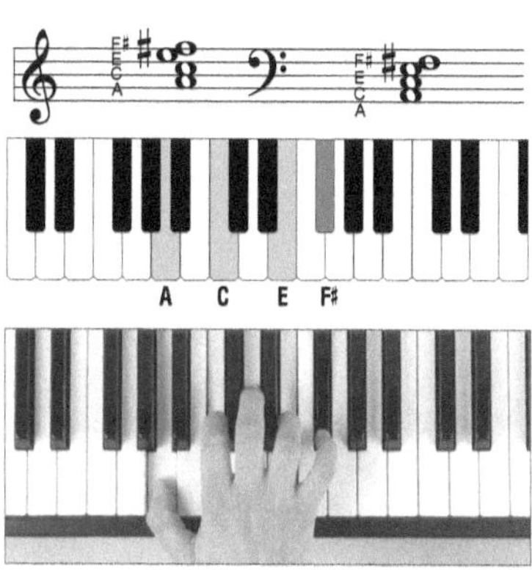

♯m7♭5 Second Inversion

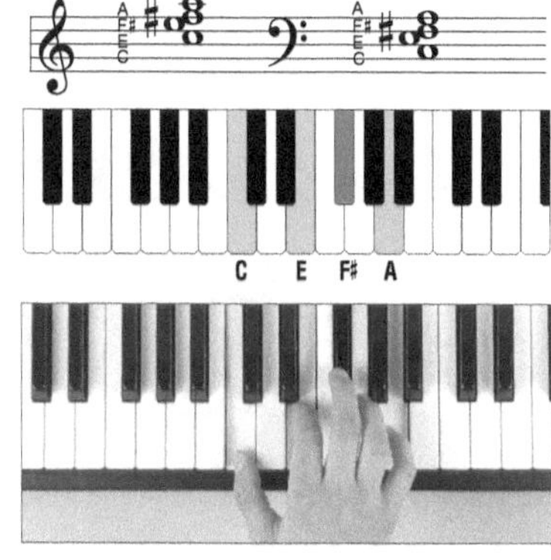

F♯m7♭5 Third Inversion

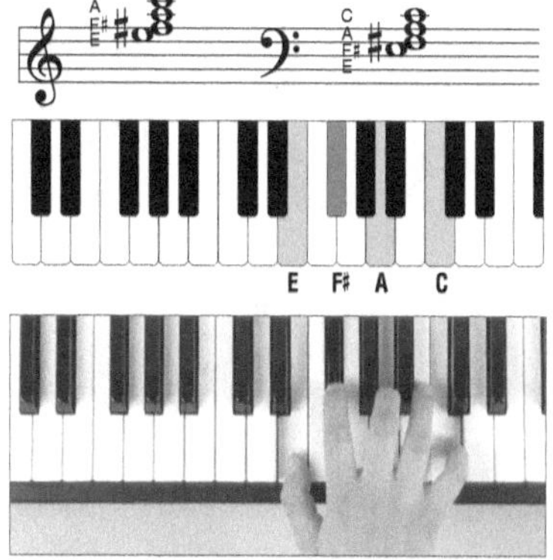

F♯dim7 Root Position

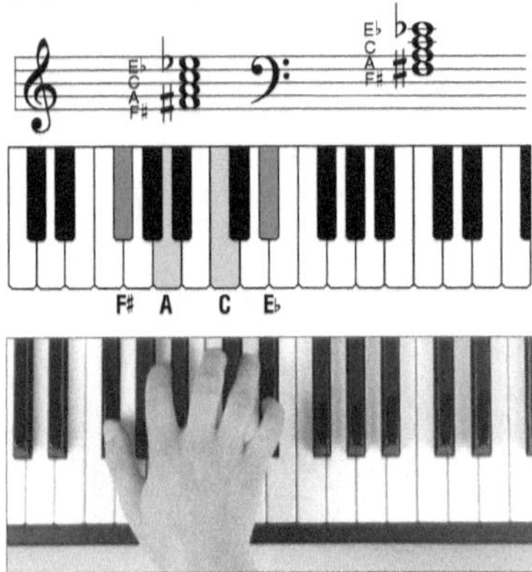

F♯dim7 First Inversion

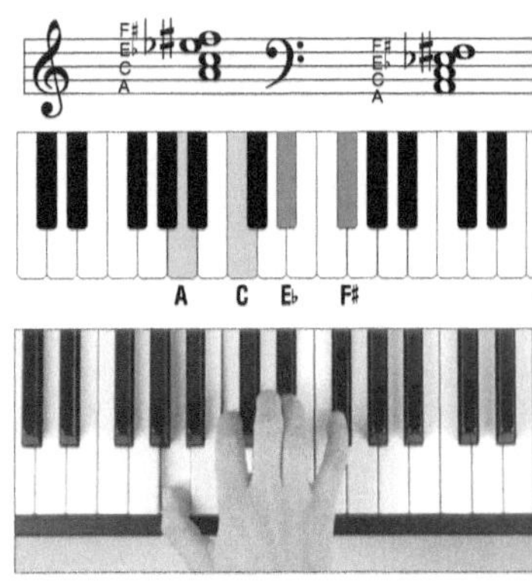

F♯dim7 Second Inversion

F♯dim7 Third Inversion

♯dim(maj7)

Root Position

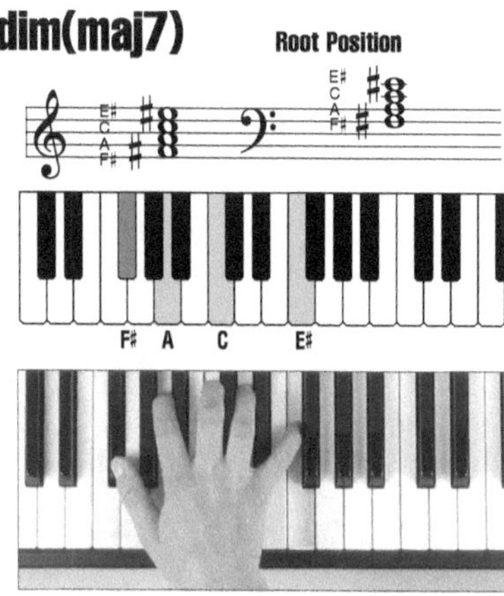

F♯dim(maj7)

First Inversion

♯dim(maj7)

Second Inversion

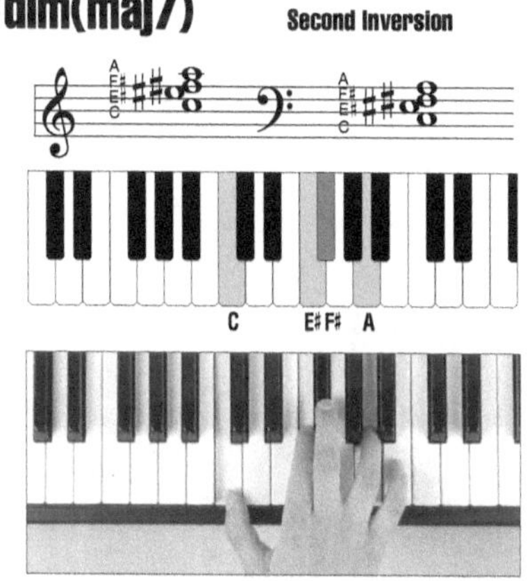

F♯dim(maj7)

Third Inversion

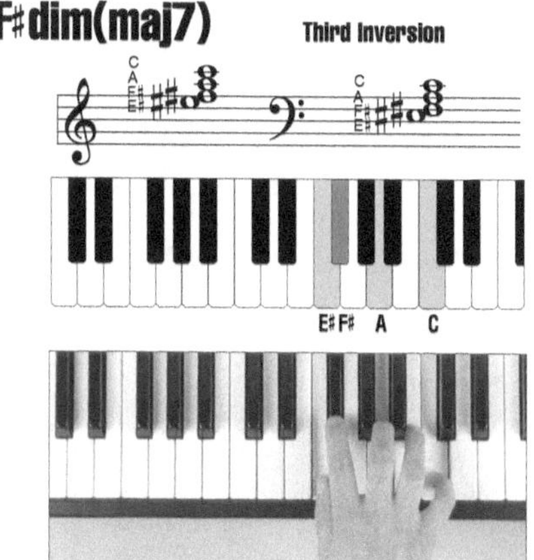

F♯5

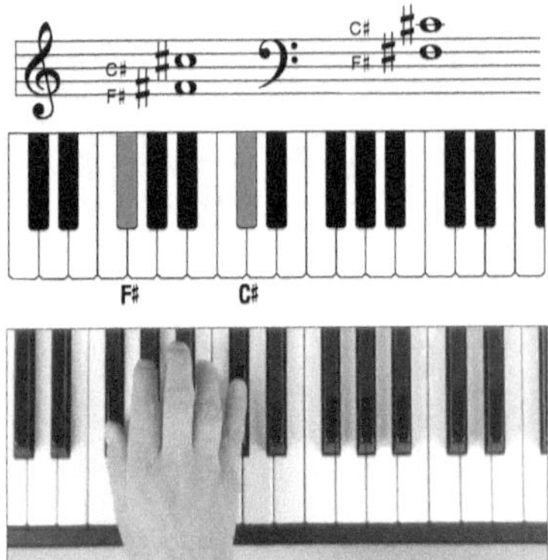

F♯$^6_9$

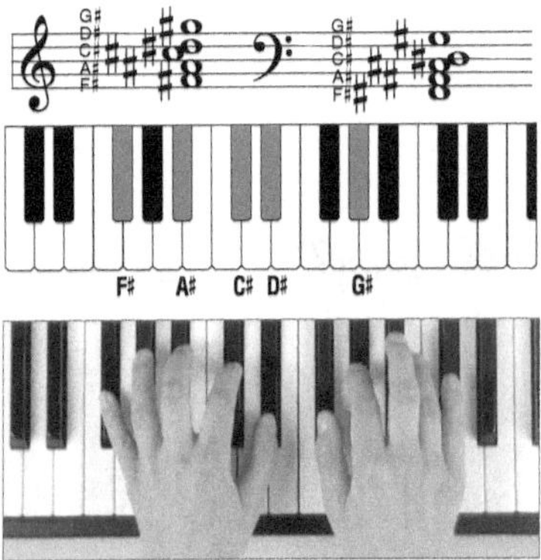

F♯maj$^6_9$

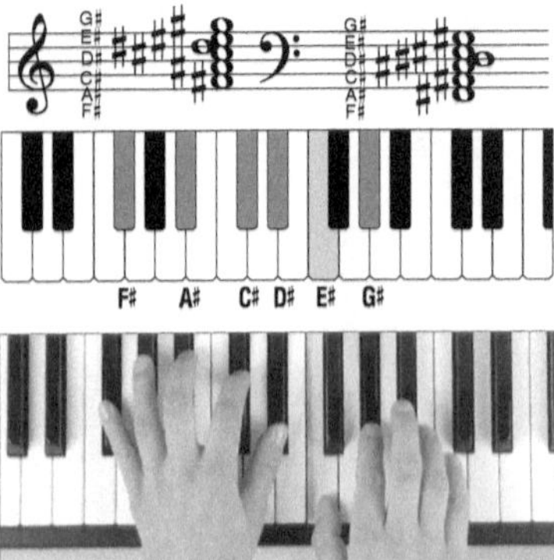

F♯maj7♯11

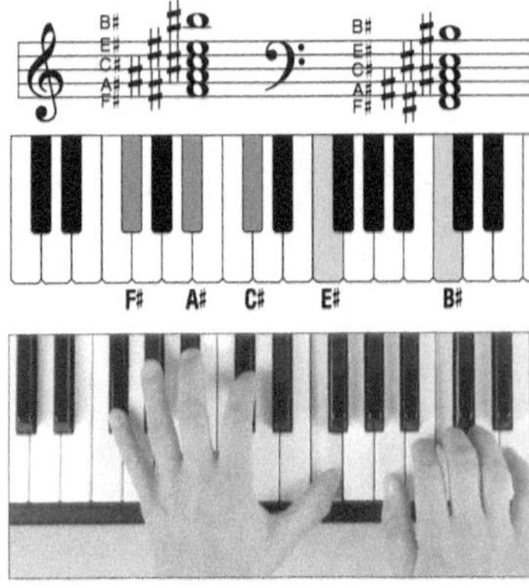

F♯maj9

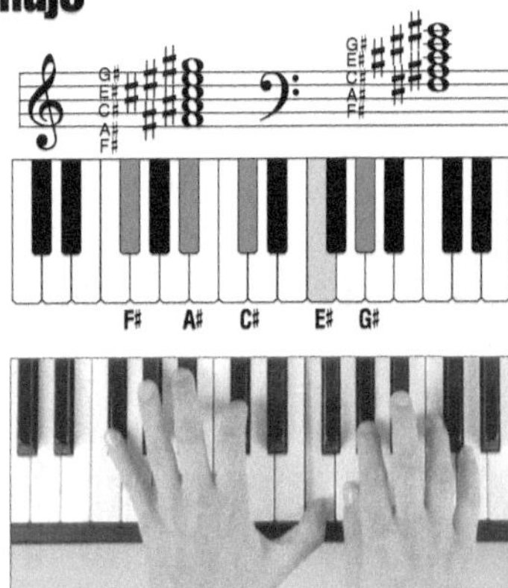

F♯maj9♭5

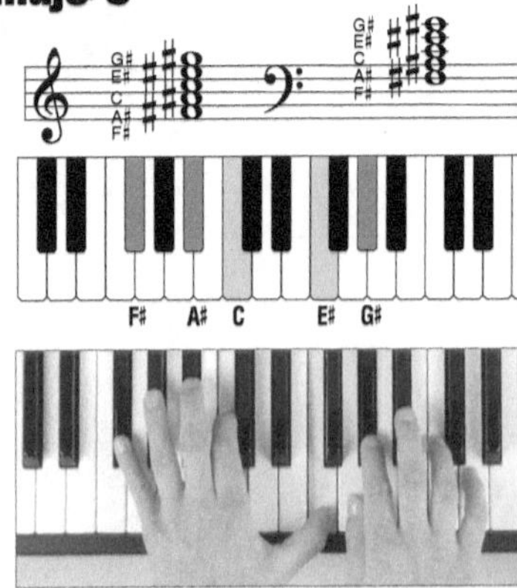

F♯maj9♯5

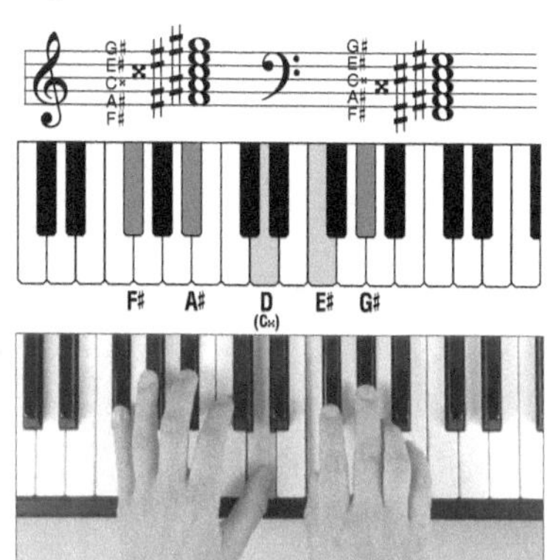

F♯maj9♯11

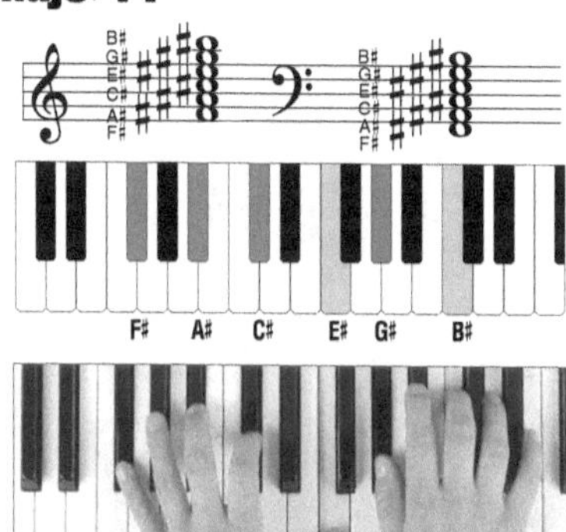

F♯maj13

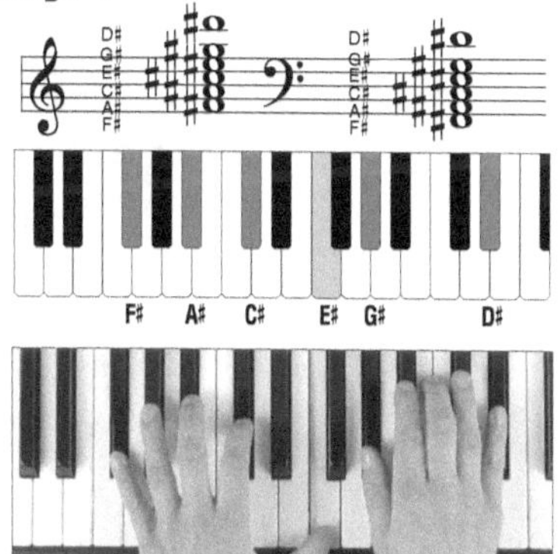

F♯maj13♭5

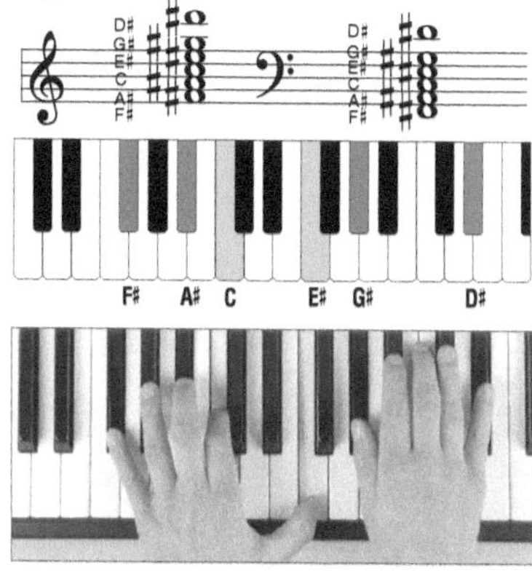

F♯maj13♯11

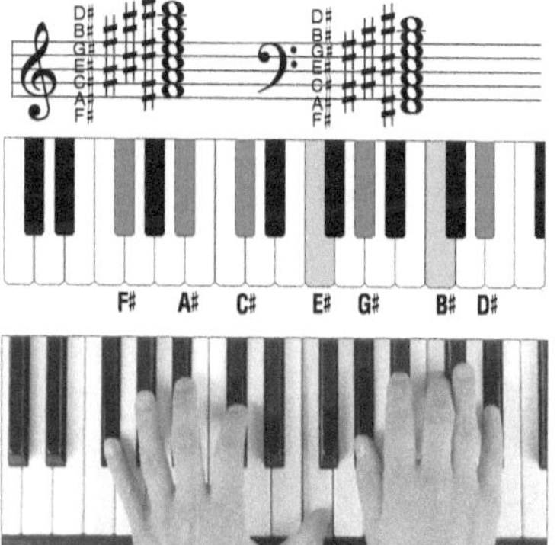

F♯7♭9

F♯7♯9

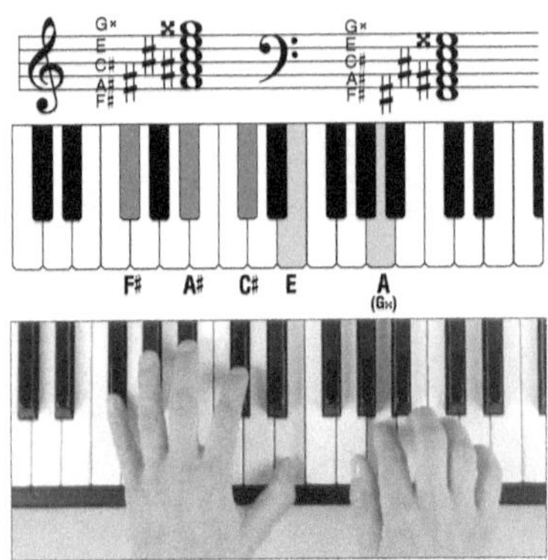

F♯7♯11

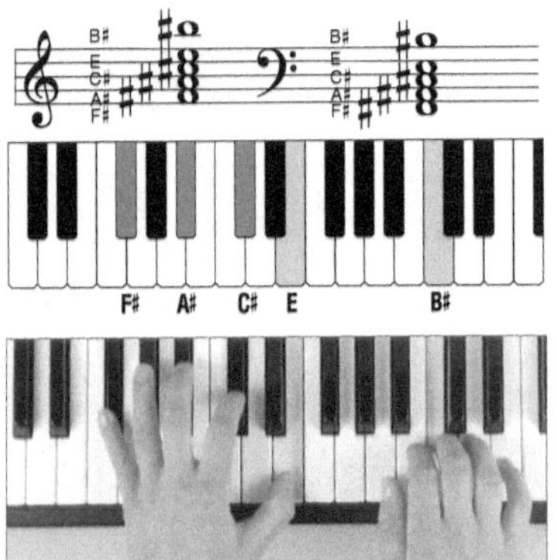

F♯7♭5(♭9)

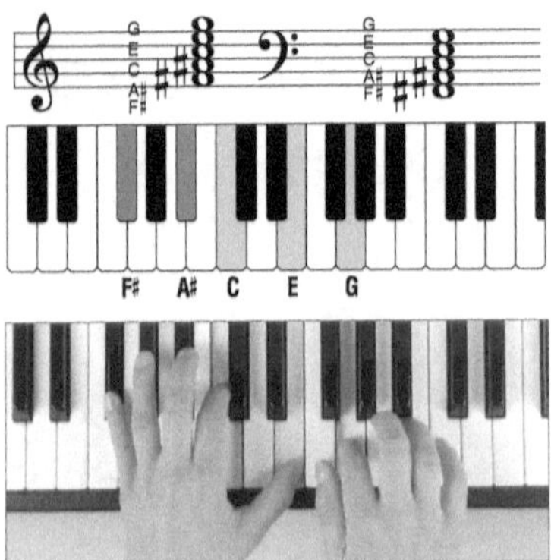

F♯7♭5(♯9)

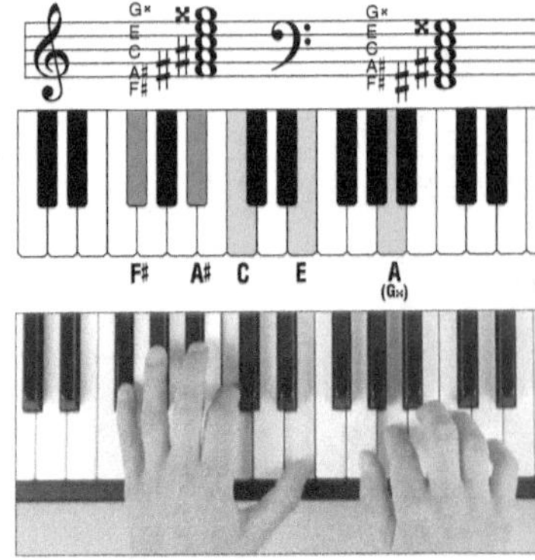

F♯7♯5(♭9)

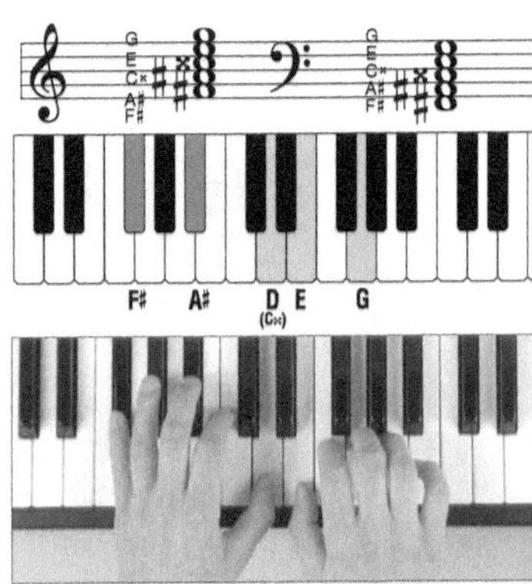

F♯7♯5(♯9)

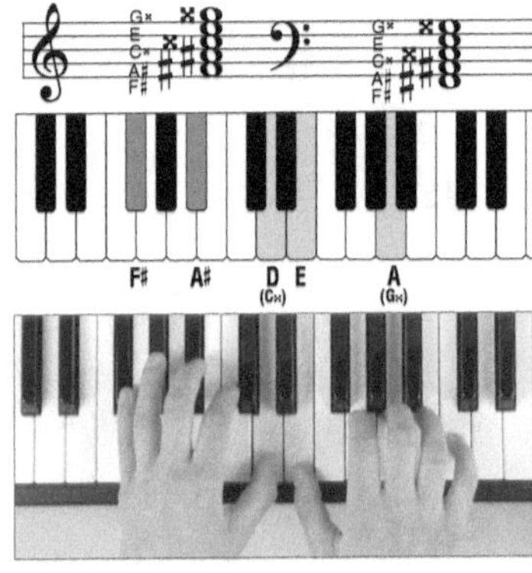

F♯7♭9(♯9)

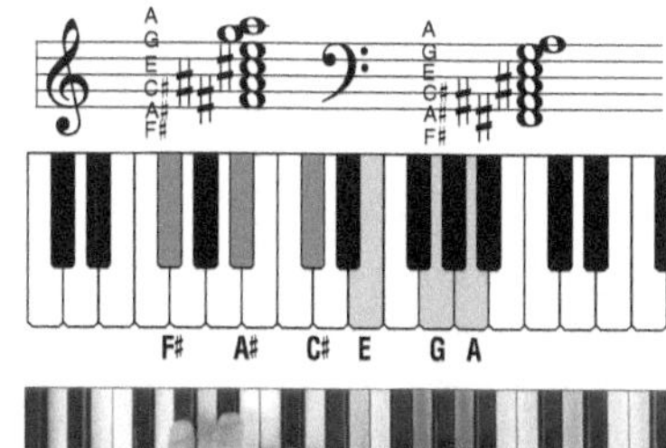

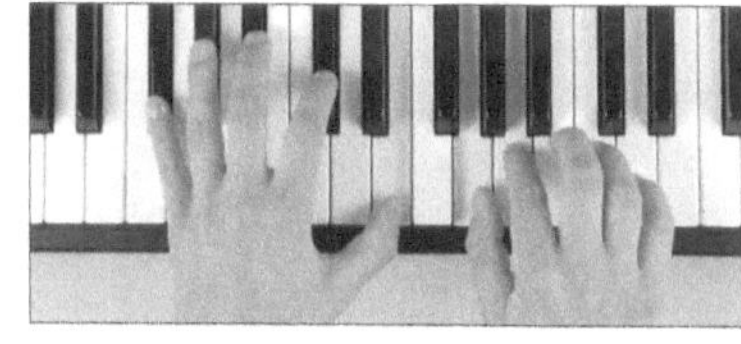

F♯7(add13)

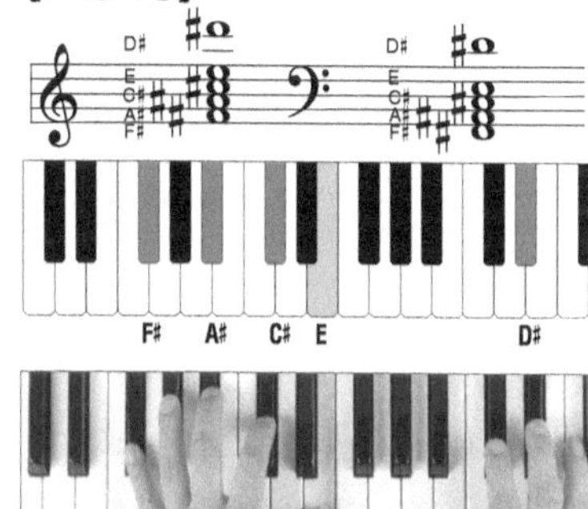

F♯7♭13

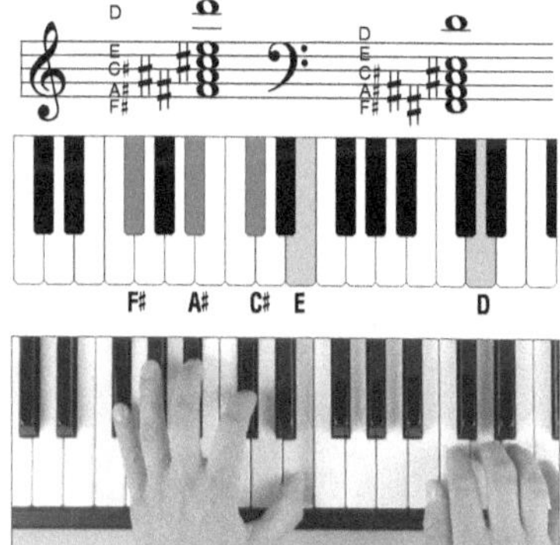

F♯7♭9(♯11)

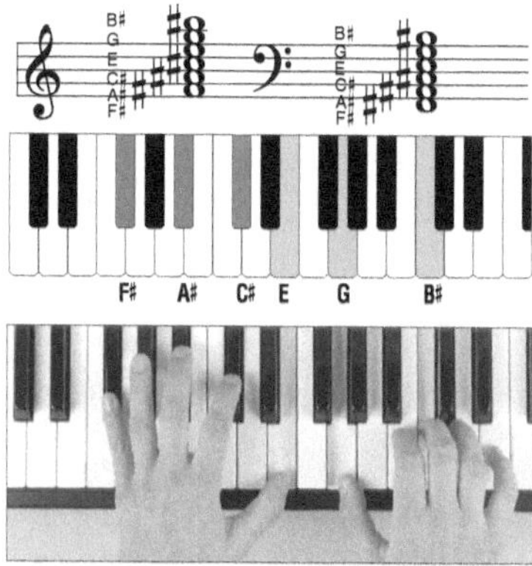

F♯7♯9(♯11)

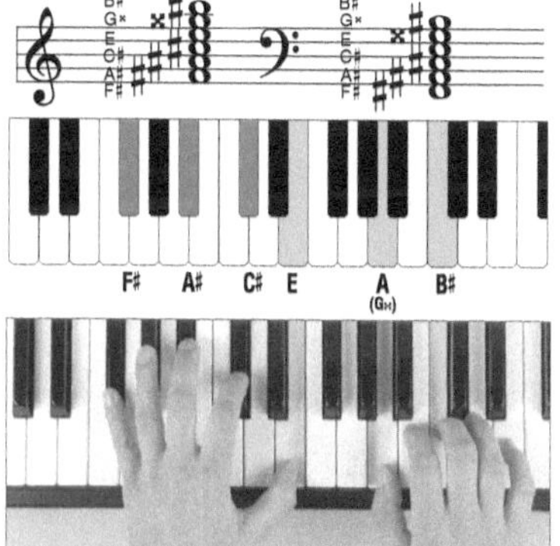

F♯7♭9(♭13)

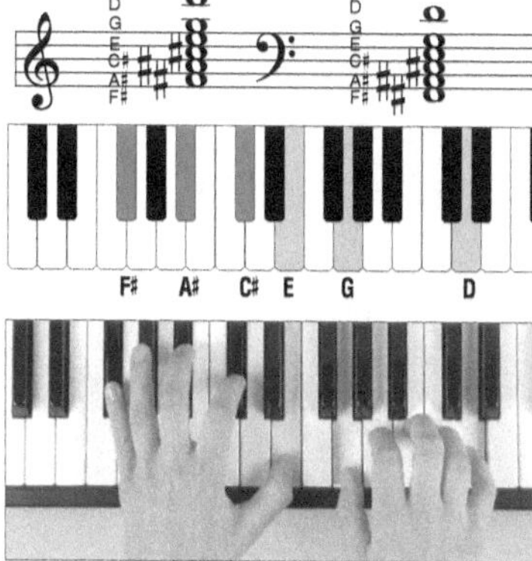

F♯7♯9(♭13)

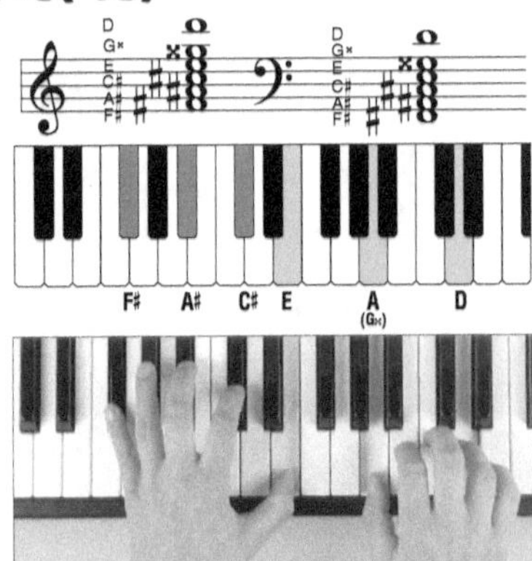

F♯7♯11(♭13)

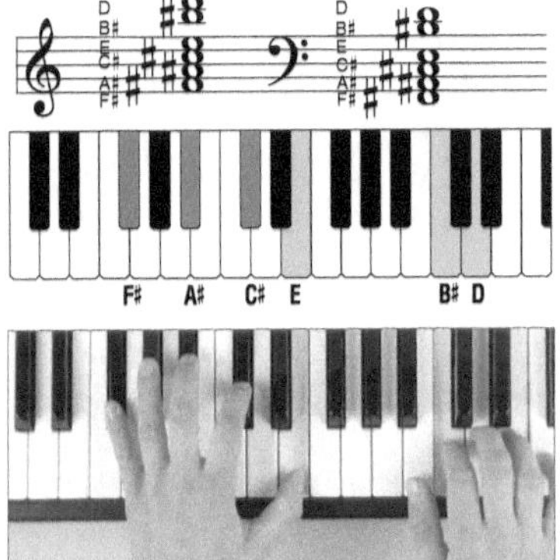

F♯7♭9(♯9, ♯11)

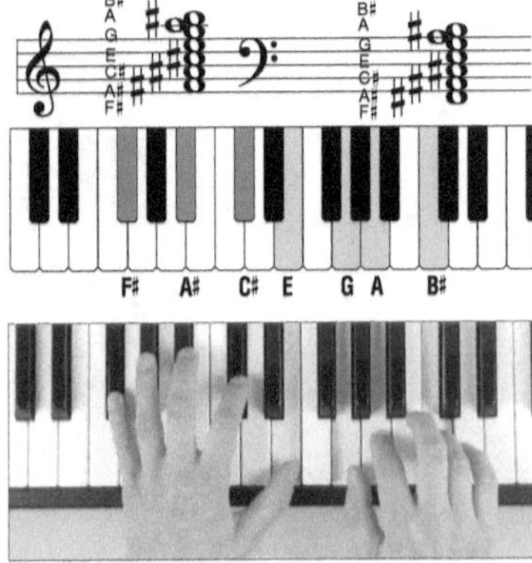

F♯9

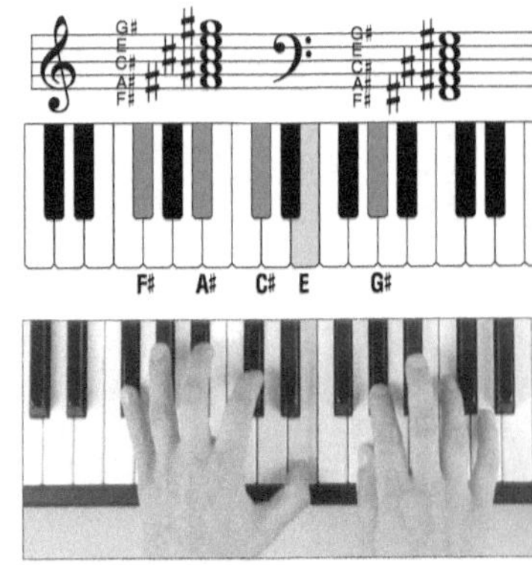

F♯9(♭5)

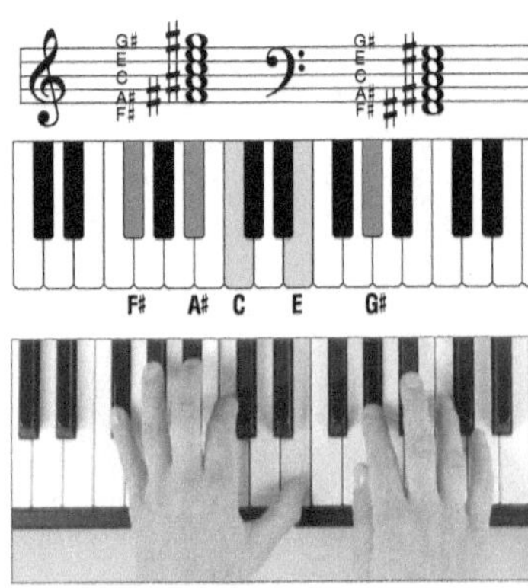

F♯9♯5

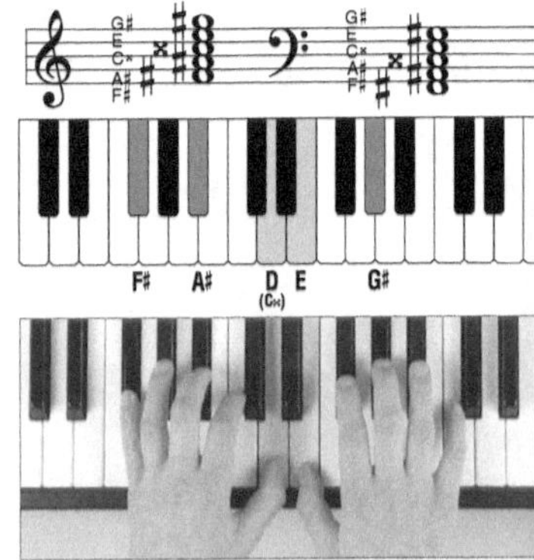

#9#11

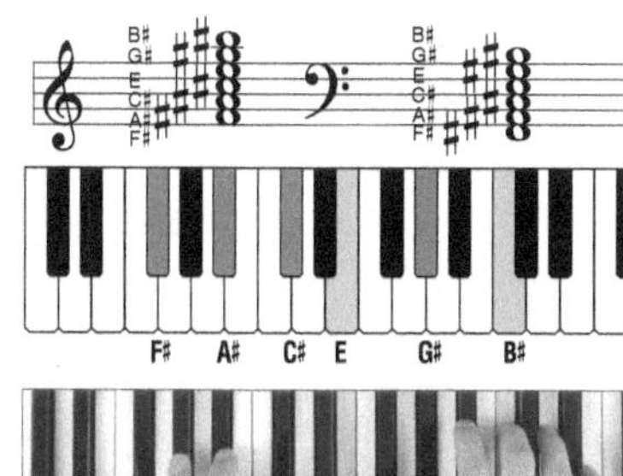

F#11, #9(sus4)

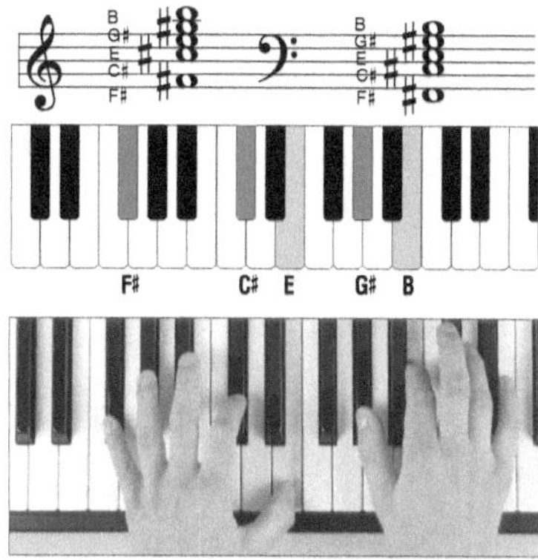

#9♭13

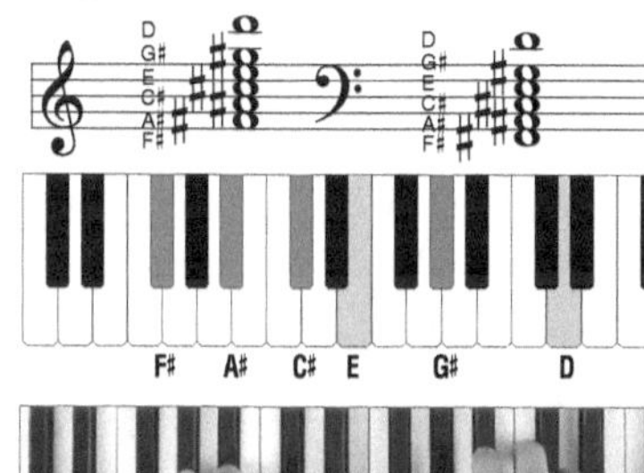

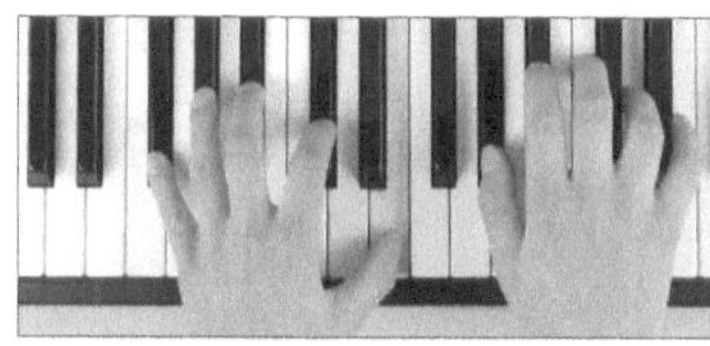

F#13

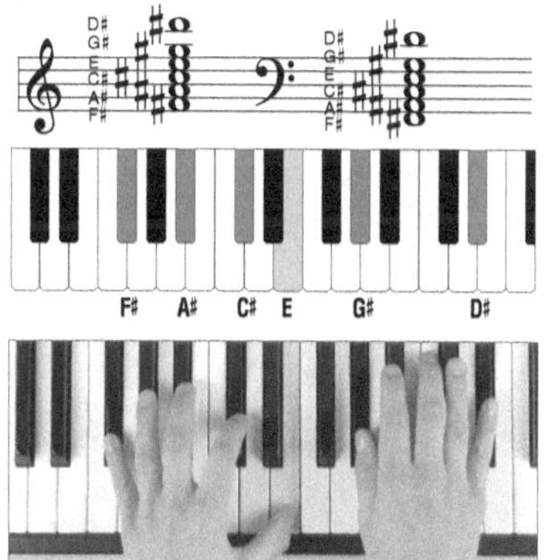

#9#11(♭13)

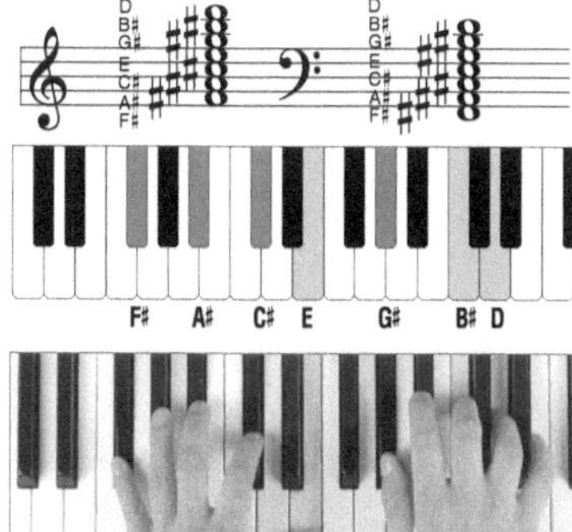

F#13♭5

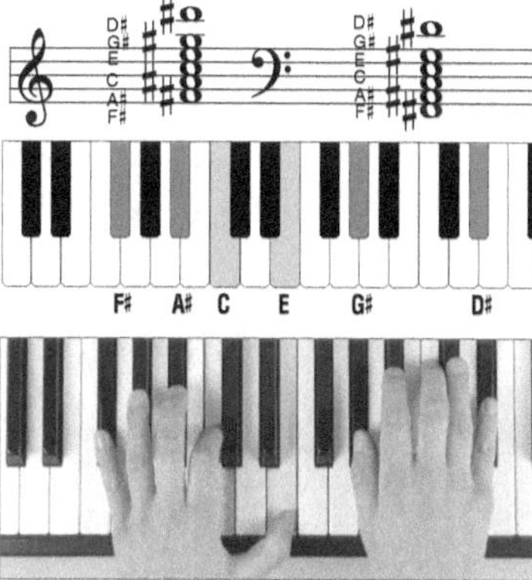

F♯13♭9

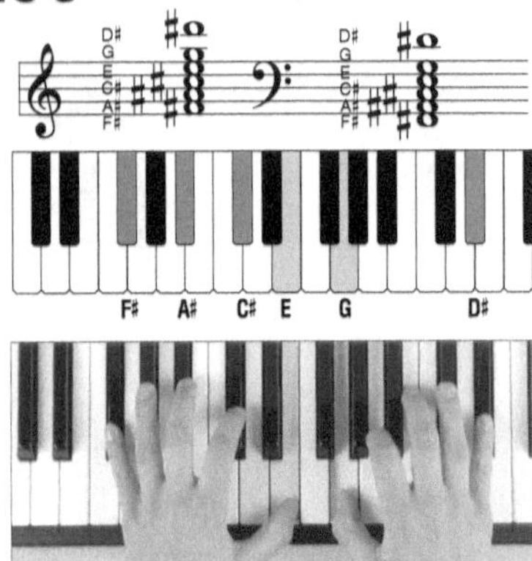

F♯13♯9

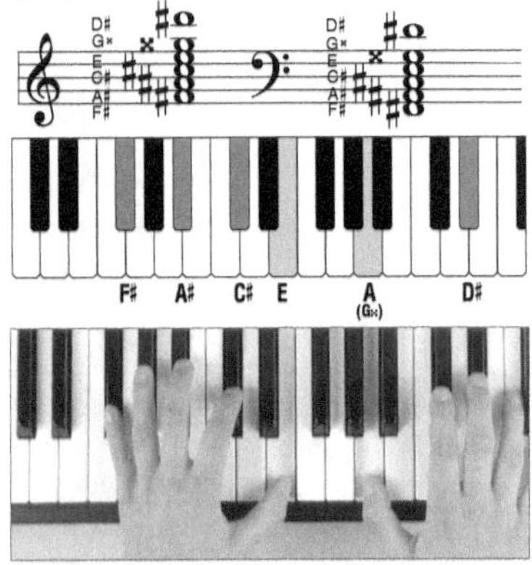

F♯13♯11

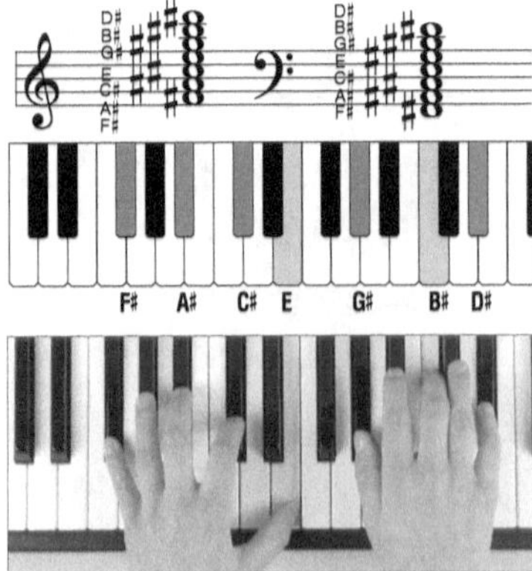

F♯13(sus4)

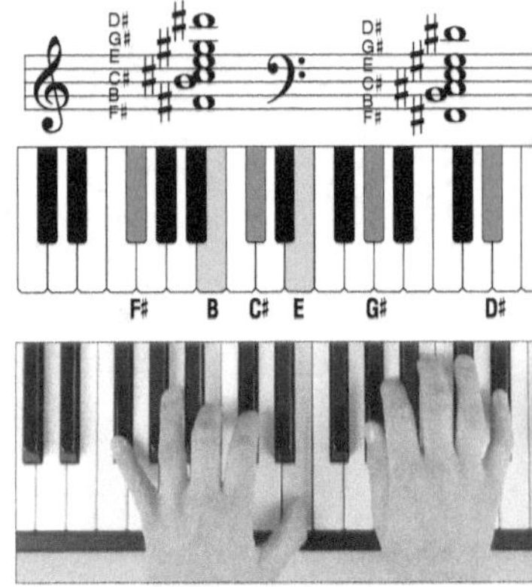

F♯m(♯5)

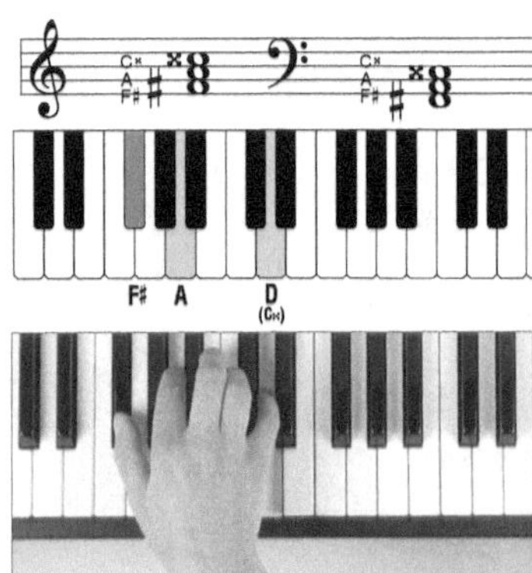

F♯m$^{6}_{9}$

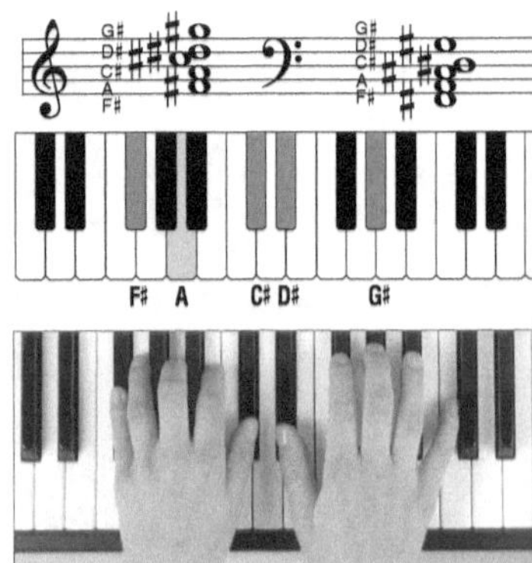

F#m7(add4)

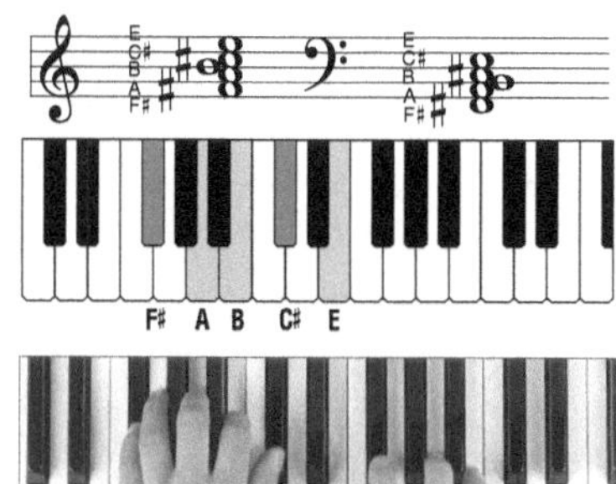

F#m9

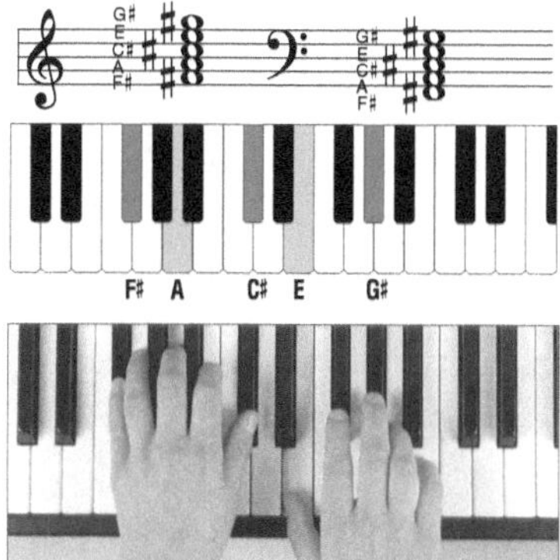

F#m7(add11)

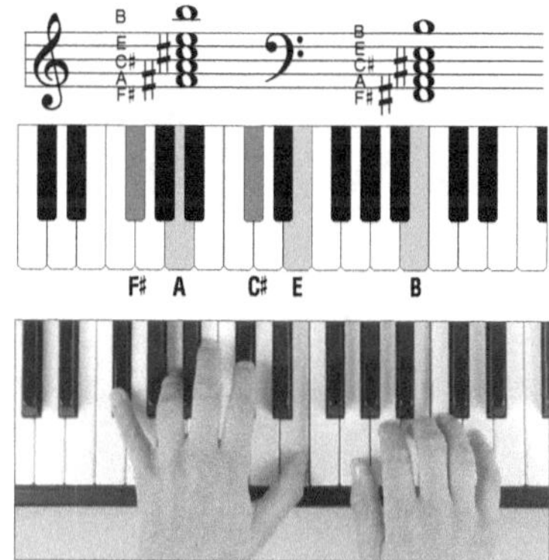

F#m9(maj7)

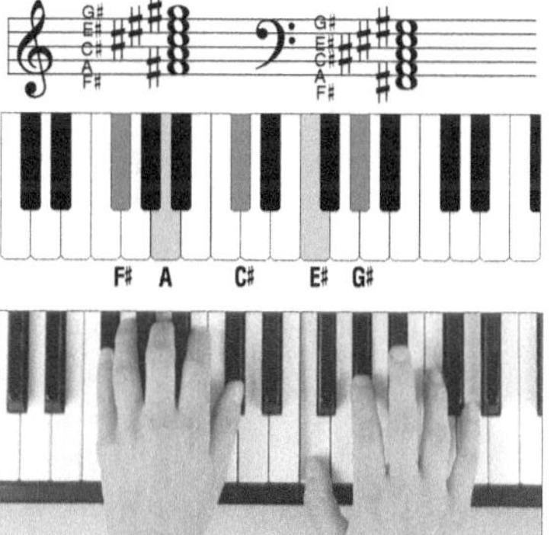

F#m7♭5(♭9)

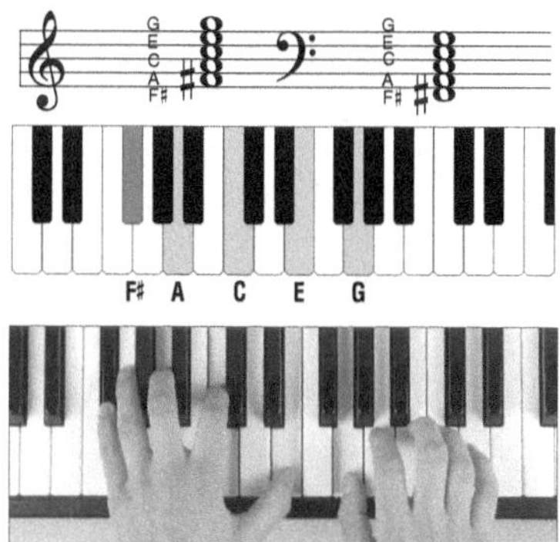

F#m9♭5

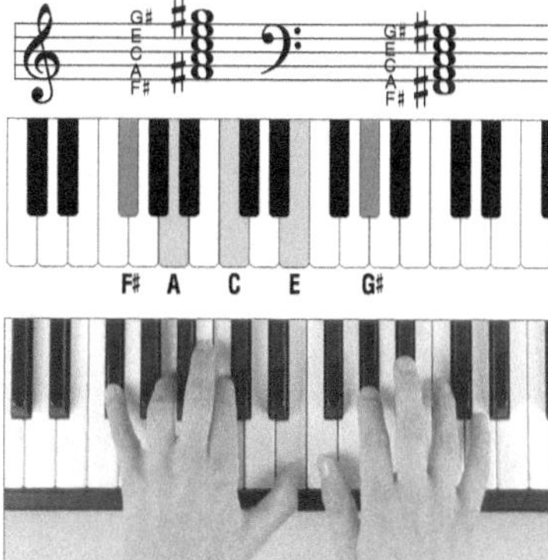

F#m11

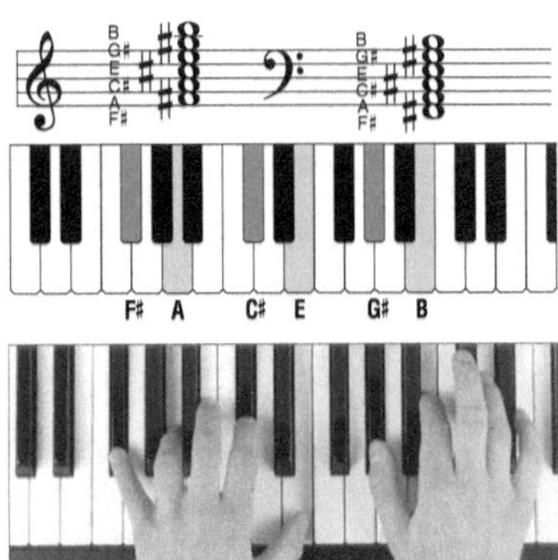

F#m13

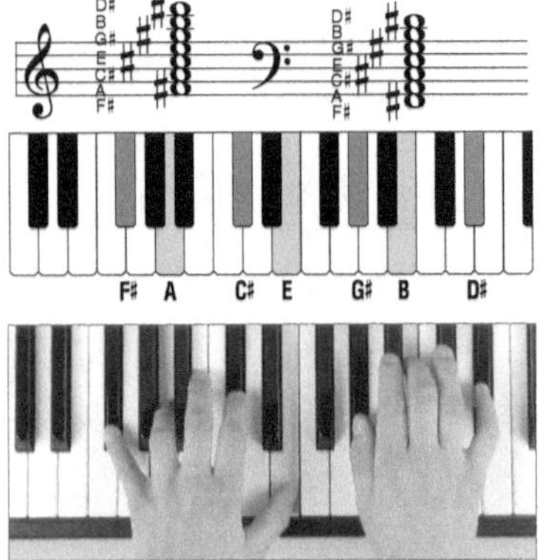

F#dim7(add9)

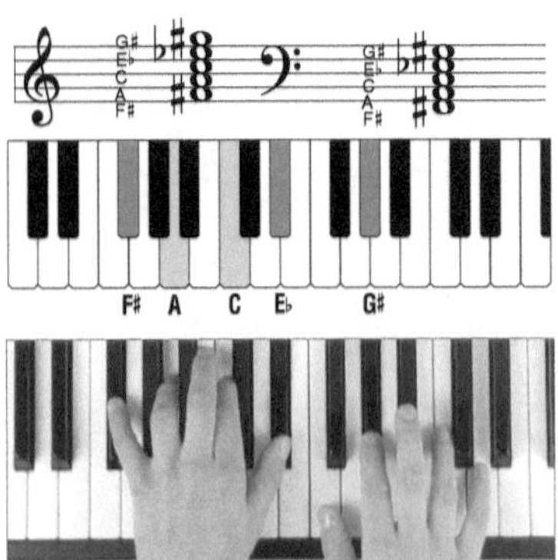

F#m11♭5

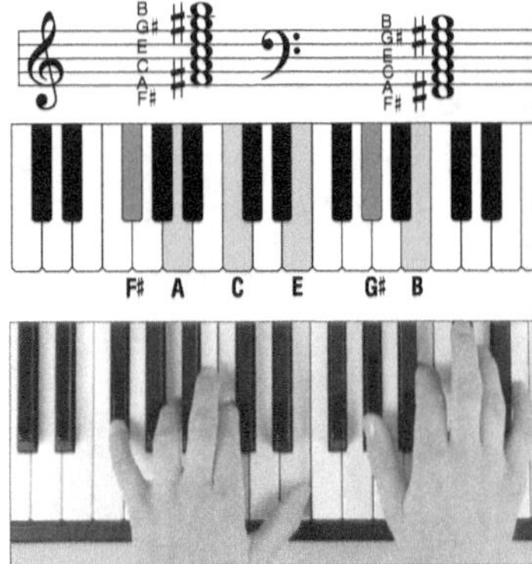

F#m11(maj7)

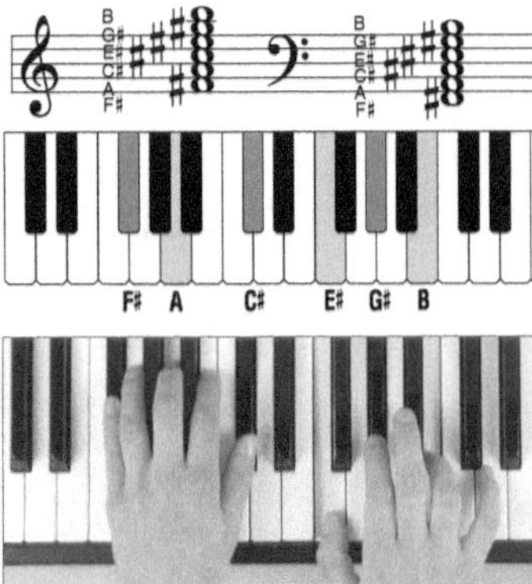

F#7alt.

G Root Position

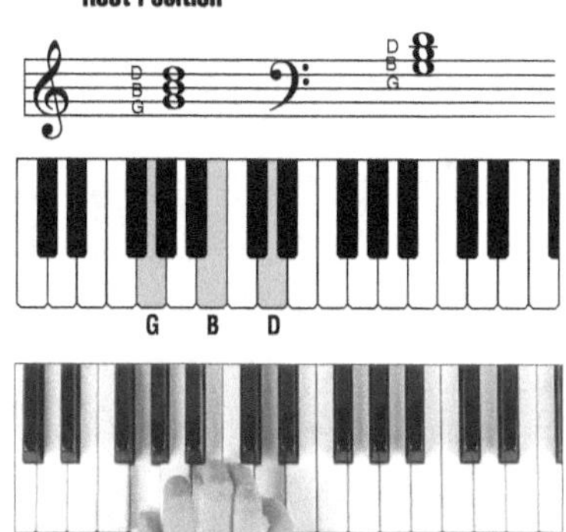

G First Inversion

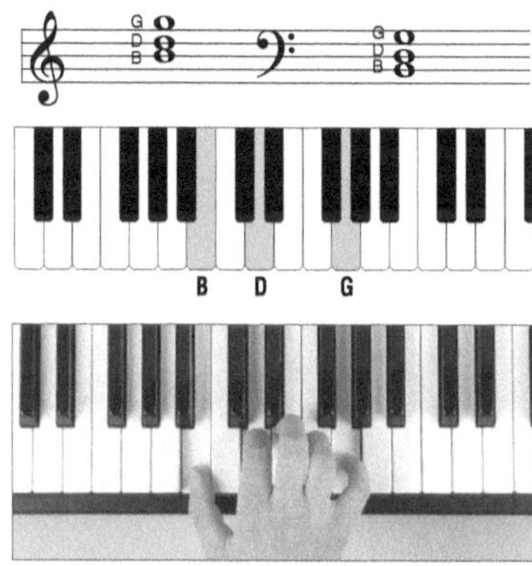

G Second Inversion

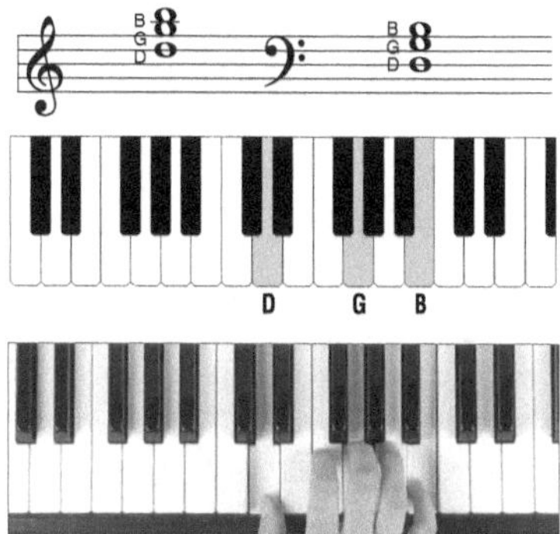

Gm Root Position

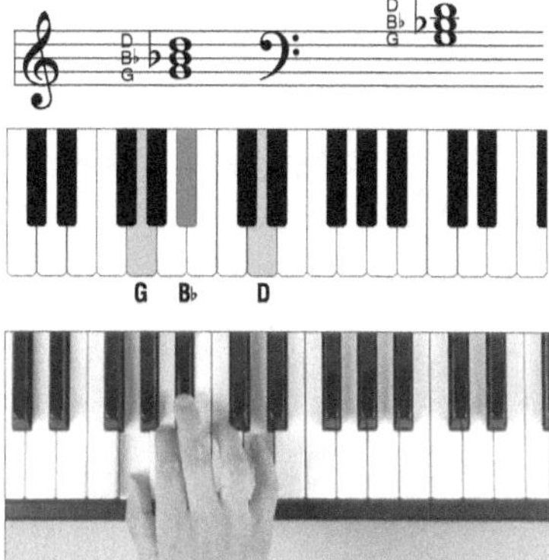

Gm First Inversion

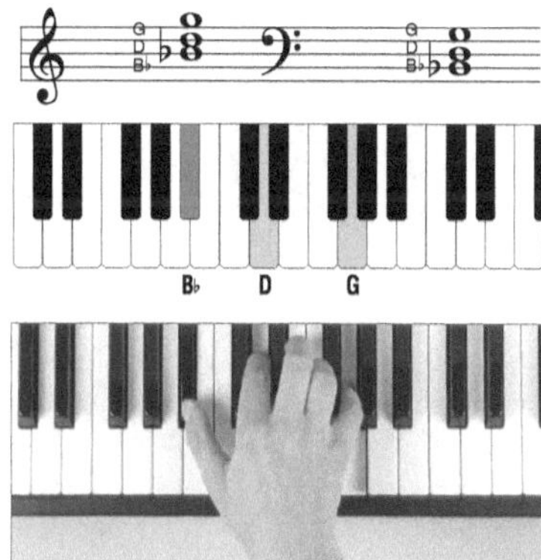

Gm Second Inversion

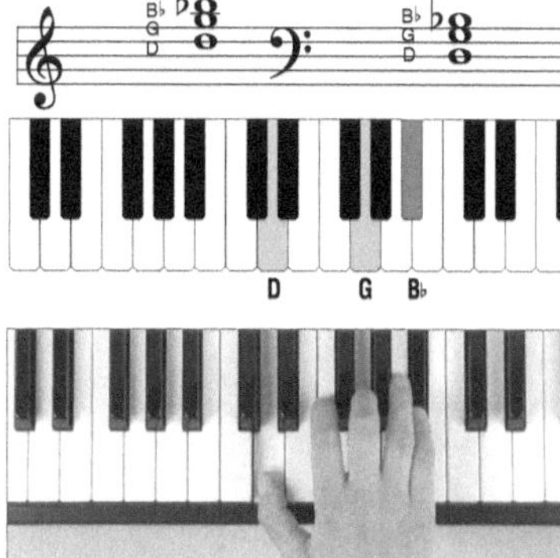

G+ Root Position

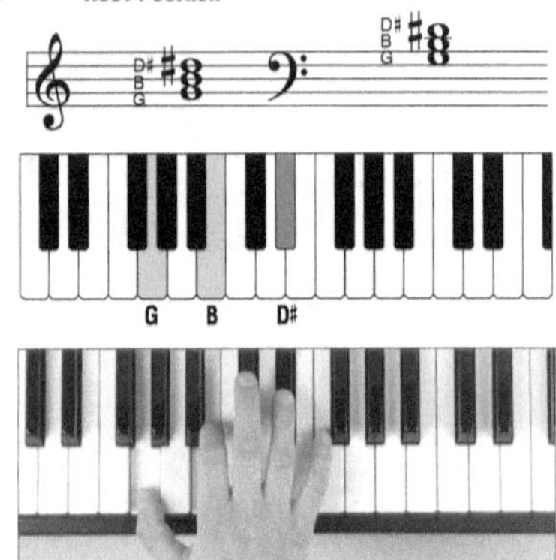

G+ First Inversion

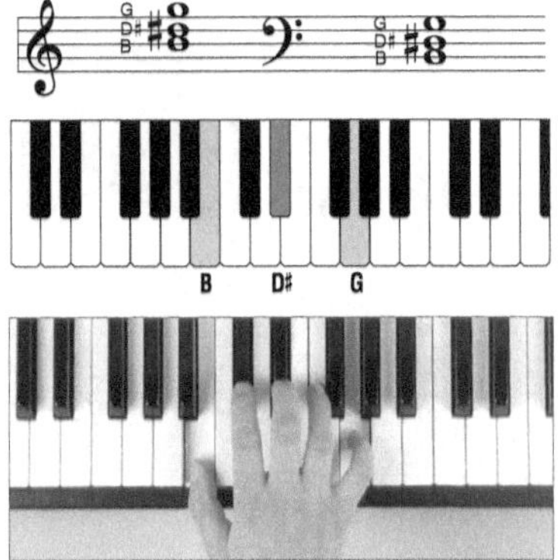

G+ Second Inversion

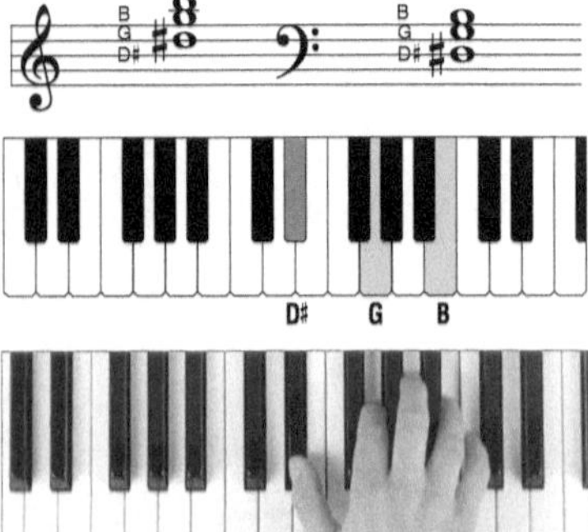

Gdim Root Position

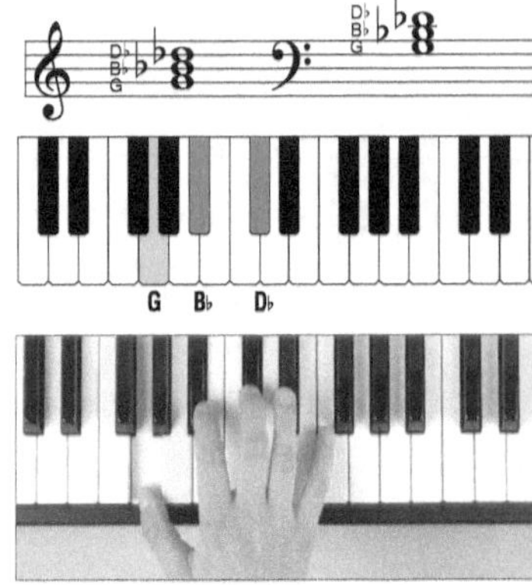

Gdim First Inversion

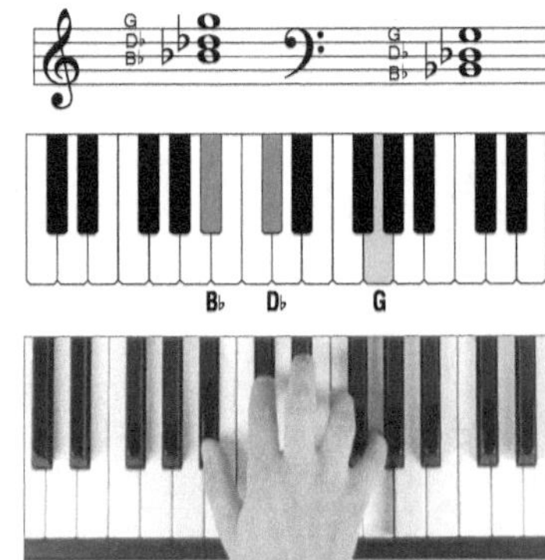

Gdim Second Inversion

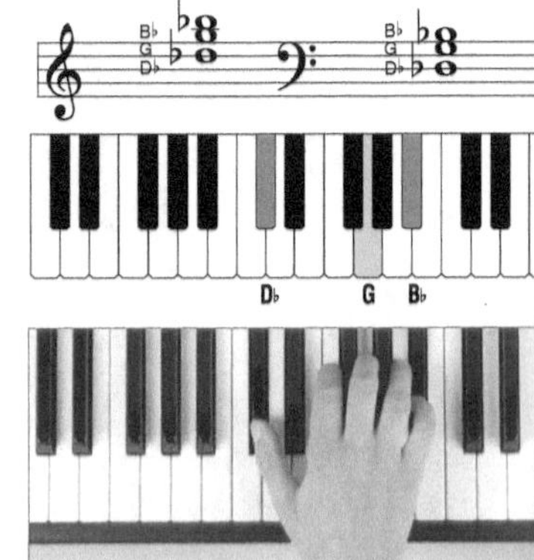

Gsus Root Position

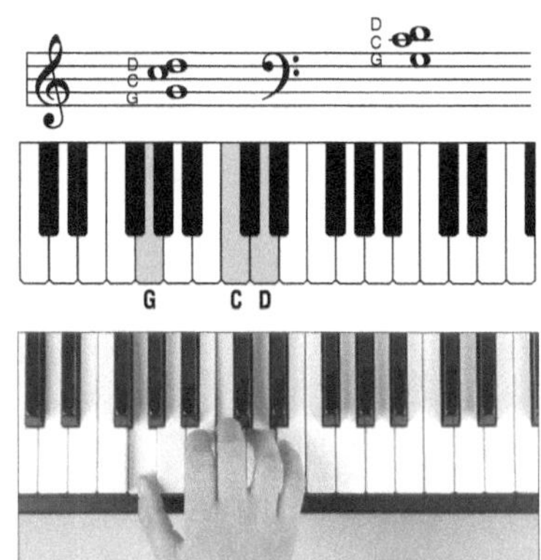

Gsus First Inversion

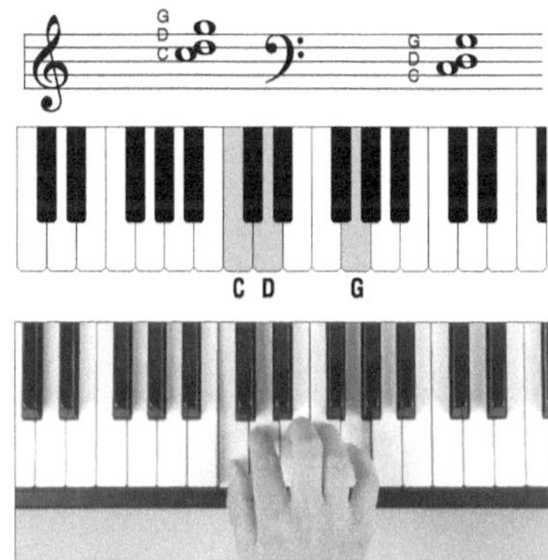

Gsus Second Inversion

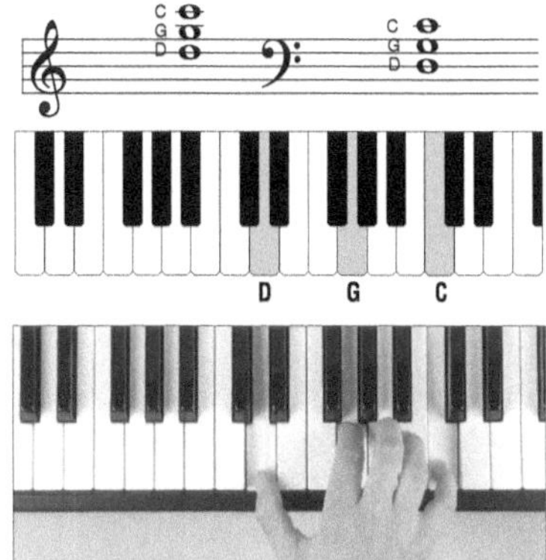

G(♭5) Root Position

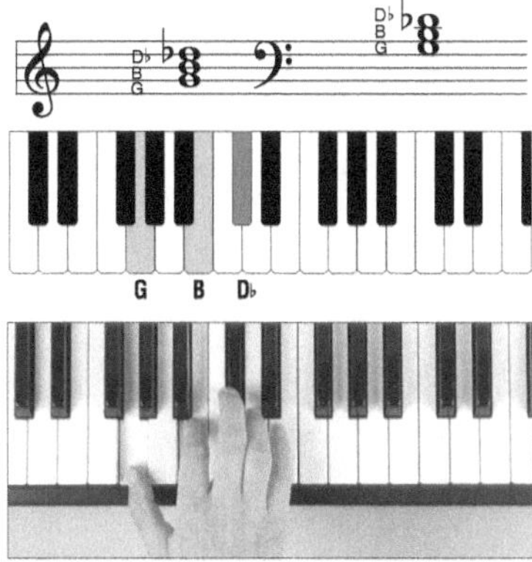

G(♭5) First Inversion

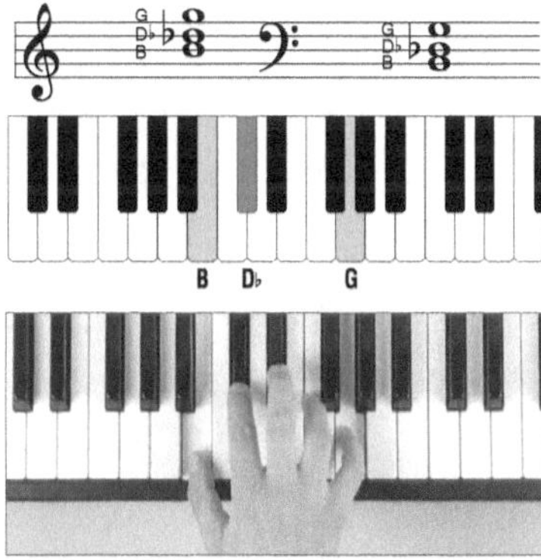

G(♭5) Second Inversion

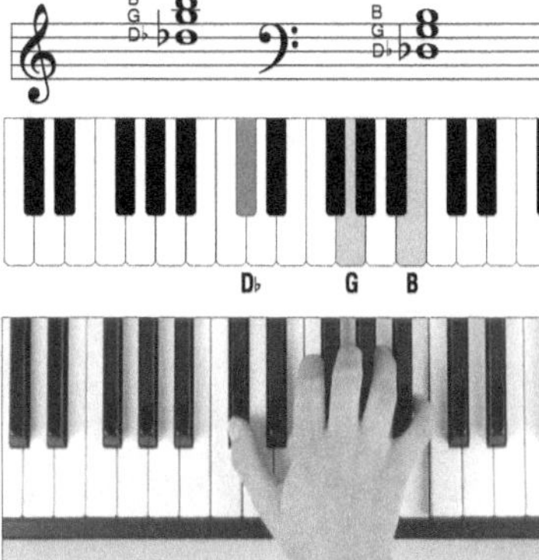

Gsus2 Root Position

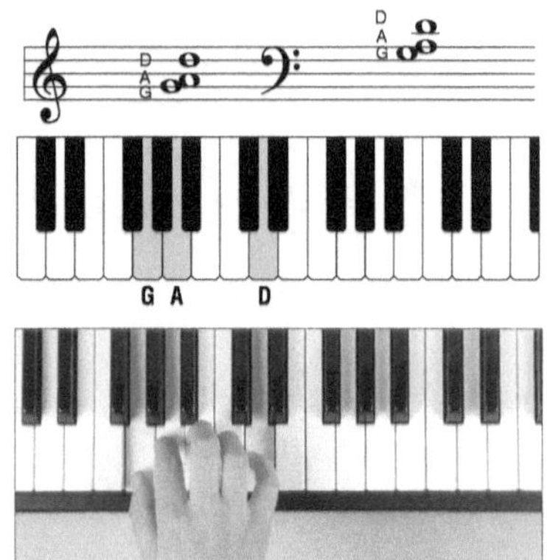

Gsus2 First Inversion

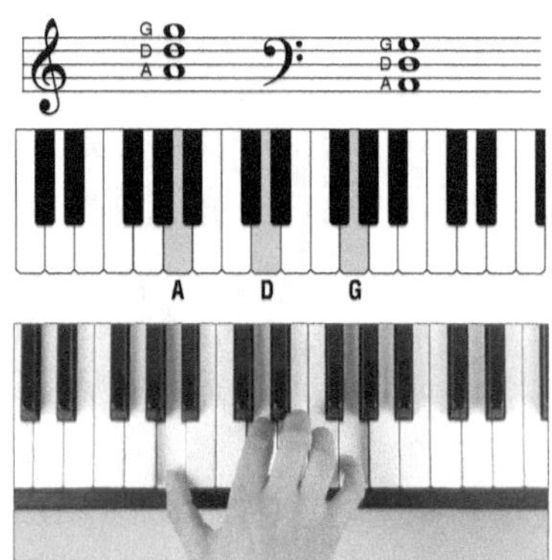

Gsus2 Second Inversion

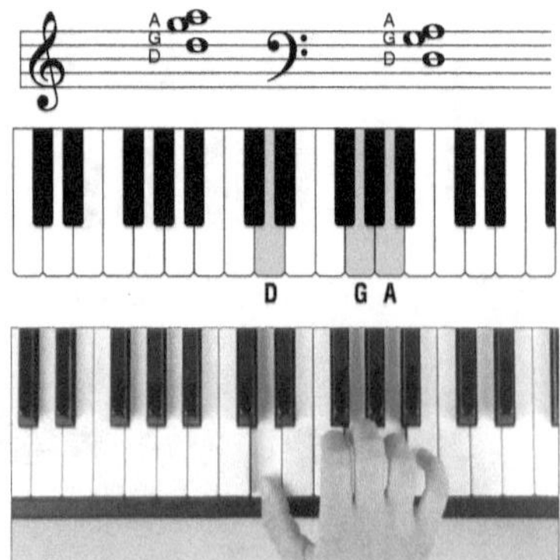

G6 Root Position

G6 First Inversion

G6 Second Inversion

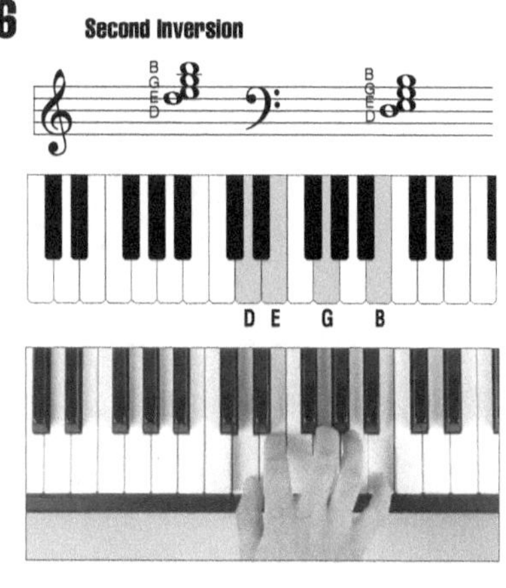

G6 Third Inversion

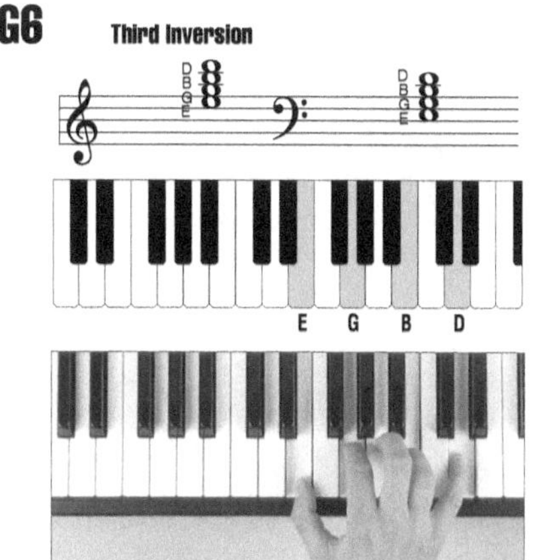

G(add2), G(add9) Root Position

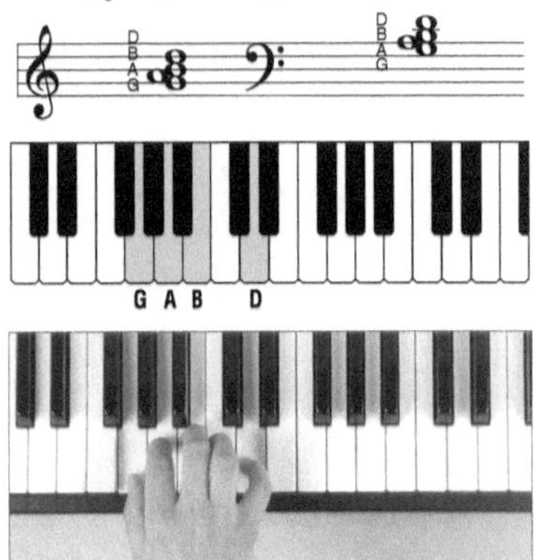

G(add2), G(add9) First Inversion

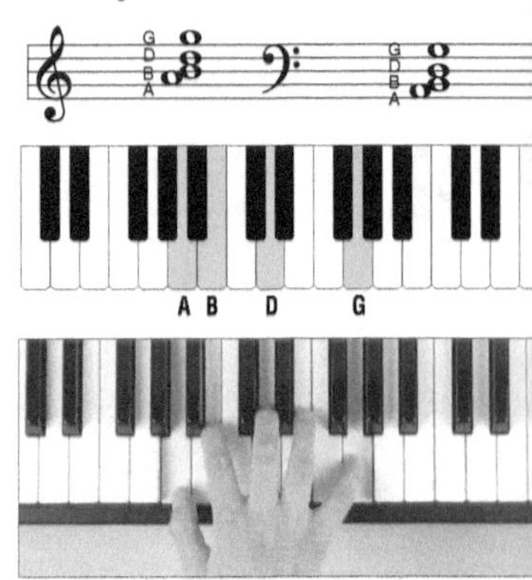

G(add2), G(add9) Second Inversion

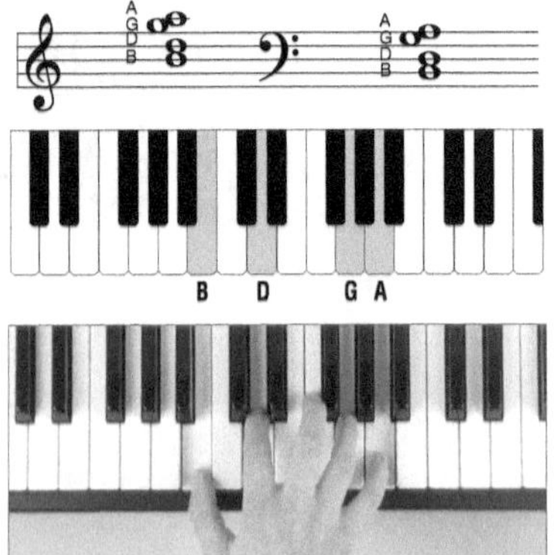

G(add2), G(add9) Third Inversion

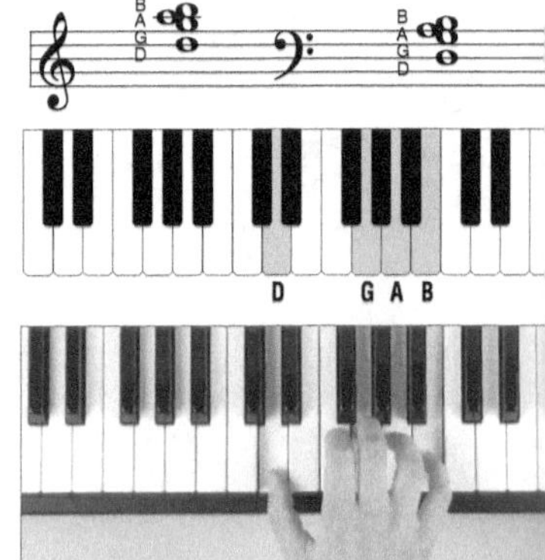

Gmaj7 Root Position

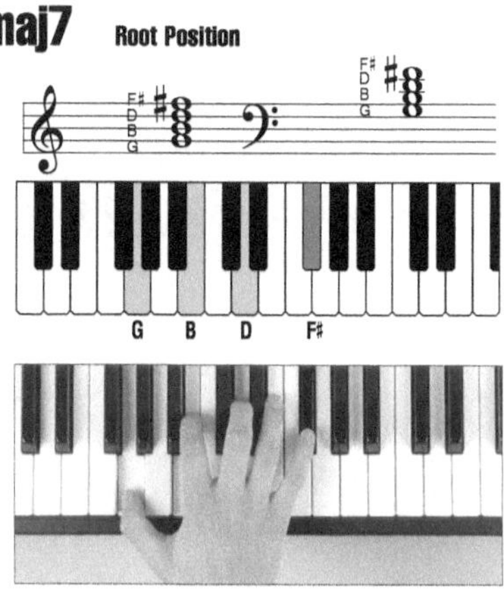

Gmaj7 First Inversion

Gmaj7 Second Inversion

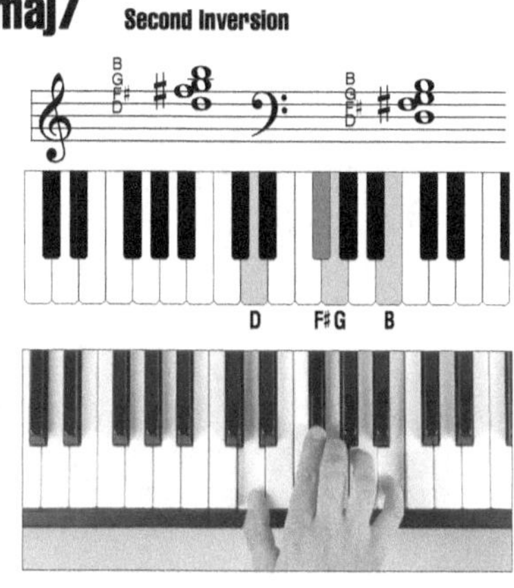

Gmaj7 Third Inversion

Gmaj7♭5 Root Position

Gmaj7♭5 First Inversion

Gmaj7♭5 Second Inversion

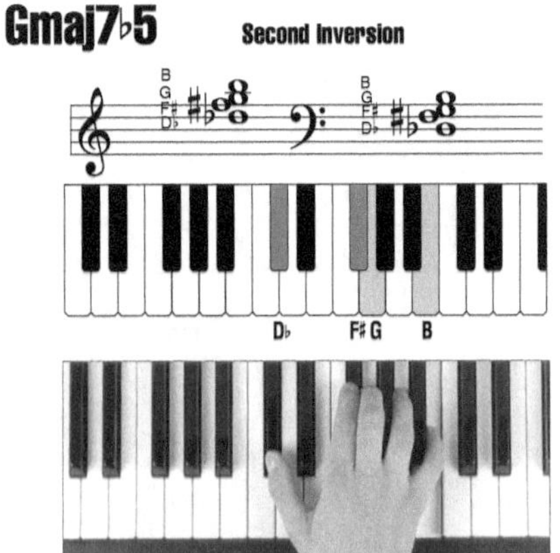

Gmaj7♭5 Third Inversion

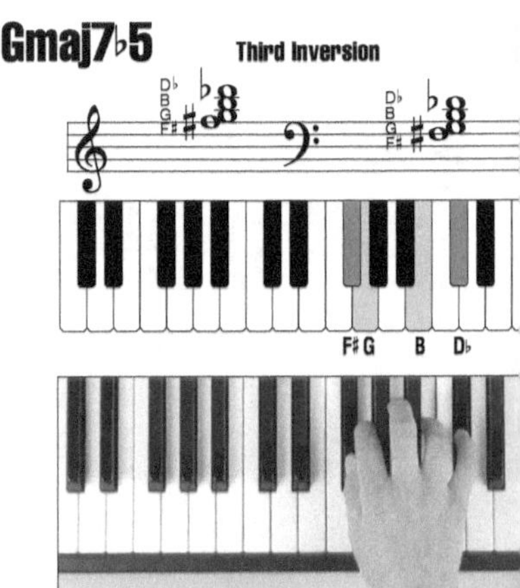

Gmaj7♯5 Root Position

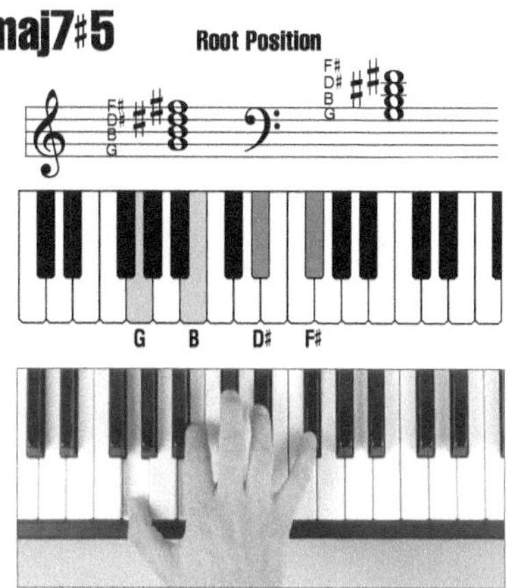

Gmaj7♯5 First Inversion

Gmaj7♯5 Second Inversion

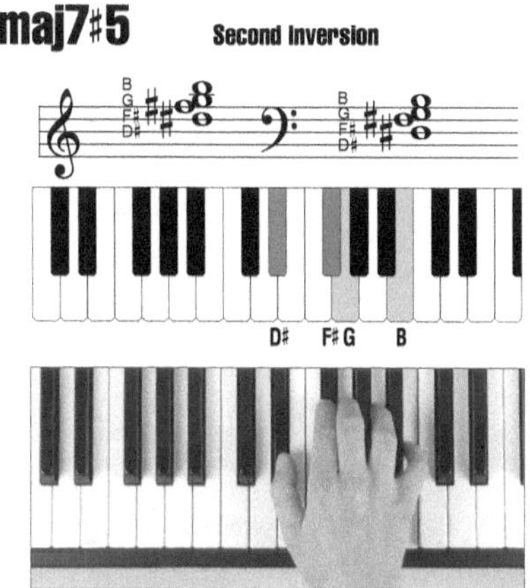

Gmaj7♯5 Third Inversion

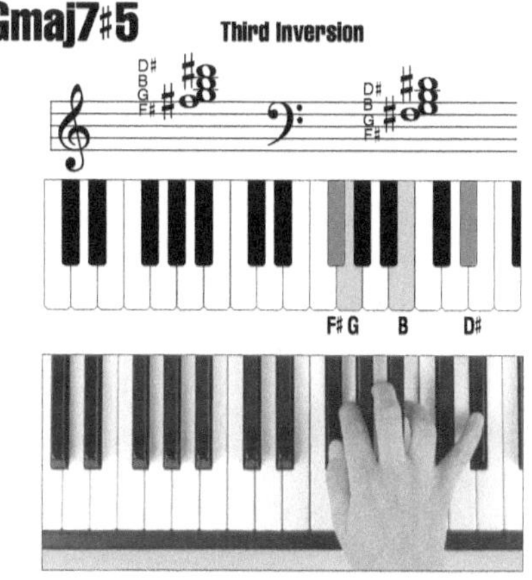

G7 Root Position

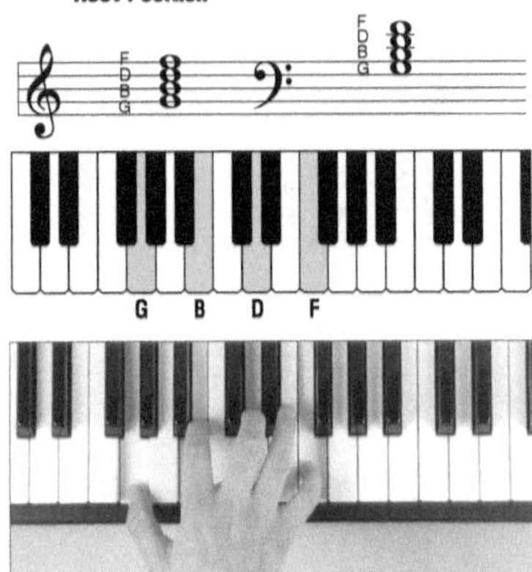

G7 First Inversion

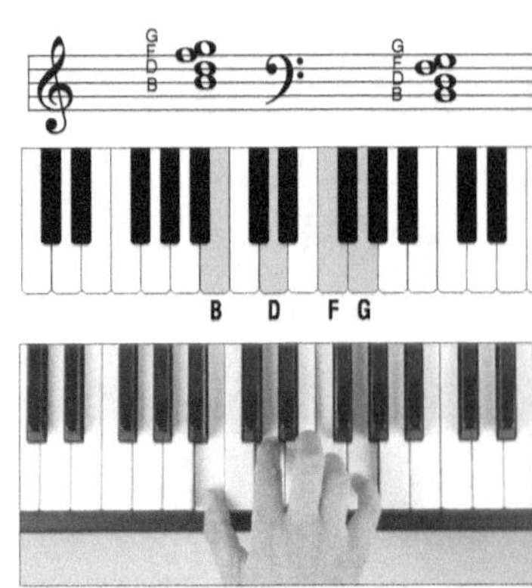

G7 Second Inversion

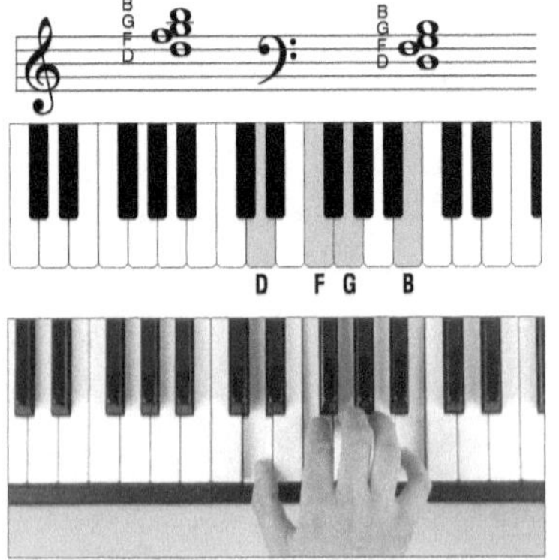

G7 Third Inversion

G7♭5 Root Position

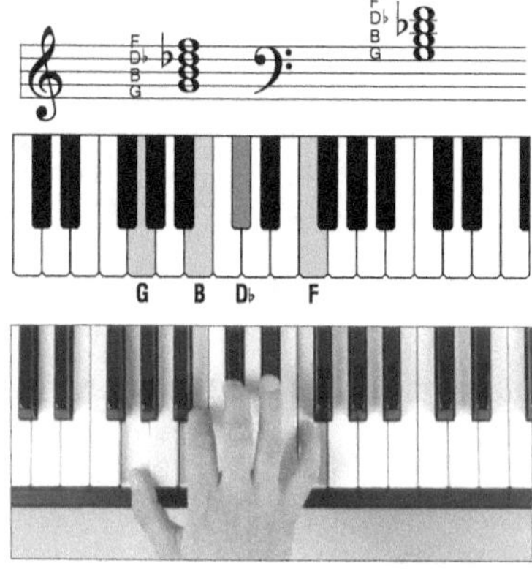

G7♭5 First Inversion

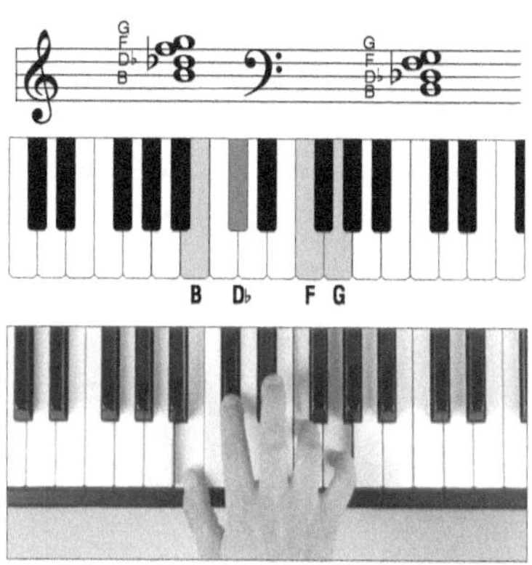

G7♭5 Second Inversion

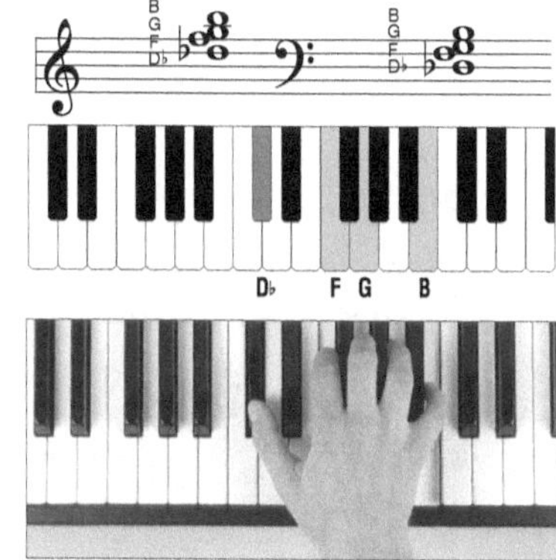

G7♭5 Third Inversion

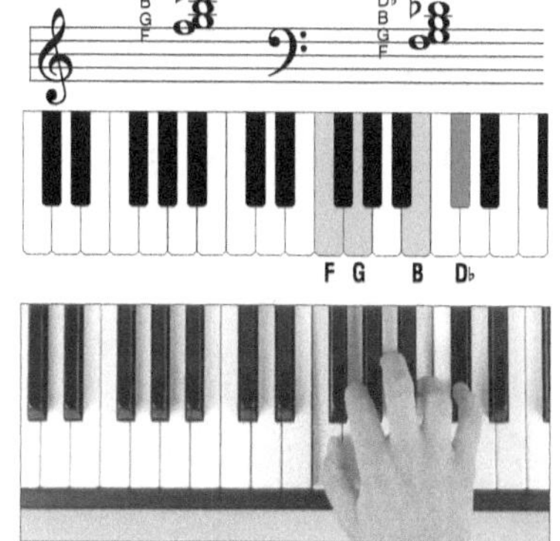

G7♯5 Root Position

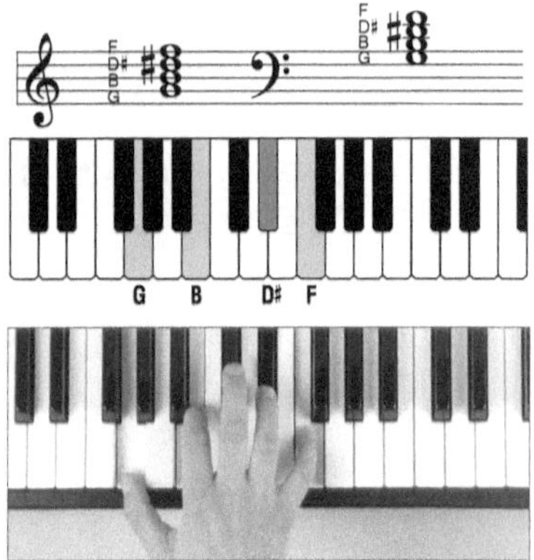

G7♯5 First Inversion

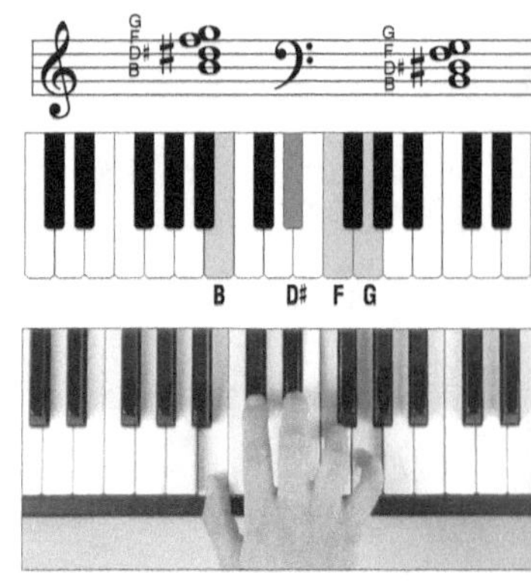

G7♯5 Second Inversion

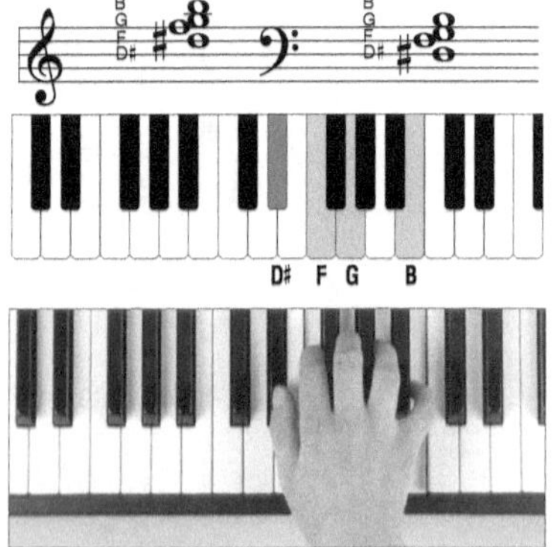

G7♯5 Third Inversion

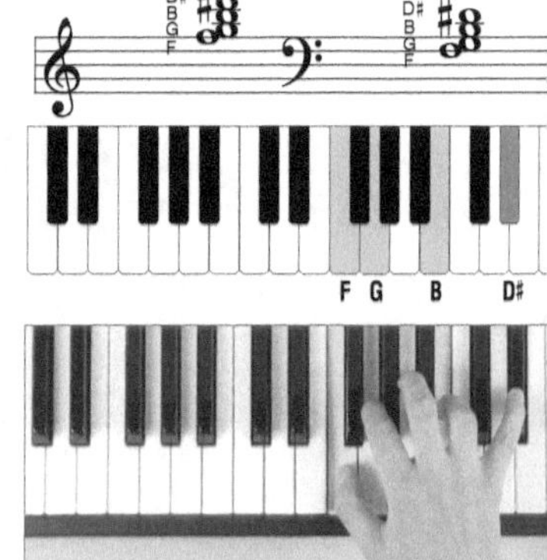

G7sus Root Position

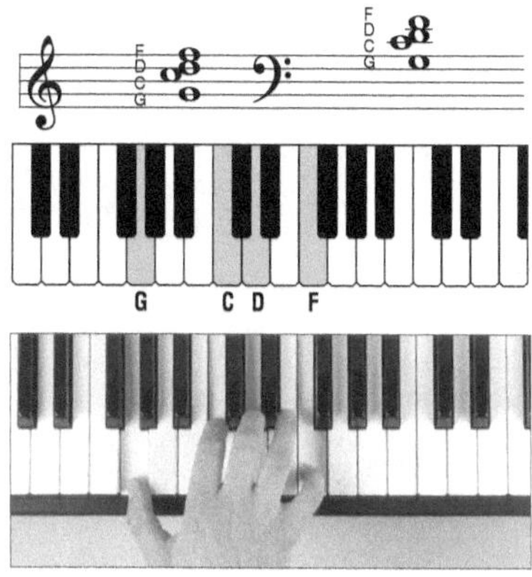

G7sus First Inversion

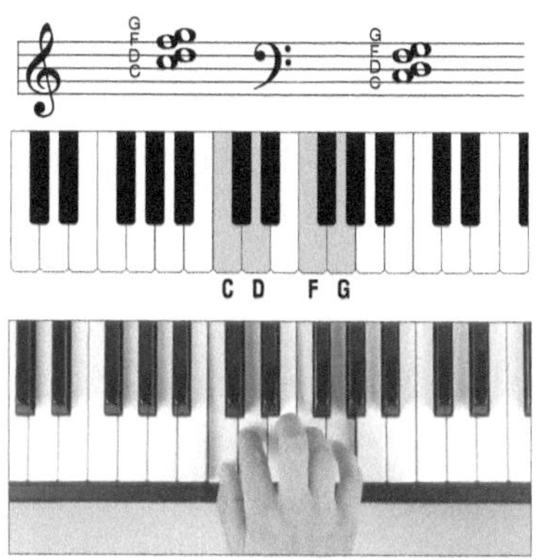

G7sus Second Inversion

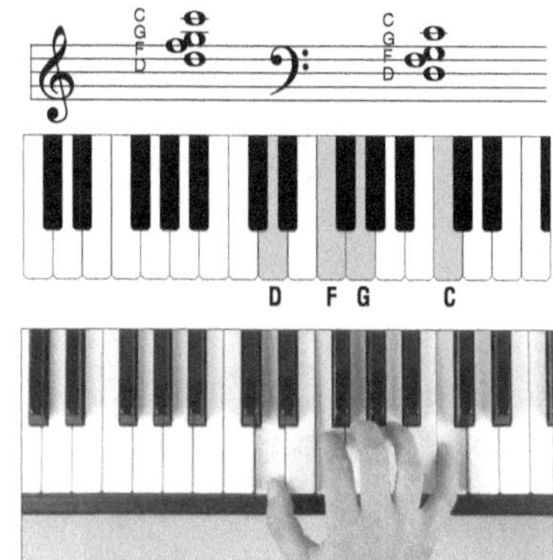

G7sus Third Inversion

Gm(add2), Gm(add9) Root Position

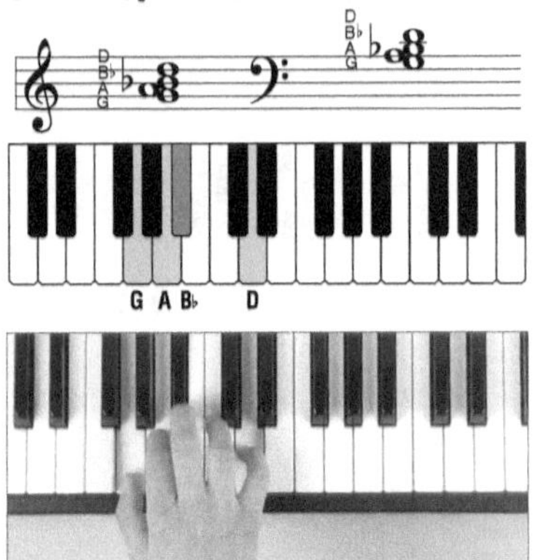

Gm(add2), Gm(add9) First Invers

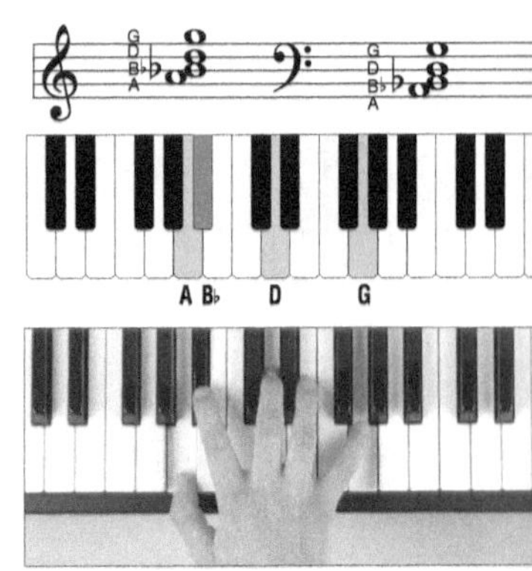

Gm(add2), Gm(add9) Second Inversion

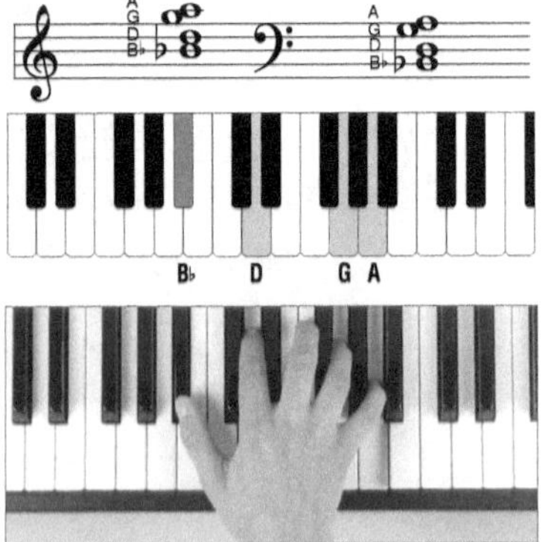

Gm(add2), Gm(add9) Third Invers

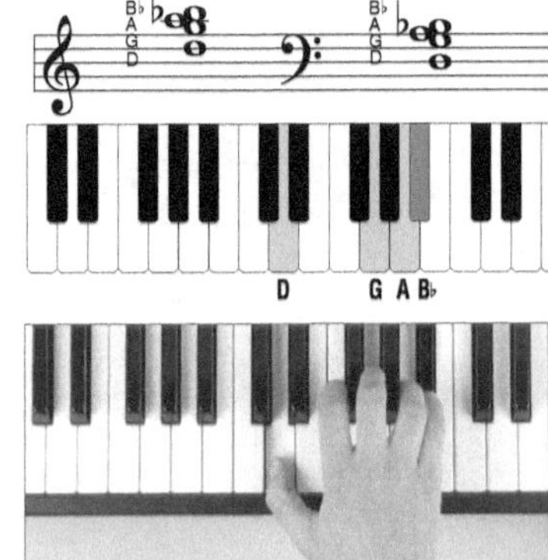

Gm6 Root Position

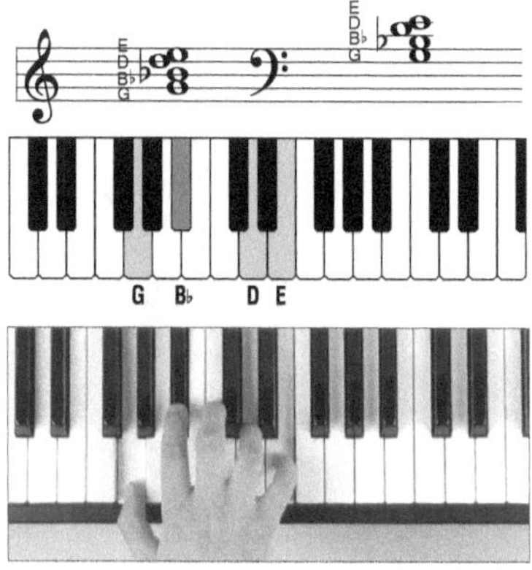

Gm6 First Inversion

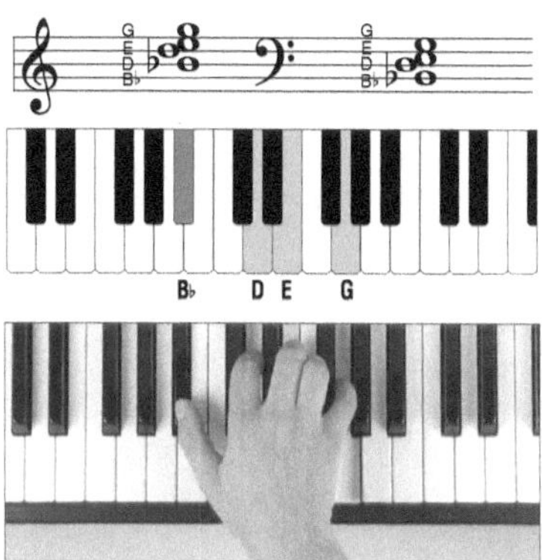

Gm6 Second Inversion

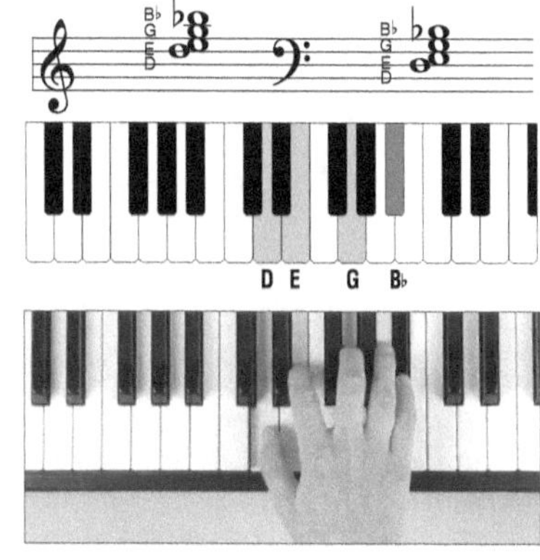

Gm6 Third Inversion

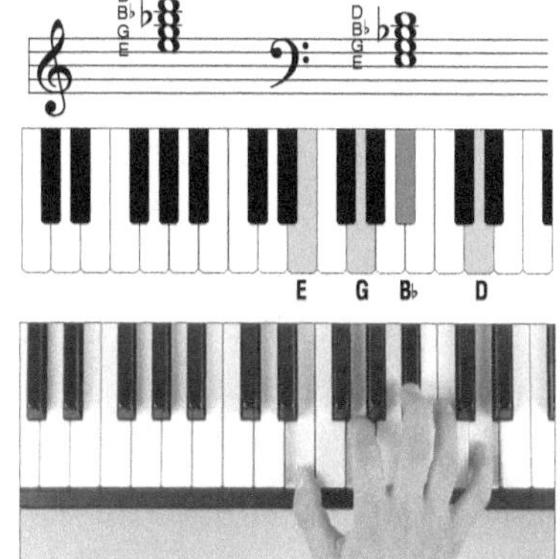

Gm7 Root Position

Gm7 First Inversion

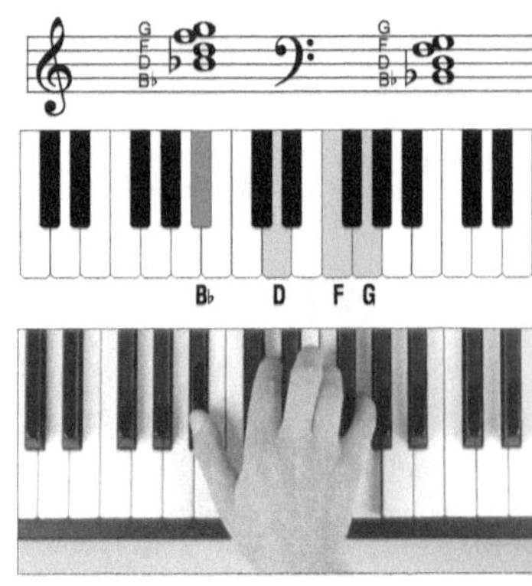

Gm7 Second Inversion

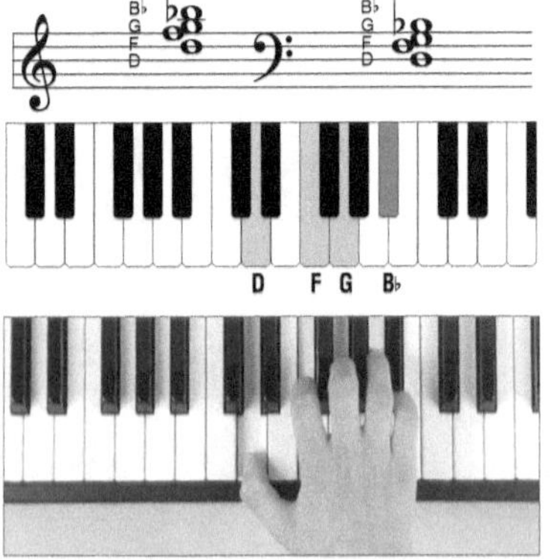

Gm7 Third Inversion

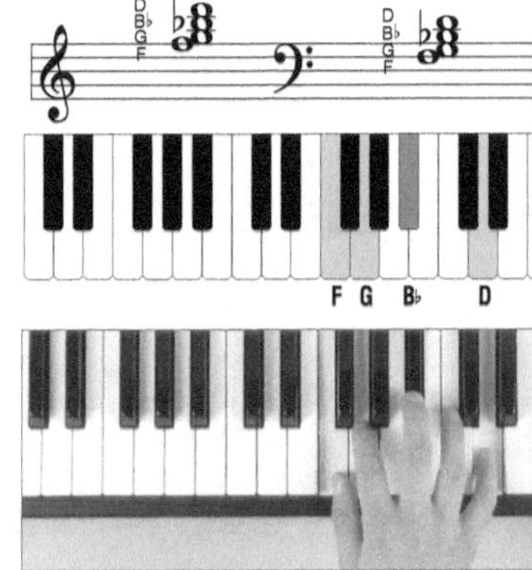

Gm(maj7) Root Position

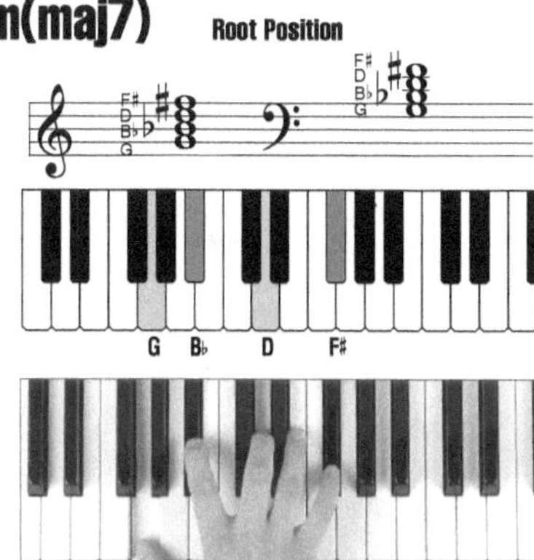

Gm(maj7) First Inversion

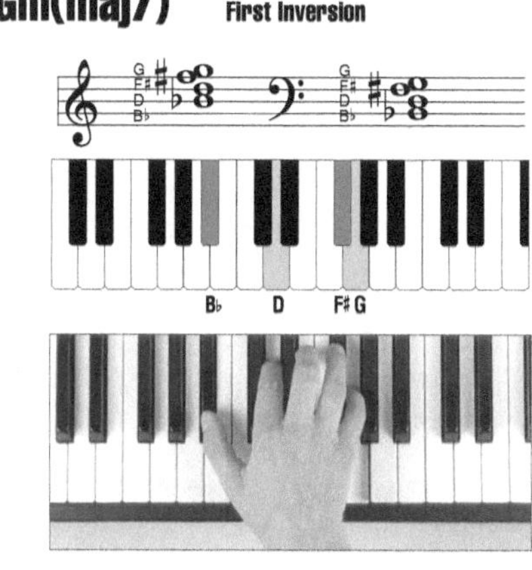

Gm(maj7) Second Inversion

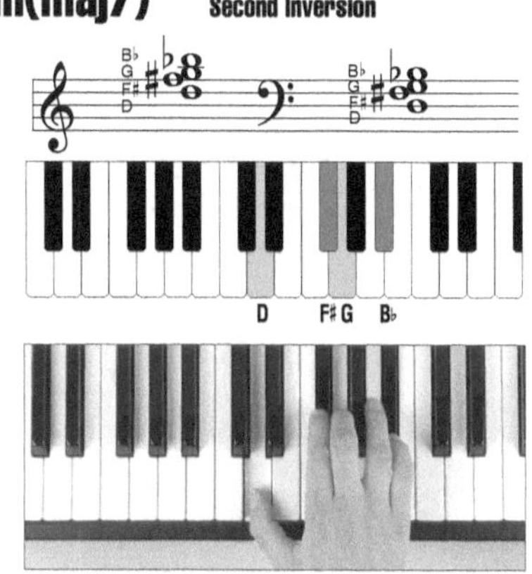

Gm(maj7) Third Inversion

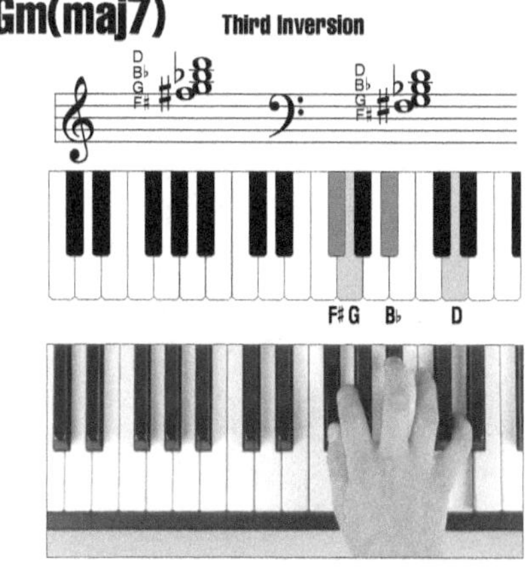

Gm7♭5 Root Position

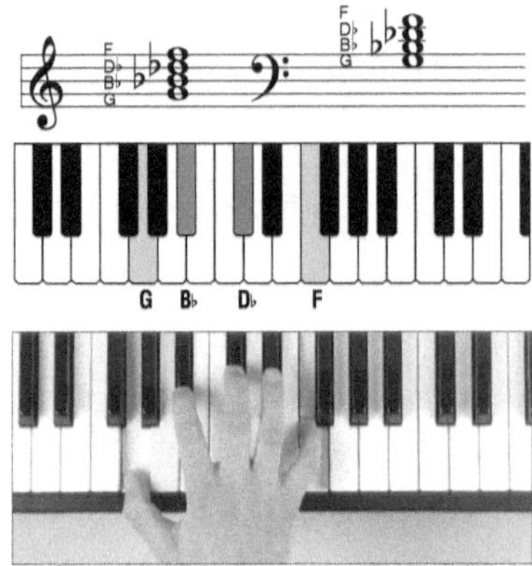

Gm7♭5 First Inversion

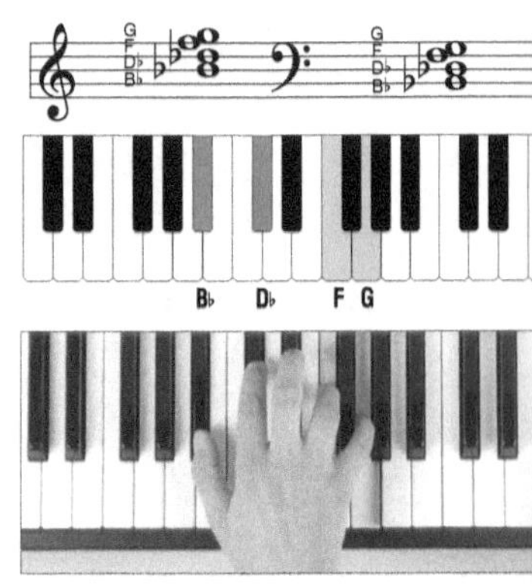

Gm7♭5 Second Inversion

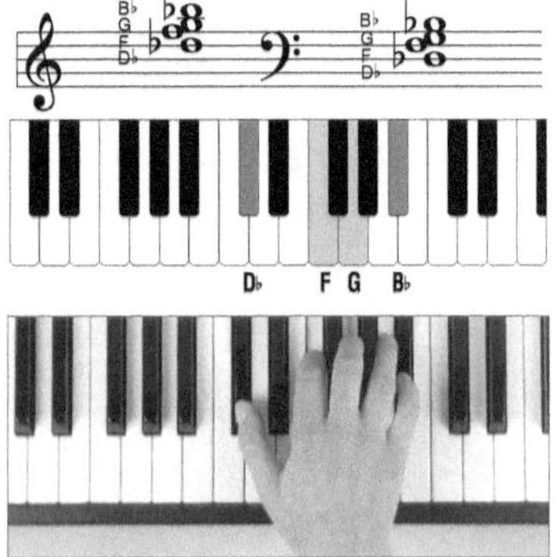

Gm7♭5 Third Inversion

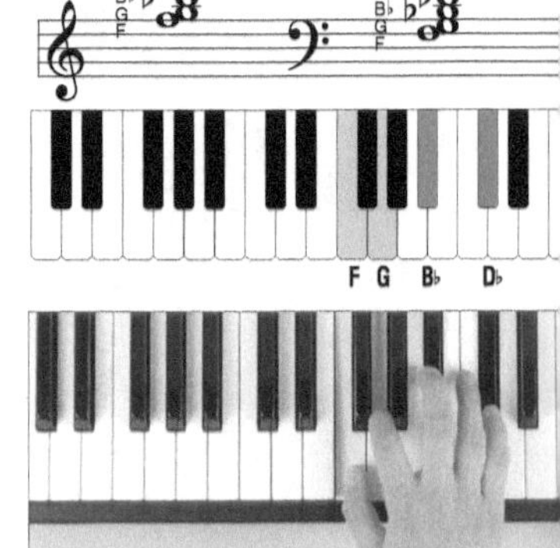

Gdim7 Root Position

Gdim7 First Inversion

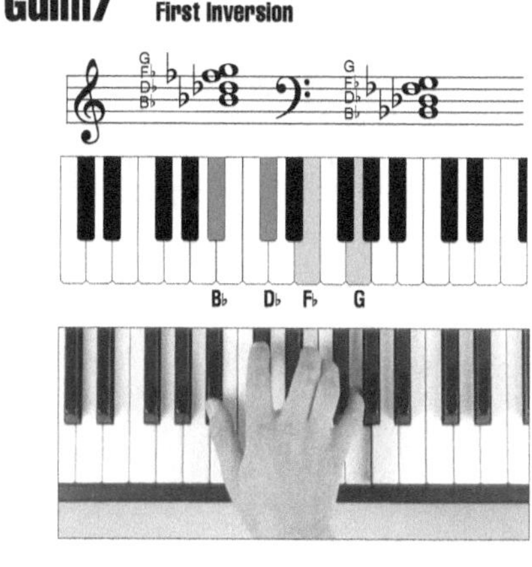

Gdim7 Second Inversion

Gdim7 Third Inversion

Gdim(maj7) Root Position

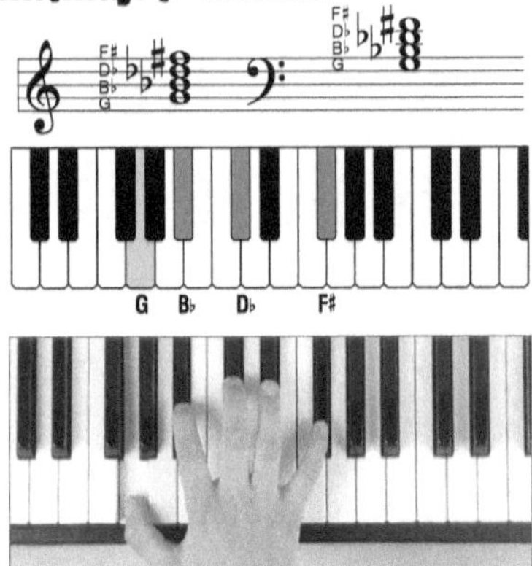

Gdim(maj7) First Inversion

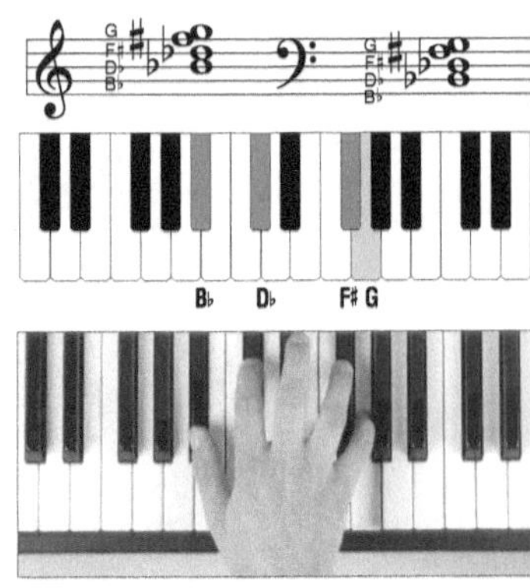

Gdim(maj7) Second Inversion

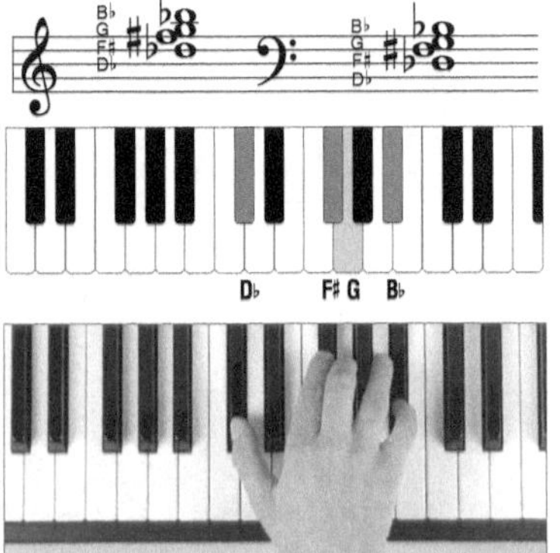

Gdim(maj7) Third Inversion

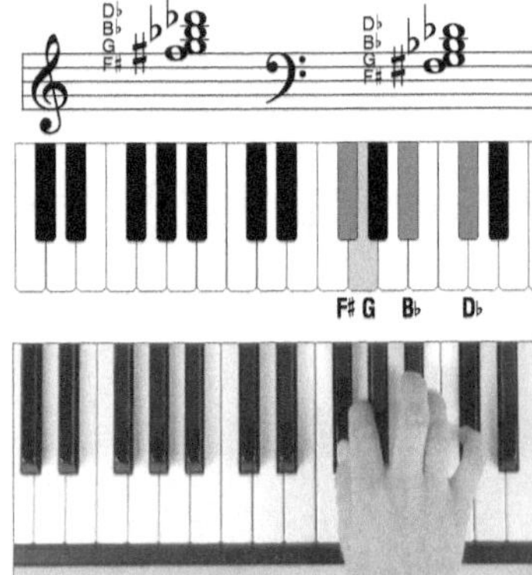

5

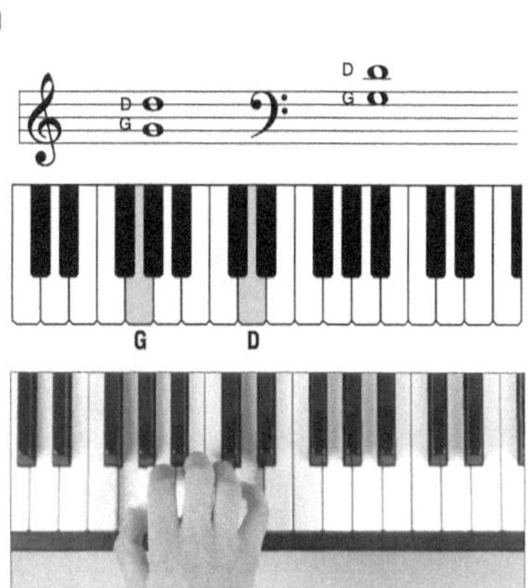

6/9

maj6/9

Gmaj7♯11

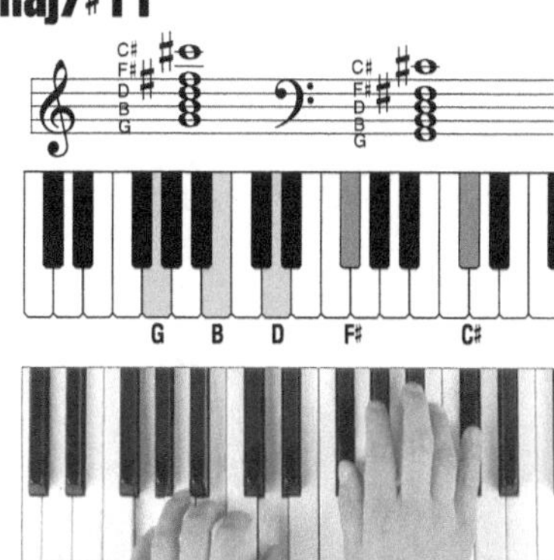

Gmaj9

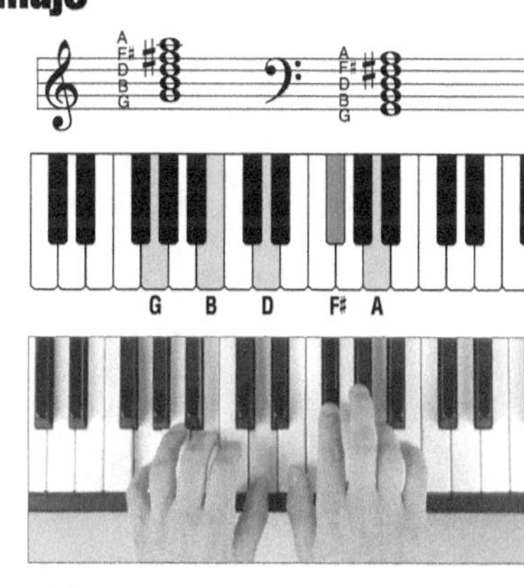

Gmaj9♭5

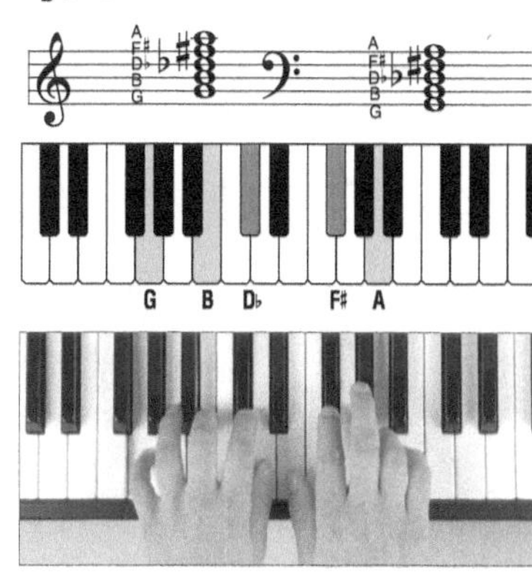

Gmaj9♯5

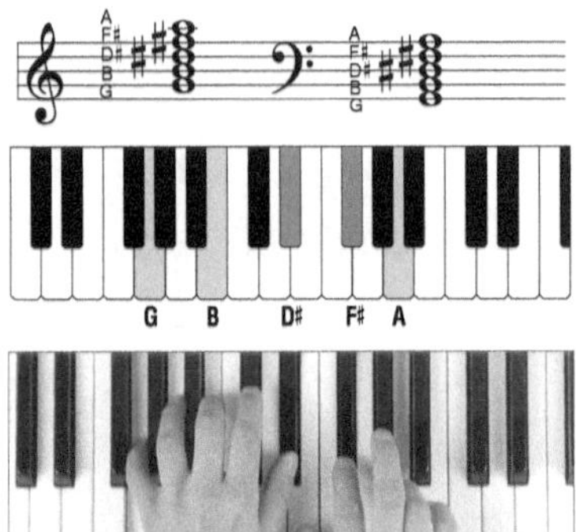

Gmaj9♯11

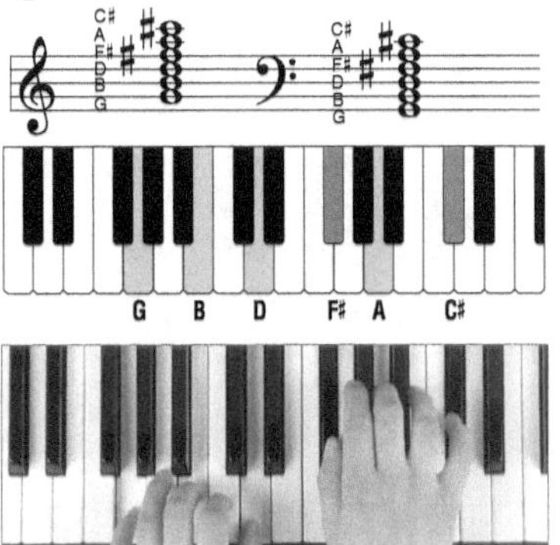

Gmaj13

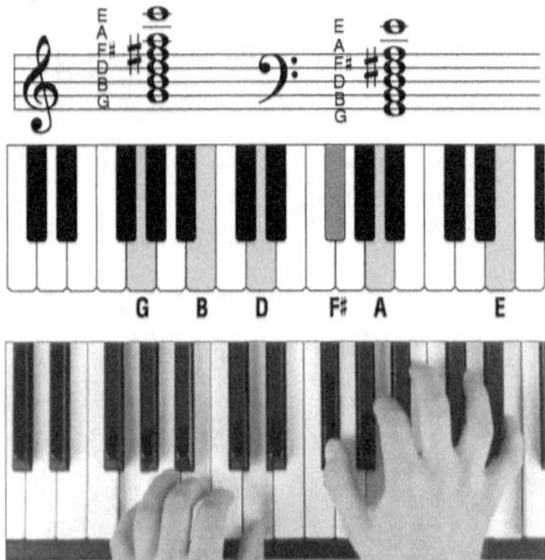

Gmaj13♭5

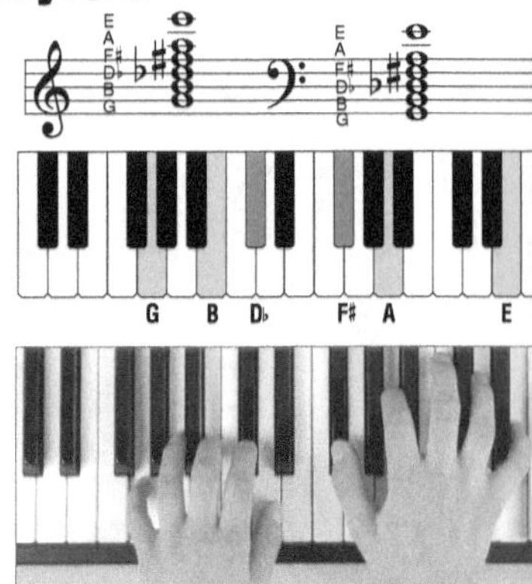

Gmaj13♯11

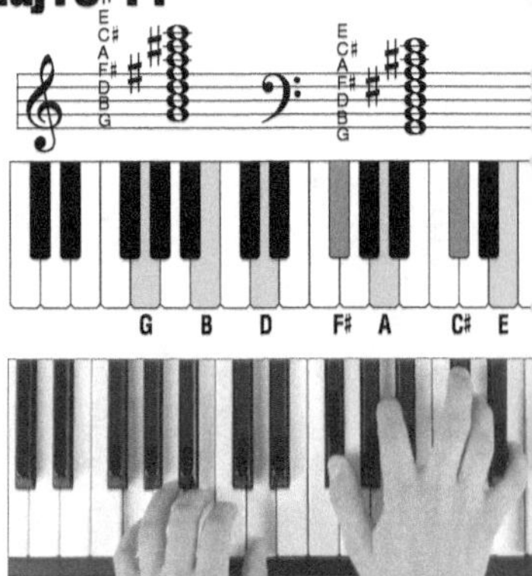

G7♭9

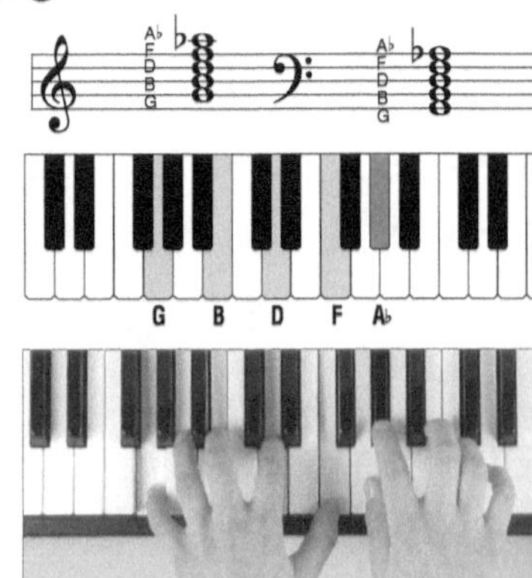

G7♯9

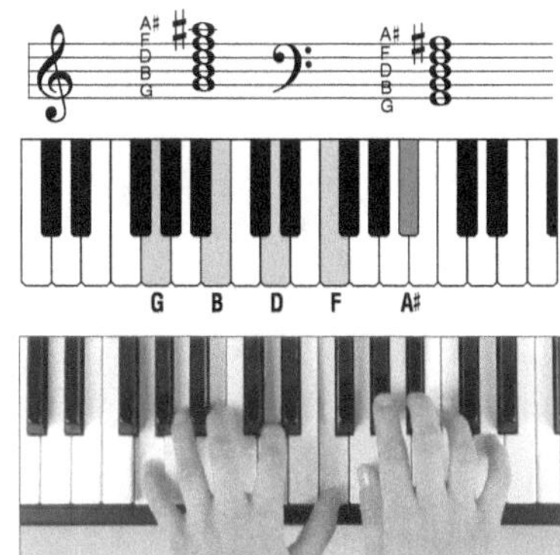

G7♭5(♯9)

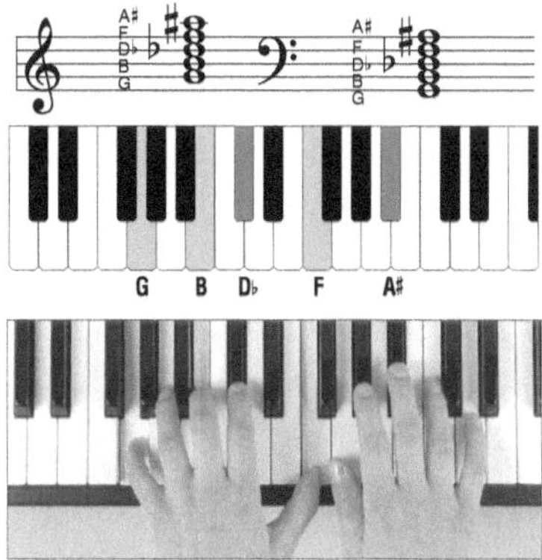

G7♯11

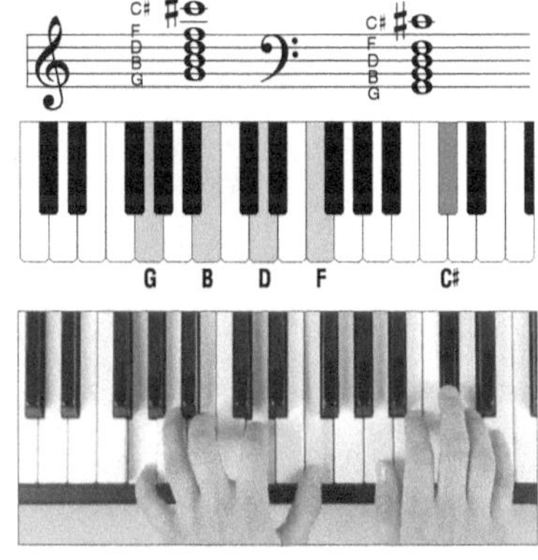

G7♯5(♭9)

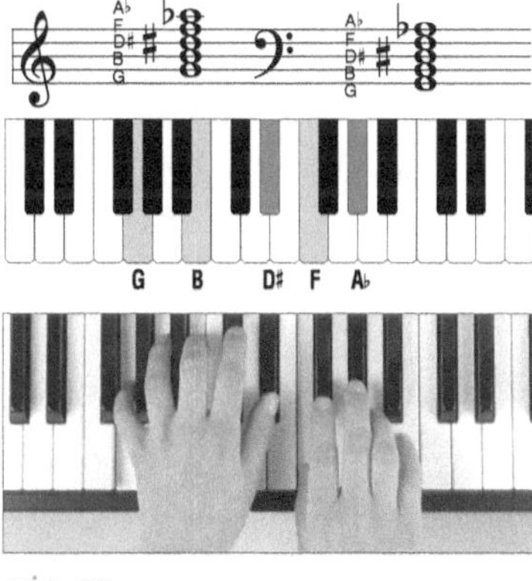

G7♭5(♭9)

G7♯5(♯9)

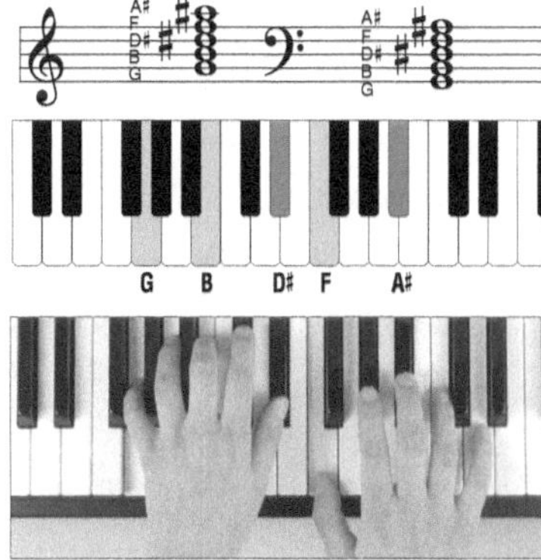

G7♭9(♯9)

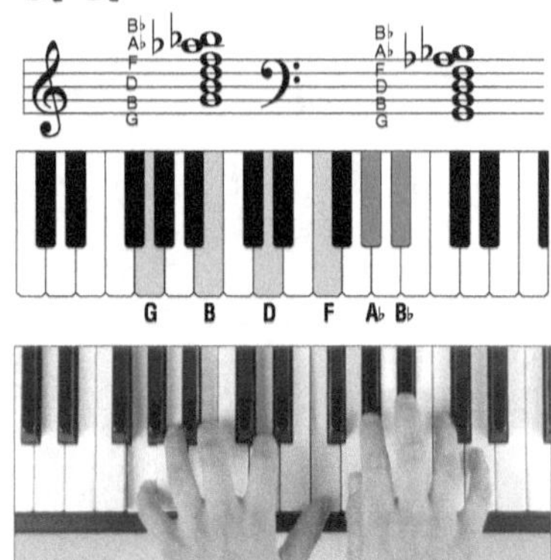

G7(add13)

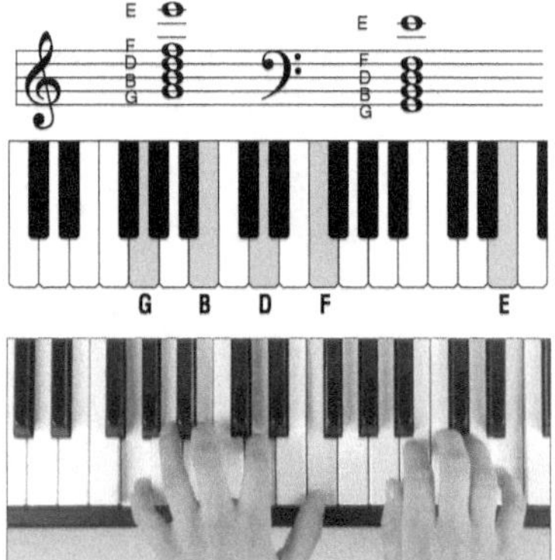

G7♭13

G7♭9(♯11)

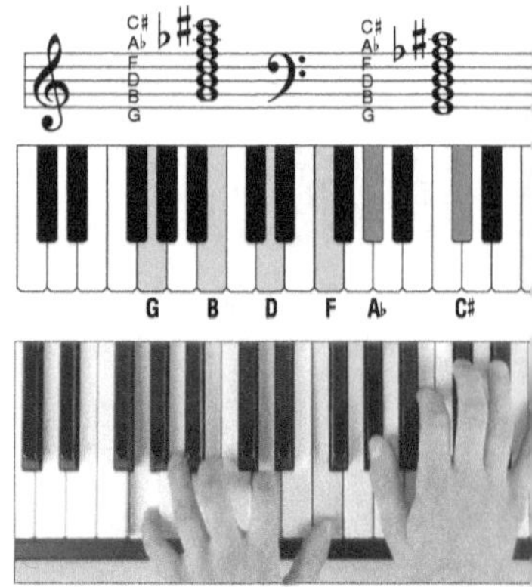

G7♯9(♯11)

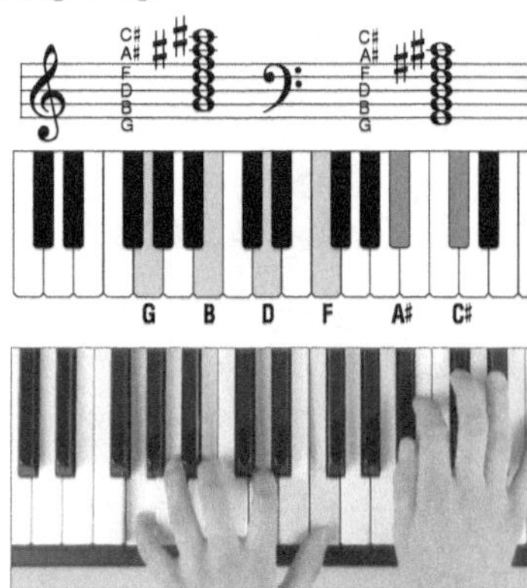

G7♭9(♭13)

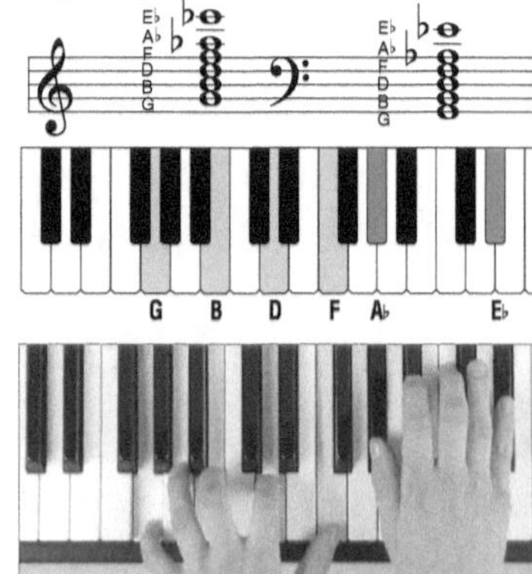

G7♯9(♭13)

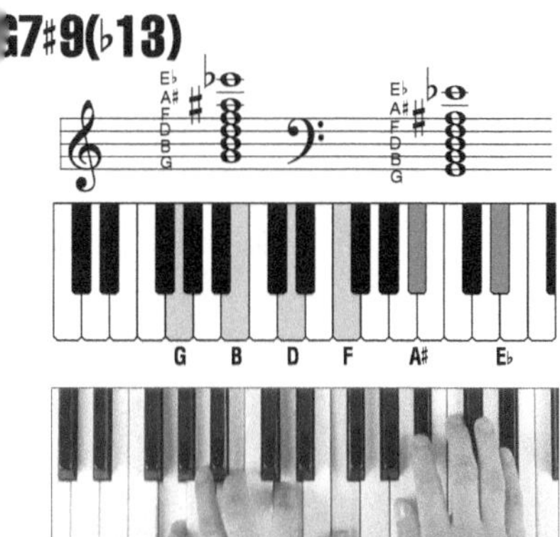

G7♯11(♭13)

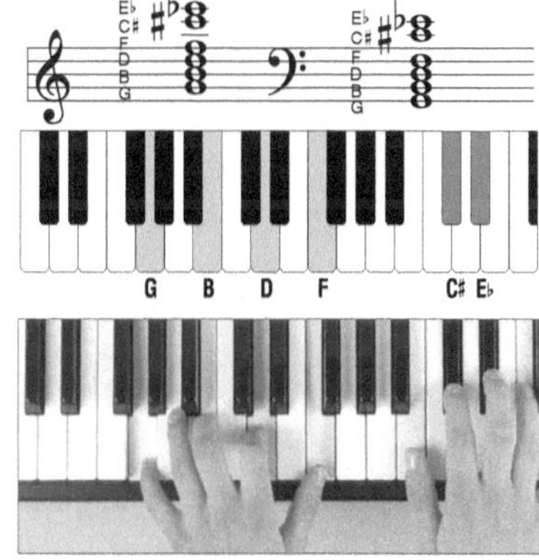

G7♭9(♯9,♯11)

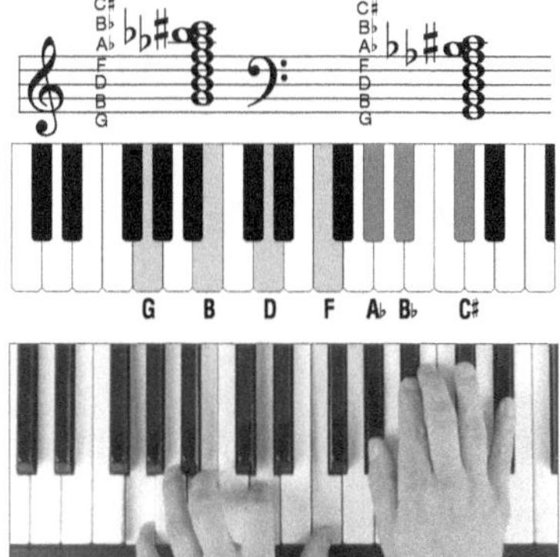

G9

G9(♭5)

G9♯5

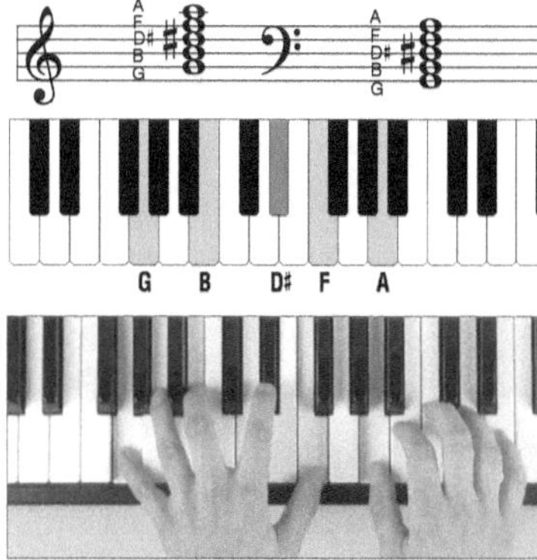

G9♯11

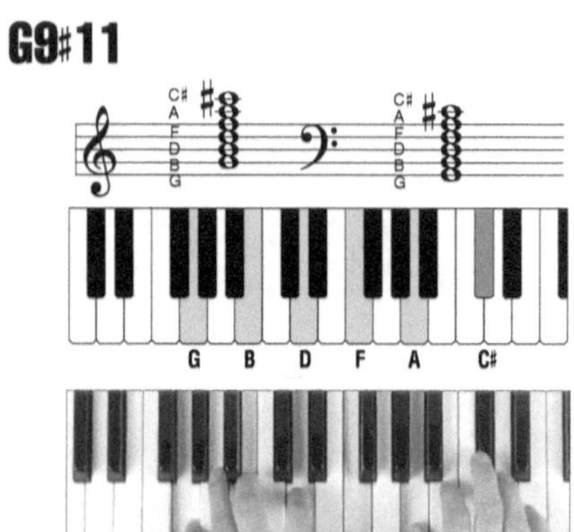

G9♭13

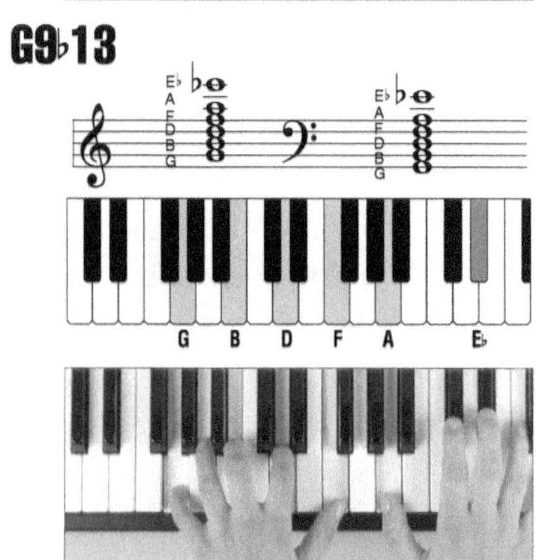

G9♯11(♭13)

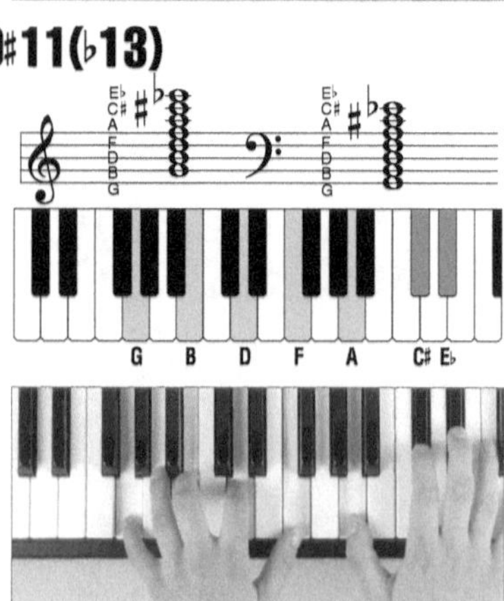

G11, G9(sus4)

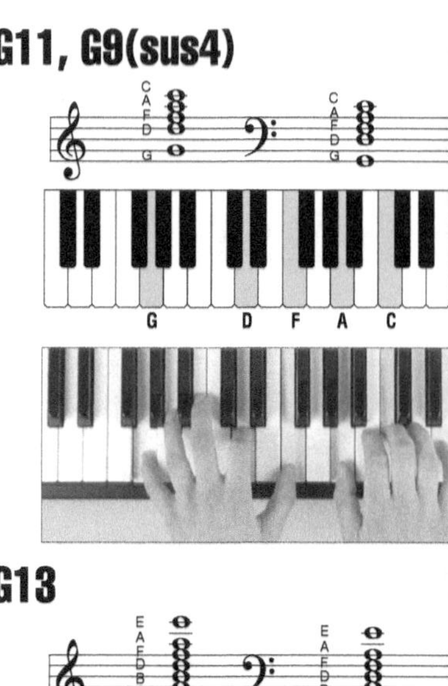

G13

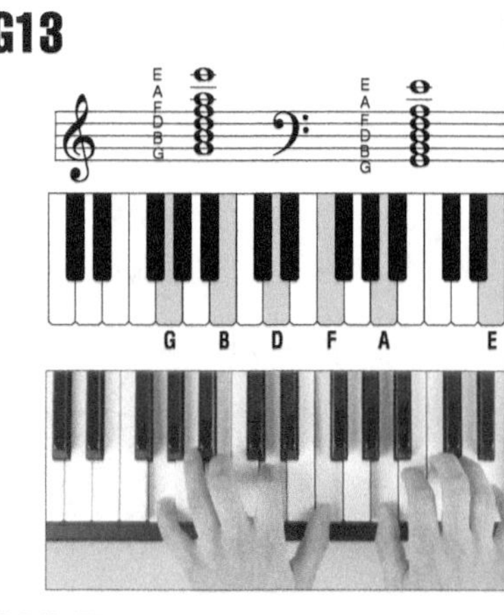

G13♭5

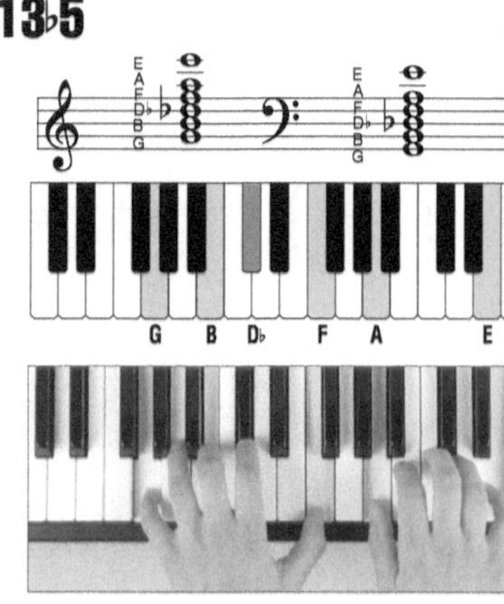

G13♭9

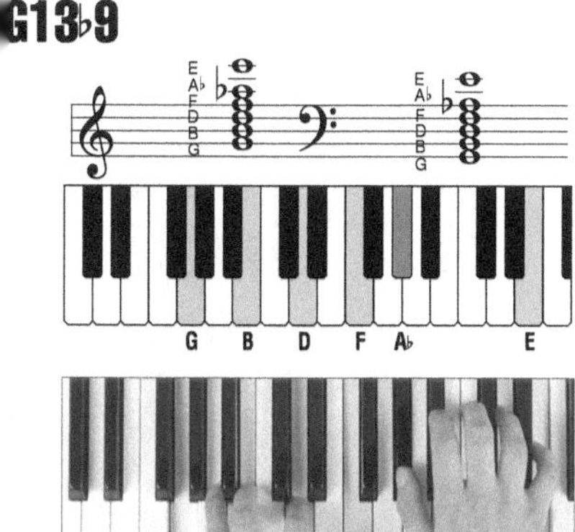

G13♯9

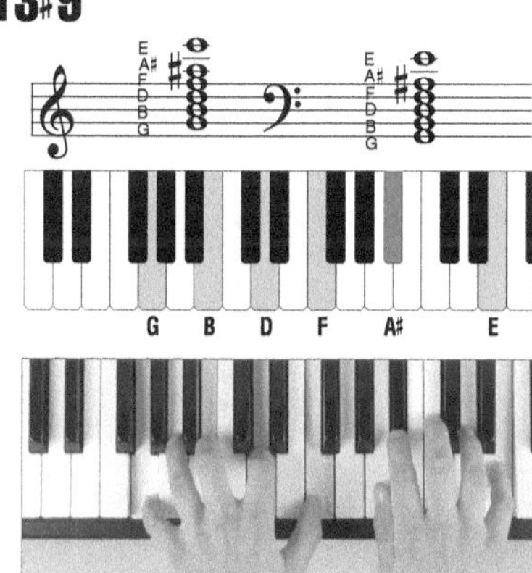

G13♯11

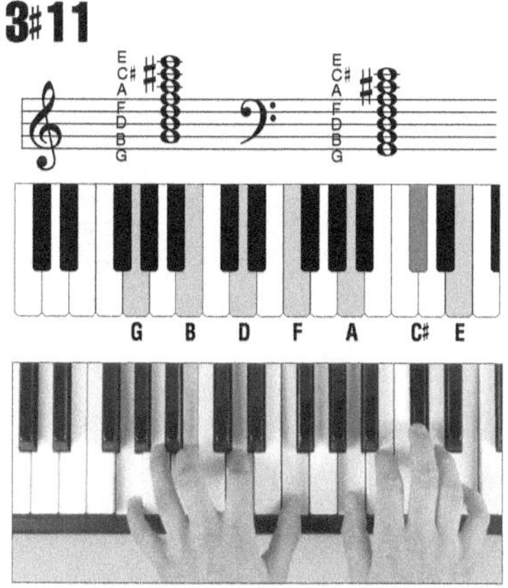

G13(sus4)

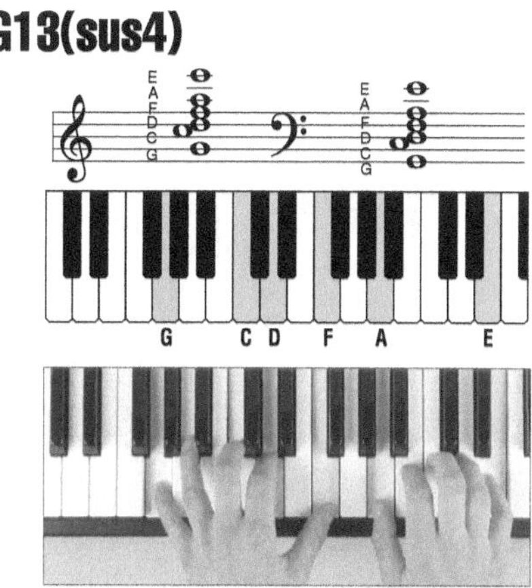

Gm(♯5)

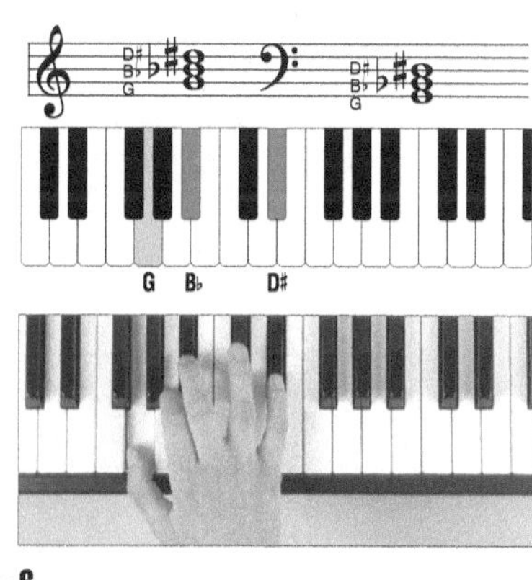

Gm$^{6}_{9}$

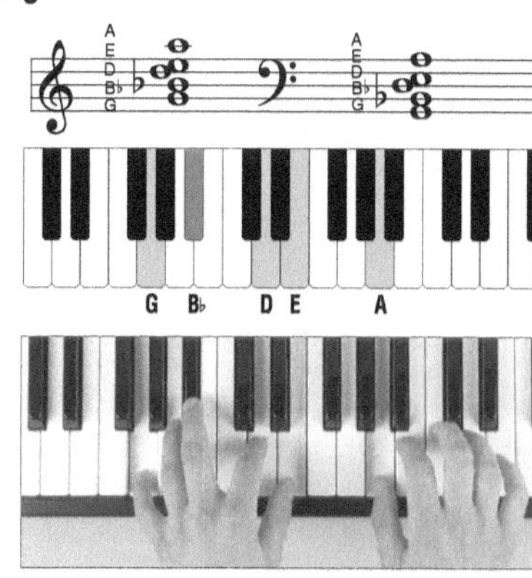

Gm7(add4)

Gm7(add11)

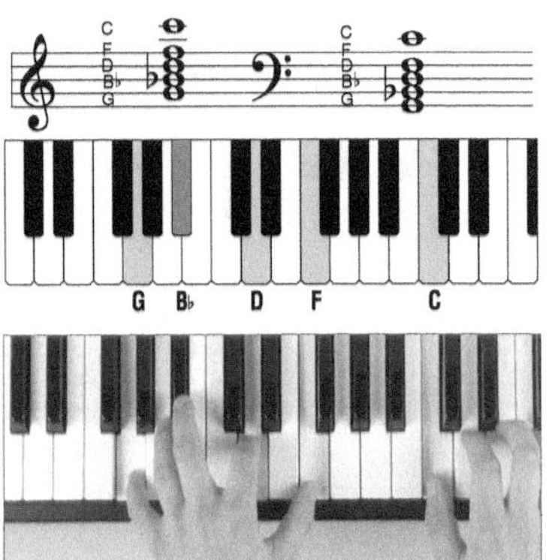

Gm7♭5(♭9)

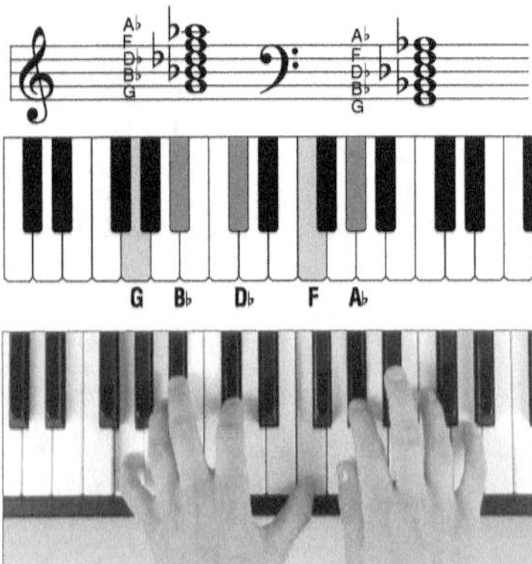

Gm9

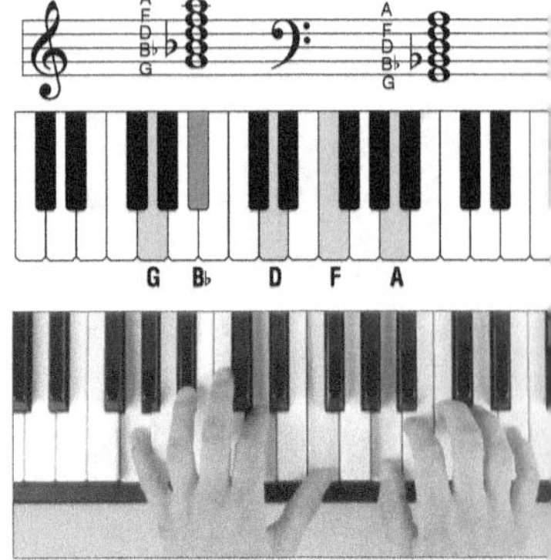

Gm9(maj7)

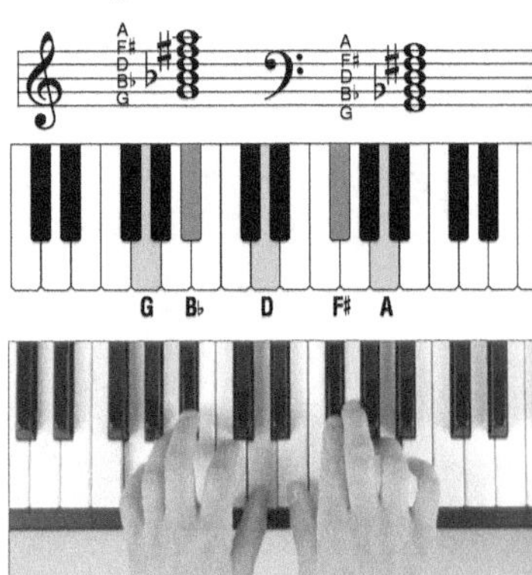

Gm9♭5

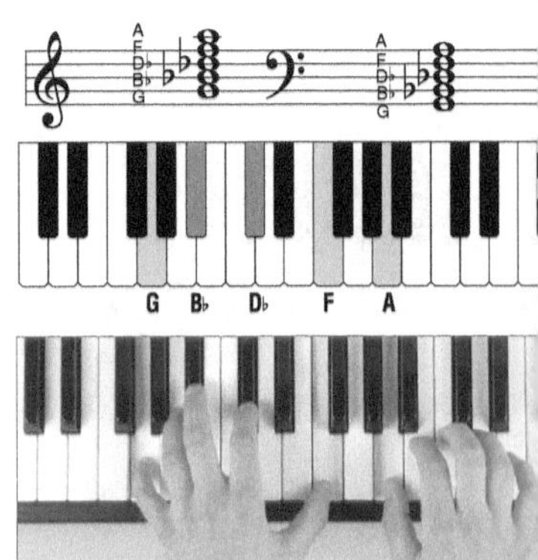

Gm11

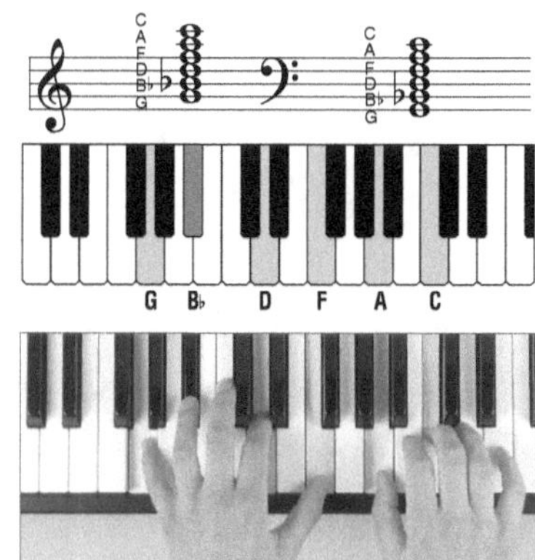

Gm11♭5

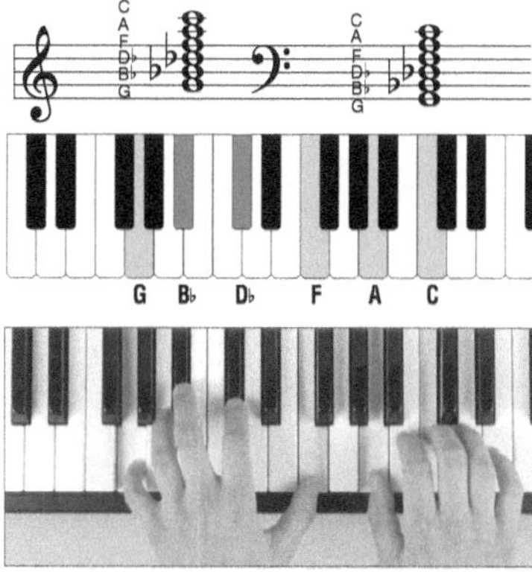

Gm13

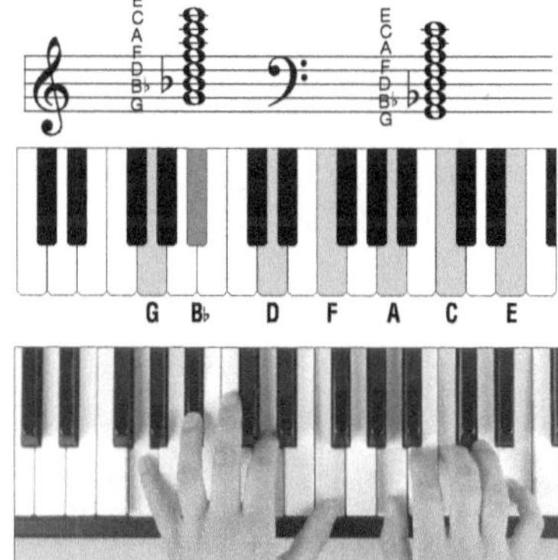

Gm11(maj7)

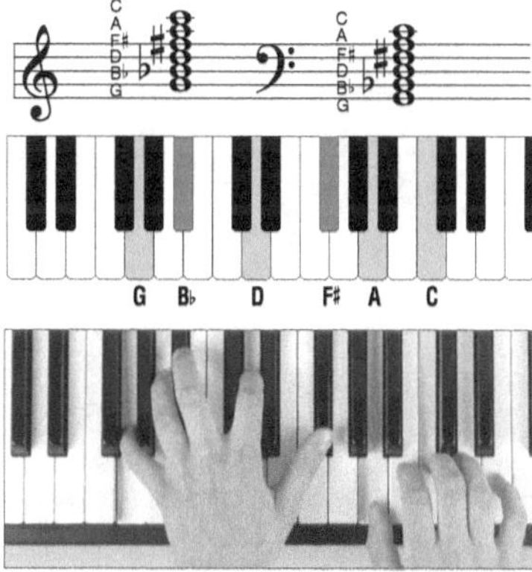

Gdim7(add9)

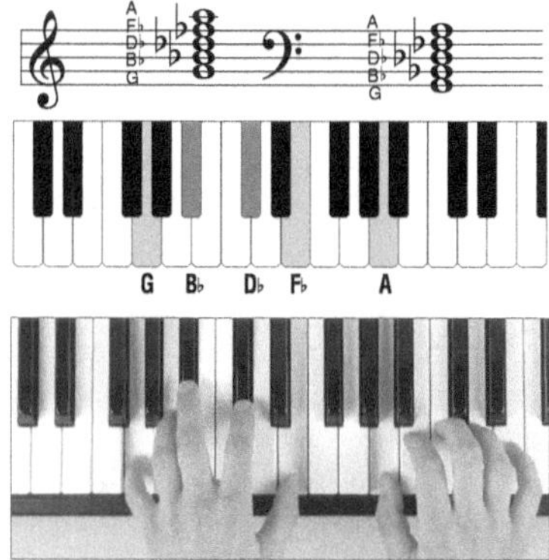

G7alt.

G

A♭ Root Position

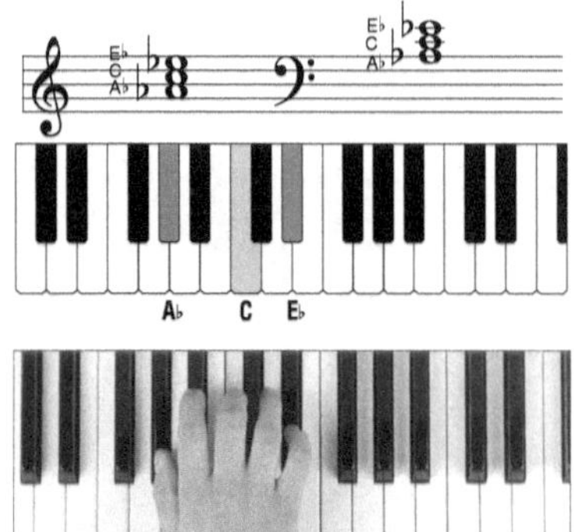

A♭ First Inversion

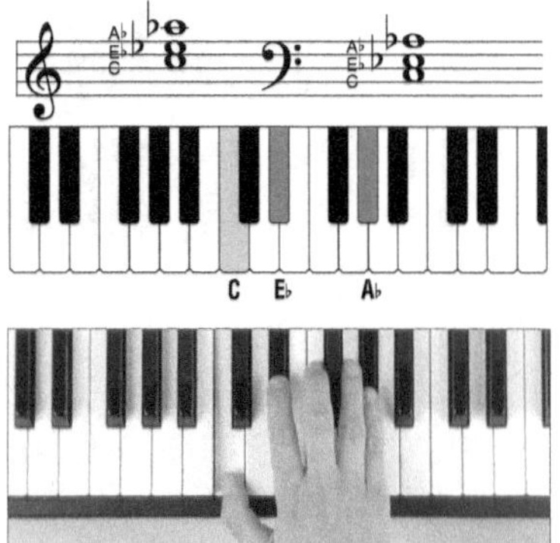

A♭ Second Inversion

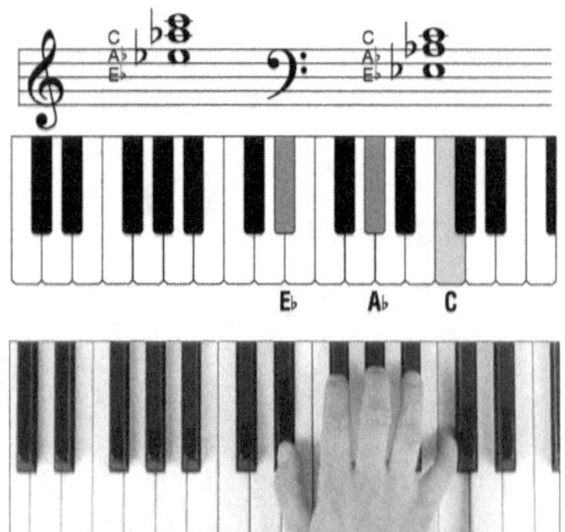

A♭m Root Position

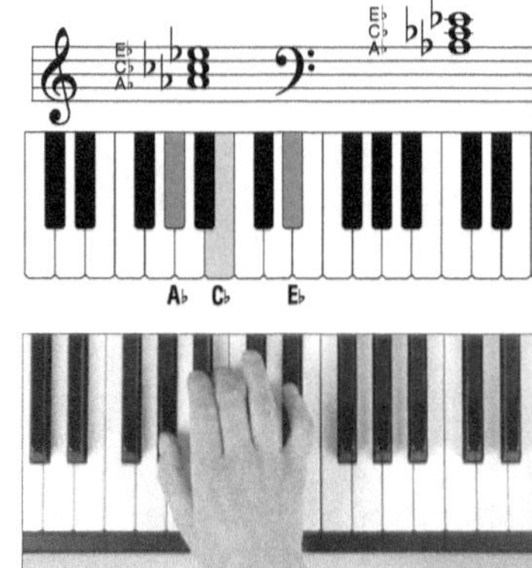

A♭m First Inversion

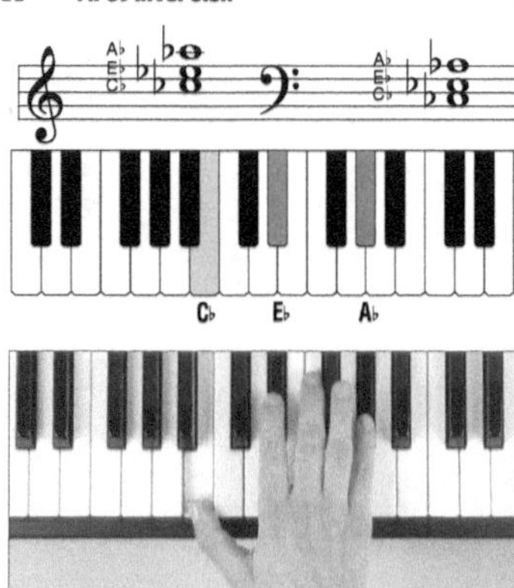

A♭m Second Inversion

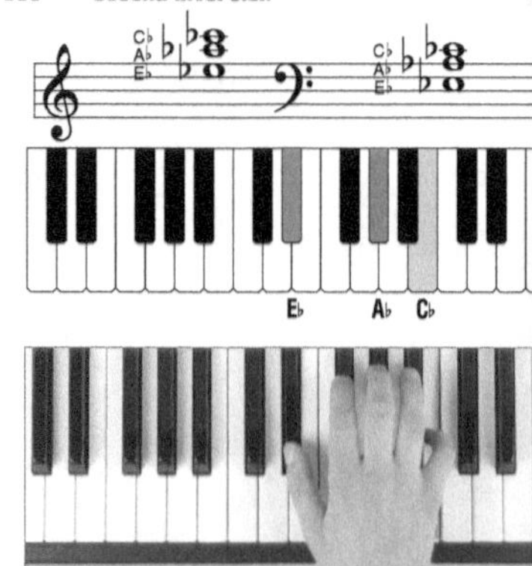

A♭+ Root Position

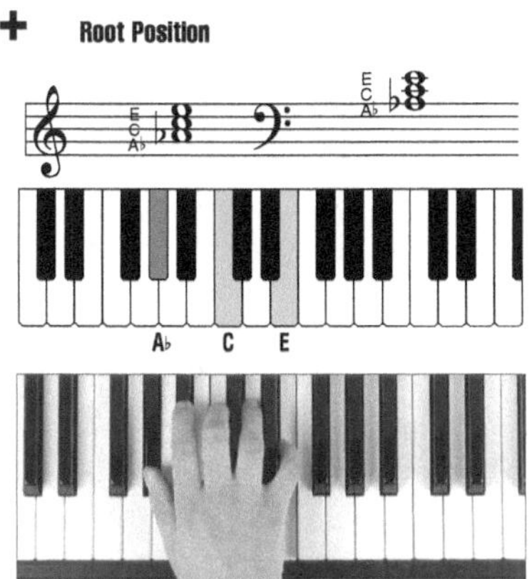

A♭+ First Inversion

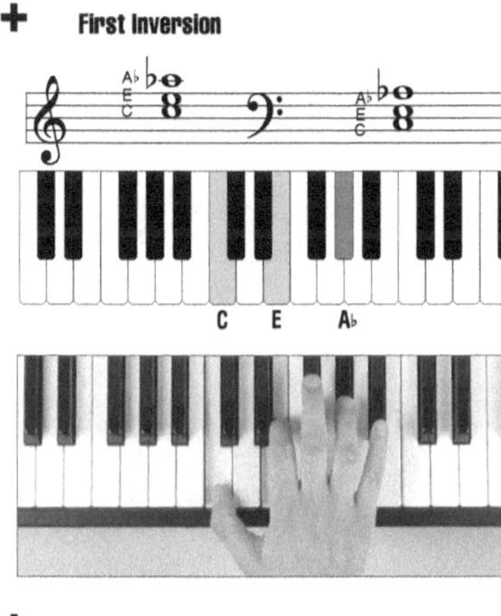

A♭+ Second Inversion

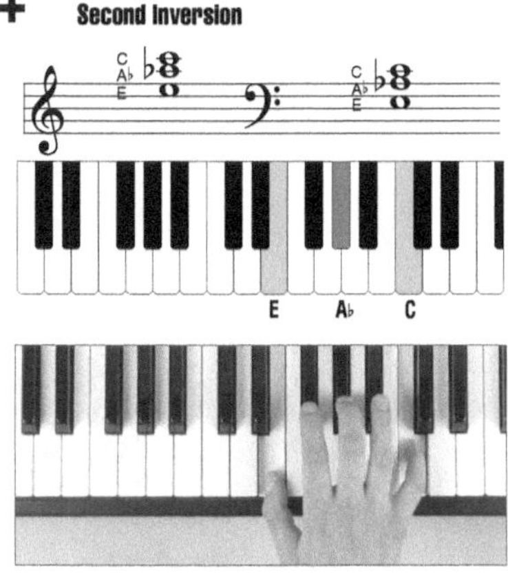

A♭dim Root Position

A♭dim First Inversion

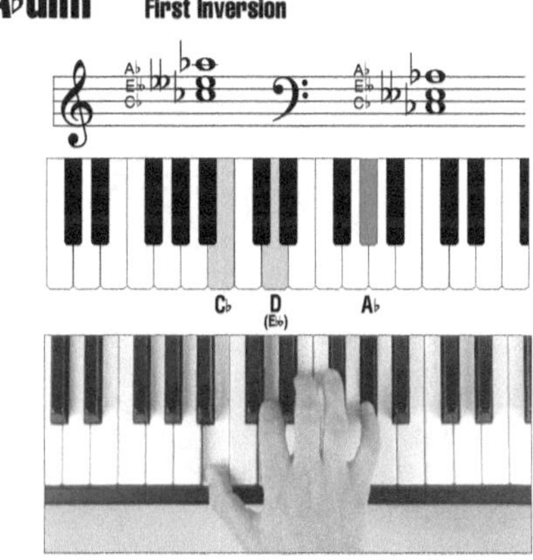

A♭dim Second Inversion

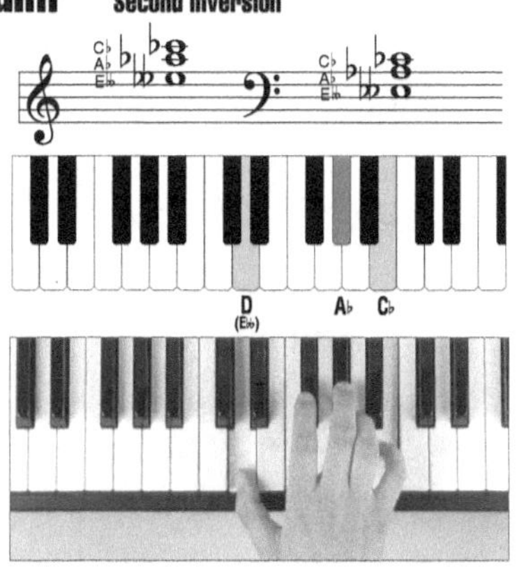

A♭sus Root Position

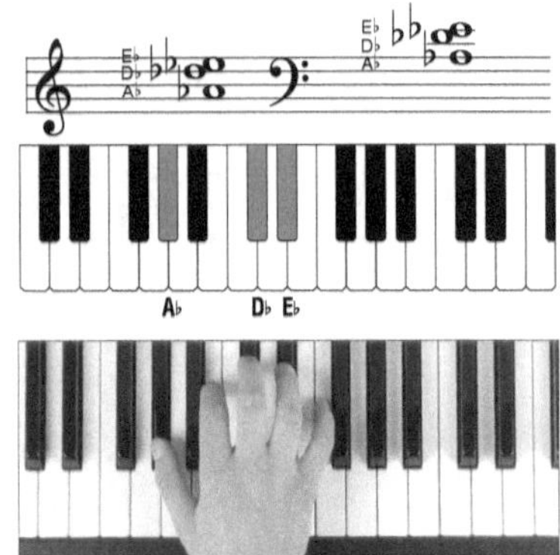

A♭sus First Inversion

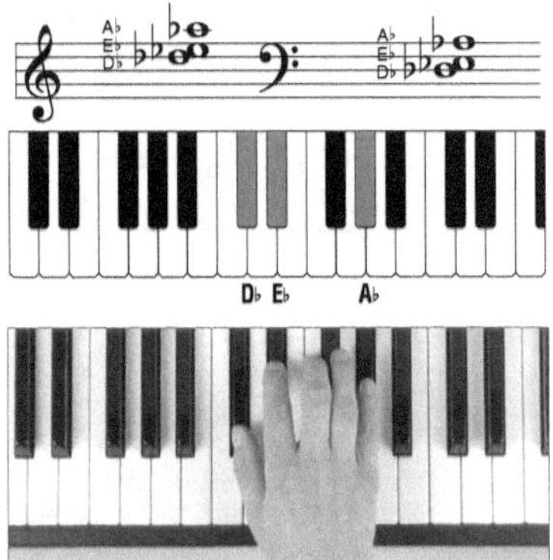

A♭sus Second Inversion

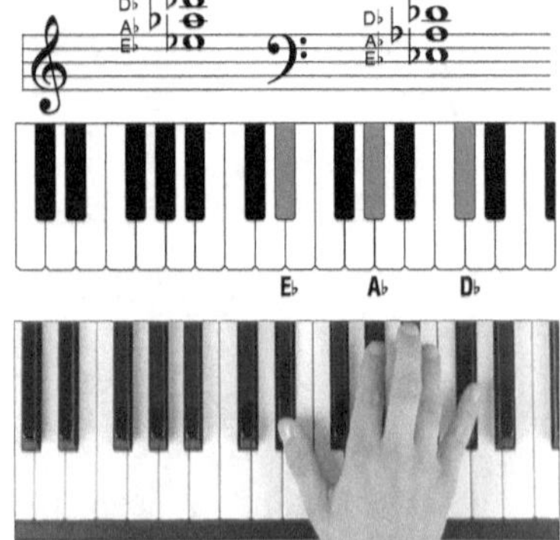

A♭(♭5) Root Position

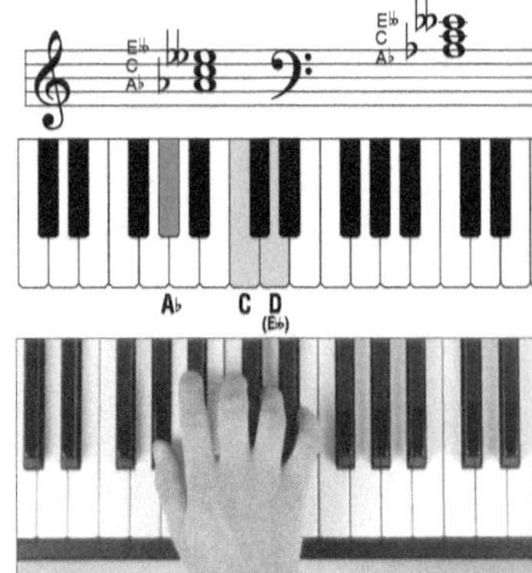

A♭(♭5) First Inversion

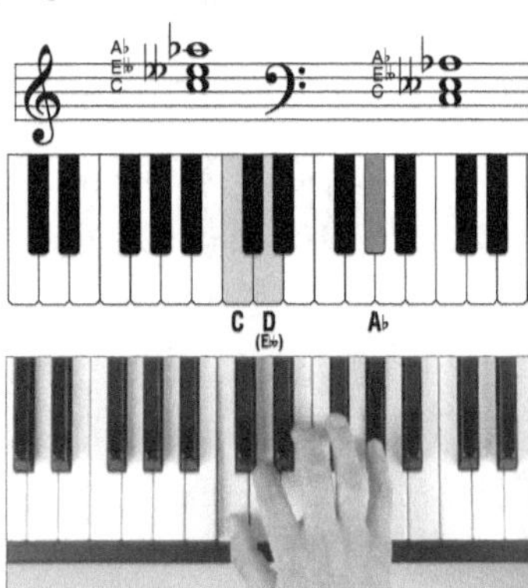

A♭(♭5) Second Inversion

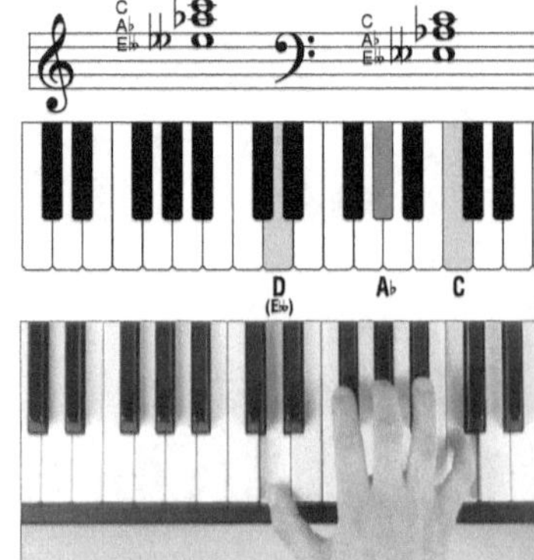

A♭sus2 Root Position

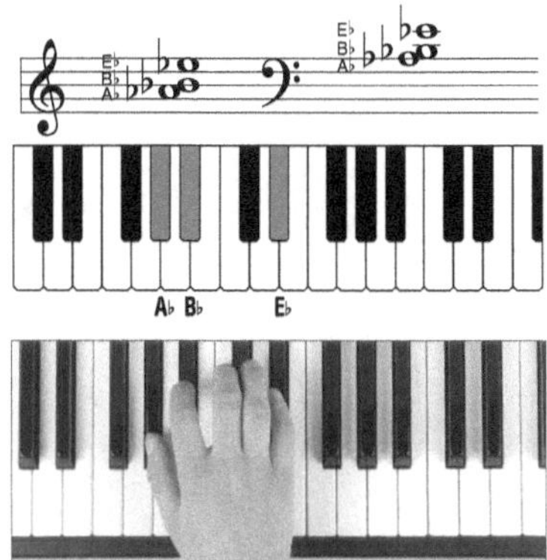

A♭sus2 First Inversion

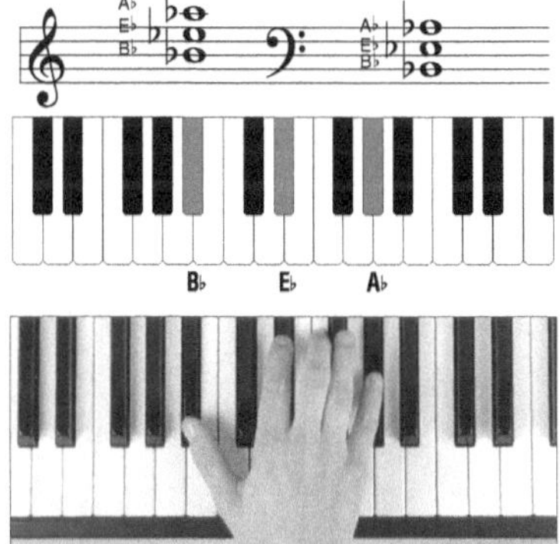

A♭sus2 Second Inversion

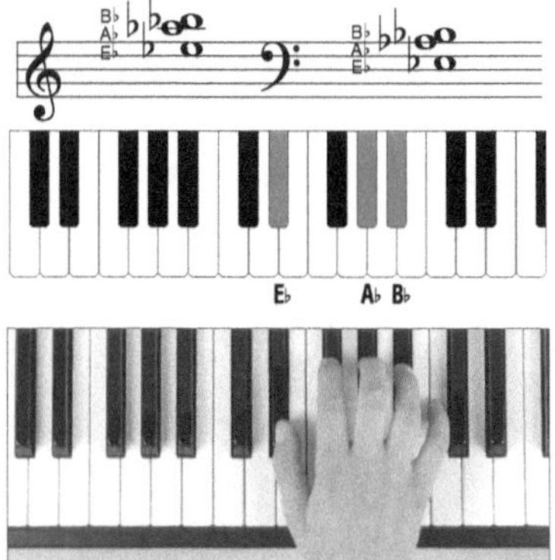

A♭6 Root Position

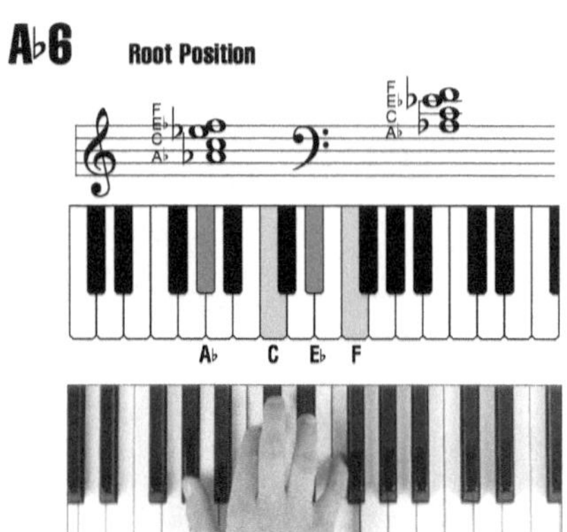

A♭6 First Inversion

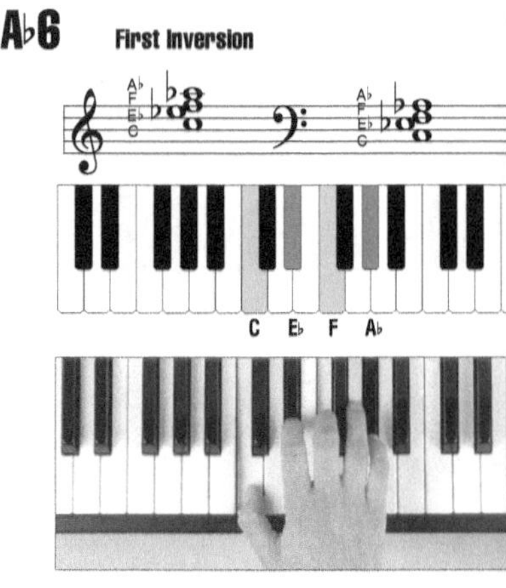

A♭6 Second Inversion

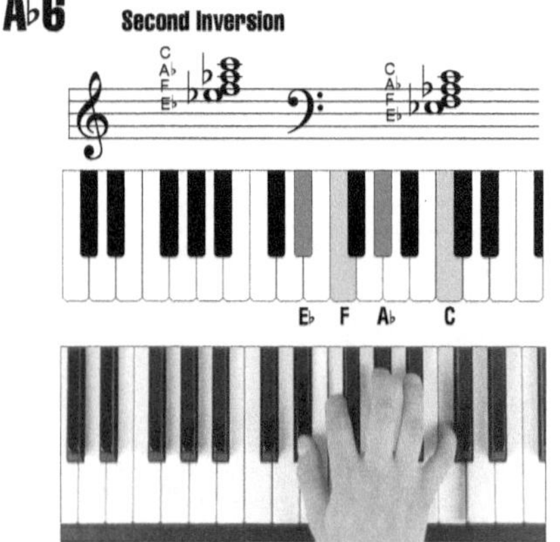

A♭6 Third Inversion

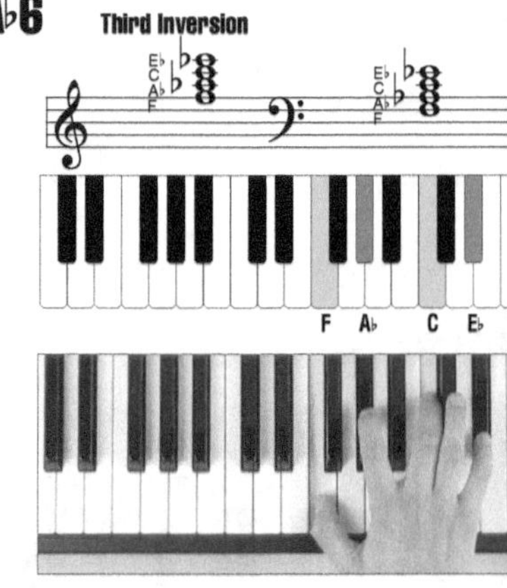

A♭(add2), A♭(add9) Root Position

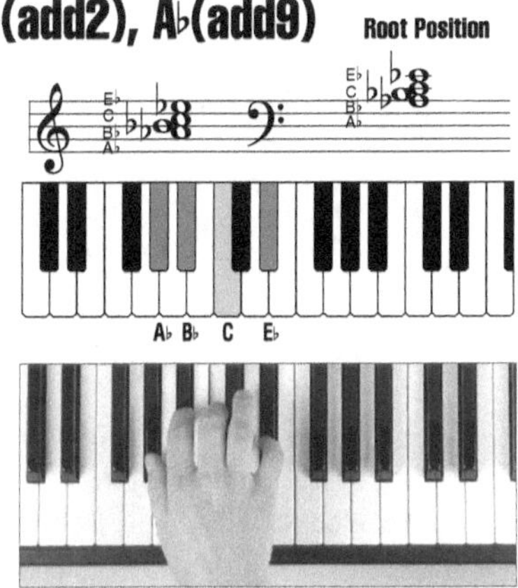

A♭(add2), A♭(add9) First Inversion

A♭(add2), A♭(add9) Second Inversion

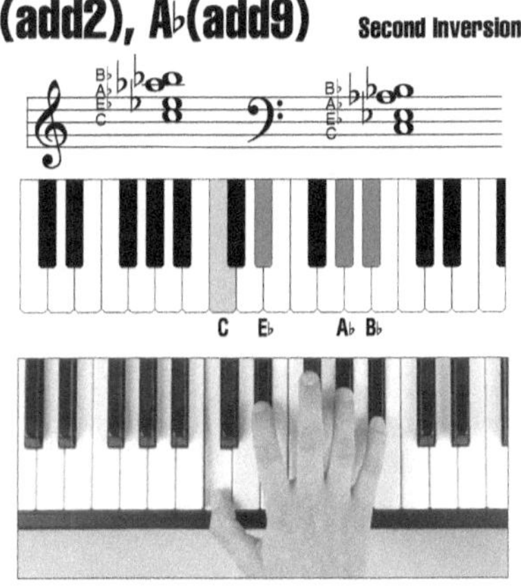

A♭(add2), A♭(add9) Third Inversion

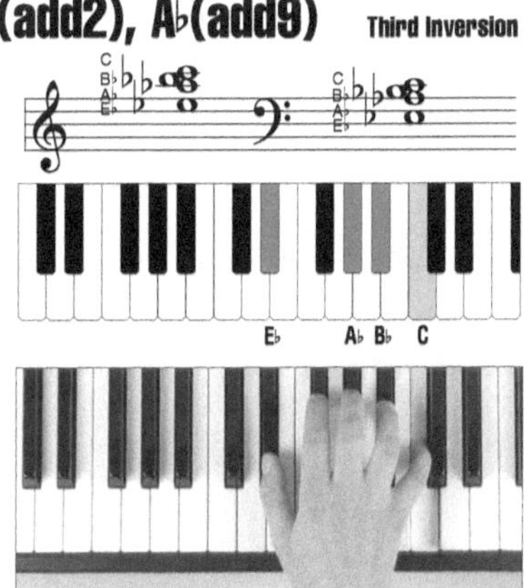

A♭maj7 Root Position

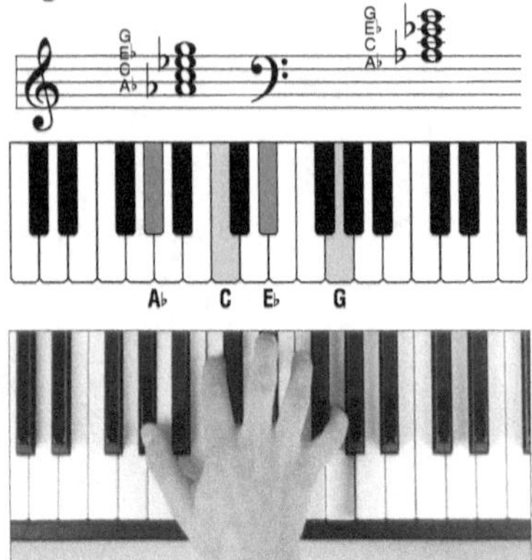

A♭maj7 First Inversion

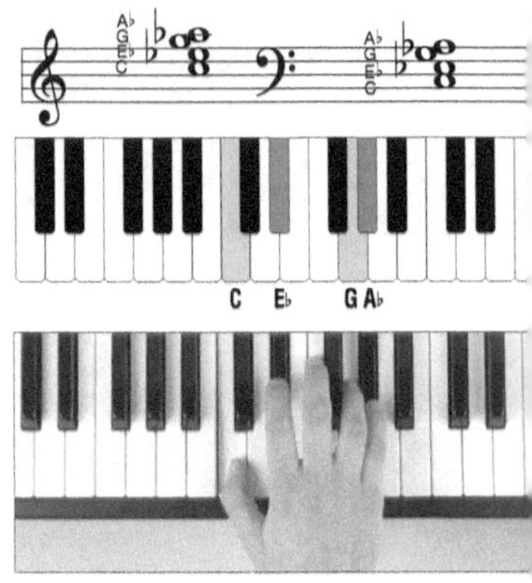

A♭maj7 Second Inversion

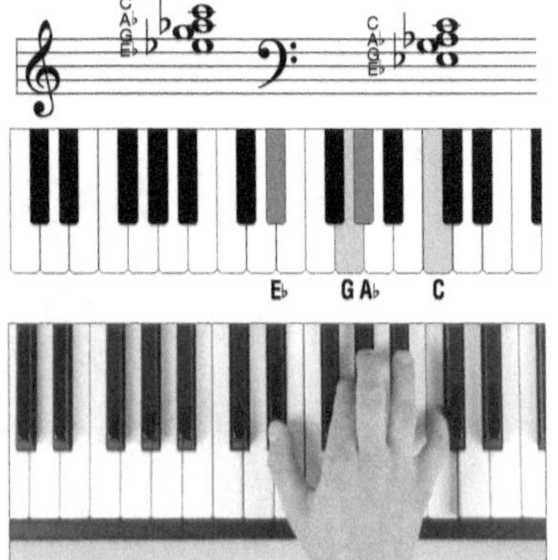

A♭maj7 Third Inversion

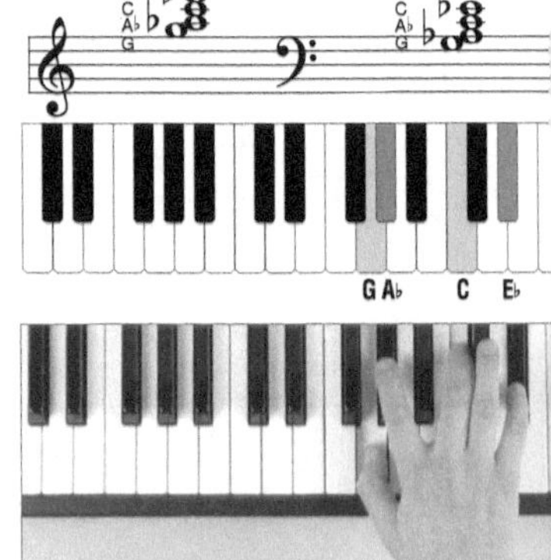

A♭maj7♭5 Root Position

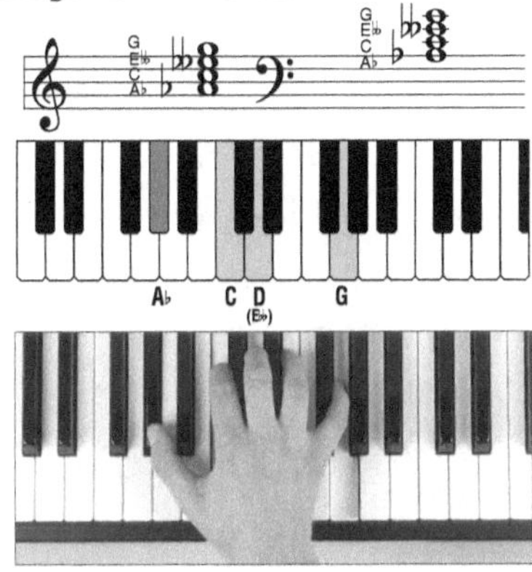

A♭maj7♭5 First Inversion

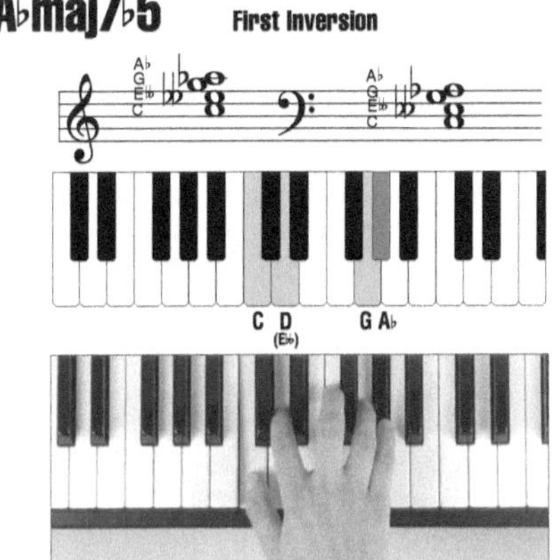

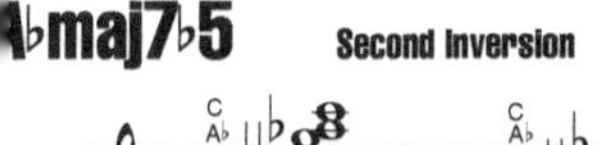

A♭maj7♭5 Second Inversion

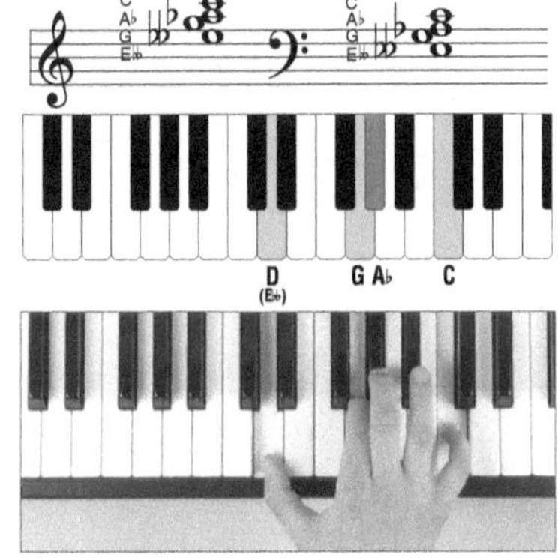

A♭maj7♭5 Third Inversion

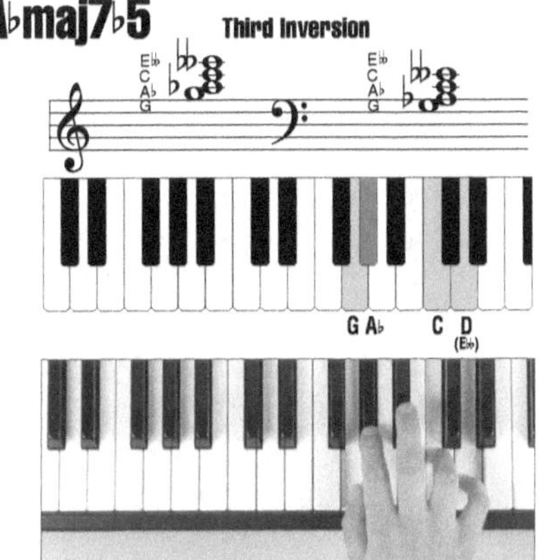

A♭

A♭maj7♯5 Root Position

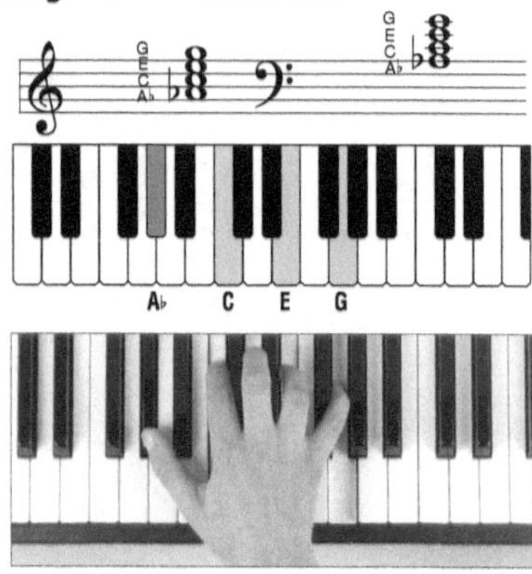

A♭maj7♯5 First Inversion

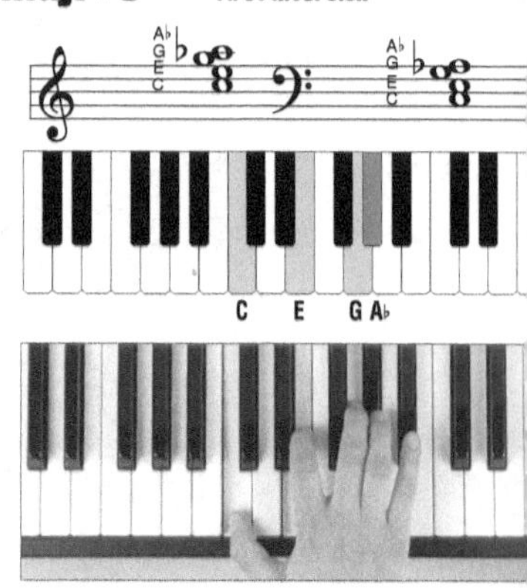

A♭maj7♯5 Second Inversion

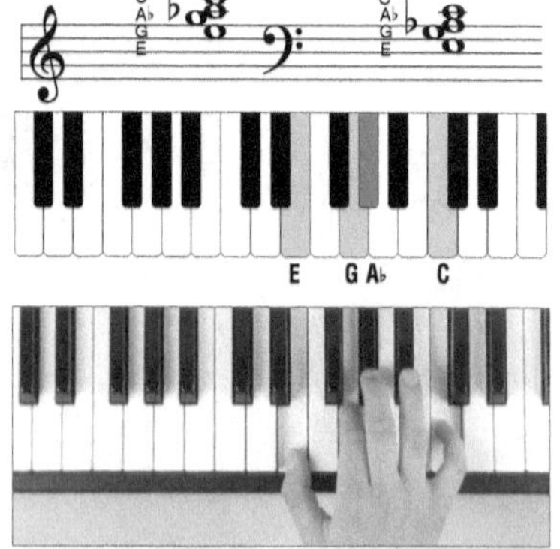

A♭maj7♯5 Third Inversion

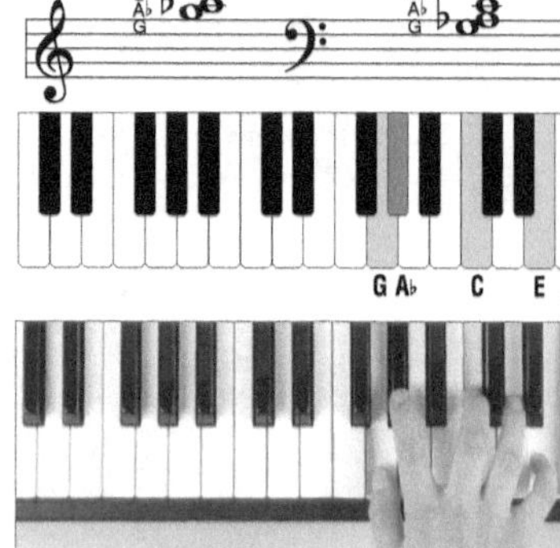

A♭7 Root Position

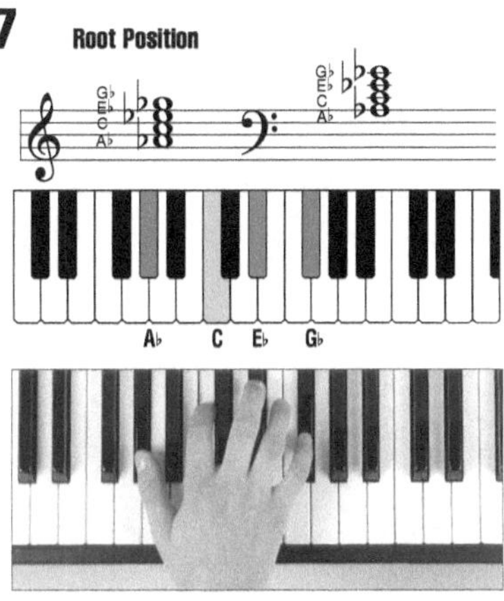

A♭7 First Inversion

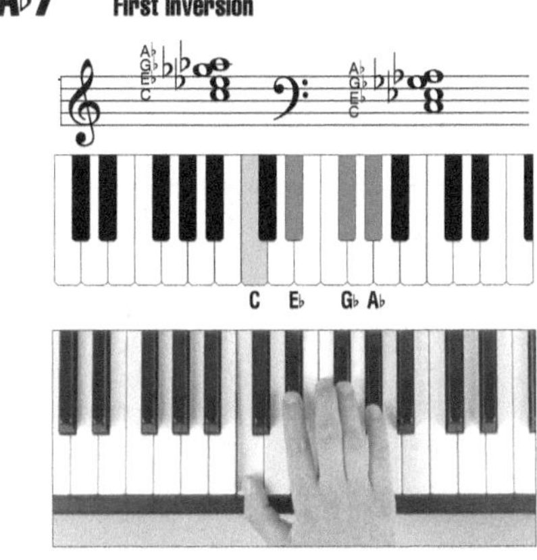

A♭7 Second Inversion

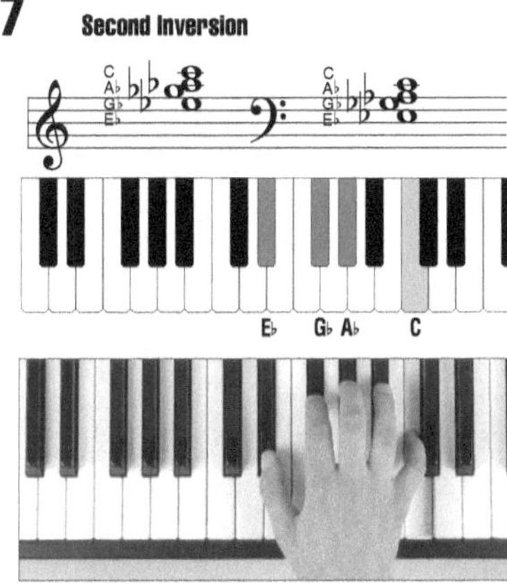

A♭7 Third Inversion

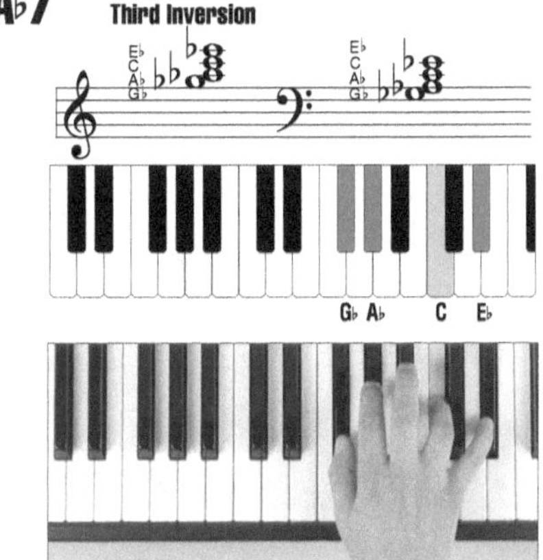

A♭7♭5 Root Position

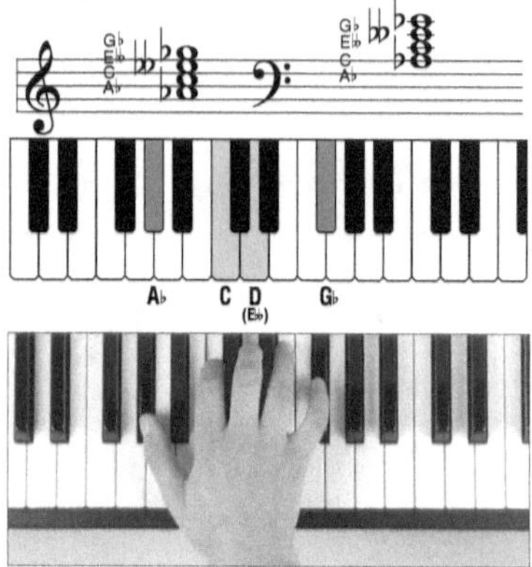

A♭7♭5 First Inversion

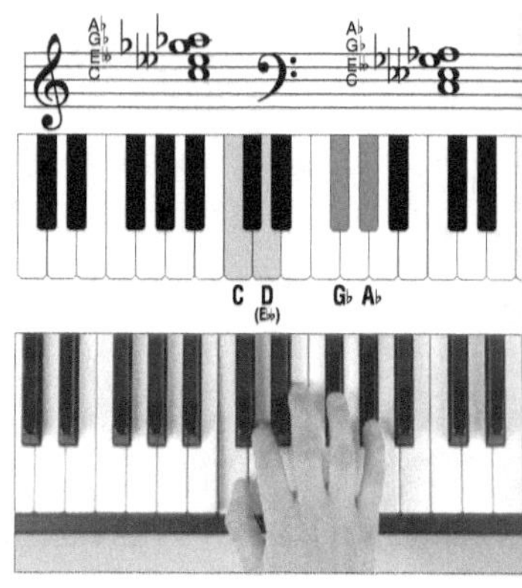

A♭7♭5 Second Inversion

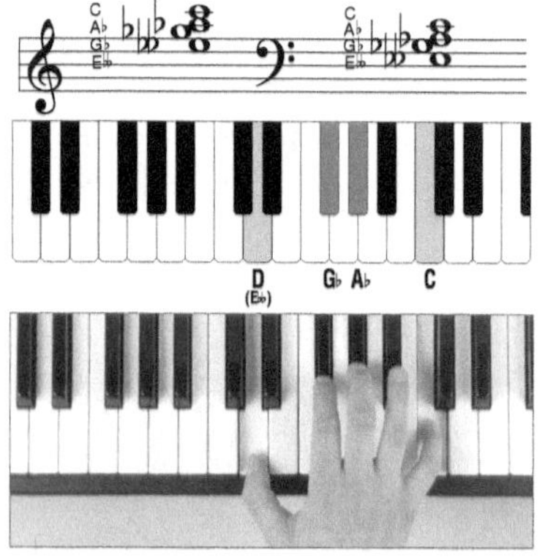

A♭7♭5 Third Inversion

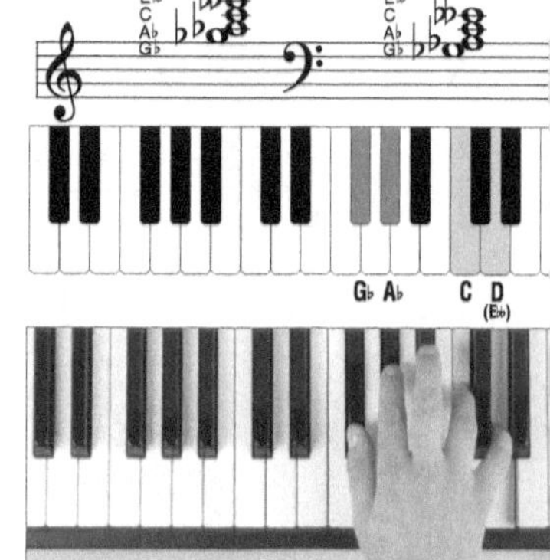

A♭7♯5 Root Position

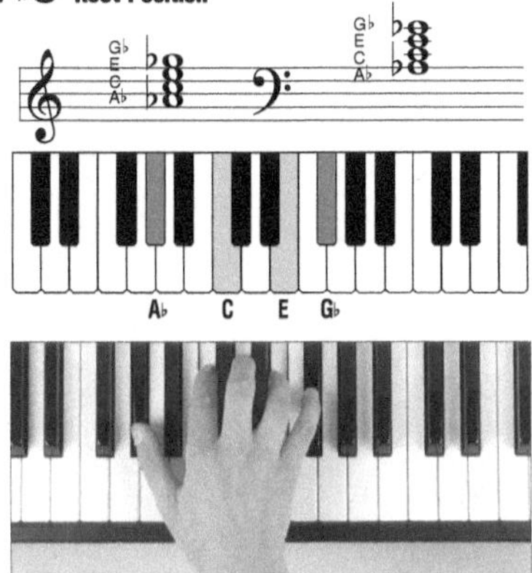

A♭7♯5 First Inversion

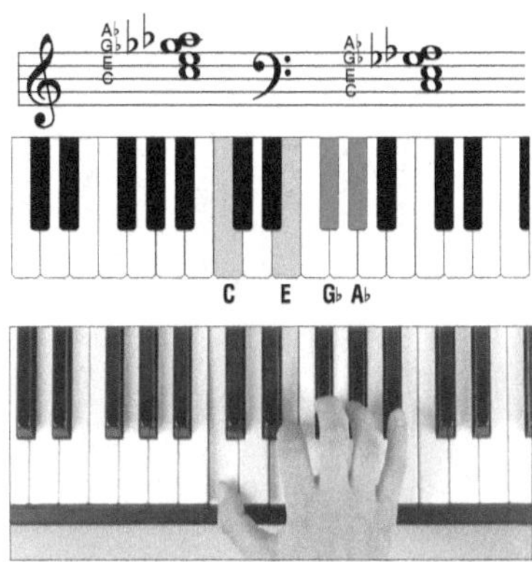

A♭7♯5 Second Inversion

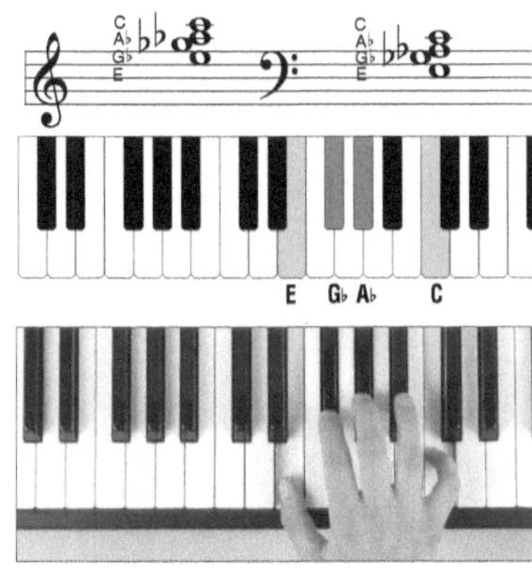

A♭7♯5 Third Inversion

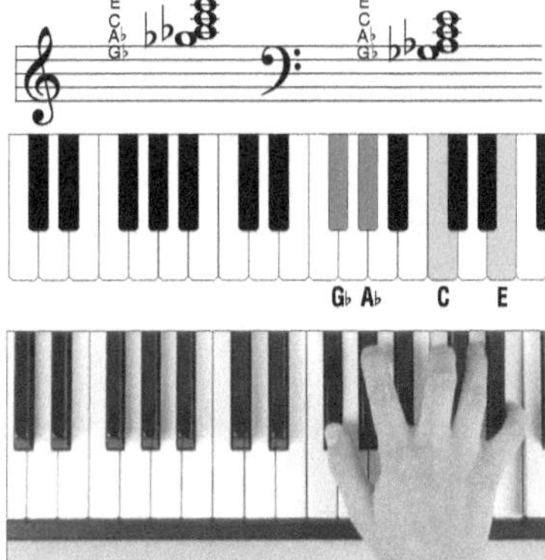

A♭7sus Root Position

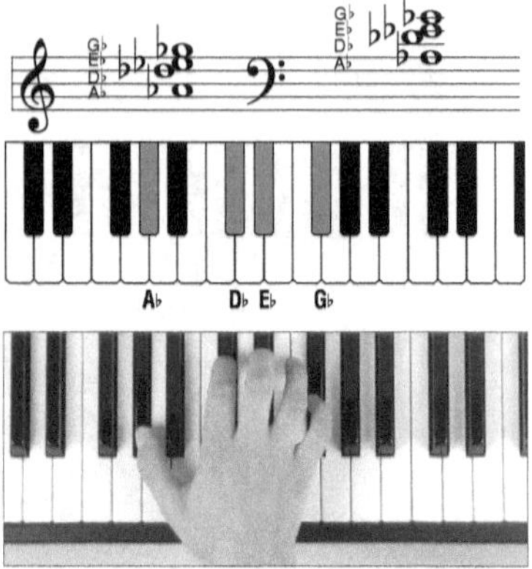

A♭7sus First Inversion

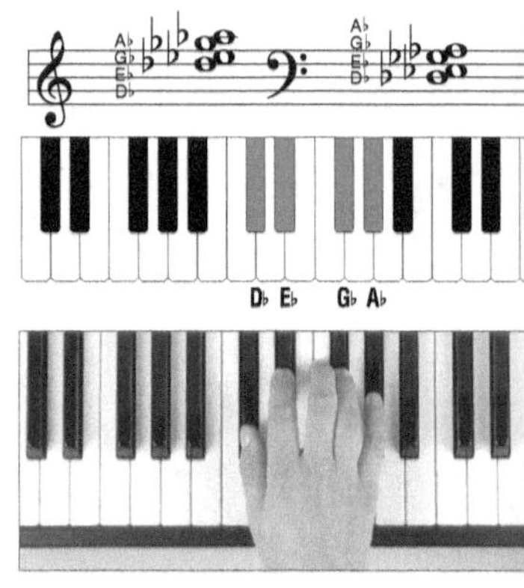

A♭7sus Second Inversion

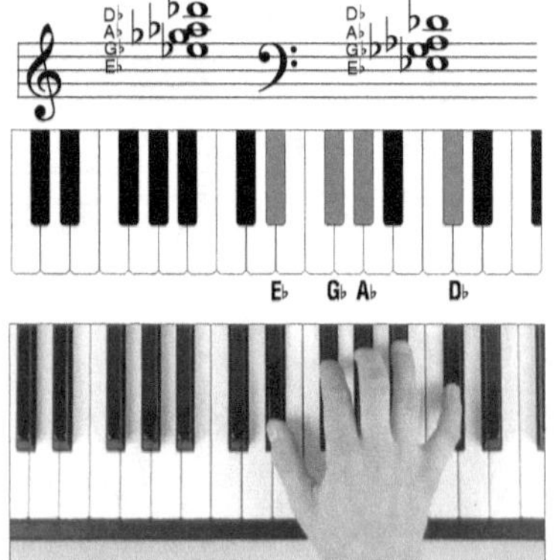

A♭7sus Third Inversion

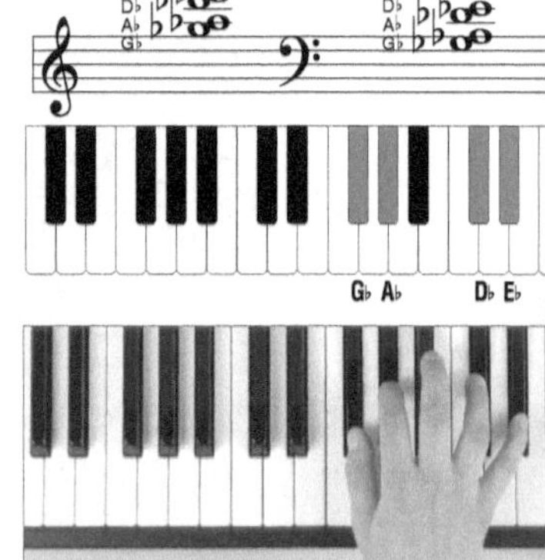

A♭m(add2), A♭m(add9) Root Position

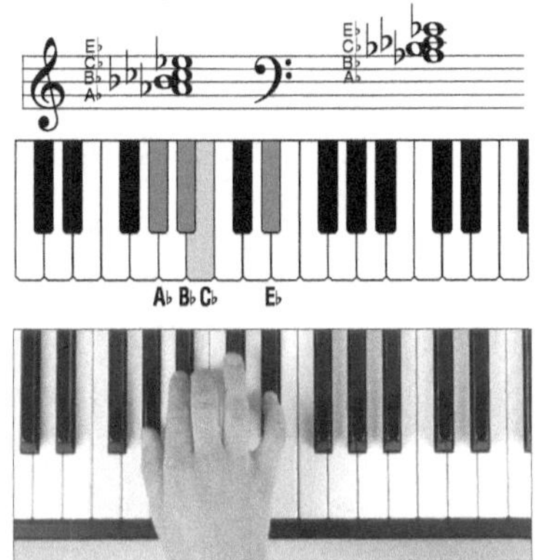

A♭m(add2), A♭m(add9) First Inversion

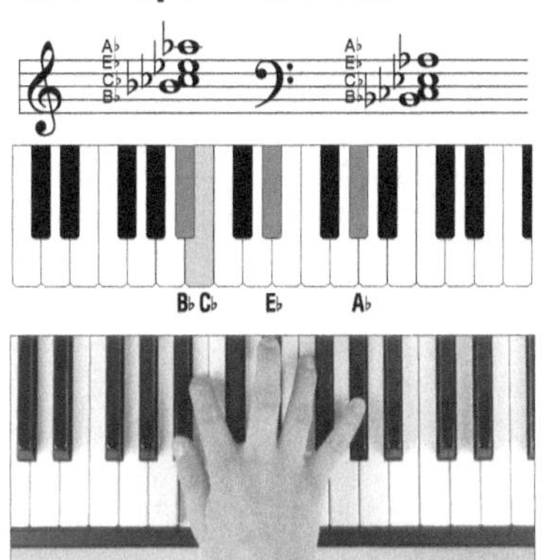

A♭m(add2), A♭m(add9) Second Inversion

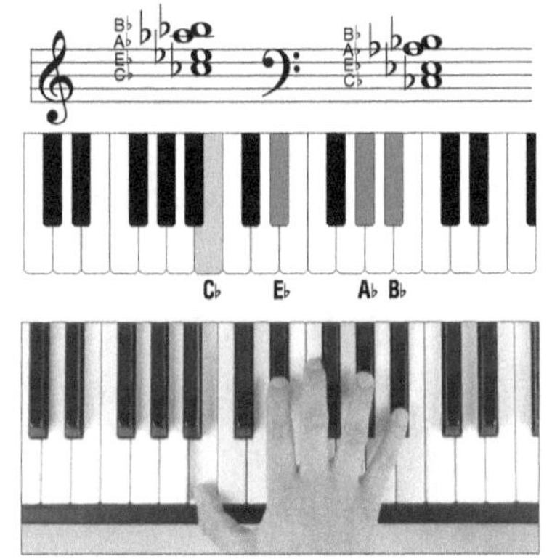

A♭m(add2), A♭m(add9) Third Inversion

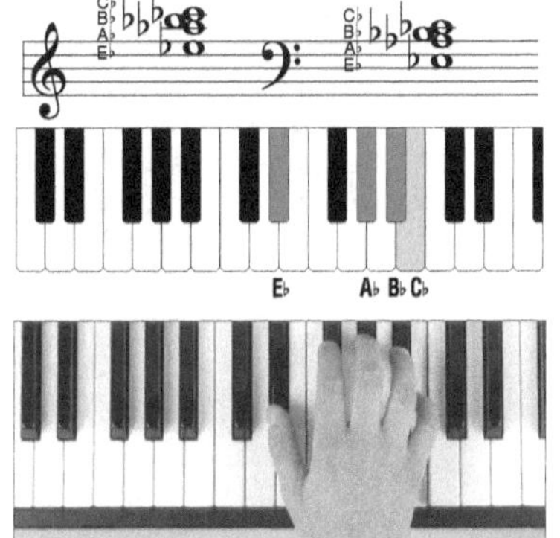

A♭m6 Root Position

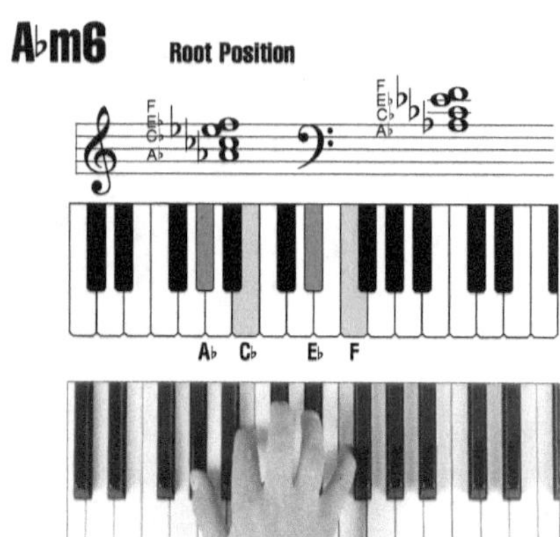

A♭m6 First Inversion

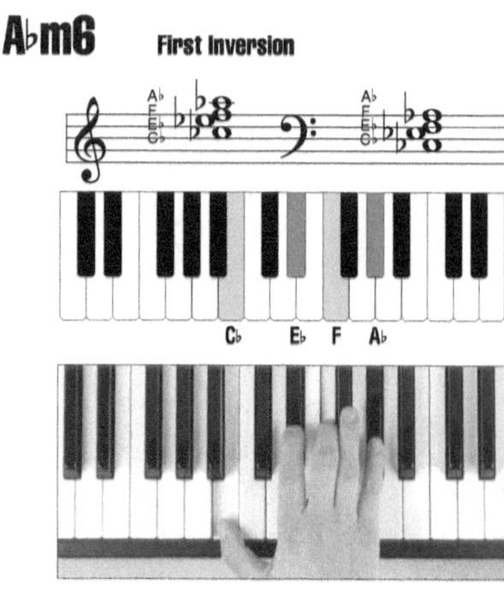

A♭m6 Second Inversion

A♭m6 Third Inversion

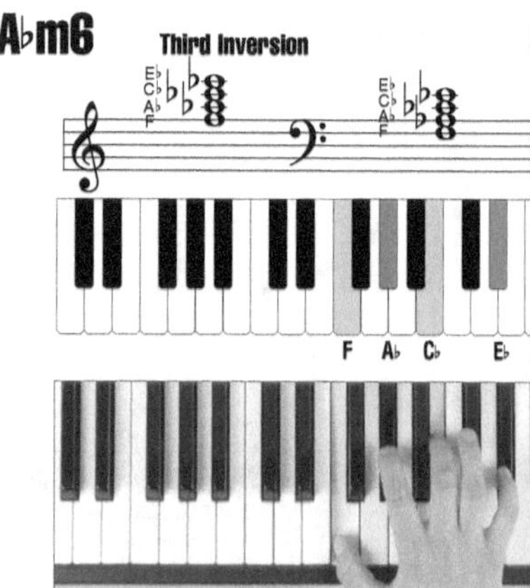

A♭m7 Root Position

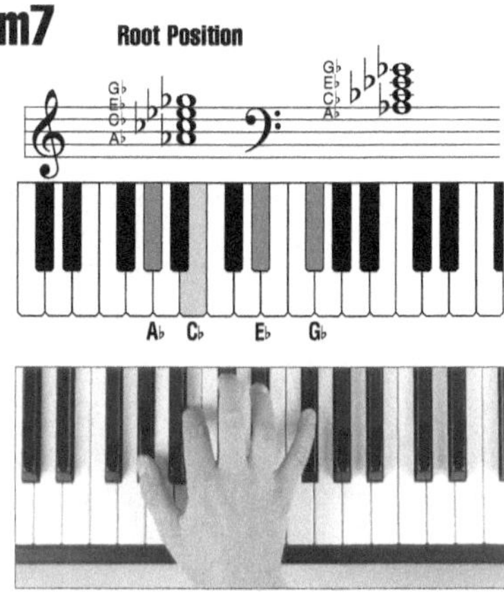

A♭m7 First Inversion

A♭m7 Second Inversion

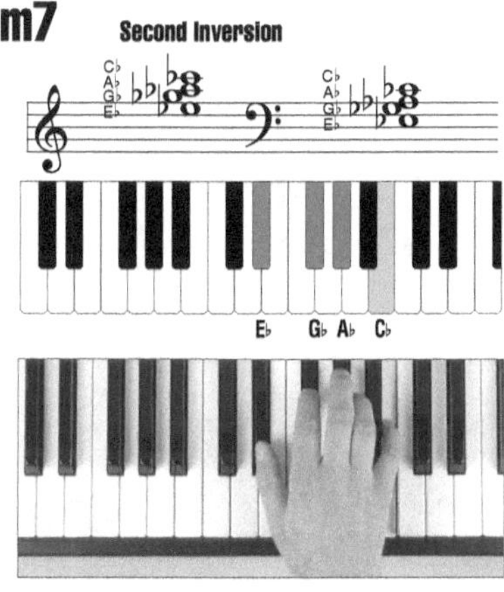

A♭m7 Third Inversion

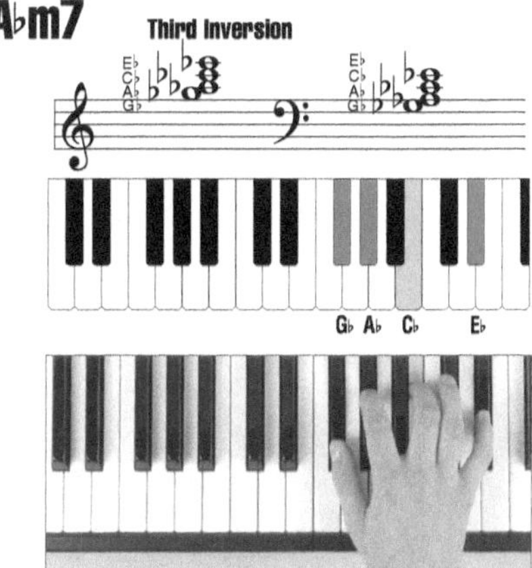

A♭m(maj7) Root Position

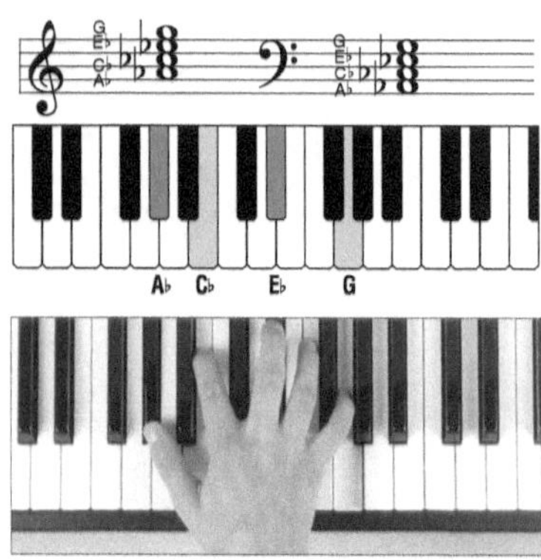

A♭m(maj7) First Inversion

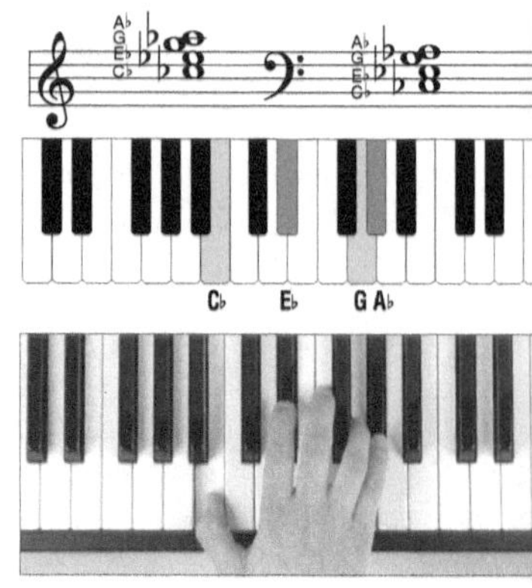

A♭m(maj7) Second Inversion

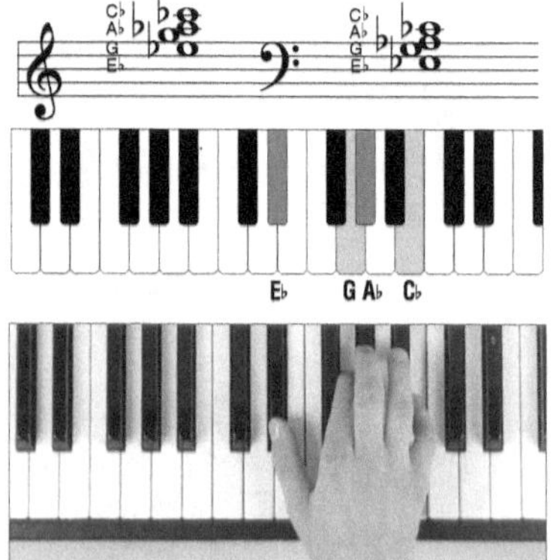

A♭m(maj7) Third Inversion

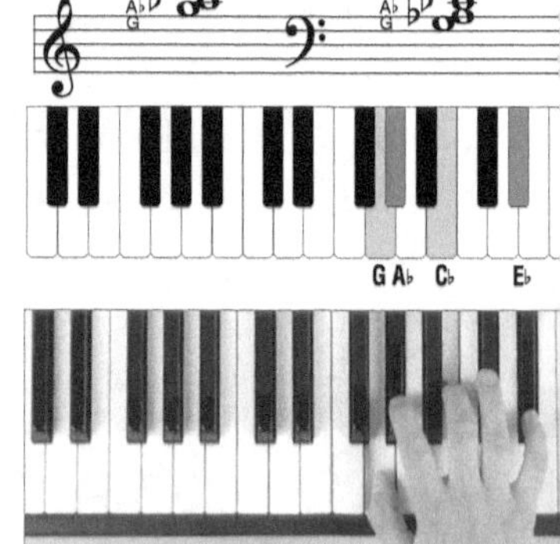

A♭m7♭5 Root Position

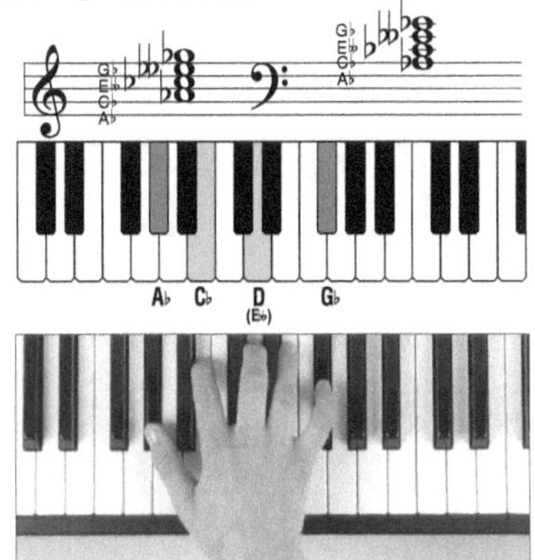

A♭m7♭5 First Inversion

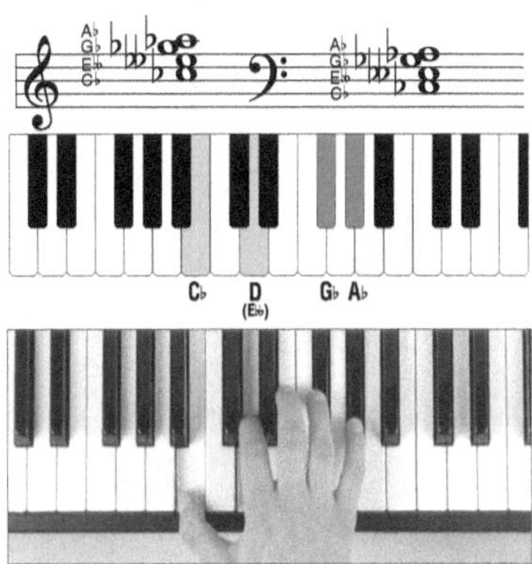

A♭m7♭5 Second Inversion

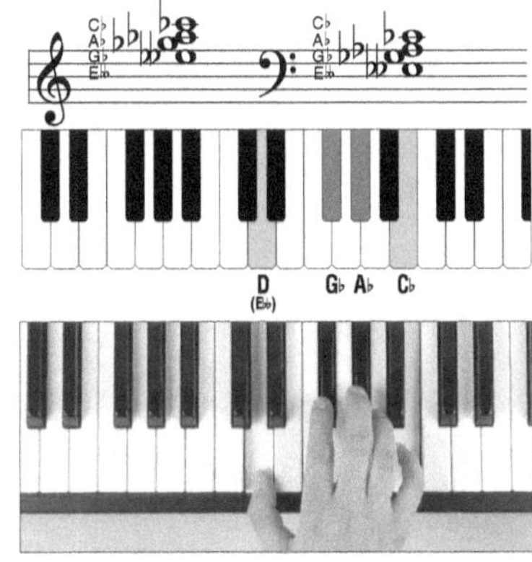

A♭m7♭5 Third Inversion

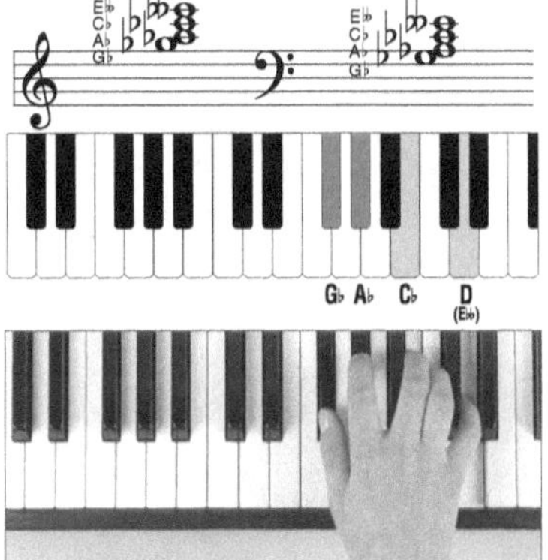

A♭dim7 Root Position

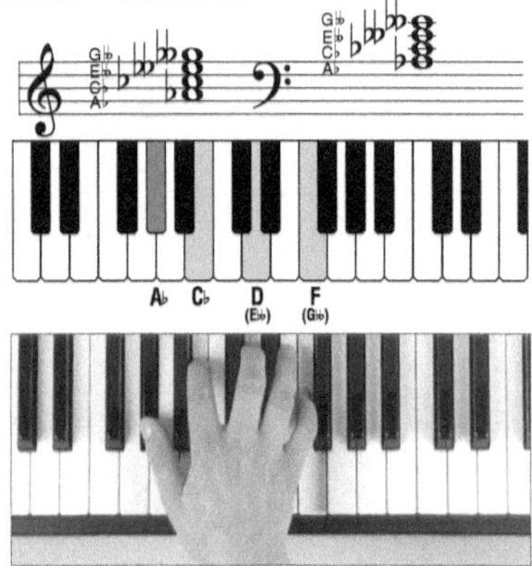

A♭dim7 First Inversion

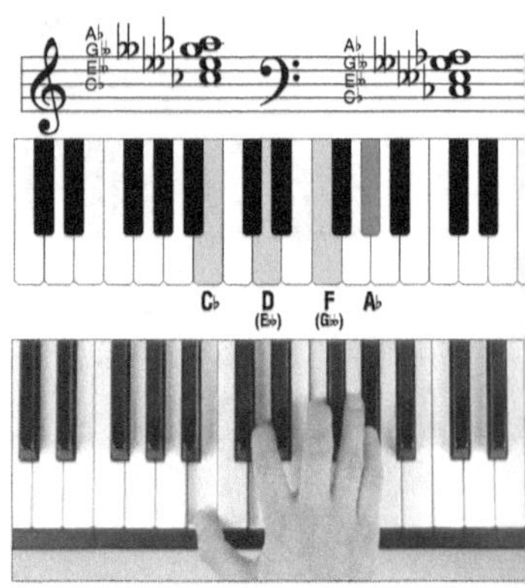

A♭dim7 Second Inversion

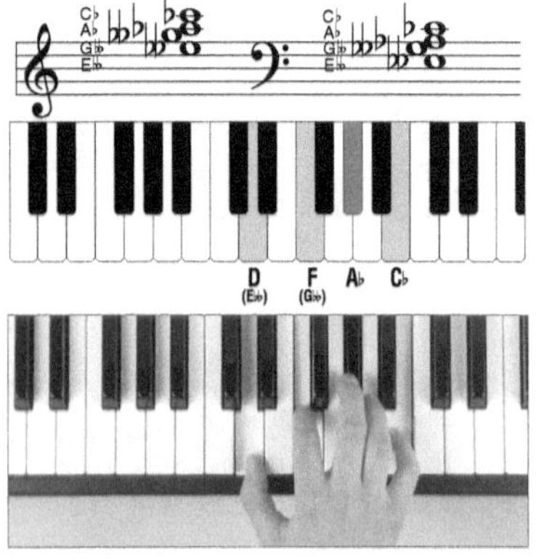

A♭dim7 Third Inversion

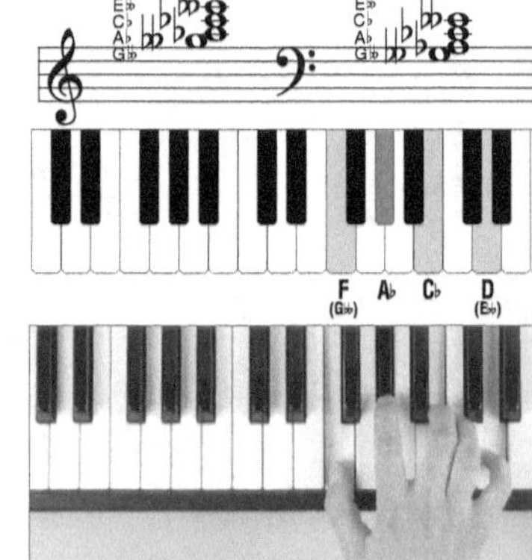

A♭dim(maj7) Root Position

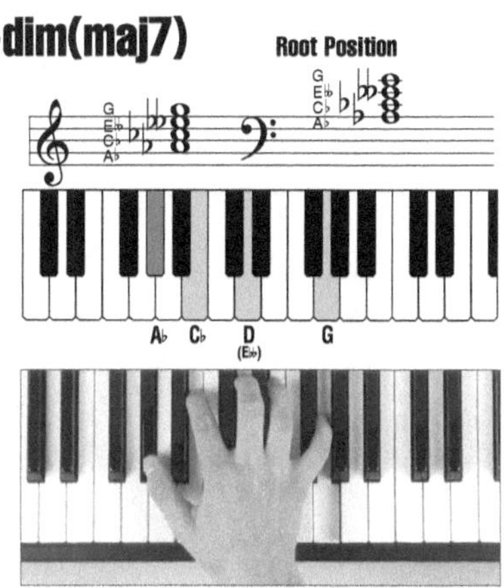

A♭dim(maj7) First Inversion

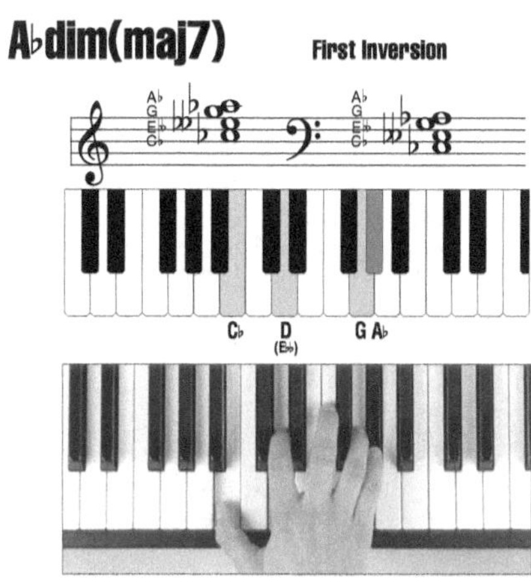

A♭dim(maj7) Second Inversion

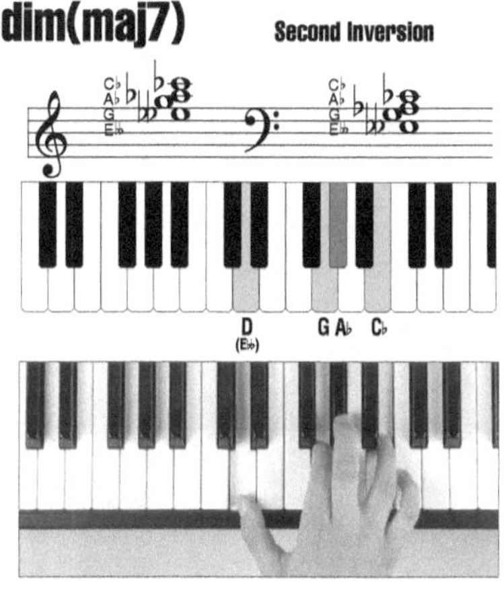

A♭dim(maj7) Third Inversion

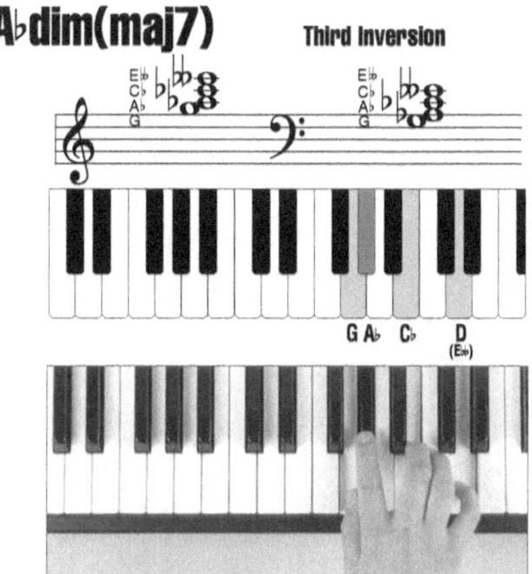

A♭5

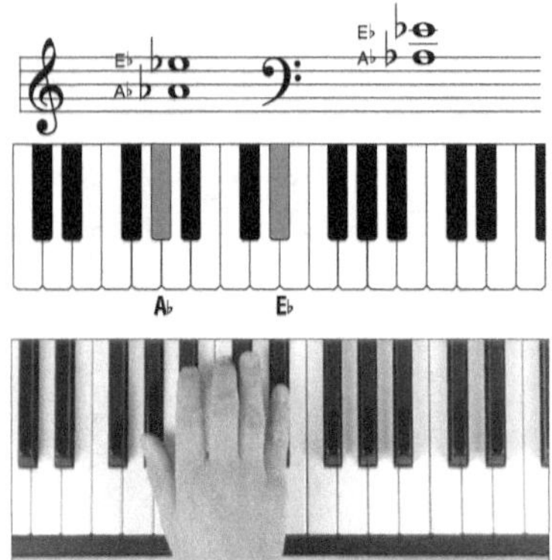

A♭maj7♯11

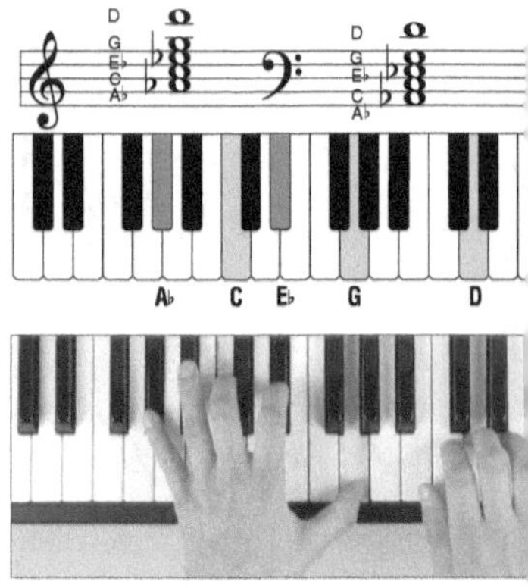

A♭$^6_9$

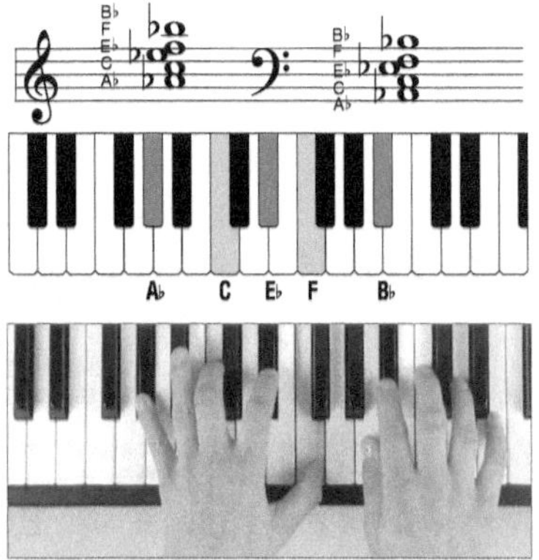

A♭maj9

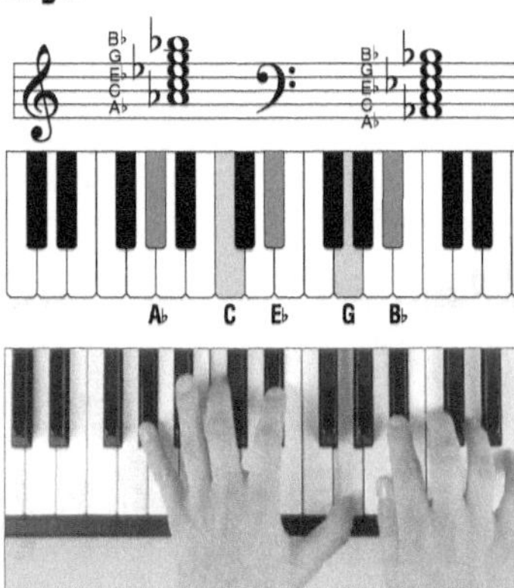

A♭maj$^6_9$

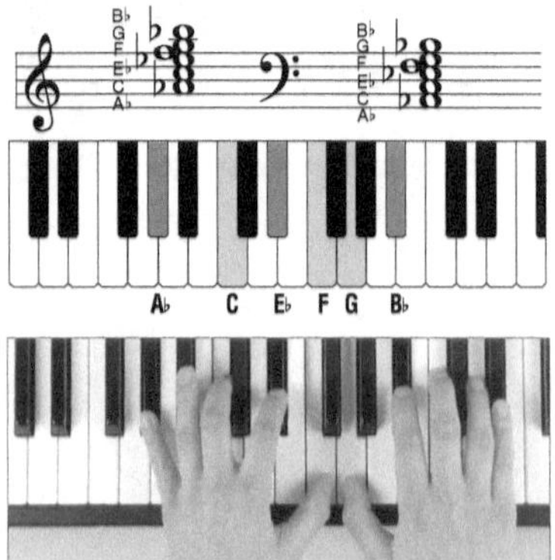

A♭maj9♭5

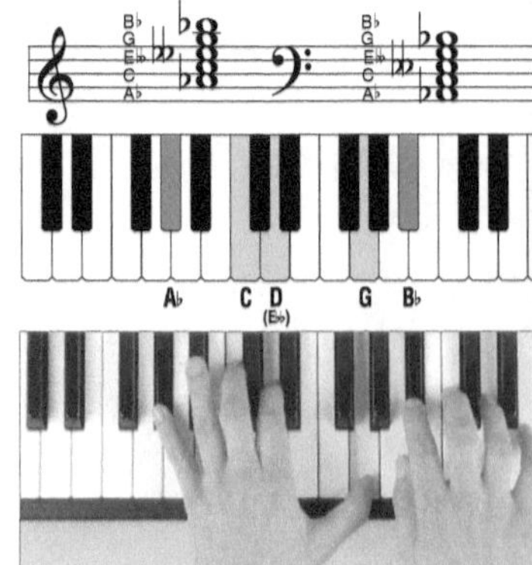

A♭maj9♯5

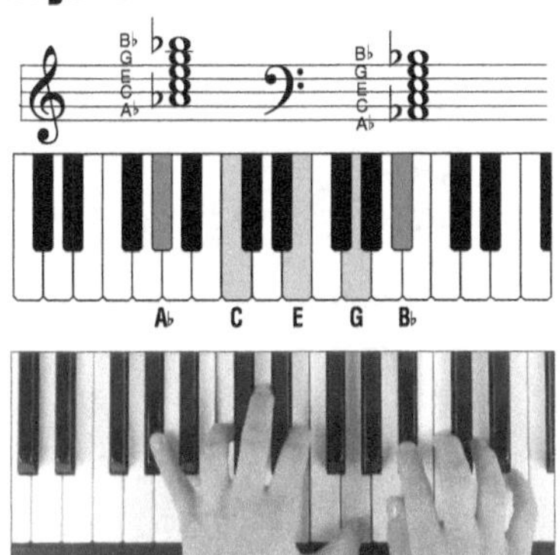

A♭maj13♭5

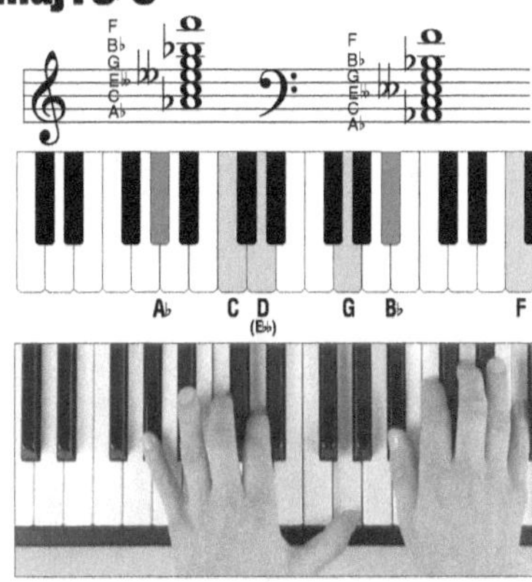

A♭maj9♯11

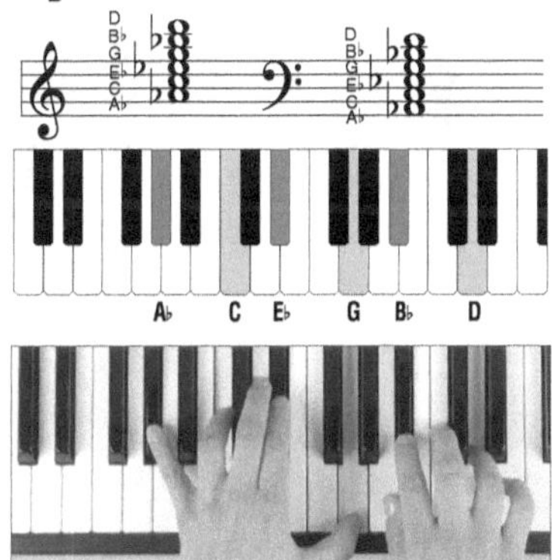

A♭maj13♯11

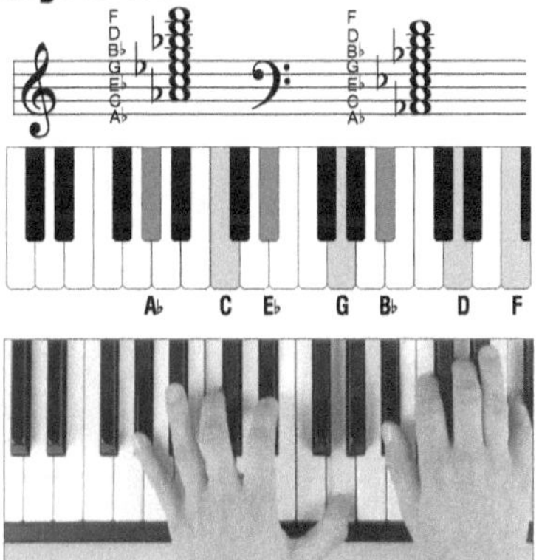

A♭maj13

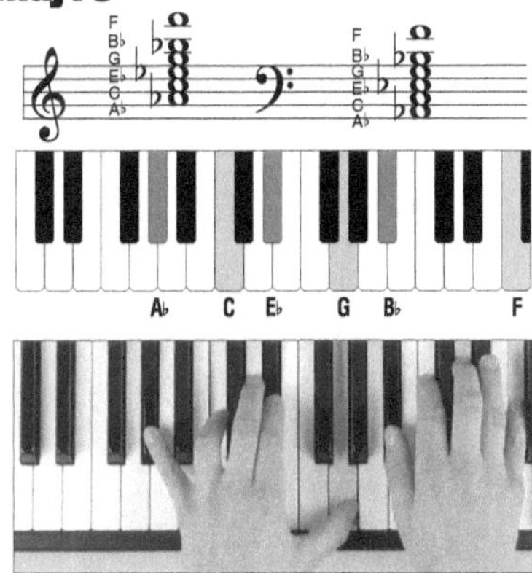

A♭7♭9

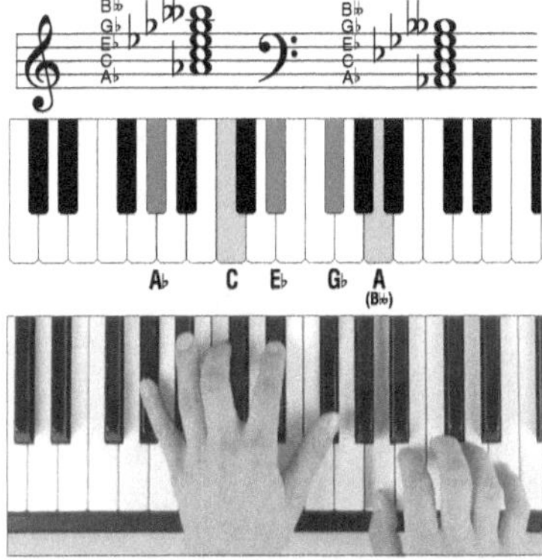

A♭7♯9

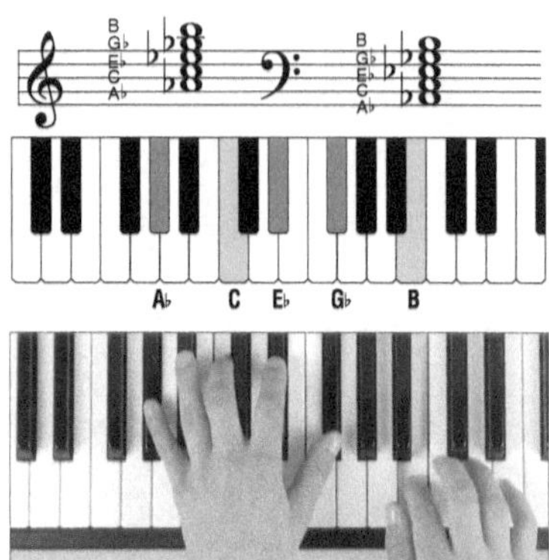

A♭7♯11

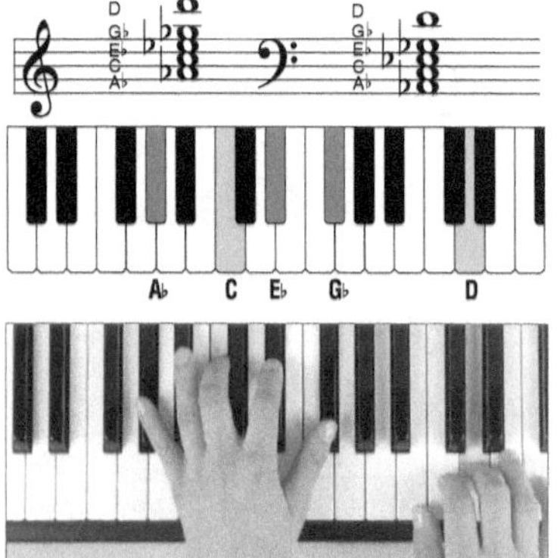

A♭7♭5(♭9)

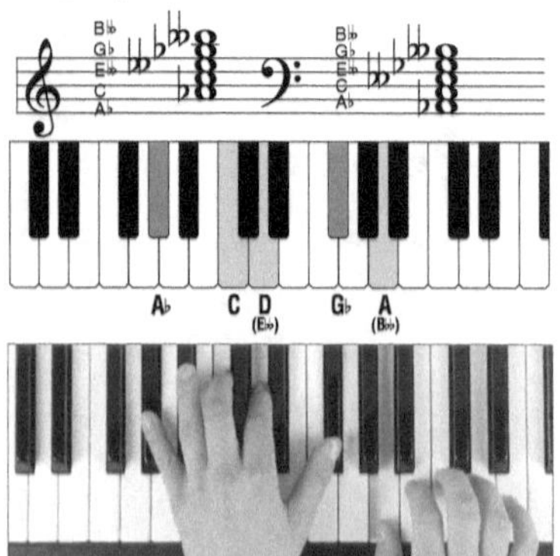

A♭7♭5(♯9)

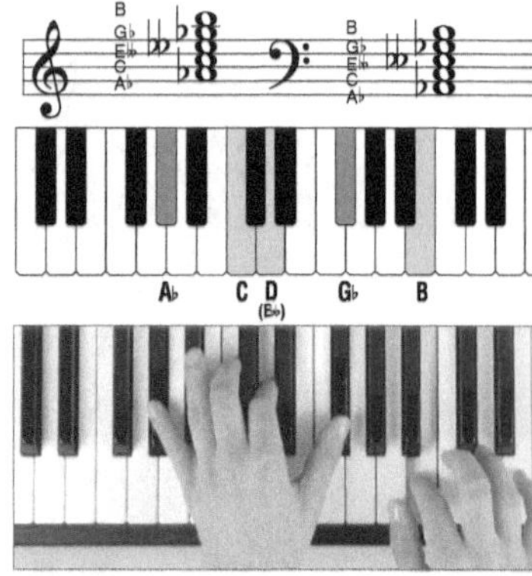

A♭7♯5(♭9)

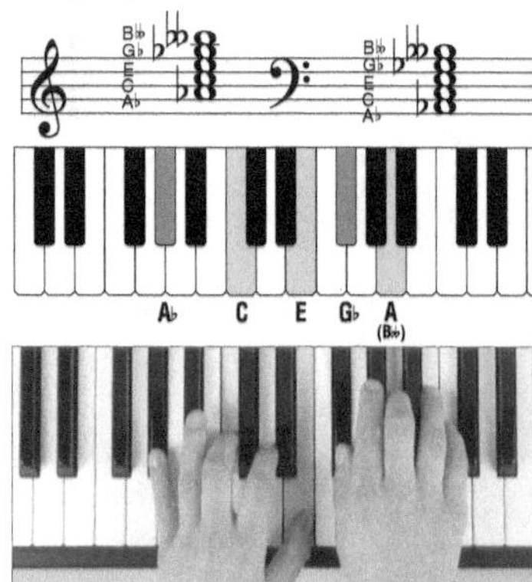

A♭7♯5(♯9)

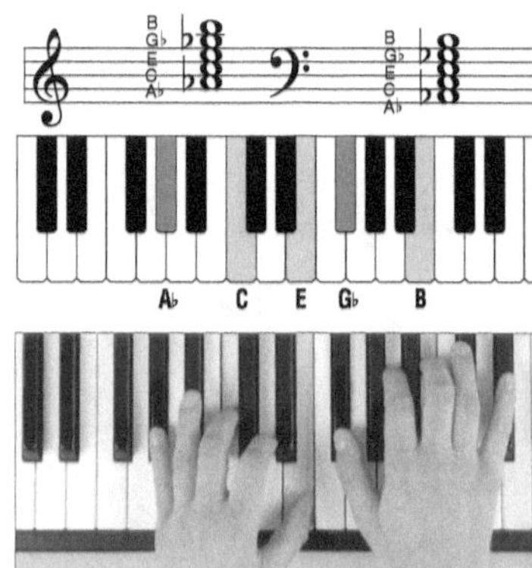

A♭7♭9(♯9)

A♭7♭9(♯11)

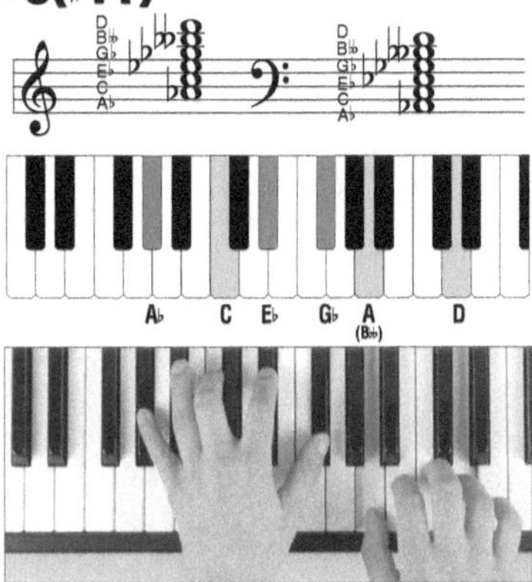

A♭7(add13)

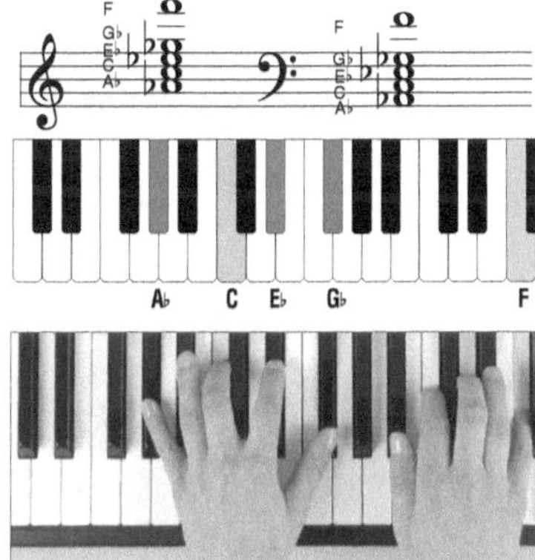

A♭7♯9(♯11)

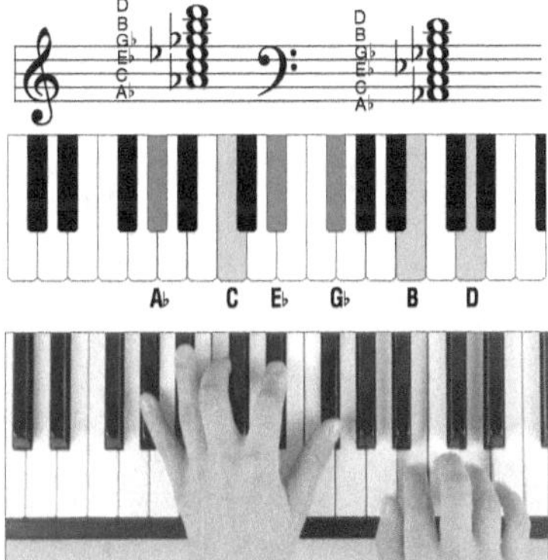

A♭7♭13

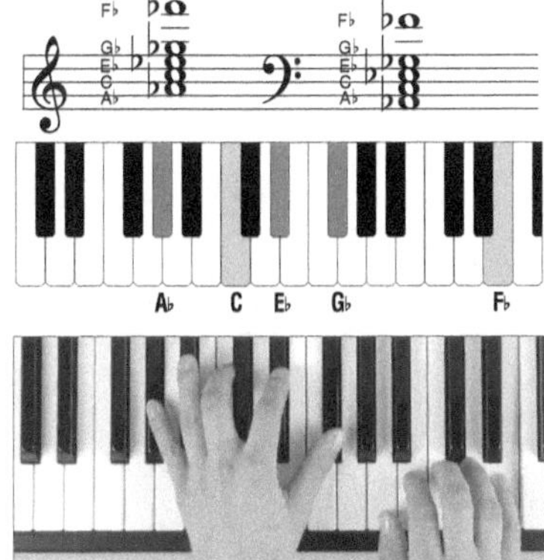

A♭7♭9(♭13)

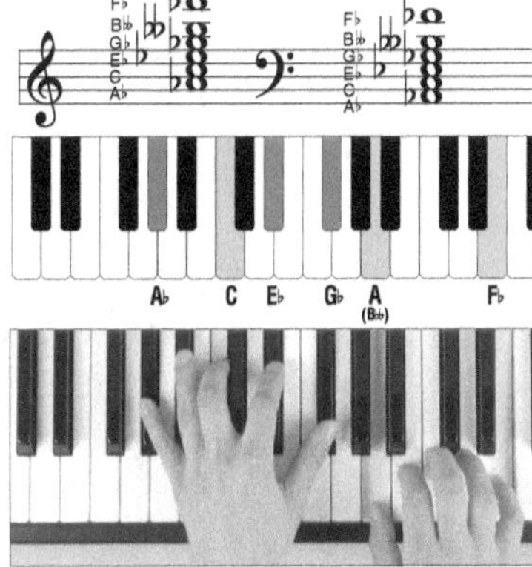

A♭7♯9(♭13)

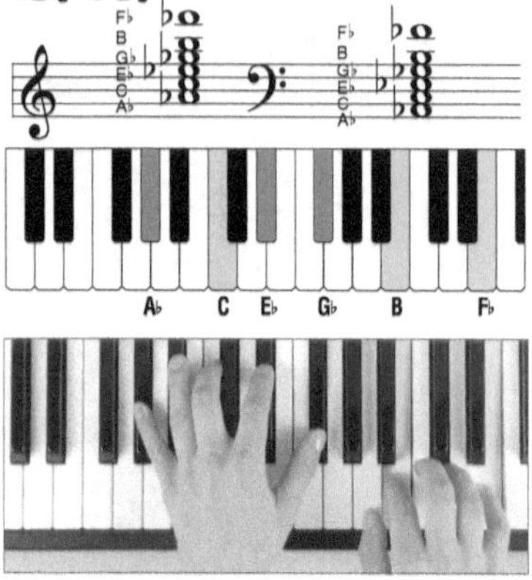

F♭
B
G♭
E♭
C
A♭
A♭ C E♭ G♭ B F♭

A♭7♯11(♭13)

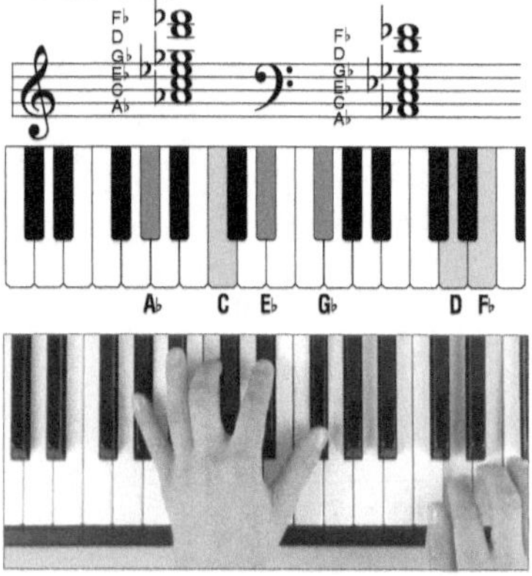

F♭
D
G♭
E♭
C
A♭
A♭ C E♭ G♭ D F♭

A♭7♭9(♯9,♯11)

D
C♭
B𝄫
G♭
E♭
C
A♭
A♭ C E♭ G♭ A (B𝄫) C♭ D

A♭9

B♭
G♭
E♭
C
A♭
A♭ C E♭ G♭ B♭

A♭9(♭5)

B♭
G♭
E𝄫
C
A♭
A♭ C D (E𝄫) G♭ B♭

A♭9♯5

B♭
G♭
E
C
A♭
A♭ C E G♭ B♭

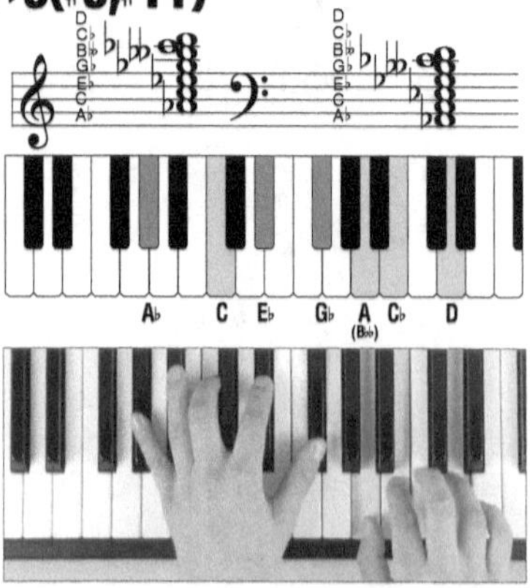

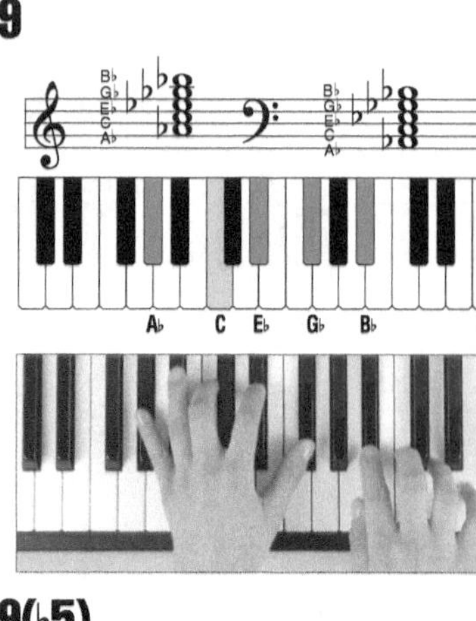

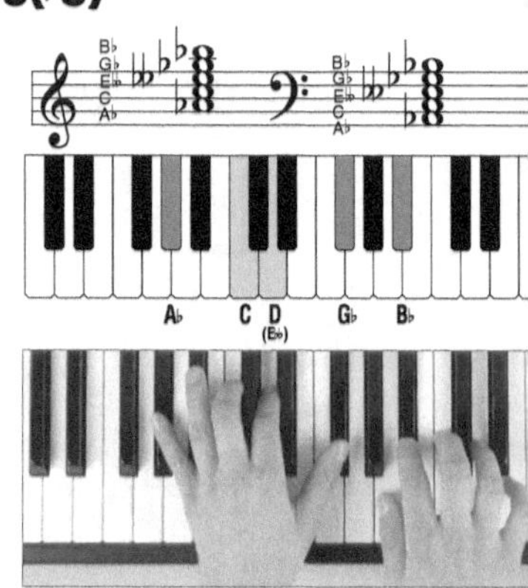

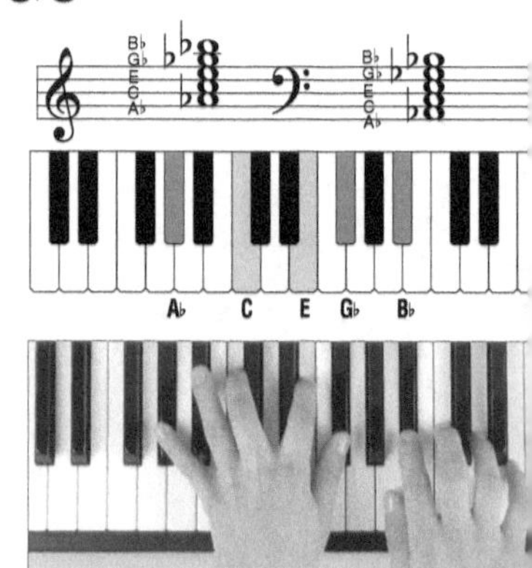

♭9♯11

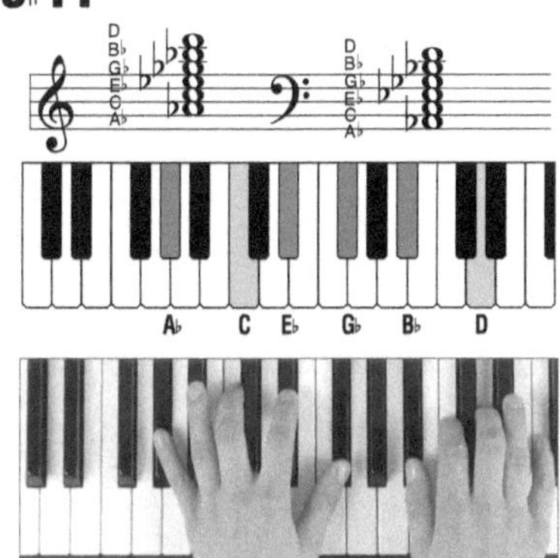

♭9♭13

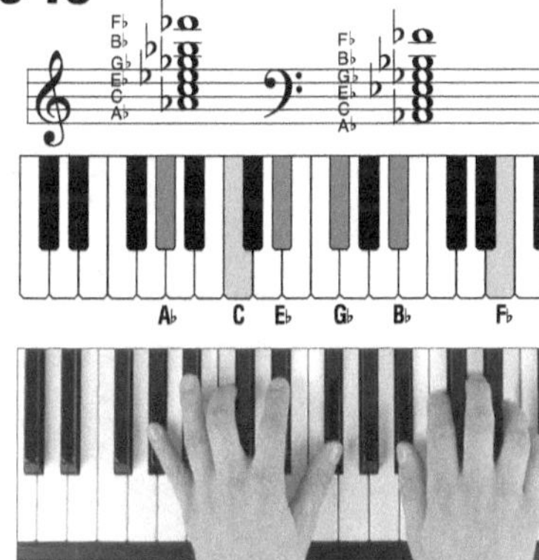

♭9♯11(♭13)

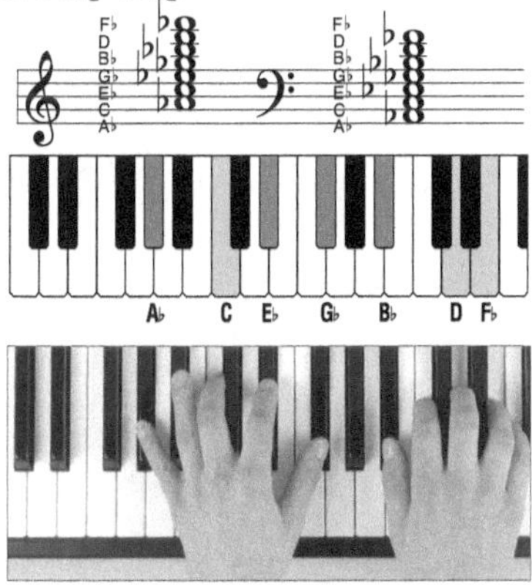

A♭11, A♭9(sus4)

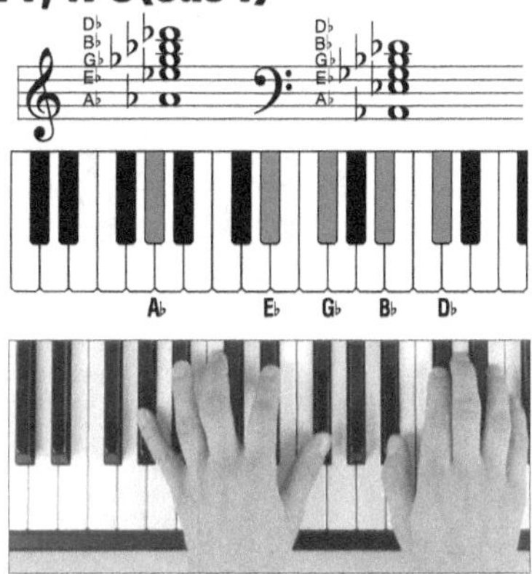

A♭13

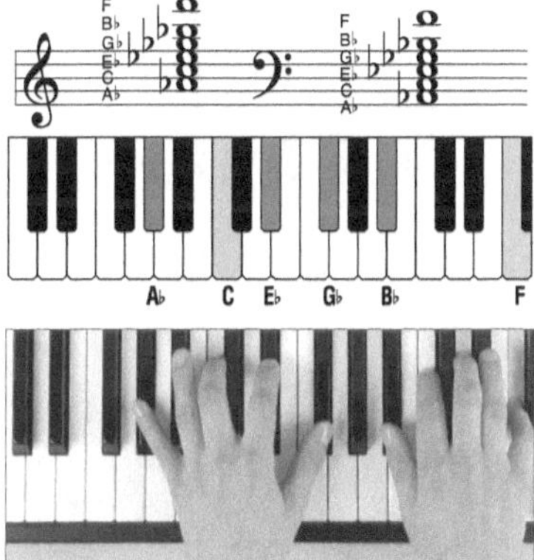

A♭13♭5

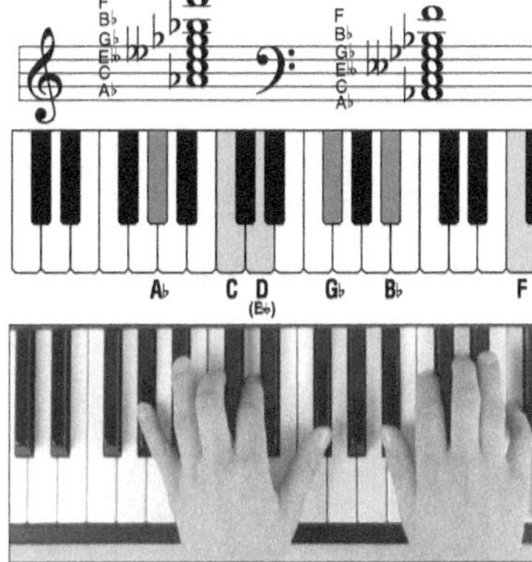

A♭13♭9

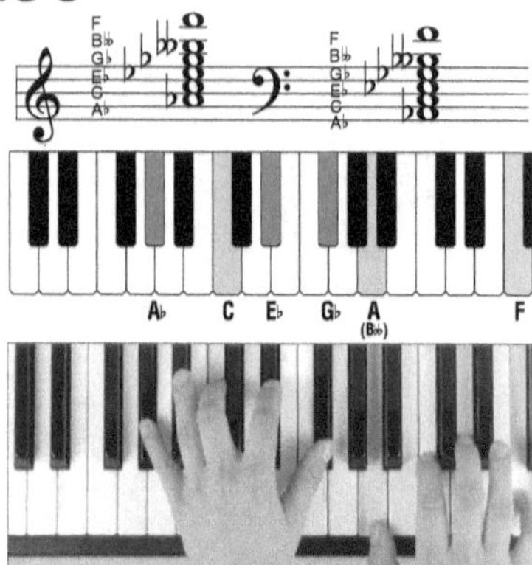

A♭13♯9

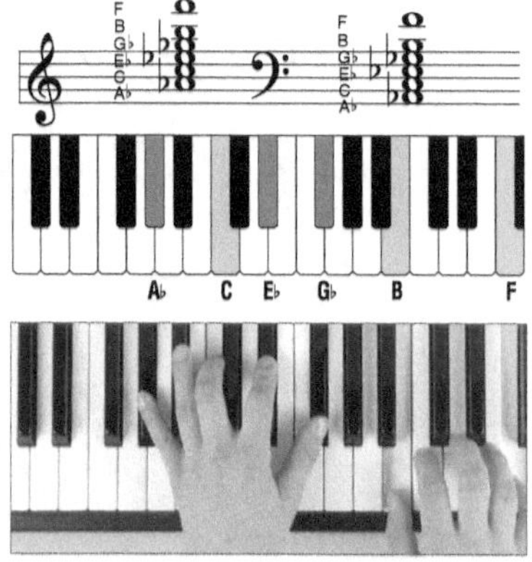

A♭13♯11

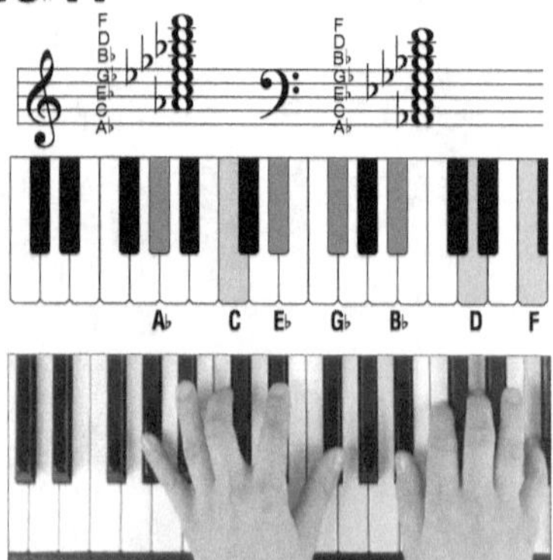

A♭13(sus4)

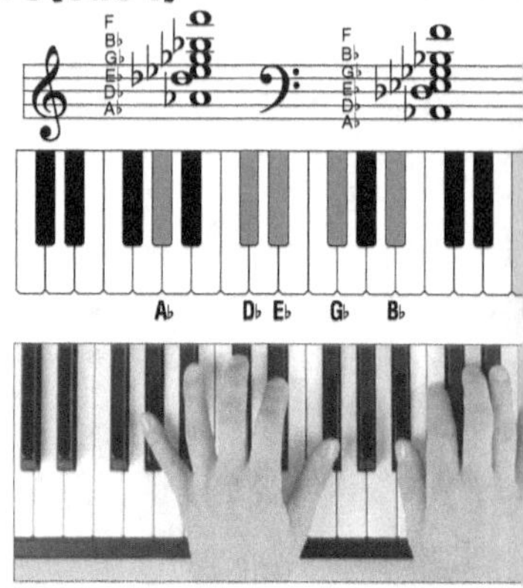

A♭m(♯5)

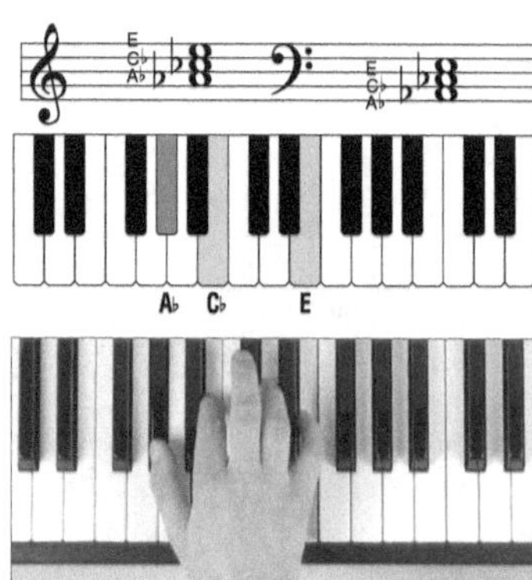

A♭m$^{6}_{9}$

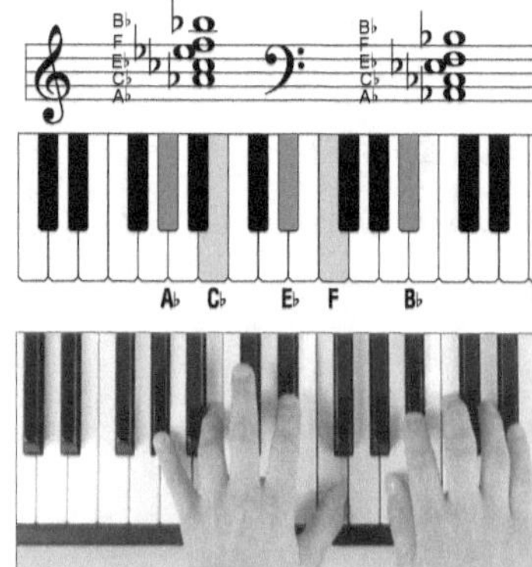

A♭m7(add4)

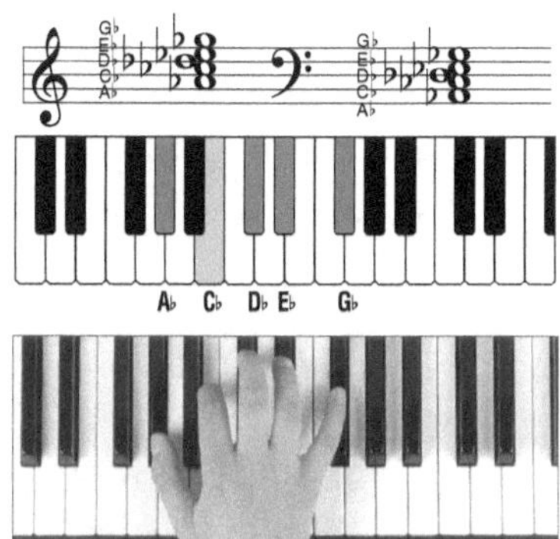

A♭m9

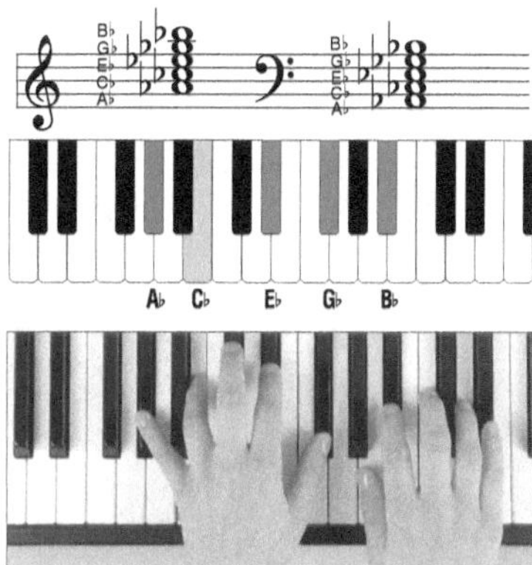

A♭m7(add11)

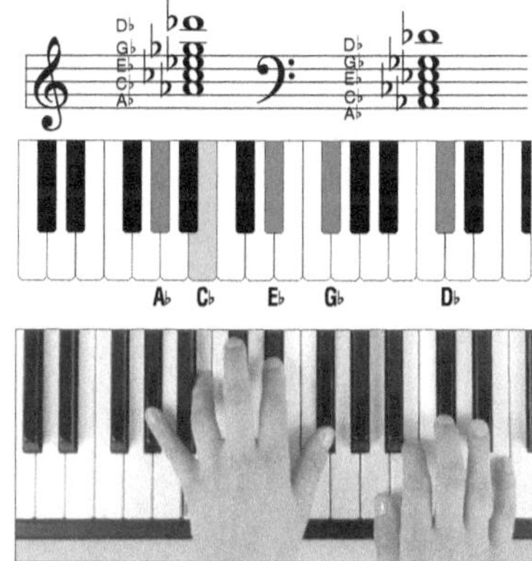

A♭m9(maj7)

A♭m7♭5(♭9)

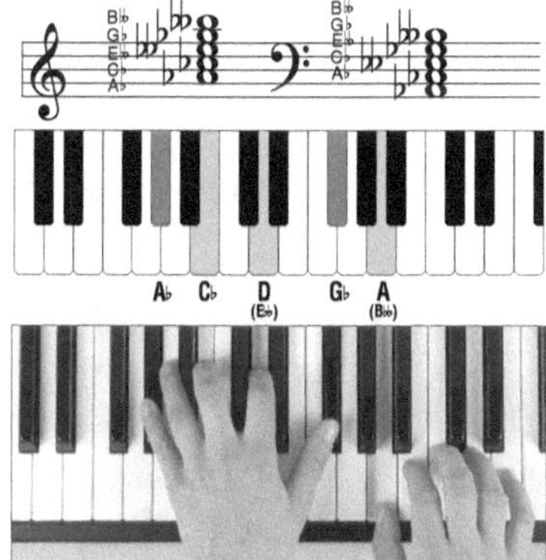

A♭m9♭5

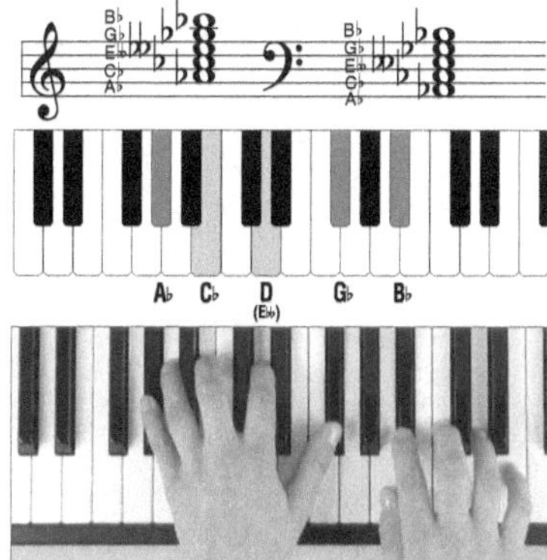

A♭m11

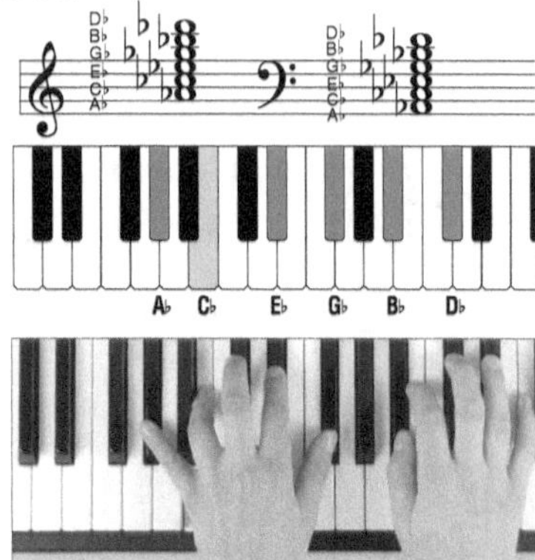

A♭m13

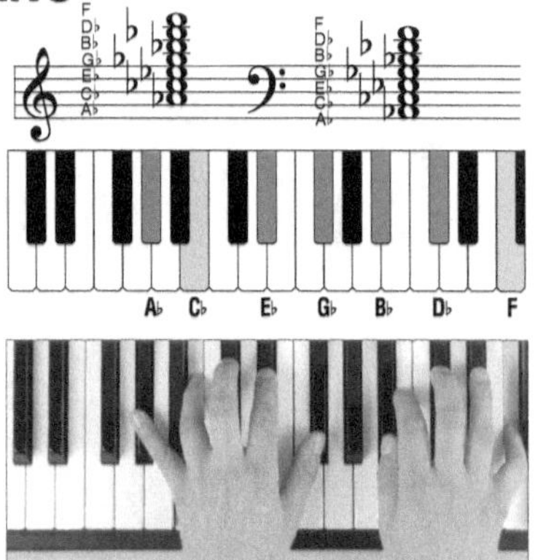

A♭dim7(add9)

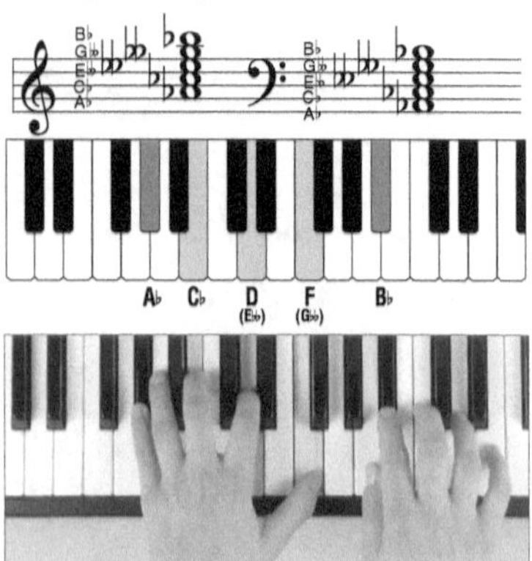

A♭m11♭5

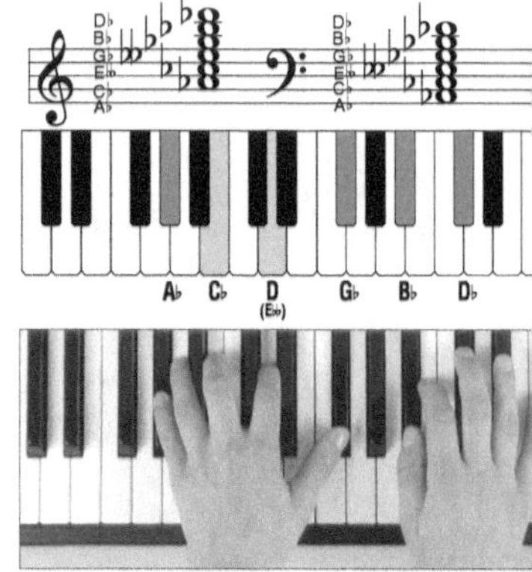

A♭m11(maj7)

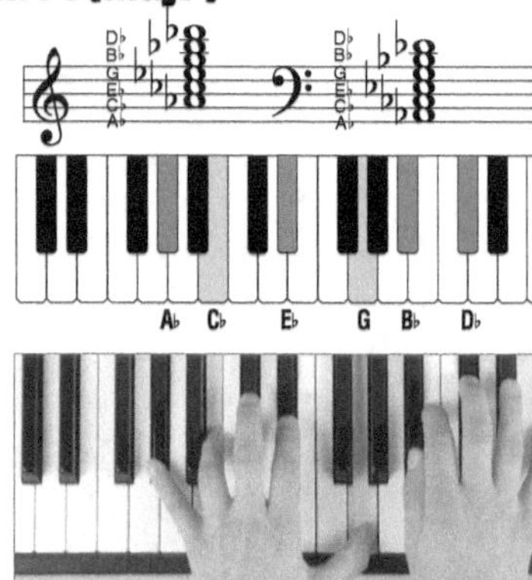

A♭7alt.

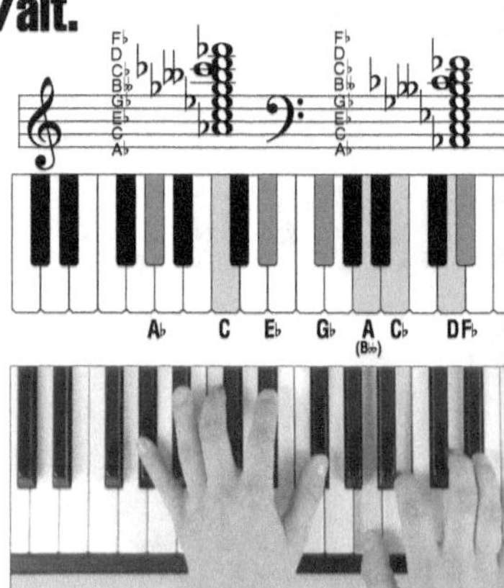

A

Root Position

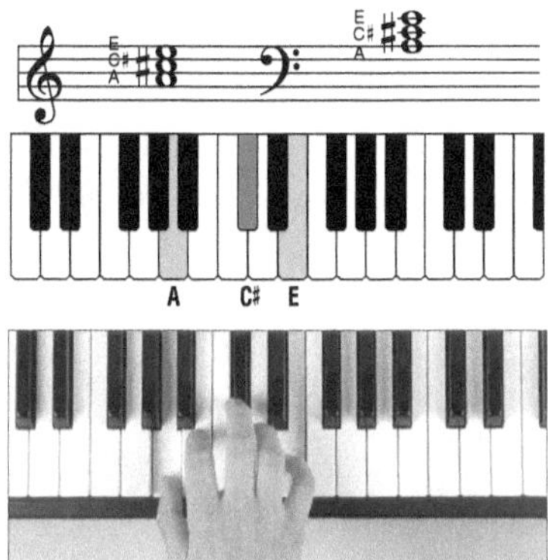

A

First Inversion

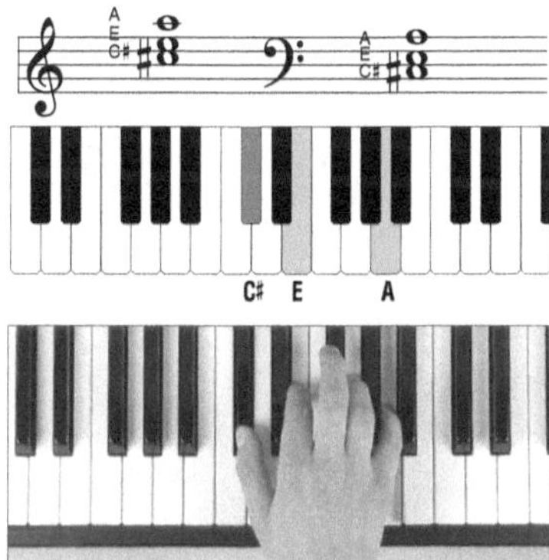

A

Second Inversion

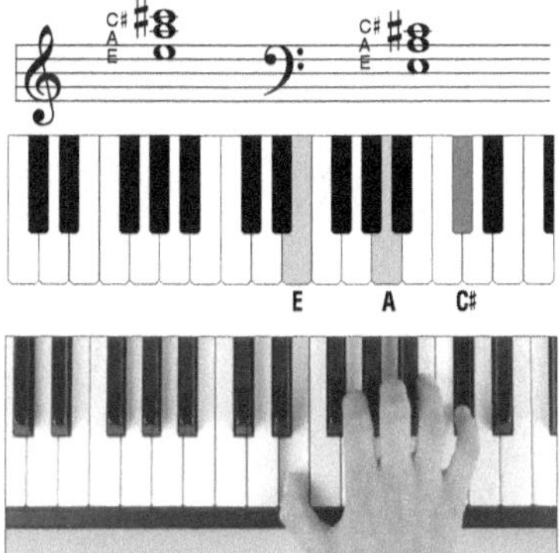

Am

Root Position

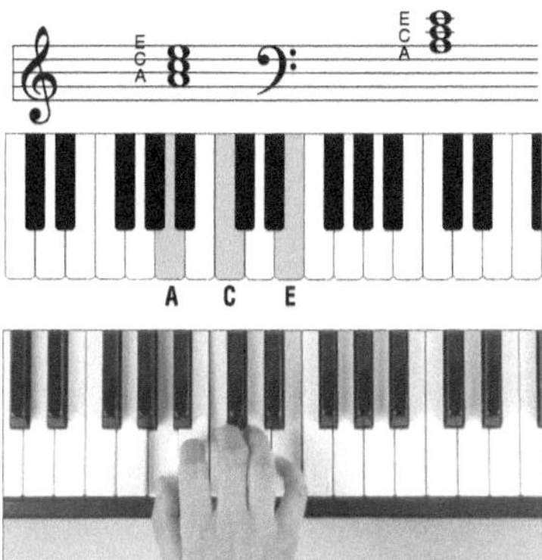

Am

First Inversion

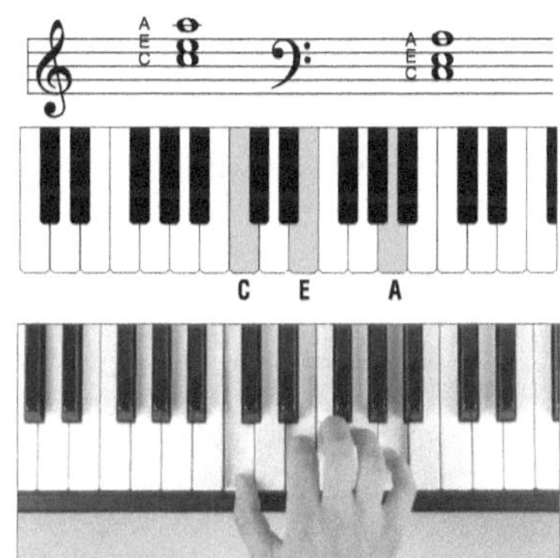

Am

Second Inversion

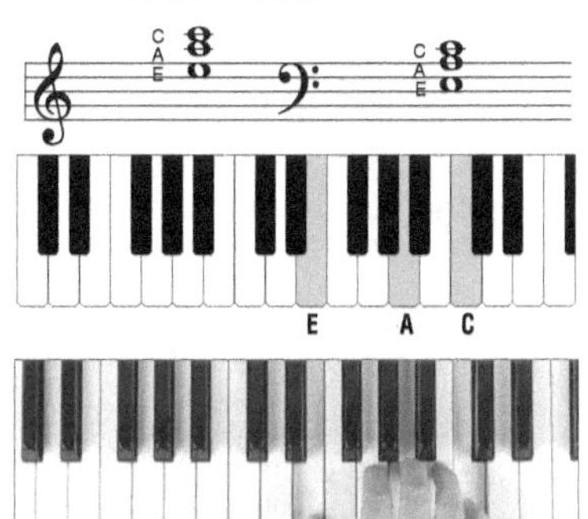

A+ Root Position

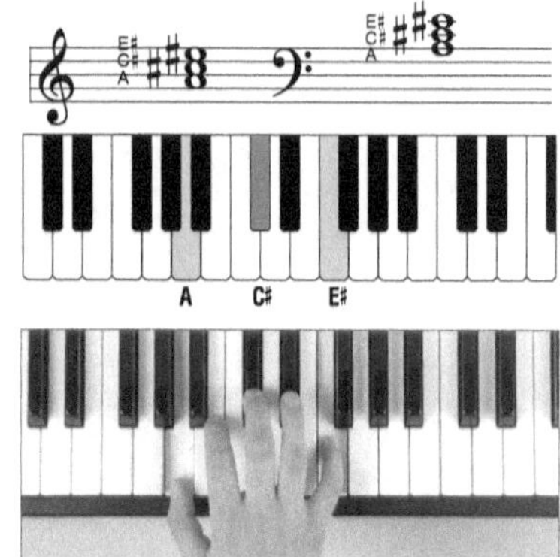

A+ First Inversion

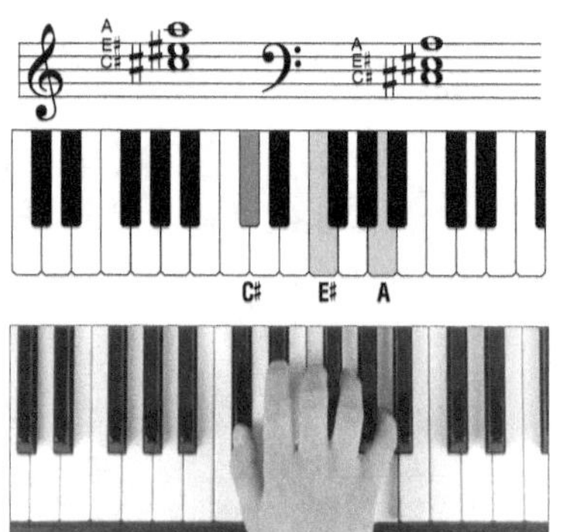

A+ Second Inversion

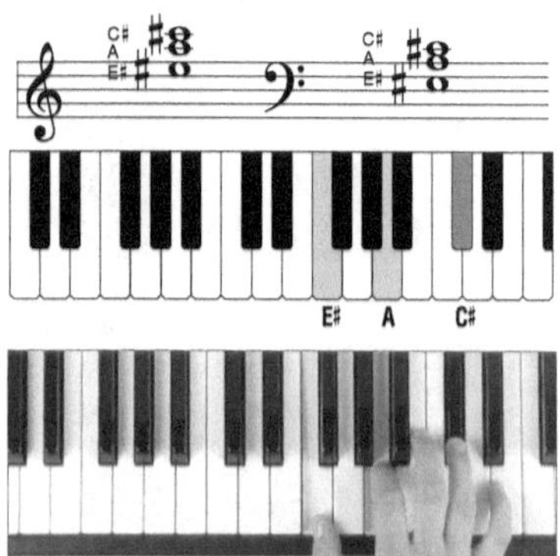

Adim Root Position

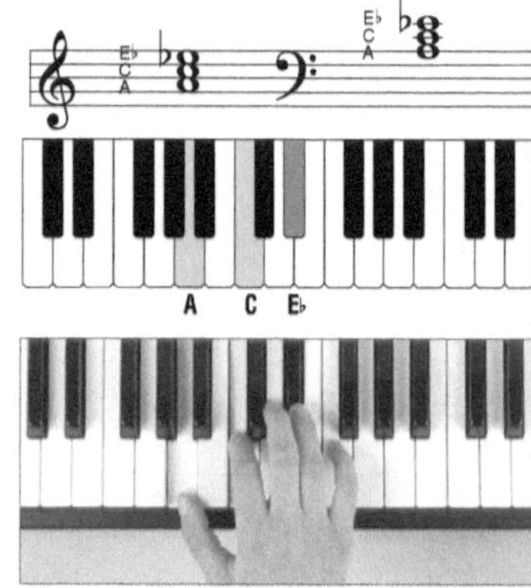

Adim First Inversion

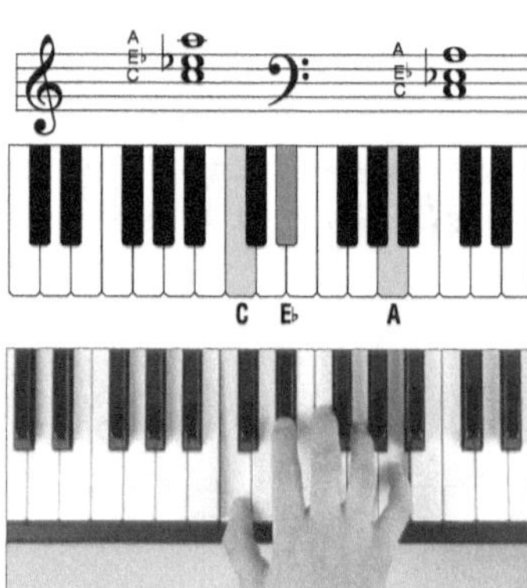

Adim Second Inversion

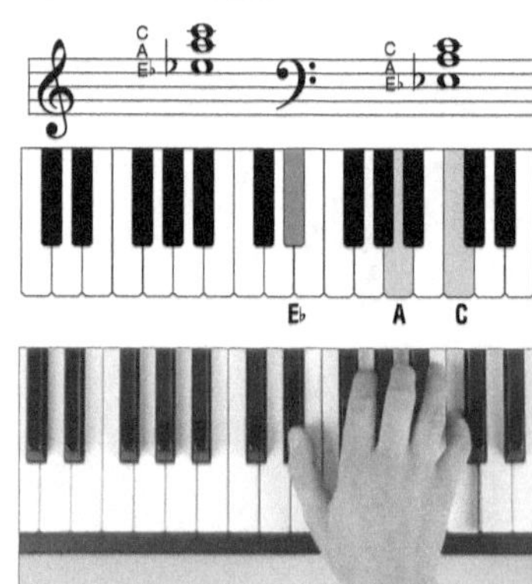

Asus Root Position

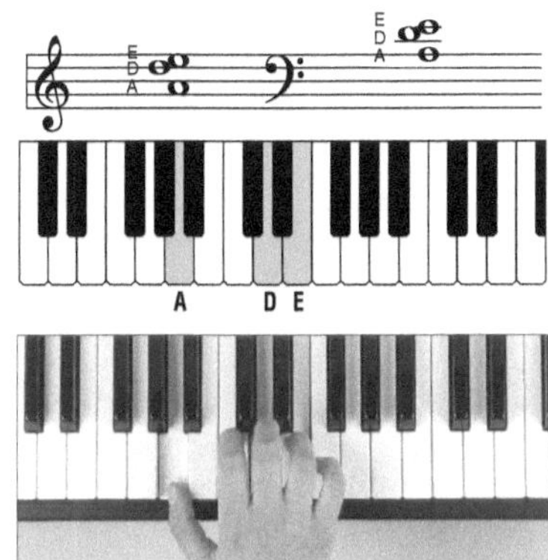

Asus First Inversion

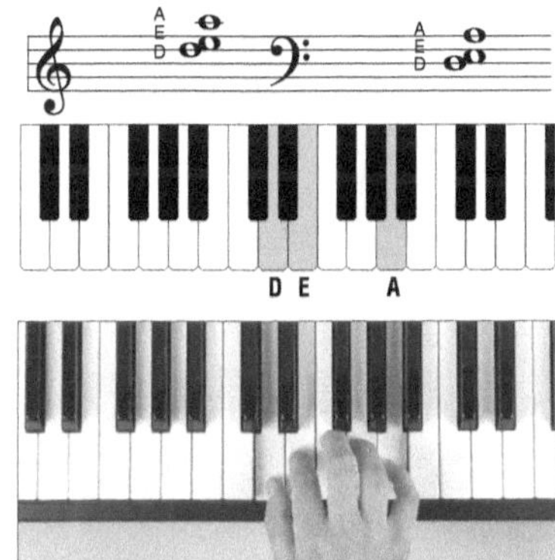

Asus Second Inversion

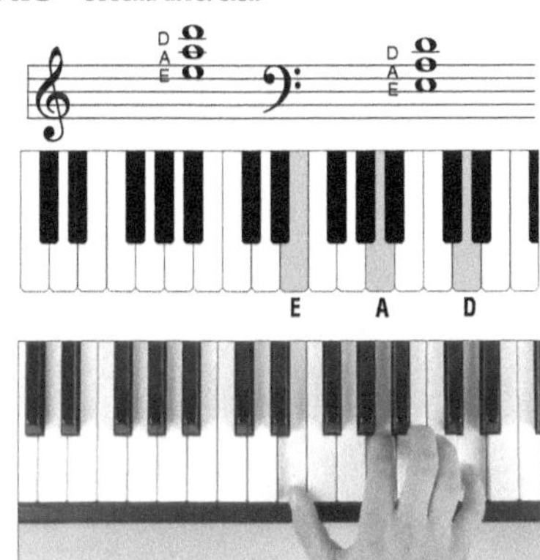

A(♭5) Root Position

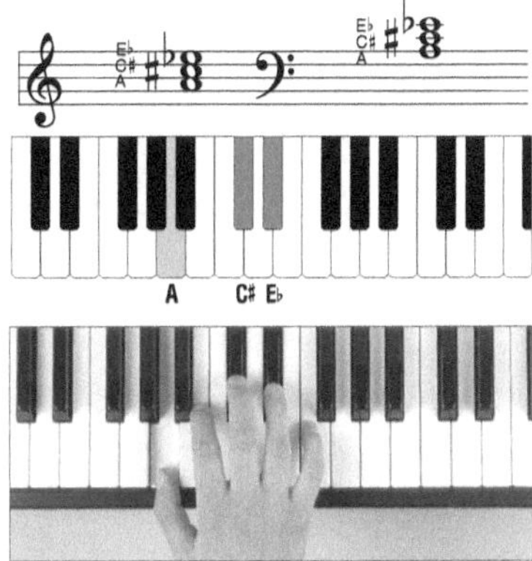

A(♭5) First Inversion

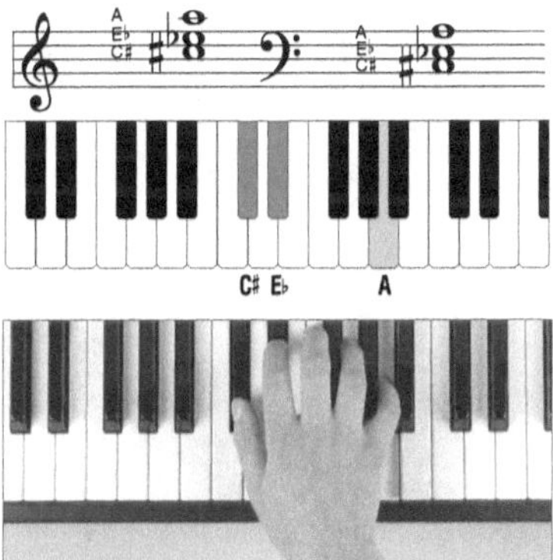

A(♭5) Second Inversion

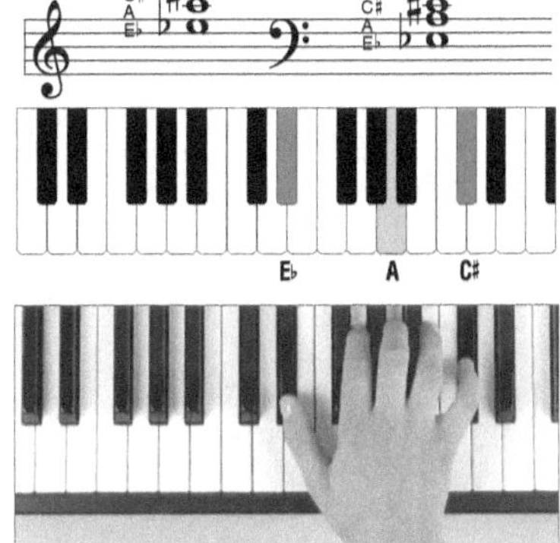

Asus2 Root Position

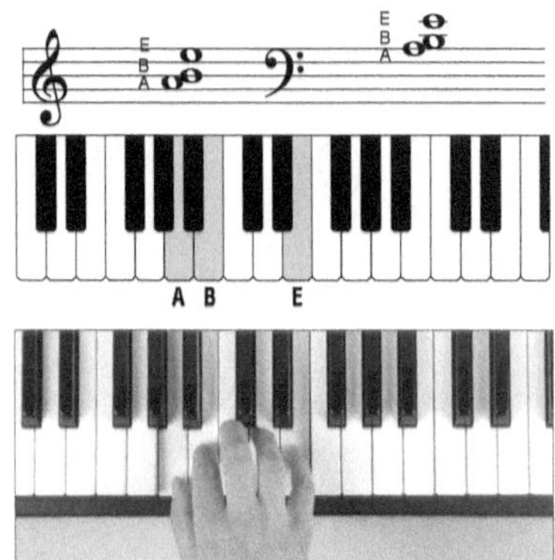

Asus2 First Inversion

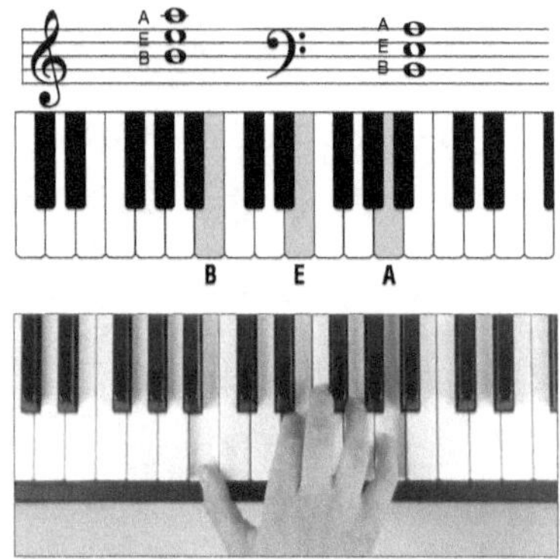

Asus2 Second Inversion

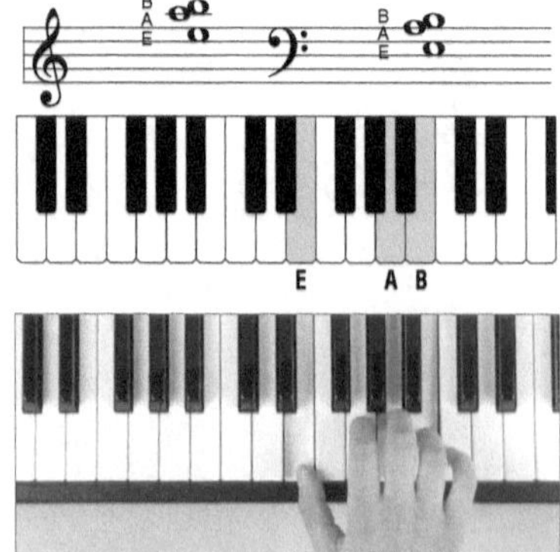

A6 Root Position

A6 First Inversion

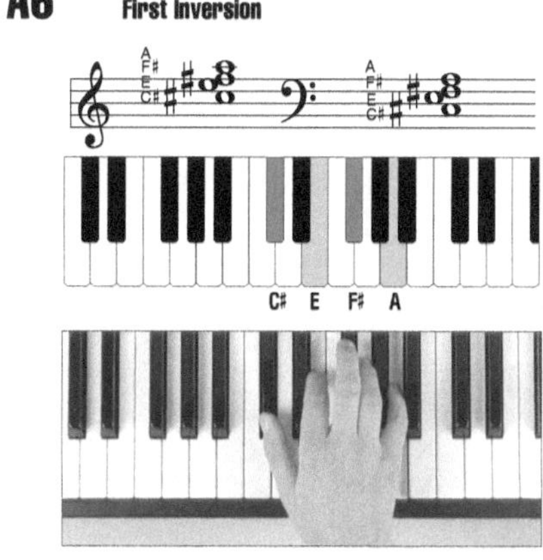

A6 Second Inversion

A6 Third Inversion

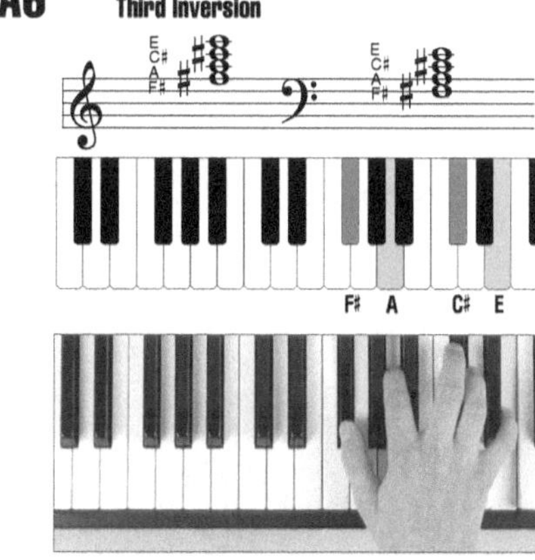

A(add2), A(add9) Root Position

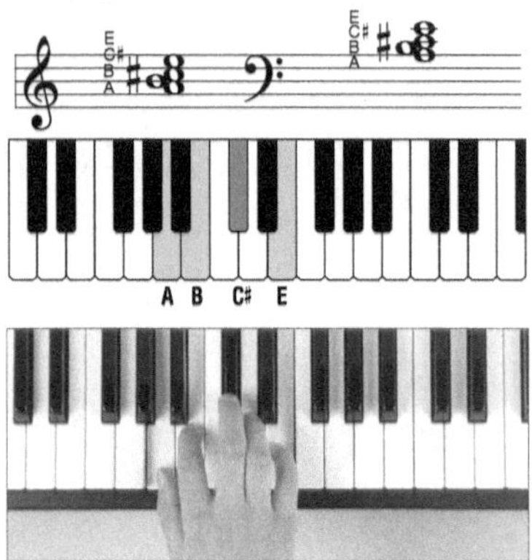

A(add2), A(add9) First Inversion

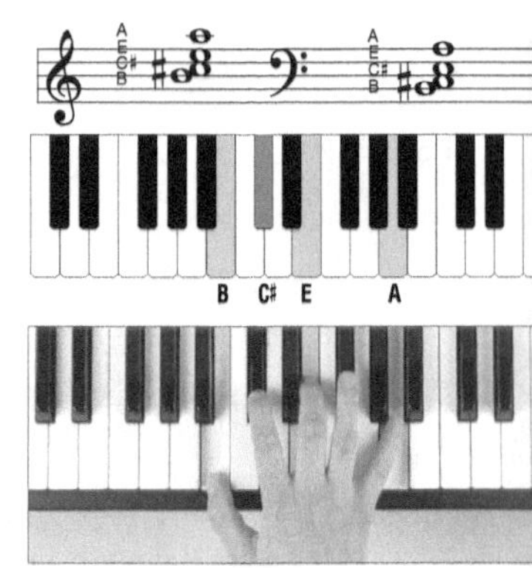

A(add2), A(add9) Second Inversion

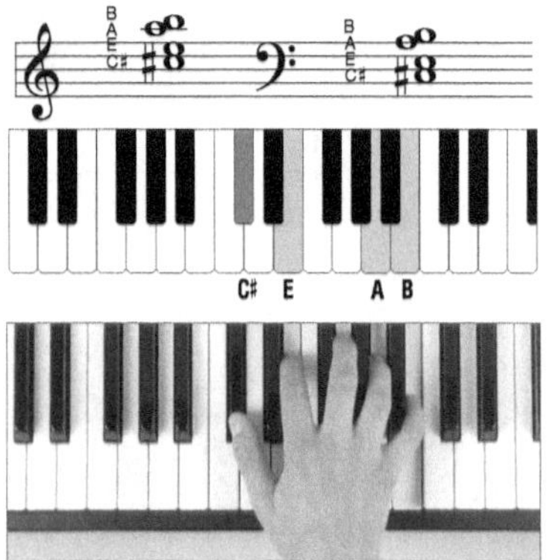

A(add2), A(add9) Third Inversion

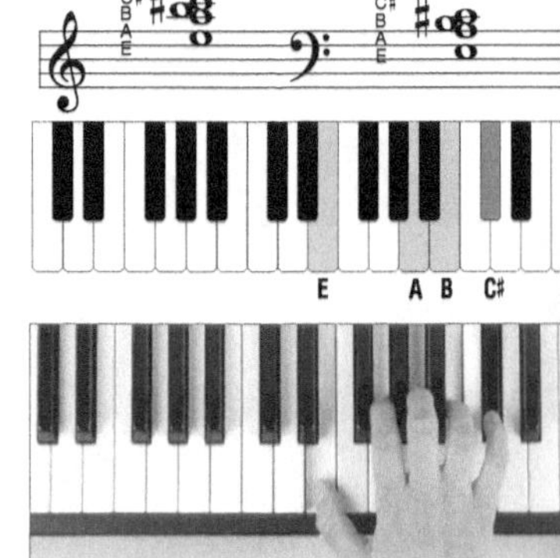

Amaj7 Root Position

Amaj7 First Inversion

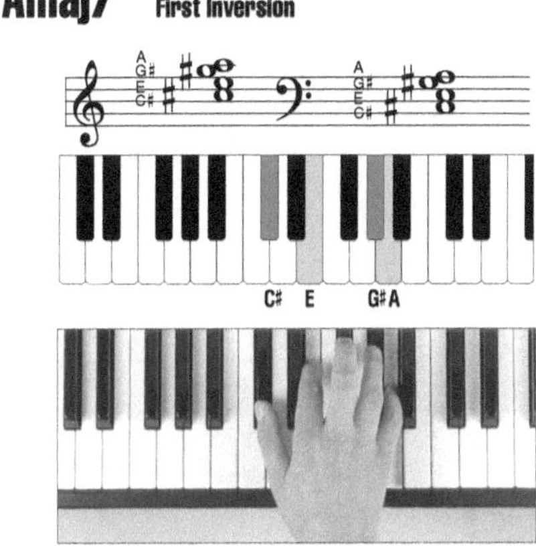

Amaj7 Second Inversion

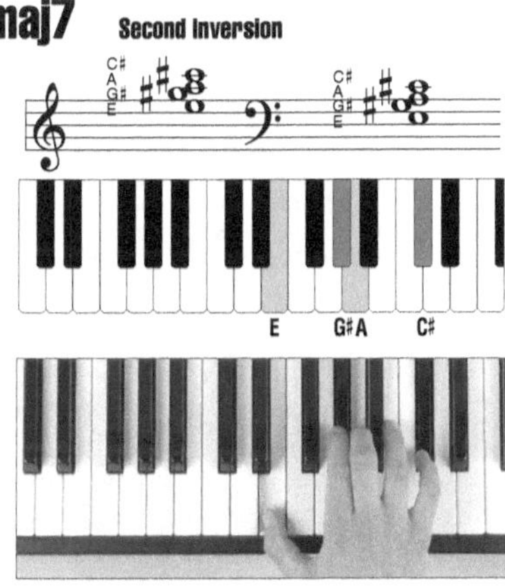

Amaj7 Third Inversion

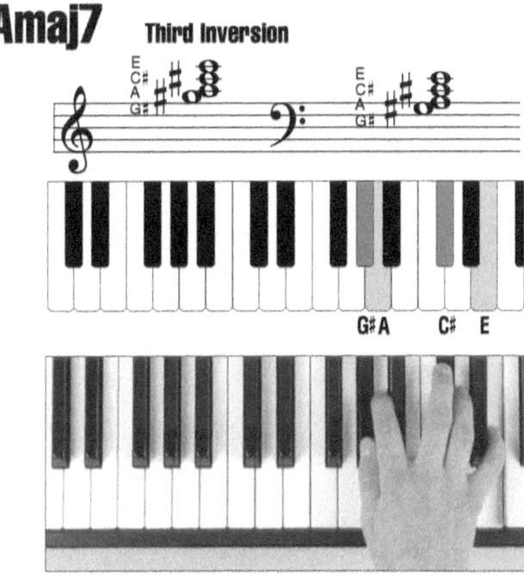

Amaj7♭5 Root Position

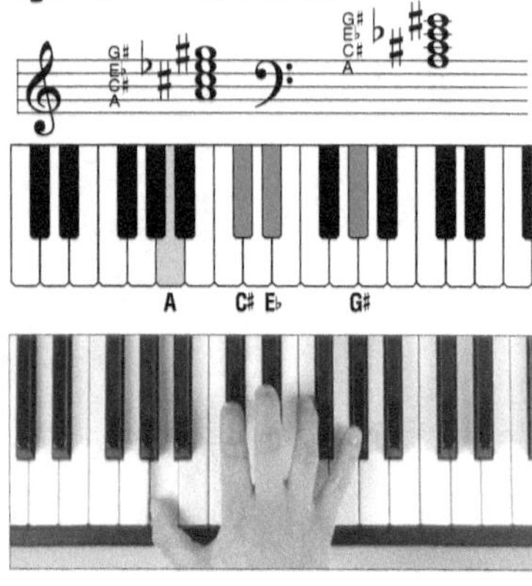

Amaj7♭5 First Inversion

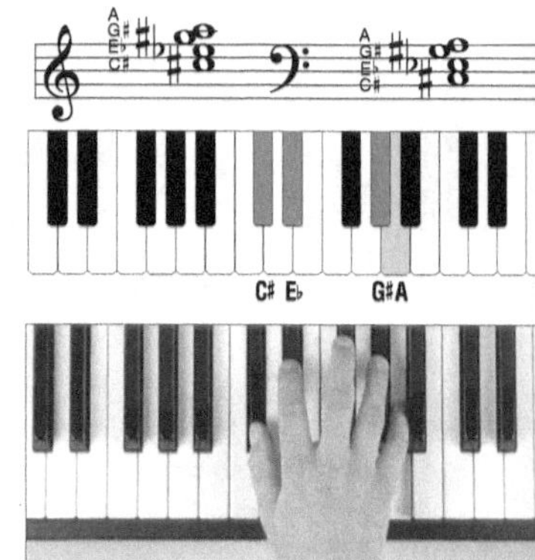

Amaj7♭5 Second Inversion

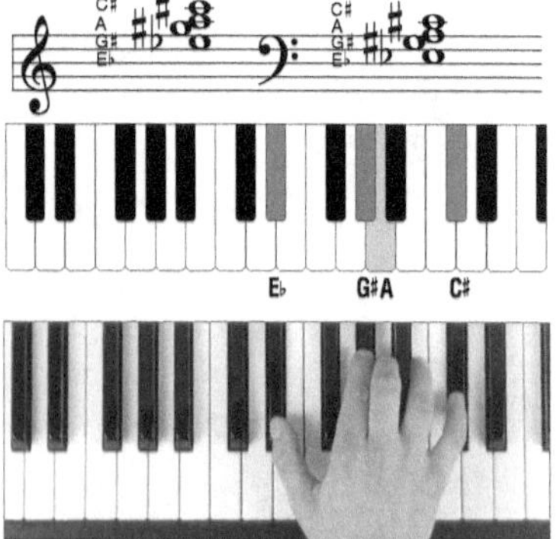

Amaj7♭5 Third Inversion

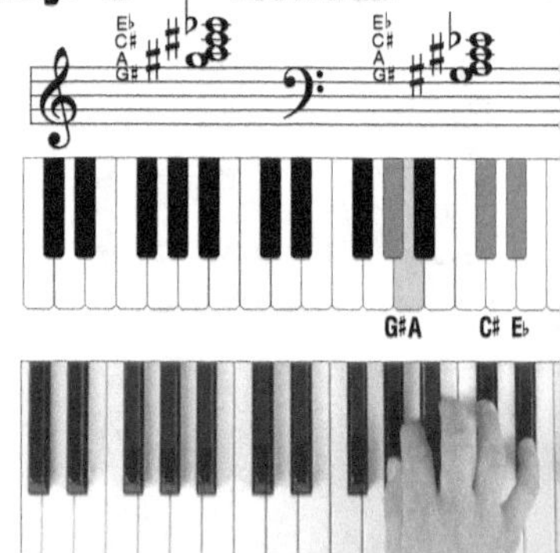

Amaj7♯5 Root Position

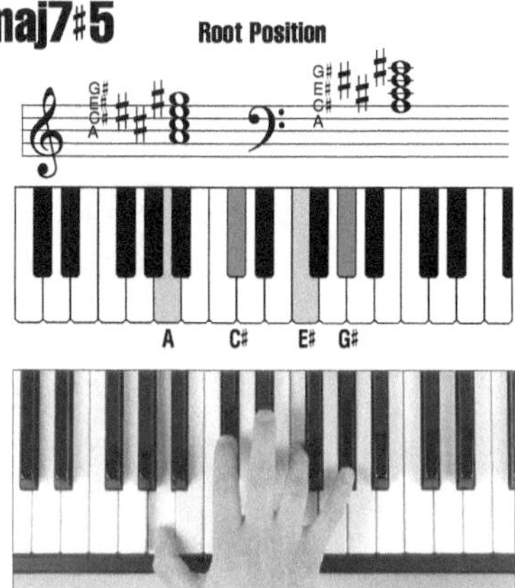

Amaj7♯5 First Inversion

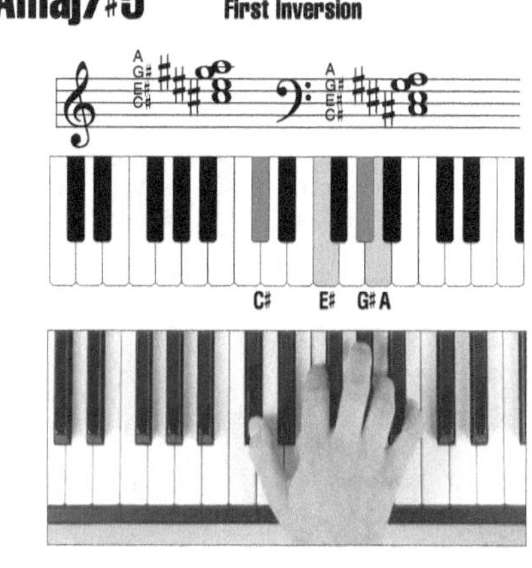

Amaj7♯5 Second Inversion

Amaj7♯5 Third Inversion

A7 Root Position

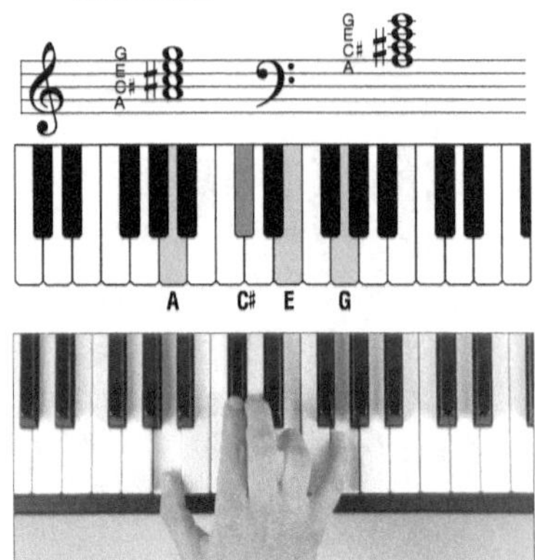

A7 First Inversion

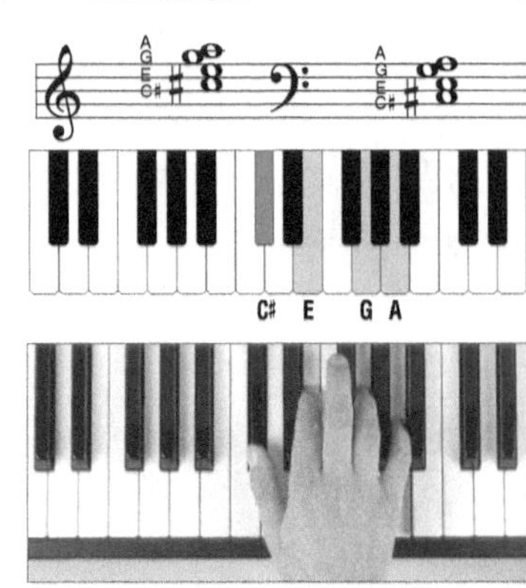

A7 Second Inversion

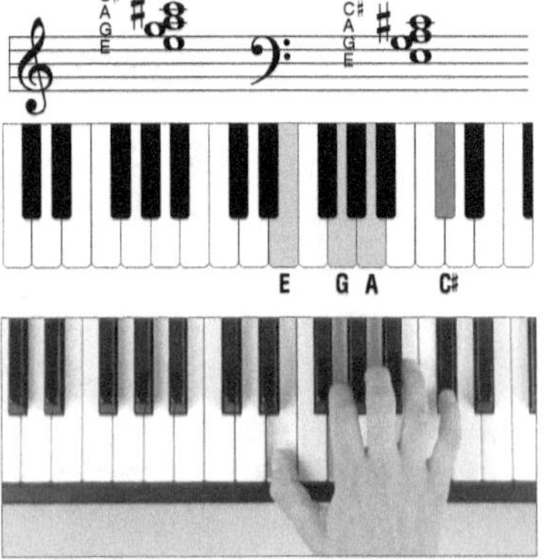

A7 Third Inversion

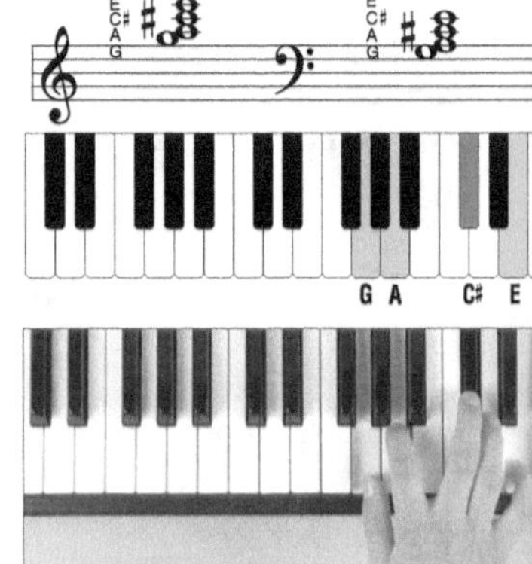

A7♭5 Root Position

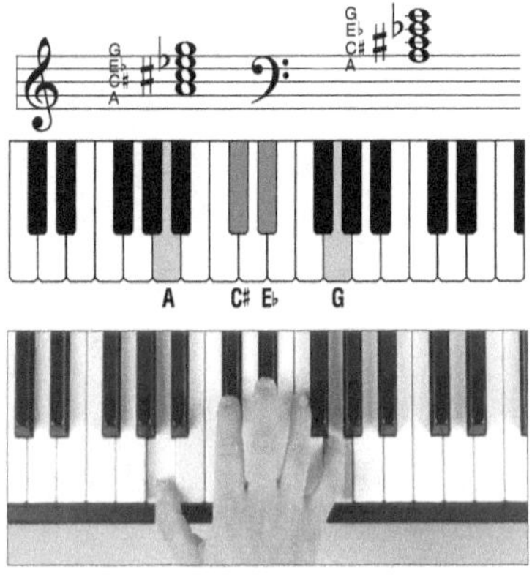

A7♭5 First Inversion

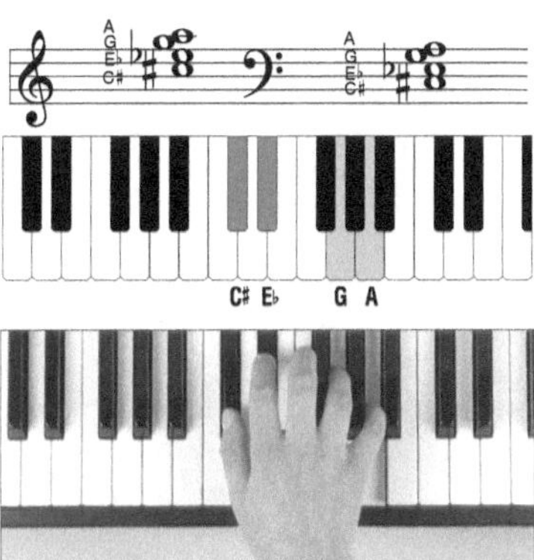

A7♭5 Second Inversion

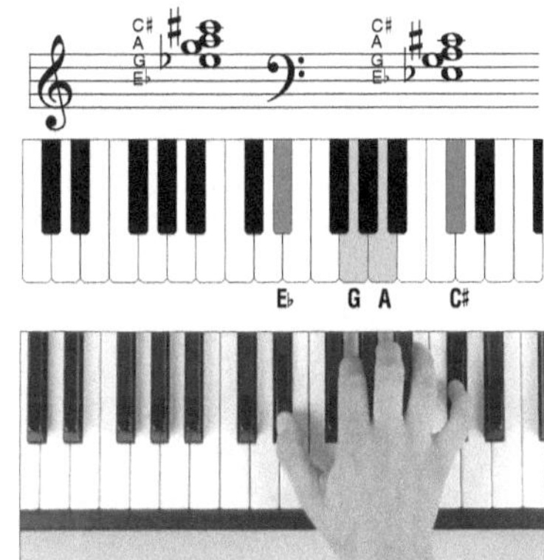

A7♭5 Third Inversion

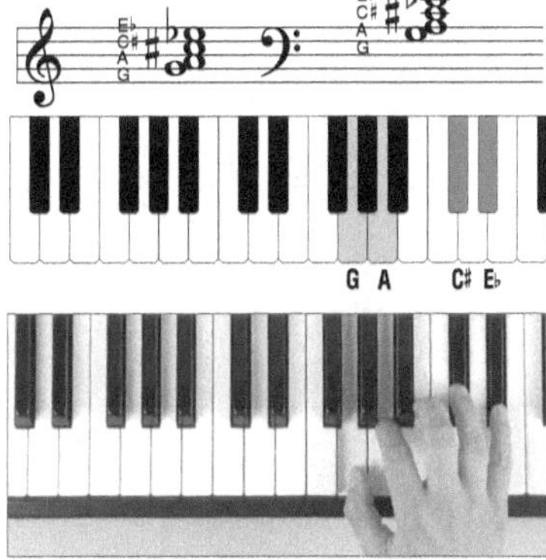

A7♯5 Root Position

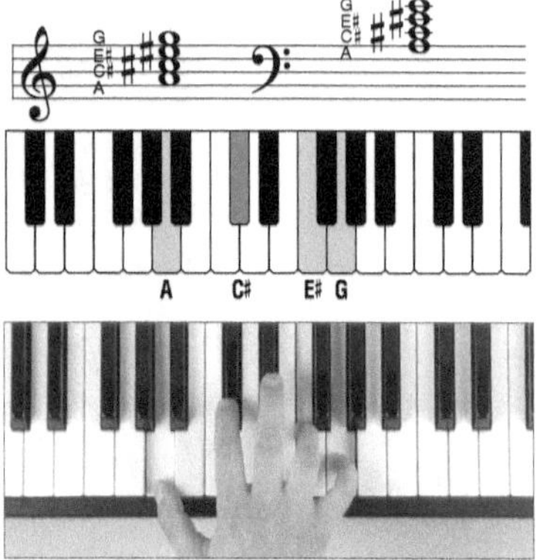

A7♯5 First Inversion

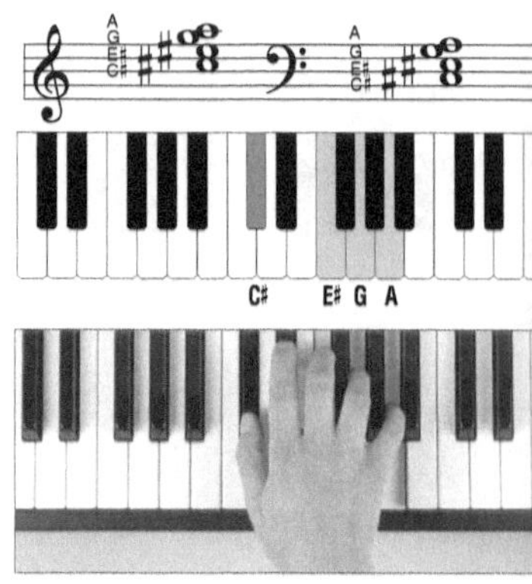

A7♯5 Second Inversion

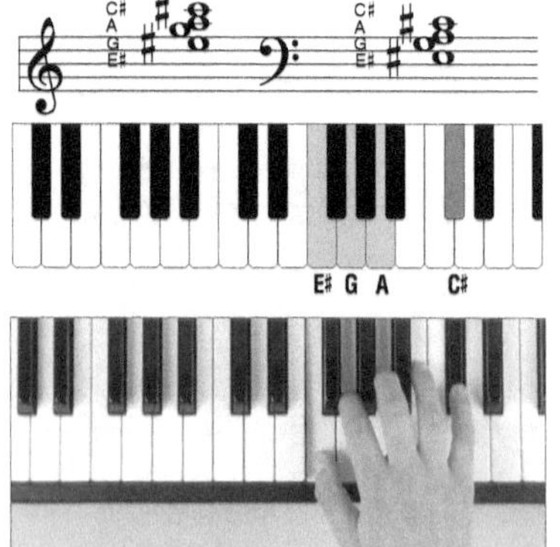

A7♯5 Third Inversion

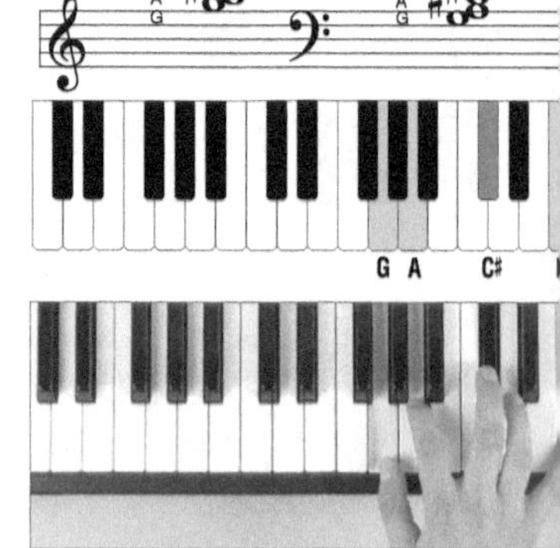

A7sus Root Position

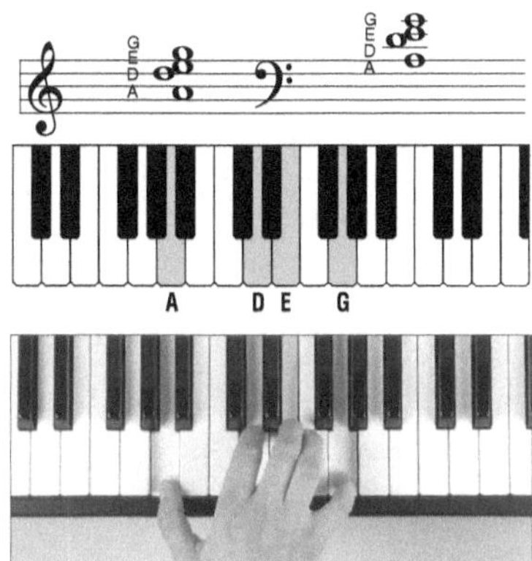

A7sus First Inversion

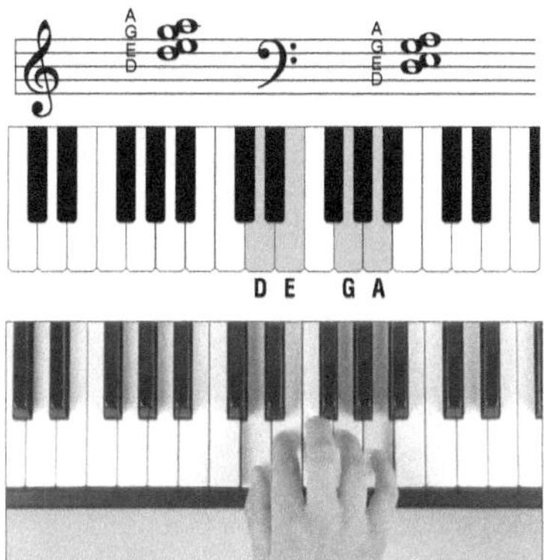

A7sus Second Inversion

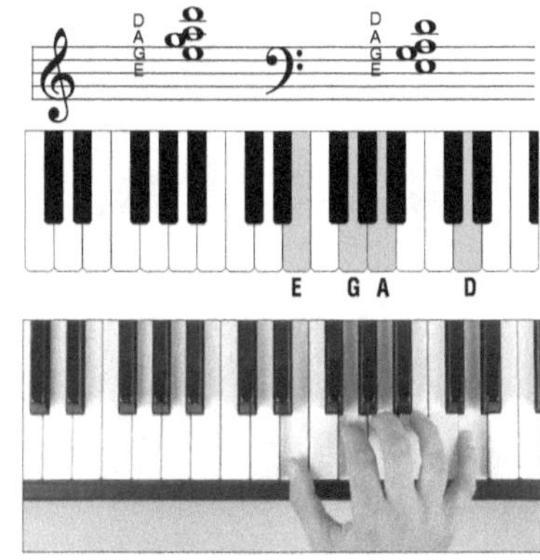

A7sus Third Inversion

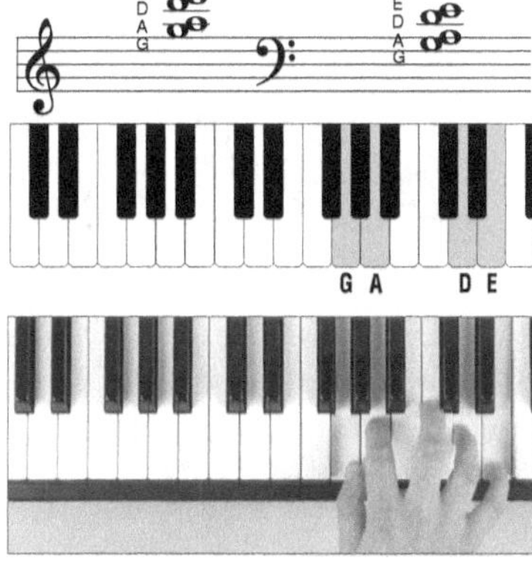

Am(add2), Am(add9) Root Position

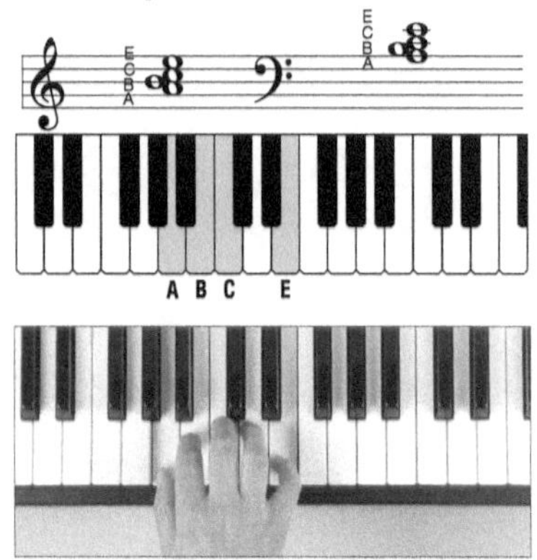

Am(add2), Am(add9) First Invers

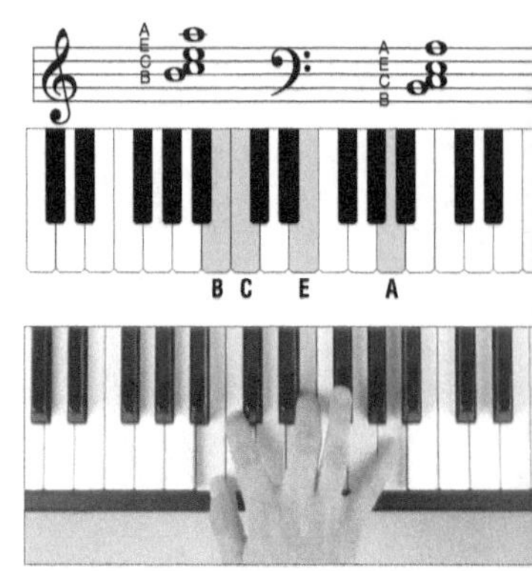

Am(add2), Am(add9) Second Inversion

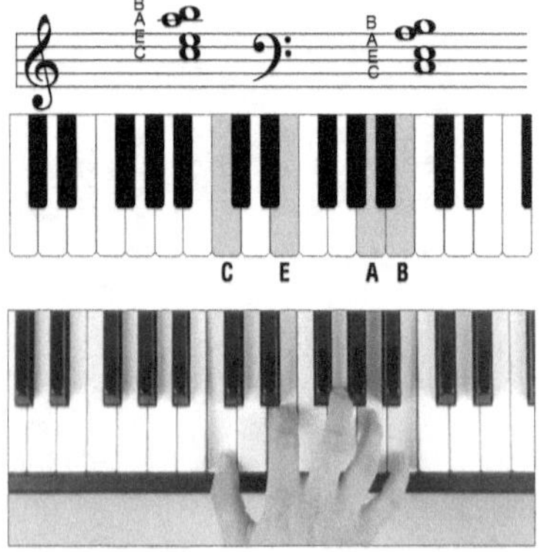

Am(add2), Am(add9) Third Invers

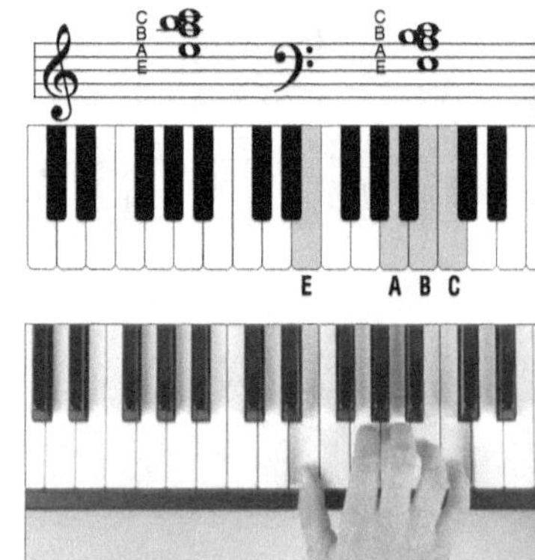

Am6 Root Position

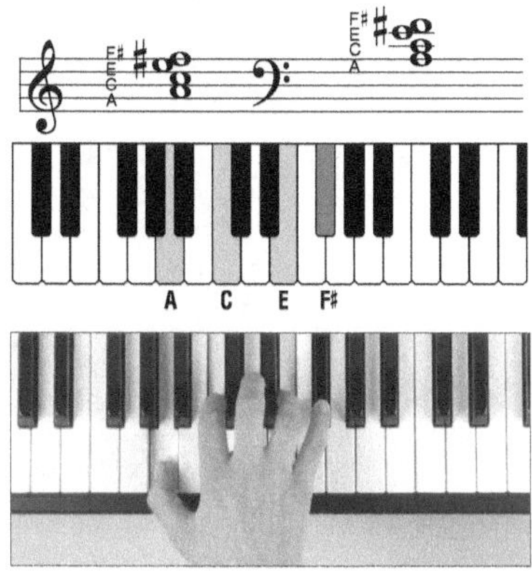

Am6 First Inversion

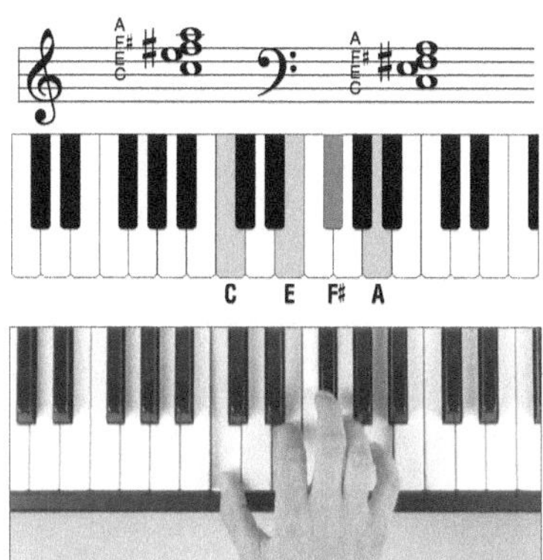

Am6 Second Inversion

Am6 Third Inversion

Am7 Root Position

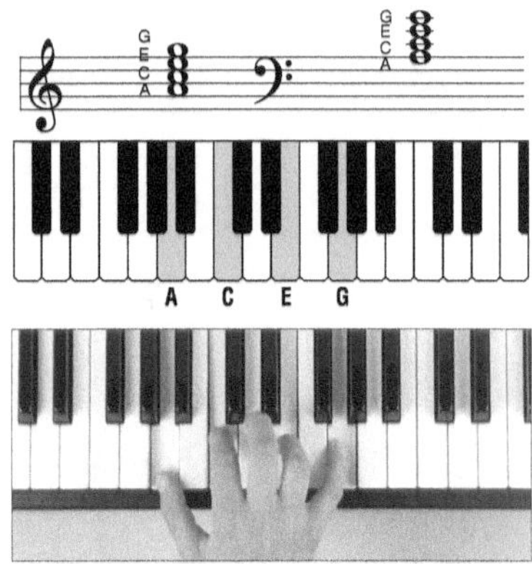

Am7 First Inversion

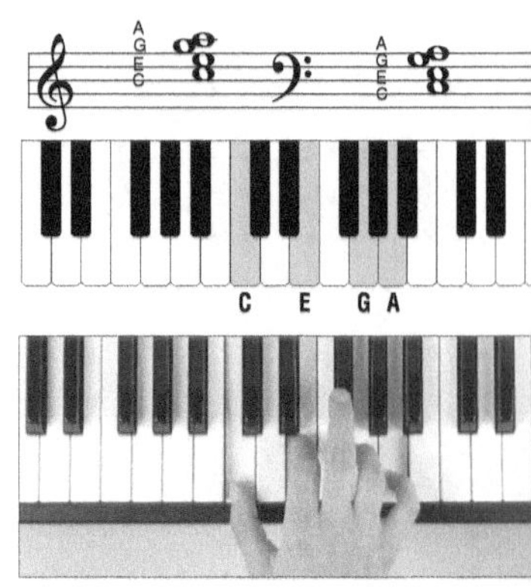

Am7 Second Inversion

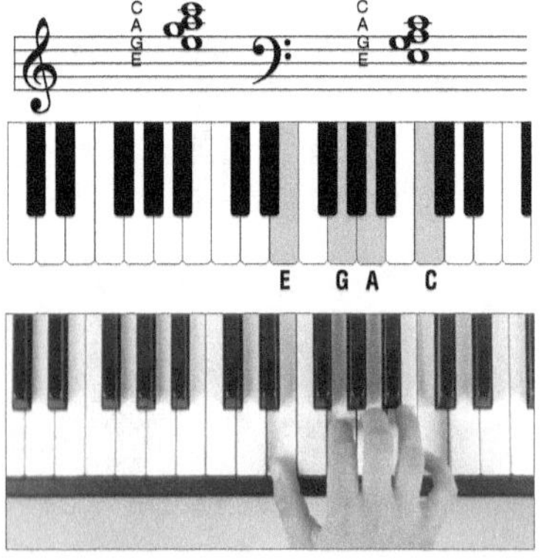

Am7 Third Inversion

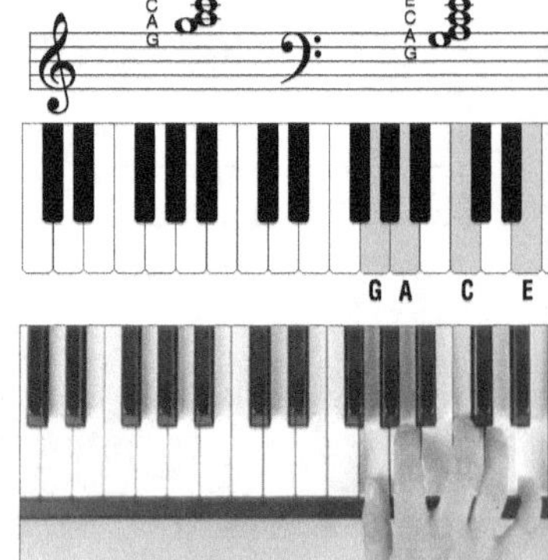

Am(maj7) Root Position

Am(maj7) First Inversion

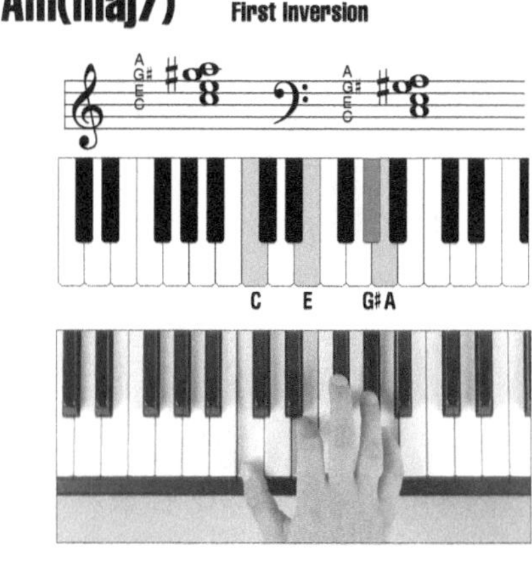

Am(maj7) Second Inversion

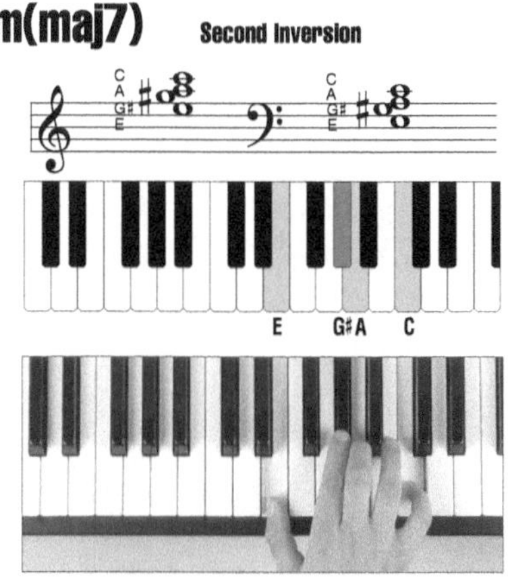

Am(maj7) Third Inversion

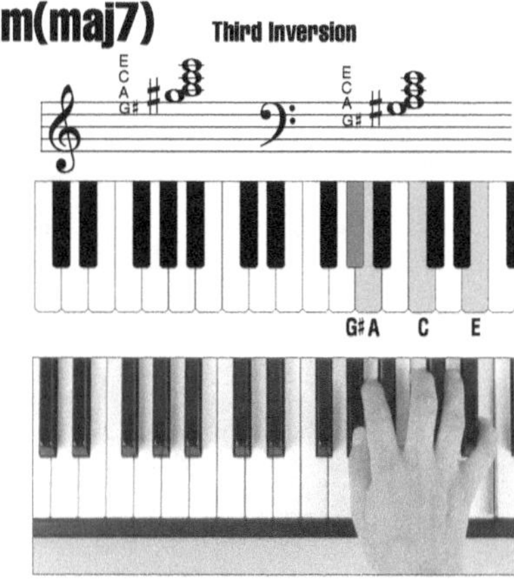

Am7♭5 Root Position

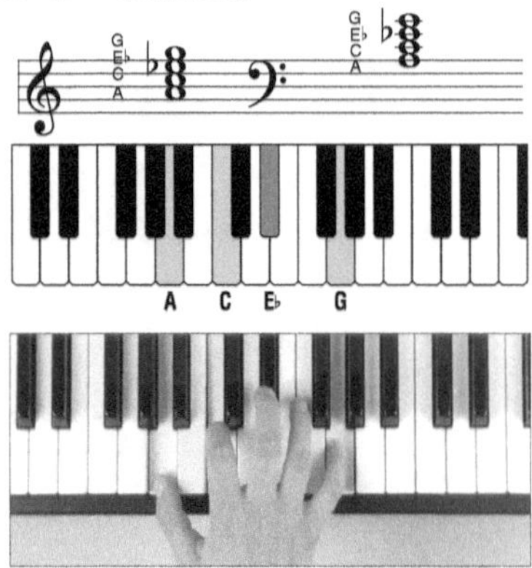

Am7♭5 First Inversion

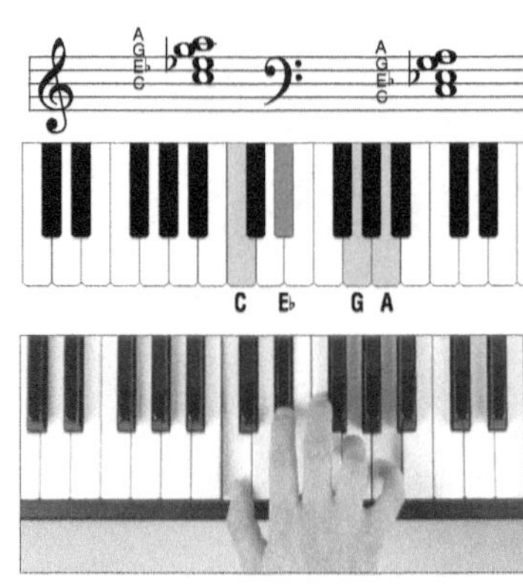

Am7♭5 Second Inversion

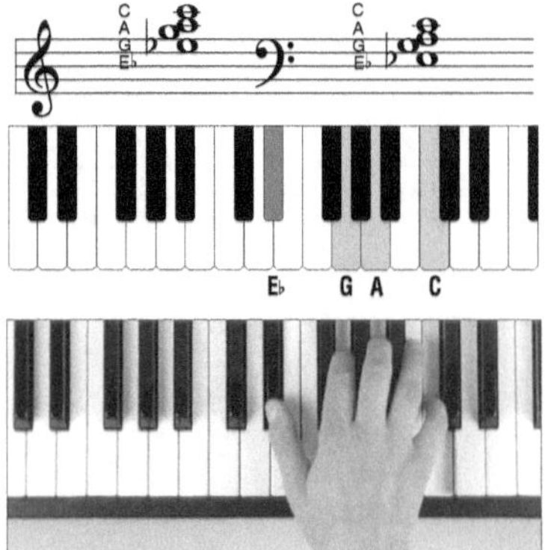

Am7♭5 Third Inversion

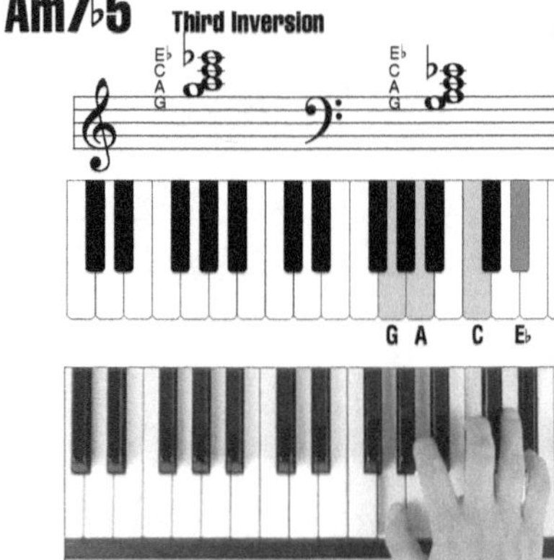

Adim7 Root Position

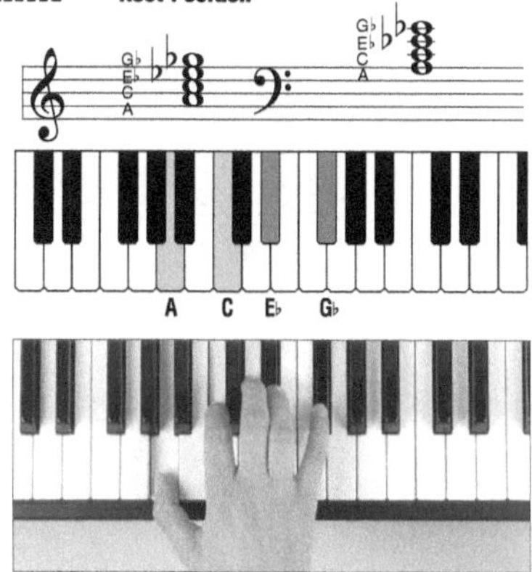

Adim7 First Inversion

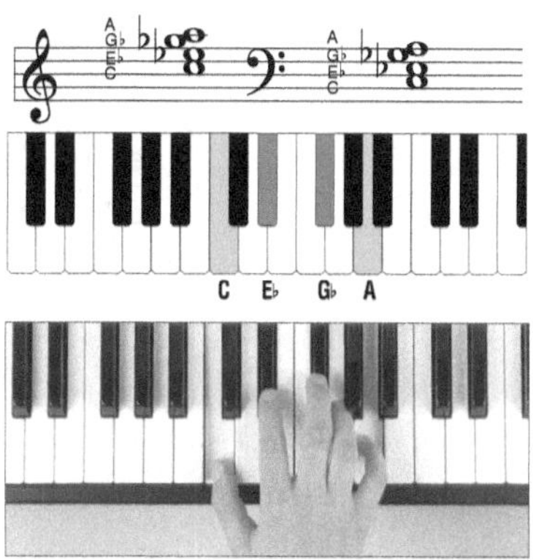

Adim7 Second Inversion

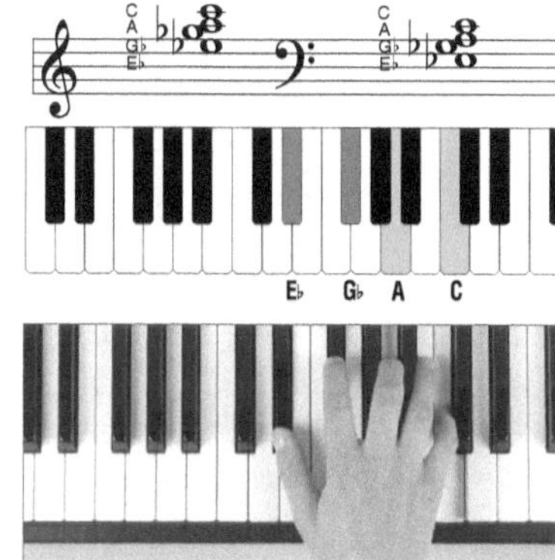

Adim7 Third Inversion

Adim(maj7) Root Position

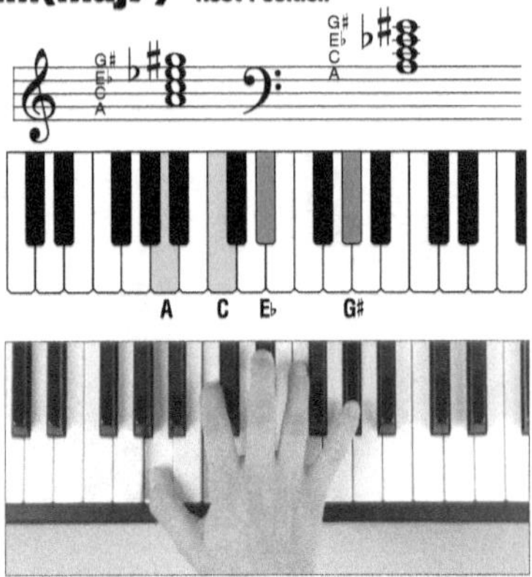

Adim(maj7) First Inversion

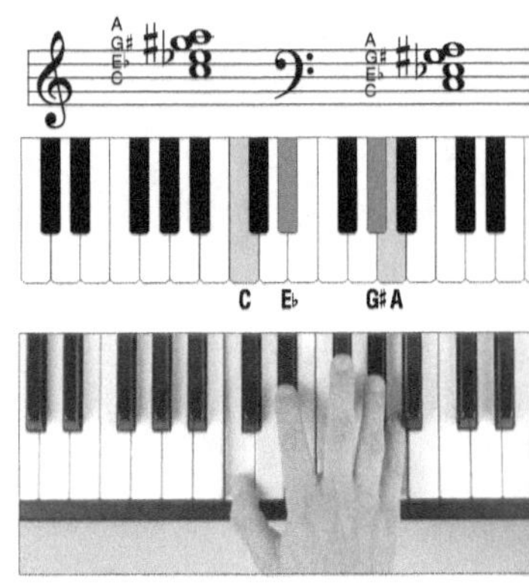

Adim(maj7) Second Inversion

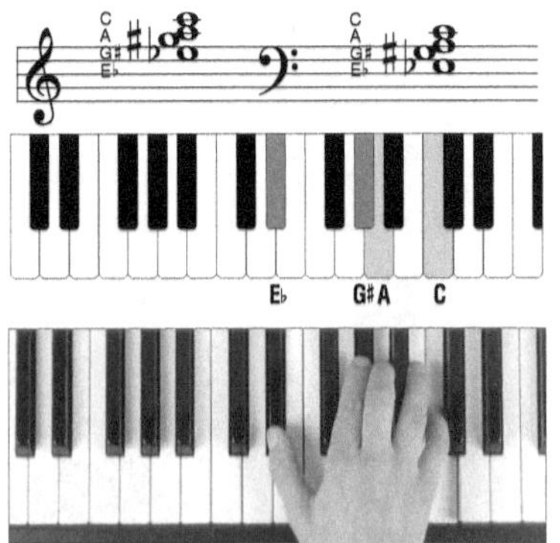

Adim(maj7) Third Inversion

A5

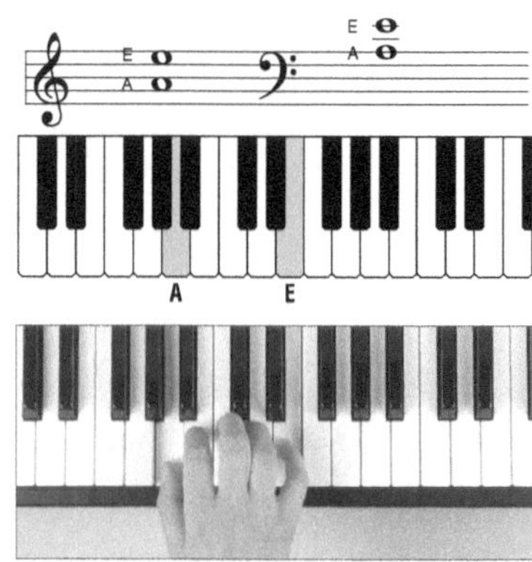

A6/9

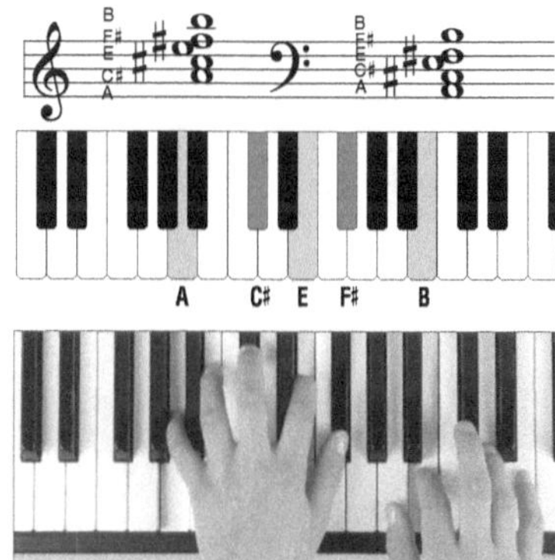

Amaj6/9

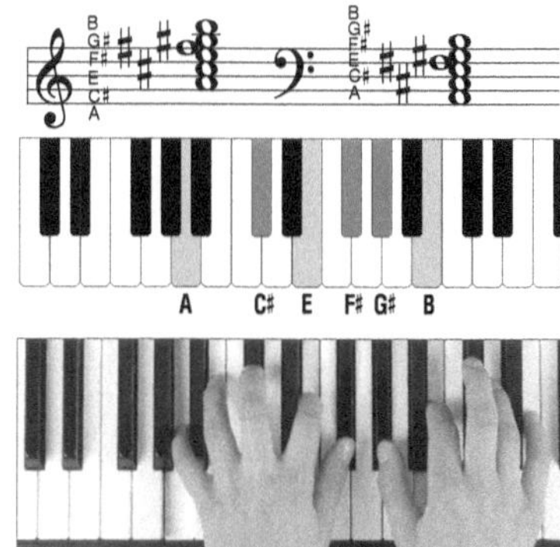

Amaj7♯11

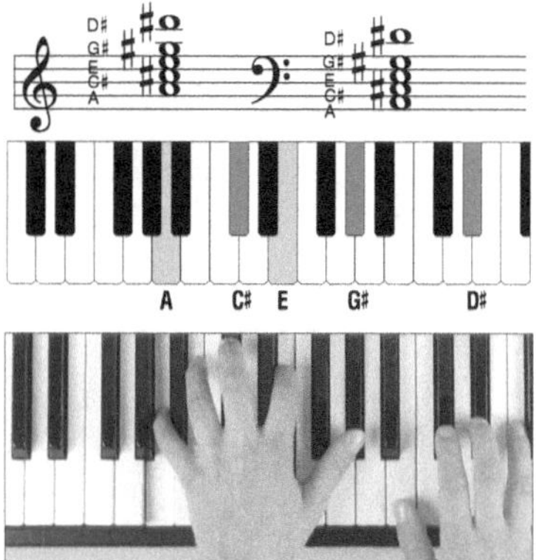

Amaj9

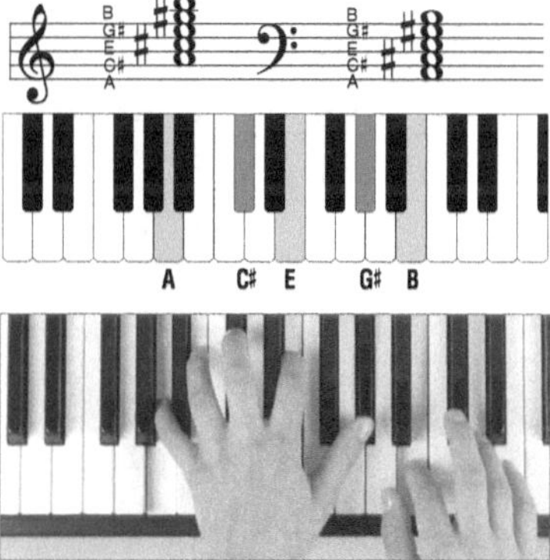

Amaj9♭5

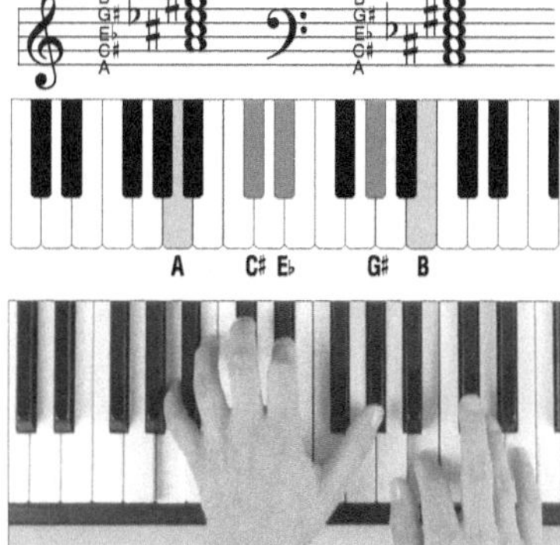

Amaj9♯5

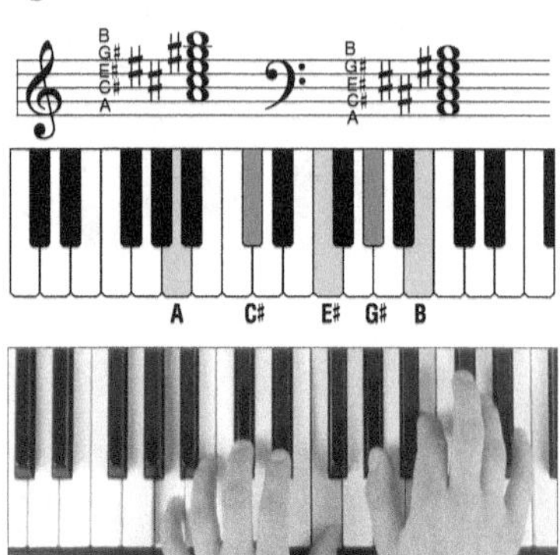

Amaj9♯11

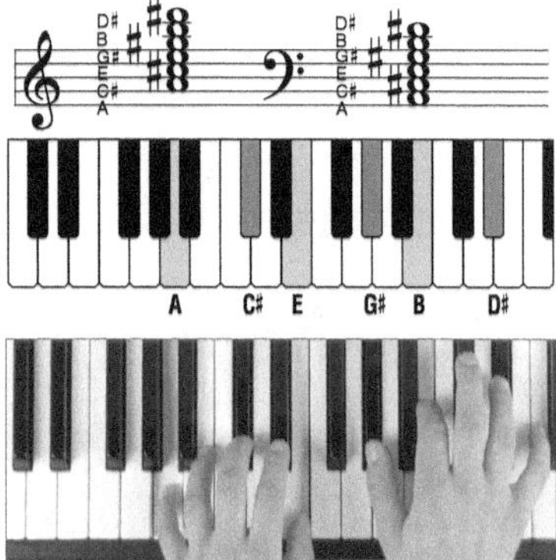

Amaj13

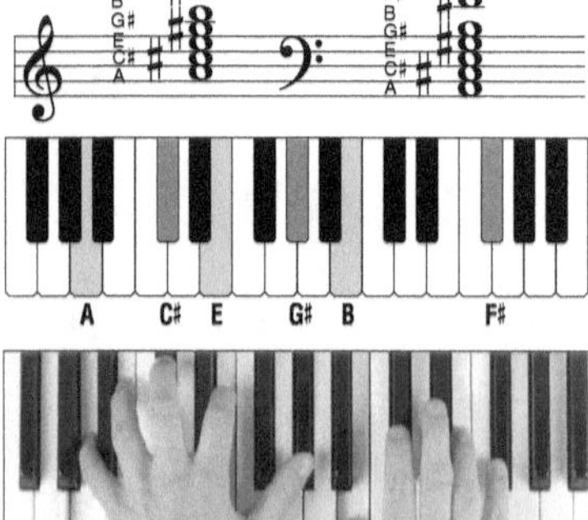

Amaj13♭5

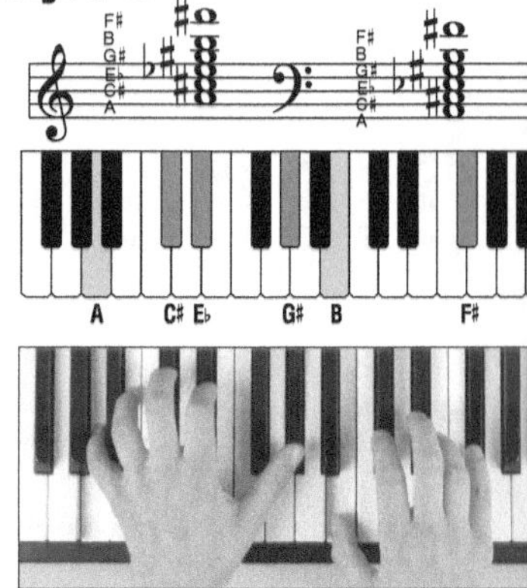

Amaj13♯11

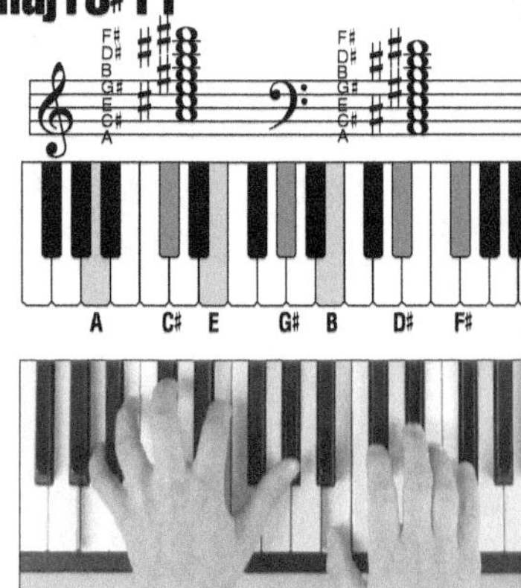

A7♭9

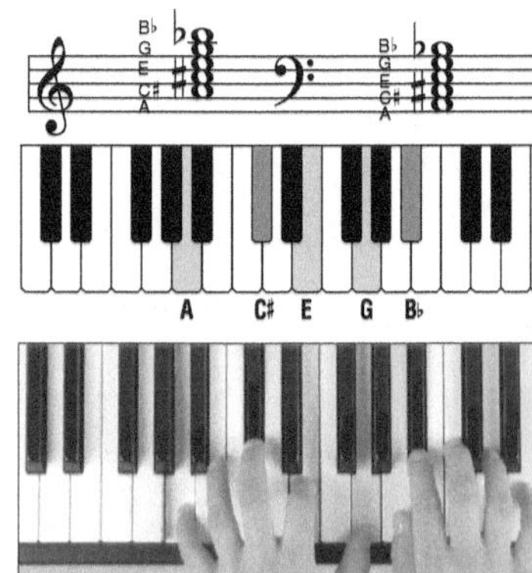

A7♯9

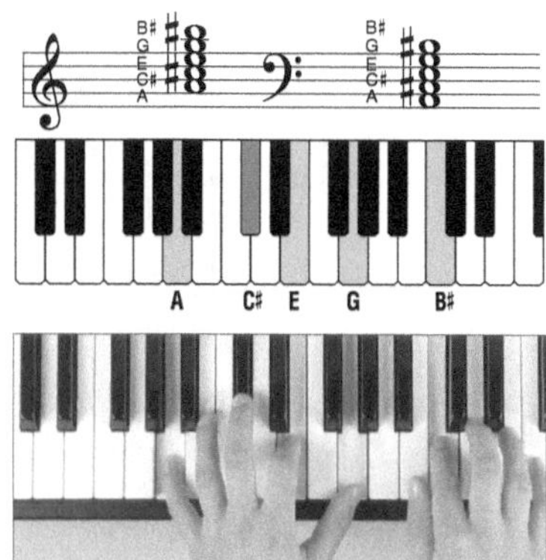

A7♭5(♯9)

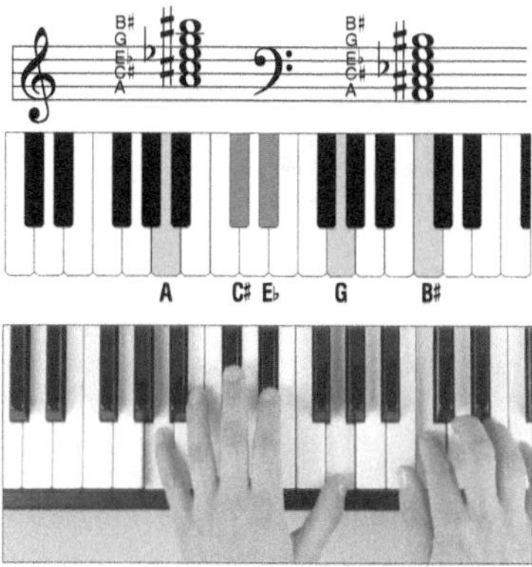

A7♯11

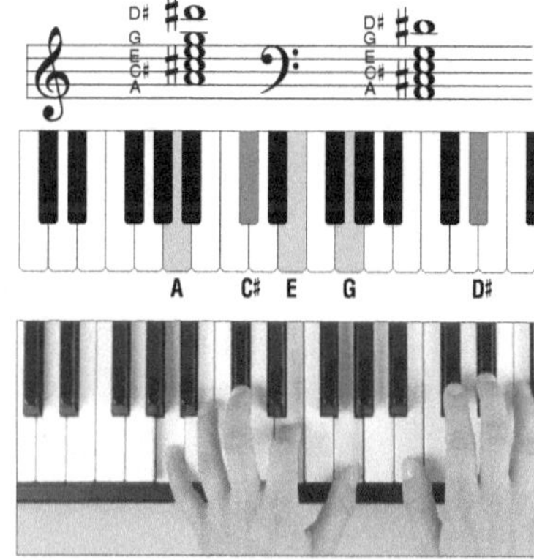

A7♯5(♭9)

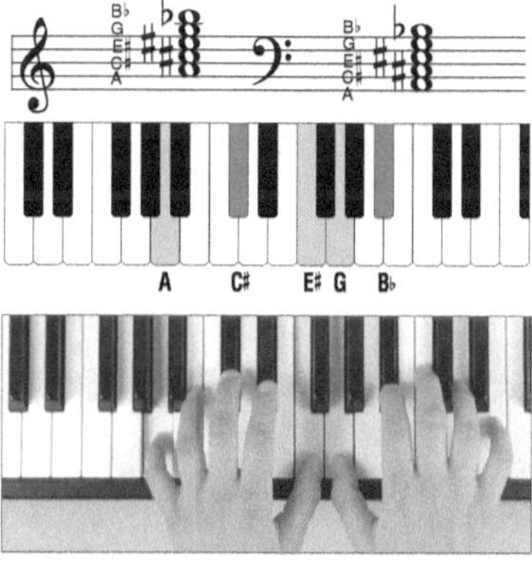

A7♭5(♭9)

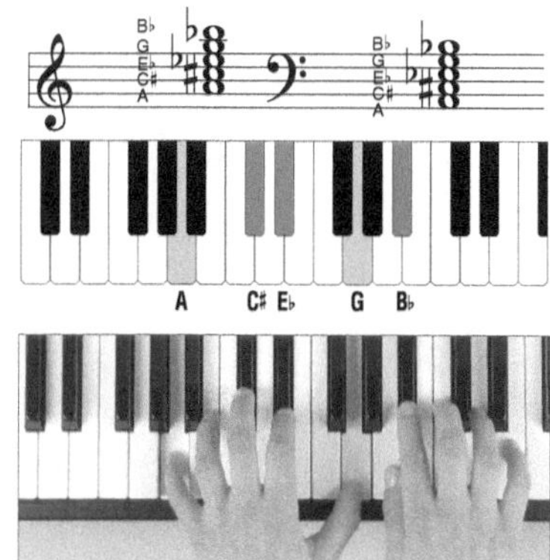

A7♯5(♯9)

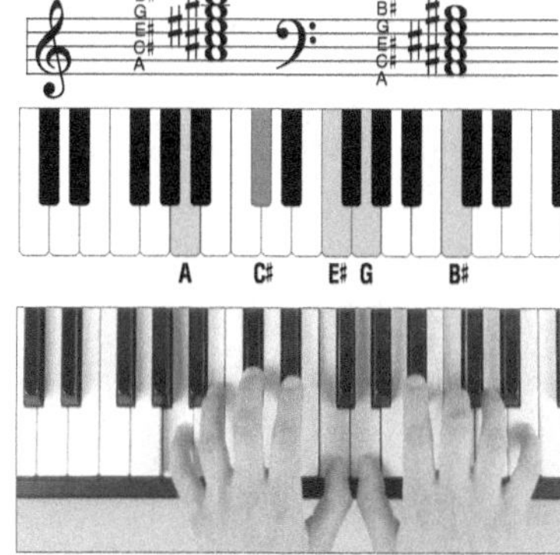

A7♭9(♯9)

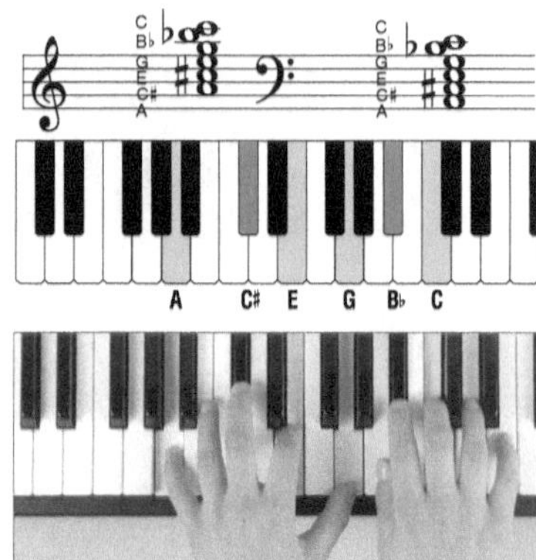

A7(add13)

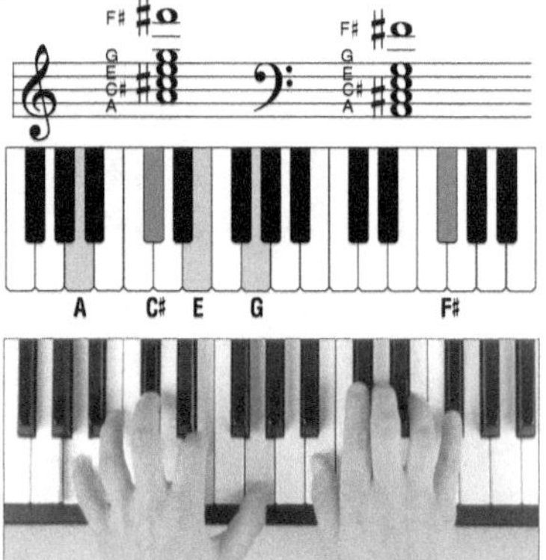

A7♭13

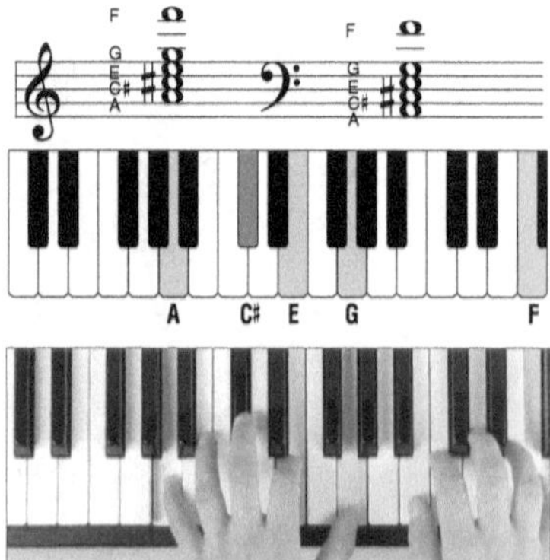

A7♭9(♯11)

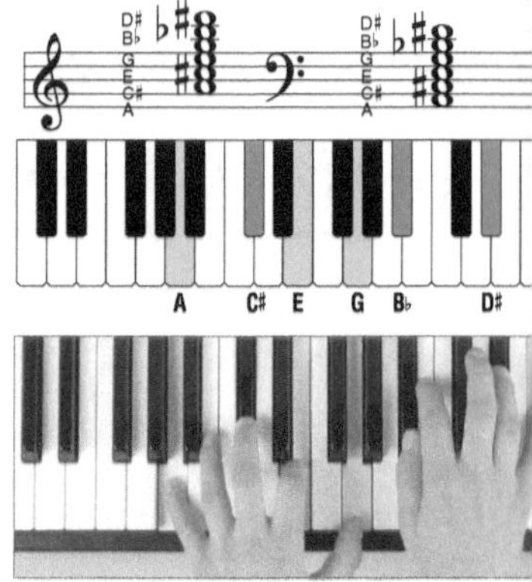

A7♯9(♯11)

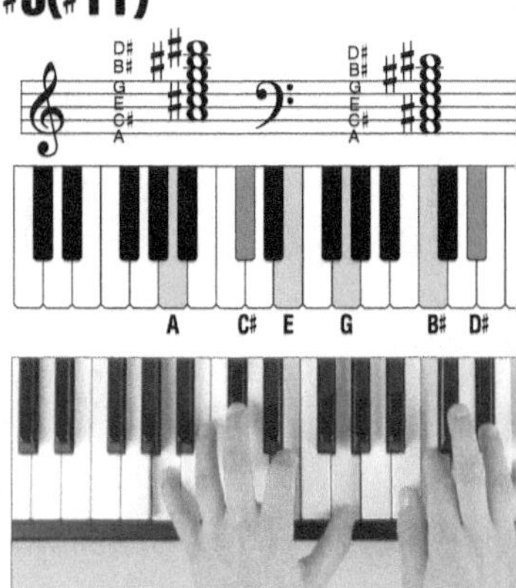

A7♭9(♭13)

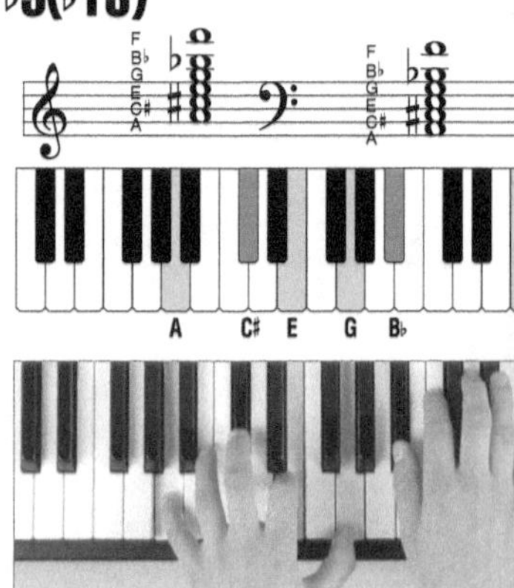

A7♯9(♭13)

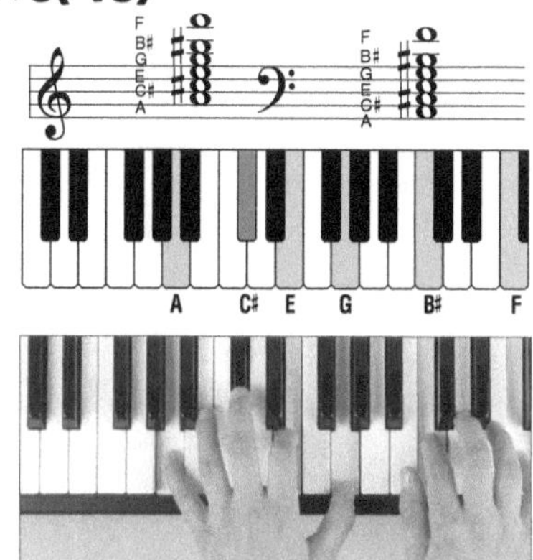

A7♯11(♭13)

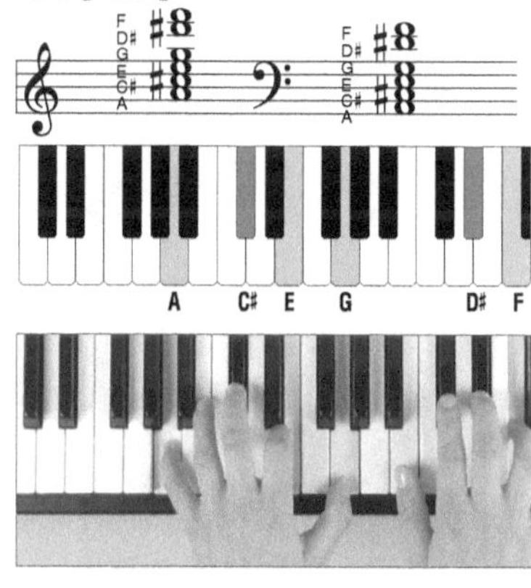

A7♭9(♯9,♯11)

A9

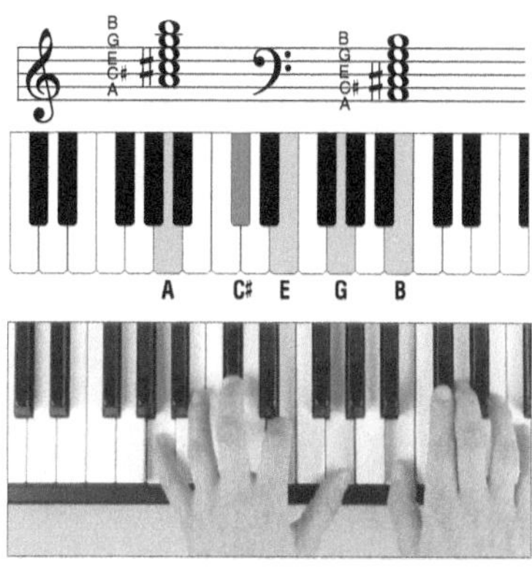

A9(♭5)

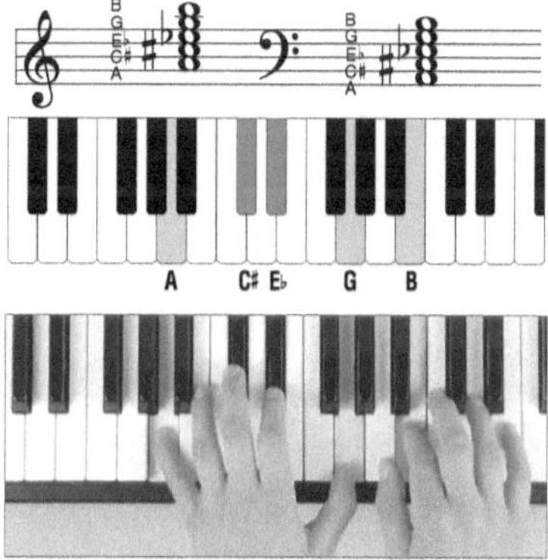

A9♯5

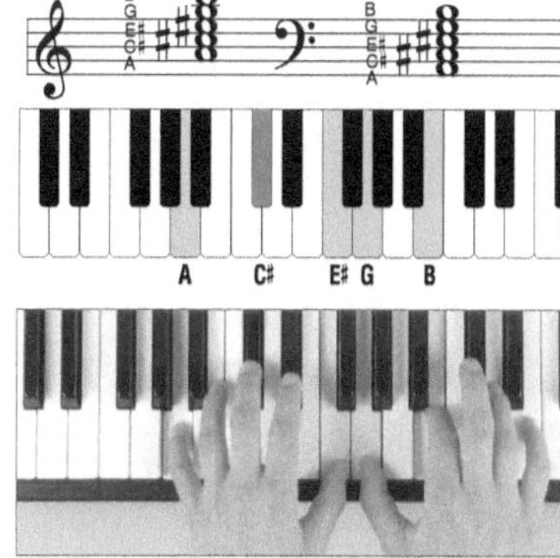

A9♯11

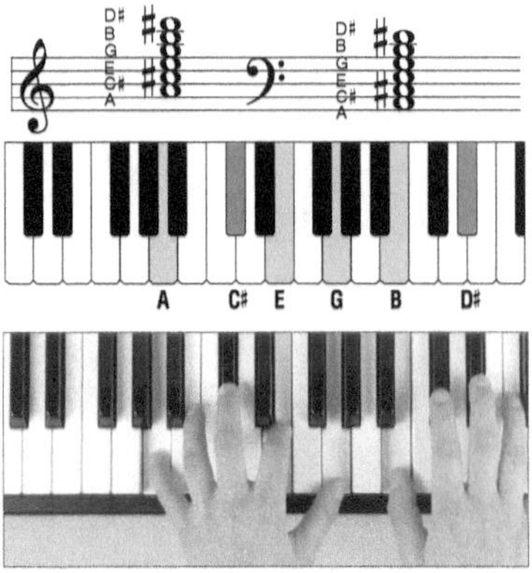
D♯ B G E C♯ A
D♯ B G E C♯ A
A C♯ E G B D♯

A11, A9(sus4)

D B G E A
D B G E A
A E G B D

A9♭13

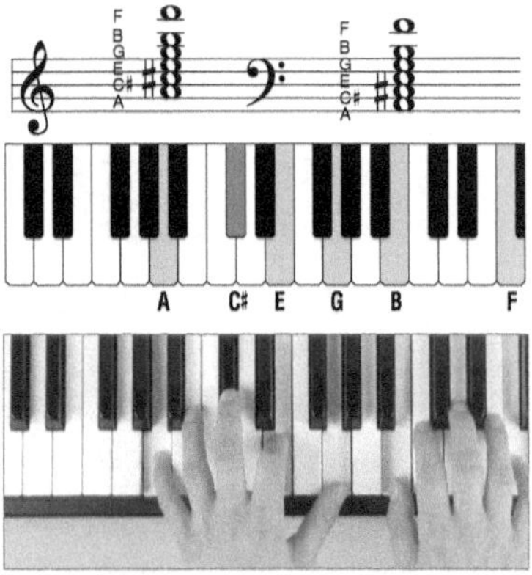
F B G E C♯ A
F B G E C♯ A
A C♯ E G B F

A13

F♯ B G E C♯ A
F♯ B G E C♯ A
A C♯ E G B F♯

A9♯11(♭13)

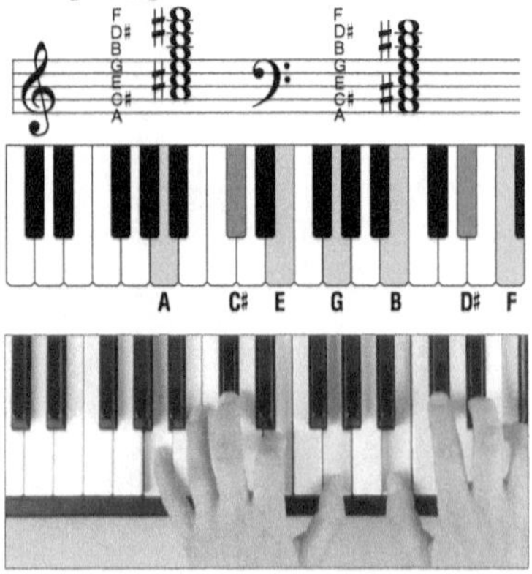
F D♯ B G E C♯ A
F D♯ B G E C♯ A
A C♯ E G B D♯ F

A13♭5

F♯ B G E♭ C♯ A
F♯ B G E♭ C♯ A
A C♯ E♭ G B F♯

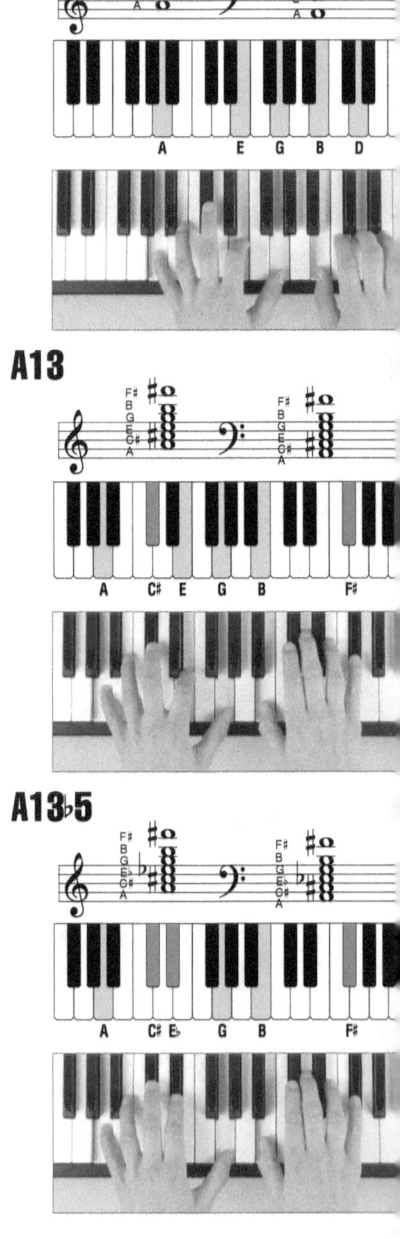

A13♭9

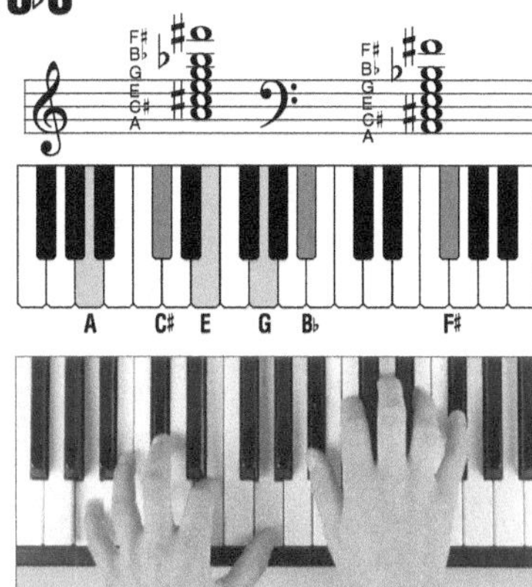

A13♯9

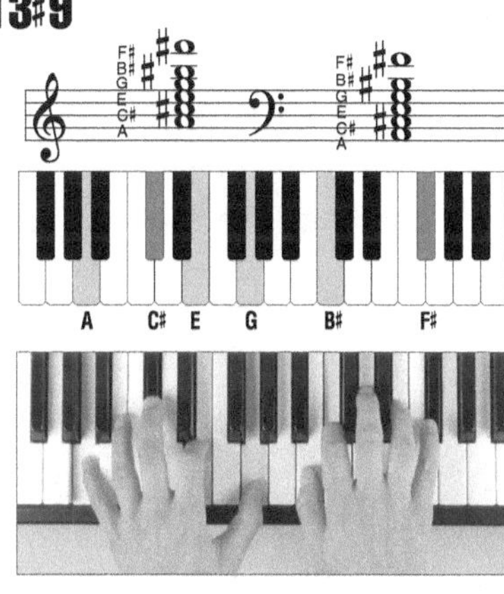

A13♯11

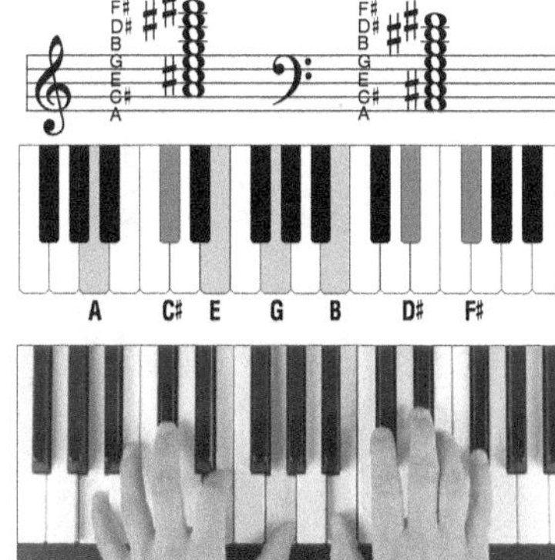

A13(sus4)

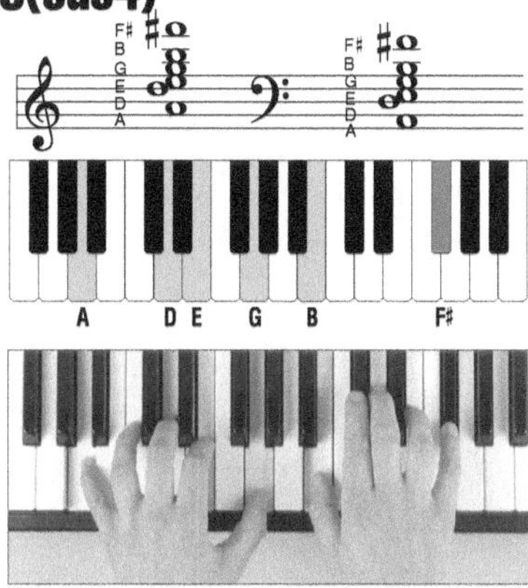

Am(♯5)

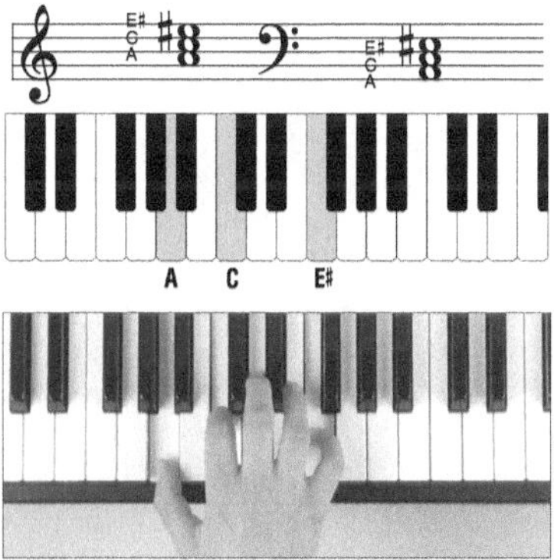

Am$^{6}_{9}$

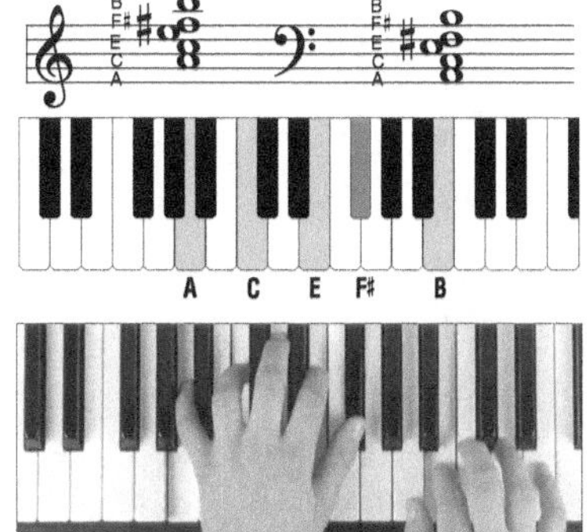

Am7(add4)

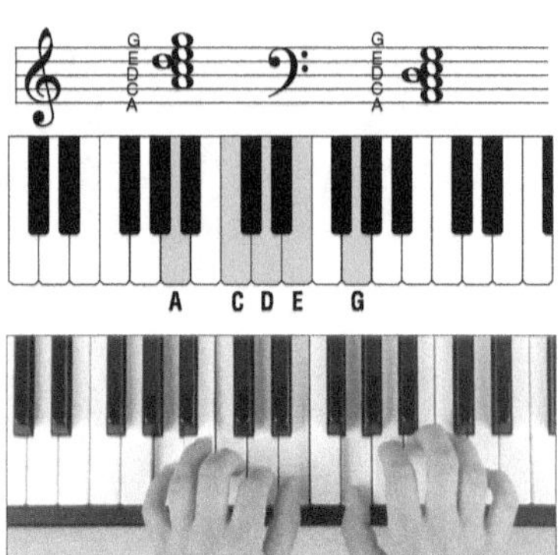

Am7(add11)

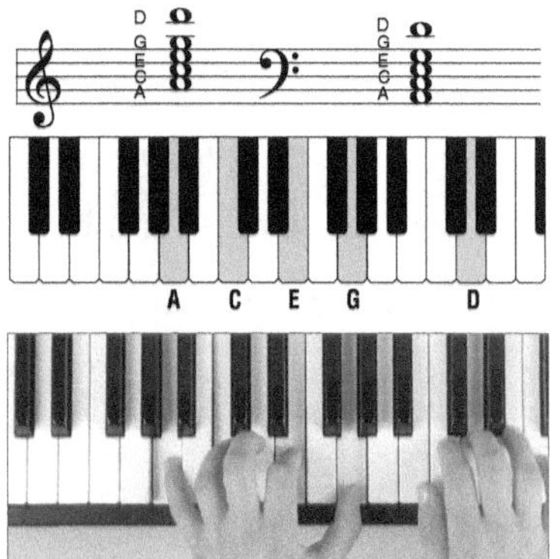

Am7♭5(♭9)

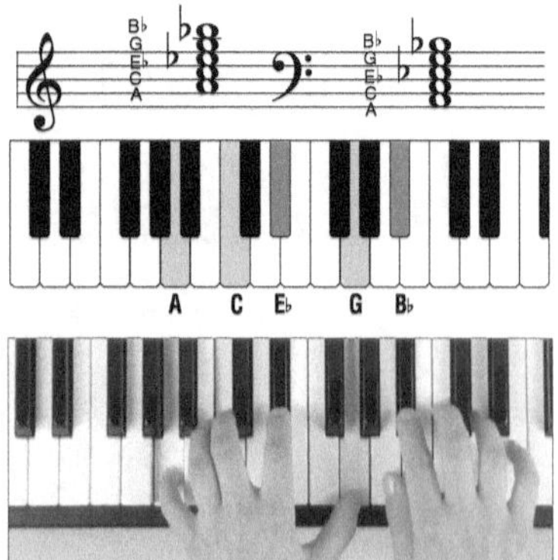

Am9

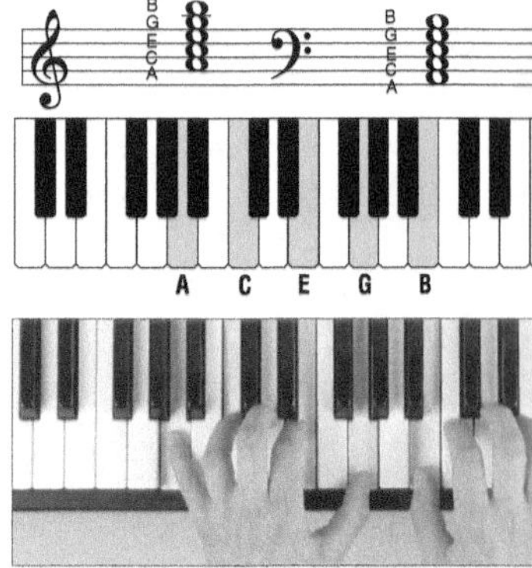

Am9(maj7)

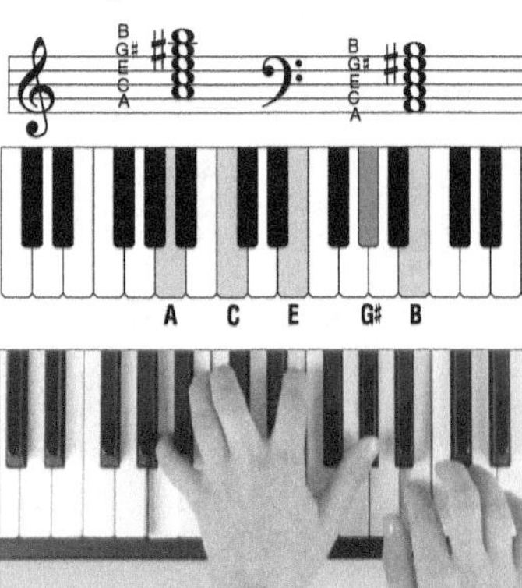

Am9♭5

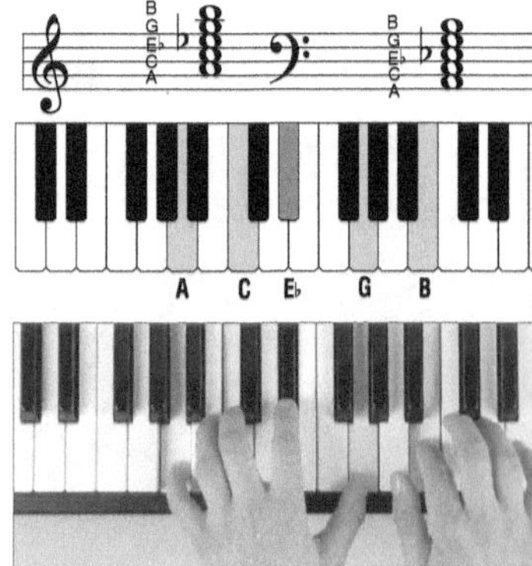

Am11

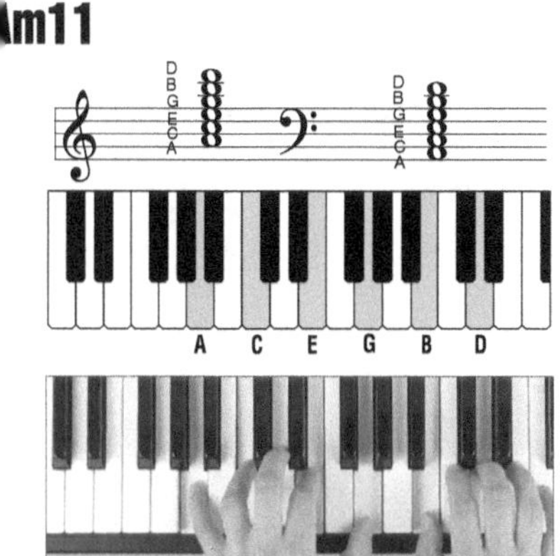

Am13

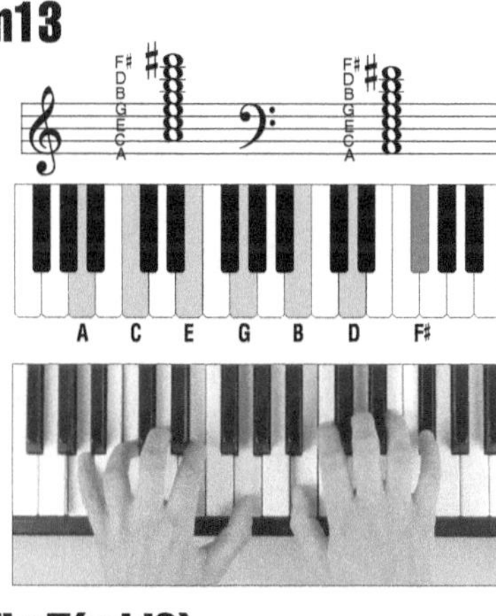

Adim7(add9)

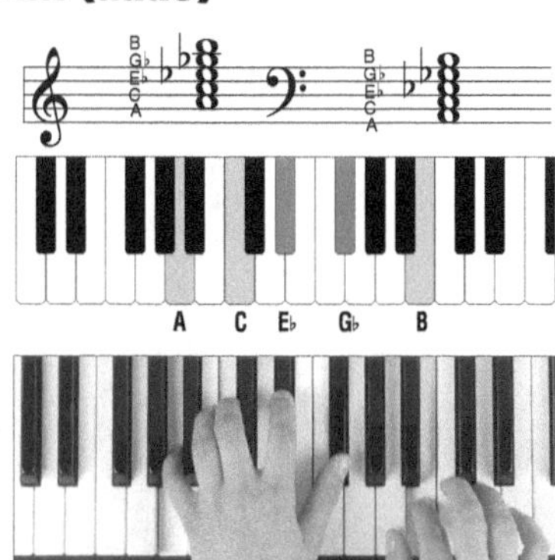

Am11♭5

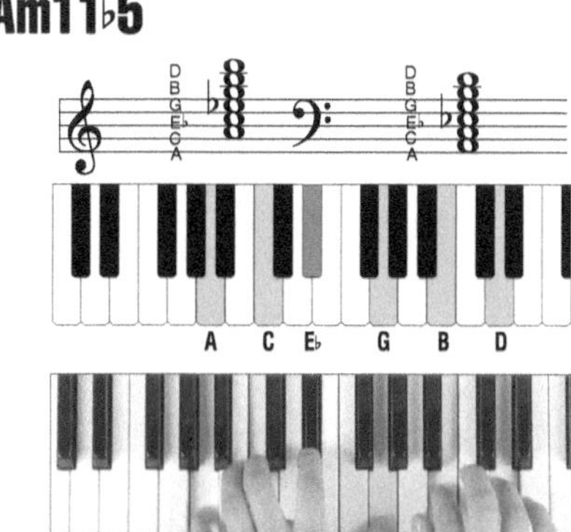

Am11(maj7)

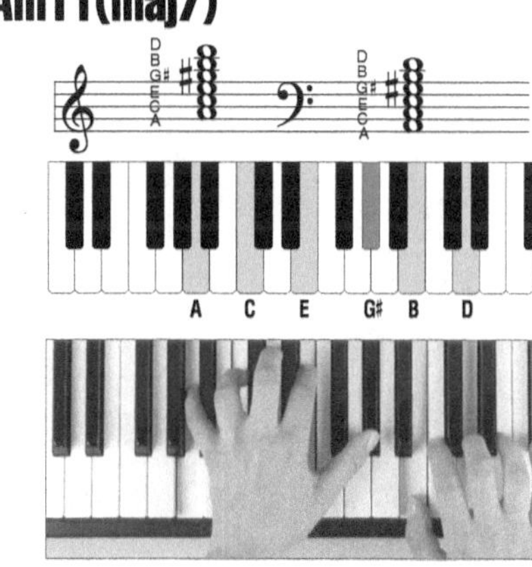

A7alt.

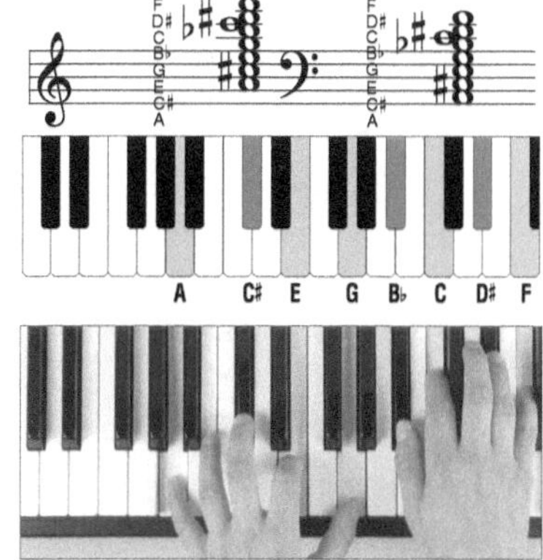

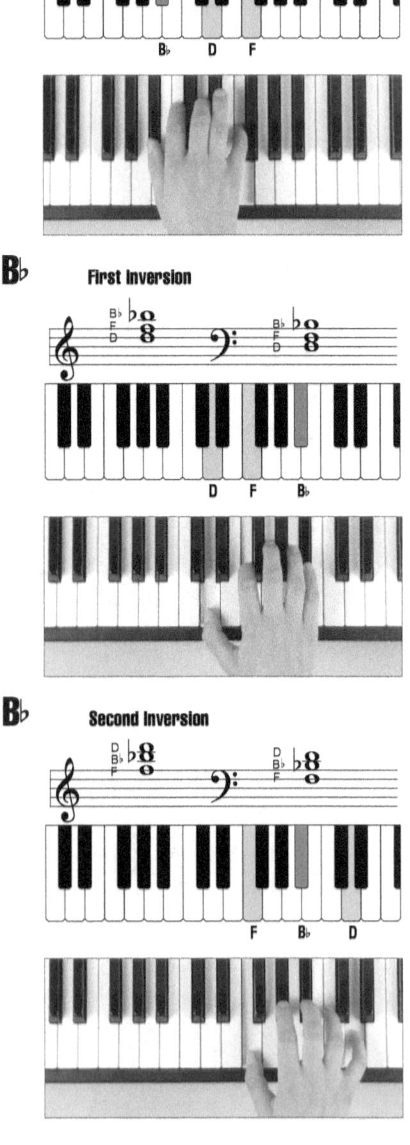
B♭
Root Position
F
D
B♭
B♭
D
F
B♭
First Inversion
B♭
F
D
D
F
B♭
B♭
Second Inversion
D
B♭
F
F
B♭
D

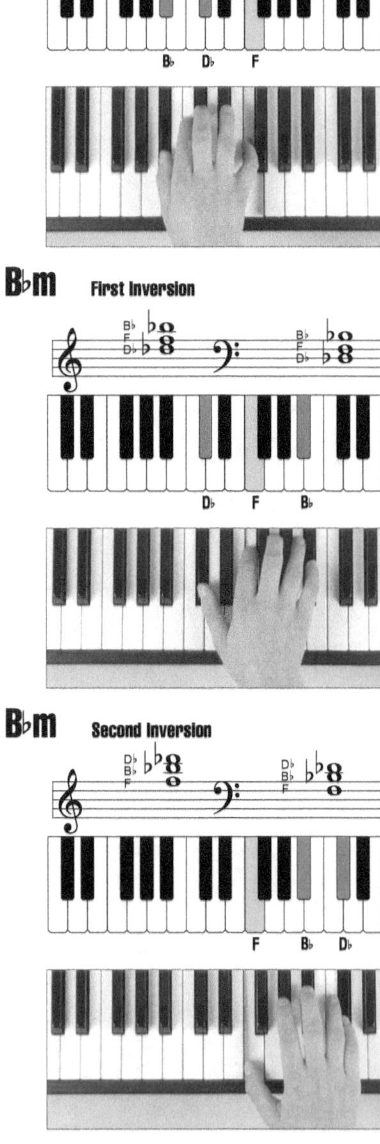
B♭m
Root Position
F
D♭
B♭
B♭
D♭
F
B♭m
First Inversion
B♭
F
D♭
D♭
F
B♭
B♭m
Second Inversion
D♭
B♭
F
F
B♭
D♭

B♭+ Root Position

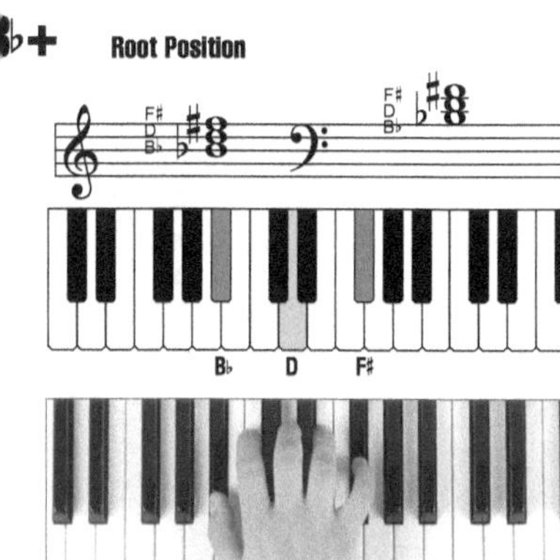

B♭+ First Inversion

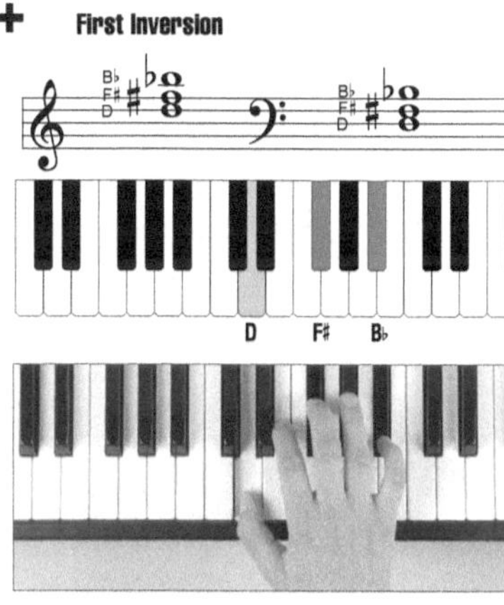

B♭+ Second Inversion

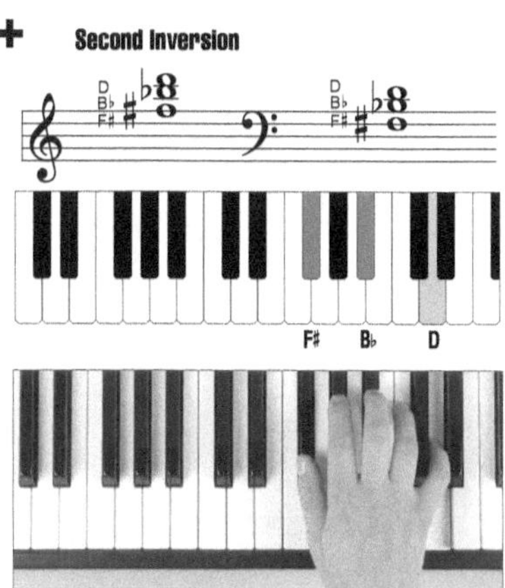

B♭dim Root Position

B♭dim First Inversion

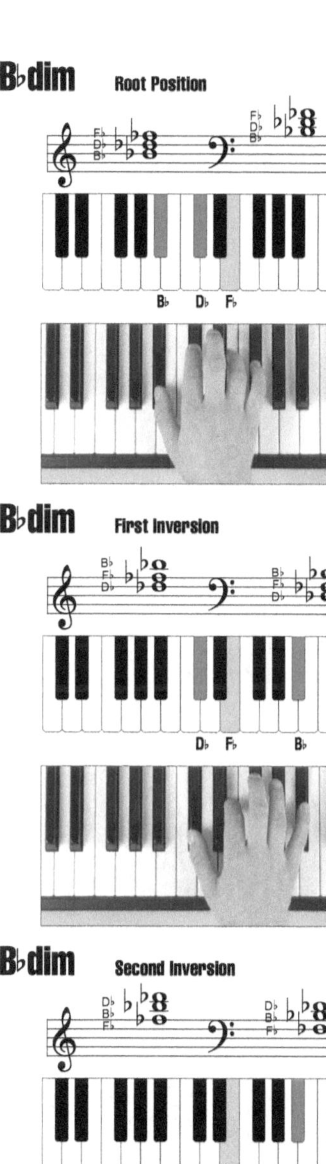

B♭dim Second Inversion

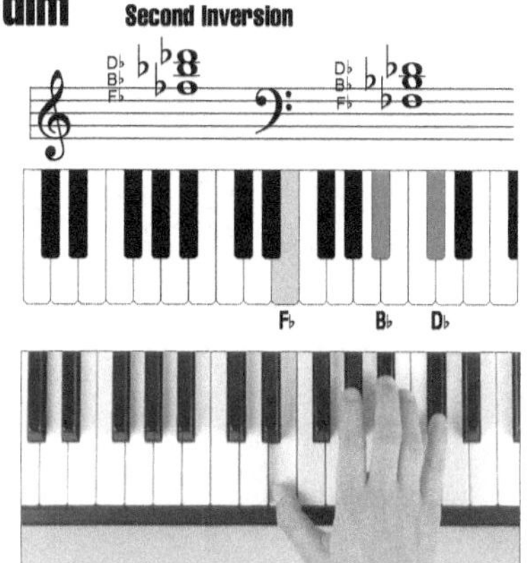

B♭sus Root Position

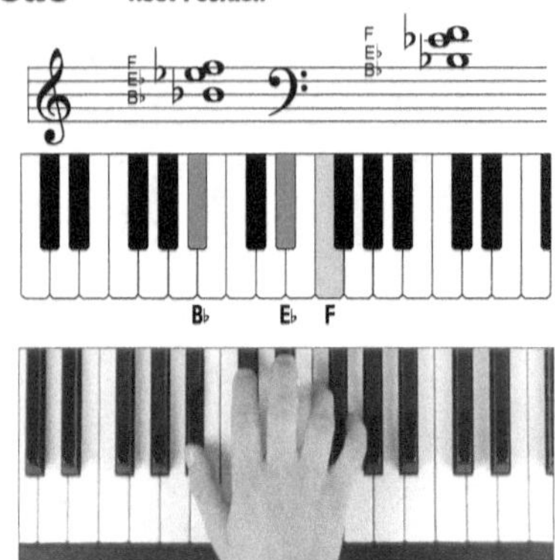

B♭sus First Inversion

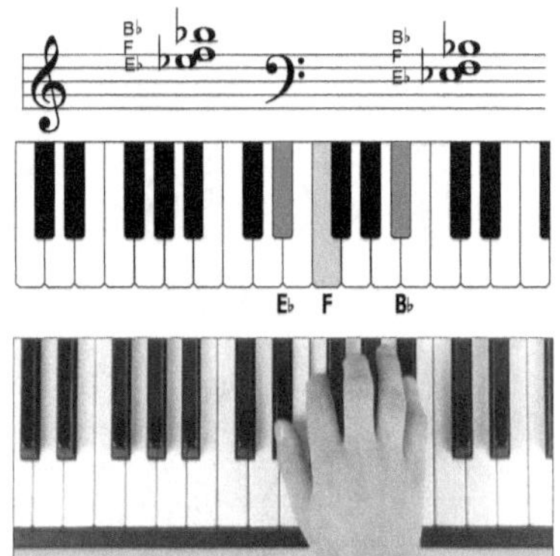

B♭sus Second Inversion

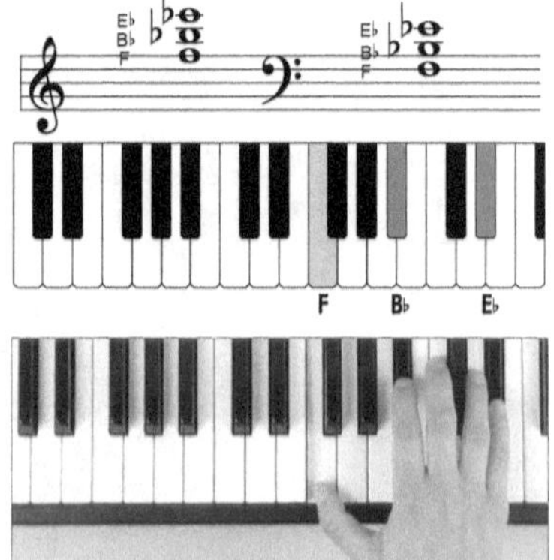

B♭(♭5) Root Position

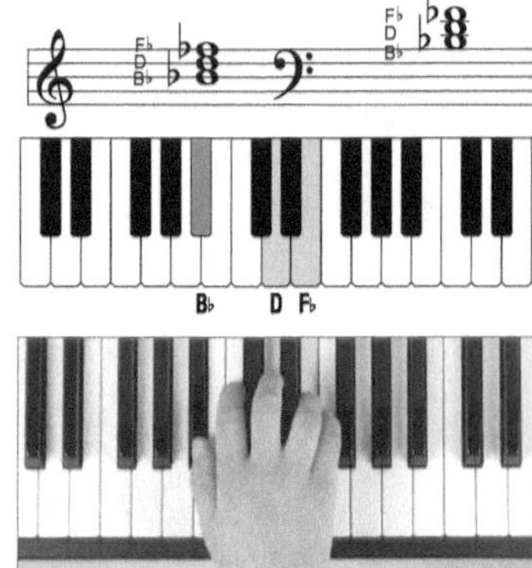

B♭(♭5) First Inversion

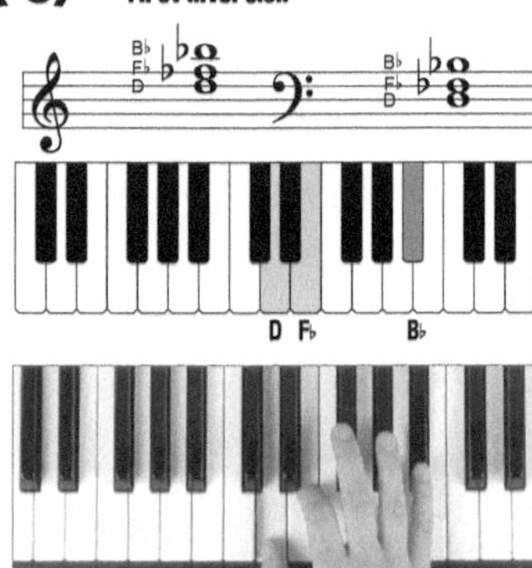

B♭(♭5) Second Inversion

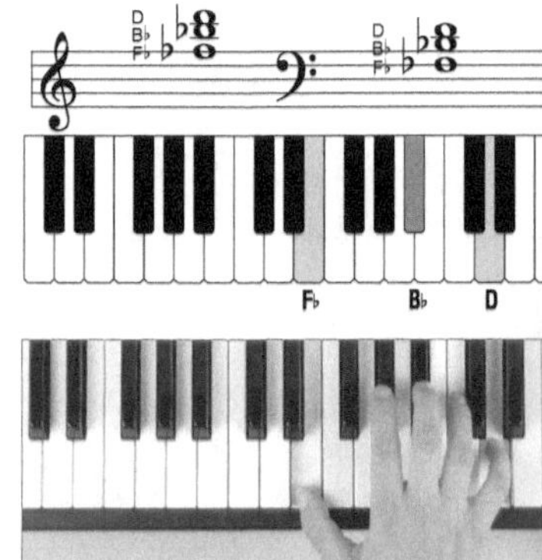

B♭sus2 Root Position

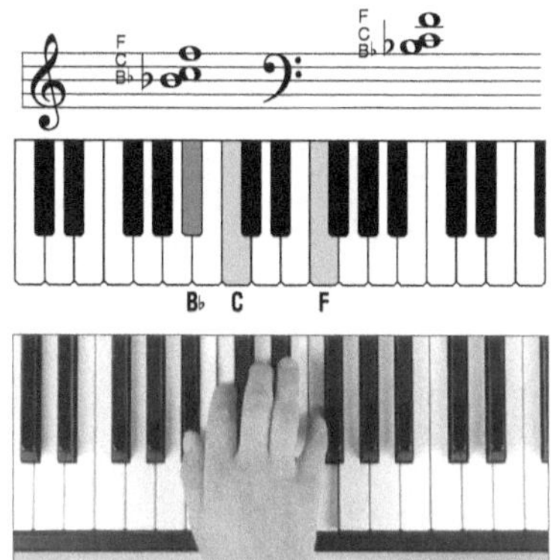

B♭sus2 First Inversion

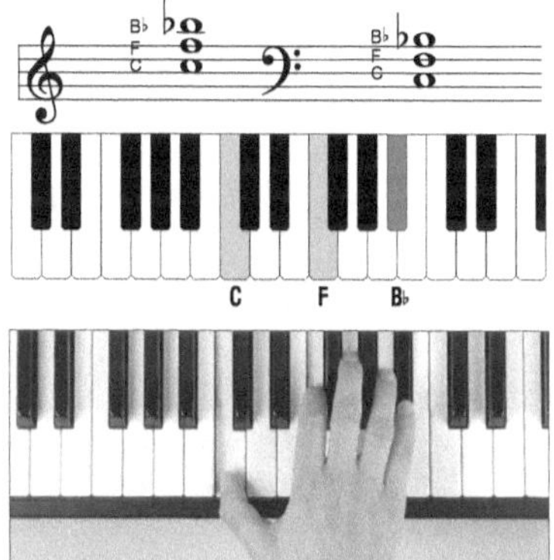

B♭sus2 Second Inversion

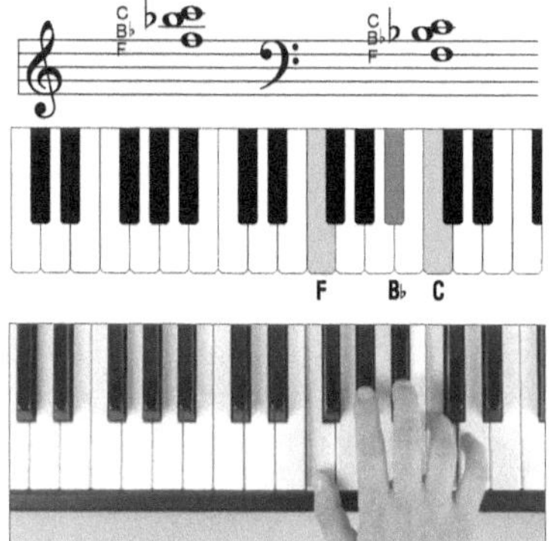

B♭6 Root Position

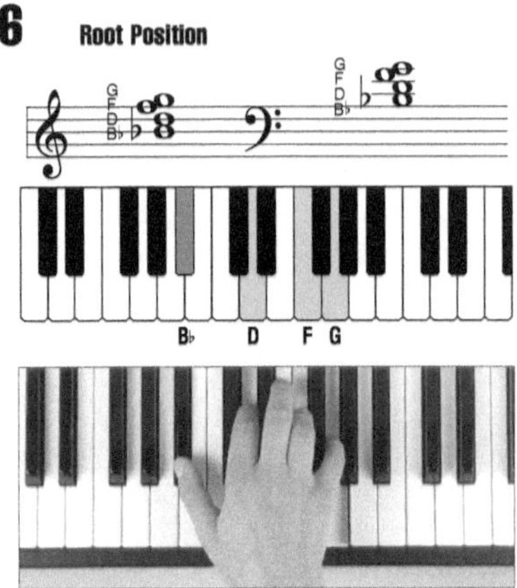

B♭6 First Inversion

B♭6 Second Inversion

B♭6 Third Inversion

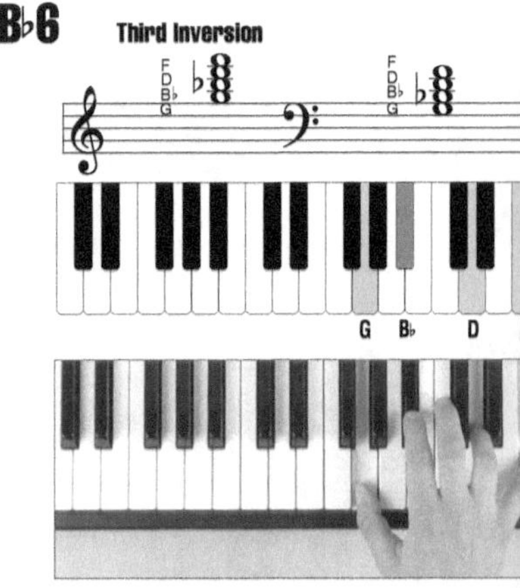

B♭(add2), B♭(add9) Root Position

B♭(add2), B♭(add9) First Inversion

B♭(add2), B♭(add9) Second Inversion

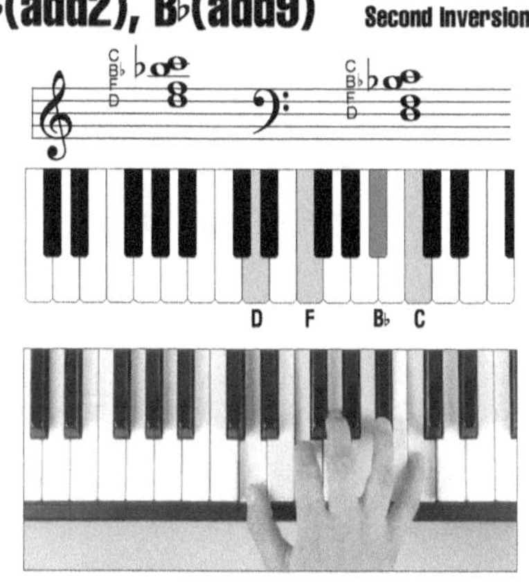

B♭(add2), B♭(add9) Third Inversion

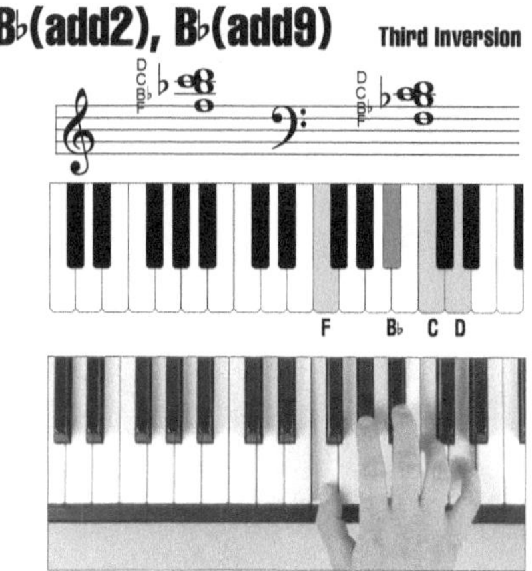

B♭maj7 Root Position

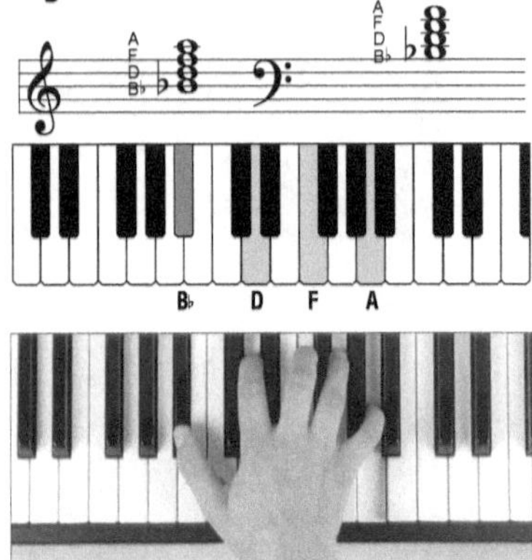

B♭maj7 First Inversion

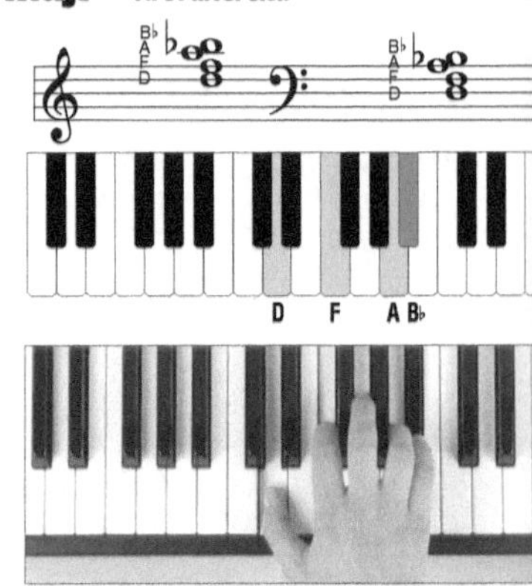

B♭maj7 Second Inversion

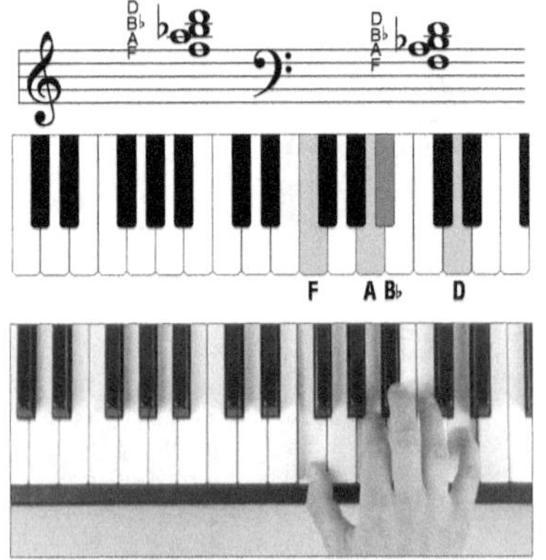

B♭maj7 Third Inversion

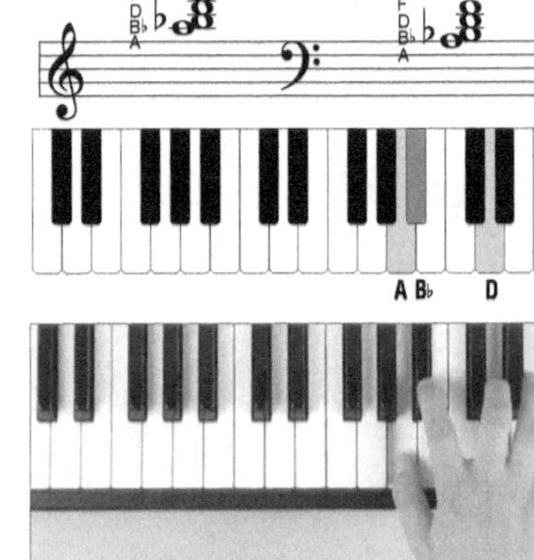

B♭maj7♭5 Root Position

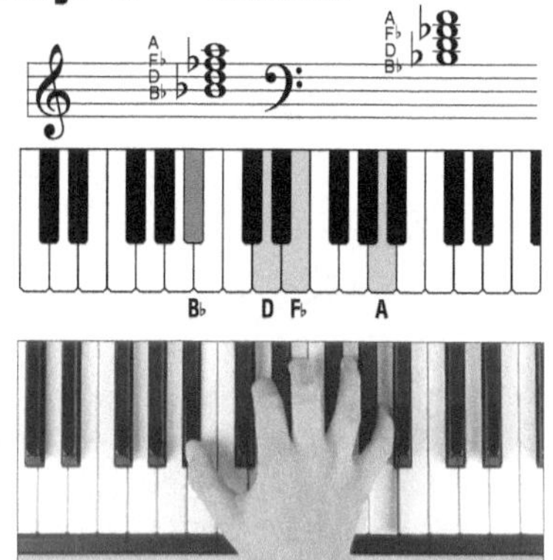

B♭maj7♭5 First Inversion

B♭
A
F♭
D

D F♭ A B♭

B♭maj7♭5 Second Inversion

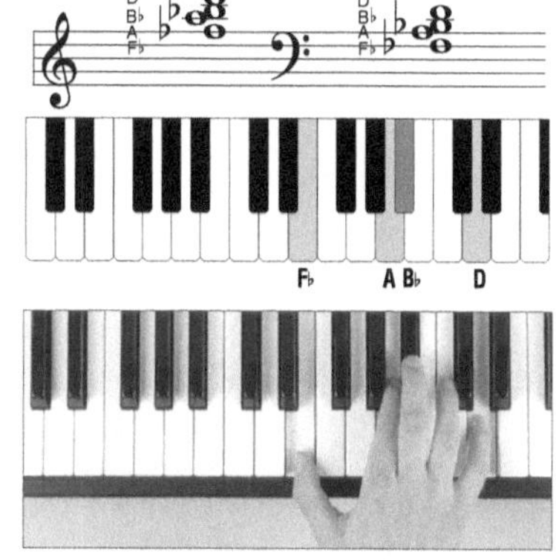

B♭maj7♭5 Third Inversion

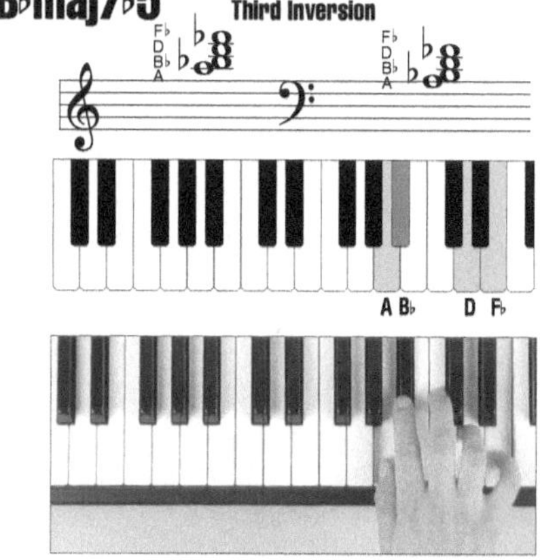

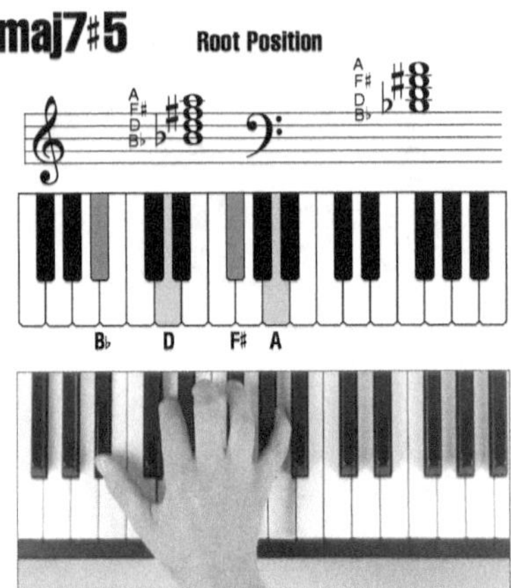
B♭maj7♯5
Root Position
A F♯ D B♭
A F♯ D B♭
B♭ D F♯ A

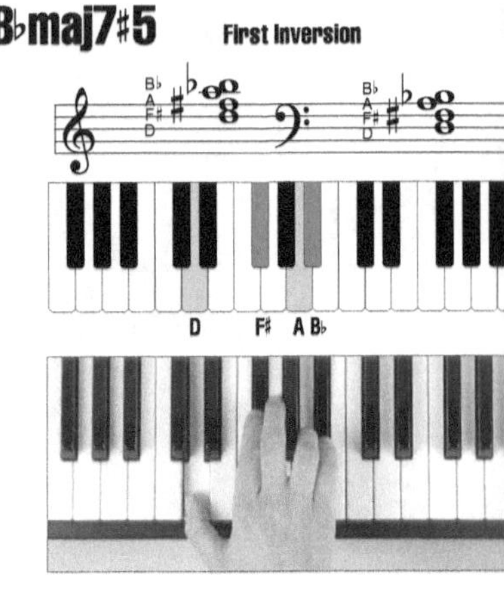
B♭maj7♯5
First Inversion
B♭ A F♯ D
B♭ A F♯ D
D F♯ A B♭

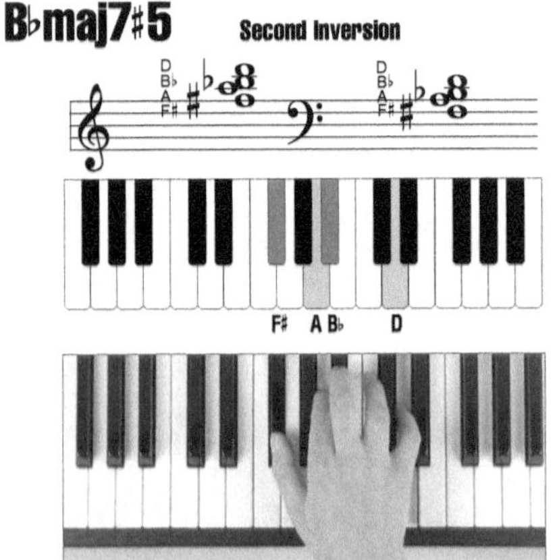
B♭maj7♯5
Second Inversion
D B♭ A F♯
D B♭ A F♯
F♯ A B♭ D

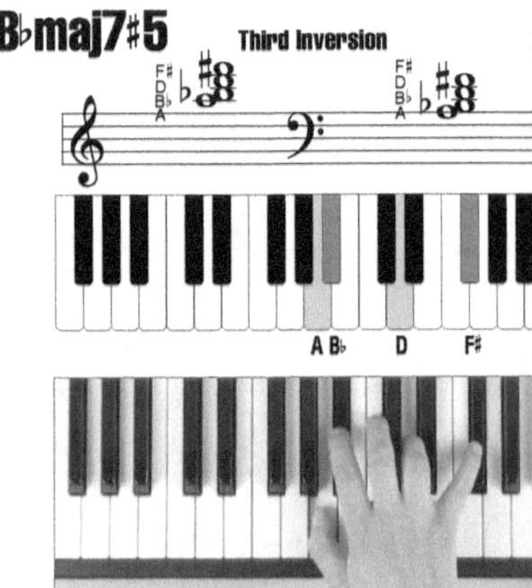
B♭maj7♯5
Third Inversion
F♯ D B♭ A
F♯ D B♭ A
A B♭ D F♯

B♭7 Root Position

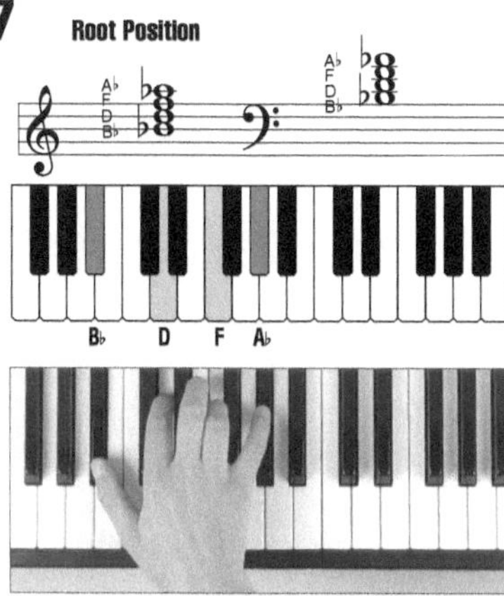

B♭7 First Inversion

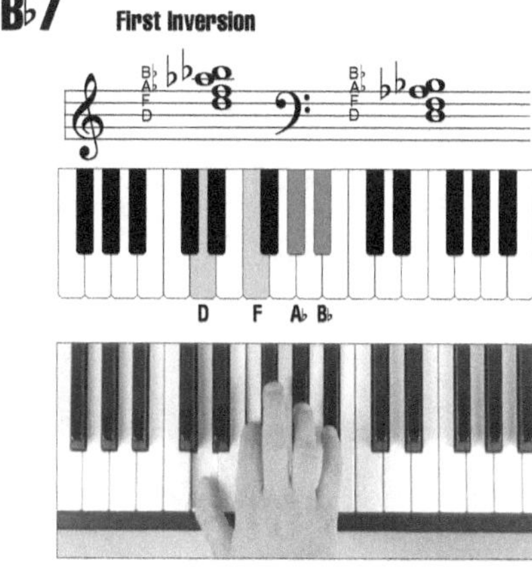

B♭7 Second Inversion

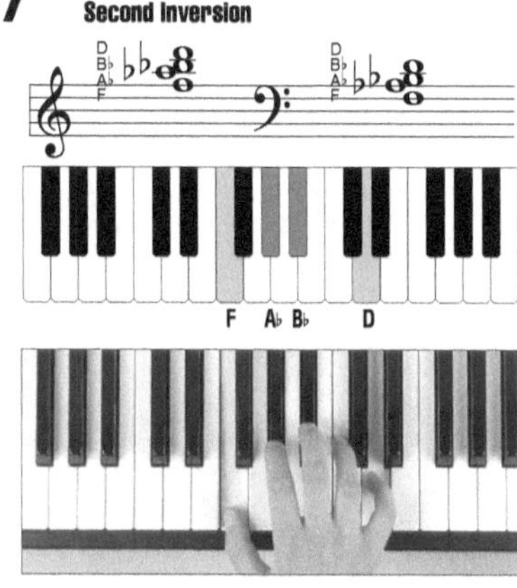

B♭7 Third Inversion

B♭7♭5 Root Position

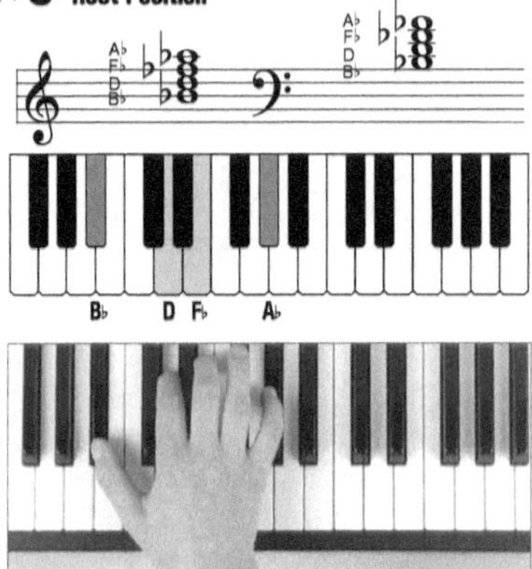

B♭7♭5 First Inversion

B♭7♭5 Second Inversion

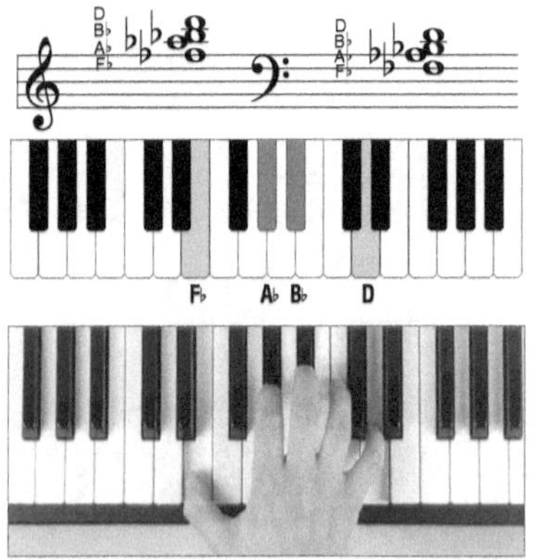

B♭7♭5 Third Inversion

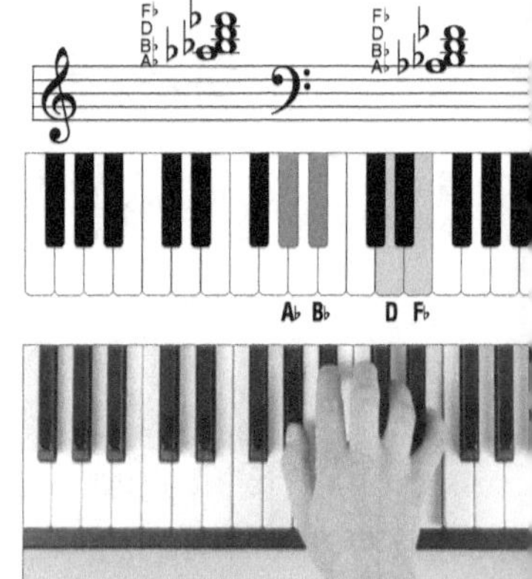

B♭7♯5 Root Position

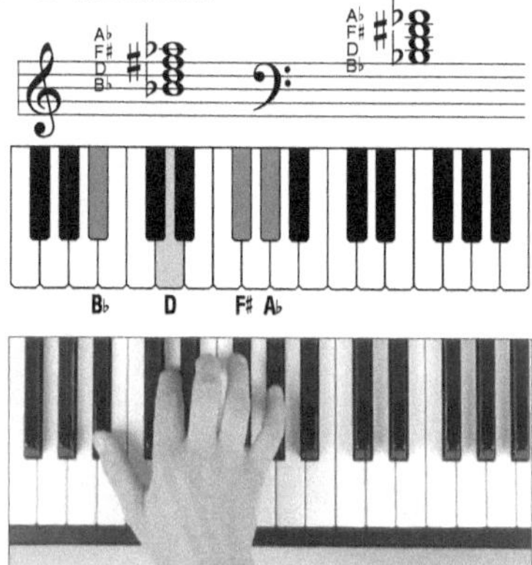

B♭7♯5 First Inversion

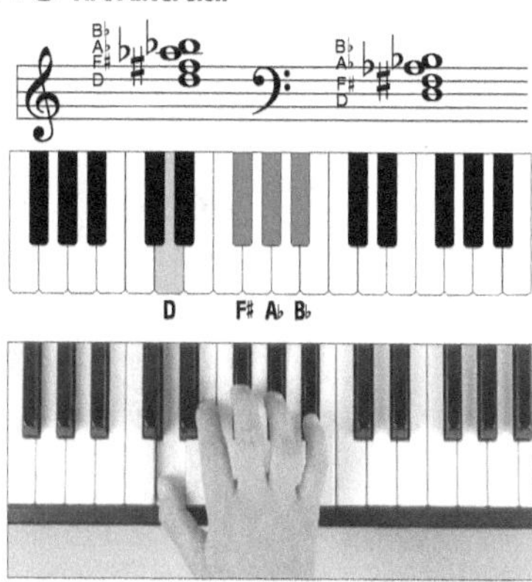

B♭7♯5 Second Inversion

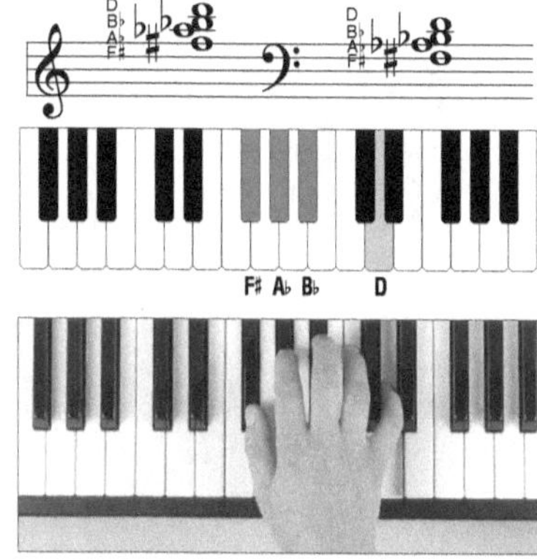

B♭7♯5 Third Inversion

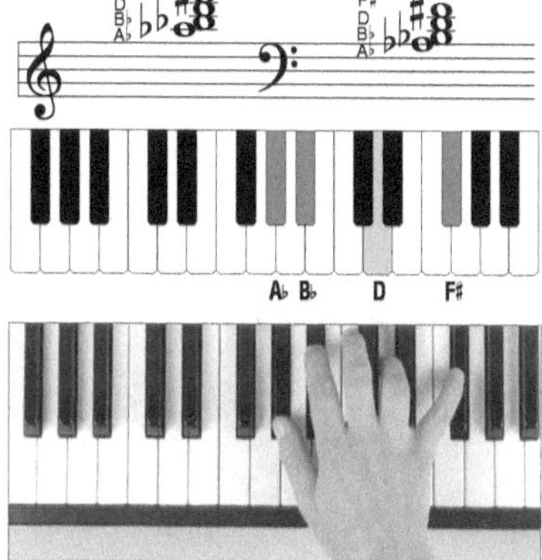

B♭7sus Root Position

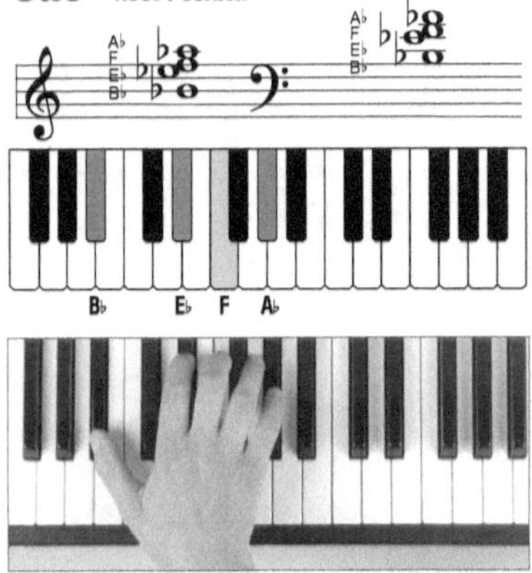

B♭7sus First Inversion

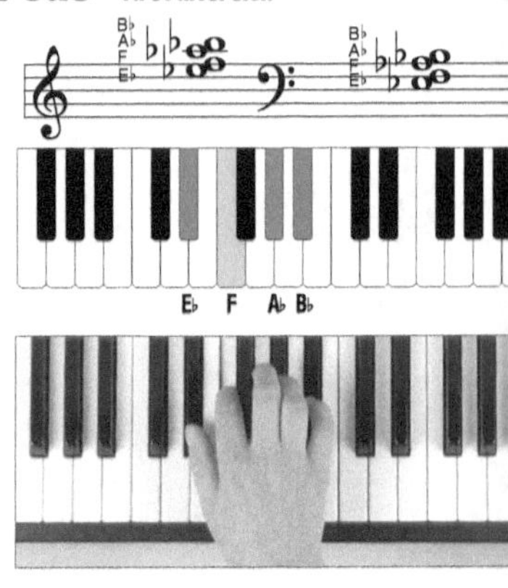

B♭7sus Second Inversion

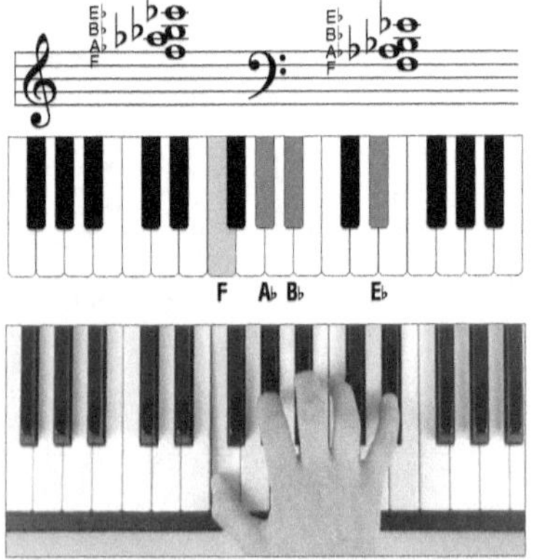

B♭7sus Third Inversion

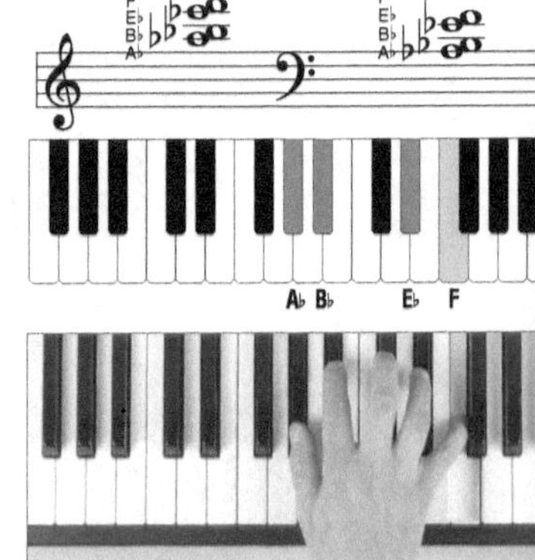

B♭m(add2), B♭m(add9) Root Position

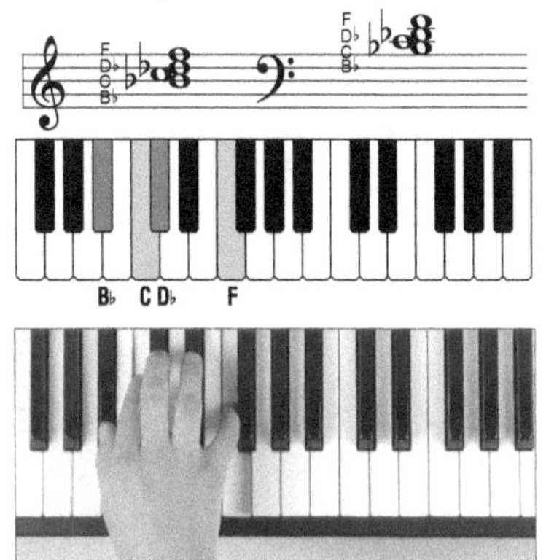

B♭m(add2), B♭m(add9) First Inversion

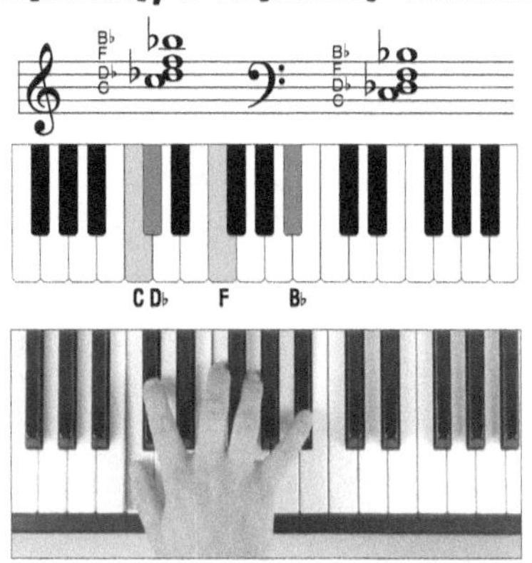

B♭m(add2), B♭m(add9) Second Inversion

B♭m(add2), B♭m(add9) Third Inversion

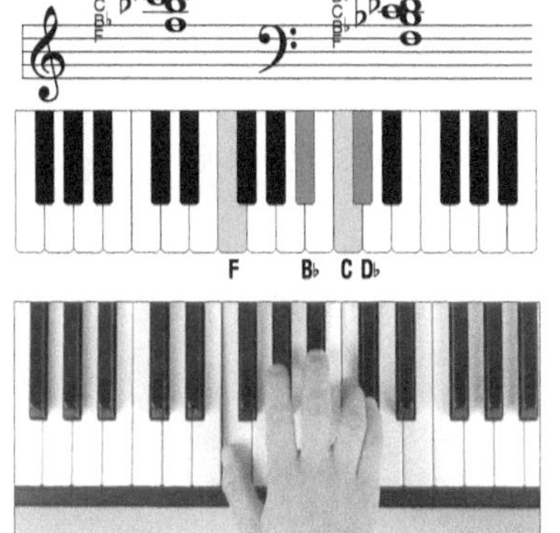

B♭m6 Root Position

B♭m6 First Inversion

B♭m6 Second Inversion

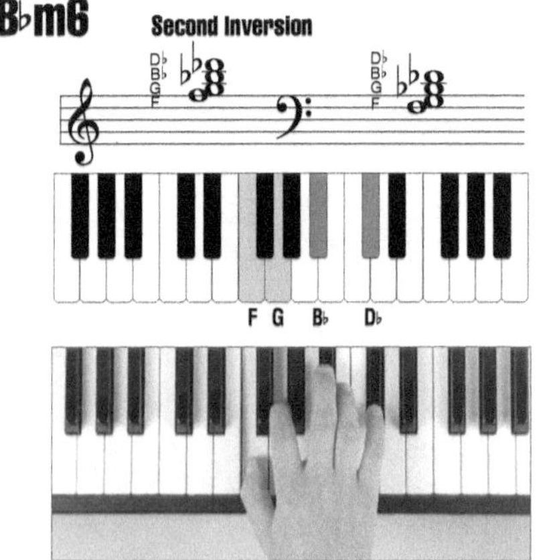

B♭m6 Third Inversion

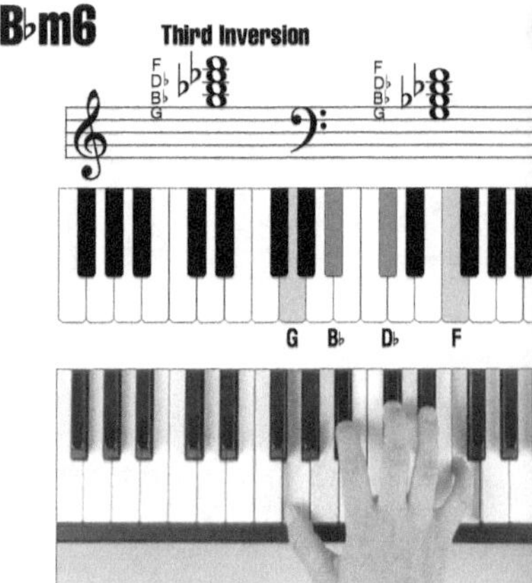

B♭m7
Root Position
A♭
F
D♭
B♭
A♭
F
D♭
B♭
B♭ D♭ F A♭

B♭m7
First Inversion
B♭
A♭
F
D♭
B♭
A♭
F
D♭
D♭ F A♭ B♭

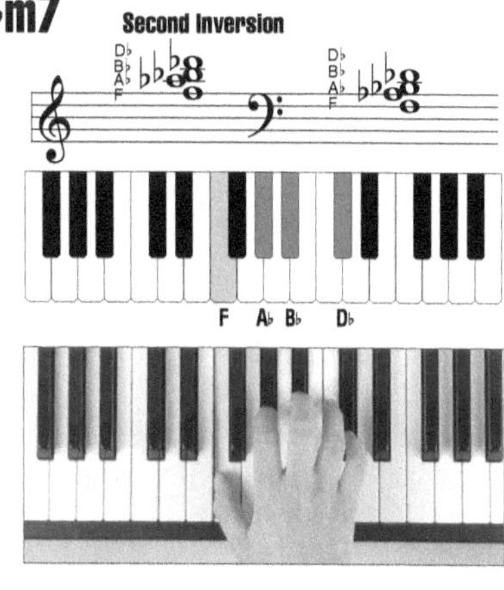
B♭m7
Second Inversion
D♭
B♭
A♭
F
D♭
B♭
A♭
F
F A♭ B♭ D♭

B♭m7
Third Inversion
F
D♭
B♭
A♭
F
D♭
B♭
A♭
A♭ B♭ D♭ F

B♭m(maj7) Root Position

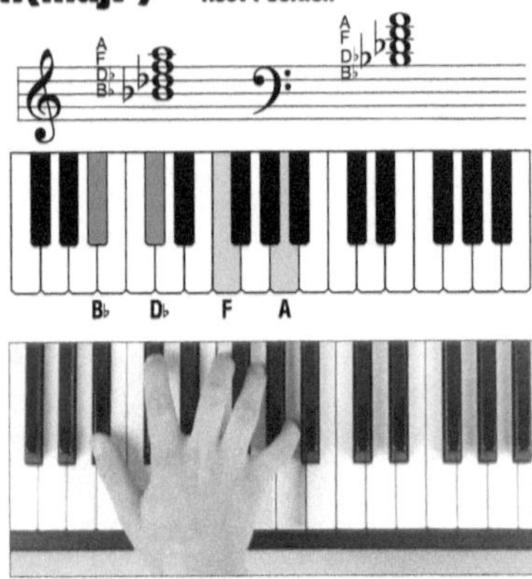

B♭m(maj7) First Inversion

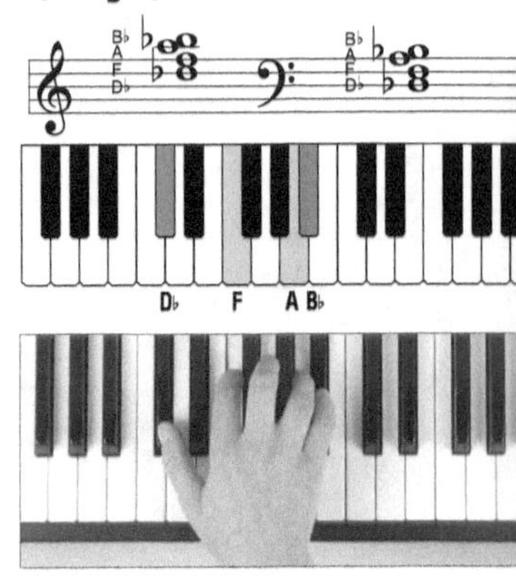

B♭m(maj7) Second Inversion

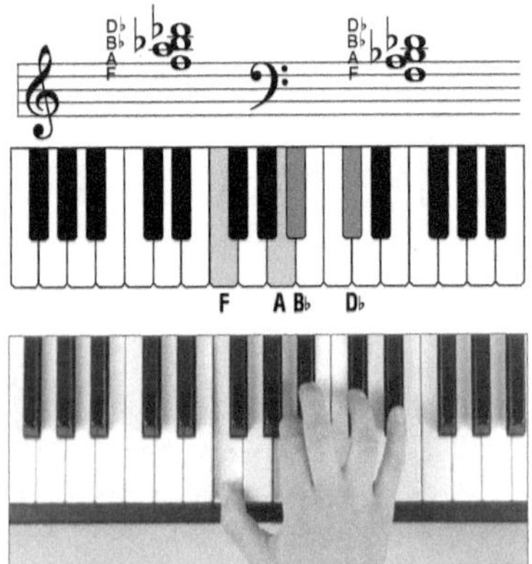

B♭m(maj7) Third Inversion

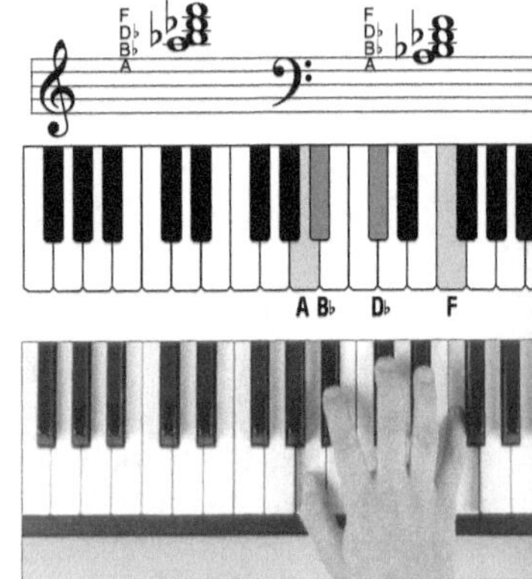

B♭m7♭5 Root Position

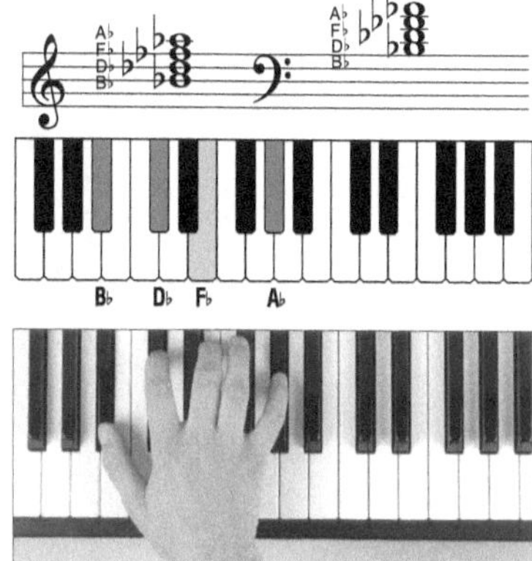

B♭m7♭5 First Inversion

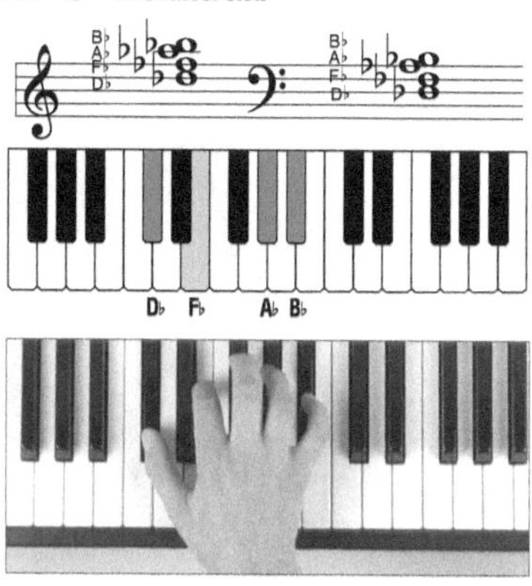

B♭m7♭5 Second Inversion

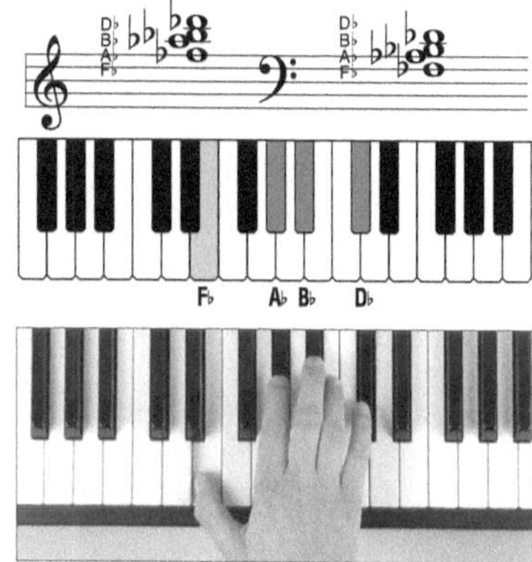

B♭m7♭5 Third Inversion

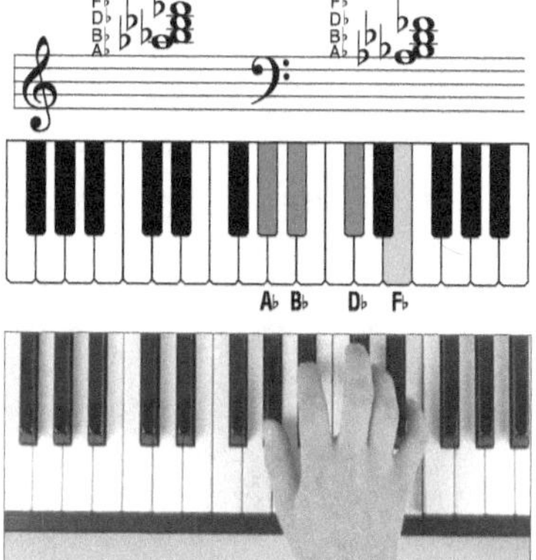

B♭dim7 Root Position

A♭♭ F♭ D♭ B♭

A♭♭ F♭ D♭ B♭

B♭ D♭ F♭ G (A♭♭)

B♭dim7 First Inversion

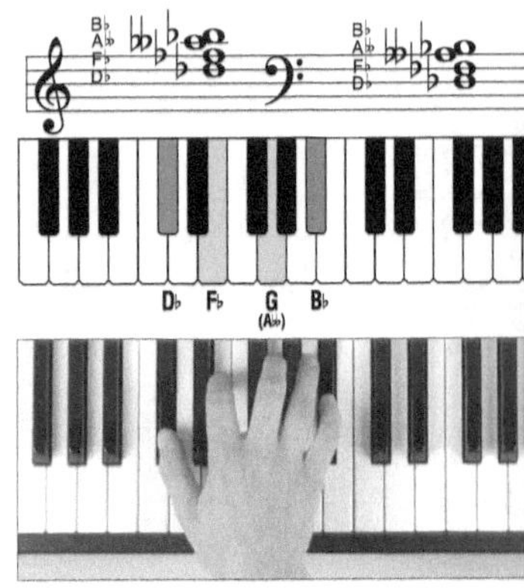

B♭dim7 Second Inversion

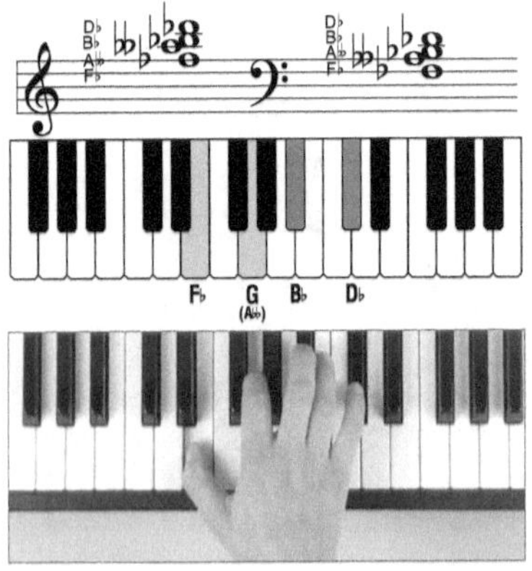

B♭dim7 Third Inversion

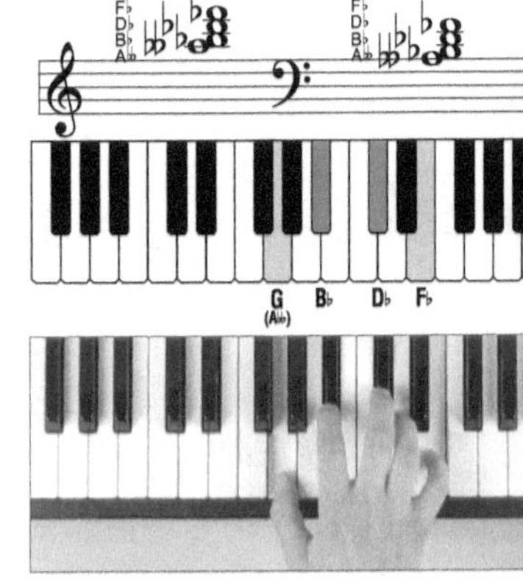

B♭dim(maj7)

Root Position

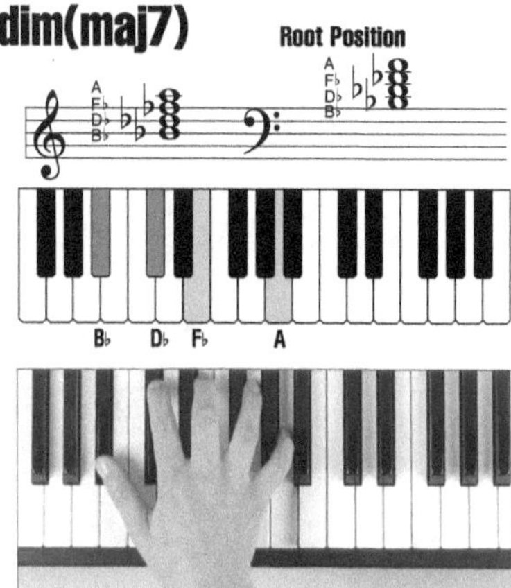

B♭dim(maj7)

First Inversion

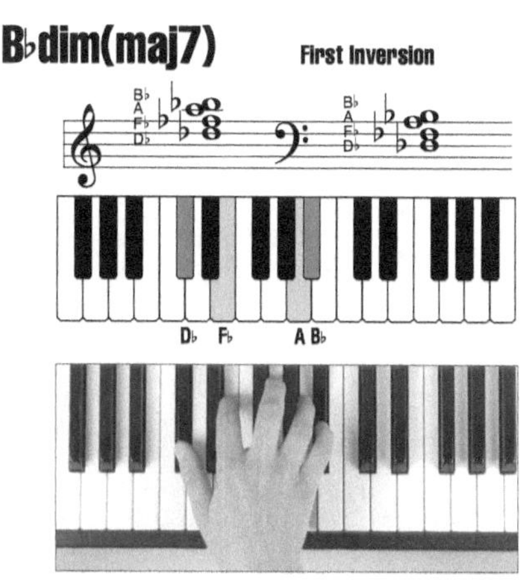

B♭dim(maj7)

Second Inversion

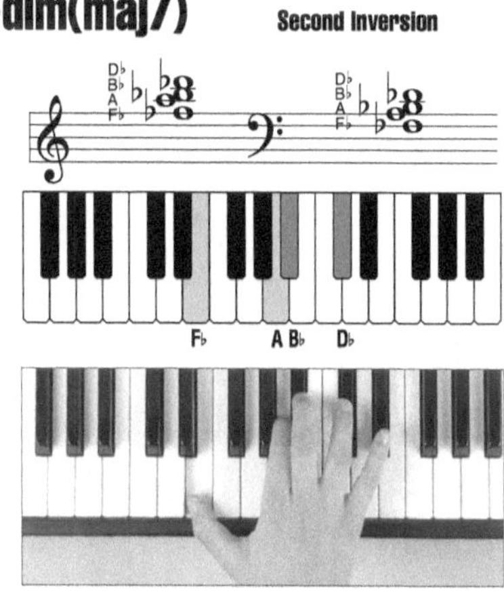

B♭dim(maj7)

Third Inversion

B♭5

B♭$^{6}_{9}$

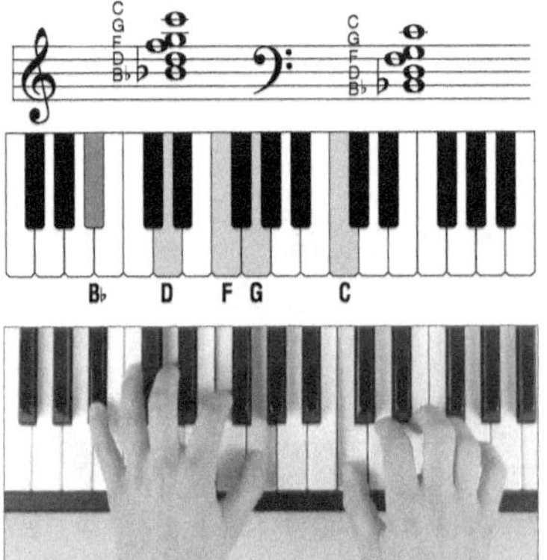

B♭maj$^{6}_{9}$

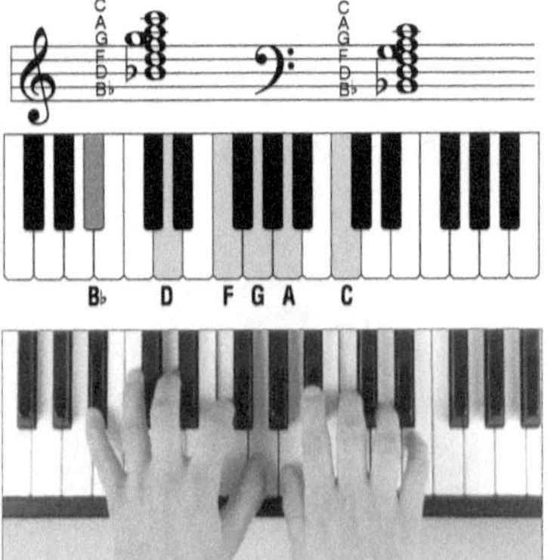

B♭maj7♯11

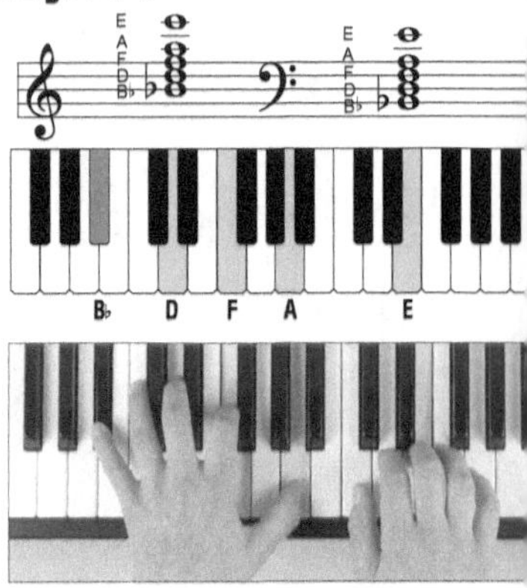

B♭maj9

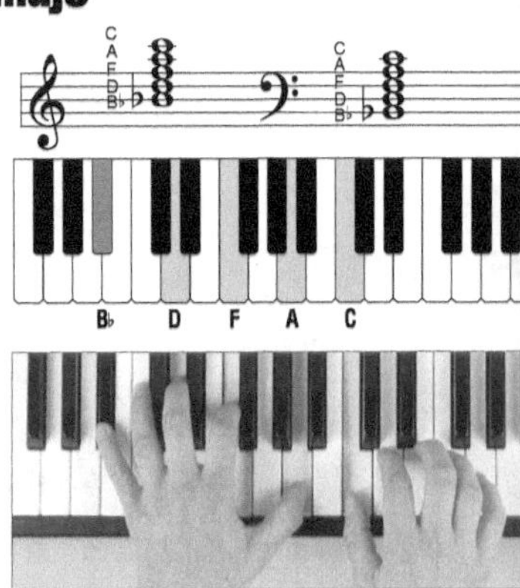

B♭maj9♭5

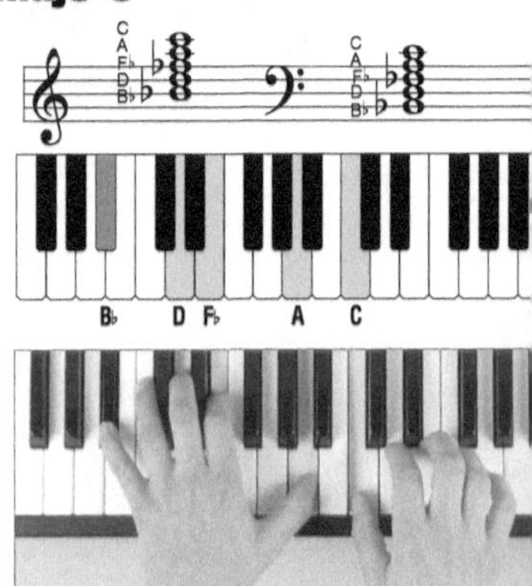

B♭maj9♯5

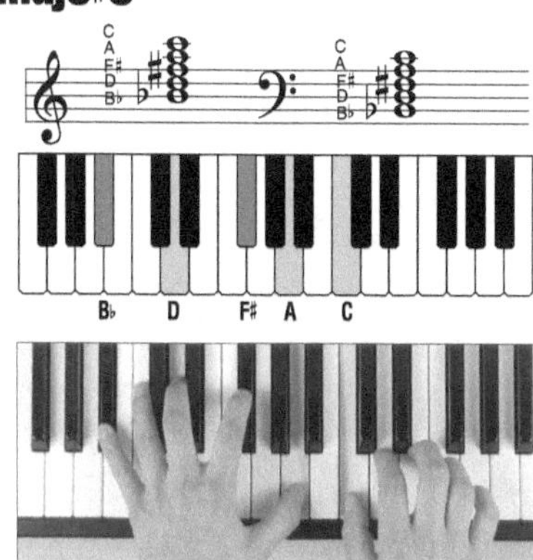

B♭maj9♯11

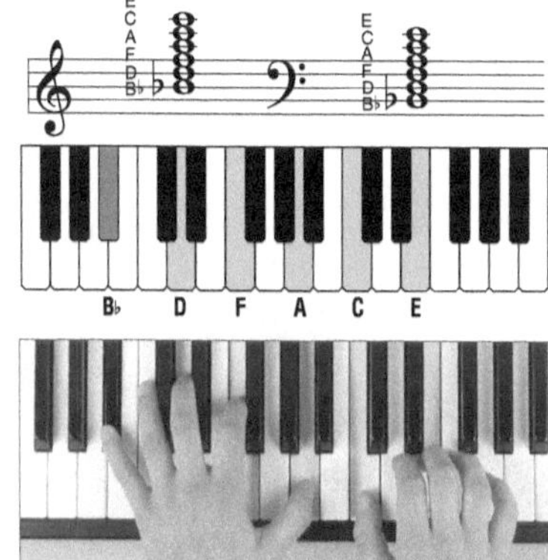

B♭maj13

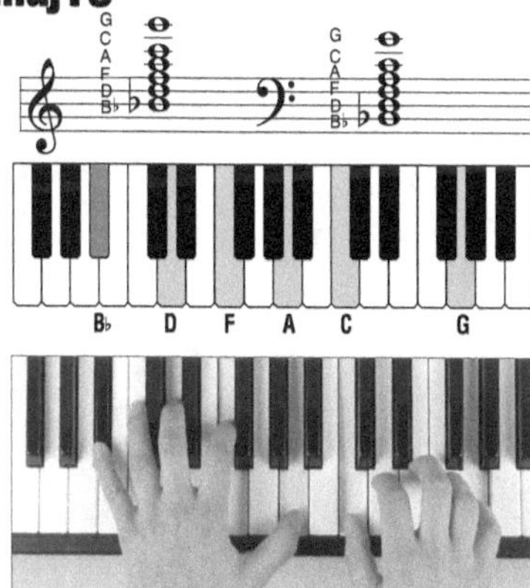

B♭maj13♭5

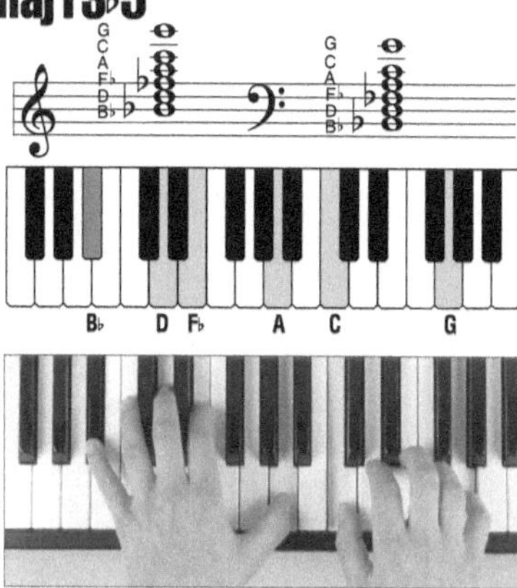

B♭maj13♯11

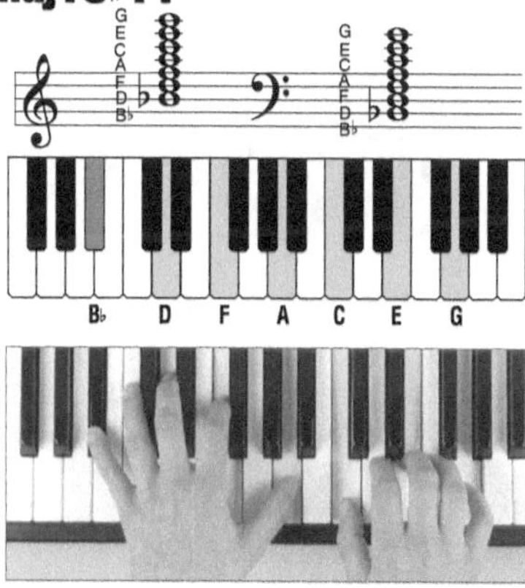

B♭7♭9

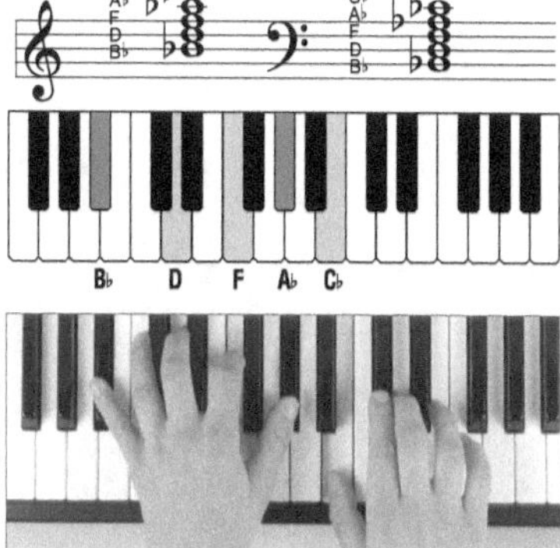

B♭7♯9

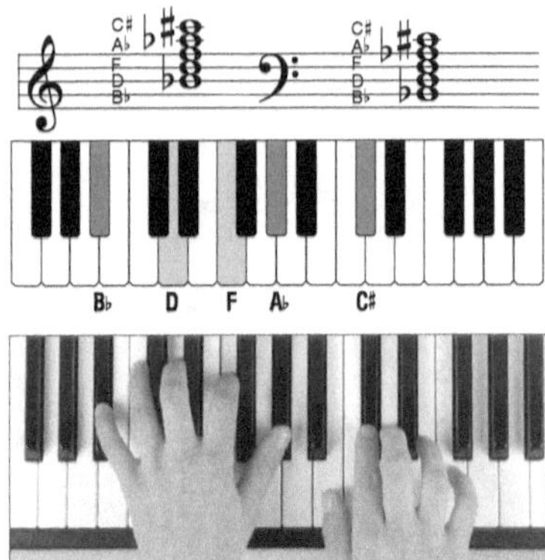

B♭7♯11

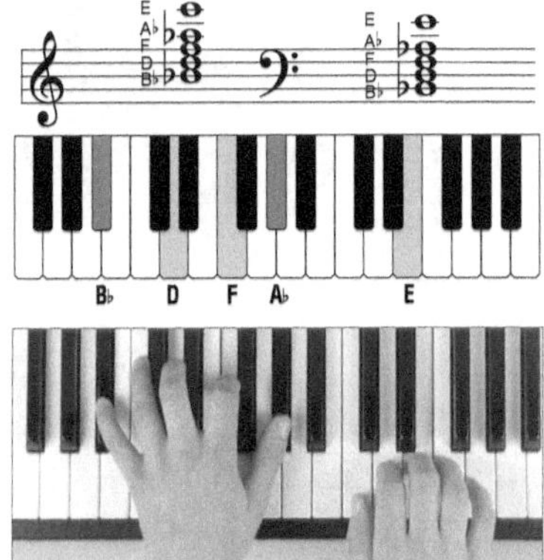

B♭7♭5(♭9)

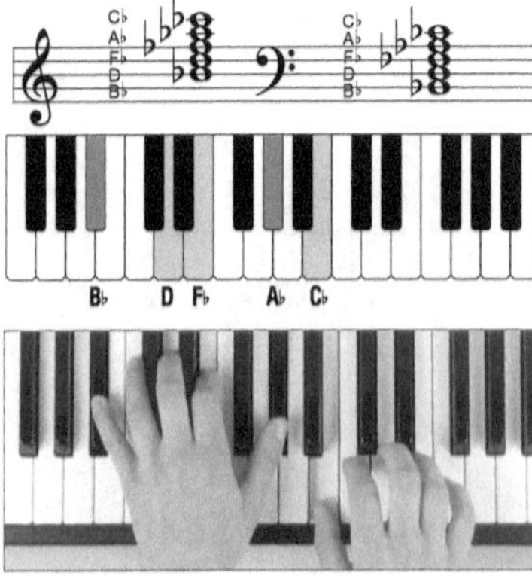

B♭7♭5(♯9)

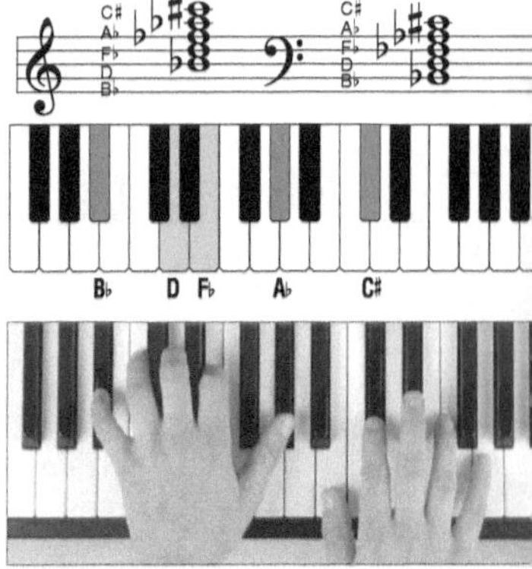

B♭7♯5(♭9)

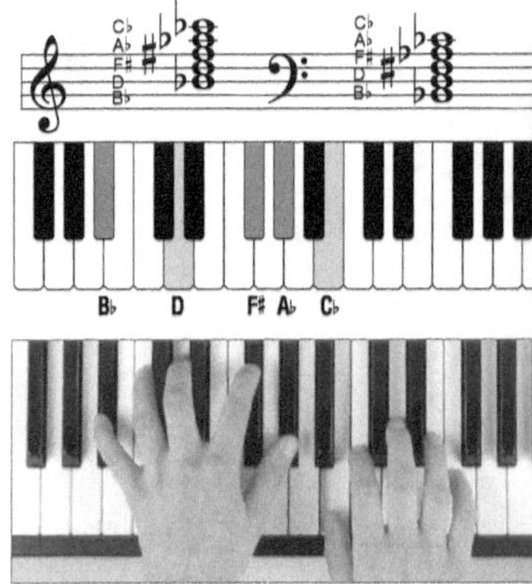

B♭7♯5(♯9)

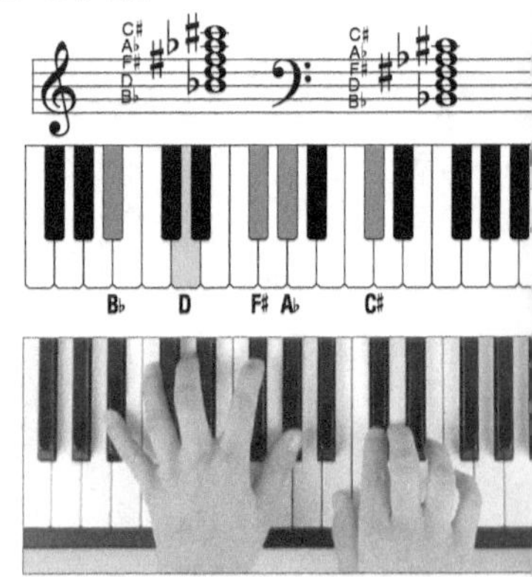

B♭7♭9(♯9)

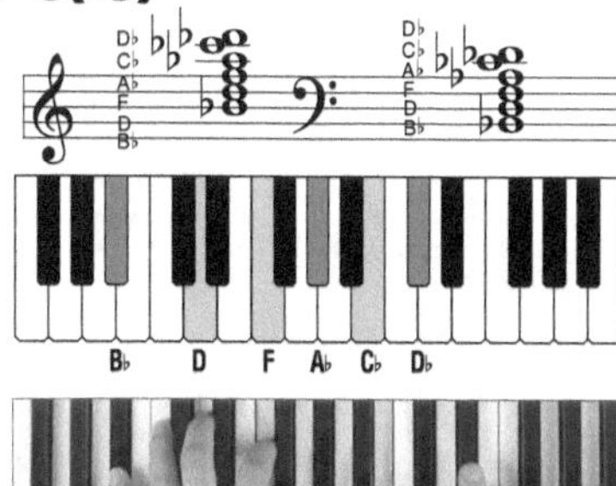

B♭7(add13)

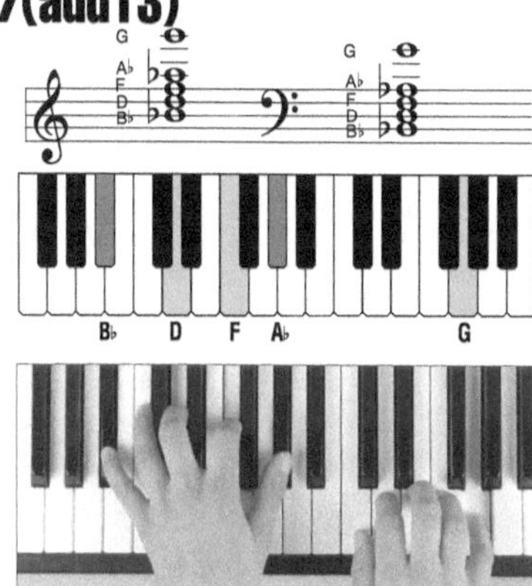

B♭7♭13

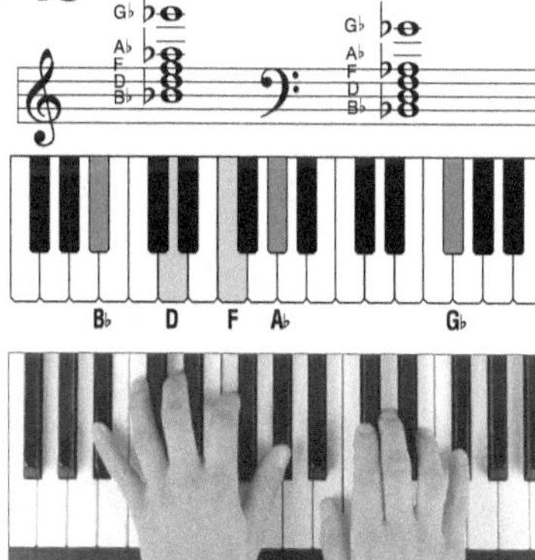

B♭7♭9(♯11)

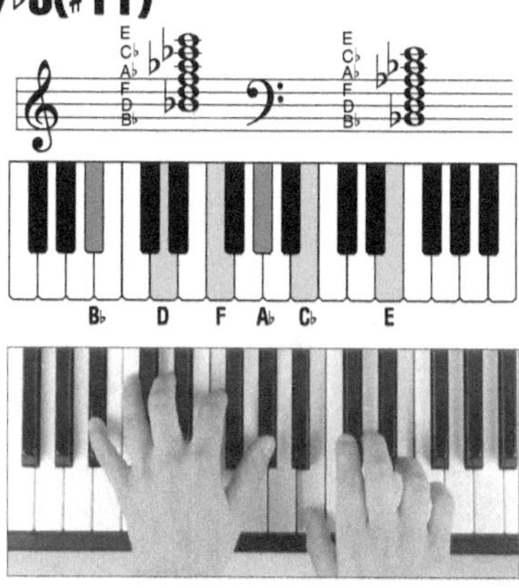

B♭7♯9(♯11)

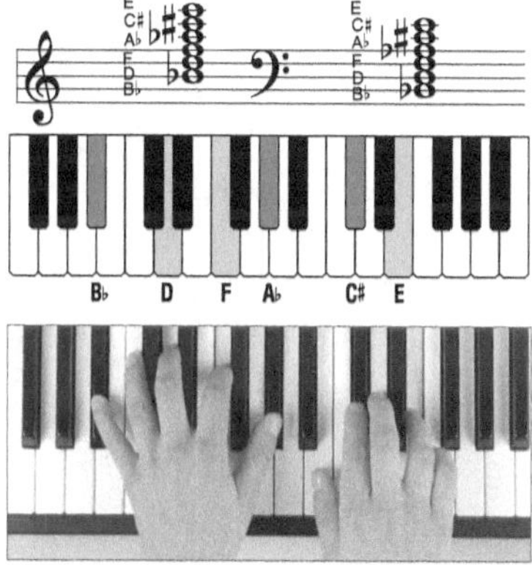

B♭7♭9(♭13)

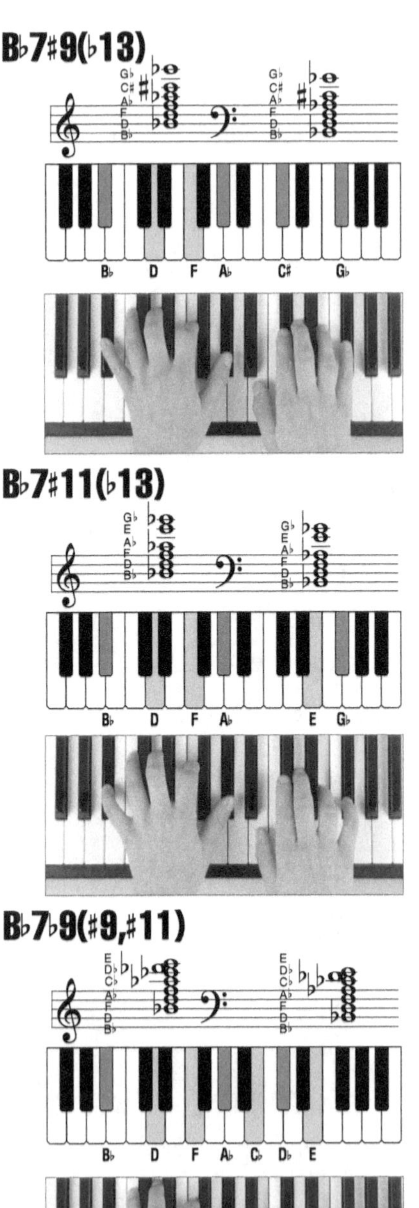
B♭7♯9(♭13)
G♭ C♯ A♭ F D B♭
G♭ C♯ A♭ F D B♭
B♭ D F A♭ C♯ G♭
B♭7♯11(♭13)
G♭ E A♭ F D B♭
G♭ E A♭ F D B♭
B♭ D F A♭ E G♭
B♭7♭9(♯9,♯11)
E D♭ C♭ A♭ F D B♭
E D♭ C♭ A♭ F D B♭
B♭ D F A♭ C♭ D♭ E

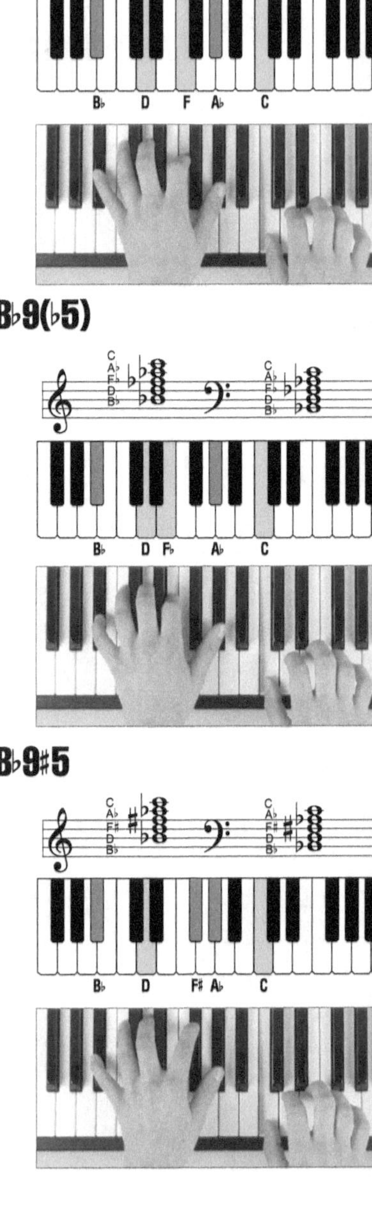
B♭9
C A♭ F D B♭
C A♭ F D B♭
B♭ D F A♭ C
B♭9(♭5)
C A♭ F♭ D B♭
C A♭ F♭ D B♭
B♭ D F♭ A♭ C
B♭9♯5
C A♭ F♯ D B♭
C A♭ F♯ D B♭
B♭ D F♯ A♭ C

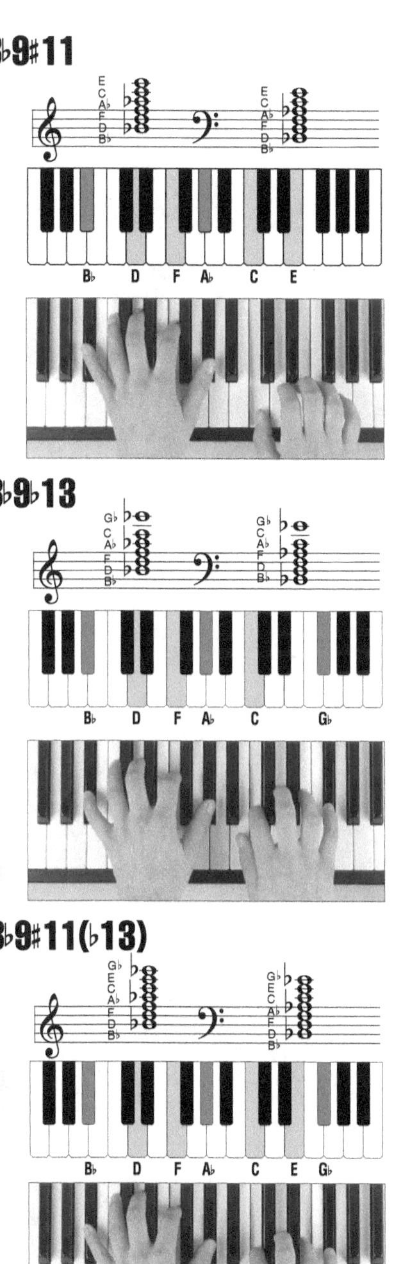
B♭9♯11
E
C
A♭
F
D
B♭
B♭ D F A♭ C E
B♭9♭13
G♭
C
A♭
F
D
B♭
B♭ D F A♭ C G♭
B♭9♯11(♭13)
G♭
E
C
A♭
F
D
B♭
B♭ D F A♭ C E G♭

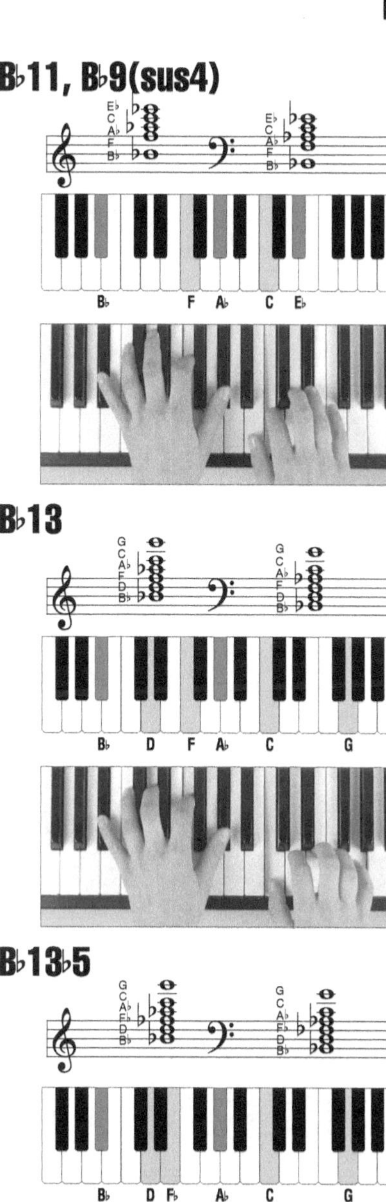
B♭11, B♭9(sus4)
E♭
C
A♭
F
B♭
B♭ F A♭ C E♭
B♭13
G
C
A♭
F
D
B♭
B♭ D F A♭ C G
B♭13♭5
G
C
A♭
F♭
D
B♭
B♭ D F♭ A♭ C G

B♭13♭9

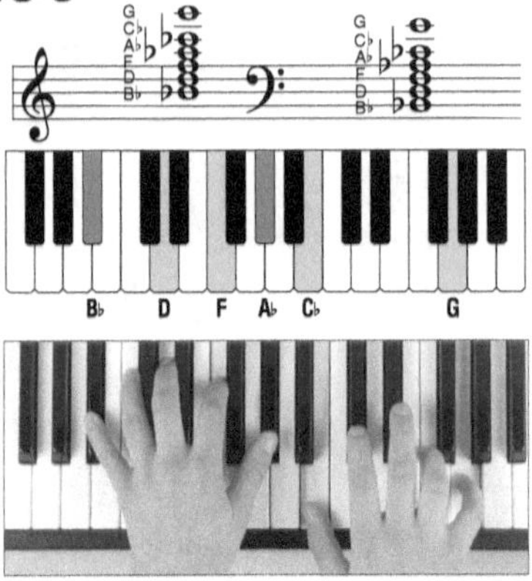
B♭ D F A♭ C♭ G

B♭13♯9

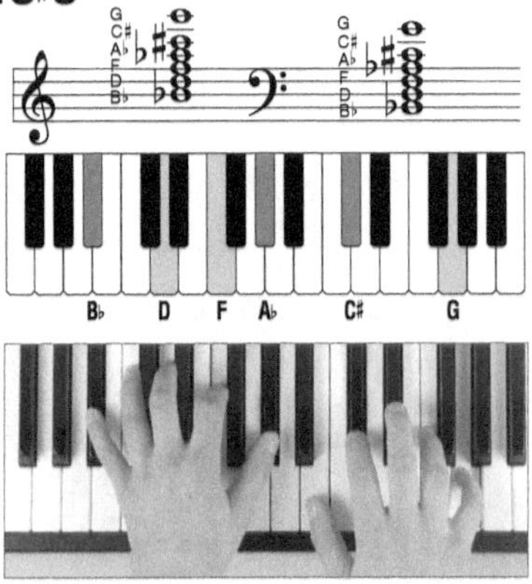
B♭ D F A♭ C♯ G

B♭13♯11

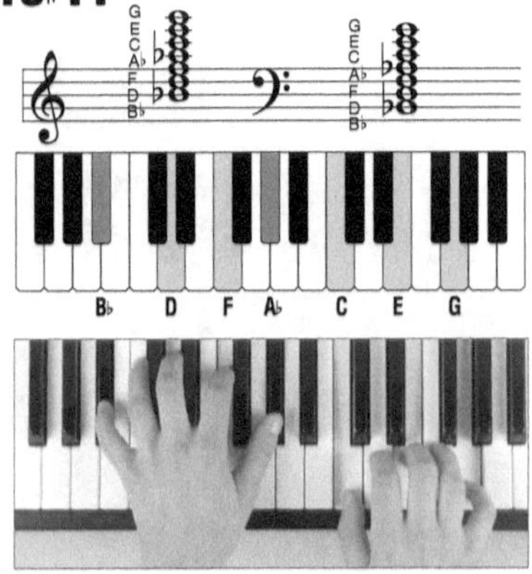
B♭ D F A♭ C E G

B♭13(sus4)

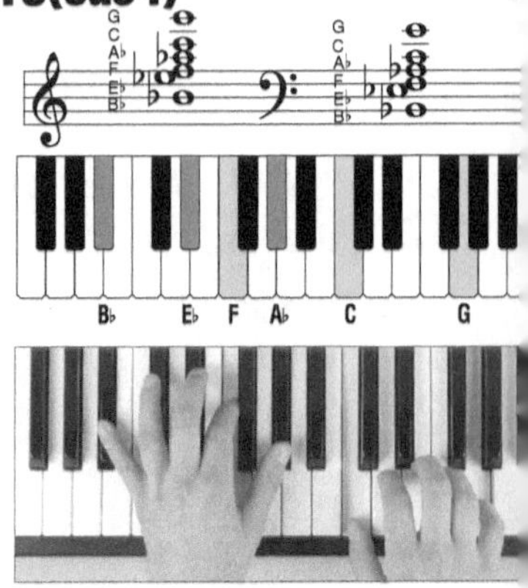
B♭ E♭ F A♭ C G

B♭m(♯5)

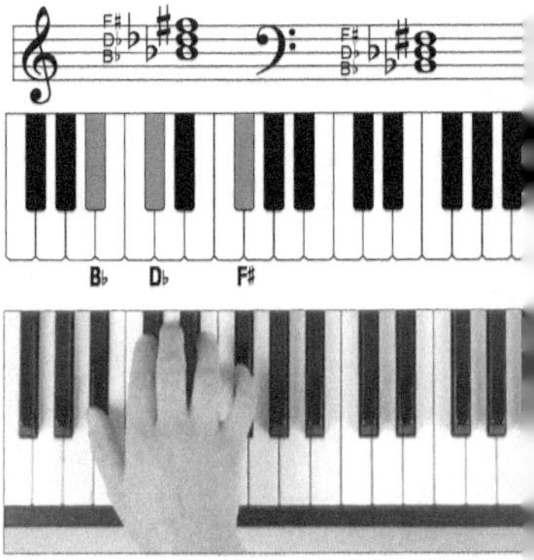
B♭ D♭ F♯

B♭m6/9

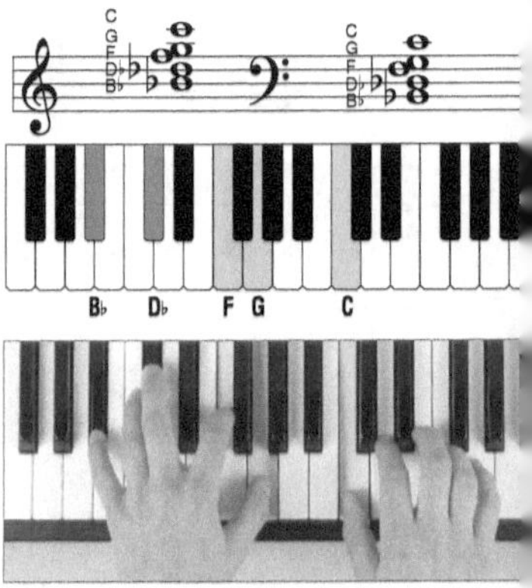
B♭ D♭ F G C

B♭m7(add4)

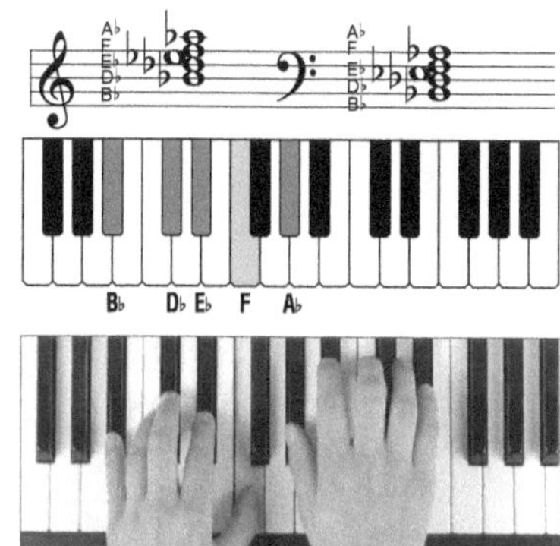

B♭m7(add11)

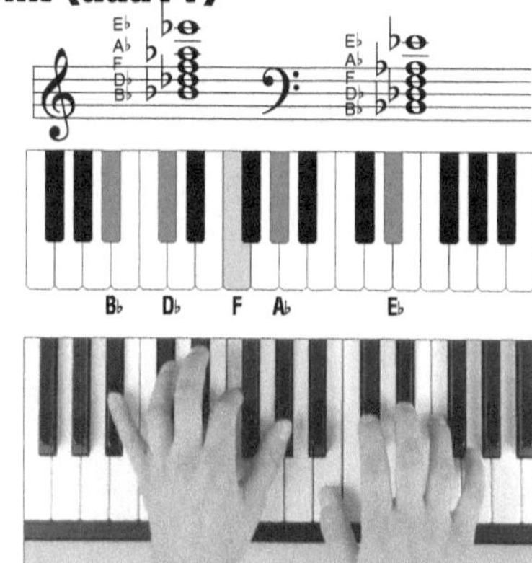

B♭m7♭5(♭9)

B♭m9

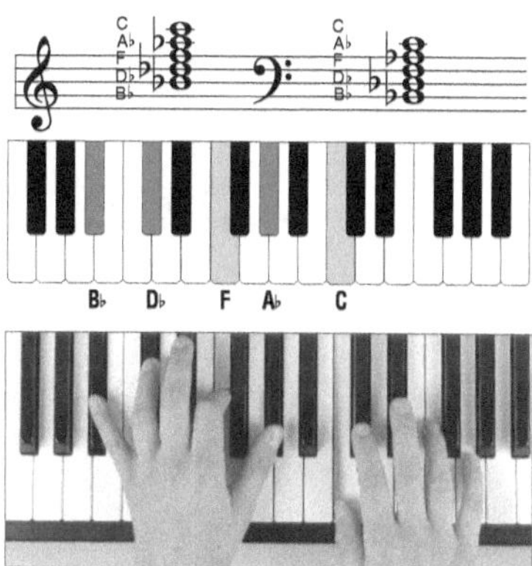

B♭m9(maj7)

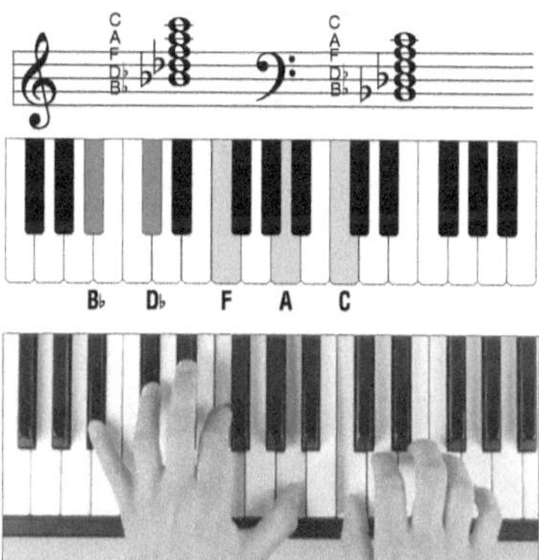

B♭m9♭5

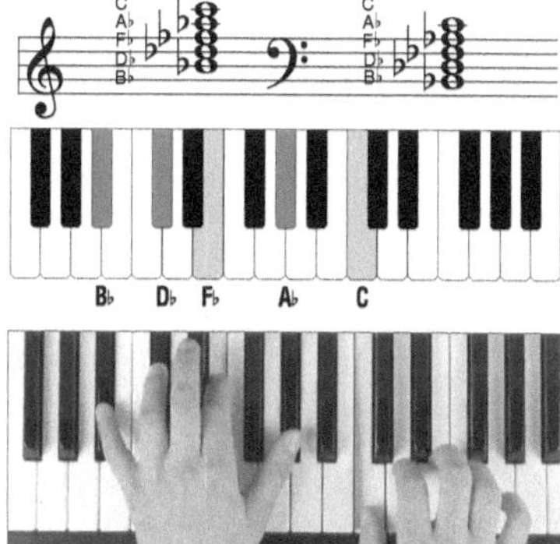

B♭m11

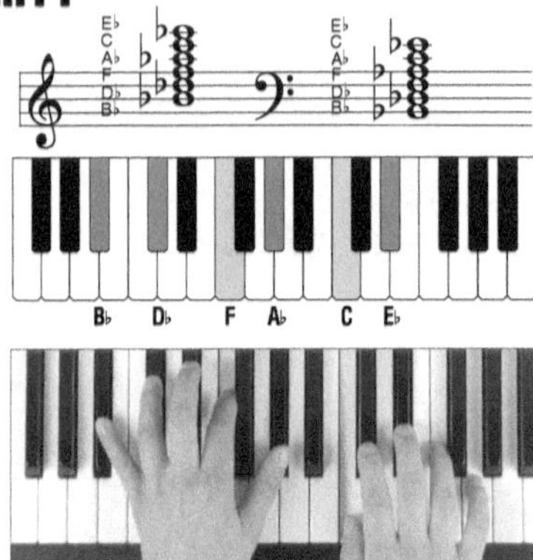

B♭m13

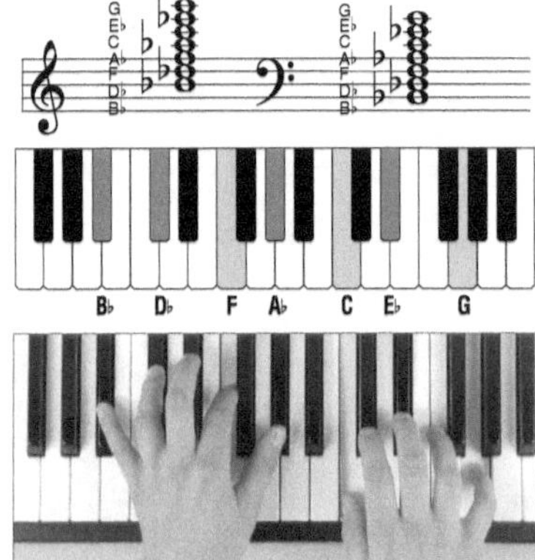

B♭dim7(add9)

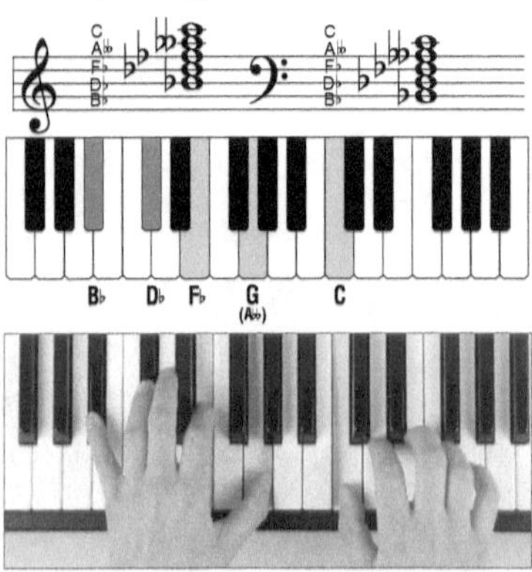

B♭m11♭5

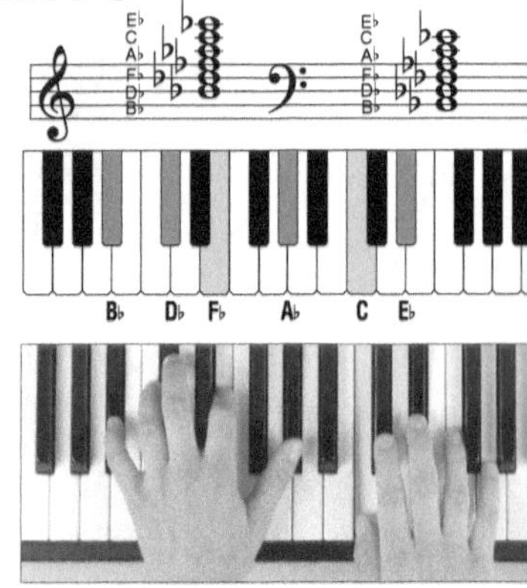

B♭m11(maj7)

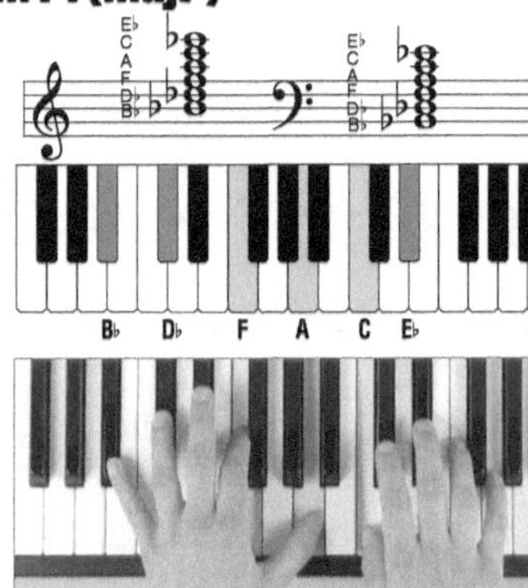

B♭7alt.

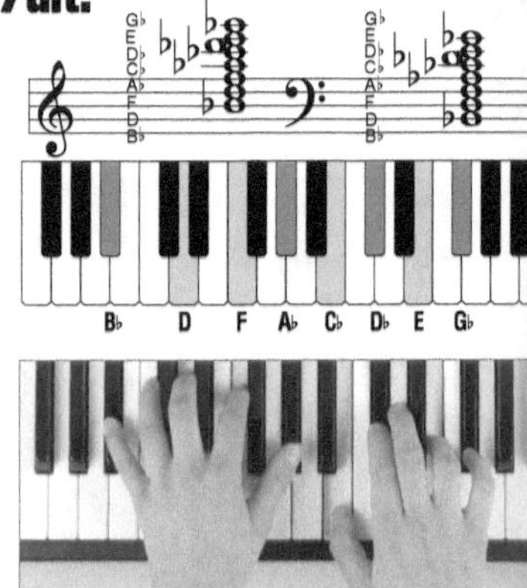

B

Root Position

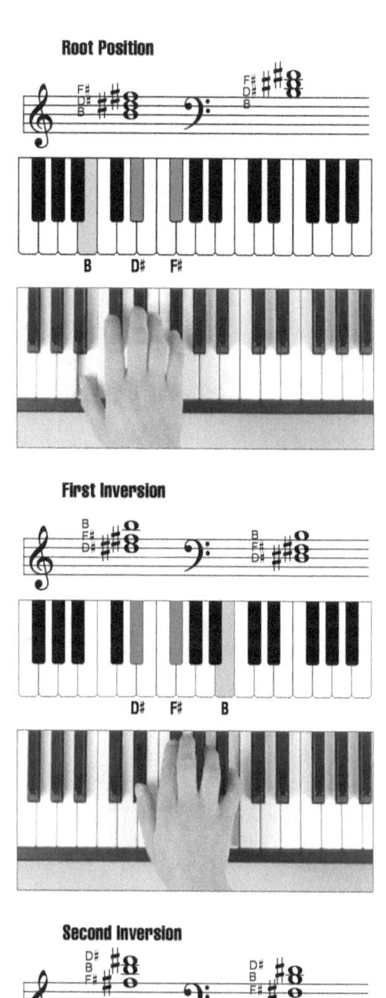

B

First Inversion

B

Second Inversion

Bm

Root Position

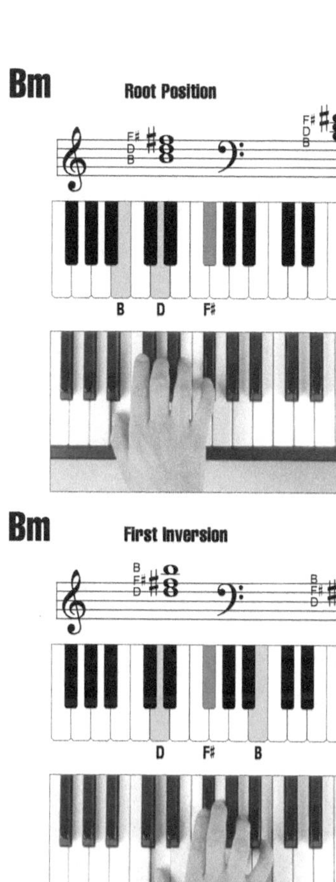

Bm

First Inversion

Bm

Second Inversion

B+ Root Position

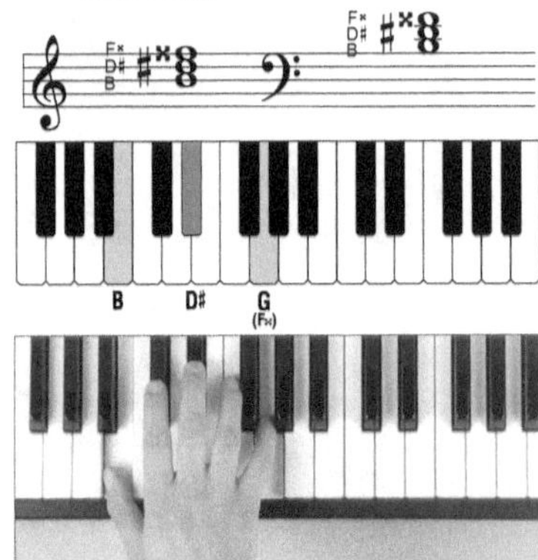

B+ First Inversion

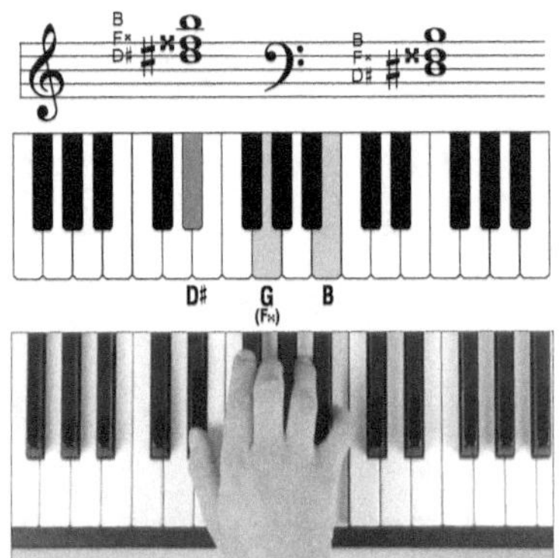

B+ Second Inversion

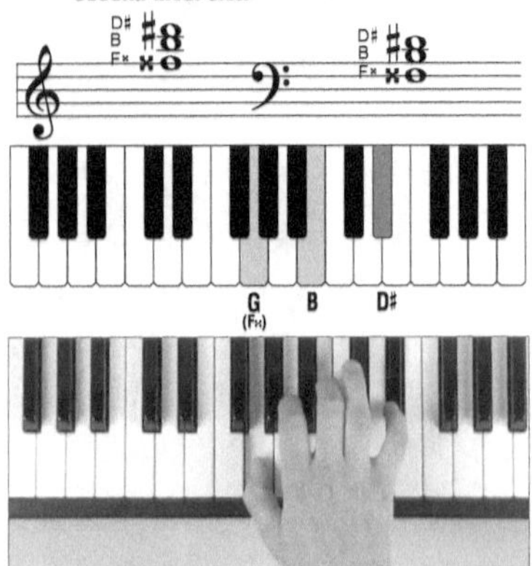

Bdim Root Position

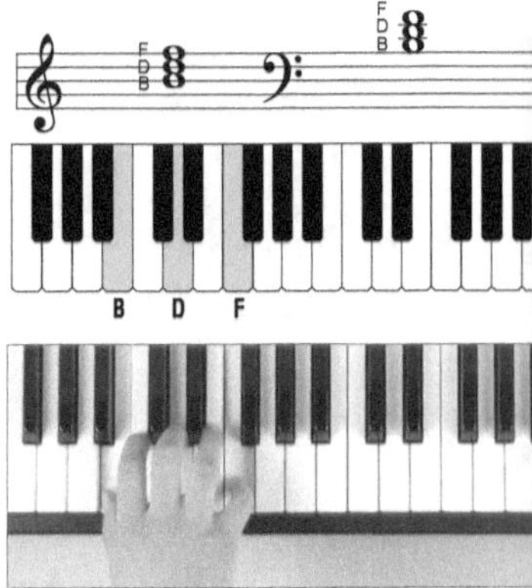

Bdim First Inversion

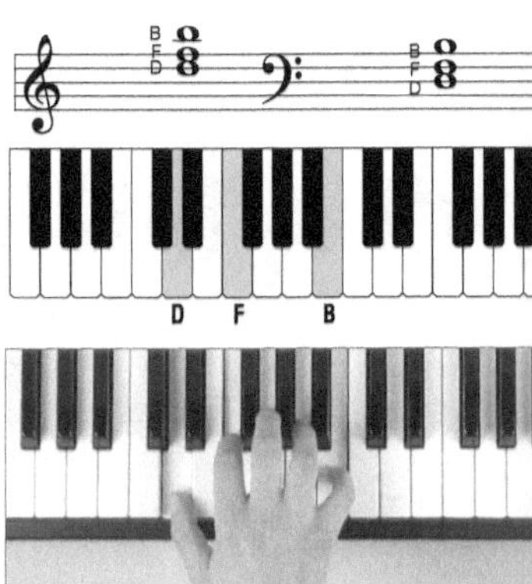

Bdim Second Inversion

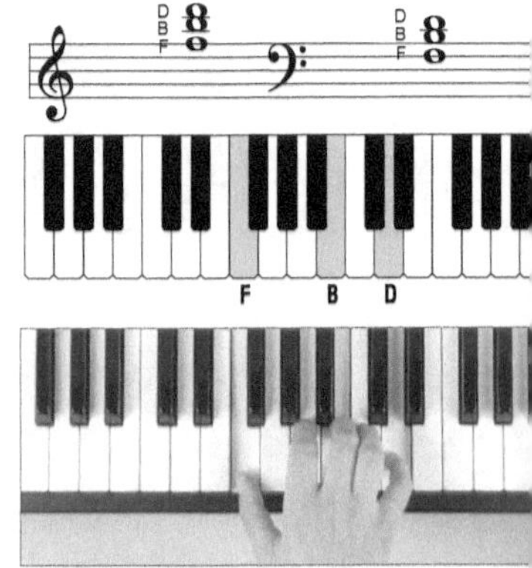

Bsus Root Position

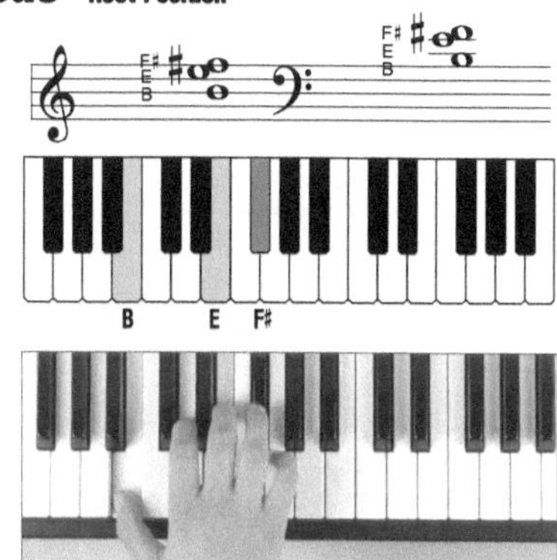

Bsus First Inversion

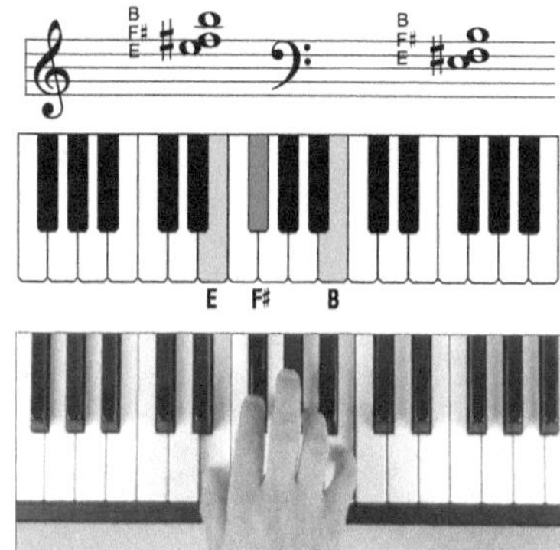

Bsus Second Inversion

B(♭5) Root Position

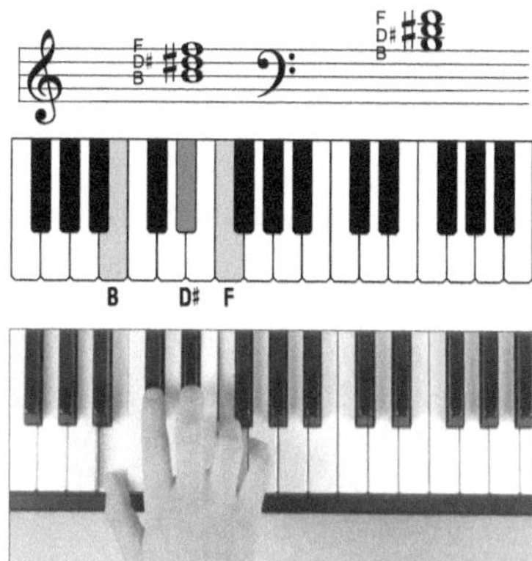

B(♭5) First Inversion

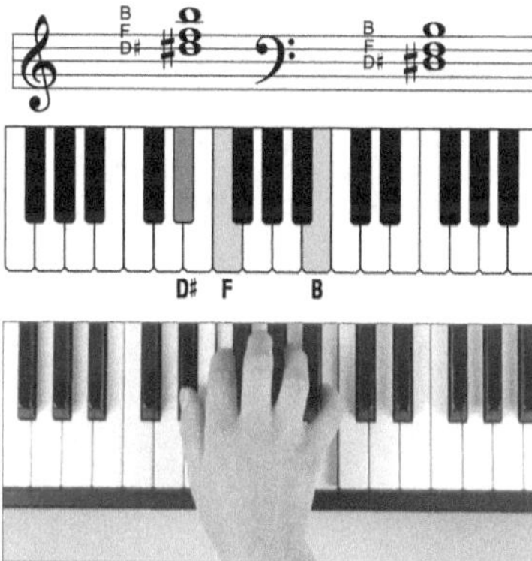

B(♭5) Second Inversion

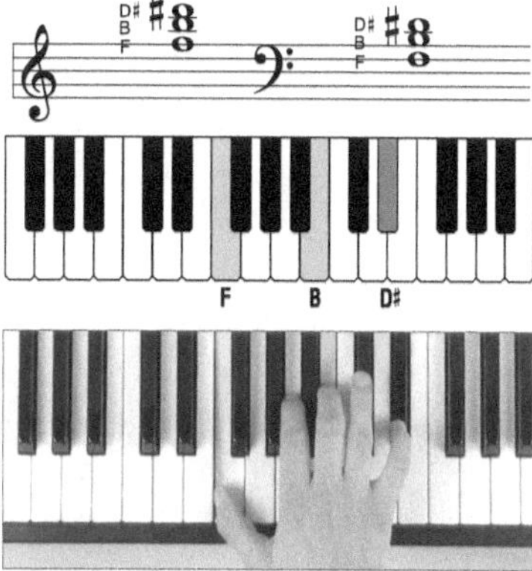

Bsus2 Root Position

Bsus2 First Inversion

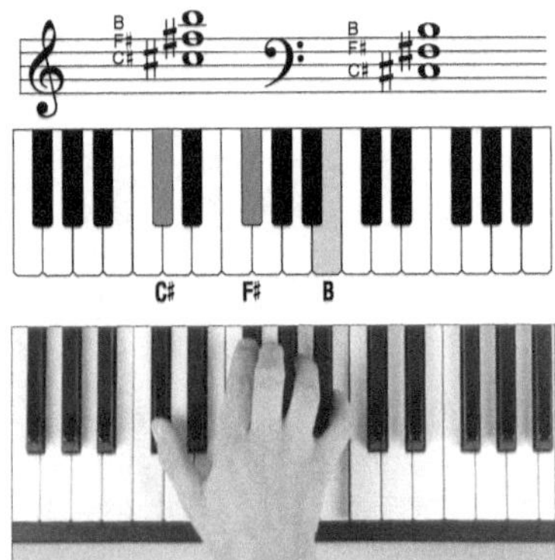

Bsus2 Second Inversion

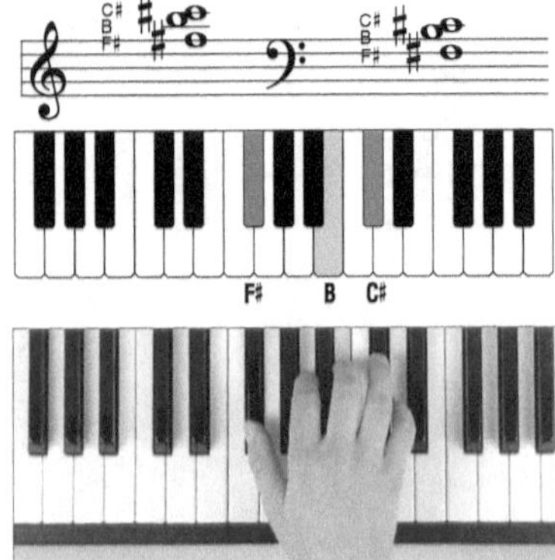

B6 Root Position

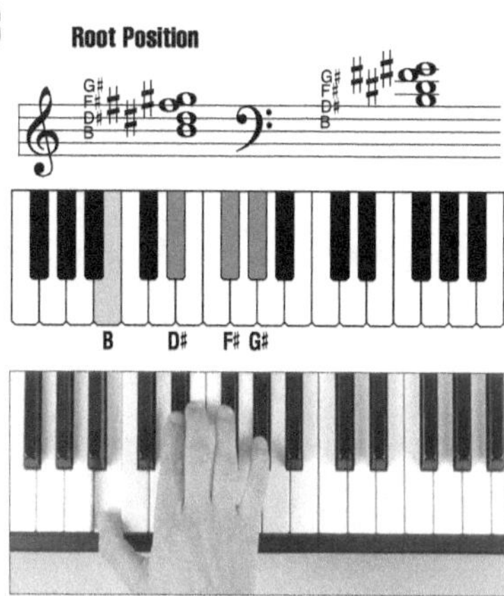

B6 First Inversion

B6 Second Inversion

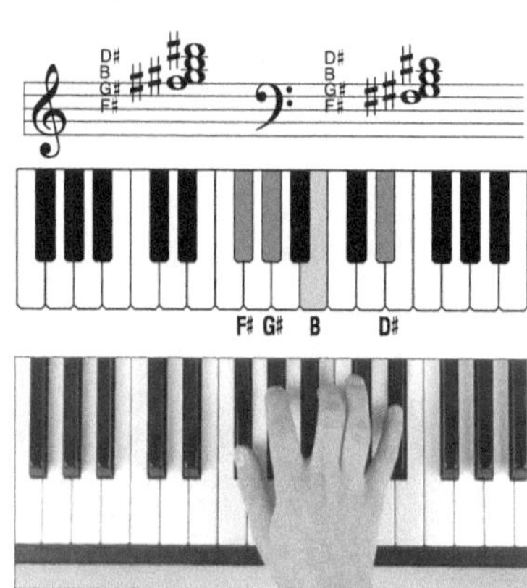

B6 Third Inversion

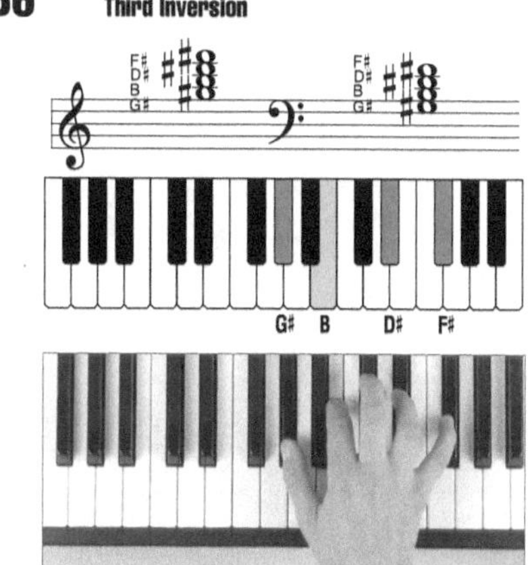

B(add2), B(add9) Root Position

B(add2), B(add9) First Inversion

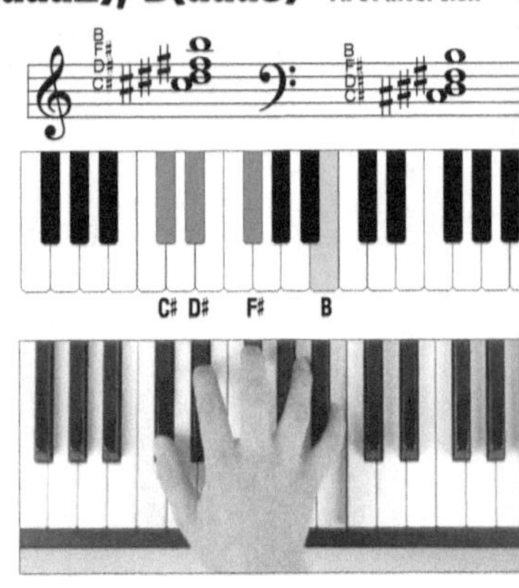

B(add2), B(add9) Second Inversion

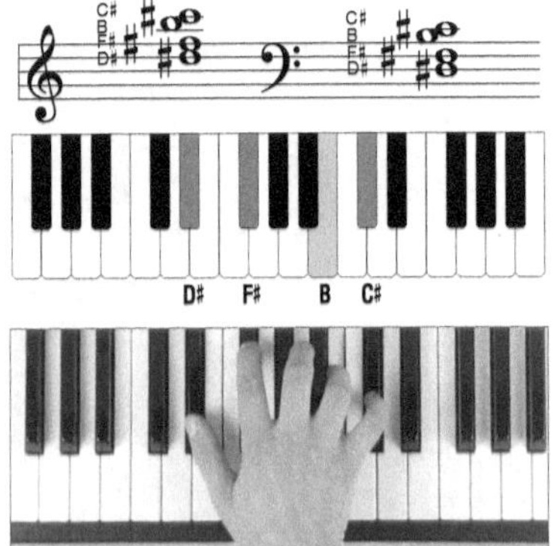

B(add2), B(add9) Third Inversion

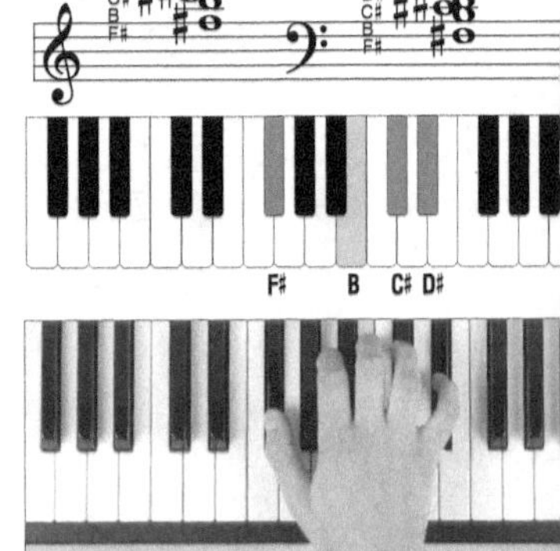

Bmaj7 Root Position

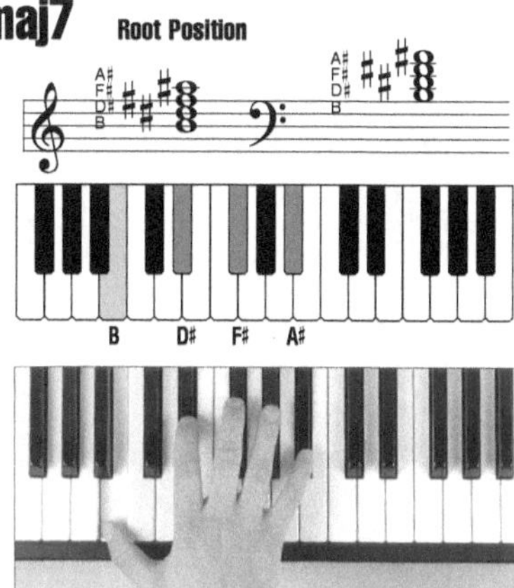

Bmaj7 First Inversion

Bmaj7 Second Inversion

Bmaj7 Third Inversion

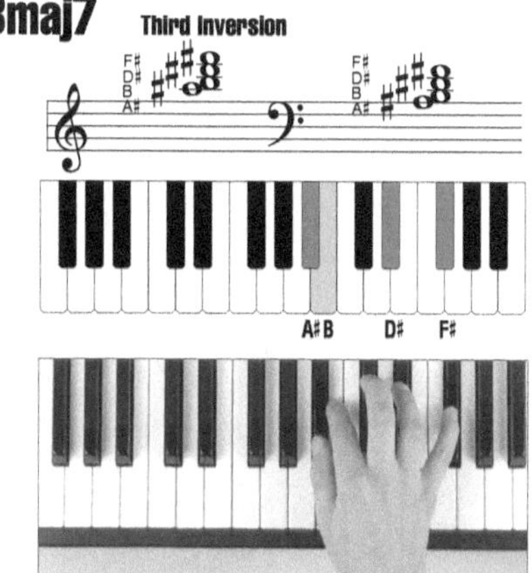

Bmaj7♭5 Root Position

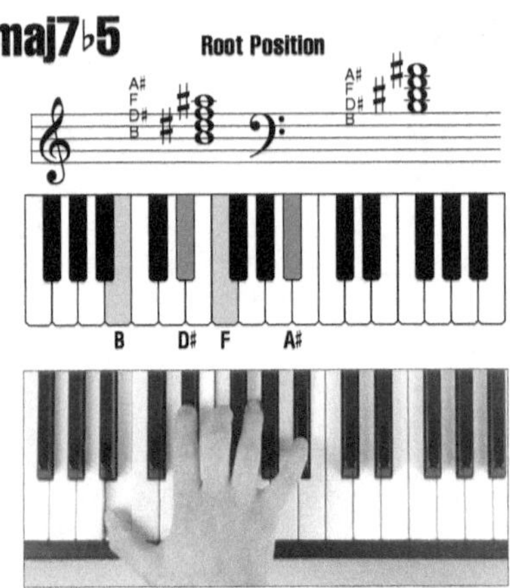

Bmaj7♭5 First Inversion

Bmaj7♭5 Second Inversion

Bmaj7♭5 Third Inversion

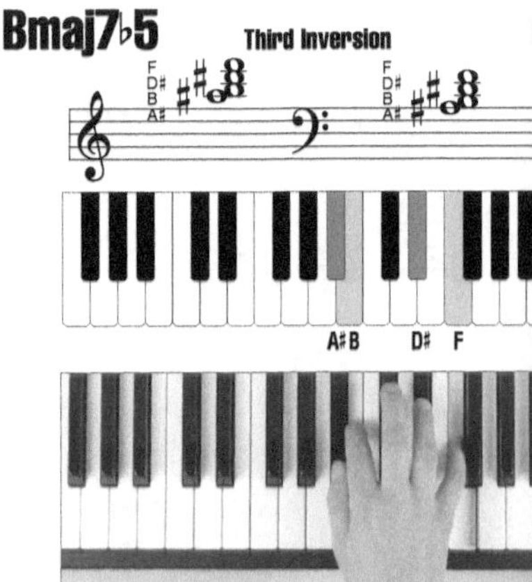

Bmaj7♯5 Root Position

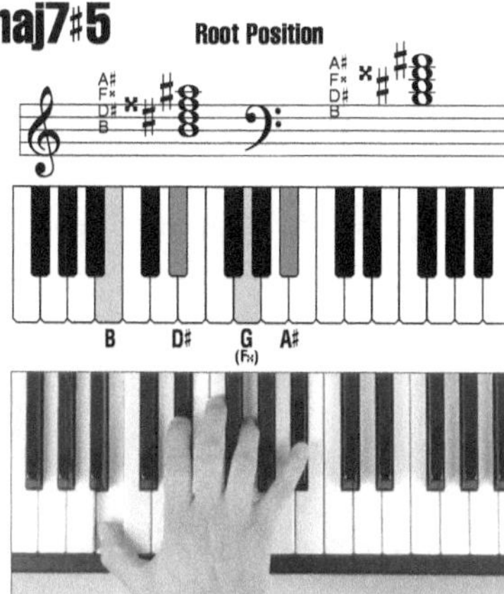

Bmaj7♯5 First Inversion

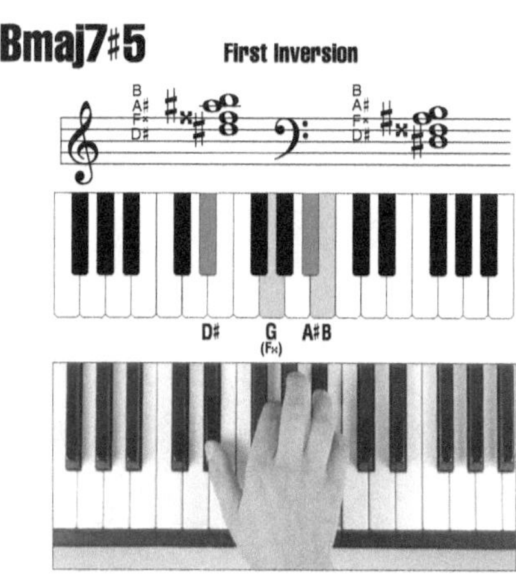

Bmaj7♯5 Second Inversion

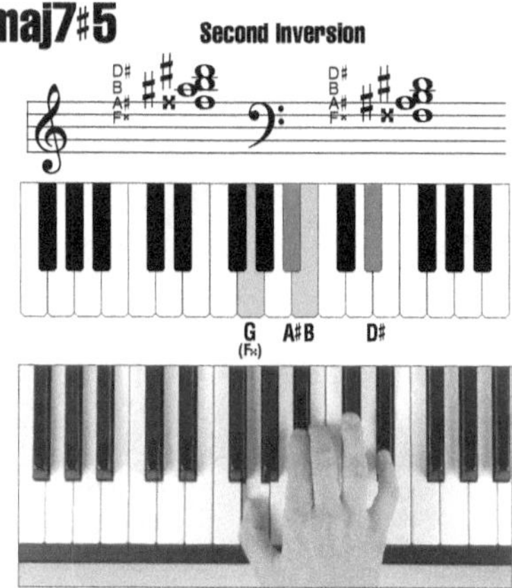

Bmaj7♯5 Third Inversion

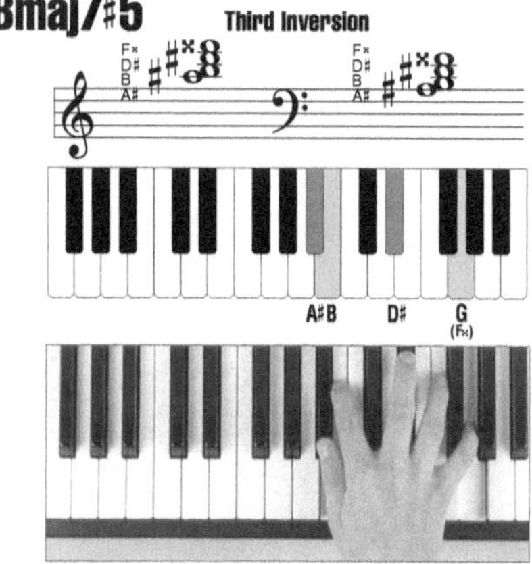

B7 Root Position

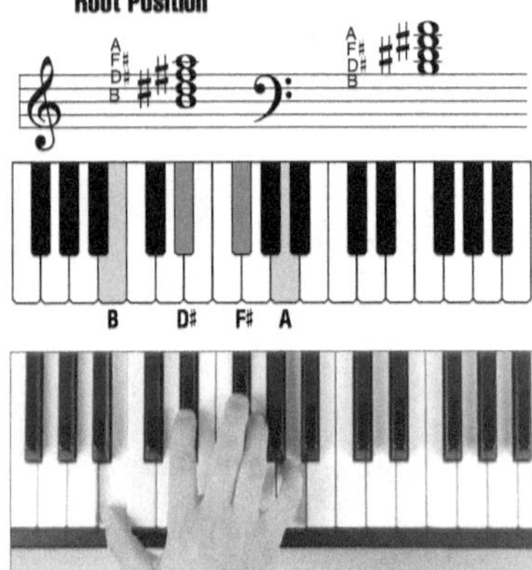

B7 First Inversion

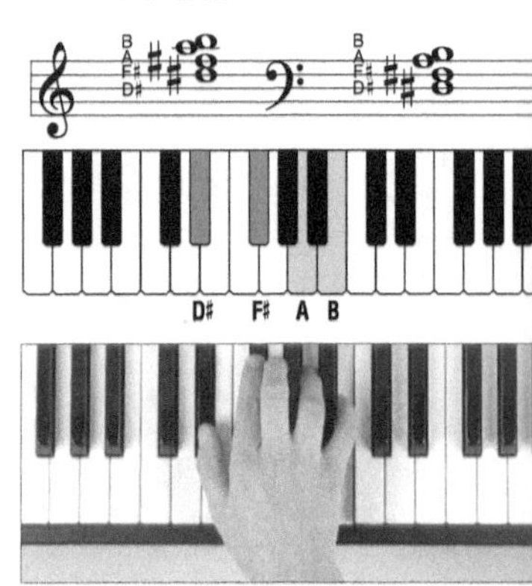

B7 Second Inversion

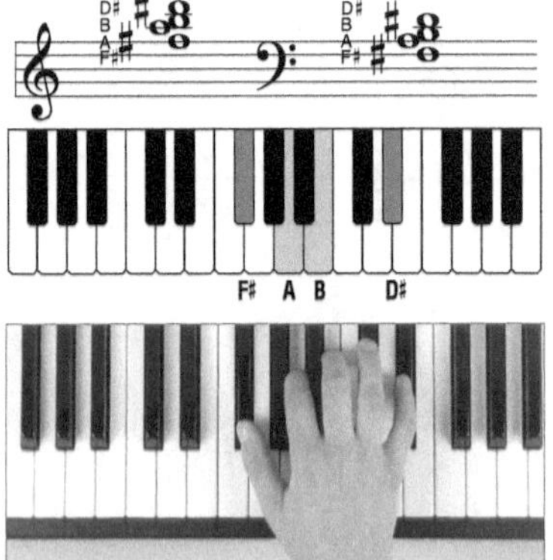

B7 Third Inversion

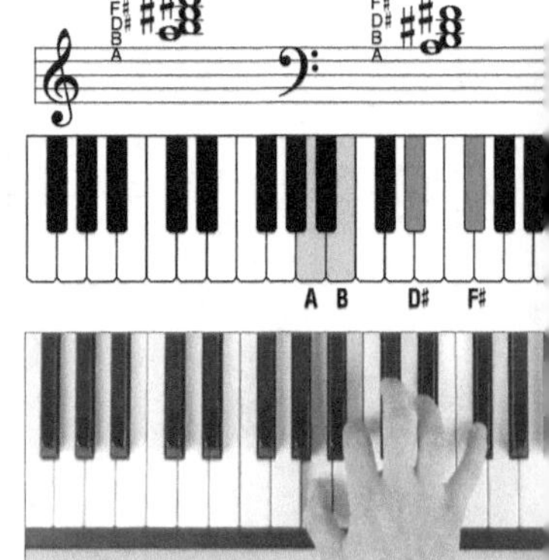

B7♭5 Root Position

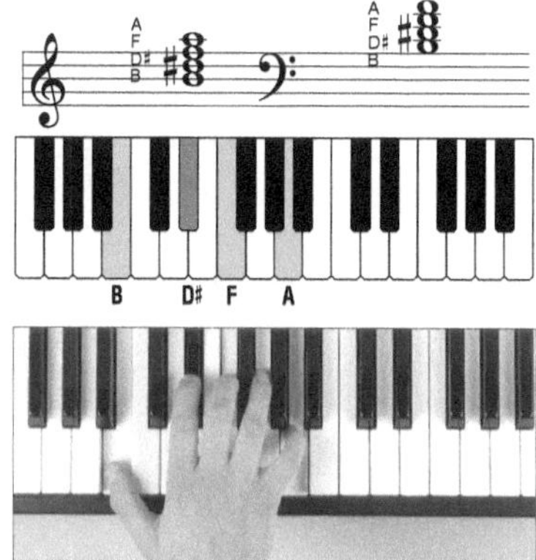

B7♭5 First Inversion

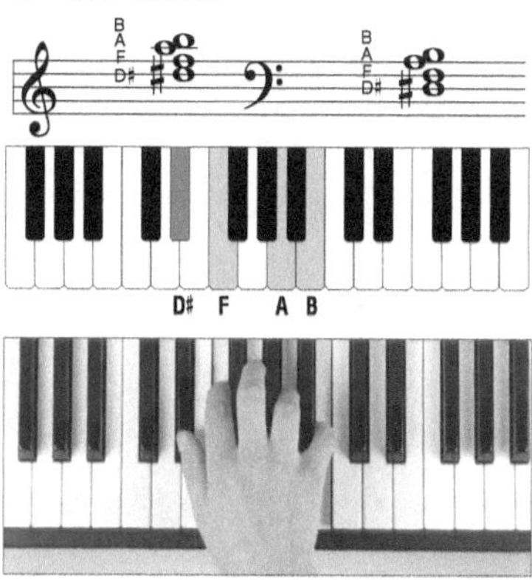

B7♭5 Second Inversion

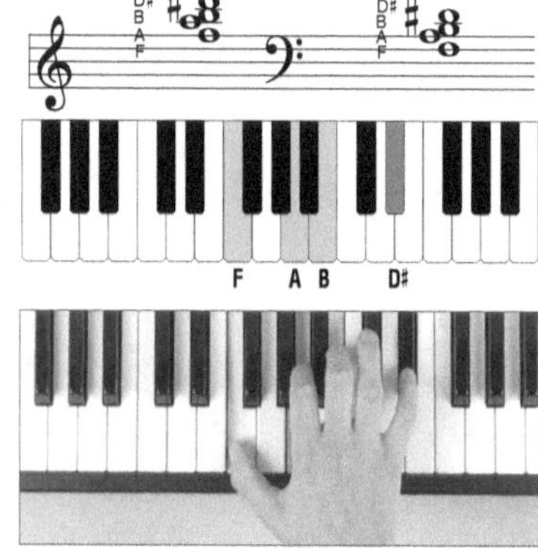

B7♭5 Third Inversion

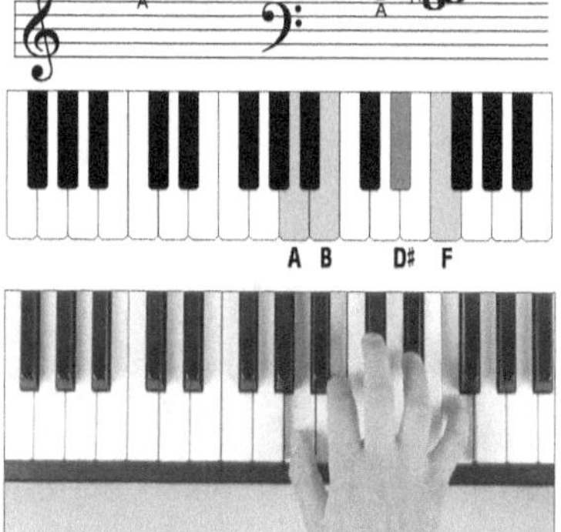

B7♯5 Root Position

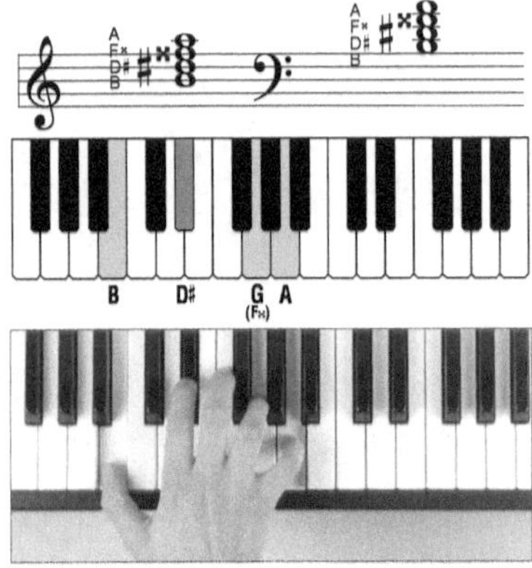

B7♯5 First Inversion

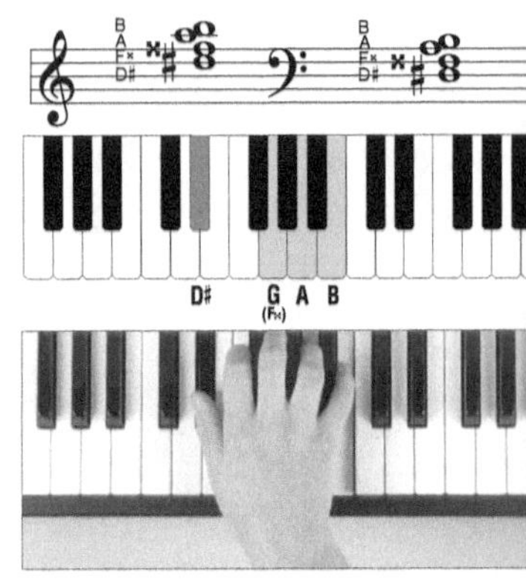

B7♯5 Second Inversion

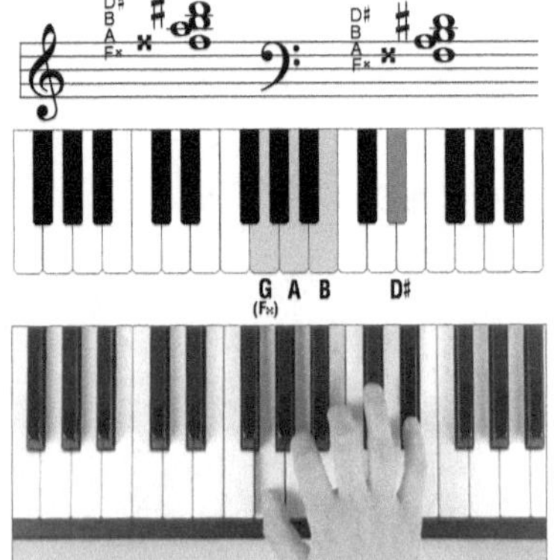

B7♯5 Third Inversion

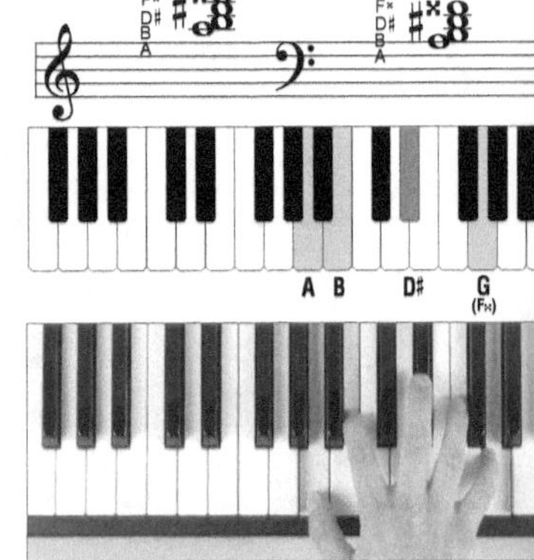

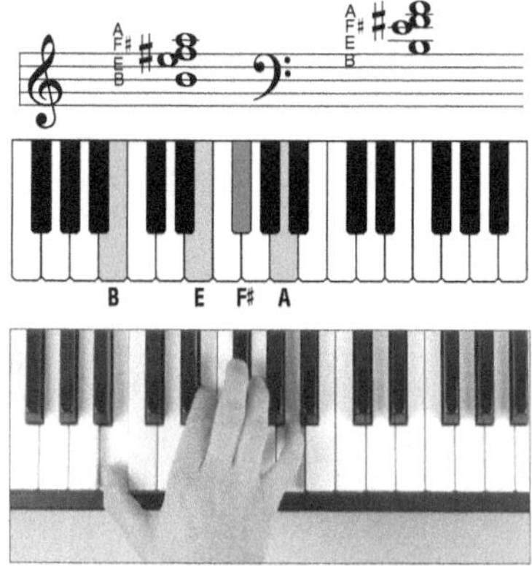

B7sus First Inversion

37sus Second Inversion

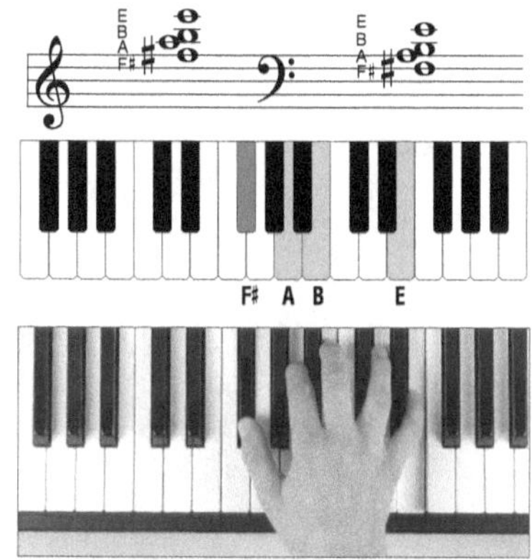

B7sus Third Inversion

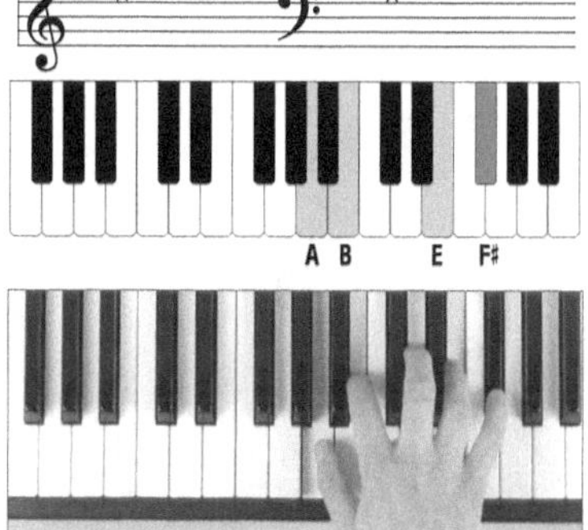

Bm(add2), Bm(add9) Root Position

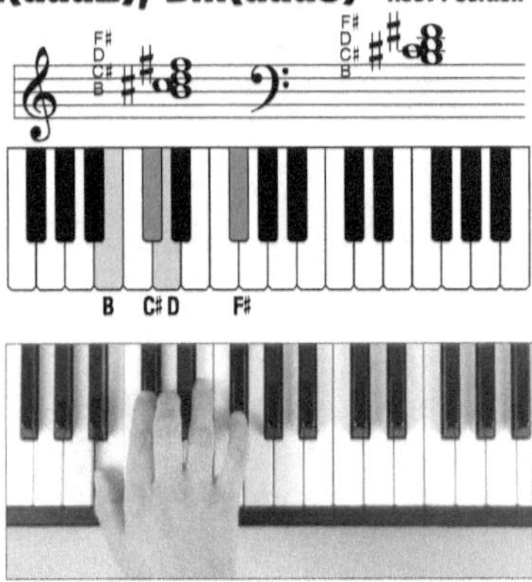

Bm(add2), Bm(add9) First Invers

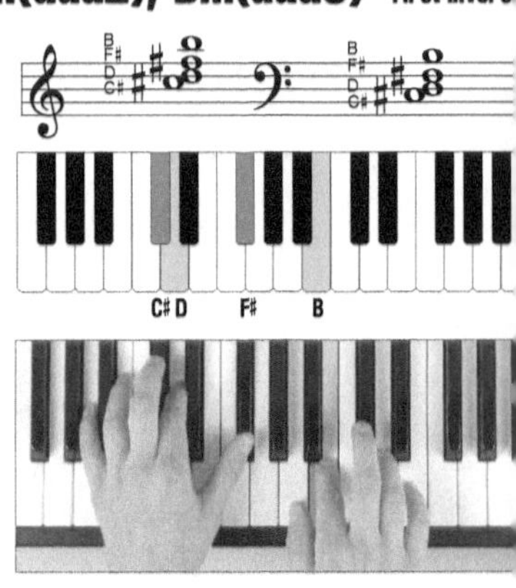

Bm(add2), Bm(add9) Second Inversion

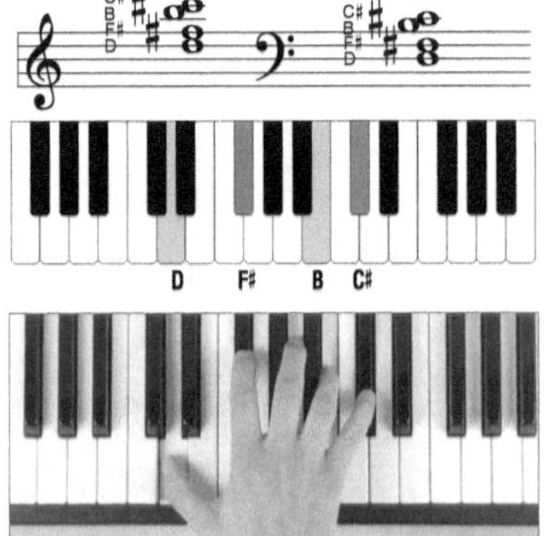

Bm(add2), Bm(add9) Third Invers

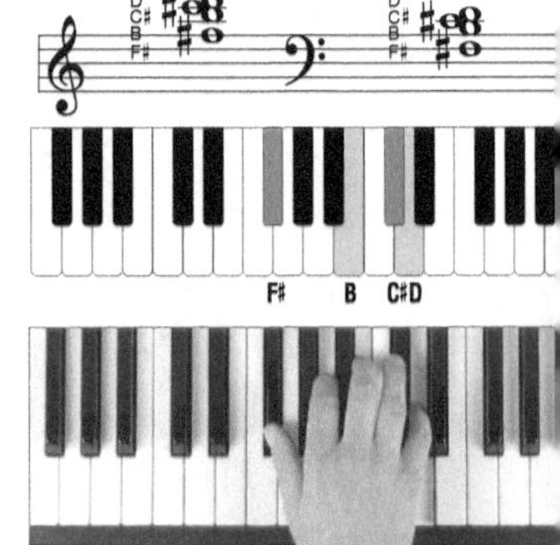

Bm6 Root Position

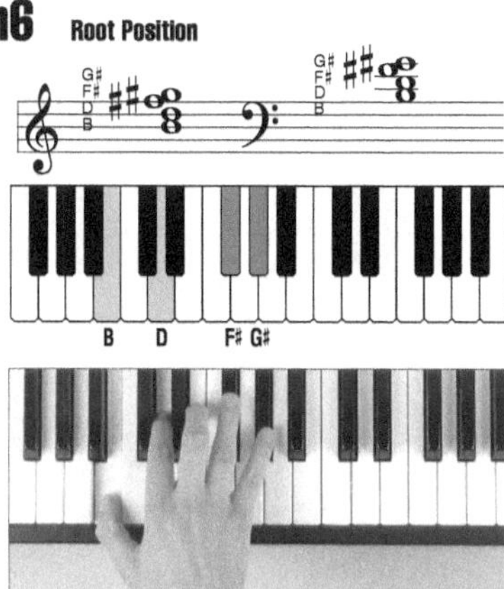

Bm6 First Inversion

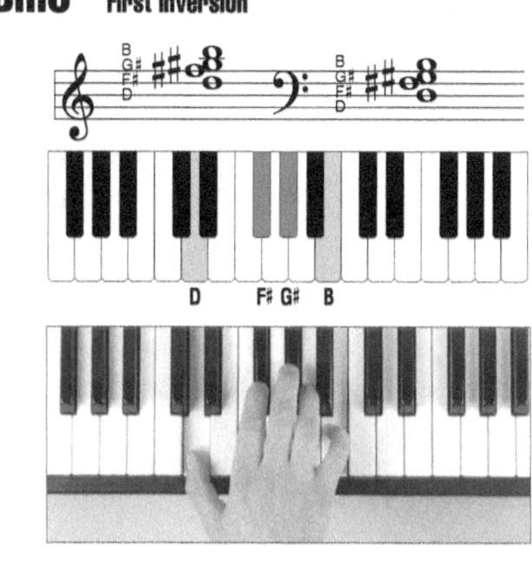

Bm6 Second Inversion

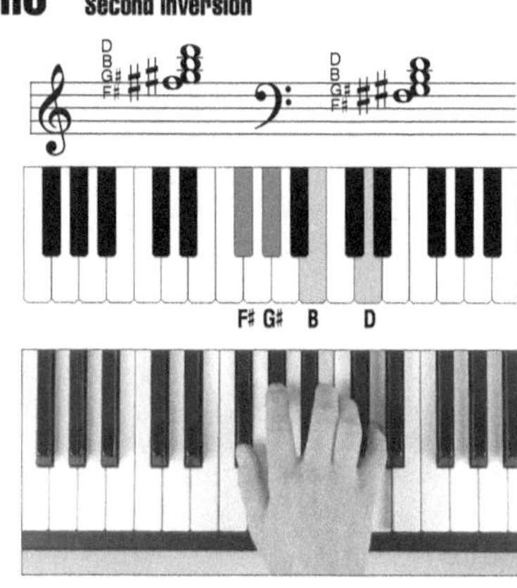

Bm6 Third Inversion

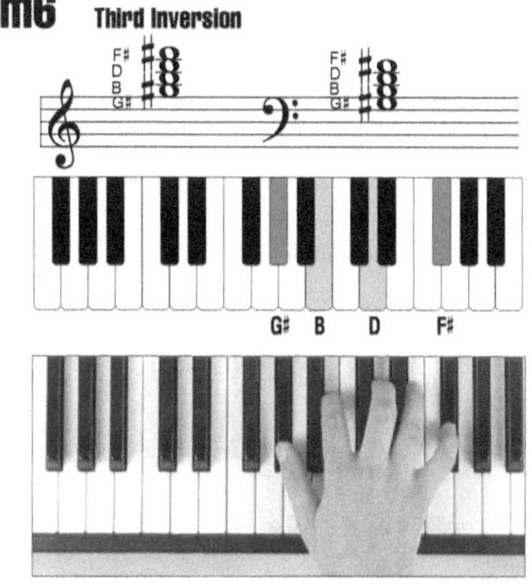

Bm7 Root Position

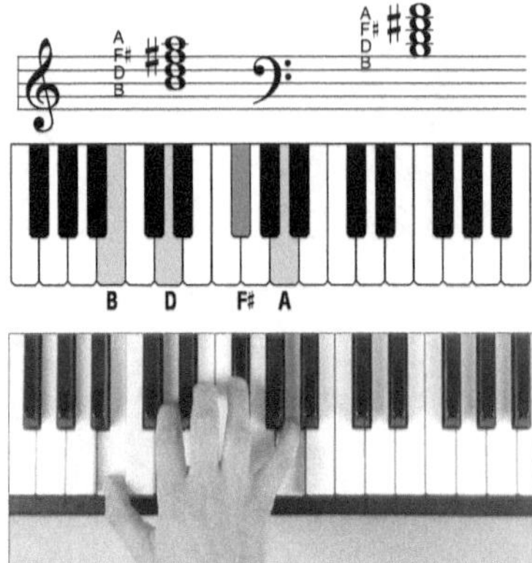

Bm7 First Inversion

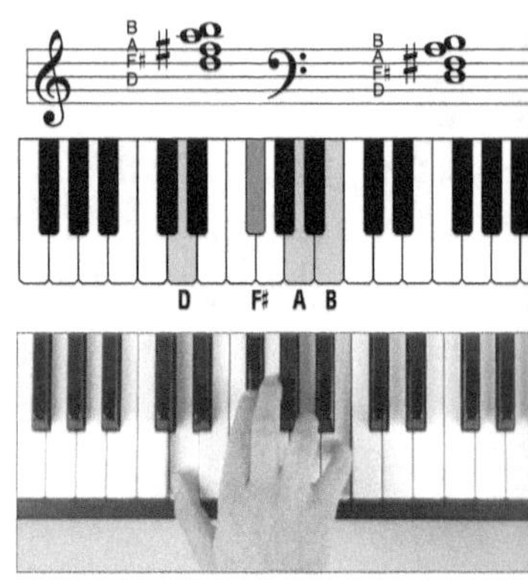

Bm7 Second Inversion

Bm7 Third Inversion

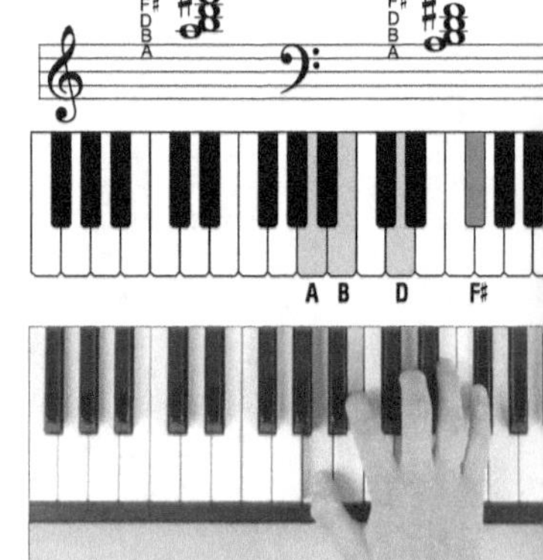

Bm(maj7) Root Position

Bm(maj7) First Inversion

Bm(maj7) Second Inversion

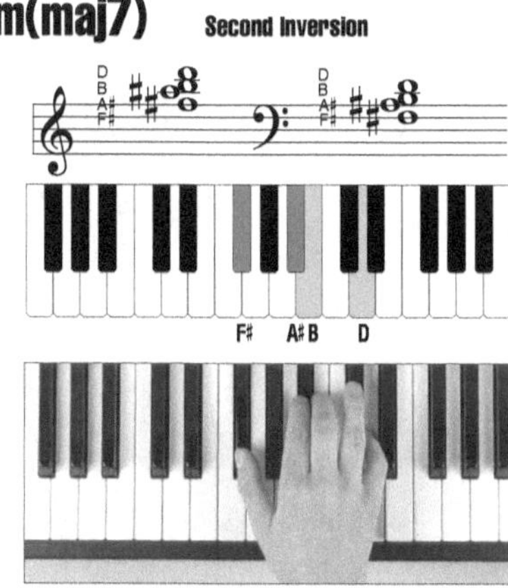

Bm(maj7) Third Inversion

Bm7♭5 Root Position

A
F
D
B

A
F
D
B

B D F A

Bm7♭5 First Inversion

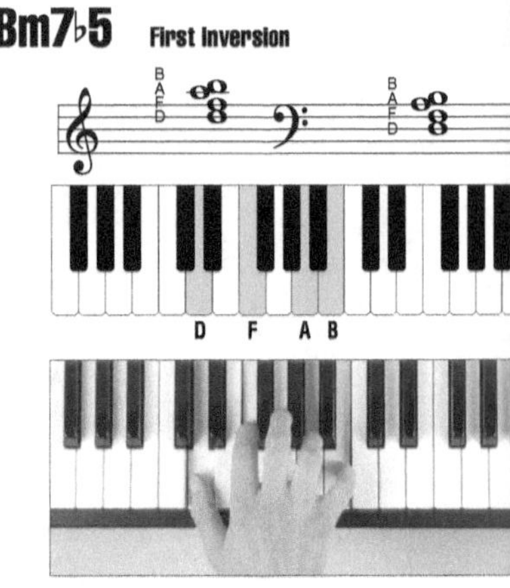

Bm7♭5 Second Inversion

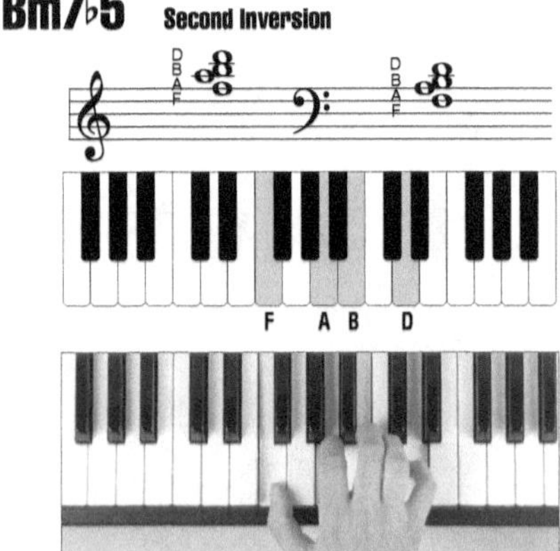

Bm7♭5 Third Inversion

Bdim7 Root Position

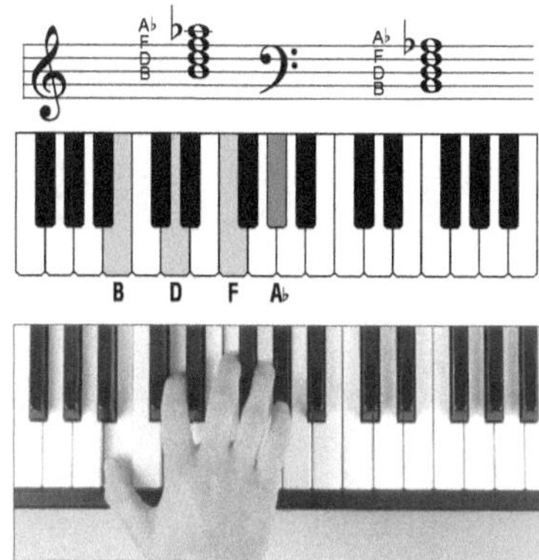

Bdim7 First Inversion

Bdim7 Second Inversion

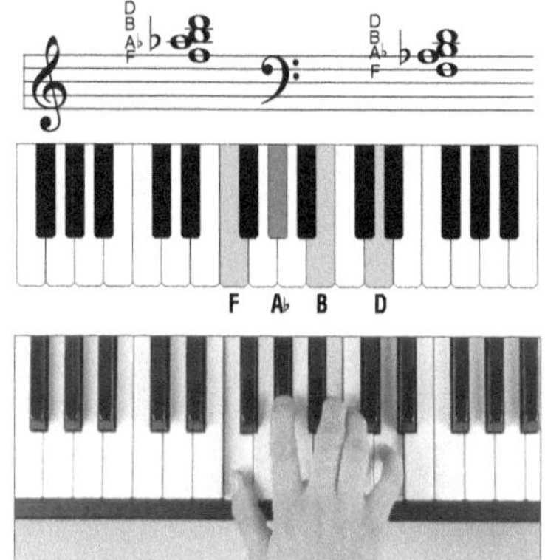

Bdim7 Third Inversion

Bdim(maj7) Root Position

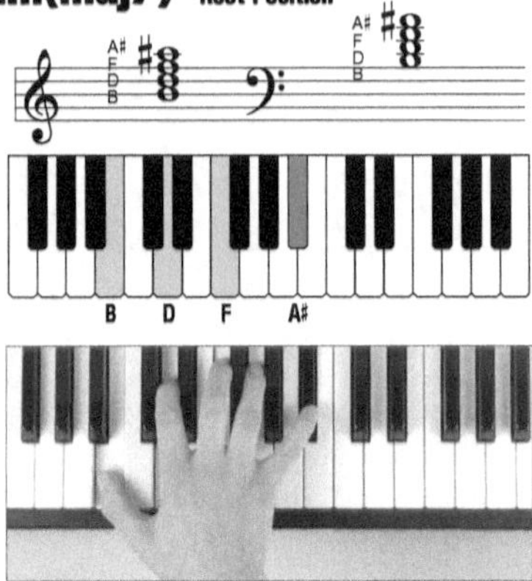

Bdim(maj7) First Inversion

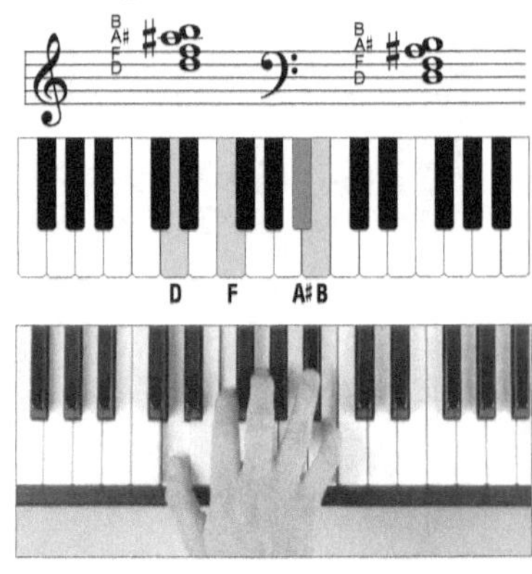

Bdim(maj7) Second Inversion

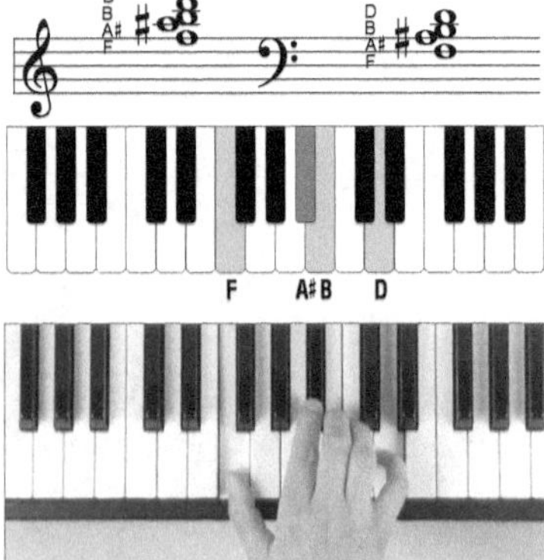

Bdim(maj7) Third Inversion

5

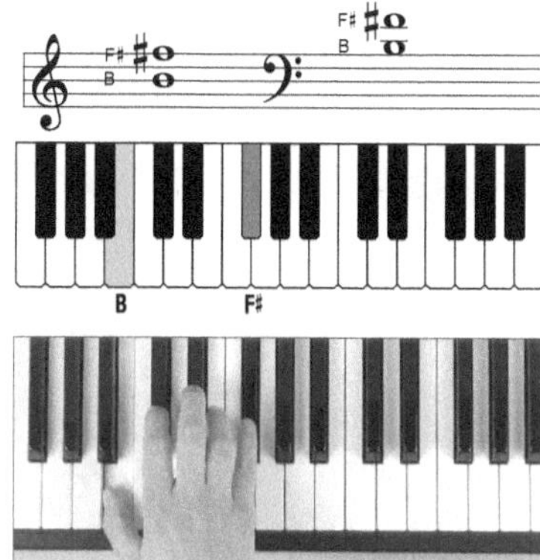

6 9

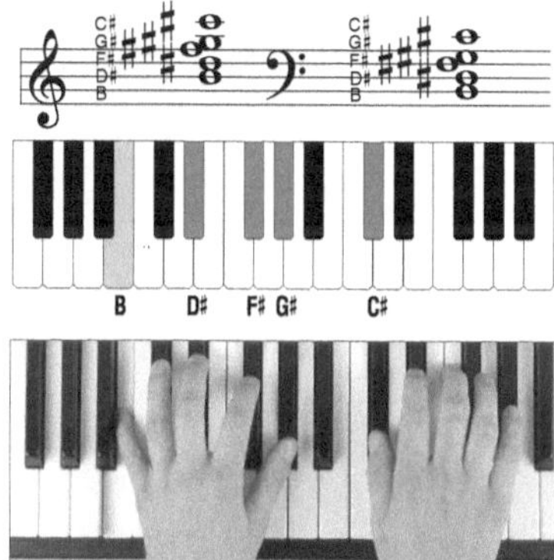

maj6 9

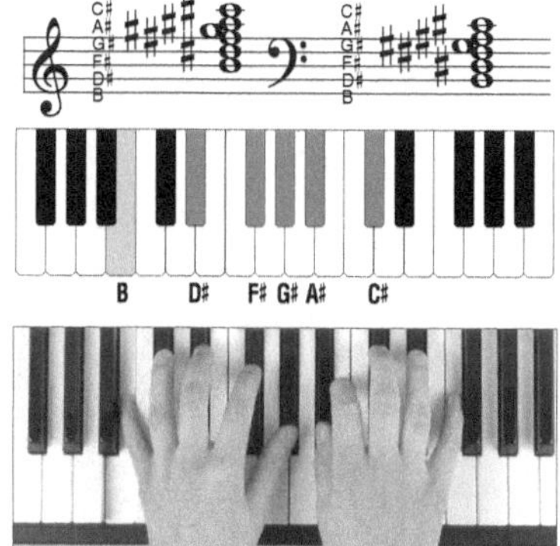

Bmaj7#11

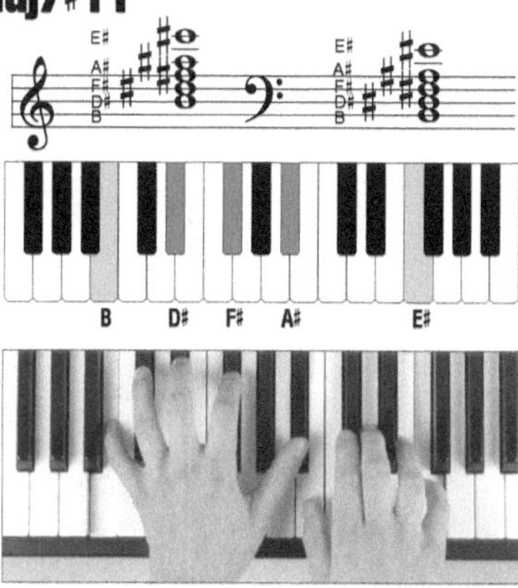

Bmaj9

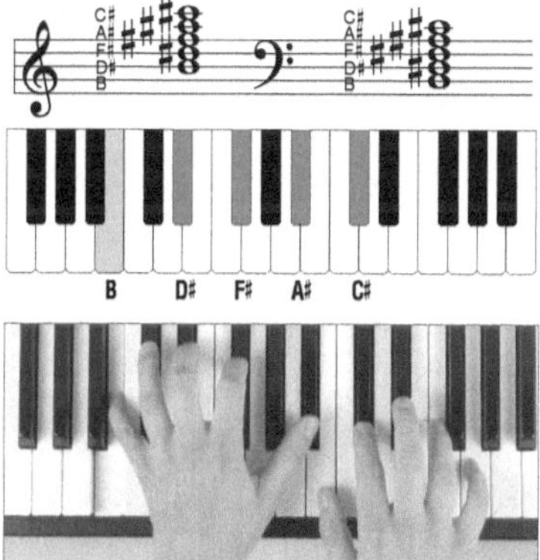

Bmaj9♭5

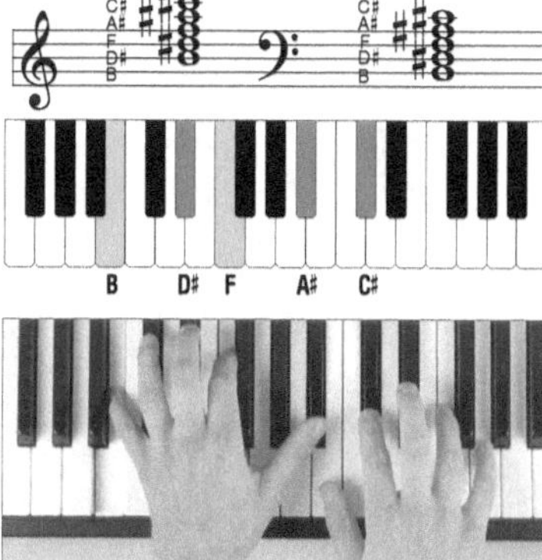

Bmaj9♯5

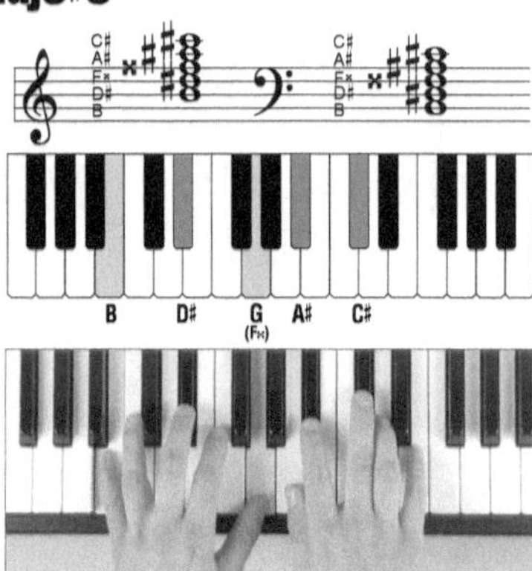

Bmaj9♯11

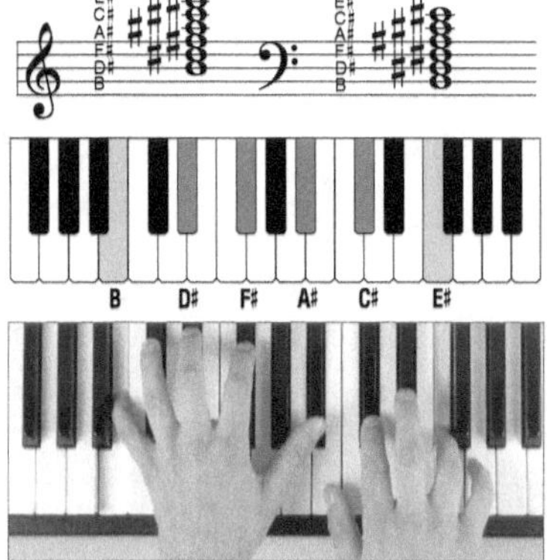

Bmaj13

G♯
C♯
A♯
F♯
D♯
B

B D♯ F♯ A♯ C♯ G♯

Bmaj13♭5

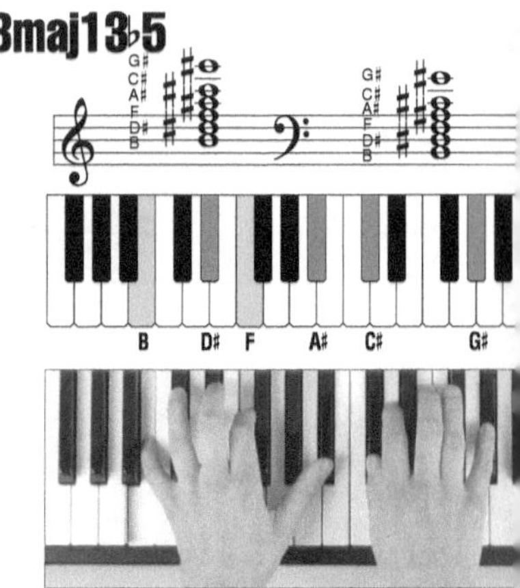

Bmaj13♯11

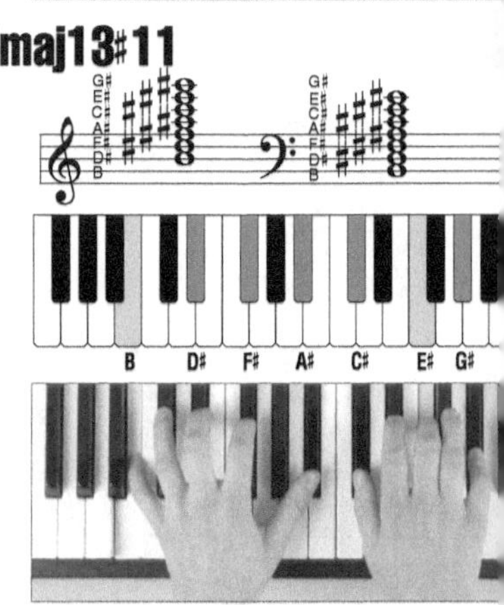

B7♭9

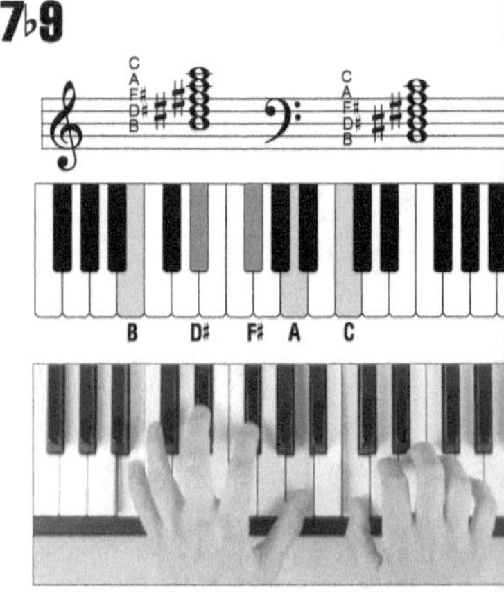

B7♯9

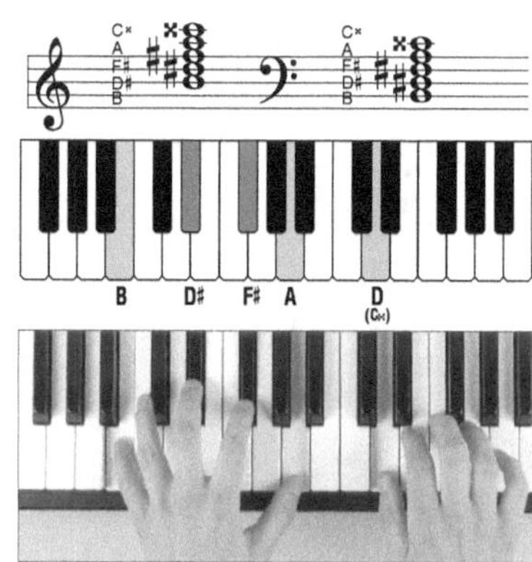

B7♯11

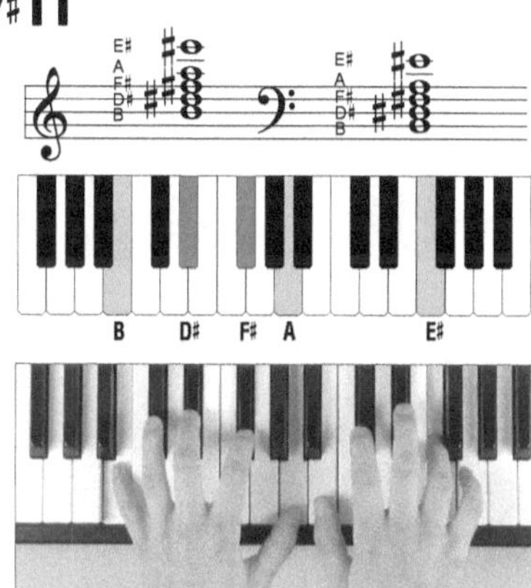

B7♭5(♭9)

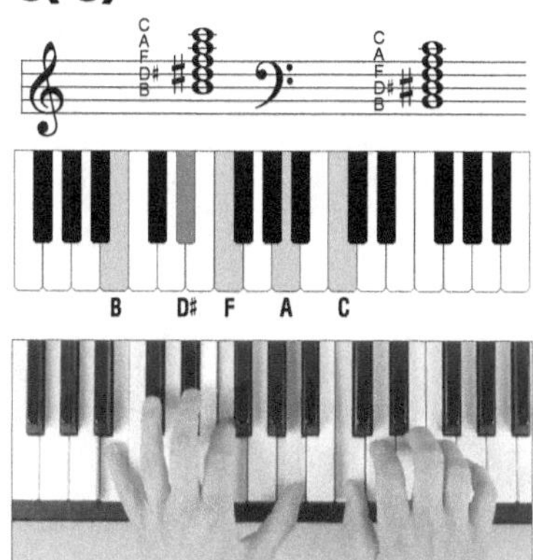

B7♭5(♯9)

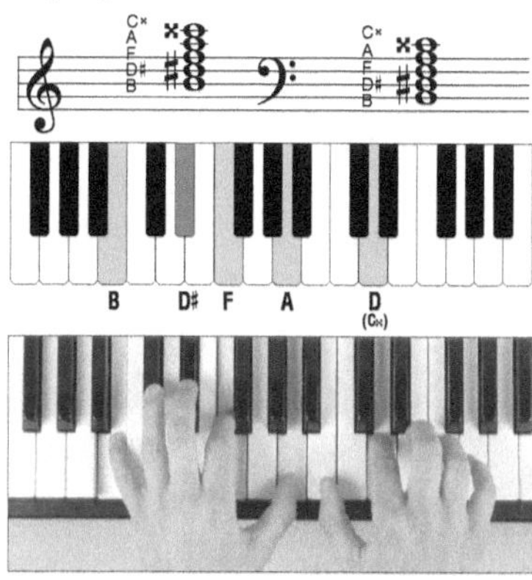

B7♯5(♭9)

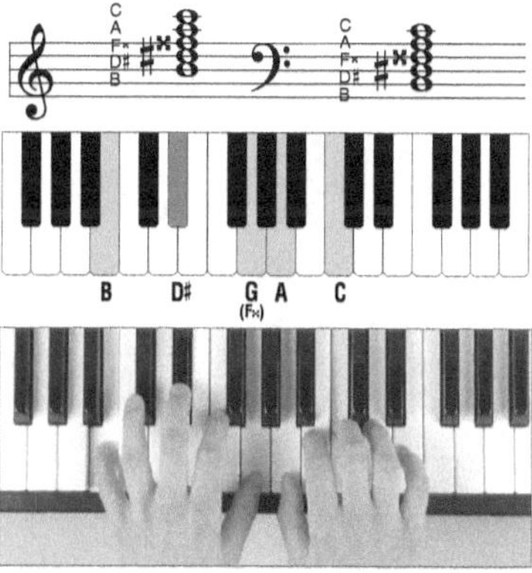

B7♯5(♯9)

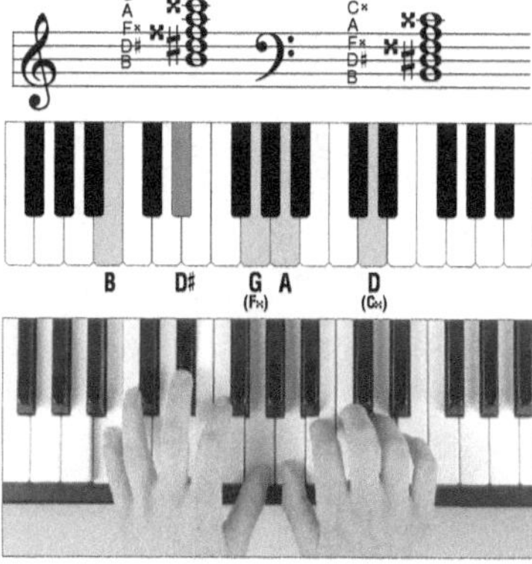

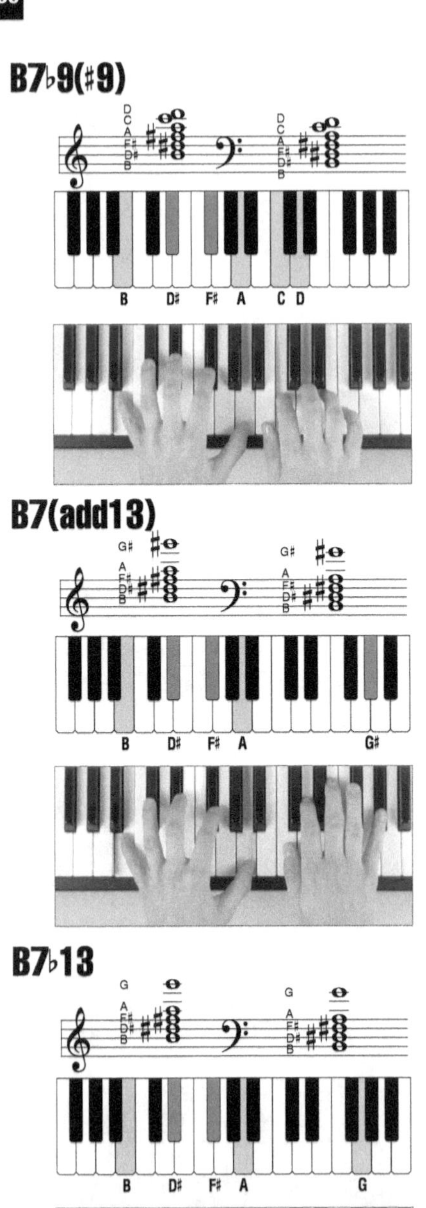
B7♭9(♯9)
D
C
A
F♯
D♯
B
B D♯ F♯ A C D
B7(add13)
G♯
A
F♯
D♯
B
B D♯ F♯ A G♯
B7♭13
G
A
F♯
D♯
B
B D♯ F♯ A G

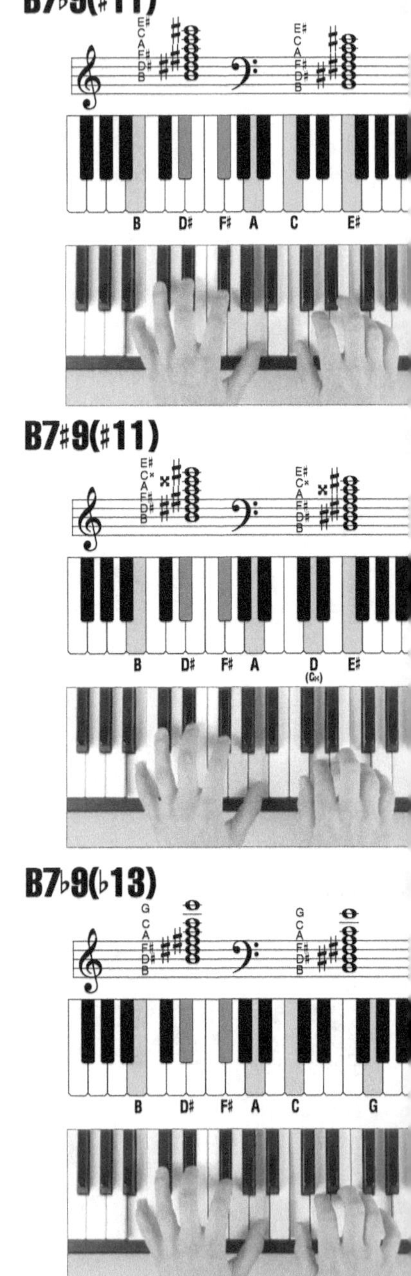
B7♭9(♯11)
E♯
C
A
F♯
D♯
B
B D♯ F♯ A C E♯
B7♯9(♯11)
E♯
C×
A
F♯
D♯
B
B D♯ F♯ A D E♯
(C×)
B7♭9(♭13)
G
C
A
F♯
D♯
B
B D♯ F♯ A C G

B7♯9(♭13)

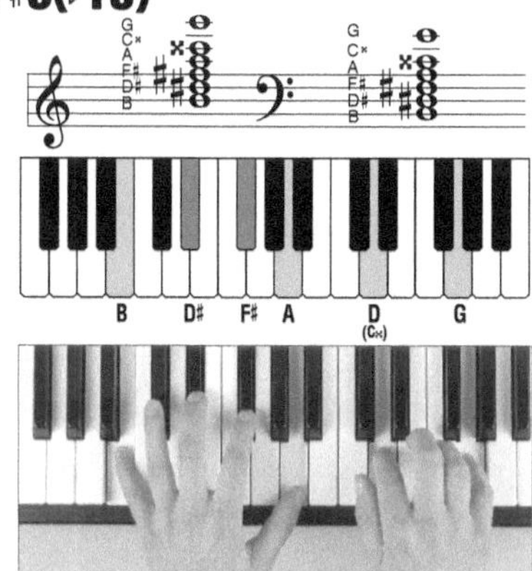

B7♯11(♭13)

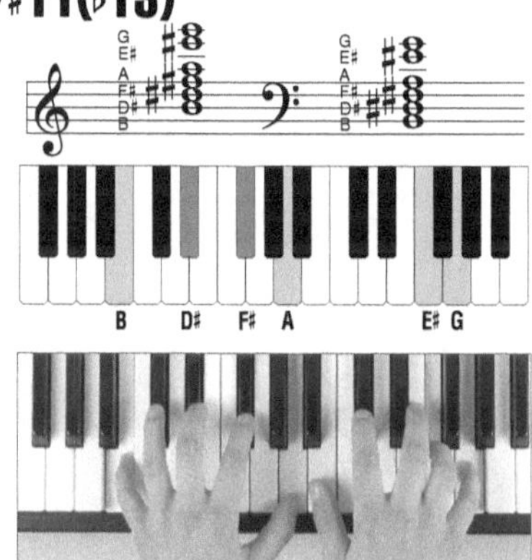

B7♭9(♯9,♯11)

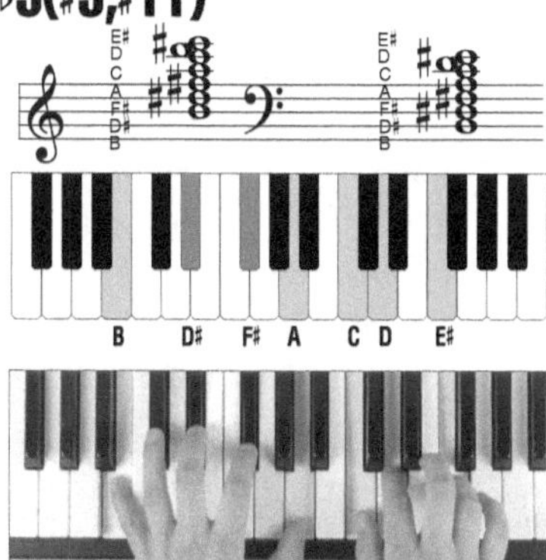

B9

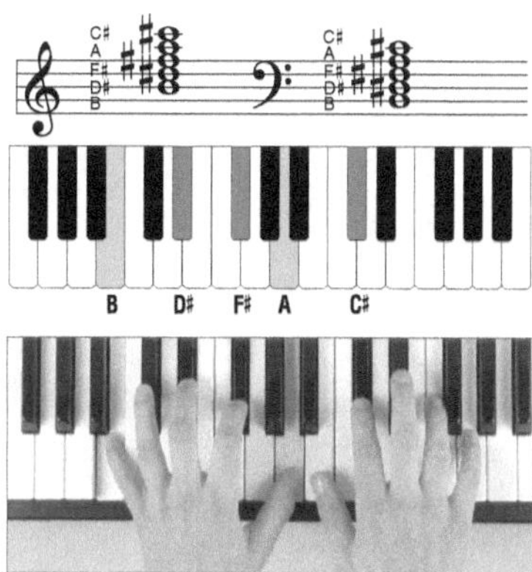

B9(♭5)

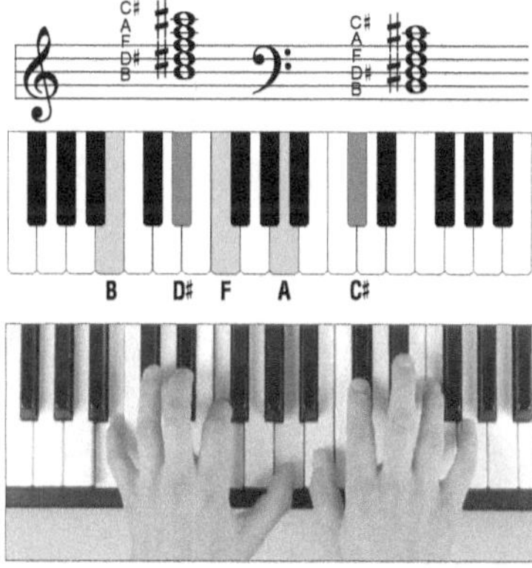

B9♯5

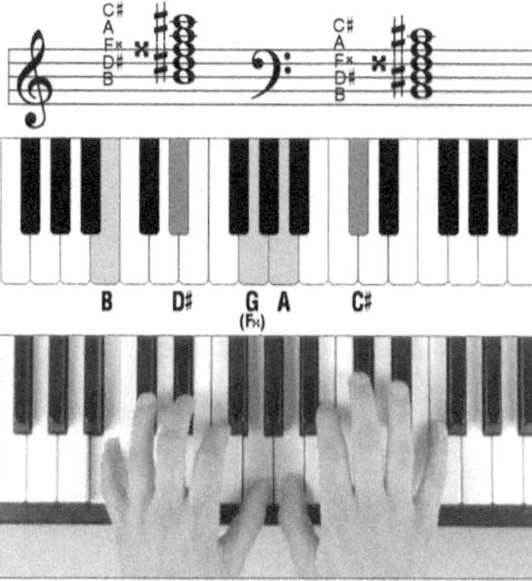

B9♯11

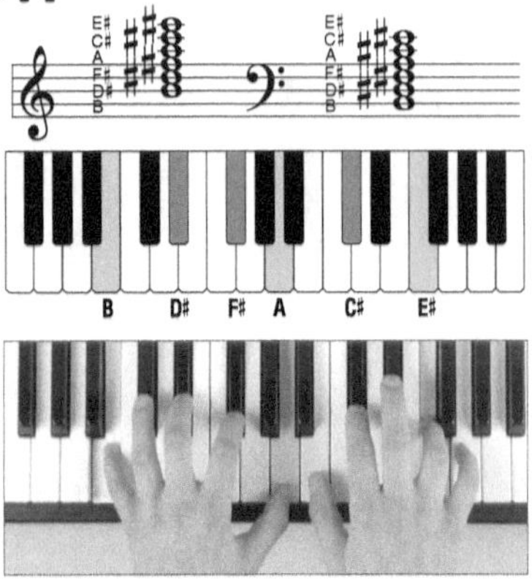

E♯ C♯ A F♯ D♯ B

E♯ C♯ A F♯ D♯ B

B D♯ F♯ A C♯ E♯

B9♭13

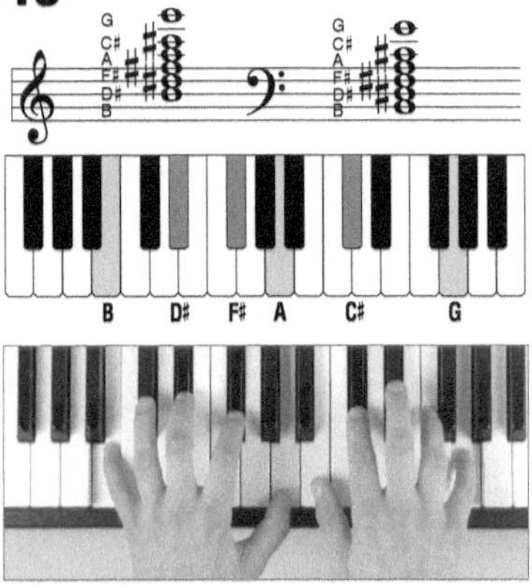

G C♯ A F♯ D♯ B

G C♯ A F♯ D♯ B

B D♯ F♯ A C♯ G

B9♯11(♭13)

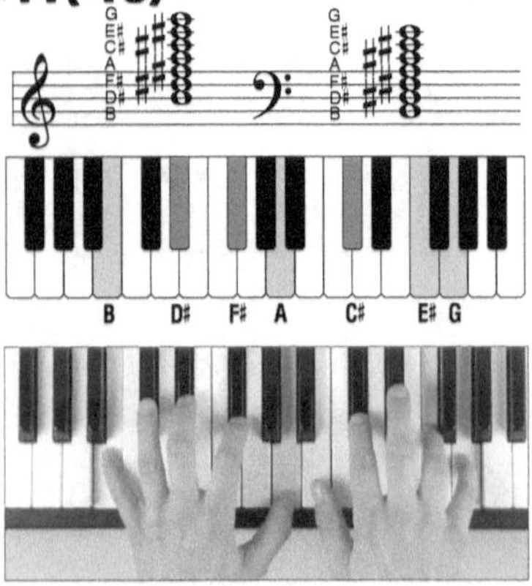

G E♯ C♯ A F♯ D♯ B

G E♯ C♯ A F♯ D♯ B

B D♯ F♯ A C♯ E♯ G

B11, B9(sus4)

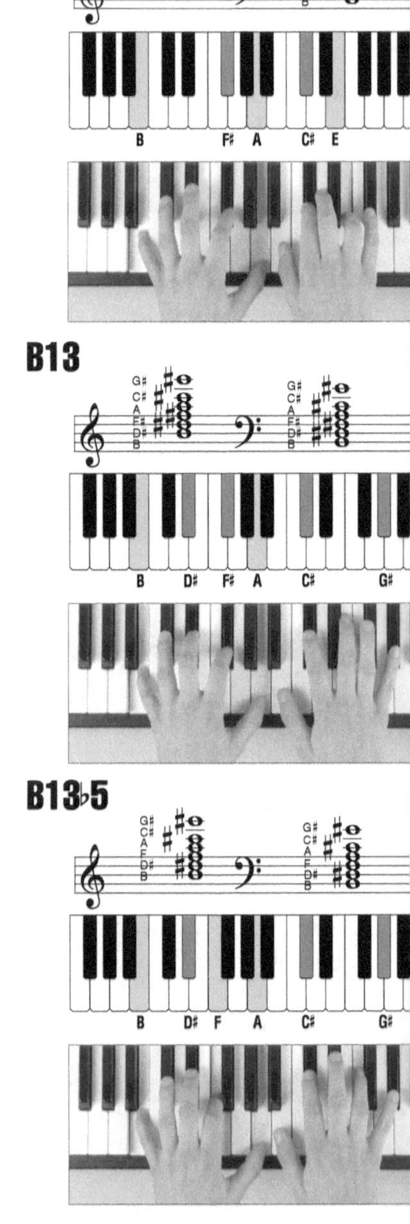

B13♭9

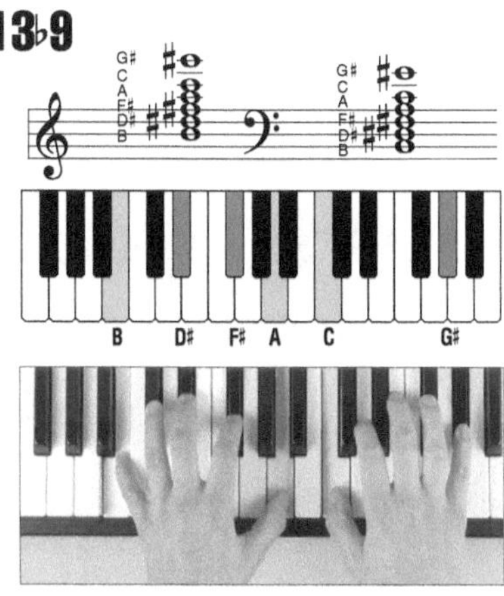

B13(sus4)

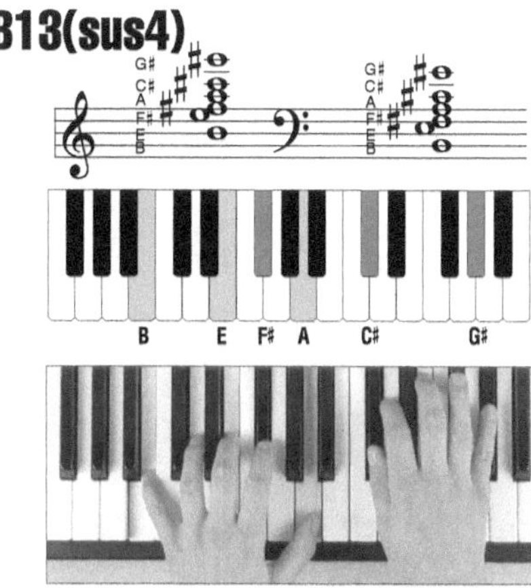

B13♯9

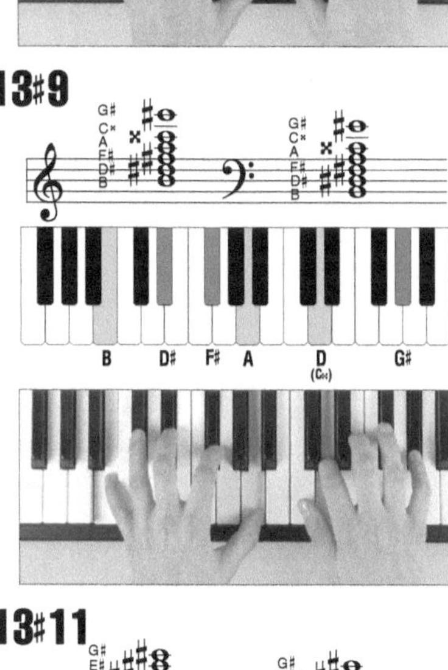

Bm(♯5)

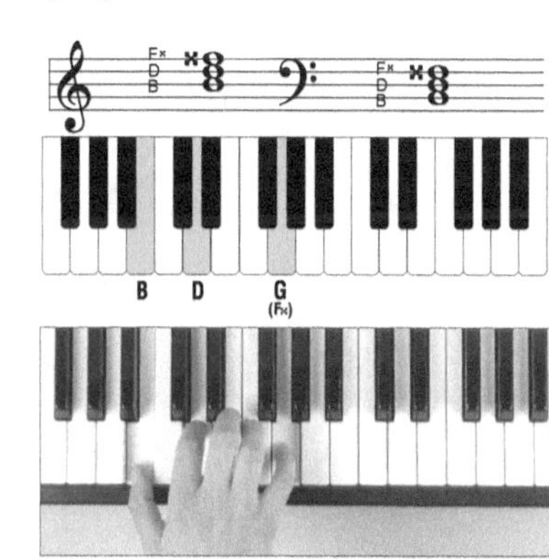

B13♯11

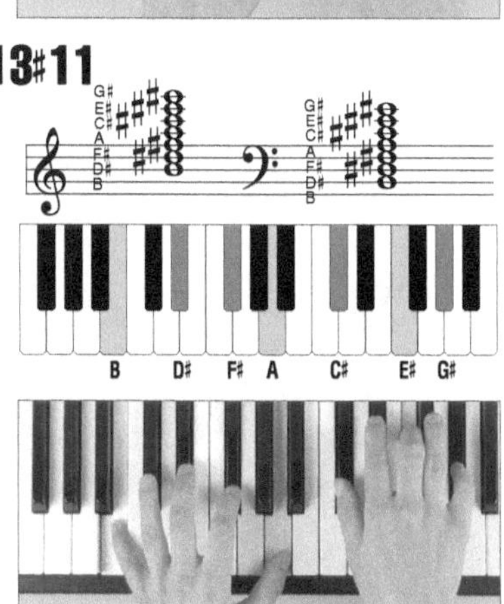

Bm6/9

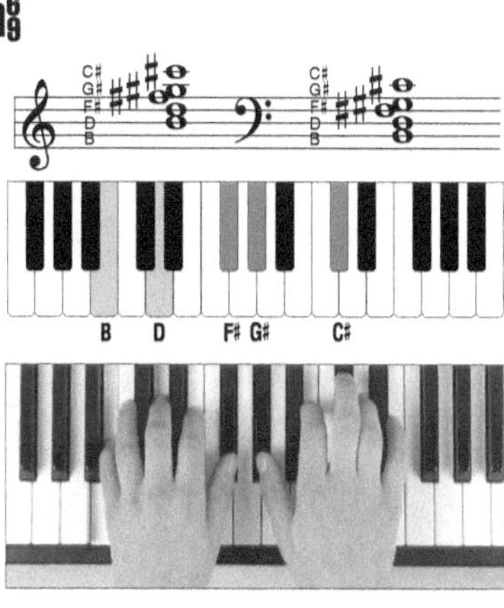

Bm7(add4)

Bm7(add11)

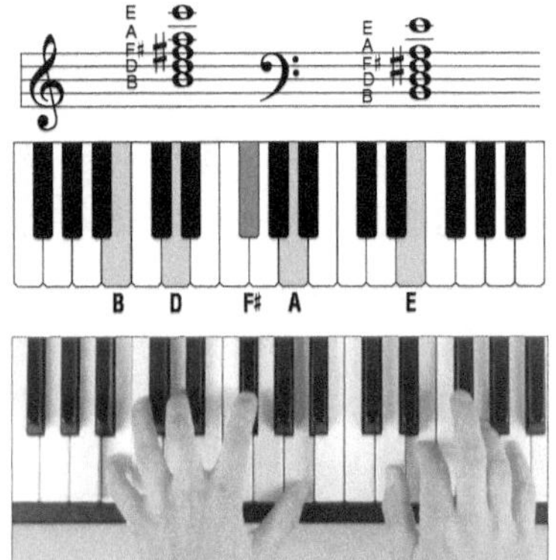

Bm7♭5(♭9)

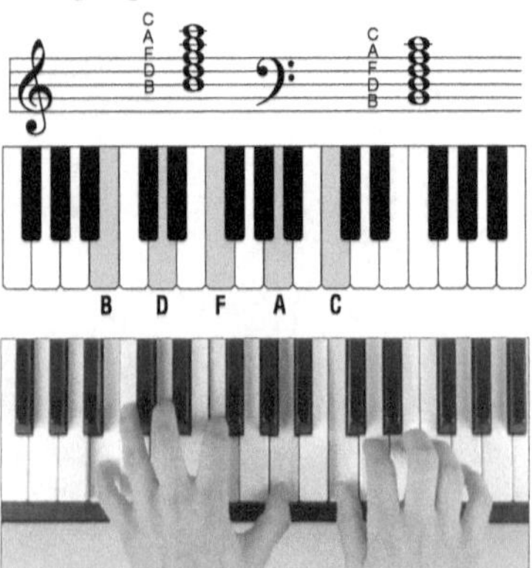

Bm9

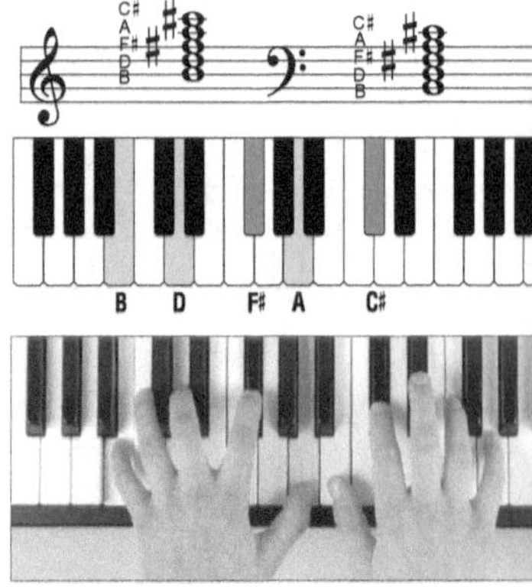

Bm9(maj7)

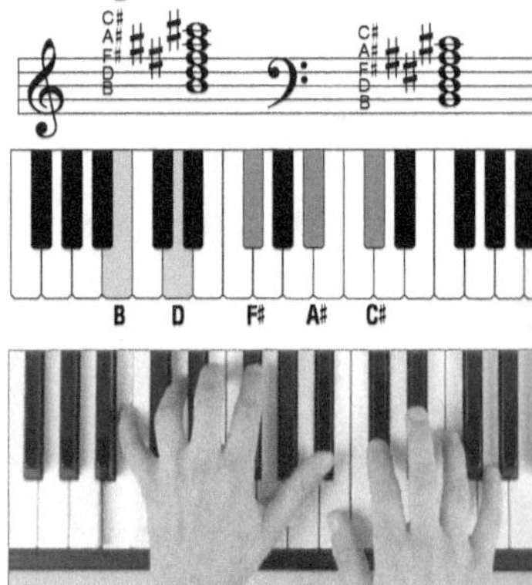

Bm9♭5

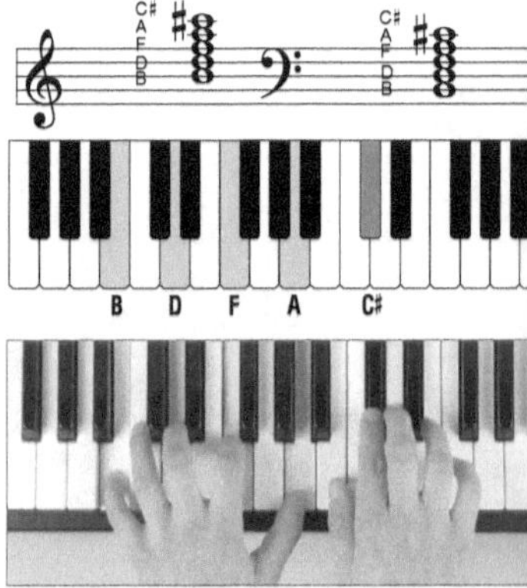

Bm11

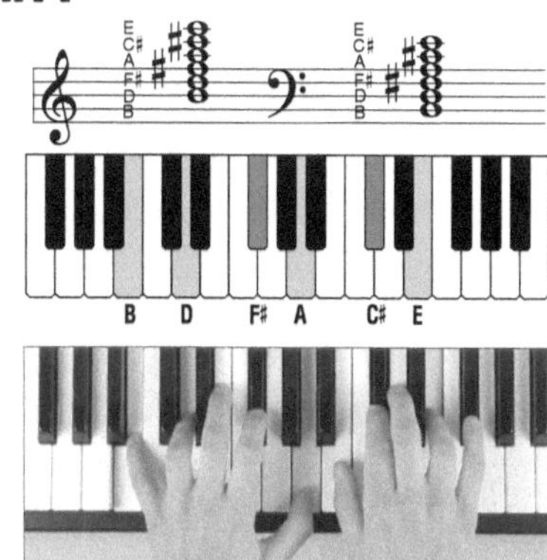

Bm11♭5

Bm13

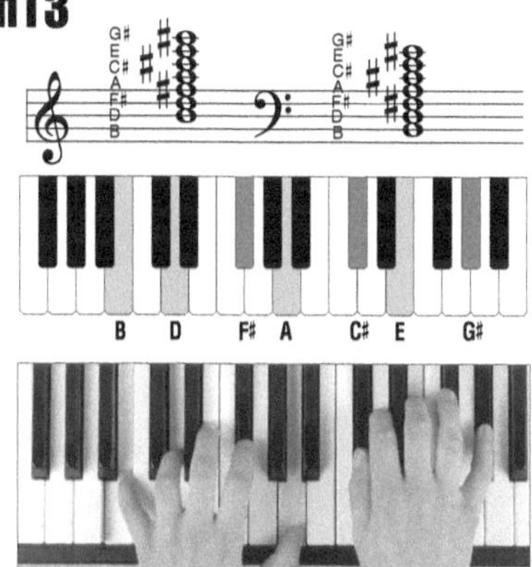

Bm11(maj7)

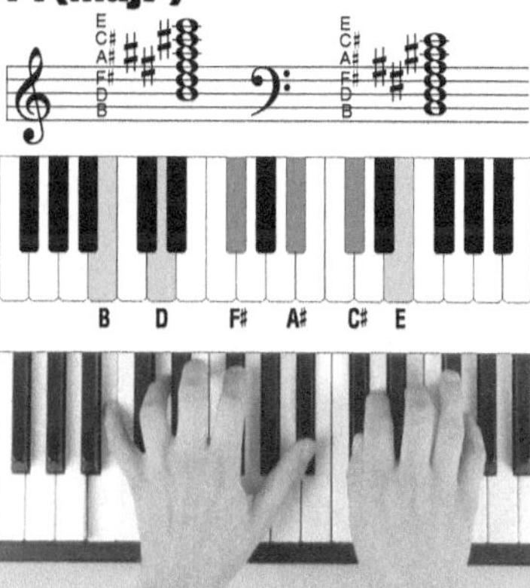

Bdim7(add9)

B7alt.

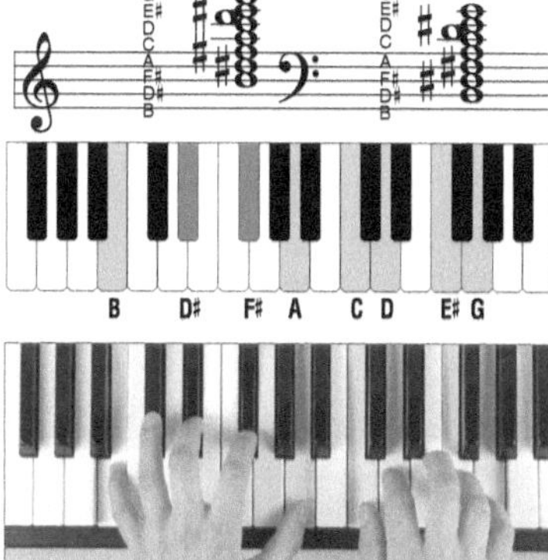